Motivation

THEORY, RESEARCH AND APPLICATION

SIXTH EDITION

Herbert L. Petri
Towson University
Professor Emeritus

John M. Govern
Towson University
Professor

WADSWORTH
CENGAGE Learning·

Australia • Brazil • Japan • Korea • Mexico • Singapore • Spain • United Kingdom • United States

WADSWORTH
CENGAGE Learning

Motivation: Theory, Research and Application, Sixth Edition
Herbert L. Petri, John M. Govern

Editor-in-Chief: Linda Ganster-Schreiber

Executive Editor: Jon-David Hague

Acquisitions Editor: Timothy Matray

Assistant Editor: Jessica Alderman

Editorial Assistant: Nicole Richards

Media Editor: Mary Noel

Senior Art Director: Pamela Galbreath

Marketing Manager: Talia Wise

Marketing Program Manager: Janay Pryor

Senior Marketing Communications Manager: Heather Baxley

Manufacturing Planner: Karen Hunt

Rights Acquisitions Specialist: Dean Dauphinais

Design Direction, Production Management, and Composition: PreMediaGlobal

Cover Designer: William Stanton, Stanton Design

Cover Image: © Greg Epperson/ shutterstock.com

For product information and technology assistance, contact us at **Cengage Learning Customer & Sales Support, 1-800-354-9706.**

For permission to use material from this text or product, submit all requests online at **www.cengage.com/permissions**. Further permissions questions can be emailed to **permissionrequest@cengage.com**.

Library of Congress Control Number: 2012935948

ISBN-13: 978-1-111-84109-6

ISBN-10: 1-111-84109-8

Wadsworth
20 Davis Drive
Belmont, CA 94002-3098
USA

Cengage Learning is a leading provider of customized learning solutions with office locations around the globe, including Singapore, the United Kingdom, Australia, Mexico, Brazil, and Japan. Locate your local office at **international.cengage.com/region**

Cengage Learning products are represented in Canada by Nelson Education, Ltd.

For your course and learning solutions, visit **www.cengage.com**.

Purchase any of our products at your local college store or at our preferred online store **www.cengagebrain.com**.

Printed in the United States of America
4 5 6 7 8 9 10 21 20 19 18 17

This book is dedicated to Jan
(HLP)
and
Monica, Mom, and Dad
(JMG)

About the Authors

Courtesy of Author, Herbert L. Petri

HERBERT L. PETRI

Herbert L. Petri received his B.A. degree from Miami University, Oxford, Ohio, and M.A. and Ph.D. degrees from Johns Hopkins University. He has taught at Towson University since receiving his doctorate and has been recognized on five separate occasions for his excellent teaching. He retired from Towson University in May 2011. Dr. Petri is Adjunct Professor in the Psychological and Brain Sciences Department at Johns Hopkins University where he teaches courses in Motivation and Evolutionary Psychology.

Courtesy of Author, John M. Govern

JOHN M. GOVERN

John M. Govern earned a B.S. in Psychobiology from Albright College and a Ph.D. in Social Psychology from Temple University. Dr. Govern's primary research interest is in social cognition. He has enjoyed teaching at Towson University since 1989.

Brief Contents

Contents

Chapter 3
Physiological Mechanisms of Arousal   61

Chapter 4
Physiological Mechanisms of
Regulation   101

Preface

We have found the study of motivation to be one of the most fascinating and complex topics in psychology. It is fascinating because people want to know why they behave the way they do—to understand the processes that activate their behavior. It is complex because it cuts across many specialty areas within psychology and draws from each of them. Thus you will find in this book physiological, learned, and cognitive explanations of behavior.

Our motives for writing this text are also complex. First, we feel that a motivation text should cover in detail the major approaches suggested by theorists of varying specialties and backgrounds. A book designed for a first course in motivation ought to put forward, as far as possible, an unbiased view of motivational theory. Therefore, we have tried to present the material in this text as objectively as possible, including both the advantages and disadvantages of each of the approaches discussed.

It is also our belief that students should be presented with the basic ideas within a given area, as well as some conclusions about those ideas. Students too often become "lost in the data" and miss the major points. For this reason, we have purposely avoided an encyclopedic presentation of the major areas. Instead, we have focused on the kinds of research conducted to test the major ideas; both older "classic" studies as well as newer studies. As we see it, a textbook on motivation should provide the basic information necessary for a good background in motivational processes, while at the same time allowing instructors the freedom to present additional material of their own choosing related to the various areas. This book is intended to provide the basic information instructors can build upon.

Motivational theory is sometimes difficult for students because it requires ways of thinking that are often quite far removed from everyday experience. For this reason, we have strived to use examples drawn from day-to-day life whenever possible. We have also tried to keep the language simple and direct.

This book is divided into three major areas: approaches to motivation that emphasize its biological components, approaches that emphasize its learned components, and approaches that emphasize its cognitive components. Within each of these areas we have tried to present the material in such a way that understanding the later chapters does not depend on having read the earlier chapters. The independence of the chapters allows each instructor to select whichever ones best fit with his or her particular approach to motivation. This independence also means that chapters can be assigned in any order that is deemed appropriate.

It hardly seems possible that more than thirty years have passed since publication of the first edition of this text and yet our understanding of motivational processes has changed greatly during that period of time. The sixth edition represents a refinement of the progression of topics found in the earlier editions. As was the case with earlier editions, the sixth edition has been updated with new information that has become available since the printing of the fifth edition. The sixth edition now contains approximately 1425 references. About 15% of these references are new to the 6th edition and include updated information as well as several new topics that have been added.

Changes in This Edition

There have been many additions to the sixth edition even though the basic flow of topics remains the same. For example, Chapter 1 presents information on research methods in motivation and then provides a rationale for most if not all motives in humans as well as animals. That theme is evolution. An argument is made for the replication of one's DNA as the primary operating principle behind motivated behaviors. Thus motives such as hunger, thirst, and sex as well as the need to achieve, gain power, affiliate, and so forth are seen as adaptive behaviors that increase the chances of successfully replicating one's genes into the next generation. Indeed, one could argue that the things that motivate us to behave exist because they have had survival value.

Chapter 2, while retaining most of the earlier information on the genetics of motivation, examines newer information from the burgeoning field of Evolutionary Psychology such as innate attraction signals in humans. Chapter 3 on Arousal updates the information on sleep and stress and includes new information on why we dream (e.g., Threat Simulation Theory and Virtual Rehearsal Theory). New to this chapter are data showing that the brain transitions from waking to sleep and from non-rapid eye movement sleep to rapid eye movement sleep much as a flip/flop switch operates. New evidence also provides strong support for the role of sleep in memory formation. Also new to this chapter is a section devoted to examining the role of placebo effects on behavior. Chapter 4 on Physiological Mechanisms of Regulation updates research on hunger, thirst, sex, and aggressive motives covering such recent topics as the role of ghrelin in signaling hunger, and the role of the pancreatic signals of insulin and amylin in glucose availability. Much new information is also noted concerning the role of hypothalamic neurotransmitters in the control of food intake. A new section on the role of habituation processes in obesity has also been added, as has a new section on the role of stress in obesity. Chapter 5 on the role of learning

in motivation includes many of the classic studies that have shown how learning influences motivation, and, in addition, examines information about the role of learning in sexual motivation and aggressive motivation. Chapter 6 on incentive motivation adds a new section on the role of pheromones in incentive motivation and new research on sexual attraction signals. Chapter 7 on hedonism includes new research on gender and pain, the modulating effects of both learning and emotion on pain, and the role of endogenous opiates in pain. Chapter 8 updates research on locus of control, social learning theory, achievement motivation, and a new section on the Theory of Planned Behavior. New research on social loafing under various conditions is also explored. Chapter 9 on cognitive consistency and social motivation has been updated and the two major concepts presented in reverse order from that in the fifth edition. They were switched because some have explained many of the social motivation topics (e.g., conformity, compliance) using a motive for cognitive consistency. Thus, it made sense to discuss consistency motivation first and then show how the motive for consistency is related to social motivation. Chapter 10 updates research on attribution (e.g., self-serving bias, false consensus effect, the actor–observer effect, fundamental attribution error). Finally, new information is included on attribution and achievement, and research showing how an entity versus incrementalist approach can explain some social behaviors. Chapter 11 presents a new hierarchy of needs proposed by Kenrick et al. (2010) that updates and revises Maslow's original model. Bandura's concept of personal efficacy is shown to be related to the development and maintenance of healthy behaviors, and a fuller discussion of positive psychology theory and research is included. In the last several years, there has been a renewed interest in the topic of emotion, and Chapter 12 reflects this new interest. In particular, progress has been made in understanding how the brain integrates the components of an emotional response. Updated coverage of the importance of the amygdala and the prefrontal cortex in this integration can be found in the sixth edition as well as an updated version of Izard's Differential Emotions Theory and the most recent circumplex model of emotions.

The sixth edition builds upon the structure of the fifth edition. Thus the instructor familiar with the fifth edition will find the sequence and topics of the sixth edition similar but updated with more recent research.

A unifying concept added in the fifth edition was the role of evolution in motivation. That approach is maintained and strengthened in the sixth edition. We have refined this thematic approach, suggesting that most (and perhaps all?) motivation can be ultimately understood as promoting the survival of all animals, including humans. An additional concept carried over from earlier editions is that many motives are best understood as complex interactions among processes that then produce behavior. For example, sexual behavior is best understood as having genetic, arousal, regulatory, incentive, and learned components. Attempting to study sexual behavior without considering this combination of factors leads to an incomplete understanding of sexual motivation. Therefore, information about sexual motivation is found in several chapters. Aggressive behaviors, and ultimately all motives, are probably also best understood as resulting from a similar interaction of factors.

As in the fifth edition, key terms are boldface in the text and summarized at the end of each chapter with the page number where that particular term was explained. Thus, the major ideas within the chapter are readily available to the student and can aid in studying, while the page numbers provide easy access to those parts of a chapter where that key idea was discussed, providing a context for learning the material.

The sixth edition also encourages exploration of motivational topics beyond those found in the text itself. Suggestions for further reading are found at the end of each chapter, often on topics that students will find of interest. Additionally, for most chapters, there are Web Resources with addresses to Web sites that provide additional information on some of the topics related to that chapter.

Acknowledgments

As is the case with any endeavor of this size, many people have contributed time, effort, and expertise to this project. We would particularly like to thank the reviewers for this and previous editions for their constructive and thought-provoking suggestions. These reviewers are Terry F. Pettijohn, Ohio State University; Steve Bounds, Arkansas State University; Samuel Clay, Brigham Young University—Idaho; Nicolle Matthews, Northeastern, University of Phoenix, Curry College and University of Massachusetts—Dartmouth.

We are also grateful to Towson University for supporting this project and providing the necessary materials for developing the manuscript of the sixth edition. To the many students in our classes who have been subjected to varying renditions of this material, we say thank you. You helped us determine what would work and what would not. Many colleagues have shared books, articles, and expertise. We thank all of them for their help.

The staff at Wadsworth provided excellent support in the production of the sixth edition. In particular, Tim Matray, Acquisitions Editor; Nicole Richards, Editorial Assistant; Jessica Alderman, Assistant Editor; Pam Galbreath, Art Director; Michelle Clark, Production Manager; Mary Noel, Media Editor and others on the Psychology team have been extremely helpful and supportive throughout the entire project. Finally, we must express our greatest appreciation to our families, who have now endured the writing process yet another time. For Herbert Petri, his wife Jan has always been there to provide support and encouragement when called upon. For John Govern, Monica Greco has done the same. It is our hope that both students and faculty alike will find the sixth edition of this text interesting and informative.

Herbert L. Petri
John M. Govern

PART I   OVERVIEW

CHAPTER 1
Overview: Conceptualizing and
Measuring Motivation and the
Role of Evolution in Motivation

CHAPTER 1

Overview: Conceptualizing and Measuring Motivation and the Role of Evolution in Motivation

Introduction

Each of us has an intuitive understanding of what it means to be motivated. We know that at some times we want to do something and at other times we do not. Essentially we know what it feels like to be motivated. Subjectively, we often talk about our motives as wants, needs, drives, or desires.

In our day-to-day living we also often talk about being unmotivated, that is, not wanting to do something. However, when one examines these situations carefully, it usually appears that it is not so much that we are unmotivated (although it sometimes feels that way) as it is that we do not *want* to behave in a particular way. For example, a student might say "I'm totally unmotivated. I can't force myself to open the book and read the chapter tonight." If 10 minutes later the same student is asked by friends to go out for pizza and beer, the formerly unmotivated student may now be motivated to engage in this alternative to study. Even though we feel totally unmotivated, it is actually the case that we are motivated to do something other than what we need to do (such as studying). So, the concept of motivation would seem best understood not as an on-again, off-again mechanism but rather as a constant flow of behavior that can be directed in many different ways (Birch, Atkinson & Bongort, 1974). Such an analysis suggests that we should be more interested in how motivation is directed first toward one behavior, then toward another than to try to analyze it as present or absent.

But from what do we derive our motivation? Let's use as a working example the hypothetical behavior of a person we will call Angie.

Angie's Problem

Angie has a problem. She is constantly anxious. As a young child, she used to get stomachaches before she performed on stage at dance recitals. As a teenager, she was moody and anxious about how others saw her. Her self-esteem could be crushed by minor comments made by friends about her looks. In college she began developing panic attacks that came on suddenly out of the blue. She became fearful that she would have an attack when she had to give presentations in class. As a result, she avoided classes that required presentations. Angie's problem is more common than you might think. Anxiety disorders are among the most common problems seen by therapists. Fortunately, today there are good ways of dealing with the kinds of problems that Angie experiences.

From a motivational point of view, we can ask what produces the kinds of anxiety experiences that people like Angie have. Research on the biology of behavior suggests that some people may have a genetic predisposition to develop certain kinds of disorders like Angie's. However, whether or not such a predisposition does get expressed often depends upon the kinds of experiences one has had. In other words, learned factors also play an important role in the development of many motives. Finally, the way in which we interpret events around us will also influence our motives. Angie's problems with self-esteem may reflect a misinterpretation on her part of how people feel about her. Given the considerations previously mentioned, a therapist might prescribe medication to alleviate some of the anxiety she constantly feels and at the same time help her relearn and reinterpret events around her by using cognitive-behavioral therapy.

The biological, behavioral, and cognitive aspects of behavior previously mentioned are a reoccurring theme throughout this text. Some motives seem best explained biologically, others appear to be primarily learned, while still others are best viewed as cognitive in nature. In addition, many motives appear to result from a combination of biology, learning, and cognition. Let us look,

then, a little more closely at the concept of motivation.

The Concept of Motivation

Motivation is the concept we use when we describe the *forces acting on or within an organism to initiate and direct behavior*. We also use the concept of motivation to explain differences in the **intensity** of behavior. More intense behaviors are considered to be the result of higher levels of motivation. Additionally, we often use the concept of motivation to indicate the **persistence** of behavior. A highly motivated behavior will often be persistent even though the intensity of the behavior may be low. For example, a hungry monkey occasionally rewarded with a piece of banana for pressing a lever on a variable interval (VI) schedule (a VI schedule "rewards" a response unpredictably, constantly changing the amount of time between one reward and the next) will press the lever very presistently but at a low rate of responding. Fast responding does not pay off, but persistence does.

Does the study of behavior need a concept of motivation? One reason often suggested by both casual and scientific observation is that "something" triggers behavior. Sometimes we behave in a certain way and at other times we do not. What was different from the one time to the others? Presumably motivation was present when we behaved, but was absent (or, more correctly, a different motive was active) when we did not. The concept of motivation helps to explain why behavior occurs in one situation but not in others. To the extent that such a concept increases our ability to understand and predict behavior, the concept is useful. As readers will discover throughout this book, many psychologists have found the concept of motivation useful.

The Measurement of Motivation

As scientists, we almost never measure motivation directly. Instead we manipulate some stimulus (S) condition and then measure some behavior in the

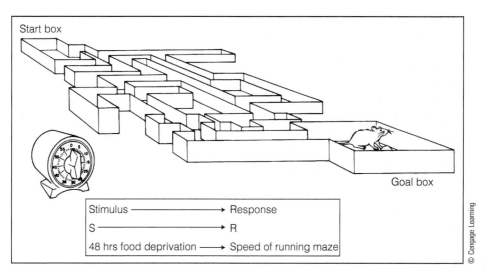

FIGURE 1.1 Stimulus-response analysis for motivation. Motivation is inferred when changes in responding follow from changes in stimulus conditions.

form of a response (R). Suppose, for example, that we take food away from a rat for 48 hours (a form of **deprivation**) as our stimulus change (S) and observe how fast that rat subsequently runs in a maze (R) in order to get food at the goal box (see Figure 1.1.). Further, suppose we observe that our rat runs faster after 48 hours of deprivation than when not deprived. In this hypothetical experiment we manipulated hours without food and measured speed of running, neither of which is motivation. Motivation, however, can be *inferred* from the change in behavior that occurred, and an indication of its strength can be observed in the rat's speed of responding in the maze. Thus the concept of motivation helps us understand the change in the animal's behavior (assuming that some other alternative cannot better explain the change), and we might label the inferred motivational state as *hunger*. The concept of motivation in this example serves as an intervening variable.* An **intervening variable** is a concept developed by a researcher that serves to link a stimulus and a response and helps to relate the

two. Thus, the concept of motivation serves to link the stimulus change (deprivation) to the behavior change (increased speed of running) and provides one possible explanation for the relationship between the stimulus and response, as shown in Figure 1.2.

The intervening nature of motivational processes is one reason motivation is difficult to study. We can only infer the existence of motivation by observing changes in the relationships between stimulus conditions and responses. A second difficulty stems from the temporary nature of motivation. Psychologists typically describe the temporary nature of motivation by pointing out that motivation is a **performance variable**. When enough motivation is present, behavior is performed; when motivation is too low, behavior is absent. Motivation as a performance variable is often contrasted with learning, where more permanent changes in behavior occur (although learning obviously also influences performance). We learn

---

*A *variable* is any factor that can have more than one value; for example, we can be a little hungry, moderately hungry, or ravenously hungry.

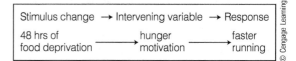

FIGURE 1.2 Motivation as an intervening variable.

many things that are not immediately demonstrated in behaviors, but the demonstration of learned behavior depends, at least in part, upon adequate motivation. Indeed every specialty area within psychology analyzes situations that involve the combination of specific processes and the performance of these processes in behavior.

Characteristics of Motivation

We have discussed motivation as if we knew what it is. As noted earlier, each of us has some intuitive feeling for what is called motivation, and yet it has proven rather difficult to define. Kleinginna and Kleinginna (1981), for example, gathered 102 defining or criticizing statements concerning motivation, so it is obvious that theorists differ in their views of motivation. Though textbooks on the topic differ somewhat in their definitions, one commonly held characteristic of motivation is its activating properties.

Activation

The activating property of motivation, or **activation**, is most easily seen in the production of behavior. Is the observed organism behaving in some way? If it is, then at least some minimal amount of motivation is assumed to be present. If no overt behavior is observed, then the motivational level of the organism may be insufficient to trigger behavior. While the occurrence of overt behavior is generally taken as evidence for motivation, its absence does not necessarily mean that no motivation is present. For example, consider a rabbit that freezes when a predator appears. Is the rabbit unmotivated by the presence of this threat? Probably not. In fact, while overt behavior may be virtually absent in this situation, behavioral indexes such as heart rate, adrenaline output, and so forth would probably be high. The moral is clear—though motivation is considered to be behaviorally activating, the behavior activated may not always be overt. We must therefore be very cautious in assuming a lack of motivation when

no overt responding is apparent; perhaps we are simply not measuring the response or responses being activated. Fortunately, for many motivational states, changes in motivation do lead to changes in overt behavior.

A second characteristic often mentioned in regard to the activating properties of motivation is persistence. Hungry animals persist in their attempts to get food. Similarly, humans often persist in behaving in particular ways even when the chances of success are vanishingly small. Observation of this continued persistence has led many psychologists to regard it as an index of motivation. This index, however, is also not free of problems. How persistent a behavior is depends at least in part on what alternative behaviors are available. Suppose, for example, that a hungry monkey has been taught to press a lever for food. For several hours each day, the monkey is placed in an experimental chamber that contains only the lever. Of course the monkey does not have to press the lever, but there is little else for it to do, and if lever pressing has been learned, it will tend to persist. On the other hand, suppose the monkey is placed in a chamber where several different responses in addition to lever pressing are possible. If these alternative responses lead to different outcomes (e.g., a peek out a window or a sip of a sweet-tasting fluid), lever pressing may become less persistent. In multiple-response situations (as often occur in naturalistic situations) continued persistence probably does accurately reflect motivational strength, but, as Beck (1983) points out, motivational research has not typically examined persistence in situations where more than one response is possible. Thus, although persistence does seem to be one index of motivation, it is important to realize that other factors may also contribute to the persistence of behavior.

Both casual observation and laboratory research suggest that energetic behavior is more motivated than hesitant behavior. One rat that runs faster than another through a maze may also be more motivated. Such an hypothesis is more likely to be true if we also know that the two rats differ in how hungry they are but not in how well they have learned to run the maze. **Vigor** of responding, then, is another characteristic typically associated with the presence of motivation. But, as with the other characteristics we have examined, vigorous responses do not always mean high motivation. It is possible, for example, to teach a rat that the correct response to obtain food is to push down a lever with a certain amount of force. Suppose that we designed an experiment where hungry rats had to press the response lever with a good deal of force for food pellets to be delivered. If someone were to observe these "forceful" rats, he or she might conclude that the rats were highly motivated as they banged away at the response lever. However, in this instance the observer would be wrong because the vigorous responding would not index motivation alone; factors such as learning to respond forcefully would also be involved.

Overt responding, persistence, and vigor are characteristics of the activation properties of motivation, assuming that other factors can be ruled out and are, under appropriate conditions, reasonable indexes of the presence of motivation. Activation is usually considered one of the two major components of motivation; however, Birch, Atkinson, and Bongort (1974) suggest that the activation of behavior should not be a major concern of motivational analyses because organisms are continuously active. These researchers propose that motivational analyses should examine the conditions that lead the organism to change from one activity to another. In other words, the *directionality* of behavior is what is important.

Direction

When we are hungry we go to the refrigerator, and when we are thirsty we go to the water faucet. How do we decide to direct our behavior in one way rather than another? Questions of this type involve a consideration of which mechanism (or mechanisms) directs behavior. Although the specific way in which this directionality is achieved is debated by theorists, many psychologists have argued that motivation is involved. **Directionality**, then, is often considered an index of motivational

state. The direction that a particular behavior takes is usually obvious, as in going to the refrigerator when we are hungry; however, when several choices are possible, directionality is sometimes not so clear. Suppose that we have two bottles, each filled with a solution of water and sucrose (table sugar) but with different concentrations. Will a rat be more motivated by one of the two concentrations? To determine which is the more motivating, we would run a **preference test**. The rat is given the opportunity to lick fluid from either bottle, and we measure the amount consumed. If we were to conduct such a test, we would discover that the rat preferred the more concentrated sugar solution (Young & Greene, 1953), and we would have some evidence that more concentrated solutions of sucrose are more motivating. In some situations, preference testing is the best way to determine which of several alternatives is most motivating because indexes such as persistence or vigor may not indicate differences. Indeed, Beck (2000) considers preference to be the most basic motivational index.

The Study of Motivation: Categories of Analysis

As you proceed through the chapters of this text, you will discover that motivation has been studied from many different points of view. In general, we can order these views along at least four dimensions, each containing points representing opposing views, as shown in Figure 1.3. Although these dimensions overlap in some respects, the following analysis attempts to provide a framework within which the student can understand these differing points of view. Certainly other frameworks are possible.

Nomothetic versus Idiographic

Research may be classified as falling along a continuum that proceeds from strictly nomothetic approaches at one extreme to strictly idiographic approaches at the other. The **nomothetic approach** involves the development of general or

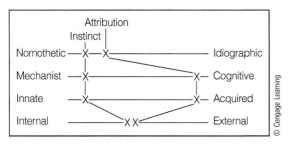

FIGURE 1.3 Categories of analysis. Four dimensions along which analysis of motivation may differ. As shown, motivation from an instinctive perspective is nomothetic, mechanistic, innate, and in response to both internal and external cues. Motivation from the point of view of attribution theory is nomothetic, cognitive, acquired, and also in response to both internal and external cues.

universal laws (*Merriam-Webster Online Dictionary*). Typically, research of this type studies groups of people or animals and determines how they are *similar*. For example, identifying brain structures such as the hypothalamus that are involved in motivation is nomothetic because research has shown that the hypothalamus is involved in motivation not only in a single rat but also in rats in general and people too. Further, it is often assumed that the general rules uncovered by studying one species will also apply to other species. Although this assumption is sometimes incorrect and is always open to critical review, the nomothetic approach attempts to discover general laws applicable to the widest range of situations. In the study of motivation the nomothetic approach predominates. In opposition to nomothetic analyses is the **idiographic approach**, which proposes that we can understand behavior by looking at how people differ from each other, that is, by examining those properties that make each person *unique*. In motivation, the idiographic approach is most clearly seen in the humanist and actualization theorists (see Chapter 11).

Innate versus Acquired

Psychologists have debated for over 100 years the contribution that innate versus acquired tendencies

make to behavior, and motivation, as a specialty area within psychology has not escaped this contention. Early theorists such as McDougall (reprinted in Russell, 1970) and James (1890) saw motivation as primarily controlled by innate motives they termed **instincts**. Although these early approaches did not last, modern research on the innate components of motivation is being pursued by animal behaviorists, ethologists, and evolutionary psychologists. During the mid-20th century, psychology was dominated by research on the factors involved in learning. Theorists and researchers have studied how behavior is acquired, and much of what has been discovered is also applicable to the acquisition of motive states. Perhaps the most important motivational notion to develop from this work was the concept of incentive motivation. We will examine incentive motivation in Chapter 6; suffice it to say here that analyses emphasizing both innate and acquired motives continue today.

Internal versus External

Another dimension along which motivation may be studied concerns the source of the motivation—that is, internal versus external sources of motivation. One prevalent approach has involved the idea that different motive states can be conceptualized as needs that, when active, promote behaviors to reduce those needs. **Needs** are usually viewed as internal sources of motivation that activate and direct behavior to items in the environment that alleviate some state of deprivation. In this context, needs are often couched in physiological terms (e.g., the need for food and water or the avoidance of pain) although some theorists also include social and psychological needs within their frameworks (see, for example, Lewin, 1936, 1938). In contrast to needs theorists, others emphasize external sources of motivation provided by **goals**. These theorists generally examine the motivating effects of either various goal objects or social relationships. According to this point of view, motivation can be activated by changes in the external environment. For example, helping behavior often depends upon the number of other people present.

Research has shown (see Chapter 9) that the presence of other people often inhibits helping responses.

Mechanistic versus Cognitive

How do the processes that control motivation work? Are they blind and mechanical, triggered automatically by changes in internal or external states, or are they controlled by rational, purposive thought? As you can probably guess, theorists have forcefully defended both sides. Some theorists argue that motives such as hunger, thirst, and sex are triggered automatically by changes in factors such as blood sugar level, fluid balance, and hormonal concentrations. Other researchers point out that learned motives may also generate behavior outside of awareness. This mechanistic approach assumes that changes in specific factors activate circuits that in turn motivate the organism to engage in behavior. Neither conscious awareness nor intent on the part of the organism is assumed. Researchers who embrace the mechanistic view are often interested in internal need states and innate patterns of behavior. In contrast, other researchers, more often interested in externally motivated states and acquired motives, believe that motivational processes are cognitive in nature. The cognitive approach assumes that the manner in which information is interpreted influences motive states. For example, attributing failure at a task to its difficulty is likely to have a different influence on future motivation than attributing failure to lack of ability. The complexity of motivation is such that it is probably safe to assume that all approaches mentioned have some validity. In certain situations, behavior seems best understood as motivated by internal states that activate the organism to respond in genetically determined ways. Other behaviors seem clearly the result of external information that is acted upon in light of acquired experiences. Various combinations of approaches fit our observations of still other behaviors. To summarize, at this time *no one approach would appear to be better than any other in explaining motivation in its entirety.* Some approaches explain particular motive states better than others; however,

depending on the motive studied, the best explanation may be nomothetic or idiographic, innate or acquired, internal or external, mechanistic or cognitive, or some combination of these.

Levels of Analysis

Before closing this discussion of the ways in which motivation is analyzed, we should mention the different levels at which it may be studied. Because motivation cuts across so many specialty areas within psychology, the number of levels (and sublevels within levels) at which it is studied is quite large. For the sake of brevity, we will group these various levels into the four main categories of physiological analysis, individual analysis, social analysis, and philosophical analysis.

Physiological Analysis

Though physiological analyses of motivation have been conducted using both humans and animals, research with animals is the most prevalent. Typically, this level of analysis is concerned with the brain's control of motivated states. Researchers, for example, are interested in the various brain structures involved in the triggering of motivation, the way in which motivationally important information is processed by groups of cells, and the neurotransmitters within the brain that are involved in the alteration of motivational states. Thus we can identify many sublevels within the physiological analysis of motivation.

Studies of the role of the nervous system in motivation often require electrical, chemical, or surgical manipulation of carefully mapped brain areas. For example, in a now classic study conducted in 1954 by James Olds and Peter Milner, thin wires called **electrodes** were introduced into various parts of a rat's brain. These electrodes were designed so that portions of the brain could be stimulated electrically by the experimenters.

The experimental situation was so arranged that if the rats pressed a lever current would be applied to the electrode. To everyone's amazement, rats with electrodes implanted in the septal region would press the lever many hundreds of times per hour in order to receive this weak electrical current. By conventional standards of conditioning, the electrical stimulation would have to be judged as a powerful reward. One rat pressed the lever more than 7,500 times in a 12-hour period while another responded 1,920 times in one hour. When the electrical current was turned off, bar pressing quickly ceased; when it was turned on again, bar pressing quickly resumed. The rats appeared to be highly motivated to obtain the electrical stimulation and worked for long periods of time to obtain it. The subjective impression one gained from observing these self-stimulating rats was that the electrical stimulation was quite pleasurable.

Since the discovery of self-stimulation sites in the brain by Olds and Milner, hundreds of additional studies have been conducted. The effects have proven to be much more complex than first supposed; for our purposes in this chapter, however, this research indicates one method of gaining knowledge about motivation. Direct manipulation of the brain by electrical stimulation has shown us that brain circuits exist that may be active when reward occurs. Circuits that appear to have a punishing effect on behavior have also been noted (e.g., Delgado, Roberts, & Miller, 1954).

Electrical stimulation of the brain is only one of several techniques used in the study of motivation at the physiological level. Researchers can also study motivation by *chemically stimulating* the brain after inserting a minute tube (called a **canula**) into a specific brain region, injecting a solution, and noting how motivation changes as a result. Additionally, researchers sometimes create a **lesion** within the brain by surgically removing some portion of it and observing how (or if) motivation is altered. These techniques have revealed that a wide range of motivated behaviors, including feeding, drinking, sexual arousal, fear, and aggression, can be altered by manipulation of specific brain areas. Finally, we should note that it is possible to **record** the brain's natural electrical activity during various motivated states. The general activity of large

groups of brain cells (called **neurons**) can be recorded by an electroencephalograph (**EEG**), while small groups of cells and even single neurons can be recorded through the use of **depth electrodes**. **Positron-emission tomography (PET) scans** and magnetic resonance imaging (**MRI, fMRI**) are also used to study the brain. Such studies have been used to see what areas of the brain are involved with various tasks. A PET scan measures the metabolic activity of different brain regions, an MRI enables one to visualize areas of the brain, and an fMRI allows one to both visualize the brain and detect differences in metabolism in various parts of the brain (Carlson, 2007).

Though a particular researcher will often use only one or two physiological techniques, data gathered by all these techniques should be consistent. If lesion techniques have shown that a brain area is involved with feeding, then chemical or electrical stimulation of this area in other experimental subjects ought to elicit food-related activities. Similarly, recordings from this brain area during feeding behavior should indicate altered activity within these cells. Unfortunately, the convergence of information from different experimental techniques has not always been as consistent as one would like. The reasons for this lack of consistency are complex and remain a problem for understanding motivation at a physiological level of analysis.

Individual Analysis

The study of motivation at the level of the individual involves research aimed at understanding motivational changes that occur to a person as a result of internal or external conditions. Analysis at this level occurs about equally often in animal and human research. In animal research deprivation is often used to alter the motivational state of the organism; for example, one might deprive a rat of food for 48 hours and observe how its behavior changes as a result. In research conducted with humans, researchers may attempt to induce a motivational state through specific instructions. In some achievement studies, for example, researchers stimulated the need for achievement by telling the participants that they had failed an important task (McClelland, Clark, Roby, & Atkinson, 1949). More simply, human participants are sometimes asked, using a survey technique such as a questionnaire, to indicate their own motives as they perceive them. One such technique developed by Rotter (1966) has provided theorists with considerable insight into how people view themselves.

Even though research at this level is conducted in order to provide insight into the important motivational factors that influence the behavior of the individual, most research of this type is actually done with groups of individuals. Testing several individuals increases the likelihood of finding an effect and taking the nomothetic approach; it is proper to presume that behavioral changes detected in several individuals (if properly sampled) are also present in people in general. An example of just such an approach is early research conducted by Bandura and his associates concerning how aggression may be learned in children (Bandura, 1973).

In a now well-known study, Bandura showed a group of nursery-school children a film in which an adult attacked a life-size Bobo doll in unusual ways. For example, the adult hit the Bobo doll with a large mallet while saying such things as "Socko!" and "Pow!" A second group of children saw the same behaviors performed by a cartoon character (actually an adult dressed up in a cat suit). A third group observed the aggressive behaviors performed by a live adult while a fourth group saw a live model behave in a calm, nonaggressive manner toward the Bobo doll. Shortly afterward, the children were led to a room containing several different toys, among them the Bobo doll. The children's behavior was observed both for the novel forms of aggression depicted by the adult and for overall aggression. Results of the experiment showed that the live model's behavior was imitated more often than the filmed or cartoon model's behavior. However, significant imitation of the aggressive behavior of both the filmed model and the cartoon character also occurred. Of

particular interest was the finding that the children not only modeled the observed aggressive behaviors but they also performed many aggressive behaviors of their own. The group that had observed the nonaggressive model, however, showed little aggressive behavior. Bandura's research is important for an understanding of motivation at the level of the individual because it strongly suggests that some motivated behaviors are learned, quite simply, through observation. Thus, if our parents or peers behave aggressively, we will learn to behave this way also. If, on the other hand, the models we observe show us that they are motivated to work hard, pursue excellence, and be successful, we are likely to be motivated in similar ways.

Social Analysis

A moment's reflection should quickly reveal that our behavior often differs when we are in the company of others. Behavior in particular situations such as the classroom is generally predictable too: students take notes, ask questions, and sometimes fall asleep; professors lecture, answer questions, and tend to write illegibly on the chalkboard. These same individuals, however, behave rather differently at parties. Students and professors may drink alcoholic beverages, argue politics, and play idiotic games that they would not even consider in other circumstances. Our motivations for engaging in these rather different sets of behavior are often studied by social psychologists. These psychologists tell us that our behaviors are considerably influenced by both **situational factors** (such as whether we are in the classroom or at a party) and by the **presence of others**. As just one example, conformity studies conducted by Solomon Asch in the mid-20th century (1952, 1965) showed that approximately 80% of the participants he tested conformed to a group decision at least once even though that decision was clearly wrong. Recent studies have confirmed that the level of conformity shown by people has not changed much today (Bond & Smith, 1996). When interviewed after the experiment, many participants indicated that they did not question the group's decision but rather wondered why they differed from the group. These participants also expressed a strong desire to conform. Studies such as those conducted by Asch indicate that the presence of others, whose opinions differ from our own, generates within us motivation to conform. Motivation, then, may be analyzed not only at the physiological or individual level but also at the level of groups. Groups can influence our motives and, in conjunction with situational variables, alter the ways in which we behave.

Philosophical Analysis

One final level of analysis should be mentioned. Motivational theory is infused with philosophical assumptions that are often subtle. Theorists sometimes view motivation in a negative way; that is, they see the presence of motivation as an **aversive state** that behavior seeks to overcome. Freud's theory perhaps represents a good example of this particular philsophy of motivation. According to Freud (1957), motivational states create a condition of tension that the individual then seeks to reduce. Further, Freud thought that individuals have little control over the innate conditions that generate this motivational tension, and, as a result, the ego must repeatedly control behavior to keep the tension low within the id.

Humanist psychologists present a sharp contrast to the negative view of motivation espoused by Freud. Unlike Freud, who regarded our behavior as the result of strong inner forces of which we are largely unaware, theorists such as Rogers and Maslow have proposed that our behavior is directed toward **self-actualization**. Motivation, from this point of view, is a **positive state** pushing the individual to become all that she or he can become. We regard the approaches of both Freud and the humanists as examples of philosophical analysis because (a) the descriptions of motivation and its effects depend upon the theorists' philosophy (humans are basically evil versus humans are basically good), and (b) the theories are couched in terms that make them difficult to test experimentally.

As a result, one must usually accept or reject their propositions based on the philosophical arguments they provide rather than on empirical data. We do not mean to imply, however, that these approaches should be dismissed because empirical data are less available; we have included them in this text because they do have something to add to the understanding of motivation.

Analysis of Angie's Problem

Let us return now to the story that began this chapter. Angie has anxiety. Why? We can analyze Angie's problem at any (or all) of the four levels we have just discussed. At the physiological level, Angie may have a genetic predisposition to be anxious. This could be due to a sensitivity to arousing stimulation or perhaps an overactive sympathetic nervous system. It is also possible that she may have an imbalance of neurotransmitters (e.g., serotonin) that increases her potential to become anxious. At the physiological level of analysis, we would look for the basis of Angie's problem in physiological changes that have disrupted the processes that normally control the expression of anxiety.

At the individual level of analysis, we might investigate the possibility that some aspects of her anxiety are learned. Perhaps sometime in school Angie was embarrassed by a teacher after making a presentation. Consequently, she has associated cues associated with school situations with the feelings of anxiety, and when those cues occur again she feels anxious (through a learning process called classical conditioning). To understand Angie's problem at the individual level, we would attempt to discover what conditions motivate her to feel anxious. Does she become anxious in some circumstances but not in others? Do past experiences play a part in her anxiety? Answers to any or all of these questions might provide insight into the reasons for her anxiety.

At the social level, we might examine Angie's family life more closely. Perhaps her mother always expected a lot from her children but was also very crital of their behavior. Angie wanted to please her mother but could never seem to measure up to her mother's standards, so Angie becomes anxious whenever she has to perform. Additionally, perhaps Angie had a brother or sister who was outstanding in everything he or she did, and seemed to do so without any effort. Angie tries to compete with her sibling but can't and this makes her anxious. The group analysis of Angie's problem would look to the interactions she has with her parents, siblings, and peers and attempt to understand her anxiety problems in relation to the social interactions she has.

From a philosophical point of view such as Freud's, Angie's problem might be viewed as a result of pent-up sexual desire. If any type of sexuality is frowned upon in her family, then her normal sexual drives might become locked up in the id. In this analysis, the anxiety she feels in performance situations could be due to her conflict between desire and conformity to the rules of her family. She feels anxious for having such desires. The humanist psychologists, on the other hand, might see Angie's problem as the result of a lack of positive regard. If Angie's parents led her to believe that she was loved only when she behaved correctly (conditional positive regard), then her tendency toward growth and full functioning would become stunted. Angie would try to channel energy normally used for this growth into defenses to protect her self-image, but the anxiety might still appear in highly stressful situations such as when she must give a presentation to the class.

As you can see, the reasons, one might suggest, for the anxiety Angie experiences depend, at least in part, on the level of analysis one chooses. In actuality, Angie's anxiety is probably the result of a complex set of physiological, individual, social, and philosophical factors. It is worth noting that most behaviors are the result of a complex interaction of motivational factors.

Major Constructs in Motivation

A number of major constructs are frequently used in motivational theory. An understanding of some of these major constructs can be useful for comparing the different theories because the theories differ in regard to the way these constructs are handled.

Energy

Many of the theories discussed in this book assume the existence of some source of **energy** that drives behavior. Some theorists have proposed that just one source of energy exists for all behavior, that the energy behind behavior is **general**. Assumptions of a general energy source require the existence of some additional mechanism that can direct this energy in different ways at different times. Other researchers have proposed that the force behind particular behaviors is **specific**. For these theorists, the energy-activating behavior can also serve a directing function because each behavior has its own energy source. During hunger, for example, food-getting behavior would be activated and directed, while water-directed behaviors would occur during thirst.

While some motivational theories do not explicitly postulate a source of energy for behavior, such a source is implied by many theories. Several theorists have proposed that an energy concept is unnecessary and that one can understand the motivation of behavior without having to assume some energy existing behind behavior. Thus the concept of energy is more important in some theories than in others.

Physiological Mechanisms

Several different physiological mechanisms have been proposed as constructs to help explain motivation. One general approach has been to assume that some motivational mechanisms are genetically programmed or "wired in" to the organism. This biological approach has usually taken one of two forms.

The instinct approach proposes that energy accumulates within the organism and leads to a motivated state. Preprogrammed behaviors then occur to reduce the motivation. The triggering of these "wired-in" or innate behaviors is usually attributed to specific stimuli in the environment that have the effect of releasing the behavior. More recently (see Buss, 2008), **evolutionary psychology** has examined motivated behaviors of humans as adaptations to environmental conditions that existed many thousands of years ago and that can lead to specific behaviors, changes in physiological states, or even cognitions. These adaptations then bias us to respond in particular ways to the conditions of our environment.

The second biological approach proposes that circuits within the brain monitor the state of the body and activate behaviors when changes are detected. The activation of these circuits then leads to the motivation of responses, which may be either innate or learned. For example, one classic theory of hunger motivation proposed that specialized detectors measured changes in blood glucose and triggered hunger motivation when glucose levels dropped.

Learning

The role of learning in motivated behavior has also been important. Clark Hull (1943, 1951, 1952) developed a theory in the late 1940s and early 1950s that attempted to outline the interrelationships of learning and motivation in generating behavior. Theorists such as Spence (1956, 1960) have stressed the role of incentives in controlling goal-directed behavior. Research has also examined the ways in which classical and operant conditioning may be involved in the development of motive states. Some motives also seem to be learned through observation; this process, termed **modeling**, may be the basis for much of human motivation behavior (Bandura, 1977).

Social Interaction

Our interactions with others can also be motivating. Research in social psychology has pointed to the power of the group in motivating us to conform and to the power of authority figures in motivating us to obey. Also, the presence of others often reduces the likelihood that an individual will provide help in an emergency situation. Social situations have a large influence on our behavior because the presence of others alters our motivation.

Cognitive Processes

The role of cognitive processes in motivation has become increasingly recognized. The kinds of information we take in and the ways in which that information is processed have important influences on our behavior. Theories such as Heider's balance theory, Festinger's cognitive dissonance theory, and Bem's self-perception theory emphasize the role of **active information processing** (i.e., thinking) in the control of behavior.

Attribution theory has also emphasized the role of cognition in the interpretation of others' (and our own) behaviors and indicates that our behavior will, to a large extent, be based on these interpretations.

The Activation of Motivation

Another major construct of motivational theory concerns the triggering of motivation. Research in this area has investigated the mechanisms that monitor the state of the organism and that trigger motivation when the body is out of balance. Early theories emphasized the role of **peripheral** (also called **local**) **receptors** in the monitoring of physical states. Thus an empty, cramping stomach or a dry mouth were once thought to be the cues that told an individual that he or she was hungry or thirsty.

As evidence against the local theories accumulated, emphasis shifted to **central receptors** in the brain that monitor conditions such as blood glucose or blood osmolarity, which might trigger appropriate motivational states. One current proposal looks at the interaction of peripheral cues such as leptin (a hormone produced by fat cells) and central receptor sites in the hypothalamus that together help to regulate eating behavior.

Homeostasis

Theorists have also presented differing views regarding the purpose for motivation. Perhaps the most commonly accepted purpose is to maintain

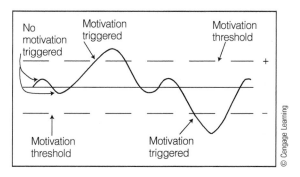

FIGURE 1.4 Homeostasis.

homeostasis (i.e., the idea that an optimal level exists for various states of the body). When the body deviates too far from this optimal level, motivational circuits are triggered by the receptors monitoring these states, and behaviors that will bring the body back to its optimal level are begun. Figure 1.4 depicts the concept of homeostasis. Certainly, some motive states seem homeostatic. As we shall see, however, others are not easily explained by the concept of homeostasis.

Hedonism

Perhaps the oldest explanation for the purpose of motivated behavior is the idea of **hedonism**, which assumes that we are motivated by pleasure and pain. We learn to approach situations that are pleasurable and similarly learn to avoid situations that are painful. Figure 1.5 depicts the idea of a hedonistic continuum. Hedonistic explanations propose that pleasure and pain exist along a continuum and that what is pleasurable or aversive will change as conditions change. For example, the offer of an additional large dinner immediately after one has just finished a large meal would not be pleasurable.

Though hedonism may explain some motive states, it does not provide a satisfactory explanation for motivations that result in self-destructive or self-painful behaviors.

Growth Motivation

Growth motivation stresses the idea that humans are motivated to reach their full potential—physically,

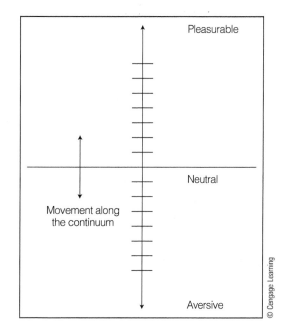

FIGURE 1.5 Hedonistic continuum. Specific situations place us at different points along the continuum.

psychologically, and emotionally. Rogers discusses this growth motivation in relation to the fully functioning individual, while Maslow uses the term *self-actualization* to describe the motivation to strive for personal fulfillment.

One aspect of growth motivation is the need to control or have an effect on our environment. This has been called *effectance motivation* by some and *personal causation* by others. By whatever name, all growth motivation theories suggest that humans are strongly motivated to test and improve their capacities.

Philosophical and Physiological Roots of Motivational Theory

Modern psychology is the product of philosophical thought that can be traced back to Greek philosophers such as Aristotle and to developments within the study of physiology, many of which occurred between 1800 and 1850 (Boring, 1950). These two approaches to understanding heavily influenced early psychological thought and indeed continue to influence our understanding of psychological processes today. As will become clearer, the study of motivation is a complex blend of philosophical and physiological concepts. While some theorists have attempted to understand motivation almost exclusively from the point of view of physiology, others have approached it from a more philosophical direction (see for example, Chapter 11). Both philosophy and physiology have much to offer psychologists who attempt to unravel the complex motives that activate and direct human behavior. Although we cannot begin to do justice to the many and complex ideas that philosophers and biologists have developed over the ages, we will briefly review a few ideas within philosophy and physiology that have influenced our understanding of motivation.

Philosophical Antecedents

Aristotle   The Greek philosopher Aristotle proposed two important ideas that even today continue to have an influence within the study of motivation. Aristotle argued that the soul is free (**free will**) and that the mind at birth is a **blank slate** (Boring, 1950). Aristotle's first idea is often contrasted to the idea of **determinism**, which proposes that all behavior is the result of conditions that precede the behavior. In psychology these preceding conditions are known as **antecedent variables**.

Each of us has some opinion about the free will versus determinism controversy, but psychology, for the most part, has chosen to disagree with Aristotle and embrace determinism. Determinism as it applies to psychology assumes that *every behavior has a cause*. If behavior Y occurs, some antecedent condition X must have caused it. Thus if you observe someone eating, you will probably assume that an antecedent condition called hunger led to the eating behavior. Though the antecedent conditions that determine behavior are often not observable, psychology nevertheless assumes that some previous condition caused those responses to occur. The

concept of motivation is often proposed as the antecedent condition that leads to responding.

Though modern psychology has generally chosen determinism over free will, Aristotle's idea that the mind is a blank slate (upon which experience writes) had a tremendous influence on psychological theory. Aristotle's concept led to the proposal that most behaviors are learned. The acquisition of behavior through experience is one side of a long-standing argument in psychology known as the **nature–nurture controversy**. Psychologists who accepted Aristotle's premise believed that experience (nurture) is the major force in the development of behavior. In opposition to the nurture psychologists, others proposed that much of our behavior is programmed into us by heredity (nature). This latter group argued that nature provides ready-made behaviors that are executed when conditions are appropriate. Psychological thought on the nature–nurture problem has swung back and forth several times, and the controversy has never been resolved to everyone's satisfaction. Most psychologists today, however, recognize that both sides were right; *behavior is a combination of both nature and nurture.*

The nature–nurture controversy is important to the study of motivation because both nature and nurture play roles in the activation of motive states. As you will discover in later chapters, some motives seem best understood as the result of genetically programmed sequences, while others are clearly learned. Further, motivation may also result from a complex blend of nature and nurture.

Descartes   Aristotle, of course, was only one of many philosophers who influenced psychological thought. Rene Descartes was equally influential. Descartes is best known for his arguments concerning the dualistic nature of humans. **Dualism** proposes that human behavior is partly the result of a free, rational soul and partly the result of automatic, nonrational processes of the body. According to Descartes, humans, being the only possessors of souls, are motivated by both the soul (motives of this type were often called **will**) and the body (motives of this type were later attributed to **instinct**). Animals, however, have no souls and are therefore essentially **automatons** (mechanical beings). This mechanistic approach and Descartes's proposal of **innate ideas** (a view similar to Plato's) became one basis for the instinct psychology that was popular around the turn of the 20th century. Thus, in many respects the nature-nurture controversy can be seen as an outgrowth of the philosophies of Aristotle and Descartes.

Locke Before we leave this necessarily brief exposition of the philosophical roots of motivation, we need to examine some contributions of the British school of philosophy. Two ideas proposed by British philosophers became especially important for psychology. These two ideas concern the importance of sensory experience and the association of ideas. We shall consider the philosophy of John Locke as representative of the British approach, although there were many other noted philosophers within this same framework. Locke proposed that ideas are the elementary units of the mind (Boring, 1950). Further, he thought that these ideas come from experience (nurture again) in one of two ways. One source of ideas is the conversion of **sensation** into **perception**. For example, the conversion of the sensation of light of 521 nanometers leads to the perception of the color green. The idea of green, then, results from experience with particular wavelengths of light, namely, those near 521 nanometers. The second source of ideas, according to Locke, is **reflection**, which occurs when the mind obtains knowledge of its own operations. Thus one can generate ideas from sensory information or from understanding how one manipulates and works with ideas. This second source amounts to "ideas about ideas and the manner of their occurrence" (Boring, 1950, p. 172).

Ideas, according to Locke, can be simple or complex. Because a simple idea is the elementary unit of thought, it is not further analyzable, but a complex idea can be reduced to simple ideas. The concept of complex ideas composed of simple ideas leads naturally to a concept of association. Complex ideas are nothing more than the association of simple ideas to one another. The concept of **association** is one of the most fundamental axioms within psychology. For example, the association of stimulus to stimulus, stimulus to response, response to response, and response to reward have all been offered as the basis for learning. Associationism is equally important to motivation because many motives, especially those peculiar to humans, appear to be learned through association. These "higher" motives are often quite complex but are assumed to gain their motivating properties through earlier association with more basic motives. Through repeated association, these motives can become so strong that the more basic motives with which they were originally paired are no longer necessary. The independence of these higher motives appears similar to Allport's (1937) concept of **functional autonomy**.

Other philosophical approaches have contributed to our understanding of motivation, many more than we have time to consider here. (For the student interested in the philosophical underpinnings of psychology, Boring [1950] is still one of the best references.) It is time to move on to a brief look at discoveries in physiology that have also affected motivational thought.

Physiological Antecedents

Sensory and Motor Nerves Modern conceptions of the role of brain mechanisms in motivation are largely outgrowths of discoveries about how the nervous system gains information and controls behavior. At one time it was thought that nerves allowed the flow of animal spirits from one part of the body to another. The concept of reflex and its close companion, instinct, are outgrowths of the idea that animal spirits coming from the sense organs along one pathway are sent back to the muscles along a separate pathway (Boring, 1950). Galen (circa A.D. 129–199) had correctly guessed that separate **sensory and motor nerves** must exist, but more than 600 years passed before Charles Bell (1811, as cited by Boring, 1950) was able to show that the sensory fibers of a **mixed nerve** (containing both sensory and motor fibers) enter the spinal cord on the posterior side, while the motor fibers exit the cord on the anterior side. In 1822, Magendie made the discovery independent of Bell (Boring, 1950). The discovery of separate sensory and motor fibers led to the study of sensation on one hand and responses on the other. Indeed one might argue that the stimulus-response analysis of behavior, once so popular in psychology, could not exist before this fundamental fact of physiology was known.

Specific Nerve Energies   Once sensory and motors fibers were shown to exist, it was only a short intellectual step to the realization that different fibers must carry different kinds of information. This idea, usually associated with Muller, eventually became known as the **doctrine of specific nerve energies** (Boring, 1950) and was important because it implied that (a) the nerves send specific coded messages rather than allowing for the flow of animal spirits, and (b) these codes determine the content of the information (e.g., different energies for different colors or tones). Thus the nervous system becomes an active, interpreting mechanism rather than a passive conduit for ill-defined and mysterious vapors.

Electrical Nature of the Nerve Impulse   In 1780, Galvani had discovered that a frog's leg could be made to twitch when the muscle of the leg was connected to what amounted to a primitive battery (Boring, 1950). Galvani's experiment suggested that the energy passing through a nerve might be electrical in nature, and somewhat later (1848–1849), DuBois-Reymond used a galvanometer to show that the energy passing along the nerve is indeed electrical. Helmholtz measured the speed of this electrical wave down a nerve and found it to be less than 100 miles per hour. As noted by Boring (1950), Helmholtz's discovery showed that it is possible to study the function of the nervous system through experimental procedures.

Localization of Function   Sometimes theories are important for the development of a science even though they are ultimately proven wrong. One such case was the **phrenology** of Gall in the early 1800s. Gall proposed the idea that particular mental abilities are located in specific regions of the brain. Any excess in a particular ability would lead to an enlargement of that portion of the brain, and as a result, a bump would be created on the skull. According to Gall, one could determine a person's special abilities by feeling the bumps on his or her head (see Figure 1.6). Though Gall's ideas concerning the "reading" of a person's abilities from bumps on the head have been thoroughly discredited, his ideas did promote the further examination of the **localization of function** within various areas of the brain. Today we know a great deal about the function of specific areas of the brain, and motivational theory has been strengthened by the discovery that activity within the **hypothalamus** (a region within the brain) is related to changes in several motivational states. Even though Gall's phrenology is no longer useful, his emphasis on the localization of function within the brain has been very important.

The study of motivation, as you can see, has roots in both philosophy and physiology. Further, motivation has been analyzed both as an act of the will and as the result of activity in specialized brain centers. In Part II of this book we examine theories that have emphasized the biological or physiological aspects of motivation. In Part III we examine theories that have emphasized the role of experience, while in Part IV we examine cognitive interpretations of motivation including social motives as well as approaches that are more philosophical in nature. Rogers and Maslow, for example, have both proposed theories of motivation that are more philosophical than experimental. The complex nature of motivation has resulted in the development of theories from many differing points of view. As we shall see, there is room within motivational

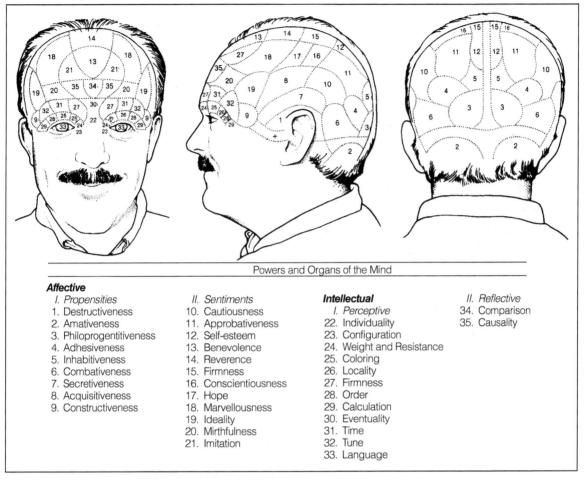

FIGURE 1.6 A phrenology chart showing the locations of presumed abilities. Adapted from Spurzheim, 1908.

theory for physiological, experiential, and cognitive approaches.

The Flow of Ideas about Motivation

In order to better understand some of the topics examined later in this book, it is useful to take a brief look at how concepts about motivation have changed across time.

As we have just seen, modern motivational theory is rooted in earlier philosophical ideas and

physiological discoveries. One final historical note, about the changing perspectives researchers have taken over the years, is worthy of our examination. In the 1800s it was common to distinguish between the behavior of animals and that of humans using Descartes's dualistic distinction. Animals, having no rationality, were instinctively motivated to behave in appropriate ways, whereas humans, having both rationality and instinctive motives, might behave as a result of either of these mechanisms.

In the late 1800s, theorists such as William James (1890) and William McDougall (1970) argued that much of human behavior could be regarded as instinctive, thus playing down the dualistic concept of a rational soul or will. Behaviorists beginning with John Watson (1914), while for the most part rejecting the instinct notion in favor of a learning analysis, also vehemently opposed what they considered the mentalistic approaches common to psychology at that time. As a result, in the early 1900s a strong behaviorist position developed that emphasized the idea that behavior was largely a reaction to the environment, and S-R (stimulus-response) psychology was born. Thorndike's (1913) studies of the importance of the consequences of a response to future behavior were a strong argument in favor of the S-R type of analysis.

The motivation of behavior, then, could be argued to result from the consequences of previous behavior: Pleasurable consequences would be sought again, while aversive consequences would be avoided if possible. The behaviorism of the early 1900s was, in many ways, a return to the concept of hedonism espoused by some Greek philosophers more than 2000 years earlier. The behaviorists, however, had experimental data to show that behaviors did indeed change as a result of their consequences.

By the end of the 1920s, the instinct theories of James and others had been roundly criticized and largely rejected (although, as we shall discover, this rejection was probably premature).

Behaviorism was the dominant theme in psychology, and a new motivational concept, known as drive theory, was touted as the primary motivational basis for behavior. The drive concept, first introduced by Woodworth (1918), proposed that motivated behavior was in response to changing bodily needs that were acted upon by finding those items in the environment that would reduce the drive.

Drive theory reached its zenith of popularity with the publications of Clark Hull (1943, 1951, 1952). Hull proposed a quasi-mathematical theory that indicated the crucial components for the activation of behavior and how these components interacted to produce behavior. In addition, Hull's theory provided the groundwork for analyzing the

contribution of learning to motivation and was partially responsible (as was Tolman and his colleagues) for the eventual development of the concept of incentive motivation.

Eventually, Hull's theory was shown to be inadequate, but the research spawned by the search for the basis of drive led to a greater understanding of how brain mechanisms control, and learning influences, behavior. Indeed, much of the initial physiological research on motivation was a search for the physiological basis of various drive states.

Although behaviorism was the dominant theme in psychology until about 1960, some psychologists took exception to the strong S-R bias during this time. Researchers such as Kohler (1925) and Tolman (1932) argued, and provided experimental data, for an analysis of behavior based on the active processing of information, rather than S-R connections. These forerunners of modern cognitive psychology led the way for those who came later to examine motivation as resulting from an organism's ability to anticipate future events, choose between alternatives, and act in a purposive way.

This alternative view of motivation has proven fruitful in a number of ways. Research on the motivational consequences of attributions of cause-effect has led to a greater understanding of behaviors associated with the need to achieve, social learning, and even emotion. Similarly, research on the purposive and goal-oriented nature of motivated behavior has led to the development of expectancy-value theory, a concept that has proven useful in understanding achievement behavior, social loafing, and the link between attitudes and behavior.

It is often convenient, when thinking about how things work, to use metaphors as a way of describing how something looks or behaves. Thus we sometimes talk of a person "working like a horse" or being as "timid as a mouse." Weiner (1991) has proposed that many of the concepts and research about human motivation can be understood as relating to two basic metaphors: the **machine metaphor** and the **Godlike metaphor**. The implications of the machine metaphor suggest that motivation is largely involuntary and reflex-like. The motivated person does not need to understand or even be aware of the reasons why he or she acts, because the reactions are predetermined. Thus, as noted by Weiner (1991, p. 922), "The behaviors are performed without conscious awareness." Much of motivational research from 1930 to 1960 fits the machine metaphor. The research described in the first half of this book typifies this approach. The second metaphor, the Godlike metaphor, derives from the belief that "humans were created by God and in the image of God" (Weiner, 1991, p. 921). Therefore, our behavior should be based on qualities associated with God, such as being all knowing, loving, merciful, and all powerful. The implications of this second metaphor for understanding human motivation suggest that people behave rationally (i.e., we make informed judgments about situations) and purposefully (we work to obtain specific, known goals). Additionally, we are aware of the reasons that we behave as we do (God as all knowing). Motivational research conducted between 1960 and 1980 often exemplifies this metaphor. As noted by Weiner, this view of motivation is probably too optimistic. People do not always behave rationally, or even in their own best interests. He suggests that another attribute (God as final judge) of the Godlike metaphor has influenced our thinking about motivational processes since the 1980s. There has been a downplaying of the idea of rationality and more emphasis placed on the role of how social situations are evaluated, with special emphasis placed on the role of emotion in those evaluations. Much of the research in the second half of this book can be viewed as illustrative of the Godlike metaphor (in its two forms).

Although no single theory can explain all that we know about motivation, one theory that appears to provide a reason for motivated behavior is evolution.

Evolution and Motivation

In this section we will argue that, ultimately, motivation for specific behaviors can be traced back to the most fundamental process of life: reproduction of genetic information.

Life

Life is defined by the Encarta 96 CD-ROM Encyclopedia (see also the Encyclopaedia Britannica) as the activity characteristic of organisms and encompasses two broad categories: reproduction and metabolism. As the term **reproduction** implies, living organisms are defined by the fact that they can replicate themselves. **Metabolism** involves the conversion of energy for use by the organism and is necessary for survival. The maintenance of life through metabolism allows organisms to live long enough to reproduce. Therefore, one can argue that the maintenance of life is in the service of reproduction. Darwin was perhaps the first person to note this, although most of his writing emphasized survival and the struggle for existence (Dawkins, 1986).

Reproduction, in turn, is the mechanism for maintaining genetic information. Richard Dawkins (1986, p. 126) states this idea even more forcefully: "... living organisms *exist* for the benefit of DNA rather than the other way around." From his perspective, organisms are simply the temporary receptacles that allow information stored in the genes to continue to exist across time. Organisms are, so to speak, the paper upon which the book of life is written.

Mitosis and Meiosis

Reproduction typically occurs in one of two ways. **Mitosis** is a process in which a single cell divides into two identical daughter cells. This type of reproduction is **asexual**; the same genetic information is contained in each of the new cells. Many bacteria reproduce in this manner. **Meiosis** is a process in which two specialized cells (each with half the number of chromosomes of a normal cell) are produced by a female and a male and are then later combined to form a new cell that includes genetic information from each of the two individual cells. The new cell multiplies and produces a new living organism that is genetically different from its parents but carries genes from both. This type of reproduction is **sexual reproduction** and the new organism so formed is not identical to either of the parent cells. Many plants and animals (including humans) reproduce sexually. Some organisms (such as certain fungi) are capable of reproducing either asexually or sexually depending upon circumstances. However, all organisms considered to be alive reproduce themselves. Viruses (which may or may not be alive) also have the ability to reproduce once inside a living cell but do not convert energy (metabolism) on their own. So, taking our cue from the life cycle of the virus, one could argue that reproduction is a more fundamental process than even metabolism. In fact, one theory of how life may have begun is that complex, nonliving chemicals somehow gained the ability to replicate themselves. Eventually, living organisms evolved from these nonliving replicating chemicals.

Because resources are limited, living organisms are in constant competition with one another. The survival of the individual is viciously and tenaciously defended at all costs because the survival of the individual's genetic information is dependent on the successful reproduction of that individual or related individuals who share some of the individual's genes.

In order to promote the survival of one's genes, life must be maintained until those genes can be replicated in a new generation. And because all living organisms must convert energy in order to live, one is again drawn to the conclusion that reproduction is the more fundamental process.

Viewed from this perspective, important primary motives such as hunger, thirst, sex, and the avoidance of pain, as well as numerous uniquely human motives such as the need for power, achievement, and so forth serve to maintain and/or enhance life in order to increase the chances of reproduction. One could say, then, that *motivation ultimately serves the reproduction of genetic information of the individual.*

However, successfully reproducing one's genes may not be enough. The future is uncertain and dangerous: Successful reproduction of multiple copies of one's genes increases the likelihood that at least one of those copies will be contained within an individual who will also live long enough to reproduce and pass that information on. Thus, sexual motivation should not diminish when successful reproduction occurs, but should continue throughout the reproductive period of an organism's life.

Sex

In mitosis, two copies of the genetic information each contained within a separate cell is produced from the genetic information of a single cell and requires no outside interaction with other cells. The sexual reproduction following meiosis, however, requires that a suitable partner cell be found so that one's genetic information can be continued. This creates a new problem: how best to find the partner. Although in single-celled organisms floating in a fluid medium one might expect couplings to take place pretty much at random, such a mechanism probably would not work well in multicelled land animals. As a result, we might predict that a mechanism would evolve by which an organism would actively seek out a partner. Sexual motivation would seem to be such a mechanism.

Furthermore, organisms with the strongest sexual motivation would be expected to be more successful in finding suitable partners and successfully mating than their less highly motivated competitors so that organisms with strong sexual motivation would eventually become the norm. The survival advantage of having multiple copies of one's genetic information should also have reinforced strong sexual motivation. The more times that one's genetic information is replicated and passed on in the form of a new organism, the more likely that that genetic information will continue to exist in the future. So, in essence, all organisms living today represent the ancestral "winners" in the competition for limited resources. But the game never ends; all organisms alive today compete to provide the players for the next round of the game.

In our species, a person might decide that he or she does not want any more children (or none at all), but this is an intellectual decision, not a biological one. The biological imperative to replicate must somehow be built into our cells, and although one might choose not to reproduce for personal reasons, the urge is still there. Humans are probably the only organism consciously able to decide not to reproduce. (Some animals appear to limit reproduction depending upon environmental conditions; however, there is no evidence that they do so intentionally.)

The Advantages of Sexual Reproduction

Because life is a continual competition both among members of a species as well as across species for a limited set of resources, any mechanism that provides an advantage should be retained. Sexual reproduction exists because it provided such an advantage.

Sexual reproduction would seem to be advantageous for several reasons. First, sexual reproduction produces a recombination of the genes of the two parents, thus providing offspring that possess new genetic combinations that provide a **greater diversity of genes** for survival in an uncertain and varying environment (Alberts, Bray, Lewis, Raff, Roberts, & Watson, 1989). In asexually reproducing species, changes to the genetic code would appear to depend primarily on mutations or errors of transcription when the cells divide. Changes would occur, but rather slowly. Because sexual reproduction involves the pairing of genetic information from two individuals, new combinations will occur more rapidly and these new combinations will then be subject to natural selection. As a result, *sexually reproducing species should evolve faster* to changing environmental conditions, giving them a competitive advantage.

A second potentially important advantage of sexual reproduction is that it can allow "repair" of genetic information within the gene pool. Individuals can carry genes that predispose them to certain diseases or problems. If these genes are recessive, they may not become apparent until the next generation when they are combined with the same recessive gene from a sexual partner. If the expression of the recessive gene is lethal early on, then the individual will die before passing the gene on through reproduction, and the probability of the lethal gene occurring in the overall population is kept relatively low. On the other hand, if the parent has one recessive gene that is not expressed and one dominant gene that is expressed, sexual reproduction with a partner who does not have the lethal gene can produce some individuals in the next generation who do not carry the lethal gene at all. For those fortunate individuals, the maladaptive gene carried by one of its parents has in a sense been "fixed" by the process of sexual reproduction (Alberts et al., 1989).

Because sexually reproducing species have two copies of each gene, it is possible for only one of the two copies to mutate. If this is a beneficial mutation then offspring will have the potential advantage of both the "old" gene's benefits as well as the "new" gene's benefits. Thus, sexual reproduction allows beneficial mutations to spread rapidly within the gene pool, without losing the benefits of the original gene, and through the additional processes of genetic duplication and recombination, both the "old" beneficial gene and the "new" beneficial gene can become separate genes (Alberts et al., 1989).

The Pleasures of Sex

In humans—and perhaps some other species as well (see, e.g., deWaal, 1995) sexual behavior can be intensely pleasurable. The pleasurable sensations produced by sexual behavior provide a means by which the chances of successful reproduction are increased; if the processes involved in conception were extremely painful, fewer people would engage in such behavior and successful reproduction would be reduced. (This same argument does not apply to the birth process; pleasure needs to be associated only with conception in order for reproduction to proceed.) Although people are most often motivated by the pleasure that sexual behavior provides, that same pleasure increases the probability that successful reproduction will occur by increasing the frequency of mating attempts.

The fact that human males often do not want to wear condoms while engaging in sexual behavior (because it reduces their pleasurable sensations) increases the chances of reproduction by those same males. Educating persons in "safe sex" behaviors, in an era of sexually transmitted diseases that can be lethal, is hampered by the evolution of mechanisms millions of years in the making that promote reproduction at all costs.

The primacy of reproduction over life itself is evident in some organisms. The male Australian Redback spider becomes a meal for the female spider after sexual behavior has occurred. Male Redback spiders that position themselves directly above the female's jaws during sexual behavior copulate longer, fertilizing more eggs, and reduce copulation by competing males (because the female is less likely to mate again after consuming the male). From the perspective of successful replication of one's genes, the male spider's behavior is adaptive because his genetic information is more likely to continue than a male spider who does not behave in this way; individually, it is a disaster and lends new meaning to the term "to die for love."

Similar tendencies to risk one's life for the next generation (of one's genes) can be seen in the aggressive behavior of many animal mothers when their offspring are threatened. Just one example of many can be found in the research of Figler, Twum, Finklestein, and Peeke (1995), which examines the factors contributing to the aggressive behavior of maternal crayfish.

Some might argue that sexual motivation is not as important as the previously mentioned analysis suggests because many animals engage in sexual behavior only rarely, and sexual behavior usually occurs only when the female is receptive. These points, however, really show just the opposite; that is, reproduction is so important that the behaviors leading to impregnation must be reserved to those times when they are most likely to produce offspring. As Emilie Rissman (1995) notes, mammals evolved in the tropics where sexual receptivity tends to be year round, but researchers most often study animals that live in temperate zones where seasonal changes in temperature, food, and so forth make successful reproduction more likely at certain times of the year than at others. As a result of these seasonal changes, it is thought that cyclic sexual receptivity evolved to restrict sexual behavior to those times when successful reproduction was most likely to occur.

In humans and perhaps some other primates such as the Bonobo (see deWaal, 1995), sexual behavior has been somewhat uncoupled (pun intended) from reproduction. Humans and Bonobos engage in sex for reasons other than reproduction; however, those reasons (e.g., reducing aggression, social bonding, gaining access to food) also increase the chances of living long enough to successfully reproduce. So even sexual behavior not directly aimed at reproduction would nevertheless seem to ultimately promote it.

In modern society, the importance of sexual motivation can be seen in yet another way. The implication that certain products increase one's chances of engaging in sexual behavior is used to sell virtually everything from deodorants to cars. The story lines of novels, short stories, poems, and other works of literature also emphasize relationships (e.g., unrequited love). These depictions probably work because the frustrations and joys of these relationships are something with which we can all connect and have some experience. But without reproduction as the fundamental motive, and sexual motivation as the means to this end, there is no obvious need for relationships at all. Incidentally, the story lines of many of the works we find meaningful often seem to fit the differing biological strategies of reproduction for men and women that have been noted by many researchers and which will be discussed later in this chapter. Finally, the prevalence of sexually explicit literature and images from ancient times through the present also speaks volumes about how strong the motive for sexual behavior is, as do the attempts that society has made to try to control it.

Interim Summary

Let us now organize what we know about motivation around the ideas mentioned earlier. The earlier mentioned analysis suggests that the most fundamental motive for all living organisms is reproduction. Other motives seem aimed at keeping the individual alive long enough for this fundamental motive to be successfully accomplished. In essence, then, the primary motive of all living organisms is to reproduce. (Motive here seems a little out of place since plants and single-celled organisms in this usage are also "motivated." Perhaps it would make more sense to speak of reproduction as the **primary operating principle** carried on by living organisms. The various motives, then, serve to increase the likelihood of this operating principle occurring successfully.)

If we assume that all motivation is, in the final analysis, aimed at successful reproduction of one's genetic information (at least through the child-bearing years), then the problem of understanding motivation does not revolve around the issue of when we are motivated and when we are not, but rather concerns how motivation (which is always present) is focused at different times. Sometimes we are hungry or thirsty. At other times we are sexually motivated or may be motivated to escape or avoid pain. Humans are also sometimes motivated by a need for power, glory, money, status, or any number of other things material or immaterial; however, all of these motives are tied to reproduction in the sense that successfully obtaining them influences one's chances of mating and successfully reproducing.

Higher Motives?

The question of higher motives, not related to reproduction, in humans is a difficult one to answer. Some writers such as Maslow (1973a,b),

Rogers (1961), and Peck (1978) have argued persuasively for them. For example, in Maslow's system, self-actualization, for those few people for whom it occurs, higher motives become a force later in life after the prime reproductive period has passed. However, since Maslow estimates that only about 1% of the population ever becomes self-actualized, one could argue that for most people these higher motives never significantly influence behavior. Furthermore, the analysis of motivation outlined earlier is consistent across animal species and seems to apply to the largest percentage of humans.

On the other hand, the prevalence of, and demand for, popular books on topics that could be loosely categorized as "one's search for meaning" suggest that for a substantial number of people meaningfulness is a significant motive. In informal class discussions of this topic, one of the authors (HP) has found that virtually all college students believe that people are motivated by more than just reproduction. The basis for this belief would be an interesting line of research in its own right. In Chapter 6 we will explore the ideas of meaningfulness (Klinger, 1975, 1977) and the idea that humans have a need to control the environment around them and to feel that they are effective in doing so. Whether such evidence is best considered separate from or subsidiary to motives serving the reproductive process remains an open question.

The replication of one's genetic information, then, would appear to be the basis for all other motives in animals and for most humans too. Let us look a little closer then at the processes involved in this replication, starting with the concept of evolution.

Evolution

Evolution can be defined as the progressive change of organisms across time (Solbrig, 1966). The theory of evolution is usually credited to Charles Darwin (1899), though Alfred Wallace independently developed the same idea. Both men presented papers on the topic at the same meeting in 1858. Richard Dawkins (1976) has noted that the theory of evolution is really another way of expressing the idea that those elements that are the most stable will continue to exist. Some members of a group of organisms will be less able to cope with the rigors of the environment in which they live and will thus die. Other members of the group will be better adapted to the environment and will be able to survive and therefore pass on their adaptive characteristics to the succeeding generation. Thus an interaction between one's genetic makeup and the environment in which one finds herself or himself leads to a process called natural selection.

Natural Selection

The environment is important in determining which members of a group survive. Through a process that Darwin termed **natural selection**, the environment influences the progression of genetic change. Those individuals who inherited genes that give them an advantage in the environment have a better chance of living long enough to reproduce, while those with inherited genes that put them at a disadvantage have a greater likelihood of dying before they have a chance to reproduce. In this way the disadvantageous genes are eventually removed from the gene pool of the species.

According to a summary by Hoyenga and Hoyenga (1984; who cite the work of Caspari, 1965), natural selection has an influence on three characteristics of genes. These three characteristics are **viability**, **fertility**, and **fecundity**.

Viability concerns whether a gene that expresses a certain behavior will increase the likelihood of the individual who possesses that gene living long enough to reproduce. Genes that increase viability will remain in the gene pool, while genes that reduce viability will eventually get eliminated from the gene pool. An example of such a situation is **distress calls** in baby chicks. When baby chicks are separated from their mother they emit a loud, high-pitched call that causes the mother hen to come looking for them. Presumably, this behavior exists in chicks today because it increased the viability of those individual chicks that behaved that way. Chicks that did not emit distress calls would have been more likely to have suffered fatal experiences and thus their genes would have been removed from the gene pool.

Fertility, according to Hoyenga and Hoyenga (1984), concerns mating success. Many species have evolved elaborate **mating rituals** that determine, at least in part, who will be selected for mating. For example, in some bird species the male engages in a dance to attract a mating partner. Females select a male with which to mate based on the dance. Genes controlling minor differences in the dance would be retained if those genes lead to a more "attractive" dance, while genes that lead to a less attractive dance will tend to be eliminated over time.

Fecundity involves the number of offspring produced. The more fecund an animal, the more offspring it produces. Any gene that increases fecundity will be retained, while any gene that reduces fecundity will eventually be removed from the gene pool. Although fecundity increases the number of offspring, many, perhaps most, will not live to reproduce (as can be observed in many species of fish that produce millions of offspring yet few survive to maturity). So the advantage of fecundity is that larger numbers of offspring increase the probability that some will survive to maturity and reproduce. Some species, such as humans, produce fewer offspring but invest heavily in those that are produced, increasing the chances that they will live to reproduce. Thus, fecundity is not the only useful strategy for continuing one's genetic information.

Although it would be difficult to prove, it seems likely that strong sexual motivation in the males of many species would increase fecundity. Male sexual behavior is often opportunistic, and the male's readiness to mate at almost any time is well known in many species. Such behavior on the part of males is probably under at least some genetic control and exists today because males that possessed this trait produced more offspring than males who were not opportunistic.

Sexual Selection

There is also a special class of natural selection processes known as **sexual selection** (Darwin, 1871). Sexual selection occurs when there is a competition for mates, or when one member of a mating pair is "chosen" by the other member of the pair. In species in which sexual selection occurs, the choice of a sexual partner is usually made by the female. Thus sexual selection is generally a **selection pressure** exerted on the genes of the males of a species. This selection pressure seems to affect primarily fertility; any characteristic, either physical or behavioral, that gives a male an advantage over his competitors in being chosen by a female will lead to greater mating success. Sexual selection would seem to be the basis for physical characteristics such as bright coloration (e.g. the male peacock's tail feathers), or a lioness's preference for males with dark manes (West & Packer, 2002; Withgott, 2002), and the sometimes seemingly bizarre behaviors observed in males of some species such as the male sage grouse strutting displays to attract female grouse (Schroeder, Young, & Braun, 1999).

Female versus Male Sexual Strategies

Why should sexual selection be a pressure that is usually exerted on the genes of the male of the species? The answer would appear to be related to the fact that the female of many species has two major concerns in attempting to insure that her genetic information is passed on. The first is that in species where sexual selection occurs, the female has a rather limited number of "genetic packets" (ova) that are available to be passed on. For example, a human female who begins to produce viable eggs at 13 years old and continues to do so to the age of 45 will have slightly less than 400 chances to pass her genetic information on to the next generation. Most of these chances will, in fact, be missed. Symons (1979) has estimated that a female in a hunter-gatherer society could expect to produce four to five offspring. Trivers (1985) argues that about 20% of these offspring will die within the first year of life, which means that, under optimal

circumstances, only about four children carrying the mother's genes might live long enough to also reproduce, assuming they do not die as a result of disease or accident.

The second concern the female encounters in trying to ensure the survival of her genetic information is the developmental period during which the offspring must be maintained before they are capable of maintaining themselves. If this developmental period is long, as it is in humans, then a great deal of time and effort must be invested to insure the survival of the offspring.

These two concerns make mate choice a more important decision for the female than the male (see the next section). The female's optimal strategy should be to select a mate who will provide her offspring (and thus her genes) with the greatest chance of survival. The female should, therefore, be very selective in choosing a mating partner. For humans, traits in the male associated with resource accumulation and investment in the young should be favored.

On the other hand, the male of many species produces millions of "genetic packets" (sperm) a day. Because production of this genetic information is so high, it may be dispersed with little concern of running out. The optimal strategy for the male, therefore, would be to mate with as many females as possible in order to pass his genetic information on to the next generation. Such a strategy would, in fact, account for the opportunistic sexual behavior noted earlier in the males of many species.

Mate Selection in Humans

The earlier considerations suggest that in our species men and women ought to be attracted by different qualities in the mates they seek. Evolutionary theory predicts that women ought to be attracted to men who possess the resources to support them and any children they produce because women have a larger investment in their offspring than do men. This evolutionary approach to attraction has come to be called the **parental investment model** (Trivers, 1972, 1985). Men, therefore, in their competition to obtain mates, ought to be motivated to engage in behaviors that **display their resources**. In a series of experiments, Buss (1988) found that men do appear to display their resources (e.g., expensive cars, stereos, buying of gifts) as predicted. Additionally, Feingold (1992) tested the parental investment model in a meta-analysis and, in support of Buss, found that women accorded more weight (than men) to socioeconomic status, ambitiousness, character, and intelligence in attraction to a member of the opposite sex. The burgeoning field of evolutionary psychology has in fact accumulated an impressive amount of evidence that resource accumulation is an important attractant for women (see, e.g., Buss, 2008).

Similarly, women might be expected to compete for men who have the best resources. It has been suggested that there is also a sexual selection pressure exerted on women by men because the selection of a mate in humans is not only at the discretion of the woman (Buss, 1988). According to evolutionary theory, such competition should revolve around **reproductive value**. Reproductive value is associated with youthfulness and health (Symons, 1979) and is generally indicated by physical appearance and attractiveness (Buss, 1988). Therefore, evolutionary theory predicts that women, competing among themselves for desirable men, will be motivated to engage in behaviors that enhance their appearance. Buss's (1988) study confirms that women do enhance their appearance as predicted. Although it is not possible, at this time, to say that mate preference in humans is genetically determined, the preferences people express do fit the evolutionary model (Bjorklund & Shackelford, 1999; see Miller, Putcha-Bhagavatula, & Pedersen, 2002, for a different point of view).

The point is that natural selection will lead to the survival of organisms that cope best with their environment. Thus, genes that control the expressions of particular behaviors will be continued in a species if the behaviors expressed are adaptive.

Of course, not all behaviors are genetically determined. Many, perhaps most, are learned through interactions of the organism with its environment during its lifetime. These behaviors are not passed on to the next generation. However, the ability to learn new behaviors during one's lifetime must surely be genetically determined. The ability to learn enabled organisms to survive because it made them more adaptable to changes in their environment. Thus we can see that even the ability to learn must have a genetic basis.

What all this means is that some types of behaviors may be genetically determined, such as a moth's attraction to light (called **positive phototaxis**), while other behaviors may be the result of experience, such as remembering where you last found food. Motivated behaviors, therefore, should include both types (i.e., either relatively fixed and rigid behaviors or relatively flexible and open behaviors easily modified), and indeed some behaviors are likely to be combinations of both genetic and learned components.

Historically, the study of genetically motivated behaviors has often been discussed under the topic of **instinct**. An instinct can be regarded as a genetically programmed bit of behavior that occurs when circumstances are appropriate and that requires no learning of the behavior. As we shall see, early instinct approaches were often vague; but later instinct theories, such as those of the ethologists, were much more carefully and clearly defined.

Instincts, Emotion, Thoughts and Behavior

James (1890), from his writings on psychology, can be interpreted as emphasizing three important components in human behavior. These are instincts, emotions, and thoughts. (These three sources of behavior could also interact with each other in various ways as noted by James.)

James's writings seem very apt today. One source of motivation comes from mechanisms built into the nervous system as a result of millions of years of evolution. He called these sources of behavior instincts. A second source of motivation is associated with the experience of emotion. We behave differently when angry than when sad, happy, fearful, or ashamed. Our motivation (and subsequent behavior) depends, in part, on our emotional state. Although James was more concerned with how emotions occurred, it is clear that he realized that emotions also influenced future behavior (James, 1994/1936). Current thinking suggests that emotions may be thought of as genetically predisposed biases to behave in a particular way that had adaptive value in our ancestral past. For example, feeling fearful when threatened by a large animal and subsequently withdrawing from the vicinity of the animal would have been adaptive because it reduced the likelihood of being injured.

Finally, James recognized the role of thoughts in our behavior. He called this process ideo-motor action. Although his thoughts about ideo-motor action are more complex than we can cover here, his ideas presaged the current emphasis on cognitive processes in the understanding of motivation.

The Authors' Bias

It is important at the outset for the reader to understand the point of view of the authors of this text, because the rest of the book will reflect our bias to a greater or lesser extent. From our vantage point, no one theory can explain all the data on motivation. Explanations of hunger will differ from explanations of achievement. It is naive to believe that one comprehensive theory can explain all motivational states. The reason is quite simply that motivation is **multiply determined**. The processes that undergird the physiologically important motives are different from the processes that undergird psychological motives. The only obvious overriding principle that is apparent in motivational research is that various systems have evolved to solve motivational concerns; however, those systems control behavior differently depending upon the motive in question. Some motives are innately expressed, some are learned, some are automatic, and some are the result of cognitive decision processes. These processes that exist in present-day organisms are there because at some point in time they were evolutionarily adaptive.

Motivation also appears to be **overdetermined**. Like the space shuttle, the human body has "backup systems" that come into play if one mechanism fails. One example of this is seen in a rat that has been lesioned in its ventromedial hypothalamus. After destruction of this part of the brain, the rat eats and eats and eats, sometimes increasing its weight by 100%. It does not, however, eat until it explodes. At some point, a new stable body weight (albeit obese) is reached, and its weight becomes regulated around this new point. The apparent conclusion is that a second mechanism regulating body weight at the new, higher level has become activated.

Finally, it is important to note that in this age of rapidly expanding information, what we know can change very quickly. For this reason, it is important to keep an open mind about how the processes underlying motivation work. As new information becomes available, motivational concepts change.

The content of this book, then, is mostly eclectic. Various approaches will be examined and supportive research cited. In addition, basic assumptions of the approaches will be noted as well as basic problems. This text is not an exhaustive review of the research literature because that is not the purpose of this book. Extensive reviews of specialized topics within motivation can be found in various journals (e.g., *Psychological Bulletin, Psychological Review*, as well as in the *Annual Review of Psychology*) and other more specialized texts. For your convenience, important terms are boldfaced here for easy review.

Because motivation cuts across so many different subfields within psychology, its study often seems rather disjointed, with the various theories having little relationship to one another. Although such a perception is in some cases at least partially correct, the unity of motivation as a field of study comes from attempting to determine how these differing motivational factors (biological, behavioral, cognitive) interact to produce behavior.

In an attempt to provide a unifying theme to the studies within this text, we will include in appropriate chapters information about sexual and aggressive motivation as understood from the point of view of theories within those chapters. It is hoped that, as a result, readers will understand that every motivated behavior has many components and that only when we understand these various components and how they interact can we hope to understand why people behave as they do.

SUMMARY

This chapter has examined how theorists and researchers conceptualize and measure motivation. As we have seen, motivation is difficult to measure because it is a complex and varied concept. Information about motivation processes indicates that some motives have an innate component, while others are learned. In addition, social processes and cognitions play a large role in determining the motivation of individuals. Needs for competence, control, and growth also influence the way we behave. Although the reasons we are motivated to behave the way we do are varied, we can generally say that motivation concerns the activation and direction of behavior and is indexed by changes in intensity and persistence. Further, one can get some idea about which of two (or more) events are more motivating by measuring preferences for those events.

The study of motivation has its roots in philosophy and physiology. Philosophical and biological concepts such as free will versus determinism, nature versus nurture, dualism, and the fact that sensory and motor nerves control different functions and that electrical coded messages are sent up and down nerve fibers have helped us to understand how the brain controls motivated behavior. The discovery that specific areas of the brain control specific types of behavior (localization of function) and especially the role of the hypothalamus in basic motives has been important to understanding motivational processes.

Motivation is studied at many different levels using many different techniques. Some researchers study the basic mechanisms of motivation by looking at how groups of cells within the brain control basic motivational processes, or how various neurotransmitters may contribute to changes in motivated behavior. Lesion studies, electrical and chemical stimulation studies, EEG and depth electrode studies, as well as PET and MRI scans, are also used to help us understand motivation. Motivation is also studied at the individual and group levels, and cognitive studies have become important windows looking into motivational processes, especially complex, human motives.

Except for the overarching principle that most, if not all, motives are ultimately in the service of replication of one's DNA, this text is largely eclectic. Theories that best explain one motive are often not the best explanation for other motives. Motivation is complexly determined, and no one explanation can account for all that we know about the processes of motivation. As a result, we have chosen to organize theory and research on motivation as falling within one of three basic categories: biological explanations, behavioral explanations, or cognitive explanations. Although such a system is clearly oversimplified, it nevertheless provides a framework within which one can think about motivation.

This chapter has also examined how the motives that impel our behavior are related to a more basic process shared by all living things—to keep their genetic information alive through reproduction. The study of evolutionary processes allows us to understand motives and their associated behaviors as ultimately serving this purpose by keeping the organism alive, healthy, capable of reproduction, and by providing behaviors to keep the next generation alive until they too can continue the process.

Evolutionary theory suggests that what men and women find attractive in a mate will depend upon an individual's need to continue his or her genes into the next generation. Research tells us that the sexual strategies of males and females often differ as does the characteristics that one looks for in a mate. Men generally appear to be more attracted by health and youthfulness, while women are more likely to be attracted by the male's available resources to help raise the children produced.

Furthermore, we have seen that the motivation of behavior will depend not only on genetically determined predispositions, but also on the conditions of the surrounding environment, learned behaviors, and interpretations of environmental events that we might loosely call thoughts (at least for humans). In the following chapters we will examine these various motives on an individual basis and will see that even for so-called simple motives the processes involved can be quite complex. However, it is useful to keep in mind that all individual motives in nonhuman animals would ultimately seem to serve the more basic goal of continuing the flow of genetic information across succeeding generations. Whether this idea is true for humans as well continues to be debated.

KEY TERMS

intensity/persistence, *4*

deprivation/intervening variable/performance variable, *5*

activation, *6*

vigor/directionality/preference test/nomothetic approach, *7*

idiographic approach/instincts/ needs/goals, *8*

electrodes, *9*

canula/lesion/record/neurons/ EEG/depth electrodes/ Positron-emission tomography (PET) scans/MRI/fMRI, *10*

situational factors/presence of others, *11*

aversive state/self-actualization/ positive state, *12*

energy/general/specific, *13*

evolutionary psychology/ modeling/active information processing/peripheral/local receptors/central receptors, *14*

homeostasis/hedonism/growth motivation, *15*

free will/blank slate/ determinism/antecedent variables/nature-nurture controversy/dualism/will, *16*

instinct/automatons/innate ideas/sensation/perception/ reflection/association/ functional autonomy/sensory and motor nerves, *17*

mixed nerve/doctrine of specific nerve energies/phrenology/ localization of function/ hypothalamus, *18*

machine metaphor/Godlike metaphor, *20*

reproduction/metabolism/ mitosis/asexual/meiosis, *21*

sexual reproduction, *22*

greater diversity of genes, *23*

primary operating principle, *25*

natural selection/viability/ fertility/fecundity/distress calls/mating rituals, *26*

sexual selection/selection pressure/parental investment model, *27*

display their resources/ reproductive value/positive phototaxis, *28*

multiply determined/ overdetermined, *29*

SUGGESTIONS FOR FURTHER READING

Bjorklund, D. F., & Shackelford, T. K. (1999). Differences in parental investment contribute to important differences between men and women. *Current Directions in Psychological Science, 8,* 86–89. This article provides evidence that the different sexual strategies employed by males and females can be understood as relating to parental investment.

Boring, E. G. (1950). *A History of Experimental Psychology*. New York: Appleton-Century-Crofts. This is still one of the best references for understanding the relationship of psychology to philosophy and physiology.

Dawkins, R. (1995). *River Out of Eden: A Darwinian View of Life*. New York: Basic Books. Dawkins provides a very readable account of Darwinian explanations for why we behave the ways that we do.

Schultz, D. P., & Schultz, S. E. (2012). *A History of Modern Psychology*, (10th ed.), Belmont, CA, Cengage Learning.

Weiner, B. (1991). Metaphors in motivation and attribution. *American Psychologist*, *46*, 921–930. Weiner provides an excellent analysis of the various ways that motivation has been conceptualized.

Wertheimer, M. (1987). *A Brief History of Psychology* (3rd ed.). New York: Holt, Rinehart & Winston. This text provides a brief and easy-to-read account of the major approaches in psychology.

WEB RESOURCE

http://www.pbs.org/wgbh/evolution/

PART II

PHYSIOLOGICAL MECHANISMS OF MOTIVATION

CHAPTER 2

Genetic Contributions to Motivated Behavior

CHAPTER PREVIEW

This chapter is concerned with the following questions:

1. Are some motives genetic in human and nonhuman animals?

2. What did early instinct theories emphasize?

3. How does classical ethology explain behavior?

4. How do more recent genetic theories explain motivated behavior?

Imagine two men competing with each other to be chosen by a mate. One has a naturally healthy complexion. The other is actually terminally ill but has recourse to bright ochers. He uses some belladonna to dilate his pupils and dabs oil of muskrat behind his ear. Through this clever sexual culture, it is possible that the ill man can outdo the healthy one in the display-and-attraction stakes and be chosen as the woman's mate. Of course, this may turn out to be bad news for the woman, as she may have to raise the child alone, but her consolation is that the child will have clever, culture-using genes on board (Taylor, 1997, p.1894).

This brief scenario can be used to illustrate the major thrust of this chapter, which is that some motivated behaviors are genetically programmed into the nervous system. In this example what is programmed in appears to be the ability to learn to use materials from the environment to enhance one's appearance, or perhaps, more generally, the ability to deceive others. Considerable research on the genetic components of behavior has been conducted by biologists. Though much of this research has studied birds, fish, and other nonhuman animals as subjects, there has been some research on genetically programmed behavior in humans. This research indicates that humans do appear to possess some genetically programmed behaviors.

For example, Eibl-Eibesfeldt (1972) found that when one human recognizes another, a set pattern of behaviors occurs. A person recognizing someone smiles and briefly raises his or her eyebrows. These behaviors signal the other person that he or she has been seen as familiar; usually that person responds similarly by smiling and briefly raising his or her eyebrows. Eibl-Eibesfeldt found that this greeting ceremony is universal across all the cultures (both primitive and advanced) he studied. It is a bit of genetically programmed behavior that communicates recognition between humans and probably serves to reduce the possible threat involved in approaching someone.

Genetically motivated behaviors have often been analyzed under the topic of **instinct**. An instinct can be regarded as a genetically programmed bit of behavior that occurs when circumstances are appropriate and that requires no learning of the behavior. In this chapter we will examine the various instinctive explanations for motivated behavior. As we shall see, early instinct approaches were often vague, but later instinct theories, such as those of the ethologists, have been much more carefully and clearly defined, and work continues today in a branch of psychology known as evolutionary psychology.

Early Instinct Theories

Instinct as an explanation for motivated behavior in both humans and animals reached its peak of popularity in the late 1800s and early 1900s. Beach (1955) noted that the popularity of the concept was due in part to its use as a theoretical bridge between humans and animals. This bridge was important for any development of the idea that evolution applied to both humans and animals and to both physical structure and mind. Thus, for some theorists, animals were seen as having some rationality in addition to instinctive behaviors, and humans were seen as having some instinctively controlled behavior in addition to a rational mind.

As the concept of instinct grew in popularity, it became fashionable to explain all behaviors as instinctive. This led to what has been called the **nominal fallacy** (i.e., simply naming something an instinct does not explain the behavior). For example, if we saw someone behaving aggressively, we might try to explain that behavior in terms of an aggressive instinct. The problem, however, is that we really have not explained anything; we have merely labeled the behavior. To explain the behavior, we must do more. We must understand what

conditions led to the behavior and what consequences resulted from it. Explanation presumes a cause-and-effect relationship, and labeling a behavior does not give causal information.

Also, instinctive behaviors were not clearly separated from learned behaviors because a confusion of definition existed. These problems, along with several others, eventually led to virtual elimination of the instinct concept.

Nevertheless, the early instinct approaches were important because they emphasized the continuity of human and animal behavior and because they provided a base from which the later ethological theories could build. In addition, the problems they encountered eventually led to the refinement of the concept of instinct.

To gain some feeling for these early approaches, we will examine the instinct theories of William James and William McDougall, noting similarities as well as problems in their approaches.

William James

William James, whose writing spanned both philosophical and psychological thought, believed that instincts are similar to reflexes, are elicited by sensory stimuli, and occur blindly the first time (James, 1890). To James, "occurring blindly" meant that the behavior occurs automatically under appropriate conditions and without knowledge of the end or goal toward which the behavior leads. He argued that "every instinct is an impulse," which puts instinct squarely into the domain of motivation (i.e., a force acting on or within the organism to initiate behavior). Though James believed that the first occurrence of an instinct is blind, he felt that memory interacts with instincts so that subsequent behavior is no longer blind; in other words, he believed that instinctive behavior changes through experience. He maintained that an instinct is not uniform but is only a tendency to act in a particular way (although, on the average, the resulting behavior will be relatively constant).

For example, James listed modesty as an instinct, and this instinct might cause you to blush and turn away automatically at unexpectedly encountering a nude sunbather on a beach. On the other hand, one who frequents nude bathing beaches might no longer automatically blush or turn away, but instead become blasé about nudity, so that one's "modesty instinct" would then be inhibited (held back) by experience. At any rate, this somewhat exaggerated example indicates that instincts, according to James, could be altered by experience.

James explained the variability of instincts through two principles. The first principle stated that habit (i.e., learning) can inhibit an instinct. The second principle proposed that some instincts are transitory, useful only at certain times or during certain developmental periods. James proposed that learning may inhibit an instinct by restricting the range of objects involved in an instinctive activity. Thus, learning was thought to limit the extent to which an instinct can develop or be used. For example, the triggering of the instinct of fear by a teacher might lead to a student's poor academic performance because another instinct, such as inquisitiveness, could become blocked (by learning) or limited to nonacademic situations. The transitory nature of instincts implies that some instincts are only present at a specific time in development and then become inactive. Thus, a newly hatched chick follows the first moving object it sees on its first day of life, but if not exposed to that object until later in life (e.g., three days of age), it will run away from the object. These two principles proposed by James were important forerunners of the ethological concepts of critical period and imprinting, which will be detailed later in this chapter.

James saw instinctive behavior as intermediate between reflexes and learning, shading into each at the extremes. Unlike some of his contemporaries, James did not propose to explain all behavior through instinctive processes. In his view, instincts provide a base upon which experience can build through the development of habits. The concept of instinct was not reserved for nonhuman animals. James believed that people possess all the instincts of other animals plus many exclusively human ones.

He proposed a classification of human instincts that included the following:

rivalry	curiosity
pugnacity	sociability
sympathy	shyness
hunting	secretiveness
fear	cleanliness
acquisitiveness	modesty
constructiveness	jealousy
play	parental love

James thought that by describing various instincts and how these might have been adaptive during the evolution of humans, he was explaining how behavior is motivated. Unfortunately, he did not clearly describe how one could distinguish between a reflex, an instinct, and a learned behavior.

William McDougall

McDougall argued that instincts are more than just dispositions to react in a particular way. He saw every instinct as consisting of three components: the cognitive, the affective, and the conative (striving) (McDougall, 1970). The cognitive aspect of the instinct is the knowing of an object that can satisfy the instinct. The affective component is the feeling (emotion) that the object arouses in the organism. The conative aspect of the instinct is a striving toward or away from the object. Therefore every behavior consists of (a) thoughts about those goals that will satisfy the motive, (b) emotions that are aroused by the behavior, and (c) purposive striving aimed at reaching the goal. Using McDougall's approach, we would expect that a hungry rat would have some understanding of an object that would satisfy its hunger, would show an emotional arousal when hungry, and would strive persistently toward obtaining the object that would relieve its hunger.

McDougall saw striving toward a goal as an example of the purposiveness of instinctive behavior. He believed that one can identify the activated instinct by determining the goal toward which the behavior is directed. For example, if one observes a monkey actively attempting to take apart a puzzle made of interlocking blocks, one can conclude that the behavior aroused was the instinct of curiosity. Such an analysis is said to be teleological. **Teleology** is the idea that a behavior serves some ultimate purpose. While this type of explanation is not entirely unreasonable for humans who can foresee or predict where their behavior is likely to lead, it has not been a very popular explanation for animal behavior; and many theorists, including Freud, have argued that even humans are often largely unaware of the reasons for their behavior.

Like James, McDougall (1970) compiled a long list of instinctive behaviors, some of which include the following:

parental care	sympathy
combat	self-assertion
curiosity	submission
food seeking	mating
repulsion	constructiveness
escape	appeal
gregariousness	

According to McDougall, an instinct can be altered in four ways. First, an instinct may be activated not only by some specific external object but also by the idea of that object or by other external objects or their ideas. Thus the kinds of objects or ideas that might elicit an instinct could change. For example, milk might initially activate food seeking in the infant. As the child grows, other foods would also activate this instinct, as would the thought of food. In fact, a good TV commercial might lead you to think of what is in the refrigerator and thus to activate your food-seeking behavior. (There are, of course, other valid explanations for this chain of events.)

Second, the movements through which the instinctive behavior occurs can be modified. The instinct of curiosity might initially involve exploring the local environment, as when an infant crawls about the room. Later this same instinct might be satisfied by reading in the sciences. Though the curiosity instinct remained, the behaviors involved in its expression changed.

Third, several instincts may be triggered simultaneously, and the resulting behavior will be a blend of the excited instincts. Thus, McDougall might argue that the sexual behavior of teenagers is a blend of curiosity and mating instincts, and the "petting" that occurs is a compromise behavior reflecting both of these instincts.

Finally, instinctive behaviors may become organized around particular objects or ideas and thus become less responsive in other situations. For example, people may sometimes be self-assertive (an instinct, according to McDougall) in their jobs but submissive (also an instinct) at home, so that the instinctive behavior occurs only in certain situations. In some respects this is similar to Freud's concept of fixation.

McDougall's method of analysis was anthropomorphic. He believed he could infer the feelings of other organisms by asking himself how he would feel in similar circumstances. For example, if McDougall saw a dog licking the wounds of another, he might conclude that the first dog was feeling sympathy for the second. **Anthropomorphism** (the attribution of human characteristics to objects or animals) is common in our everyday thinking. For example, the person who says "my cat feels guilty about killing the robin" is being anthropomorphic. Whether the cat experiences guilt in the human sense is questionable. Guilt may not be experienced at all in animals other than humans. Anthropomorphism is generally recognized today as an inadequate method of analysis. In fact, experimenters go to great extremes to avoid biasing their studies with their own subjective experiences.

In addition to the problem of anthropomorphism, McDougall (like James) did not clearly distinguish between instinct and learning. In many cases the two concepts overlapped (as in modifiable instincts), and this led to confusion. This was not a problem for McDougall, because he believed that all behavior is instinctive.

Criticisms of the Early Instinct Theories

Kuo (1921) attempted to destroy the concept of instinct completely in an article titled "Giving Up Instincts in Psychology." Of the several criticisms he leveled at the instinct concept, among the most important are the following three. First, he wrote, there is no agreement concerning what types of or how many instincts exist. He maintained that compiled lists of instincts are arbitrary and depend upon each writer's interests. Second, Kuo argued that all behaviors called instinctive are not innate but learned. He felt that behavior is built from random responses, some of which are reinforced and retained, others of which are unreinforced and extinguished. He felt that psychologists like McDougall were guilty of ignoring the responses that had to be learned in order to reach the goal toward which the behavior is directed. Finally, Kuo insisted that instincts are not the motive forces underlying behavior because behavior is aroused by external stimuli. By his emphasis on the external control of behavior, Kuo rejected the assumptions made by the instinctivists that behaviors are largely the result of genetic programming. Kuo felt strongly that the instinct concept had little usefulness, and he argued persuasively that the concept ought to be dropped.

Tolman (1923) also carefully reviewed the concept of instinct and pointed out several problems. Unlike Kuo, however, Tolman felt that the theory could be saved if the criticisms he noted were corrected. First, Tolman noted that the arbitrary designation of behaviors as instinctive robs the concept of any explanatory value. In other words, instincts such as curiosity, playfulness, and pugnacity are merely descriptive labels (the nominal fallacy) that do not explain the causes of the behavior. Second, no clear criteria exist for determining which behaviors are instinctive and which are not (unclear definitions of instinct and learning). Theorists, quite simply, had not bothered to state clearly how one could identify an instinctive behavior. Third, the concept, as presented, sounds very similar to Plato's doctrine of innate ideas (that all knowledge is present in every individual and only

awaits discovery). Tolman noted, however, that this is not a valid criticism because instinctive behavior may have evolved to such an extent that it now appears intelligent. Finally, he pointed out the confusion between instincts and habits (learning) that we have already seen in the theories of James and McDougall.

Tolman believed that the instinct concept could be saved by reconstructing it in behavioral rather than subjective terms. His emphasis was on the behavioral ends toward which the behavior is directed; he believed that those ends (goals) are fixed or instinctive but that the means of obtaining them can vary and are thus modifiable through learning. Therefore, behaving in order to get food when hungry is instinctive, but the behavior necessary to obtain the food is flexible and learned.

Unfortunately for the original instinct concept, the criticisms of Kuo, Tolman, and others proved too damaging, and the term disappeared from psychology texts for many years. However, though the concept of instinct disappeared from American psychology, it remained alive in a branch of European biology known as ethology.

Classical Ethology

Ethology, a specialized branch of biology, is concerned with the evolution, development, and function of behavior. While the ethological approach is not limited to the study of instinctive behaviors, most ethological research has emphasized instinct. Ethologists have carefully defined the concept and have analyzed the various components of such behaviors. We will therefore examine such concepts as appetitive and consummatory behaviors, fixed action patterns, key stimuli, vacuum activity, intention movements, conflict behavior, reaction chains, and imprinting. Much of the early work in ethology was conducted by Konrad Lorenz and Niko Tinbergen in the 1930s.

Lorenz argued persuasively that we must observe organisms in their natural setting if we are to understand their behavior (Lorenz, 1971a,

1971b). Ethology has done just as Lorenz suggested, stressing the careful observation of an organism's full range of behaviors before attempting to interpret that behavior. Considerable time is spent compiling lists of observed behaviors for each species studied. Such a list is called an **ethogram** (Tinbergen, 1951).

Ethological Terms

The ethological approach is firmly based on Darwin's theory of evolution. Instinctive behaviors exist because they have or had survival value for the species in question. Another important aspect of the ethological approach to motivated behavior is seen in the concepts of consummatory and appetitive behavior, first proposed by Wallace Craig (1918). Craig noted that behaviors can be divided into well-coordinated, fixed patterns of responding to specific stimuli, which he called **consummatory behavior**, and restless, searching behavior that is flexible and adaptive to the environment, which he called **appetitive behavior**. Appetitive behavior is subject to modification through learning (e.g., when a rat learns where food can be found in its environment). Consummatory behavior is innate and stereotyped (e.g., the chewing and swallowing of food).

The ethological approach also assumes that each behavior has its own source of energy called **action specific energy (ASE)**. Each behavior is inhibited from occurring, however, by the **innate releasing mechanism (IRM)**, which works much like a lock that can be opened by the proper key (Lorenz, 1950; Tinbergen, 1951). The "key" that allows the behavior to occur is a biologically important stimulus that may be either environmental or the result of the behavior of a species member. Environmental stimuli are called **key stimuli** or **sign stimuli**, while stimuli that involve behavior of another member of the species are called releasers or **social releasers** (Mortenson, 1975). Social releasers are key stimuli that serve a communicative function between species members. For example, postures, conspicuous plumage, or coloration indicating sexual readiness are often social releasers.

Key Stimuli   Key stimuli are usually simple stimuli or simple configurational relationships between stimuli. For example, the red belly of the male three-spined stickleback (a small fish that has been much studied by ethologists) releases aggressive behavior in other male sticklebacks that have set up territories; yet the same males will tolerate a female in their territories because she does not have the red coloration.

Sometimes the normal key stimulus is not the optimal stimulus for releasing a given behavior. The ringed plover (a bird), for example, lays eggs that are light brown with dark brown spots. If, however, we present plovers with a choice between their own eggs and eggs that are white with black spots, they choose to incubate the black and white eggs (Tinbergen, 1951). Oystercatchers also prefer abnormally large eggs over their own smaller eggs. These examples are particularly interesting because they show not only that an artificial stimulus may be preferred to a natural one but also that the stimuli may be **configurational** (e.g., dark spots on a light background) rather than single stimuli. Activation of behavior triggered by an unnatural stimulus also indicates the rigid nature of the behavior; the behavior occurs when a stimulus releases it and does not depend upon the organism learning about the stimulus. Stimuli that release behavior more effectively than the normal stimulus are called **supernormal key stimuli** or **super-optimal key stimuli**. An example of a supernormal stimulus is shown in Figure 2.1.

Rowland (1989c) provides an interesting example of a preference for supernormal stimuli. Sexually receptive female three-spined sticklebacks were presented with two dummy male sticklebacks, one of normal size (50 millimeters) and the other 1.5 times larger (75 millimeters). The dummy males were connected to a motorized carousel that caused them to move in a circular path, simulating male courtship movements. Rowland observed the receptive females' choices and found that the females showed a significant preference for the larger (the supernormal) dummy, even though the size of this dummy exceeded the size of any males in the natural population from which the females were drawn.

Rowland suggests that preference for a supernormal male stimulus could provide several

FIGURE 2.1 Oystercatcher showing a preference for an egg larger than its own as a result of the large egg's action as a supernormal stimulus. From "Social Releasers and the Experimental Method Required for their Study," by N. Tinbergen, 1948, *Wilson Bulletin*, *60*, 6–52. Used by permission.

advantages for a female stickleback. First of all, large males compete more successfully for breeding territories (Rowland, 1989a) and would therefore be expected to have greater success in raising offspring (male sticklebacks hatch and care for the young). Females who chose larger males should increase the chances of survival of their eggs. Second, Rowland suggests that larger males might be expected to fan the eggs more effectively (fanning provides oxygen to the eggs) and/or to defend the nest and eggs better than smaller males. Third, larger males might be less subject to predation and would therefore be more likely to survive to provide paternal care to the offspring until their independence.

In a related study, Rowland (1989b) has shown that male sticklebacks prefer dummy females with excessive abdominal distension or excessive body size. Thus it appears that mate size is an important variable in the mating behavior of sticklebacks. Rowland's research suggests that supernormal

stimulus effects may occur more often in nature than had been formerly assumed and that preference for supernormal stimuli may, in some cases, provide an evolutionary advantage.

Fixed Action Patterns The response that a key stimulus releases is called a **fixed action pattern (FAP)**. Fixed action patterns are species-specific motor patterns that are rigid, stereotyped, and, for all practical purposes, "blind." The occurrence of an FAP depends upon a key stimulus and is not influenced by learning. The FAP for ethologists is the instinctive behavior. It is hardwired into the nervous system and released by a specific set of conditions (the key stimulus).

Moltz (1965) noted four empirical properties of a fixed action pattern:

1. The fixed action pattern is **stereotyped**. Though this term implies that the behavior itself is invariable, and though this seems generally true,

some variability in the performance of FAPs does exist (Burghardt, 1973).

2. The FAP is **independent of immediate external control**. Once the FAP is activated, it continues to completion, regardless of changes in the external environment. The graylag goose, for example, retrieves eggs that have rolled from its nest. This behavior consists of two components: an FAP involving the drawing of the egg toward the nest with the bill, and lateral (side to side) movements of the bill that keep the nonsymmetrical egg from rolling off to one side (Figure 2.2). The lateral movements depend upon sensory feedback from the egg as it rolls unequally. They compensate and keep the egg in line with the nest. These lateral bill movements are a class of behavior known as taxes. **Taxes** are similar to FAPs in that they are unlearned; however, unlike FAPs they are responsive to environmental change (Mortenson, 1975). The FAP component of the behavior, however, continues to completion (even if a devious experimenter removes the egg!). Once released, the FAP appears to be independent of external changes in stimulation. But there must be some limitations of independence of FAPs from the

environment—a sparrow, when attacked by a cat, does not continue to feed on grain. Obviously some mechanism must exist that can short-circuit or stop an FAP when environmental conditions demand.

3. FAPs can be **spontaneous**. In addition to external stimulation, internal motivation is necessary for the occurrence of an FAP. The longer the interval since the last occurrence of the FAP, the more "ready" it is to occur. Spontaneity refers to the fact that when energy has built up sufficiently, the behavior may occur **in vacuo** (i.e., without being released by a key stimulus, also called **vacuum activity**). Burghardt (1973) has noted that the spontaneity of FAPs is often cited as evidence for central nervous system structures that control behavior independent of experience.

4. FAPs are **independent of learning**. Specifically, the FAP appears to be nonmodifiable through learning. Hailman (1969) has shown that this may not be entirely true. Hailman's analysis suggests the close interaction of innate and acquired patterns of behavior. For example, he believed that the gull chick has only a very rough innate representation of the parent that

FIGURE 2.2 Graylag goose retrieving an egg that has rolled from the nest. From "Taxis und instinkthandlung in der eirollbewegung der graugens," by K. Lorenz and N. Tinbergen, 1938, *Zeitschrift fur Tierpsychologie, 2,* 1–29. Used by permission.

becomes sharpened through experience. Newly hatched chicks respond primarily to the parent's bill and initially do not discriminate between models of their own parents and those of a related species. By one week of age, however, the chicks are sensitive to small differences in the details of beak and head and can easily discriminate differences between new models and models with which they were raised. This discrimination seems based on a type of learning known as classical conditioning (classical conditioning will be discussed in more detail in Chapter 5). On the other hand, it is also possible that some of the changes noted by Hailman could be due to maturational development rather than learning.

Intention Movements and Social Releasers

Lorenz (1971b) pointed out that before an FAP occurs, one can often observe **intention movements**. These movements are low-intensity, incomplete responses indicating that energy is beginning to accumulate in an instinctive behavior system. These intention movements may also become social releasers over the evolutionary history of the species. Initially, the intention movements are not communicative, but through a process termed **ritualization** they begin to serve a communicative function. For example, many threat gestures such as baring the teeth in canines seem to have evolved from attack responses and serve to indicate the motivational readiness of the organism for combative behavior (Mortenson, 1975). Intention movements that have become social releasers are usually exaggerated forms of the original response. The movements then serve as key stimuli for the release of FAPs in the conspecific (member of the same species) toward which they are directed.

Do humans make intention movements that serve as social signals? Lockard, Allen, Schielle, and Wiemer (1978) believe that they do. In their initial experiment, these researchers recorded the postural stance of persons who were engaged in conversation with another person. They found that at the beginning of a social interaction between two people, their participants tended to stand with their weight distributed equally on both legs. Near the close of the interaction, however, the subjects stood with most of their weight borne on one leg. This result suggested to Lockard and co-workers that shifts in weight may serve as an intention movement for departure.

A second experiment revealed that the frequency of unequal weight stances increased before departure, as did weight shifts in general. In addition, weight shifts that increased the distance between the individuals also occurred just prior to departure. Shifts in weight, then, are apparently intention movements that serve as a signal that an individual is about to leave.

These researchers produced additional evidence for the signal function of weight shifts from the fact that weight shifts were exaggerated in situations where people departed alone, as compared to situations where the two persons departed together. The weight shift exaggeration would be expected if it serves as a signal of imminent departure, since persons departing together would have little need to signal their coming departure to each other.

Intention movements are adaptive because they communicate motivational intent. The ability to recognize the intent of another member of your species would have been advantageous, especially if that recognition is innate so that it does not have to be learned over several exposures to the intentional behaviors. In this regard, Lorenz (1971b) has maintained that relationships between species members tend to be instinctive, with learning playing a minor role. However, some behaviors, such as individual recognition within closed groups and dominance orders, appear to be learned. Lorenz further suggested that learning is primarily useful in relationships with the external environment and that these differences are also seen in human behavior. Nonverbal cues, discussed in Chapter 12, may exemplify human intention movements that have become ritualized into social releasers.

Motivational Conflict

An interesting question arises if we consider the possibility that two or more key stimuli could be present at the same time. Which FAP would occur? Such situations involve a motivational conflict. **Conflict behavior** has been divided into four categories: successive ambivalent behavior, simultaneous ambivalent behavior, redirected behavior, and ethological displacement (Hess, 1962).

Successive ambivalent behavior involves the alternation of incomplete responses representing the two motivational states. For example, a male stickleback may alternate between attack and escape responses when it meets an intruding male stickleback at the border of its territory.

Simultaneous ambivalent behavior occurs in conflict situations where both motivational states can be expressed in behavior at the same time. For example, Leyhausen (cited in Burghardt, 1973) has argued that the arched back of the cat is the result of the simultaneous expression of the motives to attack (rear feet forward) and to flee (front feet drawn backward).

Redirected behavior is conceptually similar to the Freudian concept of displacement (Burghardt, 1973). In redirected behavior the appropriate responses (e.g., attack) occur, but not to the appropriate object, because of a conflicting motive (e.g., fear). Such redirected behavior is often focused on a nearby organism or inanimate object. The child who has been reprimanded by her mother and in turn "takes it out" on the cat instead of reacting aggressively toward the mother might be thought of as displaying redirected behavior.

Ethological displacement occurs when two equally strong motives are in conflict and are inhibiting each other. The energy associated with the two motives continue to accumulate but cannot be expressed through their normal behavioral outlets. This type of displacement behavior is a response that differs from either of the motives in conflict. The displacement activities are themselves, however, FAPs (Tinbergen, 1951). For example, the motives of attack and flight balanced against each other in the male stickleback may lead to displaced nest-building behavior, an FAP normally released by different stimulus conditions than the conflict between flight and attack. According to Tinbergen, the energy accumulating in the blocked instinctive behaviors may spark over to another instinct center and find its outlet through that center's FAPs. Tinbergen also notes that displacement behaviors may take on communicative value, just as intention movements do. Thus displacement nest building becomes a ritualized threat gesture in male sticklebacks.

Reaction Chains

We now turn from the analysis of responses released by patterns of stimuli to an examination of behavior sequences. We will discover that quite complex sequences of behavior may be built from simpler key stimuli, FAP combinations.

Most behaviors are more complex than a single FAP released by a single key stimulus. Behaviors frequently involve a sequence of responses in which each response is released by its appropriate key stimulus. Such a situation is known as a **reaction chain**. A reaction chain consists of alternating key stimuli and FAPs in a particular sequence until the behavior comes to an end, as in the case of the stickleback mating behavior shown in Figure 2.3. The release of an FAP often causes the next key stimulus to appear; thus the next part of the sequence is released, and so on. In Figure 2.3, the appearance of the female releases the zigzag dance in the male, which in turn serves as a social releaser for courting behavior in the female. Courting behavior then releases leading (to the nest) behavior in the male, and the chain of releasers and FAPs continues until fertilization of the eggs occurs. Lorenz (1970) pointed out that sometimes there are gaps in these chains of behavior that can be filled by learned behaviors such as imprinting (see next section). These special situations result in a series of behaviors, some learned and others innate. These sequences of instinctive and learned behaviors have been termed **instinct-conditioning intercalation** by Lorenz (1970).

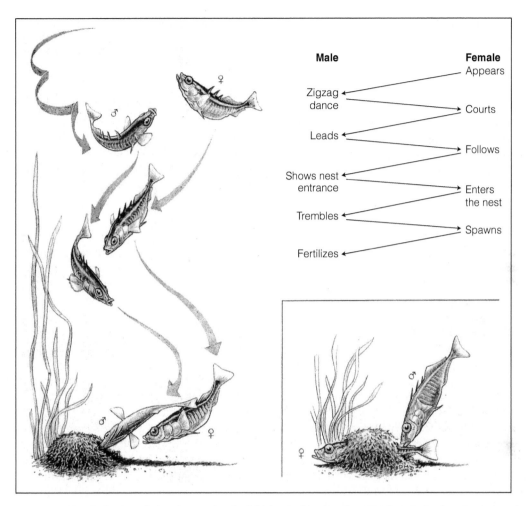

Male	Female
	Appears
Zigzag dance	
	Courts
Leads	
	Follows
Shows nest entrance	
	Enters the nest
Trembles	
	Spawns
Fertilizes	

FIGURE 2.3   Mating behavior of the three-spined stickleback showing the reaction chain that is produced when the female appears. From *The Study of Instinct*, by N. Tinbergen. Copyright © 1951 by Oxford University Press. Used by permission.

Imprinting

One area in which instinct and learning seem to intermingle is in the process known as imprinting. This process was first brought to the attention of researchers by Lorenz, although the process was recognized and described by Spaulding in 1873 (Mortenson, 1975) and, as noted by Burghardt (1973), was also described by More in 1516. Nevertheless, our understanding of the variables involved in imprinting date from the introduction of the concept by Lorenz.

Imprinting is generally considered a socialization process in which a young organism forms an attachment to its parents (Mortenson, 1975). The process of imprinting has been studied most extensively in birds (Sluckin, 1973), although imprinting occurs in other species as well, including mammals (Klopfer, 1971).

The imprinting process itself seems to include both instinctive and learned components. For example, a newly hatched chick will try to follow the first moving object it sees. Normally this is the mother hen, but it will also follow a human, a toy train, or a moving red rubber ball. The chick follows and forms an attachment to the object to which it is exposed. Thus the object of the attachment is learned; however, the process of becoming attached appears to be innate.

Lorenz described what he believed to be the major characteristics of imprinting. First, he noted that the attachment process occurs only during a very limited, critical period in the organism's life. In support of his assertion, Ramsay and Hess (1954) showed that the strength of imprinting peaks between 13 and 16 hours after hatching for mallard ducklings. The concept of critical period has been largely replaced by a related concept called the **sensitive period**. Instead of a critical period when the learning does or does not occur, there seems to be a sensitive period within which imprinting occurs more readily than before or after (Mortenson, 1975).

Second, Lorenz felt that the imprinting process is permanent and irreversible; once established, it does not extinguish. In particular, Lorenz suggested that the initial attachment formed by imprinting leads to intraspecific identification and that the sexual preferences of the adult result from this attachment. Lorenz imprinted some graylag geese on himself at the time of hatching. As adults, these geese ignored sexually receptive members of their own species but made sexual displays toward Lorenz! Most of the evidence, however, suggests that formation of an irreversible bond is the exception in imprinting rather than the rule. The reversibility of imprinting in birds may depend upon whether the species is nidifugous (leaves the nest shortly after hatching) or nidicolous (remains in the nest for an extended period). Nidicolous species show a more permanent attachment to the imprinted object, sometimes preferring that object sexually to members of their own species. Imprinting to nonspecies members in nidifugous birds, however, does not prevent them from mating with their own species (Mortenson, 1975). The extended period in the nest of nidicolous species may allow the more permanent attachment to originate from factors other than imprinting (e.g., reinforcement by parent birds).

The third characteristic of imprinting noted by Lorenz is its independence from reward. The process of imprinting occurs automatically rather than in a trial-and-error fashion that would suggest a gradual process of learning to follow. This finding has been generally supported, and several studies have shown that a response (e.g., following) is not even necessary for imprinting to occur (Burghardt, 1973). Of possible theoretical importance is the finding that, although reinforcement is unnecessary for the process of imprinting to occur, an imprinted stimulus can be used to reinforce other behaviors, such as jumping on a lever in order to obtain a brief appearance of the imprinted object (Bateson & Reese, 1969; Hoffman, Searle, & Kozma, 1966).

Not all stimulus objects are equally effective in establishing imprinting. For example, Figler, Mills, and Petri (1974), in a study of stimulus generalization in imprinting in chicks, concluded that color is a more dominant aspect of the imprinting object than shape. Other researchers have shown that the characteristic maternal call of a species is preferred over that of other species, while species-typical visual stimuli are not thus preferred (Gottlieb, 1972).

Some work has also been conducted on the effect that imprinting may have on other social behaviors. Hoffman and Boskoff (1972) obtained results suggesting that imprinting may be involved in aggressive pecking in ducklings. Other studies by Petri and Mills (1977) and Rajecki, Ivins, and Rein (1976) show that aggressive pecking in young chicks is probably due to isolation and not to imprinting per se.

Criticisms of the Classical Ethological Approach

The ethological view of motivation has been criticized both from within ethology (Hinde, 1966,

1971) and from without (Lehrman, 1970). These criticisms have been amply summarized by others (Alcock, 1975; Bolles, 1975; Burghardt, 1973), and we will note only the major criticisms.

As with the early instinct theories, the distinction between learned and instinctive behaviors is still not clear. It has become increasingly apparent that instinctive behaviors depend upon the proper developmental and environmental conditions. Basically, a behavior is considered innate if no learning has been demonstrated in its development. Hinde, however, argued that all behaviors depend upon both innate mechanisms and the environment. To say that a behavior is simply innate is to oversimplify the situation. As an example of the interaction of the innate and the acquired, Hailman (1969) has shown that the innate pecking response of the laughing gull changes developmentally, becoming more accurate and efficient, and is released by increasingly more specific objects as the chick matures. Hailman suggests that the peck appears stereotyped and innate in nature because all laughing gulls share similar environments that modify their behavior in similar ways.

Another major criticism of the ethological view involves the energy concept. Classical ethologists have argued that both displacement and vacuum activity indicate the presence of an energy buildup within the organism. Antagonists of the energy concept argue that displacement and vacuum activity can be explained by assuming a hierarchy of responses, with some responses being more probable than others. Thus, if an innate behavior is blocked from occurring, the next most probable response whose stimuli are present will occur. Displacement behavior may occur not because of energy "sparking over" but because of the occurrence of the next most probable response. Thus displacement scratching shown by fighting cocks can be analyzed as simply a highly probable response, associated with feeding, that occurs when the motives of attack and fight are balanced. Similarly, vacuum activity need not result from an overflow of energy but may result from stimulus generalization (i.e., the range of stimuli that can

elicit a response is probably wider than generally believed). Thus, for example, the female of the species is only one of a number of stimuli that may elicit sexual behavior from the male.

In summary, even though ethology has been criticized, clearly the naturalistic approach to understanding behavior has much to offer. It is also clear that some behaviors in some species have a genetic component to them.

Some Modifications to the Basic Ideas of Ethology

First, research has begun to reform our notions about the stimuli involved in releasing instinctive behavior. Konishi (1971) provided an interesting neurobiological analysis of sign stimuli in terms of stimulus filtering—the fact that our sensory systems are tuned to respond to certain kinds of stimuli and not to others. For example, the eye of the frog has receptors that respond to small, roundish, moving objects (e.g., insects) and release the response of the tongue snapping out to grasp the potential prey (Maturana, Lettvin, & Pitts, 1960). More recently, New, Tooby, and Cosmides (2007; see also Holden, 2007) have shown that humans are more likely to notice the movement of an animal than the movement of an object after a brief exposure. They argue that human attention is finely tuned to what other animals are doing. Presumably, this focusing of attention on animals evolved because it was adaptive.

Konishi noted that the concept of releasers fits well with data on filtering at the receptor level, but he argued that stimulus filtering also occurs in more central regions of the brain. He also believed that a control systems approach involving feedback and corrective action is useful in analyzing instinctive behavior. Additionally, he suggested that some behaviors are more "open" (to modification through learning) than others; such a behavioral system would compare ongoing behavior against some internal criterion (either innate or learned) and modify the response depending upon its relationship to the criterion. An example of such a feedback process is song learning in many species of birds. Song sparrows develop abnormal songs if they are deafened as chicks, yet they develop normal sparrow songs if raised only with canaries! Thus, the song of the song sparrow is apparently innate but requires auditory feedback in order to develop properly.

Konishi was not the only one to take a systems approach. Mayr (1974) provided an analysis of behavior based on what he called open and closed programs. According to Mayr, a program is a series of behaviors that are determined genetically. The difference between an **open** and a **closed program** is that an open program can be modified by experience, while a closed program (instinct) cannot. Both open and closed programs are genetically established, but only an open program is modifiable through experience. Open programs would not be considered "blank slates," however, because some types of information are more easily acquired than others. The concept of open programs is remarkably similar to the concept of **preparedness** proposed by Seligman (1970) and Seligman and Hager (1972). **Prepared behaviors** are either instinctive or very easily and quickly learned. Organisms possessing genes that allowed them to behave in this way were favored in the struggle to survive. **Contraprepared behaviors** are very difficult, perhaps impossible, to learn because they were "prepared against" during the evolutionary history of the organism. Between these extremes are what Seligman calls **unprepared behaviors**, which involve the associations between events in the environment and appropriate responding; the associations formed, however, tend to be arbitrary (e.g., teaching a rat to press a lever to obtain food), and learning will not be as quick as with more prepared responses. Seligman and his colleagues pointed out that what can be learned is biologically constrained (limited).

Mayr suggested that organisms with short life spans (and therefore less chance to profit from experience) should tend to have more closed programs, while long-living organisms would tend to have more open programs. In addition, he believed

it is possible to correlate open or closed behaviors with their function for the organism. He noted that behaviors serving a communicative function, whether within or between species, tend to be closed programs (as Lorenz has also suggested), while noncommunicative behaviors are more likely to be open programs. Thus it would be adaptive for behaviors such as threat gestures and submissive signals to be generated by closed programs, for the chance of "misunderstanding" the signals is then avoided. On the other hand, it would be adaptive for behaviors that involve interaction with the environment (such as foraging for food) to be controlled by open programs so that behaviors could adapt as conditions changed.

Baerends (1976) emphasized negative feedback as part of a system for controlling certain behaviors. Much research cited by Baerends requires the addition of a feedback system that corrects ongoing behavior or interrupts it if conditions change. This is the basis for a negative feedback system. Similarly, Hailman (1969) has shown how the improvement in the laughing gull's pecking accuracy as a chick is a result of visual negative feedback provided by the pecks that miss their mark. Thus, the original idea that a behavior once released is completely uninfluenced by external conditions seems incomplete.

Though models of innate behavior such as Baerends's are too complex for inclusion here, it is important to note that theorists such as Baerends, Mayr, and Hailman have emphasized the interaction between instinctive and learned behaviors and also the modification of instinctive behaviors through experience.

Human Ethology

Much of the original research on human instinctive behavior patterns was conducted by Eibl-Eibesfeldt, summarized in his books *Love and Hate: The Natural History of Behavior Patterns* (1972) and *Human Ethology* (1989), which point out many human behavior patterns that appear to have innate components. His conclusions were based on considerable study of both technologically advanced and primitive cultures, in addition to behaviors of blind, deaf, and severely developmentally disabled children. We will examine here just a few of his contributions.

Facial Expressions Eibl-Eibesfeldt pointed out that many facial expressions are universal and do not seem to be learned. Smiling, laughing, weeping, and frowning are observed in the appropriate circumstances across all cultures. Additionally, children born blind, deaf, or disabled also smile or laugh when happy and frown or cry when unhappy. Figure 2.4 shows some of these behaviors in a deaf-blind child.

One interesting facial behavior that Eibl-Eibesfeldt believed to be innate is the **eyebrow flick**, which consists of a very brief lifting of the eyebrow upon greeting an acquaintance. This response is shown from three different cultures in Figure 2.5. The behavior is essentially a greeting signal of recognition and perhaps a nonthreat or **appeasement gesture**. (Appeasement gestures are behaviors that inhibit aggressive behavior in social situations between a more dominant and less dominant animal. They are quite common across a variety of species).

Following Eibl-Eibesfeldt, Joseph Hager and Paul Ekman (1979) examined the ability of people to recognize specific facial signals at varying distances. They chose six emotional expressions

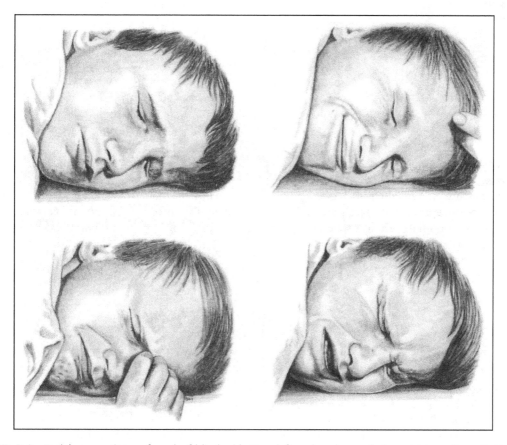

FIGURE 2.4 Facial expressions of a deaf-blind girl. Top left, relaxed mood; top right, smiling. Bottom left and right, crying. Adapted from *Love and Hate* by Irenaus Eibl-Eibesfeldt. Copyright © 1971, 1972 by Methuen and Co. Ltd. and Holt, Rinehart and Winston. Reprinted by permission of the author.

FIGURE 2.5 Examples of the eyebrow flick from three different cultures. Left, before recognition; right, after recognition. Cultures from top to bottom: Waika Indian, Papuan, Balinese. Adapted from *Love and Hate* by Irenaus Eibl-Eibesfeldt. Copyright © 1971, 1972 by Methuen and Co. Ltd. and Holt, Rinehart and Winston. Reprinted by permission of the author.

(happiness, sadness, fear, anger, surprise, and disgust) that were previously shown to be reliably associated with specific facial movements. Hager and Ekman then taught two individuals, a man and a woman, how to make these facial movements consistently. Photographs were taken of each individual making each facial movement. Then other subjects in the experiment were asked to observe either a photograph of one of the individuals (blown up to life size) or the actual individual at varying distances from 30 to 45 meters (98.4–147.6 feet). The observers had 3 seconds in which to view the facial expression before selecting the specific emotional expression they believed was being conveyed.

The results indicated that every observer performed significantly better than chance, even at the furthest distance (45 meters). Of the six expressions, happiness and surprise were the easiest to recognize. The results also indicated that, in general, the observers' judgments were more accurate for male than for female expressions, whether live or photographed. Hager and Ekman argue that their results show that the face is a long-distance transmitter of emotion. Chapter 12 examines the facial expression of emotion in more detail.

Shyness   Some behaviors that we often assume have resulted from childhood experiences may in fact have a biological basis. Kagen, Reznick, and Snidman (1988) provide evidence that extreme shyness has a genetic basis expressed in differences in arousability. Children who inherit a low threshold of arousability are more likely to become inhibited in social situations. Furthermore, the differences between these inhibited children and less restrained, socially interactive children are consistent at both 2 and 7 years of age.

Kagen and associates further suggest that this inherited tendency toward shyness requires some form of chronic environmental stress to cause it to develop. These researchers found that being later born and thus being exposed to the stress of older siblings who may take toys, tease, or yell could be sufficient stress to trigger the behavioral inhibition. Indeed, two-thirds of the inhibited children in their sample were later born, while two-thirds of the uninhibited children were firstborn.

The study by Kagen and associates is important because it points out that genetically determined predispositions to behave in a particular way often still require appropriate environmental circumstances for their expression. Stephen Suomi (Adler, 1989) has uncovered a similar set of biological-environmental interactions in rhesus monkeys. He has found that about 20% of his free-roaming colony of 200 monkeys are genetically predisposed to react to separation with depressed behavior and high levels of stress. Similar to Kagen's research, Suomi finds that the stresses of separation can be influenced by environmental circumstances. The presence of friendly peers and a nurturing foster mother can reduce the stress produced by separation from the biological mother. Genetic-environmental interactions in other behaviors have been found in other species (Greene, 1989; Oakley, 1983), so it is not too surprising that primates, humans and rhesus also should be subject to such interactions. Further study of these interactions could provide useful insights into why particular behaviors such as shyness or stress reactions occur in some individuals more than others.

Additional Innate Behaviors

Eibl-Eibesfeldt also mentioned several key stimuli that release human instinctive behavior (see also Sternglanz, Gray, & Murakami, 1977). For example, he suggested that an infant's chubby cheeks, large eyes, small mouth, and large head release "cuddling" (i.e., nurturing behaviors such as picking an infant up, rocking it, or cooing to it) behavior in adults. Toy manufacturers and cartoonists sometimes employ these characteristics to endear us to their products although they are probably not aware of why these characteristics have such qualities (see Figure 2.6). Keating et al. (2003) found that pictures of adult faces that had childlike characteristics were more likely to elicit helping behavior from others. The term used for the retention of juvenile traits into adulthood is **neoteny**, and, as it turns out, adult humans are more neotenous when compared to other primates. In humans neoteny would appear to be adaptive because it

FIGURE 2.6 Examples of stimuli that release "cuddling" in adults. Note the chubby cheeks, large eyes, and large head in relation to body. Adapted from *Love and Hate* by Irenaus Eibl-Eibesfeldt. Copyright © 1971, 1972 by Methuen and Co. Ltd. and Holt, Rinehart and Winston. Reprinted by permission of the author.

increases the likelihood of helping behavior from others.

If one considers for a moment the physical characteristics of infants of many animal species, you quickly realize that the infants often look much different than the adults of that species. Such differences are not accidental or random. The appearance of the young occurs because those differences, in the past, helped the young animal to survive. For example, differences in color from the adult often serve to protect the young from predators, providing camouflage. Differences in physical characteristics from the adults of a species also seem to inhibit aggression by adults toward the young providing them safety against a conflict they could not win. Finally, differences in the appearance of the young seems to elicit caretaking behavior from adults (usually the parents of the off-spring) in species where parental care is necessary for survival of the young.

At the adult level, female flirting was considered by Eibl-Eibesfeldt as a type of innate ritualized foreplay that involves flight as one component. He analyzed **flirting behavior** (eye contact, smile, lowering of head, and closing of eyes or looking away) as a type of ritualized flight that invites pursuit by the male. Although this may seem a little farfetched, ritualized flight is a common behavior pattern in many species during mating (Eibl-Eibesfeldt, 1972). Moore (1985) has shown that "**hair flipping**" behavior in human females is an additional type of flirting behavior. Hair flipping in females would seem to be a behavior designed to draw a male's attention to the female's hair, which has been shown to be a signal of youth and fertility (see Buss, 2008).

Eibl-Eibesfeldt also suggests that **kissing** is a ritualized form of feeding behavior derived from the feeding of the infant. Since for most of our evolutionary history baby foods did not come neatly packaged in small glass or plastic containers, it was common for parents to chew food well and then push it into the child's mouth with the tongue. Along similar lines, Eibl-Eibesfeldt noted that lovers often talk "**baby talk**" to each other. He believed that this is done to elicit cherishing behavior of the individual, much as with a child, and thus strengthens the bond between the lovers.

Eibl-Eibesfeldt (1979) has also noted that humans use many of the same basic behavior patterns used by chimpanzees when threatening attack or making fighting movements. For example, both chimpanzees and humans stamp their feet when angry, slap surfaces with the flat of the hand, and threaten conspecifics with objects such as sticks. When threatened, we also tend to stand erect and inhale, which increases our apparent size. We also sometimes use clothing for intimidation to make us look more formidable. For example, military uniforms often exaggerate the shoulders of the wearer, making them appear larger. A good example of how a change in the shoulders can alter our perception of an individual occurs when a man puts on football shoulder pads. With pads in place, the man looks much more imposing.

Staring   **Staring** is not only rude but is probably also an innate threat gesture (Eibl-Eibesfeldt, 1977, 1979; Andrew, 1965). In primates the stare is a frequently used threat gesture (Tinbergen & Tinbergen, 1972). Ellsworth, Carlsmith, and Henson (1972) conducted a series of field experiments involving an individual on a motor scooter staring at automobile drivers stopped at a red light. They found that those drivers who were stared at crossed the intersection significantly faster when the light turned green than drivers who were not stared at. While this experiment does not demonstrate that staring is an innate threat gesture, it does fit with observations of other primates. Incidentally, it is also possible that we consider staring to be rude because we innately recognize it for what it is—an intention movement indicating potential attack.

Eye contact is a complex topic; staring is only one of several types of eye contact. As summarized by Kleinke (1986), eye contact can serve a variety of functions in addition to threat, such as providing information, indicating liking or attraction, indicating competence, and communicating feelings. We must therefore be careful not to overgeneralize and assume that all eye contacts indicate threat.

The ethological method has also been successfully used in the assessment of depressive disorders. Fossi, Faravelli, and Paoli (1984) studied the behavior of 29 inpatients who were diagnosed as having a major depressive disorder. Depressed patients were found to differ in several behaviors before and after treatment. Eye contact, exploration of their environment, and social behaviors were all lower before treatment than after, whereas crying, nonsocial behaviors, and pathological behaviors were higher before treatment than after. Their data indicate that a pattern of behaviors specific to depression does exist, and it corresponds closely to the behaviors identified by clinical assessment. Fossi et al. suggest that the ethological methods of observation could prove useful in assessing maladaptive behaviors such as depression. Ethological observations also provide an objective alternative method of assessment separate from the clinical interview, which could prove useful in determining the effects of various treatments.

Speech   Other ethologists have pointed out the possible genetic character of speech (Marler, 1970; Mattingly, 1972). But ethologists have not been the only researchers to argue for a biological component to language. For example, Lenneberg (1960, 1967) had persuasively argued that language must be biologically constrained. Marler (1970) had also pointed out several parallels between song development in birds and the development of speech in humans. For example, both birds and children display a sensitive period during which the ability to learn is at its maximum, and both bird and human vocalizations are controlled by one dominant side of the brain. Both of these findings suggest a genetic component to birdsong and speech because sensitive periods are genetically determined, and the localization of vocal function within the brain is also under genetic control. Marler also noted that language is biologically constrained; children do not imitate all the sounds they hear—only the ones involved in speech. This suggests that children

innately recognize that some sounds are species-specific, and they imitate these sounds.

Additionally, Liberman and Mattingly (1989) have suggested that a specialization for the perception of speech has evolved in humans. In their terms, a **phonetic module** has evolved that analyzes auditory information and extracts the information necessary for the determination of phonetic segments (which they call phonetic gestures). Mattingly (1972) also believed that certain speech cues are innate and serve as key stimuli. He noted that synthetic speech sounds are correctly identified even though the sounds themselves are unnatural in character. That we perceive synthetic speech sounds suggests some innate recognition of these sounds. Mattingly believed that, prior to the development of language, vocalizations served as key stimuli for the release of social behavior in humans, much as they still do in many animals. Language allowed us to represent the world around us semantically, but the older social releaser system was not lost. Mattingly argued that language, therefore, serves two purposes: It provides a representation of our experiences, and it is a **phonetic social releaser system**. Perhaps the social releaser system is what allows us to sometimes "read between the lines" when we listen to someone talk, providing us with insight into that individual beyond what is being said.

Ethological Concepts Concerning Sex and Aggression

Sexual activity and aggressive behavior are viewed by ethologists as largely innate. For example, sexual behavior in many animals involves reaction chains of ritualized courtship behavior in which social releasers trigger the appropriate fixed action patterns. Ritualized feeding is often a component of these reaction chains, as seen in the domestic chicken (*Gallus gallus*) where the rooster scratches and pecks at the ground while calling to the hen. The hen, enticed by the feeding responses, approaches the rooster (Eibl-Eibesfeldt, 1970). Similarly, songbirds feed one another in a manner similar to that of an adult feeding the young. Indeed Eibl-Eibesfeldt (1970, 1972) argued that courtship behaviors, including those of humans, are derived from the parental care instinct.

In a book entitled *On Aggression*, Lorenz (1967) developed the idea that aggressive behavior has been adaptive. Two major types of aggressive behavior are noted: **interspecific** (aggressive behavior between members of different species) and **intraspecific** (aggressive behavior between members of the same species). Interspecific aggression may further be broken into the categories of predatory attack, mobbing behavior, and critical reaction. **Predatory attack** is essentially food-getting behavior and is characterized by a lack of emotionality. Lorenz suggests that an equilibrium normally exists between predator and prey so that the extinction of one species by another does not usually occur. **Mobbing behavior** occurs when the prey turn the tables on the predator and attack it as a group. Mobbing behavior can be observed in certain species of birds; for example, groups of crows have been known to attack a cat (Lorenz, 1967). The third major type of interspecific aggression, **critical reaction**, involves intense aggressive behavior motivated by fear and instigated by an inability to escape. Such behavior occurs when a cornered animal is approached closer than some critical distance. Heidiger (cited by Lorenz, 1967) pointed out that lion tamers get their lions to perform by approaching and withdrawing from this critical distance. When the tamer gets within the critical distance, the lion approaches as if to attack; when the tamer withdraws, the lion stops or retreats.

Lorenz proposes that intraspecific aggression is advantageous in three different ways. One effect of aggressive encounters among conspecifics is to **spread out members more evenly** over a given area, thereby affording each member, at least statistically, a better chance for survival. Indeed Lorenz believes that this spacing function is the most important advantage of intraspecific aggression because it provides adequate territory for breeding and food gathering. Territorial aggression, therefore, increases the chances for survival because it leads to better management of scarce resources.

A second advantage of intraspecific aggression is that it **provides the strongest animals with the best territories and the first choice of mates.** The characteristics that make the "winners" of these rival fights most dominant have a better chance of being passed on to the next generation because the conditions for their survival are better than they are for the traits of the "losers," who by losing are forced to take less desirable territories and mates. This second advantage suggests that aggressive and sexual motivation interact in complex ways to promote survival. As just one such example, Guhl (1956) has shown that the dominant rooster in a flock of chickens accounts for the greatest percentage of fertilized eggs. Obviously the rooster's dominance promotes the continued expression of this aggressive behavior in future generations. As we shall see shortly, the interaction of sexual and aggressive motives is complex.

The third major advantage of intraspecific aggression is **protection of the young** from predators. As noted above, intraspecific aggression will promote aggressiveness as a general trait within the species. Such increased aggressiveness should be advantageous in protecting the young from potential predators. Increased survival of the young, in turn, promotes the survival of the species.

Eibl-Eibesfeldt (1961) notes that intraspecific aggression very rarely leads to death or even serious injury of the opponents and, in fact, would be maladaptive if such were the case. However, it is also clear that intraspecific aggression does sometimes lead to injury of the combatants, and male animals, in particular, will sometimes kill the young of a female that they succeed in taking over. Presumably, this killing of the young of a deposed male provides the winner's progeny with a better chance of survival. Even in humans there is evidence that stepparents are more likely to kill their stepchildren than their biological children (Gibbons, 1993; see also Buss, 2008 for an extended discussion of stepparent-children interactions).

However, it is more typical for conflicts between conspecifics to involve highly **ritualized tournaments**. Animals that have specialized weapons (such as fangs) usually do not use them to full advantage during these ritualized combats. Rattlesnakes, for example, do not attempt to bite when attacking each other but rather determine the stronger by wrestling until the weaker snake is pinned.

Serious injury from intraspecific conflict is often avoided through the use of a special class of social releasers called appeasement gestures. The loser of an intraspecific conflict usually performs behaviors that inhibit further attacks by the winner. These behaviors are often submissive in appearance. For example, male cichlid fish engage in intraspecific combat with raised fins and beat at each other with currents of water directed by the tail fin. They may then "jaw lock," each fish grasping the other's mouth with its own, and a shoving match ensues. Eventually the loser submits by folding its fins and swimming away, the winner allowing the loser to escape (Eibl-Eibesfeldt, 1961). Folding of the fins appears to be a social releaser that inhibits further aggressive behavior. Dogs inhibit further aggression by rolling on their backs and presenting the vulnerable belly region to the more dominant dog, sometimes also urinating slightly at the same time. Such behaviors usually inhibit further aggression but can be disconcerting to a dog owner who is trying to get his or her pet to behave in a particular way. In such cases, genetically determined behaviors intrude and often disrupt the behaviors to be learned. Breland and Breland (1961) provide some interesting insights into those situations where learned and instinctive behaviors interact.

A particularly interesting finding in regard to dominance has been noted by Simpson and Simpson (1982). These researchers examined the relationship between the social rank of female rhesus monkeys and the sex of their offspring. They found that high-ranking females gave birth to twice as many females as males, while for lower-ranking females, male infants were more common. Further,

it was found that the daughters of high-ranking females themselves ranked high in social dominance. Though it is not at all evident how these differing sex ratios are accomplished, it is hypothesized that high-ranking females improve their own fitness by giving birth to high-ranking daughters, who remain within the colony, rather than to sons who typically migrate at puberty to other groups. Thus it would appear that aggressiveness not only may be favored as a trait but also may lead to one gender's being favored over another. Angier (2002) has also summarized data in a news article for the *New York Times*, which indicates that the presence of maternal grandmothers promotes the survival of their grandchildren. Buss (2008) has also discussed this topic at length.

From the data we have examined so far, it is apparent that aggressive and sexual motivation are intimately related. Many such relationships are known; for example, female ducks will incite males to threaten intruders (Lorenz, 1967). Eibl-Eibesfeldt (1970) has suggested that this inciting behavior acts to separate out a particular male from a group of courting males for mating. Figler and his associates (Figler, 1973; Figler, Klein, & Thompson, 1975; Klein, Figler, & Peeke, 1976; Cole, Figler, Parente, & Peeke, 1980) have provided considerable support for the hypothesis that sexual and aggressive behaviors are mutually inhibitory (see Sevenster, 1961; Peeke, 1969) in some species of fish.

In one study (Cole et al., 1980), male and female convict cichlids were exposed to either male or female target fish (behind a Plexiglas partition) for a period of 24 hours. The four groups so formed (male-male, male-female, female-female, and female-male) were all initially aggressive toward their targets; however, as the aggressive behaviors began to habituate, sexual behaviors became more prevalent. Although the two opposite-sexed groups showed the most sexual behavior, sexual behaviors were observed in the same-sexed pairs to a smaller degree. Using a sophisticated statistical procedure (principle components analysis), the researchers were able to show that these sexual and aggressive behaviors were inversely related to each other. As they point out, the most straightforward interpretation of their results is that "frequent performance of sexual behavior ... decreases the likelihood of aggressive behavior being performed and vice versa" (Cole et al., 1980, p. 13). One possible conclusion we might draw from this study is that, in order for successful mating to occur, aggressive responses toward a potential mate must first be reduced to levels that allow the emergence of sexual responses. In turn, once sexual responses have become frequent enough, aggression toward the mate is largely inhibited. Such a mechanism can help us understand how an animal that behaves aggressively toward its neighbors nevertheless lives peacefully with its mate.

Research with humans concerning the relationship of aggression to sexuality is much less clear. For example, Zillmann and his associates have found that exposure to erotic or pornographic material may lead to increased aggressiveness in individuals who have been previously provoked (Zillmann & Bryant, 1982; Ramirez, Bryant, & Zillmann, 1982). Other researchers, however, have obtained results indicating that provoked individuals are less aggressive after exposure to erotic materials (Baron, 1974a, 1974b; Baron & Bell, 1977; Donnerstein, Donnerstein, & Evans, 1975). As noted by Sapolsky and Zillmann (1981), the only point on which these different sets of studies agree is that the aggressiveness of unprovoked individuals is relatively unaffected by exposure to erotica.

The innate character of aggressiveness in humans is a matter of much debate among theorists. Most ethologists have argued that human aggressiveness is innate (see, e.g., Lorenz, 1967; Tinbergen, 1977; Eibl-Eibesfeldt, 1979). Lorenz proposes that human aggressiveness was adaptive during the early Stone Age but became maladaptive with the invention of weapons. Tinbergen, noting that some species defend group territories, has suggested that war may result from this innate group territoriality in humans. Similarly, Eibl-Eibesfeldt has proposed that war developed as a cultural mechanism of groups competing for space and raw materials but that aggressiveness as a behavior is innate. Leda Cosmides (see Gibbons, 1993) has suggested that war developed as a way for men to gain increased access to women. She and John Tooby propose that wars over women began in the Pleistocene. The male victors in these forays would have access to the women of the losers and would thus produce more children. Observations of an Amazonian tribe called the Yanomamo have shown that they sometimes organize attacks on other groups in order to capture women (Gibbons, 1993). Thus the suggestion is that certain genetic traits that produce behaviors leading to successful aggression would be promoted in the gene pool.

Some support for a genetic basis for at least some types of aggression has also been provided by Dutch researchers (Morell, 1993; Brunner, Nelen, Breakefield, Ropers, & van Oost, 1993) who have discovered a family in which outbursts of violence appear to be related to a gene defect. The mutated gene controls an enzyme called monoamine oxidase A (MAOA) that normally helps to break down the neurotransmitters dopamine, epinephrine, norepinephrine, and serotonin. These neurotransmitters are involved in the body's reaction to threatening situations. If they are not broken down by the enzyme (because the gene has mutated), the body is in a high state of readiness too much of the time. Such a situation could lead to violent overreactions in stressful situations.

The Dutch research suggests that genetic mutations can sometimes lead to an increased probability of aggressive behavior; however, one must be cautious not to overgeneralize these effects. As noted by Morell (1993), such genetic mutations are surely also influenced by social, economic, and cultural factors. While a genetic mutation might predispose an individual to violent behavior, social, economic, and cultural factors might either exaggerate or diminish such predispositions. Additionally, no one knows how prevalent such a mutation might be and, as a result, how much, if at all, this research would apply to the general population. Until more is known, research indicating a genetic basis for aggressive behavior in humans should be viewed with care.

The complexity of human sexual and aggressive behaviors is such that it seems likely that both innate and learned tendencies play a role. As we shall see in later chapters, there is considerable evidence that both physiology and environment are important influences on sexual and aggressive behaviors.

Modern Ethological Approaches

Behavioral Ecology

As Ethology itself evolved, some researchers have become interested in the relationship between behaviors and the environments in which they occur. For the most part these behaviors are at least partially under genetic control; however, learned behaviors are also sometimes studied. This area of research has become known as **Behavioral Ecology**. This approach examines how particular behaviors are adaptive within the context in which they are produced. To quote Krebs and Davies (1993, p. 10), "Behavioural ecology is concerned with the evolution of adaptive behaviour in relation to ecological circumstances."

Behavioral ecologists have studied many different aspects of animal behavior such as predator-prey relationships, competition for limited resources among species members, group membership, aggressive behaviors, sexual behaviors, and parental care, to name just a few. These behaviors are examined by behavioral ecologists in terms of their adaptiveness to the individuals involved within the specific environmental context in which they take place.

For example, many animals remain together in groups. At first glance this might seem less than an optimal strategy for any given individual within the group because there will be competition for food, mates, etc. Research has shown, however, that group membership provides an advantage to the individual despite the increased competition for resources because groups provide more protection from predators (see, e.g., Krebs and Davies, 1993, for a review of the advantages of group membership

for individuals). Within a group the probability that any given individual will become the prey of a predator is reduced because there are many other individuals who are also potential prey. Secondly, when feeding alone, an individual must also keep watch for predators, which reduces the amount of time it can feed. In a group, usually all members of the group glance around for predators so the amount of time each individual must devote to scanning the environment is less, and the fact that all members are scanning increases the chances of early detection of the predator and therefore successful escape is greater.

Group membership can also be advantageous to the individual in terms of finding new food sources. Krebs and Davies (1993) review research showing that animals that are less successful in finding food will often follow more successful individuals the next time they search for food. Since which individual will be successful will vary from day to day, such a strategy should be useful to each member within the group. When successful (and followed) an animal's total intake may be reduced somewhat, but on days following a less successful hunt, that animal will, on average, get more food by following another to their food source.

Cognitive Ethology

Some researchers (e.g., Griffin, 1984, 1992, 2001; Shettleworth, 1998) have turned their attention to how animals interpret information—what might be loosely considered the study of the animal mind. This area of research has come to be called **cognitive ethology**. They are interested in the cognitive components of animal behavior, that is, how animals take in and process information that can be later used to guide behavior. Within cognitive ethology there seem to be two main approaches. The first approach emphasizes the cognitive information processing capabilities of animals without making any assumptions about whether such processing is accompanied by conscious awareness or intent (see, e.g., Shettleworth, 1998, 2001). Although an interest in animal cognition can be traced back to early work by Romanes (1888), research by Tolman (1932) in the early part of the 1900s led to a renewed interest in the subject by the late 1970s (see, e.g., Hulse, Fowler, & Honig, 1978). Shettleworth (2001) and others (see, e.g., Heyes and Huber, 2000; Vauclair, 1996; Pearce, 1997 for reviews of this research) have continued to study animal cognition.

The second approach championed by Donald Griffin (see, e.g., Griffin, 1984, 1992, 2001) argues that animals could have some limited consciousness of what they do, although that awareness might not be equivalent to human consciousness. For example, in what has come to be called the **marking test**, some chimpanzees, after practice viewing themselves in a mirror, will touch a mark placed on their head that is only visible from the mirror (Povinelli, Gallup, Eddy, Bierschwale, Engstrom, Perilloux, & Toxopeus, 1997). Such behavior suggests that the chimp must understand that the image in the mirror is itself, indicating some degree of self-awareness. Others have used the marking test to test for self-awareness in other animals. So far self-awareness has been shown in humans, chimps, dolphins, and elephants (Reiss & Marino, 2001; Plotnik, deWaal, & Reiss 2006). As noted by Shettleworth, however, this perception of self is probably not equivalent to self-awareness as it is usually defined in humans (Shettleworth, 1998). The debate between these two approaches to cognitive ethology continues with each side presenting evidence for their point of view (see, e.g., Shettleworth, 1998; Griffin, 2001, for reviews of this research.)

Evolutionary Psychology

Not to be outdone by the ethologists, psychologists have shown a renewed interest in the genetic mechanisms of human behavior (see, e.g., Buss, 1999, 2004, 2005, 2008; Bridgeman, 2003; Ridley, 1993; Rossano, 2003). This latest round of interest in the genetics of human behavior has come to be called **evolutionary psychology**. Evolutionary psychology can be defined as "the analysis of the human mind as a collection of evolved mechanisms, the contexts that activate those mechanisms, and the behavior generated by those mechanisms"

(Buss, 1999, p. 47). In particular, evolutionary psychologists are interested in evolved mechanisms that helped resolve specific **adaptive problems** concerned with either survival or reproduction (Buss, 1999). These mechanisms evolved many thousands of years ago to deal with specific problems that our ancestors faced (Buss, 2008). Marean et al. (2007; see also McBrearty & Stringer, 2007) note that both fossils and genetic information indicate that Homo sapiens began as a species in Africa sometime between 100,000–200,000 years ago. Marean et al. provide data showing that one group of early humans occupied a cave along the coast of the Indian Ocean in Africa as early as 165,000 years ago. Moreover, they found evidence of stone tool use and pigments that could have been used for symbolic communication.

Evolutionary psychologists argue that some of the mechanisms that motivate present day behaviors first evolved to help us survive environmental conditions of those early times. Such mechanisms sample only small amounts of information that specifically concern the adaptive problem that was being faced. As envisioned by Buss (1999) the information is interpreted by a set of "decision rules" that can lead to various outputs such as physiological activity, input to other decision processes, or behavior. Finally, the various potential outputs are designed to provide a solution for that adaptive problem. Evolved psychological mechanisms in humans, then, are not as rigid as "instincts": The decision rules can produce several outcomes depending upon the context of the situation. Additionally, they propose that the brain is not a general problem solving device, but rather like a Swiss army knife that has evolved specific individual solutions for specific individual problems (Buss, 2008).

Let us consider an example. Hinz, Matz, and Patience (2001) examined the possibility that women's hair provides clues about their reproductive potential. In particular, it was proposed that both length of hair and quality of hair would serve as fertility cues. The authors of this study surveyed 230 women between the ages of 13 and 74 about their age, hair quality, marital status, hair length, children, and overall health. They found a significant correlation between hair length and age with younger women having longer hair than older women. Thus, hair length could serve as a general cue for youthfulness and, therefore, that a woman has most of her reproductive years ahead of her. In their study, hair quality was correlated with health. A healthy woman would be more likely to become pregnant and give birth successfully. Together, then, these two cues could serve as an indication of reproductive potential in a mate. Further, Moore (1985; see also Grammer, Kruck, Juette, & Fink, 2000) has shown that women use touching their hair (the hair flip) as a signal of interest when around men.

An earlier study by Barber (1995) suggested that male physical appearance communicates social dominance, which serves the double purpose of intimidating male rivals while attracting females. Characteristics that women find attractive in men (and vice versa) appear to have a genetic component and attract us because they indicate something about the quality of a potential mate. For example, women tend to prefer taller men with physical indicators of high testosterone such as a prominent chin and brow ridges and a V-shaped torso indicating upper body strength (Barber, 1995; Ellis, 1992; Johnston, Hagel, Franklin, Fink, & Grammer, 2001). Presumably, such cues are attractive because they indicate good health and the ability to protect

the woman and her children. Men, on the other hand, find young women with long hair, clear skin, full lips, and smaller, rounded chins attractive because these characteristics indicate health, high fertility, and for youthfulness, a longer period during which the woman can conceive children (Buss, 2004; Ford & Beach, 1951; Symons, 1979). Both sexes find body symmetry (especially facial symmetry) attractive because it indicates good health in a potential mate (Langlois & Roggman, 1990; Gangestad, Thornhill, & Yeo, 1994). These attractiveness cues are not conscious or voluntary; we simply know that we are attracted to some people more than others; however, these cues are attractive precisely because they predict successful reproduction.

Evolutionary psychologists have begun to study many human interactions from an evolutionary perspective, asking, and attempting to answer, how particular features or behaviors may have been adaptive in our ancestral past. To give one an idea of the breadth of studies that have been conducted from an evolutionary perspective, researchers have examined female and male mating strategies, sex differences in parenting behaviors, the adaptiveness of cooperative behaviors, and even why aggression and warfare may have been adaptive in the past. Buss (2008) provides an excellent overview of these research areas.

SUMMARY

The concept of instinct has had a long and varied career. Early formulations were often subjective and, in many cases, no more than descriptive labels. Problems also arose with the early theories because they confused learned and instinctive behaviors. Additionally, these early theories were guilty of naming behaviors without explaining them.

The ethologists helped us understand motivation from the viewpoint of naturally occurring behavior and evolution. They also attempted to define the various components of motivated behavior in ways that could be experimentally verified. Concepts such as key stimulus, FAP, innate releasing mechanism, and

action-specific energy help us understand how some behaviors are motivated by genetically controlled programs. More complex behaviors can be understood with such concepts as reaction chains, intention movements, and conflict behavior.

Newer approaches have begun to investigate these ideas in more detail, and in addition researchers are beginning to examine the role of the environment in genetically produced behavior (behavior ecology), the role of awareness in nonhuman species (cognitive ethology), and the role of genes in human behavior once again (evolutionary psychology). An interest in understanding human behavior from an evolutionary perspective has been rekindled, and many human behaviors such as language, social interactions related to sex and aggression, and even some maladaptive behaviors, such as anxiety, have been proposed to exist today because they had an adaptive component at an earlier time in the history of our species.

Though the concept of genetically programmed behaviors cannot explain all that we know about motivation, some behaviors in humans, as well as other animals, appear to have a genetic component. Genetic programming, then, is one source of the activation and direction of behavior.

KEY TERMS

instinct/nominal fallacy, *36*
Teleology/
 anthropomorphism, *38*
ethogram/consummatory
 behavior/appetitive behavior/
 action specific energy (ASE)/
 innate releasing mechanism
 (IRM)/key stimuli/sign
 stimuli/social releasers/
 configurational/supernormal
 key stimuli/super-optimal key
 stimuli, *40*
fixed action pattern (FAP)/
 stereotyped, *41*
independent of immediate
 external control/taxes/
 spontaneous/in vacuo/
 vacuum activity/independent
 of learning, *42*

intention movements/
 ritualization, *43*
conflict behavior/successive
 ambivalent
 behavior/simultaneous
 ambivalent behavior/
 redirected behavior/
 ethological displacement/
 reaction chain/instinct-
 conditioning
 intercalation, *44*
imprinting, *45*
sensitive period, *46*
open/closed program/
 preparedness/prepared
 behaviors/contraprepared
 behaviors/unprepared
 behaviors, *48*

eyebrow flick/appeasement
 gesture, *49*
neoteny, *51*
flirting behavior/hair flipping/
 kissing/baby talk/staring, *52*
phonetic module/phonetic social
 releaser system, *53*
interspecific/intraspecific/
 predatory attack/mobbing
 behavior/critical reaction/
 protection of the young, *54*
ritualized tournaments, *55*
behavioral ecology/cognitive
 ethology, *57*
marking test/evolutionary
 psychology/adaptive
 problems, *58*

SUGGESTIONS FOR FURTHER READING

Buss, D. M. (2008). *Evolutionary Psychology: The New Study of the Mind*. Boston: Allyn & Bacon. This text provides a good overview of the concepts, methods, and findings within the area of evolutionary psychology.

Crawford, C. B., & Krebs, D. L. (1998). *Handbook of Evolutionary Psychology: Ideas, Issues, and Applications*. Mahwah, NJ: Erlbaum. This edited work provides a selection of current topics of interest to evolutionary psychologists, especially sexual selection.

Griffin, D. R. (2001). *Animal Minds: Beyond Cognition to Consciousness*. Chicago: University of Chicago Press. This text outlines Griffin's position on animal behavior.

CHAPTER 3

Physiological Mechanisms of Arousal

CHAPTER PREVIEW

This chapter is concerned with the following questions:

1. Can motivation be explained as a result of the arousal of an organism?

2. Which brain mechanisms are involved in arousal?

3. What are the properties, mechanisms, and functions of sleep?

4. What is stress, and how does it influence the body?

5. Are changes in the events of an individual's life related to stress and illness?

6. How can we deal with stress?

Toward the end of each semester, an interesting phenomenon occurs. Students get sick. At first we attributed this phenomenon to attempts by certain students to avoid taking exams that would probably finalize grades lower than they desired. After observing this late-semester illness phenomenon and observing a similar phenomenon in ourselves and our colleagues during periods of acute stress, we have concluded that it is not malingering or an attempt to postpone the inevitable but a result of stress. For the student, stresses increase toward the end of the semester as exams are scheduled, projects near completion, and reports or term papers come due. For faculty, stresses more often involve deadlines for submitting articles for publication, preparing grant proposals, or preparing new courses.

Our observations are that such stresses seem to accumulate until, at some yet-unspecific point, our bodies succumb to whatever variety of flu or other such malady the year brings us. Apparently we tend to get sick precisely when we can least afford to.

Introduction

Fortunately we are not alone in thinking that stress is related to illness; numerous studies have been conducted that suggest a link between the two. We will examine some of this research toward the end of this chapter.

Stress is often conceptually located at the extreme end of a continuum of arousal. If arousal levels are too low, we sleep—or may even be in a coma. At moderate levels of arousal, we are awake and alert, while at the high end of the continuum, anxiety and stress appear. In this chapter we examine theory and research that attempts to explain motivated behavior by changes in arousal. Much of this research has focused on the brain mechanisms of arousal—about which, as we shall see, much is known.

For some reason, statistics, foreign languages, and physiological brain structures strike fear into the hearts of students. What is common to these three, perhaps, is that they require students to think (and to use strange new terms) in ways that are different from their normal approach to learning. Therefore the material in this chapter and the next is presented as nontechnically as possible, even though learning new terms and something about how changes in brain activity lead to changes in behavior will be necessary, because everything we are capable of doing, every behavior from brushing our teeth to solving differential equations, is the result of the activity of our nervous system.

In this chapter we will examine the ideas and research put forth to explain the arousal or activation of behavior. We will begin by examining early notions of how the brain accomplishes this activation and then proceed to theories and research showing that the automatic processes of the brain (the autonomic nervous system) are intimately involved. We will examine Hebb's theory of activation as representative of the thinking on arousal that was current in the 1950s. This will lead us into a more detailed examination of brain arousal mechanisms, particularly to a structure called the reticular activating system. We will examine theory and research indicating the involvement of this structure in arousal (from sleep to active attention) and then proceed to examine information on one aspect of arousal—sleep.

High states of arousal lead to stress, and we will look at research indicating that high arousal or stress influences our ability to adapt to our environment. In particular we will examine Selye's general adaptation syndrome and more recent research on stress and susceptibility to illness.

We will find that the concept of emotion weaves itself in and out of the research and that it is usually difficult to separate motivation, emotion, and arousal. A more complete discussion of the topic of emotion is found in Chapter 12; however, for the purposes of this chapter, we might say that motivation = emotion = arousal, since both motivation and emotion can be regarded as resulting from changes in arousal.

Arousal Theory

The arousal approach tends to emphasize the organism as a whole (Duffy, 1966) and argues that we can best understand behavior by understanding how the organism becomes activated. The basic idea underlying arousal theory is that we can understand motivation by viewing it on a continuum of behavioral activation. This continuum ranges from low levels of arousal (coma or sleep) to very high levels (stress). Figure 3.1 depicts how such a continuum might look although we cannot say just where these different behaviors might fall on the continuum.

Arousal theory assumes that behavior will change as we become more aroused. Some changes in arousal, as from sleep to alert wakefulness, will result in increased efficiency of performance, but other arousal changes, as from alert wakefulness to extreme arousal, will interfere with efficient responding. This reasoning suggests that an optimal level of arousal exists at which behavior will be most efficient, as depicted in Figure 3.2.

The curve in Figure 3.2 is called an **inverted U function** and indicates that increasing arousal improves performance only up to a point (the point of optimum arousal), after which continued increases in arousal actually begin to interfere with responding. This arousal–performance relationship, sometimes called the **Yerkes-Dodson Law**, is easily seen. In order to study efficiently for an exam,

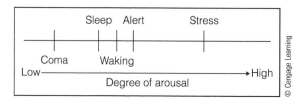

FIGURE 3.1 The arousal continuum. Different behaviors are associated with different degrees of arousal.

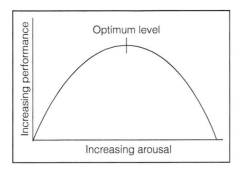

FIGURE 3.2 The inverted U function relating performance to arousal. As arousal increases, so does performance, up to a point; beyond the optimum level, increases in arousal lead to reduced levels of performance. From D. O. Hebb, "Drives and the Conceptual Nervous System," *Psychological Review*, *62*, 243–253. Copyright © 1955 by The American Psychological Association. Reprinted with permission.

we must be sufficiently aroused; on the other hand, if we become too aroused by the impending exam, the activation of the stress response may interfere with our studying to the point that we do not learn the material well.

Hokanson (1969) noted that the proposed relationship between arousal and performance holds for some types of tasks but not for others. For example, Freeman (1940) obtained an inverted U function between arousal (as measured by skin conductance) and reaction time, but Hokanson did not obtain inverted U functions for other tasks such as symbol matching or concept formation. Thus the relationship between arousal and behavior is apparently more complex and task-specific than arousal theory has indicated. Indeed there are probably numerous arousal functions that depend in part on the type of task. What is optimal arousal for one task may not be optimal for some other task.

If emotion and motivation result from activation of the nervous system, as arousal theory suggests, there should be structures in the nervous system that trigger this activation. Indeed, there are. Bremer (1937) has shown that if we cut through the brain stem of an animal between the medulla and the spinal cord (Figure 3.3), an animal continues to go through its normal sleep-wake cycle even though the body has been deprived of all its higher cortical brain tissue (Bremer called this preparation **encephale isole**). On the other hand, if we cut higher up the brain stem at the level of the colliculi, the sleep-wake cycle is abolished and the animal sleeps constantly, showing no spontaneous waking (called the **cerveau isole**). Figure 3.3 shows these two different preparations.

Taken together, the results of Bremer's two cuts suggest that some brain structure (or structures) located between the two cuts control changes in the arousal level involved in moving from sleeping

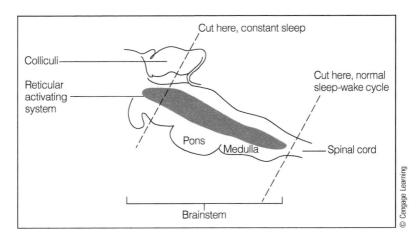

FIGURE 3.3 Brainstem cuts made by Bremer. Note location of the reticular activating system.

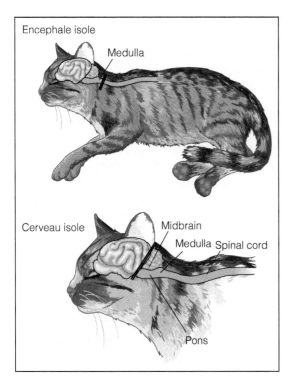

FIGURE 3.4 Bremer's study. See text for details. Straight black lines indicate the position of the cuts. From WILSON. *Biological Foundations of Human Behavior* (Fig. 10.9, p. 293). Copyright © 2001, Cengage Learning.

to waking. Further, such a structure is located in the vicinity of the **pons** (Figure 3.3).

The Reticular Activating System

Arousal theory received a big boost with the discovery by Moruzzi and Magoun (1949) of the role of the reticular activating system in arousal. The **reticular activating system (RAS)** is a group of neurons (nerve cells) located in the brain stem's central core, which runs from the level of the medulla through the thalamus, as shown in Figure 3.5 (Wilson, 2003). Moruzzi and Magoun found that electrical stimulation of the RAS led to changes in the electrical activity of the cortex (recorded by the electroencephalogram, or EEG) that were indistinguishable from changes seen when external stimuli (e.g., a loud noise) were attended. In order to understand the role of the RAS in arousal, we must briefly examine what is shown by an EEG.

An individual resting quietly shows a regular pattern of cortical electrical activity that can be measured by means of the EEG. The electrical activity of the cells in this relaxed state tends to occur around the same time (i.e., they are **synchronous**) and leads to a pattern of electrical activity known as **alpha waves**. If we make a loud sound, however, the individual will open his or her eyes and look around in an alert manner, and the pattern of the EEG during this alert behavior is very different. The cells of the cortex tend now to be active independently of one another (they are **desynchronized**), which leads to a new EEG pattern called **beta waves**. Beta waves are associated with alert, attentive, and aroused individuals ready to deal with changes in their environment.

Moruzzi and Magoun (1949) found that stimulation of the RAS led to beta wave activity just as environmental stimuli do. Therefore it seemed reasonable that the RAS is also responsible for the activation of the organism. Support for this idea was provided in a number of different ways. First, the RAS receives sensory input from the external sensory systems as well as from the muscles and internal organs (Hokanson, 1969); thus it has the necessary inputs to trigger arousal. Second, Lindsley (1951) cut all the brain structures surrounding the RAS in experimental animals and found that the animals still displayed normal sleep-wake cycles. But when he cut the RAS, leaving everything else intact, the result was a permanently sleeping animal, just as in Bremer's cerveau isole preparation. Finally, the RAS is known to send fibers diffusely to the whole cortex. Therefore, the RAS is a part of the brain circuitry that serves to arouse the organism from sleep to wakefulness and determine where on the arousal continuum we find ourselves and to what we pay attention (Kalat, 2001; Wilson, 2003).

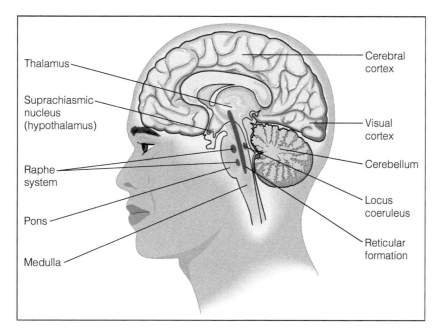

FIGURE 3.5 The location of the reticular activating system (reticular formation). From WILSON, *Biological Foundations of Human Behavior* (Fig. 9.12, p. 292). Copyright © 2001 Cengage Learning.

The discovery of the role of the RAS in arousal led activation theorists to argue that emotion and motivation were equivalent to cortical arousal (e.g., see Lindsley, 1950, 1951). Perhaps one of the best-reasoned theories was put forth by Donald Hebb (1955).

Hebb's Theory

Hebb believed that sensory information serves two purposes: to provide information, or what he termed the **cue function** of a stimulus, and to arouse the individual (the **arousal function**). If the individual's cortex is not aroused, the cue function of a stimulus will have no effect (we do not react to the sound of a passing car when we are asleep because the cortex is not aroused by the RAS).

Sensory stimuli picked up by a person are sent to both the RAS and the cortex via the thalamus. Hebb believed that the stimulus effect at the RAS level is to activate or "tone up" the cortex so that the stimulus information coming from the thalamus can be processed by the cortex. Motivation, for Hebb, is the activation of the cortex by the RAS.

It is also known that the cortex sends fibers down to the RAS (Magoun, 1963). Thus the cortex can also activate the RAS and keep arousal high even when external or internal stimulation is low. These downstream connections from the cortex to the RAS could provide a possible explanation for how thoughts might motivate behavior. For example, lying in bed and thinking about tomorrow's exam would activate one's RAS, which in turn keeps the cortex aroused, and sleep becomes difficult. Thus thoughts as well as external stimuli can lead to the arousal of an individual. More research on this aspect of arousal might prove very useful to our understanding of the way in which thoughts influence behavior.

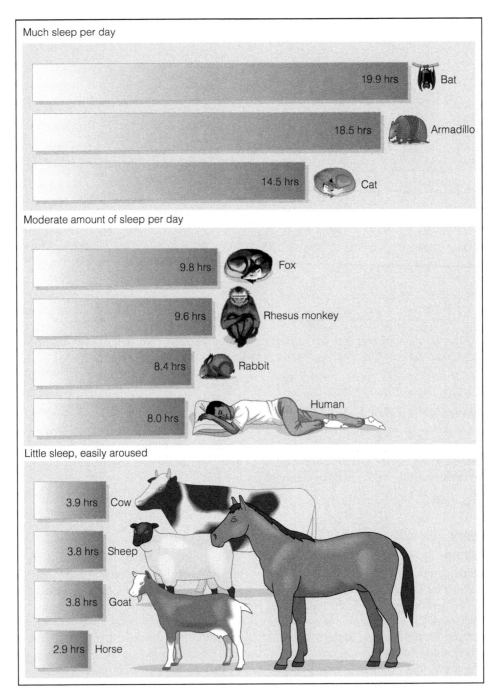

FIGURE 3.6 Hours of sleep for predators and prey. Predators generally sleep more, prey less. From KALAT. *Biological Psychology*, 7e (Fig. 9.16, p. 275). Copyright © 2001 Cengage Learning.

Psychophysiological Measures

Arousal theory is based on the assumption that one can measure arousal by monitoring the activity of the brain or changes in the autonomic nervous system and correlating these with changes in behavior. As researchers soon discovered, however, these correlations were often minimal (although usually positive). The lack of substantial correlations between different indexes of arousal has created problems for arousal theory and led Lacey (1967) to propose that more than one type of arousal exists. Thus we may see behavioral arousal as indicated by a responding organism, autonomic arousal as shown by changes in bodily functions, or cortical arousal as evidenced by desynchronized, fast brain waves. Lacey proposed that although these three arousals often occur together, they do not have to and are in fact independent. He noted, for example, that certain chemicals (e.g., atropine) produce EEG activity akin to sleep in cats and dogs, which nevertheless respond behaviorally in a normal, awake manner. Other chemicals (e.g., physostigmine) produce EEG activity like that of an alert animal, but the animal behaves as if drowsy. Comatose patients sometimes show normal EEGs, and normal responding is sometimes observed in individuals with sleeplike EEGs. Lacey also reported several studies indicating that sometimes there is little relationship between central nervous system activity and autonomic changes. As a result of these problems, he proposed that arousal is multidimensional. He believed that different situations produce different patterns of somatic responses (e.g., heart rate).

Feedback from the periphery of the body is also important in Lacey's model of arousal. For example, he reported research showing that distention of the carotid sinus (a mechanism in the carotid artery) causes EEG activity to change from alert, high-frequency activity to low-frequency activity generally associated with sleep. This change indicates that feedback from various systems of the body can directly influence the arousal system and suggests that bodily systems may also play a role in the length of arousal episodes.

To summarize, research indicates physiological mechanisms in the midbrain that are involved with arousal of the organism, the sleep-wake cycle, and alert attention to the environment (Wilson, 2003). These conclusions fit nicely with arousal theory's concept of motivation and emotion as equivalent to arousal.

Problems With Arousal Theory

Unfortunately, several problems with arousal theory remain. One major problem is the lack of a strong relationship between measures of behavioral, cortical, and autonomic arousal. A second problem specific to Lacey's theory is that it assumes different patterns of bodily responses, yet clear differences remain to be shown. Some studies have indicated that the adrenal hormone norepinephrine may be related to anger or aggression and epinephrine to fear or anxiety (Schildkraut & Kety, 1967). However, further work is needed to determine if Lacey's theory can account for different bodily response patterns. Of particular interest in this regard is a study by Ekman, Levenson, and Friesen (1983) indicating that changes in autonomic activities are discernible for the emotions of disgust, anger, fear, and sadness when careful control procedures are employed. Ekman and associates suggest that the autonomic changes may be instigated by contraction of the facial muscles into the universal signals for these emotions. Facial muscular patterns may even provide the different bodily response patterns that arousal theory dictates. We will examine the facial feedback hypothesis of emotion in more detail in Chapter 12.

Another problem with arousal theory is its general assumption that cortical arousal, as evidenced by the EEG, indicates a motivated or emotional state. As Lacey pointed out, this relationship is not always found. It is not presently clear that cortical arousal is equivalent to motivated behavior; but even if we were to make that assumption, it is also not clear how this arousal directs behavior. One final problem is the assumption that an understanding of arousal requires only an understanding of the underlying physiological mechanisms. This may be incorrect. A full understanding of arousal may also require a knowledge of environmental factors and the history of the organism.

Sleep

Many, perhaps most people regard sleep as a low state of arousal. It is also often thought of as the absence of behavior. As it turns out, both of these two conceptions are overly simplified. Anyone who has gone for any lengthy period of time without sleep realizes that sleep can become an overpowering motive, easily overriding such motives as hunger or sex. This observation is supported by research indicating that sleep shows characteristics of a motivated need state (Dement, 1972). In fact, Carlson (2007) points out that sleep is not a state, but a type of behavior, one that in fact we engage in for about a third of our lives. Additionally, during some aspects of the sleep process our brains are highly active, similar to when we are awake and alert.

Sleep research can be traced as far back as the late 1800s, but systematic research only began with Nathaniel Kleitman's studies in the early 1920s (Kleitman, 1963). Much is known about the sleep process (see, e.g., Carlson, 2007; Kalat, 2001; Long, 1987; Pressman, 1986; Wilson, 2003), yet the reasons for sleep remain obscure. It is known that the effects of sleep deprivation are specific to the type of task required of a sleep-deprived individual (Johnson, 1983). Webb (1986) found that going without sleep for approximately 48 hours led to problems of sustaining performance on a long, complex task requiring high levels of attention and cognitive processing. There were, however, no clear indications that accuracy of performance declined. Sleep deprivation also seems to increase suggestibility in humans (Blagrove, 1996). On the other hand, complete deprivation of sleep in rats causes them to die (Rechtschaffen & Bergmann, 1995; Rechtschaffen, Bergmann, Everson, Kushida, & Gilliland, 1989; Rechtschaffen, Gilliland, Bergmann, & Winter, 1983), perhaps as the result of changes in the immune system (Everson, 1995). In the following sections we will explore a little of what is known about sleep, what physiological structures seem to be involved, and what the functions of sleep are thought to be.

General Properties of Sleep

As noted earlier, we humans spend roughly one-third of our lives in the state of sleep. On that basis alone, sleep must be considered an important behavior to understand. Even though a major portion of our lives is spent sleeping, large variations exist among individuals in the amount of sleep needed. While most people sleep 7 to 8 hours per night, others are able to get along with less. Dement (1972) reported his study of two individuals who regularly slept less than three hours per night without apparent ill effects.

Common sense indicates that we sleep when we are fatigued. This cannot be the entire explanation, however, because people confined to bed 24 hours per day sleep approximately the same amount of time that they would have slept if they had been up and active. Dement suggested that we may sleep because we are least efficient at certain times. Our bodies go through cyclic changes that often approximate 24 hours in length; these cycles are called **circadian rhythms** (from the Latin circa, about, and diem, a day). Many of these circadian rhythms operate in the lowest part of their cycle during sleep, and Dement proposed that sleep may protect us from engaging in behavior at a time when we are least efficient. Webb and Agnew (1973) similarly suggested that sleep is adaptive because it keeps organisms from responding at unnecessary or dangerous times. Meddis (1975) made a similar proposal based on an evolutionary perspective. Further, several lines of research suggest that circadian rhythms and sleep are closely linked (Czeisler et al., 1989; Pool, 1989). A more complete understanding of the role of circadian rhythms in the sleep-wake cycle is beginning to be understood (see Lavie, 2001, for a review of this research). At the present time it appears that sleep is controlled by at least two separate processes: a homeostatic process that increases our likelihood of engaging in sleep the longer we are awake, and a circadian process that determines when we wake up (Kramer, et al., 2001; Lavie, 2001; Takahashi, 1999).

Different animals spend different amounts of time in sleep. The apparent universal need for sleep in animals is shown by the fact that even fruit flies appear to need their sleep (Shaw, Cirelli, Greenspan, & Tononi, 2000) and that sleep in these flies is under genetic control (Koh, Joiner, Wu, Yue, Smith, & Sehgal, 2008). Variation in sleep times seems to fit with Webb and Agnew's (1973) idea of the adaptiveness of sleep, because different animals would be expected to differ in the durations of time when responding would be disadvantageous to them. Others have suggested (see, e.g., Kalat, 2001; Lima, Rattenborg, Lesku, & Amianer, 2005) that amount of time spent asleep relates to the danger of attack: animals who are likely to be attacked (prey) while asleep generally sleep very little, while predators generally sleep much more. See Figure 3.6. Whales and some birds show a specialized form of sleep known as **unihemispheric slow-wave sleep (USWS)** where one half of the brain sleeps at a time. Whales also show little or no rapid eye movement sleep (REM) seen in other mammals (Lyamin, Manger, Ridgway, Mukhametov, & Siegel, 2008; Rattenborg, Lima, & Amlaner, 1999). The reason such a mechanism might have evolved in whales probably involved sleeping and breathing while in the water, while for birds USWS is thought to serve an antipredator function as one eye remains open during USWS (Rattenborg, Lima, & Amlaner, 1999).

In humans the length of time spent in sleep decreases with age. Infants who are three days old sleep approximately 14 to 16 hours a day, while five-year-olds sleep about 11 hours. By age 20, the average individual sleeps about $6 1/2$ to 7 hours per night. (Generally, in older adults, a further small decrease in sleep time occurs, although the most striking thing about sleep in older adults is its variability. Some older people sleep more than they did when younger, while others sleep considerably less [Webb & Agnew, 1973, but see Spielman & Herrera, 1991].) Furthermore, the sleep of older individuals appears to differ from that of the young. Ancoli–Isreal and Kripke (1991) note that older people report more awakenings during the night and more insomnia. Similarly, Buysse and colleagues (1992) found that healthy elderly subjects took more daytime naps and experienced shorter and more fragmented nighttime sleep when compared to young adults. Buysse and colleagues also found that older people went to sleep earlier in the evening. Spielman and Herrera (1991) report that older people still sleep approximately 7 hours per day but that the sleep is broken up more and often includes daytime naps. They also report that there is a decline in both Stage 3 and Stage 4 sleep (see next section) with age and that this decline appears to be more severe in men than in women.

Consider how we fall asleep. Sleep seems to come gradually; that is, we seem to "drift off" slowly into sleep. Although it was originally thought that we fall to sleep abruptly (Dement, 1972), it now appears that our intuition is correct. The movement from waking to sleep is a gradual transition that moves us from waking, through the Stage 1 of sleep to Stage 2 (see Ogilvie, 2001, for an excellent review of this transition process). Indeed, if awakened just before entering Stage 2 sleep, more than 50% of participants say that they are awake (Ogilvie, 2001)! The stages of sleep are typically defined by changes in the EEG pattern, and as we shall see, the EEG has been a powerful tool in helping researchers to study sleep. Let us look more closely at the stages of sleep.

Stages of Sleep

As defined by electrical activity of the brain, sleep proceeds through five stages during the night. The alpha wave activity that characterizes **relaxed wakefulness** occurs before Stage 1 and is replaced by fast, irregular waves of low amplitude in **Stage 1** of sleep. The EEG pattern shows theta wave activity (3.5–7.5 Hz). Then after 10 to 15 minutes in Stage 1, the EEG pattern starts to show brief periods of **sleep spindles** (14 Hz/sec waves) and **K-complexes**, and the person is now in **Stage 2** of sleep (Carlson, 2001). In **Stage 3** another wave pattern is seen called **delta waves** (< 3.5 Hz). These large slow waves occur during 20 to 50% of the sleep stage. When these slow waves occur more than 50% of the time, the person is said to be in **Stage 4** of sleep. Stage 4, in which these slow, high-amplitude waves become dominant, will be reached approximately 30 to 45 minutes after initially falling asleep. After some time in Stage 4 sleep, the EEG pattern begins to change again to Stage 3, then to Stage 2, and finally to **Stage 5**. At Stage 5 the EEG pattern is a mix of theta, beta, and alpha waves (Carlson, 2001), and the individual's eyes usually begin moving rapidly under the lids. Muscle tone, as measured at the jaw muscle, is

very low. This fifth stage of sleep is generally called **REM sleep** (rapid eye movements) and is the time during sleep when most dreaming occurs (Webb & Agnew, 1973; Wilson, 2003). Examples of the various EEG patterns of the sleep stages are shown in Figure 3.7

REM and NREM Sleep   Sleep Stages 1 through 4 are generally called **NREM** (for non-REM) **sleep** because eye movements are not evident during these stages. NREM sleep is also sometimes called slow-wave sleep to point out the predominance of the high-amplitude, slow delta waves seen in Stages 3 and 4.

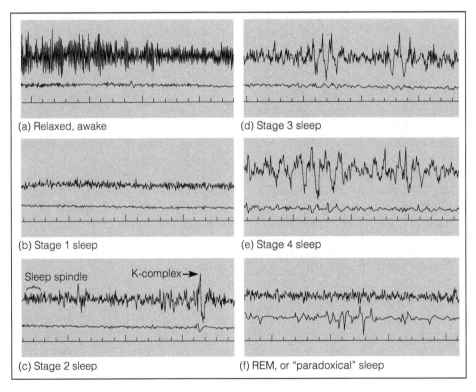

(a) Relaxed, awake

(b) Stage 1 sleep

(c) Stage 2 sleep   Sleep spindle   K-complex →

(d) Stage 3 sleep

(e) Stage 4 sleep

(f) REM, or "paradoxical" sleep

FIGURE 3.7   Polysomnograph records from a male college student. A polysomnograph includes records of EEG, eye movements, and sometimes other data, such as muscle tension or head movements. For each of these records, the top line is the EEG from one electrode on the scalp; the middle line is a record of eye movements; and the bottom line is a time marker, indicating 1-second units. Note the abundance of slow waves in Stages 3 and 4. (Source: Records provided by T. E. LeVere). From KALAT. *Biological Psychology*, 7e (Fig. 9.9, p. 263). Copyright © 2001 Cengage Learning.

Some researchers believe that NREM sleep serves a restorative function, giving the body a chance to rebuild resources. We know, however, that Stage 4 sleep decreases with age, showing a sharp decline after age 30 and in some individuals disappearing altogether by age 50 (Webb & Agnew, 1973; but see Webb, 1982, for another view). Hayashi and Endo (1982) have also found large reductions in sleep Stages 3 and 4 in healthy older persons. Their results indicate a forward shifting of REM toward earlier portions of the night, perhaps, Hayashi and Endo suggest, because of the reduction in Stages 3 and 4.

Snoring, if it occurs, typically does so during NREM sleep, and a person awakened during NREM sleep does not usually report dreaming. Typically he or she reports random thoughts, usually of a nonemotional sort, similar to waking thoughts.

Sleep time is not equally divided among the five stages of sleep, nor do the stages occur evenly throughout the night, as might have seemed to be the case from the earlier discussion of sleep stages. Across a total sleep period only about 5% of total sleep is spent in Stage 1, while almost 50% is spent in Stage 2. Stage 3 occupies only about 6% of total sleep time, and Stage 4 amounts to approximately 14%. REM sleep accounts for about 25% of sleep time on average.

Of the various stages, Stage 4 and REM sleep have been studied most extensively. A greater proportion of Stage 4 sleep occurs early in the night, while most REM sleep occurs later. Figure 3.8 shows how these stages change across a night's sleep.

REM sleep was discovered by Aserinsky and Kleitman in 1955 (see also Aserinsky, 1987). It quickly became apparent to researchers that REM sleep correlated with reports of dreaming. For example, Dement (1972) noted that reports of dreaming from individuals awakened during REM sleep are approximately 80%, while reports of dreaming from persons awakened from Stage 4 are only about 7%. Some controversy exists concerning the percentage of dreams reported in REM and NREM sleep. Goodenough (1991), noting reviews by Foulkes (1966), Rechtschaffen

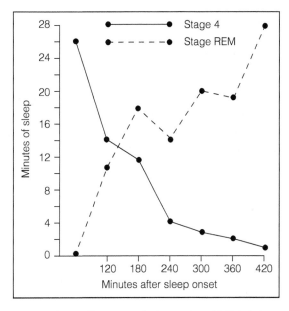

FIGURE 3.8 Time spent in Stage 4 and REM sleep as a function of time since falling asleep. As can be seen, Stage 4 occurs primarily early in the night, while REM sleep increases as the night progresses. From "Measurement and Characteristics of Nocturnal Sleep," by W. B. Webb and H. W. Agnew in *Progress in Clinical Psychology*, Vol 8., edited by L. E. Abt and B. F. Riess. Copyright © 1968 by Grune & Stratton. Reprinted by permission.

(1967), and Stoyva and Kamiya (1968), concludes that dreaming can occur during NREM and that under some conditions REM sleep occurs when dreams are unlikely (such as in decorticate individuals). Thus the use of rapid eye movements as the only index of dreaming is not totally accurate. There may, however, be a difference between dreams reported in REM and NREM sleep. REM dreams are more often bizarre, emotionally loaded, or lifelike, while dreams reported during NREM sleep are more likely to be described as nonemotional, random thoughts. Furthermore, as reported by Goodenough (1991), the works of several groups of researchers have found that eye movement frequency during REM is related to the activity reported in REM dreams. Eye movement frequency also seems to be related to dream bizarreness, and the intensity and emotionality of REM dreams.

In addition to rapid eye movements in REM sleep, there is also a loss of skeletal muscle tone. This is caused by inhibition of motor neurons in the brain and actually amounts to a temporary paralysis (Dement, 1972). The loss of muscle tone is the best indicator of REM or "dream" sleep. REM sleep normally occurs about once every 90 minutes throughout the night. REM periods become longer throughout the night, so that by morning one may be in a REM period for as long as an hour (Dement, 1972).

During REM sleep the EEG activity of the cortex sometimes appears very similar to that of Stage 1 sleep and is, in many respects, also similar to the EEG activity seen in a person who is awake and alert. REM sleep produces a mixture of theta and beta wave activity (Carlson, 2010) similar to both Stage 1 sleep and alert active behavior. In fact the EEG activity that occurs during REM sleep in cats is virtually indistinguishable from their waking EEG activity (Jouvet, 1976). But even though the electrical activity of the cortex appears to be close to that of waking behavior, the person is asleep and essentially paralyzed. For this reason, REM sleep has sometimes been called **paradoxical sleep**.

REM sleep, like Stage 4 sleep, tends to decline with age early in life; however, REM sleep stabilizes at about age 20 and drops only slightly in old age. According to Carlson (2001), newborn infants spend as much as 70% of their sleep time in REM sleep, which then declines to around 30% by 6 months of age. The percentage of REM sleep is around 22% by age eight and then declines further to around 15% in older people. The sleep of kittens, puppies, and rat pups is 100% REM (Dement, 1972) at birth. All these findings have led Dement to speculate that REM sleep may organize connections within the brain. In support of this hypothesis, Dement noted that guinea pigs, which are more mature than kittens at birth, show very little REM sleep.

The fact that animals show REM sleep in a fashion similar to humans raises the question of whether animals dream. Though we know that REM sleep and dreaming are correlated in humans, we cannot be sure that the same is true for other species. Thus, while the question is tantalizing, there is presently no good answer. Our knowledge of evolutionary processes, however, lends support to the possibility that some animals, such as primates and perhaps dogs and cats, do dream.

Clearly the most exciting aspect of REM sleep research was the finding that it generally coincided with dreaming. For the first time, sleep scientists could begin to study objectively the very subjective state of dreaming.

Dreams

Although some people do not believe that they dream, research has shown that everyone dreams. This is easily shown by having a "nondreamer" sleep for several nights while connected to an EEG apparatus and to equipment that measures eye movements and muscle tone. The adamant nondreamer falls asleep and eventually enters a period of REM activity. If awakened during this REM period, the nondreamer discovers to great amazement that he or she has been dreaming vividly!

The average individual spends about 100 minutes per night in dreaming (Webb & Agnew, 1973). Most dreams, however, are not recalled unless one awakens soon after they have occurred (Goodenough, 1991). This is probably why we tend to remember the dreams we had just before the alarm went off but do not remember dreams that occurred earlier in the night. The salience of a dream also appears to influence how likely it is that it will be remembered (Goodenough, 1991).

Research has shown that although most dreams are brief, they can sometimes last up to an hour (Dement, 1972). Most dreams occur in ordinary, everyday settings and are usually not terribly emotional. When emotion is present in dreams, however, it tends to be negative; about 65% of emotional dreams are of this sort. Dement also noted that dreams early in the night tend to draw on the events of the previous day, while later dreams draw more from stored memories.

Some research also suggests that dreams change with age (Herman & Shows, 1984; Waterman, 1991). Herman and Shows, for example, found in a large sample of 295 college graduates that younger persons recall their dreams more frequently than older persons. After reviewing several laboratory and survey studies, Waterman (1991, p. 356) concludes that "dream recall diminishes as one gets older." Furthermore, Waterman found that there were changes in dream content between young adult students and middle-aged adults. Middle-aged adults of both sexes showed significantly less aggressiveness, friendliness, and emotion in their dreams than did the students. Why these changes occur with age is unclear; however, REM sleep itself changes with age—time spent in REM is reduced with age, and REM is less stable (Woodruff, 1985)—and these changes in REM may be related in some way to the changes in the recall and content of dreams just noted.

Domhoff (2001) has proposed a **neurocognitive theory of dreams**. Based on an overview of research on brain injuries and the effects these have on dreaming, sleep lab research with young children and their dream reports, and content analysis of adult dreams, Domhoff suggests that dreaming is "… a developmental cognitive achievement that depends upon the maturation and maintenance of a specific network of forebrain structures" (Domhoff, 2001, p. 13). This network incorporates a "**continuity principle**" (see also Lortie-Lussier, Cote, & Vachon, 2000, for evidence of continuity in dreams) whereby personal concerns during the day also appear in one's dreams and a "**repetition principle**" whereby the same characters, settings, social interactions, and so forth show up again and again in an individual's dreams, sometimes across decades. He further suggests that the continuity between waking thoughts and dreams implies that we are dealing with the same basic issues during both waking and dreaming and that these issues include our conceptions of ourselves and others (Domhoff, 2001).

An alternative view of dreaming by Revonsuo (2000) proposes that dreaming functions to simulate threatening events (**Threat Simulation Theory**) and allows one to rehearse behaviors associated with perceiving threats and avoiding them. Moreover, this function is proposed to be evolutionarily ancient and evolved as a mechanism because it helped our distant ancestors survive and reproduce. This proposal maintains that dreaming is an "offline" representation of the world and various threats that would be important to the dreamer. Because it is offline, disbelief is suspended while the dreamer rehearses various solutions to the dreamed threat. Such real threats to life and limb were probably much more common in our hunter-gatherer past and nightly rehearsals (via dreaming) of possible behavioral solutions would have increased the chances of surviving actual threats that occurred during waking. Revonsuo (2000) reviews considerable evidence that is consistent with this hypothesis. For example, it is known that the content of dreams is more often emotionally negative and threatening to the dreamer than emotionally positive and rewarding. Similarly, aggression (either attacking or being attacked) is the most common form of behavior reported in social interactions within dreams. When attacked in a dream, it is usually either by a male (in both men and women) or an animal. Such content would make sense in hunter-gatherer societies where large animals and aggressive males from rivals groups were constantly a threat. Revonsuo also notes research in children showing that they dream about animals much more than adults and the animals they dream about are often not animals that they would come in contact with in their waking environment. About half of these dreams are about wild animals and in many of these dreams the child dreamer is the victim of attack by the animal. Additional research on the threat simulation theory of dreams has generally supported it (Bulkeley, Broughton, Sanchez, & Stiller, 2005; Gackenbach & Kuruvilla, 2008; Valli, Revonsuo, Palkas, Ismail, Ali, & Punamaki, 2005; Valli, Lenasdotter,

MacGregor, & Revonsuo, 2007; however see Malcolm-Smith & Solms, 2004). Franklin and Zyphur (2005, p. 59) have proposed an extension to Revonsuo's threat simulation theory by suggesting that dreams function as "a more general **virtual rehearsal mechanism** that is likely to play an important role in the development of human cognitive capacities." Thus, they suggest that dreaming may serve other cognitive processes in addition to simulations of threatening situations.

Sleep Deprivation

As noted earlier, the effects of sleep deprivation vary with the type of task. Short tasks performed under sufficient motivation often show only minor effects of sleep deprivation. Long, boring tasks requiring high motivation do, however, show deficits in sustaining attention (Webb, 1986).

Although common sense would seem to indicate that the effects of sleep deprivation are negative when they occur, research has shown that sleep deprivation can sometimes have therapeutic properties for some depressed individuals. As little as one complete night without sleep has an antidepressant effect on between one-third to half of depressed patients (Roy-Byrne, Uhde, & Post, 1986).

Dream Deprivation   William Dement pioneered research in dream deprivation. His procedure was to observe the recordings of sleeping persons for rapid eye movements and, when they occurred, quickly awaken the sleeper. Dement found that in order to deprive sleepers of REM sleep, it was necessary to awaken them more and more often. He noted that it was as if a **REM pressure** was building up that could be expressed only through REM sleep. When Dement let his subjects sleep normally, he discovered a now well-established phenomenon known as **REM rebound**. He found that when dream-deprived subjects were allowed to sleep, they dreamed much more than normal, as if the REM periods were rebounding from their imposed low level. Indeed this overshooting of the normal amount of

dreaming continued for several days after the period of deprivation. REM deprivation in animals produces several odd effects that are not well understood. For example, REM deprivation in animals produces a shift in eating patterns relative to the light-dark cycle but does not seem to change the amount of food eaten overall. REM deprivation also produces an increase in aggressiveness and sexual behaviors in animals, and REM deprivation rebound effects are reduced by intracranial self-stimulation (see Ellman, Spielman, Luck, Steiner, & Halperin, 1991; Ellman, Spielman, & Lipschutz–Brach, 1991, for reviews of these studies). Ellman and his associates propose that there may be a link between neural structures underlying REM sleep processes and other neural structures subserving motivational processes. They believe that it is likely that the link involves the neural structures responsible for intracranial self-stimulation effects. Other research, (Chemelli, et al., 1999; Lin et al., 1999) suggests that there is, in addition, a link between a neurotransmitter called hypocretin or orexin (which is also involved in feeding behavior) and sleep. In fact, a change in the metabolism of this neuropeptide appears to be responsible for narcolepsy in both mice and dogs and perhaps humans as well (Peyron et al., 2000; see also Chicurel, 2000; Siegel, 1999; Smith, 2000; Takahashi, 1999, for short reviews of this work).

Dement noted that his human REM-deprived subjects appeared irritable and anxious and had trouble concentrating. This suggested to him that REM sleep may be necessary for psychological well-being. Unfortunately, other investigators have not found anxiety or irritability in their REM-deprived subjects; therefore little can be concluded about the necessity of dreaming for psychological health.

REM deprivation can sometimes occur from drug usage. Many drugs (particularly barbiturates, if taken beyond recommended levels) suppress REM sleep. If the drugs are abruptly withdrawn, REM rebound occurs, and the person shows increased dreaming with vivid nightmares. Amphetamines, which act on the reticular formation to maintain arousal and wakefulness, also suppress REM when sleep finally occurs. Webb and Agnew (1973) noted that withdrawal of amphetamines leads to prolonged REM rebound, sometimes lasting up to two weeks, accompanied by vivid nightmares. Even alcohol, if taken in sufficient doses, leads to REM suppression. It is possible that the vivid hallucinations sometimes experienced in alcohol withdrawal (termed **delirium tremens [DTs]**) may result from REM rebound intruding on waking behavior (Dement, 1972; Webb & Agnew, 1973). It seems clear that some cures for sleeplessness, like heavy barbiturate use, may turn out to be worse than sleep loss (Palca, 1989).

Much research has been conducted on both REM and NREM sleep. Though we know a good deal about sleep characteristics, we are just beginning to gain some understanding of the brain systems involved with sleep. The research is complex and sometimes contradictory; nevertheless, several brain stem and forebrain structures have been identified as important in sleep maintenance.

Physiology of Sleep

The autonomic nervous system changes its activity during sleep. During NREM sleep, blood pressure, heart rate, and respiration decline, and the veins and arteries dilate (**vasodilation**). During REM sleep, blood pressure, heart rate, and respiration generally increase and become much more variable. There is an increased flow of blood to the brain and penile erection occurs in males and vaginal secretion in females (Kalat, 2001; Williams, Holloway, & Griffiths, 1973). In REM sleep the electrical activity of the cortex, as you remember, changes from slow, high-amplitude delta waves to fast, low-amplitude waves similar to those present during waking.

Most research has been aimed at explaining how structures within the brainstem may be related to changes in cortical activity. A considerable amount of research exists, however, that suggests forebrain areas also exert control over the sleep process.

Brain Stem Mechanisms That Promote Arousal

As noted earlier, Bremer's research showed that structures within the brain stem in the area of the pons are responsible for changes in arousal that move us from sleep to waking and back. Research has now shown that there are numerous structures within this area that contribute to the production of waking and sleep. Carlson (2010) has provided one of the most complete and clear reviews of this research and what follows is based on his overview of this complex topic.

When the reticular system is activated by sensory information or other factors, it in turn arouses the cerebral cortex along two separate pathways. One pathway goes from the reticular formation to the thalamus and from there to the cerebral cortex. The second pathway goes from the reticular formation to the lateral hypothalamus, the basal ganglia, and the basal forebrain. Connections from the basal forebrain activate the cerebral cortex and the hippocampus. Thus, information available to the reticular formation can have wide ranging influences on other structures important to arousal (e.g., motivation via the hypothalamus, learning via the hippocampus and basal ganglia, and cerebral cortex via both thalamic and basal forebrain connections). Changes in arousal and attention probably result from a complex interplay of these various subsystems.

In addition to these structural connections, four or five separate neurotransmitters appear to play a role in changes in arousal—they are acetylcholine, norepinephrine, serotonin, histamine, and orexin (Carlson, 2010).

Neurotransmitters That Promote Arousal

Acetylcholine Acetylcholine-producing cells in the basal forebrain and the pons activate the cerebral cortex and lead to a desynchronized EEG when they are stimulated. Blocking acetylcholine appears to reduce arousal levels, while procedures designed to increase acetylcholine production increase signs of arousal. Acetylcholine increases **general arousal** of the cortex (Carlson, 2010).

Norepinephrine Norepinephrine-producing cells in the **locus coerulus** of the pons activate many different areas of the brain including the cerebral cortex, hippocampus, thalamus, cerebellum, and the pons and medulla as well. Production of norepinephrine is high during waking and drops off during sleep, becoming almost zero during REM sleep (Aston-Jones & Bloom, 1981). In particular, norepinephrine appears to be important for vigilance (Aston-Jones, Rajkowski, Kubiak, & Alexinsky, 1994).

Serotonin Serotonin-producing cells in the **raphe nuclei** of the pons and medulla also connect to a large number of brain regions including the cerebral cortex, hippocampus, thalamus, hypothalamus, and basal ganglia. Research has shown that these cells are most active during waking and decrease during sleep. In addition, serotonin seems to facilitate automatic behaviors such as chewing, pacing, or grooming (Jacobs & Fornal, 1997). Carlson (2010) suggests that serotonin may, in general, be involved with maintaining ongoing activities and suppressing sensory information that might interrupt those activities.

Histamine The cells of the **tuberomammillary nucleus** of the hypothalamus produce histamine and are connected to many brain regions including the cerebral cortex, thalamus, hypothalamus, basal ganglia, and basal forebrain. Activity in these cells is high during waking and lower during sleep. The connections of these histamine-producing neurons to the cortex increase arousal directly, while the connections to the basal forebrain indirectly increase arousal via the acetylcholine-producing cells there as discussed above. Some research suggests that histamine is related to attention to environmental stimuli (Parmentier, et al., 2002; Takahashi, Lin, & Sakai, 2006). (Incidentally, early anti-histamines used to treat allergies made one feel tired or sleepy because they blocked brain histamine receptors.)

Orexin Recently, a fifth neurotransmitter, orexin produced by neurons in the **lateral hypothalamus** (Carlson, 2010), has been implicated in the arousal process. According to research by

Mileykovskiy, Kiyashchenko, and Siegel (2005), orexin-producing cells responded primarily when rats were alert and actively engaged with the environment.

As you can see from the short summary above, there are many regions of the brain and at least four or five neurotransmitters that play a role in controlling arousal levels. Let us look, then, at what we know about the regions of the brain that promote sleep.

Brainstem Regions That Promote NREM Sleep

The **ventrolateral preoptic area (VLPO)** appears to be crucial for delta wave sleep. Destruction of this area in rats led to an absence of sleep and led to death after only three days (Nauta, 1946). Stimulation of these neurons produces drowsiness and sleep in cats. (Sterman & Clemente, 1962a,b). Furthermore, when animals are deprived of sleep, and then allowed to sleep freely, VLPO neurons show an increase in firing rate (Szymusiak, Alam, Steininger, & McGinty, 1998). The locus coeruleus (LC) and raphe nuclei noted earlier appear to also play a role in sleep. Activity in these regions appears to inhibit REM sleep, and as their activity drops off during NREM sleep, REM sleep becomes possible (Carlson, 2010).

Neurotransmitters That Promote Sleep

VLPO neurons produce **GABA (gamma-aminobutyric acid)** as the neurotransmitter. GABA is inhibitory in its action. VLPO, then, promotes sleep through GABA connections that inhibit the activity of several sites already discussed, specifically the locus coeruleus, raphe, tuberomammillary nucleus, and the orexiogenic neurons in the lateral hypothalamus that have arousal properties. In light of the fact that these areas increase arousal levels, it makes sense that inhibition of these areas by VLPA neurons should promote sleep.

Brainstem Regions That Promote REM Sleep

Several groups of cells appear to be responsible for REM sleep. They are located in the upper portion of the pons (Saper, Fuller, Pedersen, Lu, & Scammell, 2010). Cell groups active during REM sleep include the **sublateralodorsal nucleus (SLD)**, the **precoeruleus region (PC)**, and the **medial peribrachial nucleus**. Cells in these regions secrete several different neurotransmitters, some of which are inhibitory, while others are excitatory (see Saper et al., 2010, for a more complete discussion). If cells within the peribrachial area are destroyed, REM sleep is greatly reduced (Webster & Jones, 1988). Further, these cells are highly active during REM sleep (El Mansari, Sakai, & Jouvet, 1989). As should be evident to you at this point, the mechanisms controlling arousal levels in sleep and waking are many and complex. Researchers are just beginning to unravel this complex web of interacting regions and their various neurotransmitters that enable us to sleep, wake, and be vigilant to the things around us.

Brainstem Neural Flip-Flops

One question that has perplexed researchers over the years is how arousal mechanisms move us from waking to sleep, and vice versa. Additionally, once asleep, what mechanisms produce the alternation between NREM and REM components of sleep? Recent progress in the field suggests that several groups of cells within brainstem work very much like an electrical flip-flop switch. When one system is active (e.g., waking) it actively inhibits the other system (e.g., sleep). Conversely, when the sleep side of the switch is active it inhibits the waking side. See Figures 3.9 and 3.10. Inputs from additional cell groups tip the action from one state to the other, and the transition from one state to the other is relatively rapid once the tipping point is reached. Saper et al. (2010) have reviewed considerable evidence for just such a system in the brain stem area of the pons. Further, a second, independent flip-flop mechanism appears to control transitions from NREM to REM states accounting nicely for the cycling between NREM (Stages 1–4) and REM (Stage 5) throughout a sleep period (Saper et al., 2010).

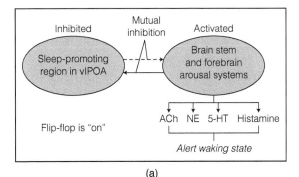

(a)

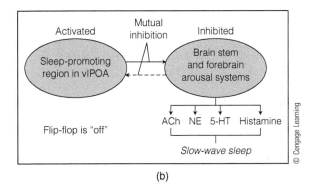

(b)

FIGURE 3.9 The major sleep-promoting region VLPA (here designated as vlPOA) and the wakefulness-promoting regions (mentioned in the text) are mutually inhibitory: when one is active the other is not. (a) The wake state: arousal systems active, VLPA inhibited. (b) The sleep state: VLPA is active, the arousal systems are inhibited. (Adapted from Carlson, 2010). solid arrow = inhibition; dashed arrow = no inhibition.

A Sleep Chemical

If you have ever gone without sleep for any length of time, you know how overpowering the desire to sleep can become. There now exists some evidence that the body produces one or more chemicals that promote sleep as a result of being awake.

Evidence for some type of sleep chemical was provided by Henri Pieron in the early 1900s (Pappenheimer, 1976). Pieron found that when he injected normal dogs with the cerebrospinal fluid of dogs deprived of sleep for 10 days or more, the recipients slept for several hours following the

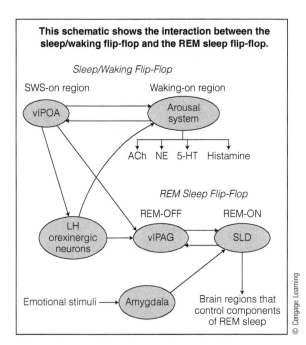

This schematic shows the interaction between the sleep/waking flip-flop and the REM sleep flip-flop.

Sleep/Waking Flip-Flop

SWS-on region   Waking-on region

vlPOA   Arousal system

ACh NE 5-HT   Histamine

REM Sleep Flip-Flop

REM-OFF   REM-ON

LH orexinergic neurons   vlPAG   SLD

Emotional stimuli → Amygdala   Brain regions that control components of REM sleep

© Cengage Learning

FIGURE 3.10 REM/NREM flip-flop's interaction with the sleep/arousal flip-flop. REM-on cells (SLD) and REM-off cells (vlPAG) take turns mutually inhibiting each other to produce periods of REM and NREM sleep throughout the sleep period. From Carlson, 2010.

injection. This suggested to Pieron that some sort of sleep-promoting chemical may develop during periods of prolonged wakefulness. Pieron's techniques left much to be desired, and although his early research was interesting, little progress was made until much later.

In 1976, John Pappenheimer at Harvard Medical School developed techniques whereby cerebrospinal fluid could easily be tapped or administered through carefully placed canulas (tubes). Pappenheimer deprived goats of sleep for 48 hours and withdrew some cerebrospinal fluid. This fluid was then injected into the cerebrospinal fluid of laboratory cats. Pappenheimer found that the cats became drowsy. In a series of experiments, Pappenheimer refined his techniques and was able to show that rats injected with cerebrospinal fluid taken from sleep-deprived goats also became significantly less active.

Recording the electrical activity of the brains in his rats revealed an increase in the slow-wave patterns seen during normal sleep. Pappenheimer's work suggests that some chemical substance that promotes sleep is generated during wakefulness.

Other research has implicated several possible chemicals in the sleep process, such as the cytokine interleukin-1 and the prostaglandin D2, as well as the neurotransmitter acetylcholine (for REM sleep) (Palca, 1989). However, the most promising work has been on the chemical adenosine. It has been shown that the neurotransmitter **adenosine**, produced by brain metabolism during waking, has an inhibitory effect on neurons in the pons that produce EEG arousal (Porkka-Heiskanen, 1999; Porkka-Heiskanen, Strecker, Thakkar, Bjorkum, Greene, & McCarley, 1997; Rainnie, Grunze, McCarley, & Greene, 1994). The work on adenosine is especially interesting because it provides a mechanism whereby prior wakefulness could contribute to the production of sleep. Adenosine is produced as a byproduct of brain activity, which is higher during waking than during sleep. Adenosine has an inhibitory effect on the neurons that maintain arousal as measured by the EEG, thus leading eventually to lowered arousal and sleep via A1 receptors (adenosine has two receptor types A1 and A2. A1 receptors are inhibitory, A2 receptors are excitatory [Saper et al., 2010]). A1 receptors appear to inhibit neurons in the arousal neuron groups mentioned earlier (locus coeruleus, raphe nuclei, tuberomammillary nucleus, basal forebrain, lateral hypothalamus). Further support for such a mechanism comes from the fact that caffeine (found in coffee) and theophylline (found in tea) block the receptor sites for adenosine, thus accounting nicely for the arousal properties of coffee and tea. The research on the chemical basis of sleep is exciting because it provides both an increased understanding of how sleep occurs and hope of a more natural cure for insomnia.

Possible Functions of Sleep

Although researchers are beginning to piece together an understanding of the brain structures involved in the sleep process, our understanding of the function of sleep is still largely a mystery. Several hypotheses have been offered, however, and some research is beginning to accumulate. The ideas are tantalizing, so let's consider a few.

What functions have been attributed to sleep? From among many proposals, probably the most common is that it provides a **restorative function** (see, e.g., Youngsteadt, 2008). Hartmann (1973) believed that Stages 3 and 4 are primarily restorative in nature. Hartmann further suggested that REM sleep may also serve a restorative function in regard to attention and emotion. He pointed out that more REM sleep seems to occur after days full of worry, stress, or intense learning. From Hartmann's point of view, REM sleep may help us cope with stressful situations by allowing us to attend to our environment more efficiently when awake. As noted earlier, several studies indicate the restorative nature of NREM sleep (Bunnell, Bevier, & Horvath, 1983; Shapiro, 1982; Shapiro et al., 1981). Further, Greenberg and associates (1983) have reported that REM deprivation decreases access to emotionally important memories but not to nonpersonal memories. Based on their results, Greenberg and associates suggest that REM sleep may be involved in making a connection between present emotionally important experiences and emotional memories related to these present experiences. Thus, it would appear that REM sleep may indeed be important in regard to emotionality. Further suggestive evidence for the importance of REM sleep in emotionality comes from research showing that depression and initial REM onset are positively correlated (Knowles, MacLean, & Cairns, 1982; Kupfer, 1976; McCarley, 1982).

A problem with any theory that argues for a restorative function for sleep, however, is that both Stage 4 and REM sleep decline with age. Many theorists have suggested that Stage 4 is primarily a restorative sleep process, yet some individuals (as noted earlier) do not show Stage 4 sleep by age 50. Any theory of restorative function must be able to deal with this discrepancy.

Dement (1972) proposed that sleep, particularly REM sleep, may be involved in the **organization of the brain**. Dement based this idea on the fact that young mammals show much more REM than adult mammals. Additionally, in humans, REM periods can be detected as early as three months before birth. Infants born up to four weeks prematurely spend as much as 75% of their sleep time in REM, while full-term babies spend about 50 to 70% of their sleep in REM. By three months of age, REM sleep periods have dropped to around 30% of sleep time (Lewin & Singer, 1991). Therefore, REM sleep could serve as an internal source of stimulation that somehow helps to "set up" the young brain correctly. REM sleep in the adult, then, might be nothing more than a vestigial (no longer useful but still existing) system that serves no real purpose. Though it is possible that REM sleep and dreaming are not necessary in the adult, additional research suggests otherwise.

Several theorists (Bertini, 1973; Dewan, 1970) have proposed that REM sleep serves as a **programming device**. New material learned during waking is seen as being incorporated into and changing the existing organization of the brain during REM sleep. Dewan has likened the process to that of a self-programming computer. During REM sleep the programs are altered and reorganized based on new information received. Part of this reprogramming, of course, requires the storing of new information in the proper location.

Broughton and Gastaut (1973), Greenberg (1970), and Pearlman (1970) have emphasized the idea that REM sleep may be involved in the **consolidation of memories**. Greenberg, for example, believed that dreaming enables material to be transferred from short-term to long-term memory. Bertini, Dewan, Greenberg, and Pearlman all believed that the storage process may be based on the emotional aspects of the information, thus explaining why emotionality occurs in dreams. The particular emotion felt during the learning process may serve as a tag or label that determines where and with what other memories a piece of information is stored. The research of Greenberg and associates (1983) also supports this notion.

Stern (1970) discussed research suggesting that REM deprivation interferes with the learning of responses and also with the retention of tasks learned prior to the deprivation. In addition, Pearlman cited evidence of interference in adaptation to anxiety-provoking events by REM deprivation. An anxiety-provoking film was shown to subjects who were then deprived of REM sleep for one night. Then they viewed the film a second time. Normal subjects showed much less anxiety on a second viewing, while the REM-deprived subjects were as anxious during the second viewing as during the first. Pearlman's results suggest that dreaming may allow us to incorporate anxiety-producing situations and thus habituate to them.

REM sleep may also play a part in the **storage of complex associative information**. Scrima (1982), for example, found recall of complex associative material to be significantly better after isolated REM periods than after either isolated NREM periods or wakefulness in a group of narcoleptics. (Narcolepsy is a sleep disorder in which the individual often falls asleep quickly during the day and in which REM can occur at sleep onset rather than after the normal NREM period.)

Chronic alcoholic patients sometimes show a set of symptoms called Korsakoff's syndrome, part of which involves disruption of memory. Greenberg (1970) studied patients suffering from Korsakoff's syndrome and found that those who had recently developed the syndrome showed increased REM states, which, however, tended to be fragmentary. Greenberg believed that alcohol-induced brain lesions interrupt both memory and dreaming processes and that the increased REM is an attempt by the brain to compensate.

Early research on the possible relationship of memory and sleep was conducted by Zornetzer, Gold, and Boast (1977). In their series of experiments, consolidation (storage time) of memory was altered by destruction of the locus coeruleus (LC). The researchers found that damage to the LC prolongs the amount of time in which new information is susceptible to memory disruption. Essentially, it appears that the LC plays a role in limiting the length of time in which memory can be interfered with. Zornetzer and associates also noted several anatomical relationships suggesting that the LC is involved in the memory process.

Two studies (Karni, Tanne, Rubenstein, Askenasy, & Sagi, 1994; Wilson & McNaughton, 1994) provide further evidence for the role of sleep in the memory process. Karni and colleagues have shown that REM sleep (but not NREM) is crucial to the development of a visual discrimination task, while Wilson and McNaughton found that cells within the hippocampus that fired together when an animal was in a particular location also tended to fire together during the next sleep period. As they note, "Information acquired during active behavior is thus re-expressed in hippocampal circuits during sleep, as postulated by some theories of memory consolidation" (Wilson & McNaughton, 1994, p. 676). The November 2001 issue of *Science* provided three reviews (and an editorial) of the roll of sleep in the learning process (Maquet, 2001; Siegel, 2001; Stern, 2001; Stickgold, Hobson, Fosse, & Fosse, 2001). All three reviewed the then available evidence of a relationship between sleep and learning mechanisms. There is growing evidence for the involvement of sleep in the learning process; however, in some cases alternative explanations cannot be ruled out (see especially Siegel, 2001, for problems with some of this research).

Robert Stickgold (2005) reviewed much of the more recent research on the role of sleep in memory consolidation. His review examined several types of learned behaviors as well as evidence from molecular studies, cellular studies, neurophysiological studies, brain imaging, and dreaming. The evidence he reports shows that several different types of memories are influenced by sleep and that several different stages of sleep contribute to the memory consolidation process. In his concluding remarks, he notes: " The past ten years have shown an explosive growth in our knowledge of the relationship between sleep and memory, providing consistent and strong support for the existence of sleep-dependent memory consolidation" (Stickgold, 2005, p. 1277). Rasch and Born (2008) provide additional evidence for a sleep—memory consolidation process for declarative memories (i.e., memories for events and facts) that requires slow-wave sleep (NREM) to reactivate and integrate new memories with old memories.

They propose a model for this process as shown in Figure 3.11. Van Der Werf et al. (2009) found that shallow sleep, involving reduced slow-wave activity and increased alpha wave activity, produced deficits in learning novel images the following day. Using fMRI technology, they found that the shallow sleep led to less activation of the right hippocampal formation. Previous studies (McDermott, LaHoste, Chen, Musto, Bazan, & Magee, 2003; Yoo, Hu, Gujar, Jolesz, & Walker, 2007) had shown that total sleep deprivation produced deficits in subsequent learning in both humans and rats; however, in the present study the participants were not sleep deprived, but were manipulated so that they spent less of their sleep period in slow-wave sleep. Van Der Werf et al. (2009, p. 123) propose that slow-wave sleep

"optimizes the hippocampus for encoding of novel information ..." Finally, Payne and Kensinger (2010) reviewed evidence supporting the idea that sleep promotes the consolidation of emotional memories. REM sleep may be especially important in this process (change to Walker & van der Helm, 2009).

Although many people consider sleep to be located at the low end of the arousal continuum, this is obviously an oversimplification especially when one considers the aroused nature of REM sleep. Sleep is an important behavior that may serve several functions—among them physical restoration and memory consolidation and perhaps other functions as well. We will now examine research dealing with the high end of the arousal continuum—what is generally called stress.

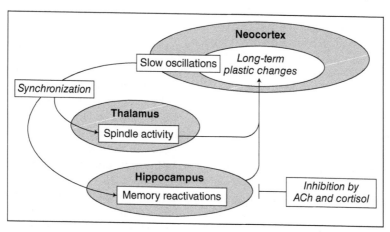

FIGURE 3.11 Model of declarative memory consolidation during sleep. During slow-wave sleep (SWS), newly encoded information in the hippocampus is repeatedly reactivated. The reactivation is driven by the "up" (excitation) State of the slow oscillations originating in neocortical networks (preferentially in those that were used for encoding during prior wakefulness) and synchronizes hippocampal reactivations with spindle activity in thalamocortical circuitry. Hippocampal output to the neocortex is normally inhibited during wakefulness because of high acetylcholine (ACh) and cortisol levels. This inhibition is released during SWS, when hippocampal acetylcholine and cortisol levels reach a minimum, thus allowing for a back-projection of reactivated hippocampal memories to neocortical networks. The hippocampal input arriving in synchrony with spindle input at neocortical circuitry supports long-term plastic changes selectively at those synapses previously used for encoding, thereby building more persistent memories of the information in neocortical networks. Note that this concept is compatible with the notion that the hippocampus does not actually store a memory but initially binds together anatomically separated neocortical sites representing the disparate parts of a memory trace. By memory reactivation during sleep, corticocortical connections are strengthened, rendering the memory increasingly independent from hippocampal regions. This strengthening of cortical connection implicates a reorganization of the neuronal representation that can be associated with qualitative changes of the memory. From Rasch and Born (2008).

Stress

When our arousal level is high, we are being stressed. Often the term *stress* is equated with distress (Arnold, 1967). It seems clear, however, that we are also stressed when good things happen to us, such as a promotion or marriage.

A more general way of looking at the concept is to think of *stress as occurring when the body is forced to cope with or adapt to a changed situation*, which may be either good or bad. Thus, any situation that causes a marked deviation from our normal state would be considered stressful.

Stress is an integral part of life; we cannot escape it, for as Selye notes, "complete freedom from stress is death" (1973, p. 693). In order to understand motivated behavior, it is important to know how stress affects our bodies and our behavior. In this section we will examine research on stress as it relates to motivation, and we will also examine ways of coping with stress.

Definition of Stress

The concept of stress has proven particularly hard to define. This is perhaps because of the multitude of situations that can trigger stress in an individual. Nevertheless, let us try to formulate a rough definition to use in examining the research on stress.

Selye (1973) defined stress as a nonspecific response of the body to any demand made upon it. Basically, Selye assumed that some optimal level of bodily functioning exists and that stressors (stimuli or situations that create stress in the person) cause a movement away from this optimal level. The stress response is seen as an adaptive behavior that attempts to return the body to its normal state. As such, stress is a homeostatic mechanism. Either systemic or psychological stress, then, can be viewed as an adaptive response designed to return the individual to a more nearly optimal condition. Research by Kemeny (2003) suggests that the stress response can be more specific than Selye thought. Some of the conditions that can

influence the stress response are its controllability, ambiguity, novelty, duration, and the demand it places on the person (Kemeny, 2003). As Kemeny notes "The issue here is not degree of activation of the sympathetic nervous system, but rather distinctive qualities of activation depending on the specific nature of the cognitive appraisal process" (2003, p. 128). Humans in laboratory experiments in which they believe that they have some control physically react less to a threat (Dickerson & Kemeny, 2004). Additionally, Creswell, Welch, Taylor, Sherman, Gruenewald, and Mann (2005) showed that the stress response can be reduced by one's personal values. Thus, it appears that the stress response may not be as nonspecific as Selye originally thought.

Systemic and Psychological Stress

Systemic stress involves a challenge to the integrity of the physical body (Appley & Trumbull, 1967). The body reacts to invasions (bacteria, viruses, heat, cold, etc.) by a generalized response that helps combat the challenge. We will soon examine this response in detail.

But stress does not require a physical challenge to the body in order to occur; it can occur for purely psychological reasons. Worry about a sick mother or anxiety about losing a job can likewise create stress. And the body's reaction to psychological stress, interestingly, is virtually identical to its systemic stress reaction. Even anticipation of the future can create stress. For example, the anticipation of a parachute jump is more stressful to an experienced jumper than the actual jump (Tanner, 1976). The presence of emotion is usually considered a sign of psychological stress, another typical sign is the disruption of ongoing behavior (Appley & Trumbull, 1967).

The effects of stress are not always bad, though we usually tend to study the negative side of stress. A certain amount of stress seems necessary for creativity and performance. Moderate amounts of stress improve performance (Tanner, 1976). We all know individuals who seem unable to accomplish anything unless stressed by an impending deadline. For these individuals, moderate stress seems to help. We should keep in mind, however, that large differences exist in the ability to tolerate stress, and it is sometimes useful to ask ourselves under what condition our own behavior is most efficient.

Endocrine System Activity and Stress

In order to understand some of the effects of stress, we must know something about the reactions of the body when a stressor is encountered. One of the major effects of a stressor is on the endocrine system.

The **endocrine system** is a set of glands located throughout the body that secrete their substances directly into the bloodstream. The substances are called **hormones** and can be thought of as chemical signals that regulate or coordinate the activity of distant organs (Selye, 1956). The major gland within this system is the **pituitary**, which has been called the master gland because of its role in controlling the other glands. The pituitary is located at the base of the brain and is controlled by the brain structure known as the **hypothalamus**. The hypothalamus is active in many motivated activities, as we shall see in Chapter 4. It manufactures hormones that have the effect of causing the pituitary to release its substances (Guillemin & Burgus, 1976; Levine, 1971).

Besides the pituitary, the other major gland of interest to us in the study of stress is the **adrenal gland**. The adrenal gland (one located on top of each kidney) is composed of two parts that serve different functions. The outer covering of the adrenal gland (called the **adrenal cortex**) secretes hormones called 17-hydroxycorticoids. While several of these corticoids exist in humans, the major secretion of the adrenal cortex is **cortisol**. The adrenal cortex also secretes small quantities of another

hormone called aldosterone, whose main effect is on water and electrolyte balance (Oken, 1967). The center portion (the **adrenal medulla**) secretes two substances, **epinephrine** and **norepinephrine**. Now let's put all this information together and try to understand what happens when we are stressed. Please refer to Figure 3.12 as you read the paragraphs below.

Information about the state of the body is constantly being gathered by external sensory systems (e.g., eyes, ears, nose) and by internal sensory systems (the condition of internal organs, blood changes, etc.). This information is monitored by the brain, and when a stressor is detected, systems within the hypothalamus are activated. The posterior portion of the hypothalamus activates sympathetic nervous system activity, which stimulates the adrenal medulla to secrete epinephrine and norepinephrine. At the same time, other systems within the anterior hypothalamus secrete a substance called **corticotropin releasing hormone (CRH)**, which causes the pituitary gland to secrete a substance into the bloodstream called **adrenocorticotropic hormone (ACTH)** (Roberts et al., 1982; Vale

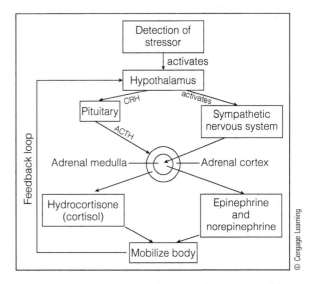

FIGURE 3.12 Flowchart of mechanisms triggered by a stressor.

et al., 1981). ACTH is important because it travels through the bloodstream to the adrenal glands, where it causes the adrenal cortex to secrete cortisol as well as small quantities of aldosterone into the bloodstream (Oken, 1967).

The release of epinephrine, norepinephrine, and cortisol into the bloodstream has the effect of mobilizing the body for action (by increasing various bodily components such as blood sugar, heart rate, and blood pressure) so that we can better deal with the stressor. Some sort of feedback mechanism also exists because, as blood levels of cortisol increase, the brain shuts off the production of ACTH and, therefore, cortisol. When the stressor is overcome or disappears, the activity of the pituitary-adrenal system is reduced, and we return to a more relaxed state. The individual most responsible for advancing the study of stress was Hans Selye (1950, 1956, 1973), who proposed a three-part system of response to stress.

The General Adaptation Syndrome

In 1925 an 18-year-old medical student named Hans Selye got his first look at the symptoms of infectious disease. It was probably his youthfulness, as he pointed out, that allowed him to see the common symptoms that all the patients possessed, rather than the specific symptoms he was supposed to see (Seyle, 1956).

Still unbiased by the current medical thinking, Selye noticed that most diseases have a common set of symptoms. The patient looks and feels sick, has a coated tongue, complains of aches and pains in the joints, and has loss of appetite and fever. Imposed on this general set of symptoms are more specific symptoms, which allow one to determine the actual disease. Though the medical practitioners of the day were interested in the specific symptoms (because they enable diagnosis of the illness), Selye was intrigued by the large degree of overlap in the general symptoms from one disease to another.

Not until 10 years later did Selye begin to fit these early observations together and arrive at the concept of stress. He had been conducting research on sex hormones and found that injecting his animals with ovarian or placental hormones caused a series of changes, including enlargement of the adrenal cortex, shrinkage of the thymus gland and lymph nodes, and ulceration of the gastrointestinal tract. He soon discovered that injections of any noxious or foreign material caused the same effects. In other words, the bodily responses that he was observing were nonspecific (they didn't change if different agents were injected), just as the symptoms he had observed in medical school were nonspecific.

These results led Selye to study the reactions of the body when subjected to stressors. He soon discovered that the changes he noted in the adrenal glands, lymph system, and gastrointestinal tract are the initial response of the body to a stressor. He named this response the alarm reaction.

During the **alarm reaction** the forces of the body are mobilized so that life can be maintained while local adaptive responses (e.g., inflammation at a point of infection) progress. The corticoids of the adrenal cortex are secreted into the bloodstream in order to help prepare the body for attack by the stressor. Epinephrine is secreted by the adrenal medulla and travels to all parts of the body, increasing the efficiency of the muscle synapses, accelerating breathing, increasing heart rate, and so on. During the early phase of the alarm reaction, our resistance to stress is actually below normal, but it quickly rises above normal.

Once local adaptive responses have been established, a second stage, which Selye termed the **stage of resistance**, develops. During this period, the processes accelerated during the alarm reaction drop back almost to normal levels (e.g., corticoid levels decrease to just slightly above normal). Rather than mobilizing the entire body for action, as in the alarm reaction, the stage of resistance mobilizes only that part of the body under attack. Ability to adapt to the stressor is greater than normal during the stage of resistance.

If, however, the local defenses are inadequate or fail to limit the effects of the stressor, resistance finally gives way to the third stage, which Selye termed the **stage of exhaustion**. In this stage the reaction to the stressor becomes general again. Corticoid levels rise very similarly to their rise during the alarm reaction. Life at this stage can continue only as long as the extra defenses brought in by activation of the whole system can last. If the stressor is not eliminated or removed, the bodily defenses are exhausted and death occurs (Figure 3.13). The three stages together comprise the body's total reaction to a stressor, and this reaction has been termed the **general adaptation syndrome (GAS)**.

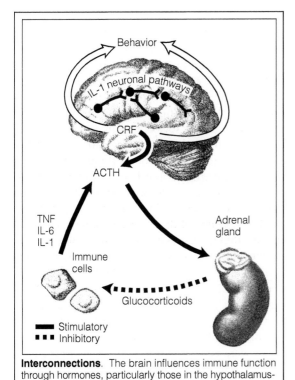

Interconnections. The brain influences immune function through hormones, particularly those in the hypothalamus-pituitary-adrenal axis, and immune messengers in turn affect the brain.

FIGURE 3.13 The interaction of the brain, hormones, and the immune system. From Sternberg, "The Stress Response and the Regulation of Inflammatory Disease." *Annals of Internal Medicine 117*:885, 1992. Used by permission.

The GAS, then, is a set of responses that is triggered by a stressor and designed to eliminate or contain the stressing element so that the body can maintain life. These physiological changes associated with the GAS are what we experience as stress (Selye, 1956, 1973).

The GAS is activated not only by physical stresses such as infection but also by psychological stresses such as anxiety, loud noises, or crowding. The body reacts in the same way (with the GAS) to all stressors. Because stressors such as anxiety cannot be easily escaped, they may cause us damage by keeping the GAS active too much of the time. In this regard, problems such as ulcers, high blood pressure, and even certain types of kidney disease may be the result of psychological stress. Thus the GAS response is not always adaptive; for some reason, the response may not be appropriate to the problem. When this occurs, we suffer, in Selye's term, diseases of adaptation.

Diseases of Adaptation

Sometimes the responses of the body may be inadequate or inappropriate to the stressor. For example, one of the most basic processes in the control of a physical stressor is inflammation. Inflammation provides a barrier that limits the spread of a stressor (e.g., infection). If, however, the body reacts to a foreign particle with inflammation, the inflammation may cause more harm than the particle. This seems to be what happens in allergic reactions to pollen. Selye believed that many common diseases are, in part, diseases of adaptation, in which the body reacts incorrectly to a potential stressor.

Selye's research has generated thousands of additional studies on stress. A thorough understanding of how physical or psychological stressors influence behavior is clearly very important. Stress, on the one hand, can motivate creativity; on the other hand, it can create high blood pressure and ulcers. One arena in which stress has been studied is its relationship to significant life changes on the one hand and to illness on the other.

Life Change, Stress, and Illness

One area of research that has attempted to untangle the web of relationships between stress and illness is the topic of life change. Life-change research, like much of the literature on stress, can be traced back to Walter Cannon (Dohrenwend & Dohrenwend, 1974). The "life charts" constructed by Adolph Meyer in the 1930s also constituted one of the earliest attempts to associate changes in the lives of patients with illness. Meyer's research pioneered modern studies of the relationship between stress and illness.

The basic idea underlying life-change research is that the events of our lives influence our susceptibility to physical and mental illness. Research has focused primarily on attempts to scale various life changes in terms of the amount of adjustments these changes require of us and then to correlate these life changes with the incidence of illness or the seeking of professional help.

Long-term studies were conducted by Hinkle (1974), who examined health and work records of telephone company employees over a 20-year span. His results showed that some people were much more likely to become ill than others. People experiencing the most missed days of work had more diseases of both a minor and major nature. Illness also tended to cluster around certain periods of an individual's life. This clustering tended to occur during times in people's lives when their social environment or interpersonal relationships made large demands on them. The stress-illness relationship was not invariable, however, because Hinkle noticed that many other people had experienced considerable stress and yet had not become ill. He suggested that healthy individuals seem able to "emotionally insulate" themselves from drastic life changes that occur to them. **Emotional insulation** would appear to involve an ability to step back from emotional events and keep them in perspective.

Thomas Holmes and his associates developed a scale of major life changes that they found to be clinically related to illness (see Holmes & Masuda,

1974; Ruch & Holmes, 1971). The 43 items of the scale (called the **Social Readjustment Rating Scale** or SRRS) were rated by people in terms of the amount of adjustment these events would require in their lives. Not all of the items were negative (although the majority were); some were positive events such as marriage or Christmas. However, all of them required some coping or adaptation on the part of the person experiencing the change.

Scaling of the 43 items led to a determination of which items required the most coping or adjustment. As can be seen in Table 3.1 (Holmes & Rahe, 1967), death of a spouse requires the most adaptation, followed by divorce, marital separation, and so on.

The SRRS has been given to various groups (adults, college students, adolescents), and agreement on the amount of adjustment required by the various life experiences is very consistent, even cross-culturally (Holmes & Masuda, 1974; Isherwood & Adam, 1976). Since the development of the original SRRS, several modifications have been made and other life–stress measurement devices developed (see Miller, 1988, for a review of modifications to the original scale and a summary of the development of several alternative life–stress inventories).

Researchers have generally found that life changes tend to cluster significantly in the two years prior to the onset of an illness. Studies showed that with an increase in the number of life-change units (termed LCUs: the measure of the amount of life change in a given unit of time, such as six months or a year) the probability of illness also increased.

Many early investigations into life change and illness were **retrospective studies**, in which individuals were asked to indicate when illnesses and life changes had occurred. The researchers then look for relationships between illness and life changes that may have preceded the illness. LCU scores ranging from 150 to 199 within one year's time were considered mild life crises, and it was found that 37% of the individuals scoring within this range reported a major health change. LCU

TABLE 3.1 The Social Readjustment Rating Scale

Life Event	Mean Value
1. death of spouse	100
2. divorce	73
3. marital separation	65
4. jail term	63
5. death of a close family member	63
6. personal injury or illness	53
7. marriage	50
8. fired at work	47
9. marital reconciliation	45
10. retirement	45
11. change in health of family member	44
12. pregnancy	40
13. sex difficulties	39
14. gain of new family member	39
15. business readjustment	39
16. change in financial state	38
17. death of close friend	37
18. change to different line of work	36
19. change in number of arguments with spouse	35
20. mortgage over $10,000	31
21. foreclosure of mortgage or loan	30
22. change in responsibilities at work	29
23. son or daughter leaving home	29
24. trouble with in-laws	29
25. outstanding personal achievement	28
26. wife begins or stops work	26
27. begin or end school	26
28. change in living conditions	25
29. revision of personal habits	24
30. trouble with boss	23
31. change in work hours or conditions	20
32. change residence	20
33. change in schools	20
34. change in recreation	19
35. change in church activities	19
36. change in social activities	18
37. mortgage or loan less than $10,000	17
38. change in sleeping habits	16
39. change in number of family get-togethers	15
40. change in eating habits	15
41. vacation	13
42. Christmas	12
43. minor violations of the law	11

Adapted from "The Social Readjustment Rating Scale," by T. H. Holmes and R. H. Rahe, 1967, *Journal of Psychosomatic Research, 11:* 213–218. Copyright ©1967 by Elsevier. Used by permission.

scores between 200 and 299 were defined as moderate life crises, and the percentage of persons reporting a major health change rose to 79% (Holmes & Masuda, 1974). Holmes believed that the onset of illness after a major life change occurs in about a year, presumably because it takes that amount of time for the stress of the life changes to show its effects. Retrospective research into these relationships, however, is hampered by problems of the subject's memory of events that may have occurred several years earlier.

Prospective studies, in which individuals supply information about recent life changes and are questioned later (usually six months to a year) about changes in health, have also been conducted. The point of such studies is to see if changes in life events can effectively predict future health changes. Holmes and Masuda cited several studies indicating that life changes do predict future illness. In one study, 86% of those individuals scoring above 300 LCUs had a major health change sometime during the next two years (48% who scored between 200 and 299 and 33% who scored between 150 and 199 had a major health change).

One of the most interesting prospective studies involved prediction of performance based on recent life-change scores in a prolonged competitive stress situation (Popkin et al., 1976). The competitive event was a dog sled race that covered 1,049 miles between Anchorage and Nome, Alaska. The researchers found that a significant negative correlation existed between life-change scores and order of finish in the race; the larger the number of recent life changes that had occurred to an individual, the poorer that person finished in the race. Though the number of subjects was small (25), the results may be revealing.

Roskies, Iida-Miranda, and Strobel (1975) studied life change and illness in a group of Portuguese immigrants to Canada. Their findings are of interest in two respects. First, 68% of the subjects fell into the moderate or major life crisis categories, yet this Portuguese sample showed no greater incidence of illness than the population of Canada as a whole. Suffering the major life change of immigration does not, then, necessarily put one into a high-risk category for illness, even though these researchers did find a significant correlation between life change and illness.

The second, more interesting finding was that significant sex differences existed in regard to life change and illness among this immigrant group. Immigrant women were more likely than immigrant men to become ill, and the correlation between life change and illness for the women was much stronger (although still only 0.24). No significant relationship between life change and illness was found for the men. And for a subgroup of the men (young or highly educated or both), the relationship was negative, indicating that for them life change was associated with health! The possibility that sex differences exist in the relationship between life change and health change needs systematic study.

Bedell and associates (1977) studied the life changes of children who attended a three-week camp for the chronically ill. These children were given a battery of personality tests and a children's version of the SRRS. The children were classified into two groups based on their life-change scores: a low-stress group whose scores approximated those of normal children and a high-stress group whose scores were far above normal. The results of the questionnaires showed that the high-stress group, compared to the low-stress group, had poorer self-concepts, perceived themselves as poorly behaved, said they were less attractive and less popular, and felt they were less successful in school. The highly stressed, chronically ill child thus tended to make negative self-evaluations.

The study also found that the high-stress group had significantly more day-to-day health problems than the low-stress group. During the three-week period of the camp, 69 episodes of illness occurred in the high-stress group, compared to only 19 in the low-stress group. Since the two groups were matched for types and severity of illness, the high-stress group was apparently more vulnerable to acute episodes of illness. One wonders whether chronically ill children are less able to adapt to the additional stresses of life change and are therefore more susceptible to acute illnesses.

A review of research by Adler and Matthews (1994) concludes that the social environment (such as life changes) can contribute to the development of disease. They cite research showing that social environments producing stress increase the likelihood of illness. As they note, the evidence is strongest for cardiovascular disease, infectious disease, and pregnancy complications.

Problems of Life-Change Research
Several studies have questioned the utility of the SRRS in predicting illness (Bieliauskas & Strugar, 1976; Bieliauskas & Webb, 1974; Caplan, 1975; Cleary, 1981; Garrity, Marx, & Somes, 1977a, b; Mechanic, 1974; Schroeder & Costa, 1984 [but see also Maddi, Bartone, & Puccetti, 1987]; Wershow & Reinhart, 1974). There seems little doubt that a relationship between life changes and health changes does exist, but the correlations, though significant, are often very small and account for very little of the total variance within the experiments. What this means is that the SRRS can predict general changes in health resulting from changes across large groups of people, but it predicts very little about the chances of illness for any particular individual as a result of life changes.

Individual differences have always been the biggest problem in attempting to understand how life events relate to illness. The same events simply do not affect people similarly. Rahe (1974) pointed out that we need to understand more about how people cope with life changes both psychologically and physiologically before we can hope to understand why life changes affect one person but not another.

Buffering the Effects of Life Change and Stress That some individuals endure numerous life changes and yet do not become ill suggests that these people may be able to reduce the stressing effects of life changes. Research examining the buffering effects of personality variables and various stress-reducing strategies has supported this idea. A number of studies have identified some of the variables that appear to play a role. Some of the suggested variables are hardiness, exercise, social support, sex-role orientation, self-complexity, humor, and optimism (Cohen & Wills, 1985; Fisher, 1988; House, Landis, & Umberson, 1988; Kobasa, Maddi, & Puccetti, 1982; Labott & Martin, 1987; Linville, 1987; Peterson, Seligman, & Vaillant, 1988; Roos & Cohen, 1987).

For example, Kobasa and associates (1982) examined the effect of two variables on the stress-illness relationship. The first variable was a personality style they termed hardiness (Kobasa, 1979). **Hardiness** is conceived as a combination of three personality characteristics—**commitment**, **control**, and **challenge**—that serve to buffer the effects of stress because they are associated with curiosity and interest in the experiences of life. Further, hardy individuals believe that they can control what happens to them and that change is natural. These attitudes seem to help buffer the effects of stress because they help individuals keep the changing life events in perspective (Kobasa et al., 1982). The second variable studied by Kobasa and associates was exercise. Though exercise has most often been examined relative to the cardiovascular system, these researchers were interested in the effect of exercise as a buffer for life-change–induced stress.

In this carefully conducted study, the researchers found that both hardiness and exercise decreased the likelihood of illness as a result of stressing life changes in a sample of 137 male, middle- and upper-level management personnel. Additionally, the buffering effects of hardiness and exercise were independent and additive. The greatest buffering effect was seen in those subjects who were high in both hardiness and exercise. These researchers propose that the buffering effect of these two variables is on differing aspects of the life-change stress-illness relationship. They believe that hardiness serves to transform the stressing events and thus decrease their stressfulness, while exercise decreases the psychological and physiological strain on the individual by these events. Thus the proposed buffering effects of these two variables are quite different; one reduces the stressfulness of the events themselves, while the other reduces the

deleterious effects of the stress on the person. As a result of their differing points of action, hardiness and exercise are additive in reducing the effect of life changes on illness.

The results of the study by Kobasa and associates (1982) are consistent with a general body of research that shows that the controllability-uncontrollability dimension of stressing life events is important in determining the effects of life change on illness. For example, Johnson and Sarason (1978) have shown that participants indicating a belief in an internal locus of control (a measure of how we view our ability to control the events of our lives) show a lower correlation between life changes and subsequent illness than participants indicating a belief in an external locus of control. Similarly, Stern, McCants, and Pettine (1982) found that items on the SRRS rated as uncontrollable by people were more highly associated with illness than were items rated as controllable. Additionally, they found that those items considered uncontrollable were also rated as more stressing. It should be noted, however, that participants' agreement on how controllable different events were was widely divergent; what one person considered controllable was often considered uncontrollable by another. Similar results have been reported by Suls and Mullen (1981), who found that undesirability and uncontrollability were related to the incidence of psychological distress symptoms. Perhaps the low correlation between life change and illness is partly due to these differing perceptions of controllability. As Stern and associates have noted, event uncontrollability may prove to be a better index of stress than life changes. The research noted above suggests that a belief that one can control the events of his or her life is an important adaptive mechanism for coping with stress.

Criticisms of the Hardiness Concept

Several researchers have questioned the role of hardiness in buffering the effects of stress (Funk, 1992; Wiebe, 1991; Wiebe & Williams, 1992; Williams, Wiebe, & Smith, 1992). Perhaps the most troubling criticism has been that measures of hardiness are confounded with measures of neuroticism (Funk, 1992; Wiebe & Williams, 1992). The scales that have been used to measure hardiness generally do so by measuring traits like alienation or powerlessness. Hardiness is then indicated by low scores on these scales. Since the absence of these negative traits is taken as evidence for hardiness, it is possible that what is being measured is a lack of neuroticism rather than hardiness per se. Funk (1992) has suggested that hardiness scales need to be modified to include more positively keyed items, and items that tap neuroticism should either be reworded or eliminated. However, a study by Maddi, Khoshaba, Persico, Lu, Harvey, and Bleecker (2002, p. 72) compared hardiness to the Millon Clinical Multiaxial Inventory III and also to the Minnesota Multiphasic Personality Inventory 2 and concluded that in both cases, "total hardiness and its components of commitment, control and challenge express vigorous mental health."

Neuroticism does appear to be related to health changes. Charles, Gatz, Kato, and Pedersen (2008) conducted a 25-year, longitudinal study on 21,676 twins from the Swedish Twin Registry. They defined neuroticism as involving symptoms of "anxiety, depression, and hostility related to emotional instability and high basal arousal" (Charles et al., 2008, p. 369) Charles et al. found that higher levels of neuroticism were associated with a greater likelihood of physical conditions such as cardiovascular, gastrointestinal, neurological, immunological, and musculoskeletal problems 25 years later. Although the effect sizes were often small, given the 25-year span between assessment of neuroticism and reports of illness, the findings are remarkable. Although some physical ailments had genetic and familial components (based on separate analyses of dizygotic and monozygotic twins), other ailments such as irritable bowel syndrome, gastroesophageal reflux disease, chronic widespread pain, and chronic fatigue-like syndrome were still associated with neuroticism when genetic and familial factors were controlled.

Clearly, some sort of relationship exists between measures of hardiness/neuroticism and health/disease. Let us now examine some additional factors that influence the life change → stress → illness relationship.

Other Buffers of Stress

Our social relationships can influence our health (House et al., 1988). It has been known for some time that death rates from all causes are higher among the unmarried than the married. Similarly, unmarried and socially isolated persons have higher rates of tuberculosis, accidents, and psychiatric disorders.

The correlation between social relationships and health has led some researchers to propose that social relationships might promote health by buffering the effects of stress (Cassel, 1976; Cobb, 1976; see Cohen & Wills, 1985; and House et al., 1988, for reviews). One buffering aspect of social interaction that has been studied is its supportive nature. **Social support theory** proposes that social relationships buffer the effects of stress through the encouragement an individual or individuals can offer to the person experiencing the stress. Social support might promote better health through practical help, emotional comfort, provision of a sense of meaning and coherence to life, facilitation of good health behaviors (proper sleep, diet, exercise, etc.), promotion of positive affect, development of feelings of self-worth, or some combination of these.

Interestingly, social support may be more effective as a buffer for men (House et al., 1988) or for persons displaying masculine sex-role orientation (Roos & Cohen, 1987). This finding might be due to the fact that women, in general, have greater social support than men (Flaherty & Richman, 1989). So that social support "appears" to have a greater effect for men. Future research will, perhaps, have more to say about this gender effect.

Other characteristics in addition to social support appear to have a buffering effect on the stress-illness relationship. Peterson and associates (1988) report that **explanatory style** (the ways we explain events) is predictive of health status 20 to 30 years later. Specifically, they found that a pessimistic explanatory style (attributing bad events to stable, global, and internal factors) at age 25 predicted poor health at ages 45 through 60. Those subjects in this study who accounted for the bad events in their lives using a more optimistic explanatory style (attributing those events to unstable, specific, and external causes) were healthier than the pessimistic group later in life. One possible implication of this study is that interpreting in an optimistic way the bad events that befall all of us may serve to buffer the stressing effects of those events. As noted earlier, Charles et al. (2008) also found a long-term relationship between health and neuroticism which, it could be argued, is a "style" of explaining events. We must, of course, be cautious in drawing such conclusions until more evidence is available. It is entirely possible that some other variable influences both explanatory style and health later in life.

One final potential buffer of the stress-illness relationship that has been investigated is **expressive style** (Labott & Martin, 1987). These investigators found that the use of **humor** as a way of coping moderated the stressing effects of negative life events, whereas emotional weeping (often thought to be cathartic) did not. In fact, their study reported that subjects who engaged in frequent weeping showed increased levels of mood disturbance when negative life events were frequent. Overholser (1992) has also found that humor is a useful method of coping with stressing situations, at least for some people. In particular, humor creativity ("... the ability to apply a sense of humor in stressful situations." [Overholser, 1992, p. 800]) was associated with better psychological adjustment.

Perhaps explanatory style (pessimistic–optimistic) and expressive style (weeping–humor) interact in their buffering effects. One might predict the least buffering when the explanatory style of pessimism is linked to the expressive style of frequent weeping. The same logic suggests that the greatest buffering would result from a combination of optimistic explanatory style and humorous expressive style. Future research may shed some light on such interactive buffering effects. Several techniques for dealing consciously with stress have also been

proposed. We will close this section by mentioning a few of them.

Selye (1956) believed that **knowledge** is a curative. If we remove some of the mystery from a process it becomes less frightening. This suggests that knowing something about our reactions to stress ought to help us deal with stress. Indeed, just realizing we are tense can often help us reduce the tension.

Hinkle's (1974) studies over many years show that some people tolerate stress better than others. He has noted that those who tolerate stress well and remain healthy seem able to **emotionally insulate** themselves from the events around them. Perhaps an ability to be objective and to accept situations that cannot be changed helps these people tolerate stress.

George Ruff and Sheldon Korchin (1967) studied the ways in which the Mercury astronauts dealt with stress. The astronauts, they found, had strong drives toward mastery and achievement, which were often frustrated by unavoidable program delays and equipment problems. Nevertheless, the astronauts were able to tolerate stress well, primarily by **looking beyond the momentary** frustrations to the future. Additionally, the astronauts tended to describe themselves in emotionally positive terms, and anticipatory anxiety (before a flight) seemed to facilitate their performance rather than interfere with it. For example, when they became anxious about something going wrong, they immediately went over the contingency plans for that emergency. Mandler (1967), in an invited commentary on Ruff and Korchin's research, noted that one of the most adaptive responses to stressors is to have **alternate plans** ready for the occasion. Perhaps we can all learn something from the astronauts and deal with our own stress situations by formulating contingency plans in advance.

Many people have become interested in **meditation** as a way of reducing the stress in their lives. Herbert Benson wrote a book, *The Relaxation Response* (1975), that analyzed many types of meditative techniques and distilled them into four steps that were common to all. According to Benson, all types of meditation promote relaxation. He believed that meditation reduces stress because it counteracts overactivity of the sympathetic nervous system at the level of the hypothalamus (Benson, 1975; Benson et al., 1977; Hoffman et al., 1982). Thus meditative techniques may result in reduced stress by activating neural mechanisms that oppose or inhibit sympathetic nervous arousal and the stress responses of the body produced by that arousal. In a more recent study, Dusek et al. (2008) were able to show that the relaxation response causes changes in gene expression in both short- and long-term practitioners of meditation that they hypothesize reduce the negative effects of stressors through molecular and biochemical processes.

Health Psychology

One outgrowth of research on stress and behavior is the development of a subdiscipline within psychology that examines the relationship between behavior and health/illness. As outlined by Baum and Posluszny (1999; see also Krantz, Grunberg, & Baum, 1985), behavior can influence health in at least three different ways: biological changes, behavioral risk, and illness behaviors.

Biological Changes Some behaviors may directly produce biological changes in the individual. These biological changes may occur as the result of emotion or other behaviors. For example becoming angry at someone or some situation can lead to an increase in blood pressure. These blood pressure changes can, in turn, eventually lead to cardiovascular changes that increase the likelihood of heart attack or stroke. Similarly, the behavior of smoking can lead to long-term changes in a number of biological processes that increase the chances of cardiovascular problems and cancer. One area within the behavior/biology relationship that is currently of great interest to psychologists is the subfield of psychoneuroimmunology. **Psychoneuroimmunology** looks at the relationships between behavior, the nervous system, and the immune system. As we shall see shortly, there is a growing body of evidence that indicates an intricate and bidirectional communication between the brain and the immune system.

The behaviors we engage in can, furthermore, influence this communication in ways that may either promote health or promote illness.

Behavioral Risk Behaviors can also influence the likelihood of health or illness in a second way by enhancing our chances of staying healthy or by impairing our chances. Although these changes are at their base, biological, this second influence is more of a probabilistic one—that is, by engaging in certain behaviors we may increase our chances of remaining healthy, while engaging in other behaviors reduces our chances. As noted by Baum and Posluszny (1999), diet and exercise are usually considered to be health-enhancing behaviors while smoking, drug use, and high-risk sexual behaviors increase the chances of health impairment. Thus, the behaviors we engage in influence our chances of remaining healthy.

Illness Behaviors A third way in which behaviors interact with health concerns the behaviors one engages in when sick or when illness is suspected. Perhaps the most obvious is simply the decision to seek medical care, however, other behaviors such as early detection and interpretation of symptoms will also play a part in determining overall health (Baum & Posluszny, 1999).

So, we may conclude that behavior and health are intimately related; the behaviors we engage in can influence our health, and, of course, our health (or illness) can have large effects on our behavior. Psychosocial factors also play a prominent role in the behavior–health relationship (see, e.g., Schneiderman, Antoni, Saab, & Ironson, 2001).

Of the three ways in which behaviors can influence health, the biological changes have been most studied. This field, as noted above, is often called psychoneuroimmunology. Let us, then, take a look at a sampling of research findings within this field.

Psychoneuroimmunology

Robert Ader has been instrumental in the developing field of psychoneuroimmunology (see, e.g., Ader, 1981). Before the mid-1970s it was generally assumed that the immune system worked, for the most part, independently of other systems (Ader, 2001). However, it is now clear that there is bidirectional communication between the brain and the immune system and that the immune system influences both the endocrine system and behavior (Ader, 2001; Exton, von Auer, Buske-Kirschbaum, Stockhorst, Gobel, & Schedlowski, 2000; Kaplan & Bartner, 2005; Masek, Petrovicky, Sevcik, Zidek, & Frankova, 2000). The brain communicates with the immune system through nervous system connections to lymphoid organs that secrete chemicals that alter immune system activity. Additionally, the brain can alter immune system activity via the endocrine system, in particular the pituitary gland (Ader, 2001). For example, as we have seen, production of ACTH by the pituitary signals the adrenal cortex to secrete cortisol, which has anti-inflammatory properties, but cortisol acts as an immunosuppressant as well.

Activation of the immune system by an **antigen** (in a general sense, any substance that produces an immune reaction, Stedman's Medical Dictionary, 1995) produces hormonal and chemical changes that are recognized by the brain. Thus, the immune system communicates to the brain something about its activity.

One of the more interesting routes of communication from immune system to brain appears to be through the production of **cytokines** (also called **interleukins [IL]**—hormone-like proteins that regulate the intensity and duration of the immune response and also cell-to-cell communication, Stedman's Medical Dictionary, 1995). The production of cytokines can cause changes in both brain activity and behavior (Ader, 2001; Kaplan & Bartner, 2005). For example, the fever and fatigue that accompanies an infection appear to be produced by one or more interleukins (specifically IL-1, IL-6, and TNF-alpha) (Pennisi, 1997). Figure 3.13 shows how this bidirectional communication between brain and immune system is thought to occur.

As shown in the figure, the brain through production of CRH (noted as CRF in Figure 3.13) stimulates the pituitary to secrete ACTH which in turn stimulates the adrenal cortex to produce

glucocorticoids. These chemicals, in turn, have an inhibitory effect on immune system cells, suppressing the activity of the immune system. These cells then communicate to the brain via IL-1, IL-6, and TNF.

Conditioning of Immune Responses

From a motivational point of view, changes in the immune system as a result of learning, can influence the body's reactions. Several studies have shown that the immune system can be altered via classical conditioning (Ader, 2001; Ader & Cohen, 1975; Exton et al., 2000). As noted by Exton et al. (2000, p. 130), "The conditioning paradigm employs the pairing of a novel stimulus (conditioned stimulus; CS) with an immunomodulating drug (unconditioned stimulus; UCS). Upon re-exposure of the CS alone, immune functioning is altered in a similar manner to that which occurs following actual drug administration."

In studies, when conditioned animals were exposed to an antigen the ones that had also been reexposed to the CS (versus those that had not been reexposed, or that had not received conditioning to the CS) had a reduced antibody response. So, if an animal is exposed to a CS just before being injected with an immunosuppressive drug (the UCS), the CS will act like an immunosuppressant (**conditioned suppression**). On the other hand, if one uses antigens as the UCS (thus producing an enhanced immune response) the CS can produce **conditioned enhancement** of the immune system as well (Ader, 2001).

Ader (2001) points out that there does not exist a great deal of information about conditioning of the immune system in humans. However, it has been shown that patients with multiple sclerosis given an immunosuppressive drug will have a conditioned reduction in white blood cells to a sham treatment. In addition, healthy subjects show an enhancement in natural killer cell activity when reexposed to a flavor associated with an injection of adrenaline (Ader, 2001). Thus, it appears that conditioned suppression and conditioned enhancement of the immune system can occur in humans (see especially Exton et al., 2000, for more evidence of human immune system conditioning).

Psychosocial Factors and the Immune System

As we have already seen, activation of the alarm reaction by a stressor produces a cascade of changes that are intended to reduce the stressful situation. This stress reaction also has effects on the immune system often acting in an immunosuppressive way (Ader, 2001; Kiecolt-Glaser, McGuire, Robles, & Glaser, 2002). Kiecolt-Glaser and colleagues (Glaser & Kiecolt-Glaser, 2005; Kiecolt-Glaser, 2009; Kiecolt-Glaser, Belury, Porter, Beversdorf, Lemeshow, & Glaser, 2007; Kiecolt-Glaser, Glaser, Gravenstein, Marlarky, & Sheridan, 1996; Kiecolt-Glaser, McGuire, Robles, & Glaser, 2002; Kiecolt-Glaser, Preacher, MacCallum, Atkinson, Marlarky, & Glaser, 2003) have shown that stress can slow wound healing, alter the body's response to vaccines, increase the chances of infection, and even trigger latent viruses.

Segerstrom and Miller (2004) note that over 300 studies on the relationship between stress and immunity have found that psychological changes can modify various aspects of the reaction of the immune system. Thus, the death of a spouse, divorce, or caring for a chronically ill person can modify immune system functions. Even milder stressors such as examinations can produce declines in natural killer cell activity (an immune system response) (Kiecolt-Glaser, Garner, Speicher, & Penn, 1984.). Segerstrom and Miller (2004), using meta-analytic techniques, found a difference in immune system response to acute versus chronic stressors. **Acute**, short-lived **stressors** (on the order of minutes) produced immune system responses that were both adaptive and maladaptive. **Chronic**, long-lived **stressors** (months, years), on the other hand, were maladaptive, producing immunosuppression. These results are similar to those of Dhabhar and McEwen (1997) who, based on research with mice, propose that acute stress enhances the immune response while chronic stress suppresses it. Especially interesting is research that suggests a link between emotional changes and immune function—specifically between depression and immunity (Olf, 1999; Leonard, 2001; Ader, 2001; Kiecolt-Glaser et al., 2002) as noted below.

Emotion and Immune Function "There is plausible evidence that the immune system has a role in the neuroendocrine and behavioral features of both depressive and anxiety disorders" (Kiecolt-Glaser, McGuire, Robles, & Glaser, 2002, p. 85; see also Miller, 1998). As noted by Kiecolt et al. there are a number of well-controlled studies that have found a relationship between depression and coronary heart disease. Some studies have also found a link between depression and cancer and even between depression and osteoporosis (see Kiecolt-Glaser et al., 2002, for a review of this research). Other negative emotions such as anxiety, hostility, and anger have also been associated with an increased likelihood of disease (Kiecolt-Glaser et al., 2002). Many diseases associated with aging such as cardiovascular disease, osteoporosis, arthritis, type 2 diabetes, cancer, and Alzheimer's disease as well as other diseases of aging have been linked to negative emotionality (Ershler & Keller, 2000) through the production of IL-6 and other proinflammatory cytokines (Kiecolt-Glaser et al, 2002). As a result, Kiecolt-Glaser et al. (2002, p. 99) argue "... that distress-related immune dysregulation may be one core mechanism behind the health risks associated with negative emotions."

Leonard (2001), has argued a similar notion: he notes that stressors activate the hypothalamic-pituitary-adrenal axis and that this activation can result in the hypersecretion of glucocorticoids that, in turn, lead to the release of inflammatory cytokines both in the periphery as well as in the brain (even though other aspects of the immune response, such as natural killer cell activity and T-cell changes are suppressed). He proposes that the hypersecretion of glucocorticoids and inflammatory cytokines leads to a reduction of noradrenaline and serotonin neurotransmitters in the brain, producing many of the symptoms of depression. Further, he proposes that the action of anti-depressant medication may be to reduce the release of the pro-inflammatory cytokines and thus allow the affected neurotransmitter systems to return to normal function. Thus, one could argue that depression is a "sickness behavior" (Dantzer et al., 1998) produced by the reaction of the immune system to stressors. If future research confirms these relationships, the effective treatment of affective disorders may require a thorough understanding of the role of the immune system.

Placebo Effects

One final area of health psychology that is influenced by motivational processes is research on placebos. As most people understand it, a **placebo** is an inert substance that people nevertheless report make them feel better. Research on placebo effects shows that while a substance may be inert, it still can have physiological effects (see Price, Finniss, & Benedetti, 2008, for a review of this literature). As they note "Placebo factors have neurobiological underpinnings and actual effects on the brain and the body" (Price, Finniss, & Benedetti, 2008, p. 565). Changes in brain activity in areas related to anxiety and pain have been noted as well as in areas related to emotion. Additionally, there is evidence that placebo effects are mediated by changes in both opioid and non-opioid processes within the brain (see Price et al., 2008, for a review of these neurobiological studies).

The effect of a particular placebo is not the result of the substance used but the context in which the placebo is given (Price et al., 2008). The **placebo response**, that is, the perceived change by an individual as a result of the administration of a placebo, is influenced by the person's expectations, desires (motivation), and emotion. Price et al. (2008) summarize research showing that social interactions such as verbal suggestions or the behavior of medical personnel administering the placebo influence the placebo response. For

example, pain reduction is greater when an analgesic is given openly and the suggestion of pain relief is made than when it is given by a hidden machine. (The placebo effect here is the greater pain reduction when the pain medication can be seen and one is told that it will help.) Verbal suggestion is important. Conversations that imply a reduction in pain produce larger effects than more neutral conversations.

Prior experience has also been shown to be a factor. Previous positive or negative experience with a placebo influences how large the placebo response is in a later test of the placebo (Price et al., 2008). Thus, learning plays a role in how effective a placebo is. Placebo effects are influenced by memories of past effects and expectancies. Price, Milling, Kirsch, Duff, Montgomery et al. (1999) found that people tend to overestimate the amount of previous pain they experienced, and this influences their expectation of pain relief (from a placebo) in the present. Thus, our memories interact with our present situation in determining our expectations about the effect of a placebo treatment.

Apparently, some people show much larger placebo effects than others. As Price et al. (2008) point out, there are **placebo responders and non-responders**. This is a potentially important point because group averages are often used in placebo research. If a group is composed of both responders and nonresponders then the group average will be an average of the two types of responders and will influence the magnitude of the placebo response measured. When responders are separately analyzed from nonresponders, the average placebo response for responders is much greater (Benedetti, 1996).

Price et al. (2008) propose that a **desire-expectation model** can account for many of the observed placebo effects. As they note "... placebo responses seem to relate to feeling good (or less bad) about prospects of relief (avoidance goal) or pleasure (approach goal) that are associated with treatments or medications. These feelings can be separately influenced by desire and expectation or by the combination of both factors. In this model desire is the motivation to feel differently (e.g., less pain) and expectation is the belief that the treatment (placebo) will allow one to reach that goal.

Sexual Arousal

Let us conclude this chapter by returning to the general notion of arousal, specifically the role of arousal in sexual behavior. For practical purposes, sexual motivation may be equivalent to sexual arousal. It is useful, therefore, to examine research on sexual arousal. Much of the work on sexual arousal was initiated as a result of the pioneering research of Masters and Johnson (1966, 1970, 1974; see also Luria, Friedman, & Rose, 1987, for an overview).

The initial research of Masters and Johnson involved a study of the sexual responses of 694 people, 382 women and 312 men. During the 12 years covered by this research, over 10,000 orgasms were directly observed. Based on these data, Masters and Johnson report that human sexual responses can conveniently be described as consisting of four stages. Both men and women go through these four stages, but in slightly different ways.

Stages of the Human Sexual Response Cycle

Two basic physiological responses that occur during sexual behavior are similar in both men and women. These two responses are vasocongestion and myotonia. **Vasocongestion** is the concentration of blood in certain portions of the body. In the male, vasocongestion produces penile enlargement and erection; in the female, vasocongestion produces clitoral enlargement. **Myotonia** is an increase in muscle tone throughout the body. In both men and women, sexual behavior leads to increases in body muscle tone that are maintained until orgasm.

Excitement The first stage of the sexual response cycle is excitement. Sexual excitement may be induced by physical stimuli such as a touch or a caress or by psychological stimuli such as erotic pictures or fantasies. During the excitement phase, the penis of the male becomes erect due to vasocongestion, and the vagina of the female lubricates and lengthens. This phase, and the last (resolution), compose the greatest amount of time spent in the sexual response cycle.

Plateau During this second phase of the sexual response cycle identified by Masters and Johnson, many of the changes that have already occurred during the excitement phase continue: Sexual arousal is intensified during plateau, perhaps in preparation for the climax of orgasm that follows this phase.

Orgasm Orgasm is a sexual climax during which the building sexual tension is dramatically reduced. In the male only one orgasm, during which ejaculation takes place, typically occurs per cycle, whereas in the female, orgasm may occur once, several times, or not at all.

Resolution Immediately following orgasm there is a refractory period in men during which further sexual behavior does not occur. In young men this refractory period usually lasts 10 to 30 minutes. In older men the refractory period is longer. Following orgasm, women do not have a definable refractory period and are capable of continued sexual activity and multiple orgasms. During the resolution phase the body returns to its prearoused state in reverse order through the stages.

Other Bodily Changes During Sexual Behavior

Female Bodily Changes During the sexual response cycle several bodily changes occur in women. In addition to myotonia, respiration typically increases from 12 to as many as 40 breaths per minute. Heart rate also increases from around 60 beats per minute to as many as

100–180 beats per minute. Blood pressure rises and reaches a peak during the late plateau stage just prior to orgasm. Sometimes, involuntary contractions of the hands and feet occur (called **carpopedal spasm**), causing the toes to curl up or the hands to close.

The breasts and nipples change in both size and color; nipples become erect, and the size of the breasts increase as a result of blood flow to the breasts. An increased blood flow to the skin causes a reddening of the skin (called the **sex flush**) that may cover the upper abdomen and breasts and spread to other parts of the body including the face, thighs, buttocks, and back. The uterus increases in size and rises up and away from the vagina. This elevation increases the length of the vagina. The vagina also expands. During the sexual response cycle, the clitoris initially swells and lengthens due to vasocongestion. Later in the cycle, but before orgasm, it retracts out of sight under the clitoral hood. The inner lips of the vagina (labia minora) turn bright red in some women just prior to orgasm as a result of increased blood flow to the area.

During orgasm, the vagina contracts rhythmically (at about 0.8-second intervals) for up to 15 contractions. The more intense the orgasm, the greater the number of contractions; however, the intensity of the orgasm does not appear to depend on these contractions (Luria et al., 1987). The uterus also rhythmically contracts during orgasm, and the anal sphincter may sometimes contract.

Male Bodily Changes Myotonia occurs during the late excitement and plateau phases. As with women, men show increases in respiration and heart rate and may also experience the sex flush, nipple erection, and carpopedal spasms of the hands and feet. Male sexual arousal is first evidenced by penile erection, although erection of the penis can occur for other reasons as well (e.g., during dream sleep and in fear- or anxiety-producing situations [Luria et al., 1987]).

During the excitement phase the testes elevate and rotate. The testes also increase in size, and the scrotum increases in thickness and contracts. When the testes are fully elevated, orgasm occurs. During the plateau phase, the skin of the penis may become deep red or purple as a result of vasocongestion. Fluid from the Cowper's gland (sometimes containing sperm) may also seep from the penis during the plateau phase. A woman could thus become pregnant even though the male did not ejaculate while in her vagina.

Men report that orgasm is sometimes felt even before the contractions associated with ejaculation occur. They also report that orgasm is experienced as a two-stage process. In the first stage the orgasm is felt as imminent and unstoppable. In the second stage semen is ejaculated. During the second stage, the prostate, seminal vesicles, and vas deferens contract rhythmically and involuntarily. The urethra also contracts, expelling the semen containing the sperm. Contractions, as in the female, occur at about 0.8-second intervals initially, but then lengthen to as much as several seconds apart. The force and volume of the ejaculation depend on how long it has been since a previous ejaculation (Luria et al., 1987).

Sexual motivation would seem to be the clearest example of the close relationship between changes in arousal and motivated behavior. For all practical purposes, it would seem that sexual behavior results from changes in sexual arousal. Some researchers, however, have suggested that prior to sexual arousal (as outlined above) sexual desire is necessary (Kaplan, 1978). **Sexual desire** may be likened to appetite; that is, one must first want to be sexually aroused before arousal can occur. Kaplan has noted that some people lose their sexual appetites, a condition she terms **hypoactive sexual desire**, and as a result become uninterested in sexual behavior.

Furthermore, a distinction can be made between reaching orgasm and satisfaction as a result. Some individuals report reaching orgasm but do not find it satisfying (Zilbergeld & Ellison, 1980). Luria and associates (1987) have suggested that a more complete description of the human sexual response cycle ought to include both desire and satisfaction. Their model suggests that the human sexual response cycle occurs in the following order: desire, excitement, plateau, orgasm, resolution, satisfaction, refractory period.

Certainly there remains much to be understood about human sexuality. Although we have learned a great deal about the physiological changes that occur during sexual behavior, we still know very little about the psychological components. Arousal theory has proven useful in understanding many of the physical changes that occur during sexual behavior; future research on the psychological aspects of sexual behavior may or may not support an arousal perspective.

SUMMARY

In this chapter we have examined theories and research suggesting that motivation and emotion can be understood in terms of arousal. Arousal theory was strengthened by the discovery of brain mechanisms that serve to activate the cortex (the reticular activating system of the midbrain), and this led to the development of theories proposing that arousal is motivation. It soon became clear, however, that arousal is not a unitary process but consists of several types of arousal (cortical, autonomic, behavioral). Arousal theory has far to go in regard to motivation. If we grant that an aroused organism is motivated, what determines whether it eats, drinks, copulates, or falls asleep? General arousal theory has little to say about the activation of specific motives or the direction that behavior will take.

Sleep was originally thought to involve little arousal. We now know that this too is an oversimplification. Recordings of the electrical activity of the brain show definite changes at different stages of sleep and also show similarities between cortical activity during REM sleep and during waking. Physiological studies have begun to trace the systems involved in sleep and show that brainstem mechanisms and specific neurotransmitters play a major role in both sleeping and dreaming.

Large deviations above our normal level of functioning may lead to an aroused state called stress. Stress is conceived as being the body's attempt to cope with or adapt to a changed environment. Stress can occur from both physical and psychological causes and leads to a generalized reaction called the general adaptation syndrome. Much of the stress reaction involves the pituitary and adrenal glands of the endocrine system. Activation of the pituitary-adrenal axis is triggered by the perception of a stressor, resulting in mobilization of the body to cope with the stress.

Considerable research conducted on the relationship of life change and illness indicates an association between the two. The major problem with life-change research has been that individuals vary greatly in their ability to withstand stress. These individual differences in the effects of life change and illness now appear to result from buffering agents that reduce the effects of the stress. The personality styles of hardiness, physical exercise, and controllability have all been implicated as factors reducing the association between life change and illness. Research in health psychology has led to a better understanding of how behaviors can be related to health and illness. In particular, the field of psychoneuroimmunology has found links between the brain, behavior, the endocrine system, and the immune system that show that these are intimately linked to one another and influence each other. Some of this research has shown that affective disorders, such as depression may be related in some way to changes in the immune system, although our understanding of those relationships is still rudimentary. Research on placebo effects has shown that a response to a placebo is influenced by the context of the situation and one's desires and expectations. Despite the fact that placebos are inert, they do produce changes in brain activity.

Most people would like to be able to reduce the amount of stress they experience. Research indicates that knowledge of the body's reactions to stress and the preparation of alternate plans to combat frustration leading to stress are effective means of reducing stress. Some people may also be more immune to stress because they can emotionally insulate themselves from the life changes they experience. Meditative techniques may be effective in reducing stress because the meditative experience triggers mechanisms within the hypothalamus that inhibit overactivity in the sympathetic nervous system. Much work, however, remains here too before we can fully understand the processes involved.

KEY TERMS

inverted U function/ Yerkes-Dodson Law, *62*

encephale isole/ cerveau isole, *63*

pons/reticular activating system (RAS)/ synchronous/ alpha waves/ desynchronized/beta waves, *64*

cue function/arousal function, *65*

circadian rhythms, *68*

unihemispheric slow-wave sleep (USWS)/relaxed wakefulness/ sleep spindles/ K-complexes, *69*

delta waves/REM sleep/ NREM sleep, *70*

paradoxical sleep, *72*

neurocognitive theory of dreams/continuity principle/repetition principle/Threat Simulation Theory, *73*

virtual rehearsal mechanism/ REM pressure/ REM rebound, *74*

delirium tremens (DTs)/ vasodilation/general arousal, *75*

locus coerulus/raphe nuclei/ tuberomammillary nucleus/ lateral hypothalamus/ ventrolateral preoptic area (VLPO)/GABA (gamma-aminobutyric acid), *76*

sublateralodorsal nucleus (SLD)/ precoeruleus region (PC)/ medial peribrachial nucleus, *77*

adenosine, *78*

restorative function/organization of the brain/programming device/consolidation of memories, *79*

storage of complex associative information, *80*

endocrine system/hormones/ pituitary/hypothalamus/ adrenal gland/adrenal cortex/ cortisol/adrenal medulla/ epinephrine/norepinephrine/ corticotropin releasing hormone(CRH)/ adrenocorticotropic hormone (ACTH), *83*

alarm reaction/stage of resistance, *84*

stage of exhaustion/general adaptation syndrome (GAS), *85*

emotional insulation/ Social Readjustment Rating Scale/retrospective studies, *86*

prospective studies, *87*

hardiness/commitment/control/ challenge, *89*

social support theory/ explanatory style, *90*

expressive style/humor/ knowledge/emotionally insulate/looking beyond the momentary/alternate plans/ meditation, *91*

psychoneuroimmunology, *92*

antigen/cytokines/ interleukins [IL]/conditioned suppression/conditioned enhancement, *93*

acute stressors/chronic stressors, *94*

placebo/placebo response/ placebo responders and non-responders/desire-expectation model, *95*

vasocongestion/myotonia/ carpopedal spasm, *96*

sex flush/sexual desire/ hypoactive sexual desire, *97*

SUGGESTIONS FOR FURTHER READING

Carlson, N. R. (2010). *Physiology of Behavior (10th ed.).* Boston: Allyn & Bacon. This advanced text provides an excellent overview of the physiology of sleep and waking. For the advanced student.

Kiecolt-Glaser, J. K., McGuire, L., Robles, T. F., & Glaser, R. (2002). Emotions, morbidity, and mortality: New Perspectives from psychoneuro-immunology. *Annual Review of Psychology, 53,* 83–197. This review examines the relationship between negative emotions such as depression and changes in the immune system.

King, B. M. (2009). *Human Sexuality Today (6th ed.).* New York: Vanga. A good overview of human sexuality.

Price, D. D., Finniss, D. G., & Benedetti, F. (2008). A comprehensive review of the placebo effect: Recent advances and current thought. *Annual Review of Psychology, 59,* 565–590.

CHAPTER 4

Physiological Mechanisms of Regulation

CHAPTER PREVIEW

This chapter is concerned with the following questions:

1. Which brain structures appear to control hunger, thirst, sexual motivation, and aggression?

2. What do anorexia and bulimia suggest about the homeostatic control of eating?

3. What factors have been proposed as important in the development of obesity?

As I sit in front of my computer, munching on a sandwich and contemplating how to begin this discussion of the physiological mechanisms of regulation, it occurs to me that the topics of hunger, thirst, and sexual motivation are terribly complex. The bulk of the research that has been conducted on hunger and thirst has taken the view that homeostasis is the primary mechanism controlling ingestion of food or water. That is, it has generally been assumed that we eat food to maintain our energy balance and drink water to maintain our fluid balance. However, it is becoming clearer that we often eat for reasons that are not related to energy need and therefore are not homoeostatic. Similarly, we often drink fluids for properties other than water balance such as taste (e.g., sodas), or the effects those fluids have on us (alcohol, coffee). Engaging in sexual behavior, likewise, often has less to do with reproduction than pleasure.

What Do We Eat: Taste and Smell as Gatekeepers

Receptors on your tongue and in your nose provide initial information about food. **Sweet**, **sour**, **bitter**, and **umami** (savory) (Berthoud & Morrison, 2008) tastes give us information about whether to ingest food that is in our mouth. Taste, then, acts as a guardian for our internal state. Sweet-tasting foods are calorically dense and therefore, in our ancestral past, would have been highly valuable. Bitter-tasting foods are more likely to contain toxins that could make us sick or even kill us, so bitter tasting foods are better avoided. Sour tasting foods might be on the verge of going bad, so it might be best to avoid them too (e.g., sour milk), although some sour-tasting substances (e.g., lemonade) when combined with sweetness are liked. **Salt** is essential for life, and substances containing salt are preferred. Taste receptors on the tongue appear to be a first line of defense, and when a bitter or sour taste is encountered, we often spit the food out, or gag to prevent the substance from being ingested (Buss, 2008). Similarly, bad-smelling foods may be spoiled and best avoided, while the smell of ripe fruits indicate readiness to eat.

Why Do We Eat?

At a superficial level the answer to that question is obvious—we eat to provide energy to our bodies. However, the question of what initiates eating is a more difficult one. Certainly part of the reason we eat is a result of **cues** in our environment that signal the availability of food. You walk into the kitchen and **smell** your favorite dish simmering away on the stove and you immediately want to know how long until dinner. Other cues such as time of day, taste, and even effort may contribute to your desire to eat (see the section on the externality theory of obesity later in this chapter).

However, Rozin, Dow, Moscovitch, and Rajaram (1998) provide evidence that a major determinant of when we eat is **memory** of when we last ate and how much we ate. Rozin et al. gave amnesic patients a meal and then shortly afterward (within 30 minutes) offered them another meal and again within 30 minutes offered them a third meal. The same procedure was used with a control group of nonamnesic individuals. Interestingly, the amnesic patients offered a second or third meal were likely to accept and to eat at least parts of the second and even the third meals. The nonamnesic persons refused the second and subsequent meals. The results of this clever study suggest that one trigger for eating may simply be the memory of how long it has been since when one last ate. The amnesics, unable to remember anything longer than a minute or so, accepted and ate the additional meals because they had no information available to them to

indicate how long it had been since they previously ate. Data such as the Rozin et al. study also suggest that we may often stop eating before the satiating effects of food have had a chance to occur—that is, we seem to often stop eating as a result of cues that tell us that the meal is over such as the food being gone, rather than to internal cues that indicate that sufficient energy has been taken in.

What Determines How Much We Eat?

A second question is what determines how much we eat at a meal. In a general sense, we want to balance energy intake with energy use, taking in an amount equivalent to what we are burning up so that we do not have to access energy stored in our fat cells. Raynor and Epstein (2001), in a review of studies on factors influencing obesity, found that the variety of food available influences how much we eat. They found that studies consistently showed that in animals and humans greater variety in the foods available led to larger amounts of food being consumed. For example, Rolls, van Duijvenvoorde, and Rolls (1984) gave people in one group sausage, bread and butter, chocolate dessert, and bananas in four separate courses, one item per course. A second group got four courses also, but only one of the four foods was used and the food was the same in each course. They found that the group that had the varied four-course meal ate 44% more food and took in 60% more energy. Thus, a variation in diet leads to greater consumption and energy intake.

Sensory Specific Satiety

Why do people and animals consume more when the diet is varied? One possibility is that consuming the same foods over and over reduces the hedonic value of that food. The idea, first proposed by Hetherington and Rolls (1996), proposes that eating a particular food until one is satiated reduces the value (or in humans, the perceived pleasantness) of that food compared to other foods. Thus an animal or person exposed to an unchanging diet will eat less than if they have access to a varied diet because the constant diet is less rewarding. This effect has been labeled **sensory specific satiety**. As noted by Raynor and Epstein (2001), sensory specific satiety seems to be related to the characteristics of food such as taste, or the feel of food in the mouth. Exposure to these sensory characteristics of food promotes the development of sensory specific satiety. When the same foods are eaten again and again, these stimulus qualities of food lead to faster satiation by these foods. A varied diet, therefore, may lead to extended eating because the variation in diet prevents or retards the development of sensory specific satiety.

Further, LaBar, Gitelman, Parrish, Kim, Nobre, and Mesulam (2001) have shown using fMRI techniques that hungry individuals showed increased activity in the amygdala and other structures when shown pictures of food, but no such increase in activity occurred when shown pictures of tools. Their results suggest that the salience of food-related stimuli is increased when hunger motivation is present. Thus the motivation to eat influences our reactivity to food stimuli in the environment.

Additionally, Harris, Gorissen, Bailey, and Westbrook (2000) have found that motivational state influences learned flavor preferences. In a series of seven experiments they showed that rats would develop a learned preference for an almond odor when paired with either sucrose or saccharin when not hungry; however, if motivated by hunger, a preference for the odor was formed only with sucrose. LaBar et al. interpret their results as indicating that in hungry animals the learned preference for the almond odor is due exclusively to an association between the odor and the caloric value of the sucrose. Thus it appears that learned preferences in rats can be based on taste alone (if not hungry) and on caloric value (when hungry).

If similar processes are at work in human eating, it would mean that eating could be initiated or maintained by both attractive tastes (regardless of hunger) and caloric value (when hungry). At least on a commonsense level these findings would seem to fit with experience. Sometimes we are attracted to and eat food even though we do not need the calories (i.e., the food tastes good), and at other times we are attracted to and eat food because we need the energy the food provides. Obviously, the reasons we eat are exceedingly complex.

Now that we have seen that the motivation to eat is especially sensitive to cues associated with food and that these cues may instigate eating, let us look at research that has examined the homeostatic mechanisms involved in eating. We will first present some background research and early ideas about hunger motivation and follow that with more recent findings that hormonal signals and brain neurotransmitters play a large role in the regulation of hunger.

Basic Metabolism

Food is composed of **carbohydrates**, **fats**, and **proteins**. As shown in Figure 4.1, carbohydrates are broken down into **glucose** as a result of the activities of the digestive system. Glucose can then be used to provide energy to the brain, the muscles, and the body (in the presence of **insulin**) or can be converted to **glycogen** by the liver (with insulin). The liver and muscles provide a temporary store of glycogen that can be rapidly converted back into glucose by the pancreatic hormone **glucagon**. This short-term energy store contains about 300 calories of energy (Carlson, 2010). Excess glucose taken in is stored in fat cells as **triglycerides** (a form of fat). Fats consumed during a meal are converted to triglycerides and also stored away in the fat cells. Proteins are first converted to **amino acids** and then, while some are used as building blocks for protein synthesis, excess proteins are also converted to triglycerides and stored in the fat cells. As Carlson (2010) points out, the short-term store of 300 calories or so is used primarily to feed the brain because although the muscles and the body can use fatty acids for energy, the brain cannot; it must have glucose.

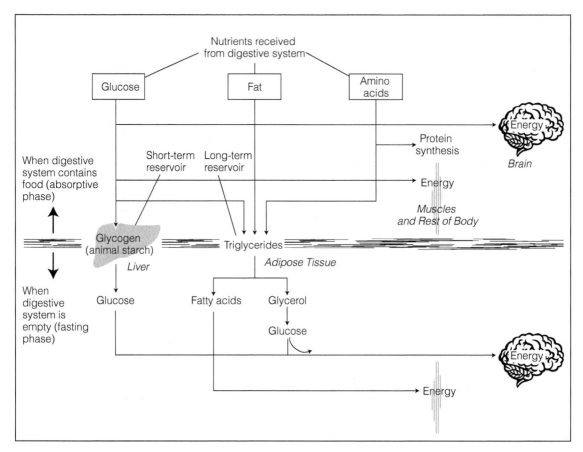

FIGURE 4.1   Relationships and uses of glucose, fat, and amino adds in fueling the body. From N. R. Carlson, *Physiology of Behavior*, 7th ed., figure 13.2, p. 395. Published by Allyn and Bacon, Boston, MA. Copyright © 2001 by Pearson Education. Reprinted by permission of the publisher.

When energy availability falls, the long-term energy stores within the fat cells are called into action. The triglycerides are broken into **fatty acids** and **glycerol**. As already mentioned, the fatty acids can be used by the muscles for energy. Glycerol is converted by the liver into glucose, which is then also available to the brain. In examining these various processes for providing fuel to the brain and body, one is struck by the prevalence of glucose. As we shall see shortly, theorists have proposed that detection of changes in glucose serves as a cue for regulating energy balance within the body, but first let's look at some of the earliest ideas on hunger.

Local Theories

Early approaches suggested that changes in stomach contractions were the signals that initiated eating. For example, Cannon and Washburn (1912) reported that stomach contractions are associated with hunger in humans. Washburn swallowed a balloon that was inflated and then

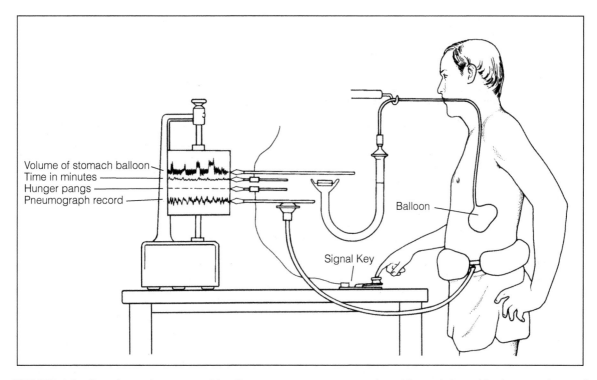

FIGURE 4.2 Experimental setup used by Cannon to measure stomach activity and the subjective experience of hunger. Adapted from "Hunger and Thirst," by W. B. Cannon in *Handbook of General Experimental Psychology*, edited by C. Murchinson. Copyright © 1934 by Clark University press. Used by permission.

attached to a marking pen that recorded Washburn's stomach contractions on a moving piece of paper (Figure 4.2). Washburn was also instructed to indicate when he felt subjectively hungry. His hunger pangs tended to line up with his stomach contractions, leading Cannon and Washburn to assume that stomach contractions are the basis of hunger signals and, as a result, of eating.

The Cannon and Washburn theory was known as the **local theory** of motivation because it assumed that the signals that control motives such as hunger and thirst are produced in the peripheral organs of the body (as opposed to the brain). The local theory of motivation, however, turned out to be inadequate. For example, severing the nerve that carries information between the central nervous system and the stomach does not eliminate the experience of hunger. The **vagus nerve** is the major source of this information; when severed it causes stomach contractions to cease but not the experience of hunger in humans (Grossman & Stein, 1948). Morgan and Morgan (1940) had earlier shown that severing the vagus does not eliminate food intake in rats given insulin, so it appeared to researchers that changes in the periphery of the body are unnecessary for the experience of hunger (see Cofer & Appley, 1964, for a more complete discussion of this research). Because the early peripheral explanations appeared unable to account for motivated states such as hunger, it was natural for researchers to begin looking to the brain as the possible site of control.

Central Theories

Central theories of motivation emphasized the idea that specialized cells in the brain detected changes in the body's state and triggered appropriate motivation. Such models deemphasize the role of the periphery in the regulation of eating and drinking. Several areas of the brain have been implicated in the homeostatic control of motivated behavior, but the greatest amount of research has focused on a small structure, buried deep within

the brain, called the **hypothalamus**. As its name implies, it is located below the thalamus. Figure 4.3 shows the location of the hypothalamus in relation to other brain structures.

Although the hypothalamus represents only a very small portion of the entire brain, cells lying within this area and fibers coursing through it are involved with many important functions. For example, the hypothalamus controls the activation of both the sympathetic and parasympathetic portions of the autonomic nervous system as well as the

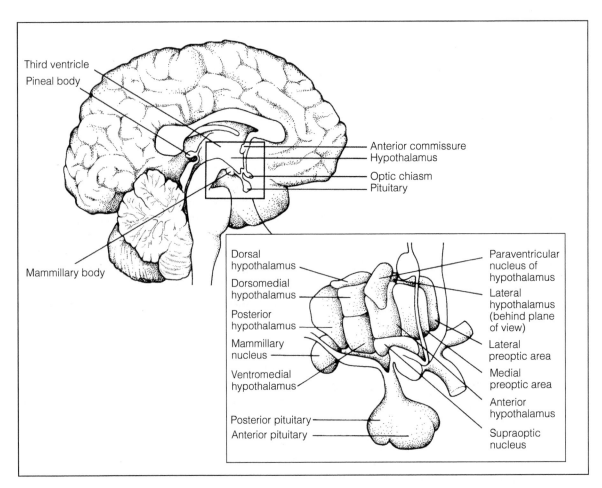

FIGURE 4.3 Relation of the hypothalamic to other brain structures and its major cell groups. Adapted from *Biological Psychology* by J. W. Kalat Copyright © 1984 by Wadsworth Publishing Company.

pituitary gland and, as a result, the rest of the endocrine system (Carlson, 1977; Guillemin & Burgus, 1976). Changes in feeding, drinking, sexual behavior, aggressiveness, and fear have all been reported as a result of experimental damage to or stimulation of this area. The hypothalamus is also richly endowed with blood vessels, which makes it well suited to sample changes in blood components (blood glucose, water content, hormone levels, etc.).

Homeostatic Regulation

The homeostatic model assumes that regulatory mechanisms exist within the body that sample the internal environment; when changes move the body away from some optimal value, these mechanisms trigger circuitry within the brain that generates motivation to return the organism to a balanced state. Figure 4.4 outlines a simple version of how such mechanisms might work. Much of the

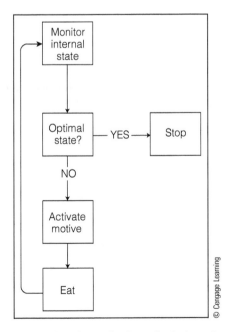

FIGURE 4.4   Flowchart of a hypothetical mechanism maintain energy homeostasis.

research directed at understanding the regulation of motivational states has concentrated on the hunger motive and, in particular, on the role of the hypothalamus in hunger.

Regulation of Hunger

Hunger motivation has been generally assumed to be homeostatic in nature. When an imbalance exists, say, in the levels of sugar in the blood (**blood glucose**), this change is detected by specialized cells called **glucoreceptors** that trigger the motive to eat. As blood glucose levels rise, these (or perhaps other) glucoreceptors inhibit further eating because energy levels are now adequate. Some homeostatic mechanism like the one just outlined have usually been assumed to control **short-term regulation** of energy intake—that is, a mechanism that controls when we eat a meal (intermeal interval)—and how much we eat (meal size). Generally, a second homeostatic mechanism, which controls **long-term regulation** of energy reserves, has also been assumed. The mechanism controlling long-term regulation is involved with maintaining adequate energy stores so that if short-term energy intake proves inadequate, these stores can be called on to maintain normal functioning. This long-term regulation is usually thought to involve the detection of changes in the amount of energy stored as fat within the adipose tissue and the activation of hunger if the stores fall below some optimal amount. Thus, we are motivated to eat not only to replace energy we have expended, but also to stockpile adequate energy for the future. Although it is convenient to analyze hunger motivation as consisting of short- and long-term components, the processes concerned with managing energy intake are extremely complex and interact intensively (see Berthoud & Morrison, 2008, for a more complete view of these myriad interactions). For convenience, however, we will continue to examine the available research using the concepts of short- and long-term regulation of hunger motivation.

Short-Term Regulation

Short-term regulation involves the control of eating over periods of time, such as from one day to the next or from one meal to another. Because short-term regulation was thought to function primarily to balance energy intake with energy expenditure, it was assumed that this system monitored some aspect of energy availability and triggered eating when available energy began to drop. The question of interest is, Where is this short-term system, and how does it work?

A clue to the possible location of the system was provided in a study by Hetherington and Ranson (1940), who found that lesions of the hypothalamus produced obesity in animals. Later research localized the obesity effect to damage in the region of the **ventromedial hypothalamus (VMH)**. When this area of the hypothalamus was damaged, the affected animal would begin eating large quantities of food, a condition known as **hyperphagia**. Figure 4.5 pictures a rat made obese by damage to this area. Hyperphagic animals can eat enormous amounts of food, sometimes increasing their body weight to twice that of normal (Stevenson, 1969); however, they do not eat until they burst. Eventually these extremely obese animals stabilize their weight at this elevated level and maintain themselves around this new weight.

A second clue concerning the operation of this system was provided by Anand and Brobeck (1951), who found that lesions in a second region, called the **lateral hypothalamus (LH)**, caused animals to stop eating.

Figure 4.3 shows the location of the lateral hypothalamus. These LH–damaged animals would neither eat nor drink (conditions called **aphagia** and **adipsia**, respectively) and would die unless the experimenter intervened. If the animals were kept alive by the experimenter, however, they would eventually recover (Teitelbaum & Stellar, 1954) and maintain themselves, though at a weight considerably below normal.

The discovery of areas within the hypothalamus that have specific and opposite effects on the eating behavior of animals led to the concept of

FIGURE 4.5 An obese (hyperphagic) rat. The dramatic weight increase is due to a lesion in the ventromedial hypothalamus. The rat actually weighs more than 1000 grams (the dial has gone beyond the capacity of the scale). Photo courtesy of Neal Miller.

centers that work together to regulate hunger (Stellar, 1954; Mayer, 1955). The VMH was considered to be a **satiety center** that "turns off" eating when energy intake is sufficient. If this center was damaged, then the animal could not inhibit its eating and thus became obese. Conversely, the LH was thought to be an excitatory or **hunger center** that "turns on" eating when new sources of energy are needed. According to the **center hypothesis**, damage to the LH should lead to a lack of eating because the cells that would normally initiate eating are damaged. The concept of excitatory and inhibitory centers within the hypothalamus that regulate food intake generated a tremendous amount of research. A major thrust of this research was an attempt to determine what changing conditions within the body signal the LH to initiate eating and, conversely, what conditions signal the VMH to inhibit eating. Changes in blood glucose provided a likely candidate.

The Glucostatic Theory of Hunger

In 1955, Mayer proposed that receptors in the hypothalamus are sensitive to changes in the ratio of blood glucose in the arteries to that in the veins. A decrease in blood glucose detected by glucoreceptors in the LH was thought to trigger eating (a so-called hunger center), while an increase in blood glucose detected by glucoreceptors in the VMH (a so-called satiety center) was thought to inhibit further food intake. Mayer's theory was based, in part, on a report by Brecher and Waxler (1949) showing that injections of a chemical called gold thioglucose killed cells in the VMH. It was presumed that these cells were killed because they absorbed the chemical as a result of its similarity to glucose.

The glucostatic theory enjoyed considerable popularity for many years, but its credibility came upon hard times. Several lines of research suggested that although glucoreceptors may exist in the VMH and LH, they are not the primary mechanisms responsible for normal short-term regulation. For example, it has been shown that gold thioglucose damages the VMH because it destroys the capillaries feeding the VMH rather than being absorbed by the cells because it is like glucose. Other chemicals that destroy capillaries also damage the VMH even though they do not contain glucose as part of their makeup (Carlson, 1977; Mogenson, 1976). The destructive action of gold thioglucose on capillaries rather than on the VMH cells cast doubt on the presence of glucoreceptors in the VMH.

Further doubt was created by Gold's (1973) study showing that lesions that are restricted entirely to the VMH and do not damage adjacent fiber bundles do not result in obesity. When the adjacent bundles are damaged, however, the VMH obesity effect is found. Gold's results question the role of the VMH in the turning off of food-motivated behavior and suggest that fibers passing near the VMH may be responsible for the obesity, because these fibers are often damaged when VMH lesions are made.

The role of the LH in the activation of eating behavior is also not as certain as the early research seemed to indicate. Evidence for glucoreceptors in the LH does exist (Oomura, 1976), and the area does seem to be involved with eating as a result of changes in glucose (Epstein & Teitelbaum, 1967); however, the role of the LH in normal eating seems doubtful (Blass & Kraly, 1974; Grossman, 1976; Kraly & Blass, 1974; Zeliger & Karten, 1974). For example, Blass and Kraly noted that depriving LH cells of glucose must be extreme before feeding is induced in normal rats. As a result, they suggested that the LH may be part of an emergency system that is triggered only under extreme conditions.

The most damaging evidence to the idea that the LH normally initiates eating is a group of studies showing that LH lesions result in a general motivational deficit of which eating is only a small part (Marshall & Teitelbaum, 1974; Stricker, Friedman, & Zigmond, 1975; Stricker & Zigmond, 1976; Wolgin, Cytawa, & Teitelbaum, 1976). Stricker and his associates have shown that LH–damaged animals do not react appropriately to highly stressful situations. Similarly, Teitelbaum and his colleagues have found that LH–damaged animals do not react to stimuli normally associated with motivated behaviors and also show large deficits in normal arousal levels. The LH–damaged animal is therefore handicapped in many ways unrelated to hunger motivation. Lack of eating in such an animal probably reflects these more general deficits rather than damage to a glucose-sensitive, short-term regulatory system.

What does all this research mean with respect to the theory that the hypothalamus contains glucose-sensitive receptors that control feeding and satiety? It seems clear that the VMH and LH are involved in hunger motivation in some fashion. There is evidence that glucoreceptors exist in the brain; injection of glucose into it suppresses feeding, and intense glucose deprivation will initiate feeding. But glucoreceptors in the brain are probably part of an emergency system that comes into play only when glucose levels drop drastically. It is also known that both the VMH and LH are involved in various behaviors in addition to eating; damage to either, therefore, results in complex behavioral changes of which eating (or lack of eating) is only a part. Consequently, the concept of a dual system of excitatory and inhibitory centers within the hypothalamus that monitor glucose levels and turn hunger on or off seems incorrect. The conclusion that glucoreceptors in the brain do not control normal feeding behavior led some researchers to look again to the periphery of the body for the signals that initiate and inhibit eating.

Peripheral Detectors for Short-Term Regulation

What peripheral mechanisms might trigger feeding behavior, and what mechanisms might stop feeding behavior? Though a single mechanism could both start and stop eating behavior, several systems are probably involved. If we think of the body as similar to a NASA rocket, in which several backup systems become active as conditions change, we should not be surprised to discover that the triggering and interruption of feeding result from more than one type of signal. Indeed researchers have found evidence for several signaling systems. (For a review, see Berthoud & Morrison, 2008.)

When we eat, enzymes in the saliva begin to break down the food into its components. This process is continued by the stomach, which then empties its contents into the upper small intestine, called the **duodenum**. The products of digestion, such as simple sugars and amino acids, are absorbed by the duodenum and enter the bloodstream, where they travel immediately to the liver; fats take a different route (Carlson, 1977).

Stomach   Several mechanisms in the stomach may act as satiety signals to turn off eating. Two such mechanisms are stretch receptors in the stomach wall, which serve to limit intake, and nutrient detectors, which inform the brain of the presence of specific nutrients (Carlson, 1977, 2010). Apparently, a feedback loop also exists between the stomach and the brain because stomach activity is modified by its contents. In fact, the entire gastrointestinal tract sends and receives information to the brain via the vagus nerve, the sympathetic nervous system, and various hormones (Berthoud & Morrison, 2008). The stomach does not appear to regulate by itself, however, because individuals whose stomachs have been removed still report hunger and still regulate.

Ghrelin and Obestatin   One recent discovery about the communication of the stomach with the brain is the hormone **ghrelin** (Kojima, Hosoda, Date, Nakazato, Matsuo & Kangawa, 1999). Ghrelin is secreted primarily by the stomach and rises sharply before a meal is eaten and is suppressed by food eaten. See Figure 4.6 for an example of ghrelin increases before meals. As the figure shows, ghrelin levels rise before meals and drop after meals. Further, ghrelin levels rise again in the early evening (perhaps stimulating snacking?) then decrease throughout the night. In addition, ghrelin levels are higher after weight loss than before weight loss. Finally, ghrelin levels do not change in persons who have had gastric bypass surgery. These findings are all consistent with the hypothesis that ghrelin serves as a short-term hunger signal produced by the stomach.

The rise in ghrelin levels before meals provides reasonable evidence that it is an appetite stimulant, and in fact, it is the only gut hormone so far identified as producing an increase in appetite (Cummings, 2006). Interestingly, Schmid, Held, Ising, Uhr, Weikel & Steiger (2005), found that injections of ghrelin not only produced an increase in appetite but also produced an increase in thoughts about food in humans.

In animals, ghrelin injections quickly produce an increase in food intake as a result of increases in feeding behaviors (Cummings, 2006). Ghrelin is suppressed most effectively by proteins, second best by carbohydrates, and least by fats (Foster-Schubert,

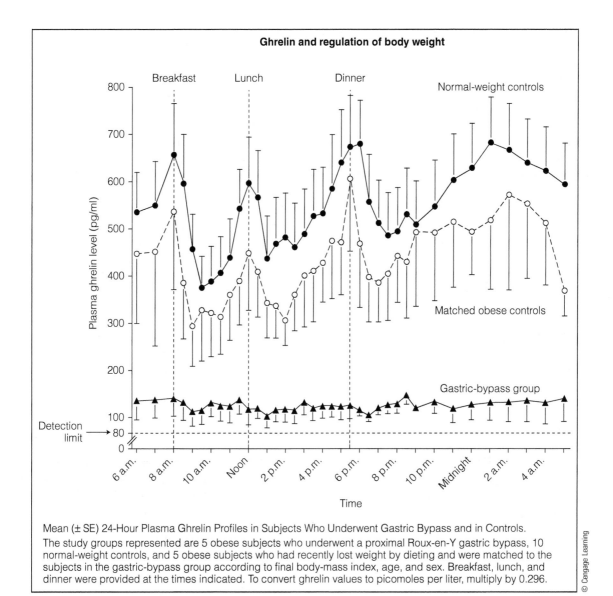

Mean (± SE) 24-Hour Plasma Ghrelin Profiles in Subjects Who Underwent Gastric Bypass and in Controls. The study groups represented are 5 obese subjects who underwent a proximal Roux-en-Y gastric bypass, 10 normal-weight controls, and 5 obese subjects who had recently lost weight by dieting and were matched to the subjects in the gastric-bypass group according to final body-mass index, age, and sex. Breakfast, lunch, and dinner were provided at the times indicated. To convert ghrelin values to picomoles per liter, multiply by 0.296.

© Cengage Learning

FIGURE 4.6 Ghrelin's role as a short-term hunger signal.

et al., 2008). Recently, another gut hormone, obestatin, has been found to have effects on appetite that are opposite that of ghrelin (Karaoglu et al., 2009; Soares & Leite-Moreira, 2008). **Obestatin** appears to be an appetite suppressant.

Duodenum The duodenum is a possible site of glucoreceptors because injections of glucose directly into the duodenum suppress eating in free-feeding rabbits (Novin, 1976). Further, Raybould (2007) and Thorens (2008) have reviewed considerable evidence for glucose sensing in the intestine. Additionally, the intestine secretes two hormones as a result of glucose absorption named GIP and GLP-1 (Thorens, 2008), which may inform the brain about glucose availability as well as a third hormone called **cholecystokinin (CCK)**. We will concentrate here primarily on the role of CCK.

Numerous studies have provided evidence that CCK, secreted by the upper intestine in response to food, signals the brain to halt eating (Gibbs, Young, & Smith, 1973; Houpt, Anika, & Wolff, 1978; Kraly, 1981b; Kraly et al., 1978; Saito et al., 1982; Schallert, Pendergrass, & Farrar, 1982; Straus & Yalow, 1979). One line of research involved a comparison of CCK concentrations found in the brains of obese and nonobese mice. This study, conducted by Straus and Yalow (1979), showed that genetically obese mice have only about 25% of the amount of CCK present in their brains as normal mice and suggests that overeating by these obese mice may result from a lowered concentration of CCK. Saito and associates (1982) have demonstrated an association between CCK receptor sites in the brain and obesity, but it is not clear how their results relate to those of Straus and Yalow (1979). Nutrients (particularly fats and proteins) reaching the duodenum stimulate the production of CCK by cells in the lining of the duodenum (Geary, 2004; Raybould et al., 2006).

Liver   The liver receives nutrients from the gastrointestinal tract via the portal vein. Thus, only the portal vein and some parts of the liver are directly in contact with these nutrients and any hormones produced by the gut that might be transported by the portal vein (Berthoud & Morrison, 2008). As a result, the portal vein or some parts of the liver are a potential source of both hunger and satiety signals (Novin, 1976; Thorens, 2008; Vanderweele & Sanderson, 1976). Some early research indicated that this was the case. For example, injections of glucose into the **hepatic portal vein** suppress feeding, while injections of glucose into the jugular vein (which supplies the brain) have no effect. The satiating effect of portal glucose injections is eliminated, however, if the vagus nerve is cut. This suggests that glucoreceptors exist in the liver and transit their information to the hypothalamus along the vagus nerve. In support of this liver–hypothalamus relationship, Schmitt (1973) has shown that portal

infusion of glucose changes the rate of neuron firing in the hypothalamus. It thus appears that the portal vein or liver is a source of satiety signals sent to the brain to suppress feeding.

On the other hand, evidence also exists that the hepatic portal vein or liver initiates feeding. For example, Novin (1976) reported experiments in which a chemical called **2-deoxyglucose (2-DG)** was infused into the hepatic portal vein. Because 2-DG blocks glucose utilization, this should fool the liver receptors into functioning as if blood glucose were low and thus initiate eating. That is precisely what happened, with the onset of feeding being very rapid. Novin's results suggest that the sensors in the hepatic portal vein or liver monitor glucose availability and send this information to the hypothalamus, which either initiates or suppresses feeding. Thorens (2008) reviews more recent evidence that provides broad support for a glucosensing system in the hepatic portal vein or the liver. However, as noted also by Thorens, considerable evidence suggests that glucose-sensing systems also exist in the brain stem (e.g., the nucleus of the solitary tract), and the hypothalamus.

Pancreas   The beta cells of the **pancreas** are responsive to changes in glucose and their hormone products, **insulin** and **amylin**, can potentially serve as signals of glucose accessibility too (Berthoud & Morrison, 2008). Insulin helps transport glucose into cells, while amylin slows down nutrient intake in a number of different ways that are related to meal size and satiation (Wookey, Lutz, & Andrikopoulos, 2006). Thus, both insulin and amylin could serve as signals of glucose availability. As we shall see momentarily, insulin serves as a signal for long-term regulation as well.

Long-Term Regulation

Studies in long-term regulation of feeding behavior examine the mechanisms that control feeding so as to keep body weight stable. Though many of us complain about being overweight, our body weight appears to be relatively well regulated; that is, although our weight may not be what we would prefer, we do maintain a particular weight quite consistently, varying only a pound or two over long periods of time.

What are the mechanisms that allow an organism to regulate its body weight? Most theories of long-term regulation assume that some receptor system (or systems) acts to monitor body fats and then regulate food intake to keep body fats fairly constant. Such theories are called **lipostatic theories** (fats are lipids).

Set-Point Theory: A Lipostatic Theory of Hunger   Richard Keesey and his colleagues (Keesey et al., 1976; Keesey & Powley, 1975; Powley & Keesey, 1970) argued that each of us has a normal level of body weight that is rather consistently maintained. They viewed the LH as concerned with proper regulation of the body's normal weight or **set point**. If the LH is damaged, the lack of eating and drinking observed in such cases is not a deficit in the ability to eat but rather a change in the body's set point to a new, lower level. Lack of eating, then, is the way in which the organism reduces its body weight to the new set point.

Keesey and Powley noted results that support this kind of interpretation. When LH–damaged animals recover, they begin eating again in an apparently normal manner, except that they maintain themselves at a lowered body weight. Recovered animals also maintain this weight against various dietary challenges. For example, if they are given a concentrated diet, they eat less to maintain the new set point while dilution of their diet leads to increased eating in order to maintain their weight.

If the alteration of feeding behavior evidenced by such animals is their way to reduce body weight to a new set point, then depriving these animals prior to lesioning the LH ought to eliminate their typically observed lack of eating and drinking. Indeed, Keesey found that previously deprived, LH–lesioned animals began to eat almost immediately, supporting the idea that the LH is involved with the determination of a body weight set point.

Keesey and Powley noted that the VMH may also control the body's set point. (Damage to the VMH, you will recall, causes overeating and obesity.) It is possible, they argued, that lesions of the VMH lead to a raising of the body weight set point to a new, higher level. They noted that VMH–damaged animals defend their new, higher body weights against dietary challenges in much the same way, though not as completely, as LH–damaged animals defend their lowered body weights. Further, VMH–damaged animals tend to be finicky eaters.

The most likely stimulus for regulation around a set point is body fat. Keesey and associates proposed that the LH and the VMH work in a reciprocal fashion to determine a set point for adipose (fatty) tissue. What then is the stimulus to which the set point is sensitive? One way in which the set point might work is to monitor some aspect of the fat cells. Some monitoring of fat cells does occur; Faust, Johnson, and Hirsch (1977a) found that adipose tissue surgically removed from 3-week-old rats was replaced very precisely. Results of this research indicated some type of developmental regulation of the number of fat cells within the body. Regeneration of fat cells occurred only during a very limited developmental span, however, for the researchers found that by 15 weeks of age, regeneration no longer occurred. These researchers noted, too, that diets high in fat content led to greater regeneration of fat cells than diets low in fat, suggesting that dietary content may also play a role in the development of fat cells in young organisms. The study by Faust and associates is important because it shows that fat cell number is genetically regulated but can also be influenced by diet in young organisms.

More importantly, Faust, Johnson, and Hirsch (1977b) found in a second study that surgical removal of adipose tissue (without regeneration) led to an increase in size of individual fat cells. The amount that these enlarged cells could increase was clearly limited, however, indicating some sort of regulatory mechanism.

How might the brain determine how much energy is available in the fat stores? Some signal or signals must be detected by specialized receptors that can tell the brain how much stored energy is available. Research using new molecular biology techniques has provided us with a partial answer.

Leptin and Insulin   The information that is briefly summarized here comes primarily from a review of the literature by Woods, Schwartz, Baskin, and Seeley (2000). In 1994, a signal produced by fat cells was discovered (Zhang et al.) and named leptin. **Leptin** is a hormone produced by fat cells and released into the bloodstream in direct proportion to the amount of energy available in the fat stores. Thus, lean individuals have lower leptin levels and obese individuals have higher levels.

Additional research has led to the conclusion that circulating levels of leptin regulate the amount of energy stored in the fat cells (Woods et al., 2000). The regulation of fat stores is extremely complicated and not yet completely understood (see, e.g., Berthoud & Morrison, 2008); however, research indicates that leptin is detected by specialized receptors in the **arcuate nucleus** of the hypothalamus. These neurons that are sensitive to changes in leptin produce additional neurotransmitters that then trigger other brain areas responsible for energy intake (e.g., eating) and energy usage (e.g., metabolic rate). Interestingly, neurons in the arcuate nucleus are sensitive to changes in insulin levels as well.

Insulin levels are related to both glucose availability and fat storage, so insulin circulating in the blood appears to be an additional signal relaying information about energy stores to the brain (Woods et al., 2000).

When one goes on a diet or weight is reduced for other reasons, leptin and insulin levels drop. This change is detected by the arcuate neurons, which alter the neurotransmitters they secrete. One of the most important of these neurotransmitters is **neuropeptide Y (NPY)** (Berthoud & Morrison, 2008). NPY is a potent appetite stimulant probably through its action on neurons in the **paraventricular nucleus (PVN)** of the hypothalamus. When PVN neurons are stimulated by NPY, food intake is increased, weight gain occurs, and energy expenditure is reduced. These changes may account in part for the often observed problem with maintaining weight loss. The brain is programmed to protect one's energy stores; when they are reduced, strong hunger is produced and energy usage is lowered, making it easier to regain the lost weight.

Another important neurotransmitter in the control of energy storage is **alpha-melanocyte-stimulating hormone (α-MSH)**. α-MSH is produced from its precursor proopiomelanocortin (POMC). POMC is produced by arcuate neurons close to those that produce NPY (Cowley, et al., 2001). α-MSH is a neurotransmitter that has anorexic effects—that is, it reduces energy intake (Berthoud & Morrison, 2008). When fat stores drop, leptin levels decrease, and as a result, NPY levels increase, stimulating hunger while α-MSH drops, also increasing hunger.

When fat stores are increased, leptin levels and insulin levels increase and as a result, NPY levels decrease while α-MSH levels increase. The information previously noted is, however, a bare outline of a much more complex system. Numerous studies have shown that additional neurotransmitters within the hypothalamus also play a role in the regulation of energy stores (Abu-Elheiga, Matzuk, Abo-Hashema, & Wakil, 2001; Berthoud & Morrison, 2008; Wang et al, 2001; Woods et al., 2000; Yamada, et al., 2001) and fat cells secrete additional energy-regulating hormones as well (Steppan et al., 2001), as may also the stomach (Tschop, Smiley, & Heiman, 2000). Leptin has even been shown to regulate the **endocannabinoids** (more neurotransmitters which, as you may suspect, are stimulated by cannabis), accounting nicely for the well-known fact that cannabis users often get "the munchies" (Di Marzo et al., 2001; Mechoulam & Fride, 2001).

Energy Regulation: Two Processes or One?

Historically, most theorists have viewed hunger motivation as a two-process system—a short-term process that monitors glucose and a long-term process that monitors lipids. There have been dissenters, however. Friedman and Stricker (1976) proposed an exception to this general approach. Briefly, they suggested that hunger is best understood as a single mechanism that monitors the availability of all fuels, both external (food) and internal (fats). Hunger signals, according to this model, are sent to the brain from the liver when fuel from the intestines and adipose tissue "is inadequate for maintenance of bodily functions without significant hepatic contributions" (Friedman & Stricker, 1976, p. 423).

The Friedman and Stricker model does not need to make distinctions between short-term and long-term regulation or between glucostatic and lipostatic mechanisms. Additionally, it does not require the concept of set point because it assumes that hunger "appears and disappears according to normally occurring fluctuations in the availability of utilizable metabolic fuels, regardless of which fuels they are and how full the storage reserves" (p. 424). These researchers further conclude that the central control of feeding behavior by the hypothalamus is incorrect as it stands; their evidence suggests that LH lesions influence all motivated behaviors rather than just eating and that VMH lesions cause changes that make it difficult for animals to use stored fuels and as a result, they must overeat. As we have just seen in the last section other areas of the hypothalamus—especially the arcuate nucleus and the PVN—are indeed important components in energy regulation.

Furthermore, Woods et al. (2000) have proposed that the initiation of eating is not due to changes in available fuels but rather eating occurs when it is convenient or food is readily available. They note that animals fed at specific times of the day come to produce hormones and neurotransmitters at those times. In addition, animals learn to associate particular cues in the environment with caloric intake and that these cues may influence how much is eaten. The researchers also cite studies showing that satiety cues can be changed as a result of learning (see, e.g., Goodison & Siegel, 1995). It may be more useful, therefore, to consider meal initiation dependent on a number of individual factors that can differ from one animal (or person) to another and that glucose-driven hunger may be triggered only in rare or emergency situations. Such a point seems reasonable given the fact that most animals, and humans as well, eat *before* conditions produce low glucose levels.

Continuing research has shown that the mechanisms that control hunger motivation are both behavioral and metabolic. As we learn more about the interactions between behavioral and metabolic systems, the control of eating becomes ever more complicated. Bethoud and Morrison (2008) have provided a comprehensive account of much of this research, and those who want a more complete account of this increasingly complex topic may want to consult their review.

As noted previously, humans often eat before changes in energy balance are great enough to trigger such behavior. In fact we often seem to eat in order to avoid the loss of homeostasis. Such behavioral strategies suggest that homeostatic regulation of feeding can be easily overridden and that factors in addition to homeostasis must be at work in normal eating behavior. Several examples of nonhomeostatic eating in humans are discussed in the next section.

Nonhomeostatic Eating Behavior

Although the primary concern of the motivation to eat is to maintain energy balance, it is also quite clear that people often eat when energy is not an issue or refuse to eat in spite of the fact that energy is needed. In this section, we will examine several examples of eating that appears to be nonhomeostatic. As we shall see, one theme that runs through all of these examples is that food can be rewarding in its own right: this hedonic aspect of food can modulate eating behavior independent of the homeostatic processes discussed earlier.

Failure of Regulation

Anorexia Nervosa

Anorexia nervosa is a condition in which an individual severely restricts food intake, in some extreme cases to the point of starvation or death. The condition is most common in adolescent or young adult women, with an estimated occurrence of about 0.5% to 1% of the female population (American Psychiatric Association, 1994). It also appears to be on the rise in the elderly (see Hsu & Zimmer, 1988). Examples of male anorexia nervosa are also known but are rare (see Bruch, 1973, Chapter 15). Women are at the greatest risk of developing anorexia between the ages of 15 and 29 (Polivy & Herman, 2002). Examples of anorexia nervosa were clearly described in the medical literature more than 100 years ago by Gull in England and Laségue in France (Gull, 1874; Laségue, 1873; both as reported by Bruch, 1973) and, though the condition was once thought to be extremely rare, the incidence of anorexia has increased dramatically in the last 50 years (Bemis, 1978; Herzog & Copeland, 1985; Polivy & Herman, 2002).

The primary symptom of anorexia is a large reduction in weight as a result of the individual's restriction of food intake. Fifteen percent below expected body weight is the minimum for a possible diagnosis of anorexia. See Table 4.1 for the diagnostic criteria found in the *Diagnostic and Statistical Manual of Mental Disorders, Revised Fourth Edition* (American Psychiatric Association, 2000).

A second major symptom in women is **amenorrhea**, the absence of menstruation, which can sometimes occur before weight loss. A third symptom is a distorted attitude toward eating that often includes denial of the need to eat, enjoyment in losing weight, and a desired body image of extreme thinness. Some researchers have emphasized this last symptom particularly, noting that patients suffering from anorexia nervosa often insist that they are fat even when severely underweight (Bemis, 1978). Such insistence suggests a possible disturbance in how the individual views his or her own body.

TABLE 4.1 Diagnostic Criteria for Anorexia Nervosa

A. Refusal to maintain body weight at or above a minimally normal weight for age and height (e.g., weight loss leading to maintenance of body weight less than 85% of that expected; or failure to make expected weight gain during period of growth, leading to body weight less than 85% of that expected).

B. Intense fear of gaining weight or becoming fat, even though underweight.

C. Disturbance in the way in which one's bodyweight or shape is experienced, undue influence of body weight or shape on self-evaluation, or denial of the seriousness of the current low body weight.

D. In postmenarcheal females, amenorrhea, i.e., the absence of at least three consecutive menstrual cycles. (A woman is considered to have amenorrhea if her periods occur only following hormone, e.g., estrogen, administration.)

Specify type:

Restricting Type: during the current episode of Anorexia Nervosa, the person has not regularly engaged in binge-eating or purging behavior (i.e., self-induced vomiting or the misuse of laxatives, diuretics, or enemas)

Binge-Eating/Purging Type: during the current episode of Anorexia Nervosa, the person has regularly engaged in binge-eating or purging behavior (i.e., self-induced vomiting or the misuse of laxatives, diuretics, or enemas)

The importance of a disturbance of body image in the diagnosis of anorexia has been questioned. A review article by Hsu (1982) found that anorexics typically overestimated their body width, especially the face and waist; however, normal weight individuals also overestimated their body width, in most cases by as much as the anorexics. Obese individuals and pregnant women were also found to overestimate their body widths. As Hsu notes "Thus, overestimation of body width cannot be held to be unique among anorexics" (Hsu, 1982, p. 306).

Adding to the confusion concerning the importance of distorted body image as a symptom of anorexia is a study by Probst, Van Coppenolle,

Vandreycken, and Goris (1992). These researchers found that both an anorexic group and a normal control group reliably underestimated their body measurements when asked to alter a distorted video image of themselves so that it correctly depicted their body. Since anorexics and controls in the Probst and associates (1992) study once again did not differ, and in fact gave distorted measurements in the opposite direction of those noted by Hsu (1982), one begins to question the usefulness of disturbance of body image as a basic criterion of anorexia. Furthermore, cases of anorexia in non-Western societies (Lee, 1991) often show little or no body image distortion. However, **body dissatisfaction** does seem to be a consistent characteristic of both anorexia and bulimia nervosa (Polivy & Herman, 2002).

Cross-Cultural Evidence of Anorexia

A question of considerable interest is whether anorexia is primarily a phenomenon associated with Western society or can also be found in other cultures. Although the evidence is sketchy at best, reports of anorexia in other cultures have been noted (Dolan, 1991; Lee, 1991). What few studies have been conducted appear to suggest that the incidence of anorexia is lower among non-white populations. Additionally, Lee (1991) has noted that the symptomology of anorexia is somewhat different in a sample of Chinese anorexics studied in Hong Kong. He found that these anorexics did not show a fear of obesity nor a distortion of body image, but rather reduced food intake because eating made them feel bloated. The Chinese anorexics also showed lower levels of depression than found in most Western samples and tended to come from lower socioeconomic classes rather than higher socioeconomic classes as has been reported in past Western samples (but see Polivy & Herman, 2002, who suggest that socioeconomic class differences are not as pronounced as has been the case in the past). Lee (1991) suggests

that the differences in symptomology follow logically from differences in the sociocultural backgrounds of Western and Chinese societies. At present, it seems clear that anorexia does occur in non-Western societies; however, the prevalence of anorexia appears to be lower (although true prevalence rates are very difficult to ascertain in these societies), and the symptoms differ somewhat as a result of sociocultural differences (Lee, Lee, Ngai, Lee, & Wing, 2001).

Clearly the anorexic patient is no longer maintaining a homeostatic energy balance, and as energy reserves in the body are depleted, body weight drops. The question of interest here is why anorexic patients no longer maintain energy homeostasis. Historically, opinion concerning the reasons for this lack of homeostasis has alternated between physical and psychological explanations. The origin of the term *anorexia* (*a + orexis,* meaning "no appetite") implies that the individual does not experience hunger (anorexia—lack or loss of the appetite for food; *Dorland's Illustrated Medical Dictionary,* 1965); however, it is not clear that anorexic patients have a true loss of appetite because these individuals often demonstrate bizarre eating habits as well as refusal to eat. For example, anorexics will sometimes binge-eat, hoard food, and show a preoccupation with food or cooking. As noted by Bemis (1978, p. 595), "Most accounts emphasize that the curtailment of intake is more often motivated by the desire for an extremely thin appearance than by genuine 'anorexia' or lack of hunger." In addition, many anorexic patients show perfectionism, obsessive-compulsive behaviors, and depressed mood and/or anxiety, the precursors of which are often evident in childhood before any eating abnormalities are apparent (Kaye, 2008).

As originally described by Gull and Lasègue, anorexia was thought to be psychological in origin; however, considerable doubt was cast on this analysis when Simmonds (1914; as noted by Bruch, 1973) described the case of an emaciated woman who at autopsy was discovered to have lesions of the pituitary gland. This led many researchers to assume that anorexia involved a malfunction of the endocrine system. But in the 1930s the emphasis began to swing back toward psychological causes of anorexia, an emphasis that has remained to the present (see, e.g., the review by Polivy & Herman, 2002). The debate concerning the causes of anorexia is far from resolved, however, several cases initially diagnosed as anorexia nervosa have later been shown to result from brain tumors of various sorts (Ahsanuddin & Nyeem, 1983; Heron & Johnson, 1976; Kagan, 1951; Swan, 1977), although in the larger number of cases, no physical pathology was detected (Bemis, 1978).

Neurobiology of Anorexia

Ploog and Pirke (1987) have described some of the physiological changes that occur during anorexia. Metabolic and somatic changes are often first indicated by amenorrhea (the loss of the monthly menstrual cycle in women). During bouts of anorexia, blood pressure can drop to dangerously low levels, and heart rate may decrease to as few as 30 beats per minute. Computed Tomography (CT) scans of the brains of anorexics reveal evidence of brain atrophy and an enlargement of both external (widening of the sulci) and internal (enlargement of the lateral ventricles) cerebrospinal fluid-filled spaces. In other words, the brain seems to shrink. Ploog and Pirke found morphological changes in the brains of about 82% of the anorexics studied. After weight gain, about 42% of those demonstrating initial enlargement of the external cerebrospinal fluid spaces showed a return to normal or markedly reduced widening. Witt, Ryan, and Hsu (1985) have found that anorexic patients show learning deficits on a difficult paired-associated learning task. These researchers also found that the longer the patients had been anorexic the more poorly they performed on the task. Considering the findings of Ploog and Pirke noted earlier, it is possible that the learning deficit is in some way associated with the morphological changes in the brain that occur during anorexia.

Impairment of the sympathetic nervous system occurs in anorexia, as do endocrine malfunctions. Most prominently, cortisol levels are elevated during anorexia and appear to be an adaptation to starvation. Gonadal function is also impaired. The endocrine changes noted earlier appear to result from hypothalamic dysfunction occurring during the acute phase of anorexia. Finally, Ploog and Pirke argue that anorexia results in changes in the hunger drive. Specifically, they view the hunger drive as being perverted by the anorexic condition to the point that the consequences of hunger, such as weight loss, are pleasurable to the individual. Similarly, Kaye (2008) argues that refusal to eat food is highly rewarding because it provides a brief escape from the anorexic's depressed mood.

The rewarding effects of non-eating creates an ambivalent situation for the anorexic in which hunger motivation creates an obsession with food but the weight loss and improved mood from not eating is strongly rewarding. Ploog and Pirke suggest that this ambivalence may account for the bulimic behavior that often occurs in anorexics, and for the commonly observed obsession with food while not eating.

The Serotonin Hypothesis

Research on the physiological changes associated with anorexia has implicated the possible role of serotonin, a neurotransmitter in the brain, in the development of eating disorders. In regard to anorexia, it has been suggested that increased serotonin activity may be associated with the lack of eating and changes in mood (Kaye, 2008; Kaye & Weltzin, 1991a; Pinheiro, Root, & Bulik, 2009; Scherag, Hebebrand, & Hinney, 2010). As noted by Kaye and Weltzin, there is considerable evidence from both animal studies and human clinical studies of psychiatric groups that serotonin levels can influence appetite, mood, personality variables, and neuroendocrine function. It is therefore of some importance to the understanding of eating disorders such as anorexia to determine whether changes in serotonin levels contribute to the symptoms of those disorders.

Studies reported by Kaye and Weltzin show that underweight anorexics tend to have lower levels of the major metabolite (CSF 5-HIAA) of serotonin, suggesting that serotonin levels are below normal. When anorexics regain weight in the short term (e.g., 2 months), this metabolite returns to normal levels even when weight is still about 15% below normal body weight. In long-term (longer than 6 months) weight gain, anorexics' metabolite levels were above normal. This pattern of changes in CSF 5-HIAA suggest that serotonin levels are higher than normal in anorexics when they are at normal body weight and that restricting food leads to a reduction in the production of serotonin. Since increased serotonin levels have been associated with mood disorders such as rigidity, anxiety, inhibition, and obsessive-compulsive behaviors, Kaye and Weltzin speculate that it is possible that anorexics restrict food because restriction lowers serotonin levels and thus reduces these feelings, that is, food restriction becomes highly rewarding because it reduces negative mood states. Interestingly, anorexics say that they feel better when they don't eat (Kaye & Weltzin, 1991a). More recent research has supported the role of serotonin in anorexia as well as other neurotransmitters such as dopamine, norephinephrine, and perhaps others (see Kaye, 2008; Scherag, Hebebrand, & Hinney, 2010, for reviews of much of this work).

Heredity Factors

Studies of the families of anorexics indicate that there is a 5%–10% increased prevalence in first-degree relatives of anorexics (reports 18 and 19 in Holland, Sicotte, & Treasure, 1988; see also Pinheiro et al., 2009; Scherag, et al., 2010). Although a study by Rastam, Gillberg, and Wahlstrom (1991) found no evidence for chromosomal abnormalities in anorexics when compared to a normal population, twin studies (Holland, Sicotte, & Treasure, 1988; Pinheiro et al., 2009; Scherag, et al., 2010) suggest a strong genetic factor in the development of anorexia. In the Holland and associates study, when a female identical twin (monozygotic twins) was diagnosed as anorexic, 56% of the time the other twin was also diagnosed as anorexic. Their study found that for nonidentical twins (dizygotic twins) when one female twin was diagnosed as anorexic only 5% of the time was the other twin so diagnosed. Since both types of twins were raised in the same homes, the differences in

prevalence would appear to be due to genetic (monozygotic twins having the same genetic structure) rather than environmental factors. These researchers also found that 4.9% of first-degree female relatives and 1.16% of second-degree relatives had had anorexia. Thus, first-degree relatives have an increased chance of becoming anorexic, although second-degree relatives have approximately the same incidence of anorexia as in the population as a whole.

Using three different methods of analysis, Holland and associates (1988, p. 567) conclude "that heritability accounts for at least 80% of the variance" within their study. Wade, Bulik, Neale, and Kendler (2000) found a heritability rating of 58% in their study. Assuming that these results cannot be explained in some other way, it would appear that there is a genetic factor to anorexia.

Current research as reviewed by several different groups (Kaye, 2008; Pinheiro et al., 2009; Scherag, 2010) are consistent in implicating genes that influence neurotransmitters, their receptors, or their transport mechanisms. Genes controlling these mechanisms for serotonin, dopamine, and norepinephrine, have received considerable attention.

Brain Structures Involved in Anorexia

Kaye (2008), in a comprehensive review of the literature, has proposed that several limbic brain structures are involved in the eating dysregulation that occurs in anorexia. Although numerous structures are involved in feeding behavior, Kaye singles out the insula as especially important. He proposes that the **insula** integrates information about various body senses and how these stimuli may be important in particular situations.

Our current understanding of the various factors that play a role in producing anorexia has been summarized well in the following quote from Pinheiro et al. (2009): "Beliefs about the etiology of anorexia nervosa (AN) have undergone remarkable change. For decades, AN was considered to be a culture-bound disorder in which family and sociocultural factors were thought to play a major role, but research suggests that genetic factors are relevant in the vulnerability to this disorder (1). AN is a complex disorder resulting from a combination of genetic and environmental factors. Accordingly, it is important for clinicians and researchers to integrate knowledge of the role of genetics as well as social, psychological, and familial factors into understanding risk for AN" (Pinheiro, et al. 2009, p. 153).

Bulimia Nervosa

Anorexia nervosa patients are unwilling to eat, even to the point of self-starvation. People suffering from **bulimia nervosa**, on the other hand, binge-eat large quantities of food in a very short amount of time (see Table 4.2). During these binges, the person can consume an enormous number of calories, in one study ranging from 1,000 to 55,000 calories per episode (Johnson et al., 1982). Two early studies found the incidence of bulimia in college populations to range between 3.8% and 13% (Halmi, Falk, & Schwartz, 1981; Stangler & Printz, 1980). Rand and Kuldau (1992), using a structured interview with a random sample of 2,115 adults, found the prevalence to be 1.1%. This large sample included individuals between the ages of 18 and 96. One interesting finding from this study was that there were more cases of bulimia among the older population than expected, although bulimia was still much more common in younger women. Among women aged 18 to 30, the prevalence of bulimia was 4.1%.

The bulimic individual cannot stop eating once the binge begins and feels guilt, depression, and panic after the binge. Persons suffering from bulimia report a great sense of **loss of control** after a binge-eating episode and as a result **purge**—induce vomiting, abuse laxatives, or go on severely restrictive diets to regain a sense of control and maintain their weight.

Johnson and associates (1982) surveyed 316 cases that met the diagnostic criteria for bulimia established in 1980 by the American Psychiatric Association. They found that the typical bulimic

---

TABLE 4.2 Diagnostic Criteria for Bulimia Nervosa

A. Recurrent episodes of binge eating. An episode of binge eating is characterized by both of the following:
   (1) eating, in a discrete period of time (e.g., within any 2-hour period), an amount of food that is definitely larger than most people would eat during a similar period of time and under similar circumstances
   (2) a sense of lack of control over eating during the episode (e.g., a feeling that one cannot stop eating or control what or how much one is eating)

B. Recurrent inappropriate compensatory behavior in order to prevent weight gain, such as self-induced vomiting; misuse of laxatives, diuretics, enemas, or other medications; fasting; or excessive exercise.

C. The binge eating and inappropriate compensatory behaviors both occur, on average, at least twice a week for 3 months.

D. Self-evaluation is unduly influenced by body shape and weight.

E. The disturbance does not occur exclusively during episodes of Anorexia Nervosa.

Specify type:

Purging Type: during the current episode of Bulimia Nervosa, the person has regularly engaged in self-induced vomiting or the misuse of laxatives, diuretics, or enemas

Nonpurging Type: during the current episode of Bulimia Nervosa, the person has used other inappropriate compensatory behaviors, such as fasting or excessive exercise, but has not regularly engaged in self-induced vomiting or the misuse of laxatives, diuretics, or enemas

Reprinted with permission from *the Diagnostic and Statistical Manual of Mental Disorders*, Fourth Edition, Text Revision. Copyright © 2000 American Psychiatric Association. Used with permission.

---

was female, white, college educated, and in her early twenties. Further, these women tended to come from middle- and upper-class families that had more than one child. Although bulimia has been shown to be related to anorexia—40% to 50% of women diagnosed as anorexic will develop bulimia at some time during their time of disordered eating (Johnson & Larson, 1982)—in the bulimic women sampled by Johnson and associates, the majority were of normal weight. Purging behavior to control weight gain from the

TABLE 4.3 Precipitating Factors for Binge-Eating Behavior

N = 316	Percentage
Difficulty handling emotions	50%
Restrictive dieting	34
Interpersonal conflict	7
Loss or separation	6
Other	8
Uncertain about onset	5

Adapted from "Bulimia: An Analysis of Moods and Behavior," by C. Johnson and R. Larson, 1982, *Psychosomatic Medicine, 44,* 311–351. Copyright © 1982 by Wolters Kluwer Health. Used by permission.

binge-eating episodes was very common in the sample. As reported by Johnson and associates, the most common purging method was self-induced vomiting; the second most common method was the use of laxatives.

Table 4.3 presents the most commonly reported factors that led to the binge-eating episodes by these women. As can be seen in the table, the two most frequently mentioned factors were difficulty handling emotions and restrictive dieting. A study by Waters, Hill, and Waller (2001, p. 883) has once again found a "clear link between negative emotional states and bulimic behavior." Waters et al. further hypothesize that emotion-produced binges can be understood as an interplay between three psychological processes—classical conditioning, operant conditioning, and escape from awareness. They acknowledge that binges can also be initiated by severe caloric deprivation (see, e.g., the model developed by Fairburn & Cooper, 1989); however, their model accounts for binges initiated by food cravings (not hunger).

A study by Johnson and Larson (1982) examined the emotion factor by having bulimic women and a sample of nonbulimic women wear electronic pagers that signaled them to fill out a questionnaire concerning their emotional state and what they were doing at the time of the signal. The signals were sent out randomly, one signal per 2-hour period, between the hours of 8 A.M. and 10 P.M.

Bulimic women reported significantly more negative states than did the normal women on six of the eight mood items. Women in the bulimic group were sadder, lonelier, weaker, more irritable, more passive, and more constrained than those in the nonbulimic group. The bulimic sample also reported more fluctuations in mood and wider oscillations, indicating that their emotional state was less stable than that of the normal sample.

It had been suggested that anorexia and bulimia were variants, of the then current, DSM III category of major affective disorder (Cantwell et al., 1977). In particular, depression was associated with both anorexia and bulimia. Laessle and associates (1987) sought to determine whether anorexia and bulimia were best conceived as variants of major affective disorder. They interviewed 52 patients with a history of anorexia or bulimia, using a standardized interview technique. These researchers found that 44.2% of their sample were diagnosed as having the DSM III characteristics of major affective disorder (depression); however, in the majority of these cases the affective disorder developed after the onset of the eating disorder. The study by Laessle and associates therefore implies that the depressive symptoms commonly seen in anorexia and bulimia are secondary to the eating disorder and would seem to provide evidence contrary to the idea that anorexia and bulimia are variants of major affective disorder. Indeed Laessle and associates suggest that changed patterns of eating in anorexia and bulimia could produce depressive symptoms by causing changes in neurotransmitter systems involved with depression. *The Diagnostic and Statistical Manual of the American Psychiatric Association* (American Psychiatric Association, IV-TR, 2000) does not consider either bulimia nervosa or anorexia nervosa to be variants of major affective disorder.

Several other factors have been examined concerning their association with bulimia. One such factor is **life events**. Sohlberg and Norring (1992) studied the relationship between life events and the course of recovery in a group of Swedish bulimic patients over a 3-year period. They suggest that bulimics who have a higher frequency of major negative life events occurring during the first year of treatment are slower to recover; however, life events across the 3-year span of the study had little effect. One early life event that has been associated with the development of bulimia is childhood **sexual abuse** (Abramson & Lucido, 1991; Lacey & Dolan, 1988). Abramson and Lucido (1991) report that it is the nature of the childhood sexual experience that is crucial; they found that bulimic patients reported a significantly greater number of sexual experiences with their fathers and brothers. Additionally, these researchers noted that none of the bulimics had discussed their sexual experiences with their parents, suggesting a lack of trust and communication within their families. The authors note, "While the present findings do not allow causal inferences to be drawn, they do suggest that the dysfunctional familial patterns associated with bulimia may include child sex abuse" (Abramson & Lucido, 1991, pg. 531).

Finally, it has been reported that bulimic behavior is associated with seasonal changes, especially **hours of darkness** (Blouin et al., 1992). Blouin and associates found that binge-eating behavior increased during the winter months and decreased during the summer months in a group of 31 bulimics in Ottawa, Canada. Interestingly, photoperiod, as indexed by hours of darkness, influenced only bingeing behavior, not purging or depression. The authors speculate that the effects may be due to seasonal changes in serotonin, a neurotransmitter also associated with anorexia and, as we shall see in the next section, also implicated in bulimic behavior.

Theories of Bulimia   Several categories of explanation have been proposed for understanding bulimia. They include the **sociocultural approach**, the **clinical/psychiatric approach**, and the **epidemiological/risk factors** approach. In addition, social contagion theory combines some aspects of these three approaches to explain bulimia (Crandall, 1988). Escape theory (Heatherton & Baumeister, 1991) proposes that binge eating can provide an **escape from self-awareness**, while considerable evidence has accumulated suggesting

that bulimia may also have a physical basis (Goldbloom & Garfinkel, 1990).

The sociocultural approach suggests that changing societal norms have put an increasing emphasis on thinness for women at the same time that such norms are almost unattainable. The biological necessity to eat is put into conflict with unrealistic social norms of body shape and appearance and as a result abnormal eating patterns (binge-purge) may develop.

The clinical/psychiatric approach suggests that bulimia is associated with clinical symptoms such as impulsiveness, low self-esteem, problems with parental psychological health, or major affective disorder (Hudson et al., 1987; but see Hinz & Williamson, 1987, for a different point of view). Disordered eating, then, is often viewed from this perspective as symptomatic of psychological distress.

Unlike the first two approaches, the epidemiological/risk factors approach makes no underlying assumptions about the causes of bulimia, such as unrealistic cultural norms or psychological distress, but rather attempts to determine what factors put an individual at risk for developing bulimia. Factors that have been identified include unrealistic body image, emotional lability, stressful family relationships, hormonal changes, rigid sex roles, stress, and genetic predispositions (see Striegel, Moore, Silberstein, & Rodin, 1986, for a review).

Crandall (1988) has combined several aspects of the approaches just mentioned in a **social contagion theory** of binge eating, which proposes that norms provided by social groups (the sociocultural approach) will be especially contagious to an individual experiencing psychological distress (the clinical/psychiatric approach). The symptoms identified by the epidemiological/risk factors approach are also relevant: some risk factors may increase the likelihood of social influence (genetic predispositions, stress), while other risk factors may be understood as resulting from social learning (body image, sex roles).

Crandall's ideas are based on a study of the social aspects of binge eating. In an ingenious study, Crandall measured the eating behavior and friendship patterns of women belonging to two separate sororities at a large state university. The results of her study showed that binge eating was subject to social pressures. In one sorority, the more a woman reported bingeing, the more popular she was judged to be by her sorority sisters. In the second sorority, popularity depended on bingeing "the right amount" (p. 588). That is, women who binged near the mean amount for the group as a whole were judged to be the most popular. Furthermore, Crandall found that individuals became more like their friends over time. The bingeing behavior of an individual could be predicted from the bingeing behavior of her friends. This result did not appear to be attributable to similar individuals gathering together (assortative grouping), because the bingeing behavior of an individual changed across time, becoming more similar to the bingeing behavior of the group.

Even though binge eating is quite common on college campuses, most individuals do not binge. How can one explain the fact that persons are not equally susceptible to social contagion effects? Crandall proposes that women who experience distress (e.g., feelings of low self-esteem) are more open to social influence than those not distressed. If the norm within a group is to binge-eat and a woman receives support and approval from that group, she is more likely to adopt the norms of that group and binge-eat also. Crandall suggests, therefore, that binge eating is an acquired behavior pattern that may be adopted through modeling and social control processes.

After an extensive review of the literature on binge eating, Heatherton and Baumeister (1991) suggested that such behavior is the result of attempts to escape from self-awareness. They propose that binge eating serves to narrow one's focus of attention to the immediate environment and thus avoid aversive self-perceptions that trigger anxiety and/or depression. These self-perceptions are aversive, according to the escape hypothesis, because binge-eaters tend to have very high standards and expectations (which they cannot maintain) and are also very sensitive to what they perceive to be the demands of others. According to this proposal, they become acutely aware of their shortcomings and to avoid thinking about these (perceived) failures, they eat. The act of eating serves to narrow the binge-eater's attention to the immediate and, thus, allow a temporary escape from the self-awareness and its associated anxiety and depression.

Johnson and Larson (1982) suggested that bulimic individuals actually become addicted to eating because eating serves to moderate mood swings. However, because the binges lead to huge increases in caloric intake, these individuals develop purging as a mechanism that allows them to binge-eat without becoming fat. Johnson and Larson further suggested that a combination of factors, both physical and psychological, leads some individuals to use food as a means of tension regulation, as contrasted to such other means as alcohol or drug abuse. Thus, it is clear that researchers have a wide divergence of opinion about the psychological causes of bulimia. Still other researchers provide evidence that physical causes contribute to bulimia as well.

Some **physical factors** that may contribute to bulimic behavior include familial or inherited characteristics predisposing one toward bulimia (Strober, Freeman, Lampert, Diamons, & Kaye, 2000) and changes in several brain neurotransmitters. Among the neurotransmitters implicated in bulimic behavior are serotonin, norepinephrine, dopamine, CCK, beta-endorphin, and neuropeptide PYY (Kaye & Weltzin, 1991b). The majority of the research, however, has looked at the possible role of serotonin and norepinephrine in bulimic behavior (see Goldbloom & Garfinkel, 1990; Jimerson, Lesem, Kaye, & Brewerton, 1992; Kaye & Weltzin 1991a, b, for overviews of this research).

The **serotonin hypothesis**, as outlined by Goldbloom and Garfinkel (1990), suggests that bulimic behavior results from underactivity of serotonin in the brain. Experiments using animals have found that decreasing the level of serotonin in the hypothalamus leads to increased carbohydrate intake and an impairment in the satiety mechanisms that normally limit intake (Leibowitz & Shor-Posner, 1986). Further, Jimerson and associates (1992) found decreased concentrations of the metabolites of serotonin (and also dopamine) in the cerebrospinal fluid of patients who had severe symptoms of bulimia. The reduction in the metabolites suggests that serotonin (and dopamine) levels also may have been low. Further, Kaye et al. (2001) have found that serotonin changes in the orbital frontal cortex are associated with bulimia.

Kaye and Weltzin (1991b) review evidence indicating that norepinephrine levels are also disturbed in bulimia; however, for this neurotransmitter, the level appears to be too high. Kaye and Weltzin suggest that high levels of norepinephrine stimulate eating and that low levels of serotonin impair the satiety response that would normally limit eating.

The evidence just discussed seems to indicate a relationship between bulimic behavior and several neurotransmitters. What is not clear, however, is which is cause and which is effect. Do changes in serotonin and norepinephrine lead to the production of the bulimic behaviors, or does bulimic behavior produce a disruption in these neurotransmitters? There is even a third possibility. It is possible that bulimic behaviors are an attempt to increase the amount of tryptophan (a precursor of serotonin) available to the brain in order to produce a short-term increase in serotonin (Goldbloom & Garfinkel, 1990; Kaye & Weltzin, 1991b). At this point in our understanding it seems best to assume that some combination of neurotransmitter changes is associated with bulimia; however, more research is needed to unravel the complicated relationship between these physical changes and bulimic behavior.

As the preceding theories show, there is a diversity of ideas about why bulimic behaviors occur. It seems probable that some combination of factors is involved in the development and maintenance of this bulimic behavior. Strober et al. (2000) have suggested just such an interaction. As more research on this topic is completed, it is hoped that the interrelationship of these various factors will become apparent.

In a manner somewhat similar to the anorexic, the bulimic seems able to override the normal homeostatic control of eating. For the anorexic

the normal cues for initiating eating are in some unknown manner either ignored or unfelt, while for the bulimic the cues associated with the end of an eating episode are ignored or unfelt. In both cases the homeostatic control of energy balance is disrupted. For the bulimic, however, an approximate balance is achieved through purging behaviors. The research on the eating disorders of anorexia nervosa and bulimia nervosa shows that the homeostatic control of hunger can be overridden; research on obesity also suggests that it is not especially difficult to override these controls.

Obesity

Obesity involves the long-term imbalance between energy intake and energy usage. Whenever intake exceeds usage, the excess energy is stored in the form of fat (Kuczmarski, Flegal, Campbell, & Johnson, 1994). Obesity is a major problem in America. Though definitions vary somewhat, **obesity** is usually defined to be 20% above the tabled values for the person's height and build (e.g., The Metropolitan Life Insurance Tables). Using this definition, it has been estimated that 25% to 45% of American adults are obese (Grinker, 1982). A study by Kuczmarski and associates (1994) found that 33.4% of adults in the United States were obese.

Today, weight categories are often determined by using the Body Mass Index (BMI) which is a reliable measure of fatness for the majority of people. See Table 4.4 for a chart of BMI for height and weight. A BMI of 18.5 is considered underweight. Normal weight encompasses a BMI between 18.5 and 25. The overweight category includes individuals having a BMI between 25 and 30, and a BMI of 30 or above is considered obese. The most recent data available from the Center for Disease Control (CDC, 2010) found that in 2007–2008 32.2% of adult American men were obese and 35.5% of adult American women were obese. If one combines the overweight and obese categories, the prevalence rates were 72.3% for men and 64.1% for women. Obviously the United States population has a weight problem.

TABLE 4.4 Body Mass Index Table

	Body Mass Index Table																																		
	Normal						**Overweight**				**Obese**										**Extreme Obesity**															
BMI	19 20 21	22	23	24	25	26 27 28	29	30	31 32 33	34 35	36 37	38 39	40 41 42	43 44 45	46 47	48 49 50	51 52 53 54
Height (inches)	Body Weight (pounds)
58	91 96 100 105 110 115 119 124 129 134 138 143 148 153 158 162 167 172 177 181 186 191 196 201 205 210 215 220 224 229 234 239 244 248 253 258
59	94 99 104 109 114 119 124 128 133 138 143 148 153 158 163 168 173 178 183 188 193 198 203 208 212 217 222 227 232 237 242 247 252 257 262 267
60	97 102 107 112 118 123 128 133 138 143 148 153 158 163 168 174 179 184 189 194 199 204 209 215 220 225 230 235 240 245 250 255 261 266 271 276
61	100 106 111 116 122 127 132 137 143 148 153 158 164 169 174 180 185 190 195 201 206 211 217 222 227 232 238 243 248 254 259 264 269 275 280 285
62	104 109 115 120 126 131 136 142 147 153 158 164 169 175 180 186 191 196 202 207 213 218 224 229 235 240 246 251 256 262 267 273 278 284 289 295
63	107 113 118 124 130 135 141 146 152 158 163 169 175 180 186 191 197 203 208 214 220 225 231 237 242 248 254 259 265 270 278 282 287 293 299 304
64	110 116 122 128 134 140 145 151 157 163 169 174 180 186 192 197 204 209 215 221 227 232 238 244 250 256 262 267 273 279 285 291 296 302 308 314
65	114 120 126 132 138 144 150 156 162 168 174 180 186 192 198 204 210 216 222 228 234 240 246 252 258 264 270 276 282 288 294 300 306 312 318 324
66	118 124 130 136 142 148 155 161 167 173 179 186 192 198 204 210 216 223 229 235 241 247 253 260 266 272 278 284 291 297 303 309 315 322 328 334
67	121 127 134 140 146 153 159 166 172 178 185 191 198 204 211 217 223 230 236 242 249 255 261 268 274 280 287 293 299 306 312 319 325 331 338 344
68	125 131 138 144 151 158 164 171 177 184 190 197 203 210 216 223 230 236 243 249 256 262 269 276 282 289 295 302 308 315 322 328 335 341 348 354
69	128 135 142 149 155 162 169 176 182 189 196 203 209 216 223 230 236 243 250 257 263 270 277 284 291 297 304 311 318 324 331 338 345 351 358 365
70	132 139 146 153 160 167 174 181 188 195 202 209 216 222 229 236 243 250 257 264 271 278 285 292 299 306 313 320 327 334 341 348 355 362 369 376
71	136 143 150 157 165 172 179 186 193 200 208 215 222 229 236 243 250 257 265 272 279 286 293 301 308 315 322 329 338 343 351 358 365 372 379 386
72	140 147 154 162 169 177 184 191 199 206 213 221 228 235 242 250 258 265 272 279 287 294 302 309 316 324 331 338 346 353 361 368 375 383 390 397
73	144 151 159 166 174 182 189 197 204 212 219 227 235 242 250 257 265 272 280 288 295 302 310 318 325 333 340 348 355 363 371 378 386 393 401 408
74	148 155 163 171 179 186 194 202 210 218 225 233 241 249 256 264 272 280 287 295 303 311 319 326 334 342 350 358 365 373 381 389 396 404 412 420
75	152 160 168 176 184 192 200 208 216 224 232 240 248 256 264 272 279 287 295 303 311 319 327 335 343 351 359 367 375 383 391 399 407 415 423 431
76	156 164 172 180 189 197 205 213 221 230 238 246 254 263 271 279 287 295 304 312 320 328 336 344 353 361 369 377 385 394 402 410 418 426 435 443

Adapted from Clinical Guidelines on the Identification, Evaluation, and Treatment of Overweight and Obesity in Adults: The Evidence Report.

Information collected since the early 1900s shows that, for both men and women, weight (for a given height) has increased since the early part of the 20th century. Some of this increase is probably due to changing work patterns that now require less physical activity and to the generally sedentary lifestyle of Americans. For example, Kuczmarski and associates (1994) review a study by the CDC that found 58.1% of adults reported either irregular or no leisure-time physical activity. Changes in activity patterns are also suggested by the fact that the average daily caloric intake has remained relatively constant since the early 1900s (Grinker, 1982). However, more recently the CDC has found that average caloric intake has increased in both men and women (CDC, 2004). For women the daily intake has risen from 1542 kilocalories to 1877 kilocalories, while for men it has risen from 2450 kilocalories to 2618 kilocalories. In some individuals body weight tends to increase with age, although body weight is remarkably stable for many others (see Grinker, 1982, for a review of studies).

Despite the fact that body weight remains stable, people still get fatter with age. Two factors contribute to the increase in body fat. The first is a reduction in basal metabolic rate with age. **Basal metabolism** is the energy we consume just to maintain bodily functions at rest. Approximately

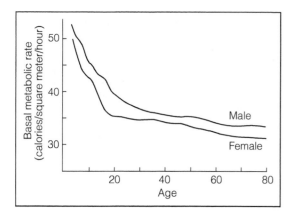

FIGURE 4.7 Decrease in basal metabolic rate with increasing age. From *Slim Chance in a Fat World* by R. B. Stuart and B. Davis. Copyright © 1972 by R. B. Stuart. Used by permission.

two-thirds of the energy we expend is consumed by basal metabolic processes; the remaining one-third is expended as a result of exercise (Franken, 1982; Rodin, 1981). As we get older our basal metabolism slows down; we need less energy to maintain bodily processes. Figure 4.7 shows the decrease in metabolic rate that occurs with age. If we continue to take in the same amount of calories daily as we did earlier in life and do not change our pattern of exercise, then we can gain weight simply because we expend less energy to maintain our basal metabolism.

A study by Roberts and associates (1994) indicates that healthy older men show an impairment in the ability to compensate for both weight gain and weight loss. Older men who were overfed maintained the additional weight longer than younger men, and older men who were underfed did not regain weight as quickly as younger men. Their results suggest that weight gain (and loss) in older individuals may result, in part, from a change in the mechanisms that normally control energy balance in younger individuals.

A second factor that contributes to increased fat is a change in the composition of the body with age. **Lean body mass (LBM)**—the weight of muscle and bone and so on—decreases with age,

while body fat increases with age (Grinker, 1982). Approximately 15% of the body weight of a young adult of normal weight is stored fat; this fat storage is equivalent to about one month's supply of calories. As a result, even if our weight remains constant, our percentage of body fat will increase and we will be fatter as we age. It seems from this information that everyone, overweight or not, is predisposed toward increasing stores of body fat. The question of interest here is what other factors might lead to and maintain obesity in some individuals.

Obesity Explanations

Adaptiveness Gone Wrong   Certainly our ability to store energy in the form of fat for future use has been adaptive. For most of our evolutionary history, food resources have been unreliable. Because the individual of normal weight already has approximately one month's supply of stored energy, some researchers have viewed obesity as the continued storage of energy, beyond the normal reserves, for famines that are no longer frequent (Margules, 1979; Pi-Sunyer, 1994). Because the energy reserves are not drawn down by lack of adequate food, the storage system continues to add to already adequate reserves. In the past, the control of obesity may have been primarily environmental. When times were hard and food was scarce, the reserves were called upon to maintain life; when conditions improved, energy was again stored away.

If this line of reasoning is correct, then humans may not have well-developed mechanisms for limiting fat storage beyond some minimum level, because nature usually limited the storage through periods of famine. Though such a hypothesis is logical, it is difficult to prove and does not explain why so many individuals who have easy access to food do maintain normal weight. Margules (1979) has suggested that the reason some people become obese while others do not results from genetic differences in the production of beta-endorphin (a chemical found in the brain). For example, Margules and associates (1978) found elevated levels of beta-endorphin in genetically obese rats and mice. Beta-endorphin has several effects, one of which is the reduction of the arousing properties of stimuli, which in turn results in lowered activity and consequently conservation of energy.

Genetic Predisposition Evidence also exists that some people are genetically programmed to carry more fat than others. Hirsch and Knittle (1970) found severely obese individuals had more than twice as many fat cells as normal-weight individuals and that the fat cells of the obese were larger than those of normal-weight individuals. Because dieting does not reduce the number of fat cells (but reduces individual fat cell size), persons with a large number of fat cells may be genetically programmed to carry more weight than the normal individual (Grinker, 1982). Because several strains of genetically obese animals exist (e.g., the Zucker rat, and the ob/ob mouse), it seems likely that genetic differences in fat cell numbers would also exist within humans. In fact, one would expect that fat cell number in the human population would distribute along a normal curve: most individuals having about the same number of fat cells but a few individuals showing extreme differences in fat cell numbers. A normal distribution of fat cell number within the population should provide a greater likelihood that some people would survive in an ever-changing environment.

One particularly interesting finding by Jones and Friedman (1982) suggests that undernourishment of female rats during their first two weeks of pregnancy leads to obesity and enlargement of fat cells in male offspring (female offspring did not become obese but did show some fat cell abnormalities). Their research was prompted by a report by Ravelli, Stein, and Susser (1976), who analyzed the body weights of 300,000 Dutch army draftees whose mothers had been subjected to undernourishment during World War II. Ravelli and associates reported that men whose mothers had been exposed to famine conditions during the first two trimesters of their pregnancy had a higher incidence of obesity than the population in general. It is possible, therefore, that intrauterine conditions during the development of the individual, as well as genetic predispositions, may play a part in obesity.

Obesity as Maintaining Obesity Judith Rodin (1981) pointed out that one consequence of being obese is that it is harder to lose weight. Several factors contribute to this side effect of obesity. First of all, the more fat that one has stored away, the greater the potential to store even more fat. This occurs because obese persons usually have higher than normal levels of insulin, a situation called **hyperinsulinemia**. Insulin increases the amount of energy stored away as fat because insulin is involved with the fat storage process—the more insulin, the more energy that can be stored away as fat. Moreover, hyperinsulinemia also seems to induce hunger, so the obese person is hungrier and stores more energy in the fat cells than does the normal-weight person.

Obesity also has an impact on **activity levels**. Obese persons are usually less active than slender persons (Bullen, Reed, & Mayer, 1964), so they burn fewer calories, thus partially maintaining the obese state through lowered activity. Energy consumption is influenced by obesity in yet another way. Fat tissue is **metabolically less active** than lean tissue (Rodin, 1981). Because a larger percentage of body weight is fat in obese individuals, they need fewer calories to maintain their weight as a result of this lowered metabolism. Incidentally, regular exercise benefits weight loss in at least two ways—exercise builds muscle, which is metabolically more active and thus needs more energy to maintain itself, and when regular exercise burns more calories than are taken in, the fat stores gives up energy (and weight decreases).

Finally, it has been proposed that **dieting** may itself promote obesity. Metabolic rate is reduced during food deprivation, which in turn makes losing weight more difficult; to add insult to injury, each successive dieting episode was thought to lead to larger reductions in metabolic rate, making weight loss ever more difficult (Rodin, 1981). However, the idea that cycles of dieting and weight gain (the so-called yo-yo dieting) can lower metabolic rate now appears to be incorrect. In a review of the literature on weight cycling, the National Task Force on the Prevention and Treatment of Obesity (1994) has found that cycles of dieting-produced weight loss followed by weight gain do not adversely affect metabolic rate. A review by Wing (1992) came to a similar conclusion.

The Role of Habituation in Obesity

Habituation is a well-established learning process in which an often repeated stimulus produces a weaker response each time the stimulus is presented. Habituation is adaptive in many circumstances where a repeated stimulus provides little or no new information and can, thus, be ignored. Epstein, Temple, Bouton, and Roemmich, in a 2009 review of the available literature, propose that obesity can be explained in part, as a result of habituation processes. One of those processes is dishabituation. **Dishabituation** occurs when a response that has become habituated (i.e., the response is no longer occurring) starts occurring again as a result of a new stimulus being presented. The new stimulus dishabituates the response so that it occurs again. Epstein et al. (2009) propose that overeating often occurs as a result of such dishabituation. There are many stimuli associated with eating food that after repeated presentations should habituate and make eating that food less likely. However, if a dishabituating stimulus occurs it should restore the eating behavior, even though caloric intake may not be needed. Suppose, for example that someone places a plate in front of us with a big steak on it. We begin eating the steak piece by piece and habituation of the stimuli associated with eating the steak is presented again and again (e.g., the smell, taste, texture of the steak). Each bite of steak makes us less likely to take an additional bite because of habituation, and perhaps we stop eating when we start to feel full. Now suppose that the plate put in front of us has steak, a baked potato, and a vegetable. We take a bite of steak, then maybe a bite of vegetable and then a bite of the potato. By varying what we eat, we

reduce the buildup of habituation to each of the foods, and as a result, eat more than we would otherwise. Each bite of a different food provides different stimuli which serve to dishabituate the eating response. Thus eating a variety of foods should lead to more eating behavior than just eating one food does.

Food variety is not the only thing, however, that might serve to dishabituate eating. Consider eating something while watching television (TV). The stimuli associated with the chips you are eating would serve to habituate the eating response; however, every time you turn your attention to the stimuli on the TV, the effect may be to dishabituate the eating response so that you continue to eat, even though under other circumstances you would probably stop. Epstein et al. (2009) present considerable evidence from both animal and human studies that support the role of habituation and dishabituation in eating behavior.

Obesity as Addiction

Earlier, when discussing bulimia nervosa, we saw that binging behavior is similar in some ways to drug addiction (Johnson & Larson, 1982). Let us briefly look at research suggesting that obesity is a type of addictive behavior.

Perhaps the best way to think about eating as a potentially addictive behavior is to point out that eating food is controlled not only by a need for energy, but also by the palatability of food (Lutter & Nestler, 2009). That is, we eat both to gain energy and because some foods just taste very good. Thus, highly palatable foods are rewarding.

The pleasurable or rewarding quality of food appears to result from a different control system than the homeostatic system discussed earlier in this chapter. It is this second system, associated with the hedonic qualities of food, that appears to promote "addiction-like" behaviors (Lutter & Nestler, 2009; Volkow & Wise, 2005). As Lutter and Nestler (2009, p. 629) note "Considerable evidence in rodents and humans now supports the theory that both drugs of abuse and the consumption of highly palatable foods converge on a shared pathway within the limbic system to mediate motivated behaviors." In particular, both drugs and highly palatable foods produce a release of dopamine which has the effect of increasing arousal, and activation of food-related memories and behavior. For example, Johnson and Kenny (2010) found that dopamine D2 receptors were involved in compulsive eating in rats while Stoeckel, Weller, Cook, Tweig, Knowlton, and Cox (2008) found that obese women, when presented with pictures of high-energy foods, showed increased activation in several limbic structures. Volkow and Wise (2005) note that the endogenous opioid system also appears to be involved in the reward value of foods high in palatability. Thus, drug addiction and food addiction leading to obesity appear to share common circuitry within the brain's motivational systems.

Stress

In Chapter 3 we examined the role of stress in motivated behavior. One additional point not covered there is that psychological stress appears to influence feeding behavior and, thus indirectly, the development of obesity (Lutter & Nestler, 2009). One clue to the role of stress in overeating is the fact that there is an association (approximately 25%) between mood disorders and obesity (Simon et al., 2006). In mice, chronic stress induced by social defeat led to an elevation of ghrelin levels that in turn led to increased eating and body weight gain (Lutter et al., 2008). Other researchers have shown that stressed mice have lower levels of leptin (which should increase hunger), and stress increases the preference for high fat diets under some conditions in mice (Lu, Kim, Frazer, & Zhang, 2006; Teegarden & Bale, 2008).

Hunger Regulation Reconsidered

The examples of nonhomeostatic eating behavior just examined tell us that hunger motivation is more complex than previously thought. Although homeostatic mechanisms of eating behavior exist, other factors, such as the reward value of high palatability foods, can alter homeostatic eating dramatically. In particular, external cues associated with food (taste, smell, texture, etc.) can often seem to stimulate eating behavior in the absence of any real need. Americans' preference for junk food is probably a good example of how such cues can lead to eating behavior in the absence of any homeostatic imbalance.

It is also possible that eating behavior is not rigidly regulated. In our evolutionary past, food resources were considerably more unstable than at present. The sight, smell, taste, and other external cues associated with food might lead to eating, even in a nonhungry person, because the next opportunity to eat might not occur for several days. It would be adaptive, therefore, to be responsive to external, food-related cues and to eat when food is available even if homeostasis is currently being maintained. A good deal of research suggests that humans eat in response to various cues other than those associated with homeostasis; and as Rodin (1981) has noted regulation is poor when only internal cues are available. So it is possible that specific homeostatic mechanisms are less important to the initiation of eating than the cues associated with the availability of food. Perhaps, given the availability of food and the relative lack of other strong motivation, we eat. Eating, like grooming behavior in the rat, may have a very high probability of occurrence, and as a result, specific internal mechanisms triggering eating may be of secondary importance.

For the present it seems best to leave open the possibility that hunger motivation is homeostatically controlled under certain conditions, but that humans also eat *before* homeostasis is disrupted; and sometimes *refuse to eat* when they should: people also eat when stressed and can become addicted to food in much the same manner as others become addicted to drugs. So, our motivation to eat is not exclusively controlled by homeostatic imbalance.

Regulation of Thirst

We have just seen that the evidence for the homeostatic regulation of hunger is less clear than might have been expected. We will now examine research concerning the homeostatic regulation of **thirst**. Our examination of these data will reveal that homeostatic regulation of water balance does occur but that, once again, nonhomeostatic mechanisms also play a role in drinking.

According to Saltmarsh (2001) about 50% of a woman's weight is from water, while about 60% of a man's weight is from water. About two-thirds of our body water is contained within the cells themselves and is known as **intracellular fluid**, while the other one-third resides outside of the cells and is termed **extracellular fluid**. The extracellular fluid can be further divided into **interstitial fluid** that accounts for about 70% of the extracellular fluid and **intravascular fluid** that accounts for about 30% of the extracellular fluid (Saltmarsh, 2001). Interstitial fluid is the fluid between the cells, while intravascular fluid is the fluid within the blood. The various fluid compartments can be seen in Figure 4.8.

Most of the water in our bodies comes from fluids we drink or water in the foods we eat. However, some water is actually made by the body as a result of the breakdown of fats and carbohydrates. The body produces about a half liter of this **metabolic water** every day (Saltmarsh, 2001).

We are constantly losing water every day as well. Aside from the obvious loss of water through urination, we also lose water in our feces, and from evaporation from the skin (this is not the same as sweating), and in our exhalation of moist air from the lungs. Interestingly, we lose about the same amount of water from breathing as we gain from metabolic processes, about a half liter per day (Saltmarsh, 2001). We can also lose large amounts of water (and salt) as sweat when body temperature (such as in fever or strenuous exercise) or environmental temperatures rise. As the sweat evaporates it cools our bodies to help regulate body temperature. Water balance must be carefully regulated because **dehydration** can be fatal if more than 15% of body weight (in water) is lost (Saltmarsh, 2001).

Mouth Factors

Early theorists regarded thirst to be the result of peripheral changes such as a dry mouth, because it was known that dehydration reduces the flow of saliva (Cannon, 1929). Dryness of the mouth, however, cannot account for the regulation of water balance (Fitzsimons, 1973), although it may be involved in special circumstances associated with eating dry foods (Kissileff, 1973; Kissileff & Epstein, 1969). Brunstrom, Tribbeck, and MacRae (2000) have provided evidence that the termination of drinking is at least partially controlled by changes in mouth dryness. Their data suggests that saliva production increases as a result of drinking and that the increased saliva reduces the sensations associated with a dry mouth, which in turn leads to a cessation of drinking. So it would seem that mouth factors may be involved in some aspects of drinking behavior after all.

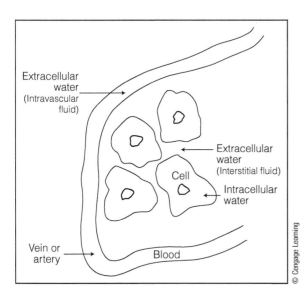

© Cengage Learning

FIGURE 4.8 Intracellular and extracellular spaces.

Extracellular and Intracellular Mechanisms

Research indicates that separate mechanisms are activated by changes in the water content of the cells (termed **intracellular mechanisms**) and in the water content of the fluid surrounding the cells (termed **extracellular mechanisms**). For example, it is known that extracellular fluid is lost as a result of diarrhea or loss of blood, yet cellular water changes do not occur. Because this loss of extracellular fluid leads to thirst, any strictly intracellular explanation of thirst must be incomplete. (Incidentally, thirst resulting from the extracellular fluid loss of bleeding explains why a common cry of the wounded on the battlefield is for water.) Extracellular thirst occurs when fluids are lost from the extracellular spaces, while intracellular thirst results from fluid loss within the cells.

Evidence for these two systems can be seen in a study by Eliot Blass (1968). Blass showed that damage to the frontal area of the brain in rats leads to a deficiency in the maintenance of proper water balance when the cells of the body are dehydrated (lack water) but not when the extracellular fluid is reduced. The control mechanisms for maintaining intracellular fluids, therefore, are independent of those that control extracellular fluids. Two motivational mechanisms have been proposed: the first, associated with intracellular fluid balance, is known as **osmometric thirst**; the second, associated with extracellular fluid balance, is known as **volumetric thirst**. To understand the research on thirst, we must briefly examine the action of the kidneys in the retention of fluid.

The Kidney

Normally we drink more water than we need, and the excess is excreted by the kidneys. The kidneys function to absorb sodium dissolved in the fluids of the body and to remove waste products of metabolism. In the process of absorbing sodium, about 99% of the water filtered by the kidneys is reabsorbed.

Because control of water balance is intimately tied to proper sodium balance, it has been suggested that thirst is controlled by sodium detectors (Andersson, 1971) and, in fact, evidence for sodium receptors in the liver that are involved in water balance has been found (see Stricker & Sved, 2000).

The kidney's ability to reabsorb both sodium and water can be altered. For example, when the flow of blood through the kidney drops, a substance called **renin** is secreted. (Renin can also be secreted when the kidney is activated by the sympathetic nervous system.) Renin interacts with a chemical produced by the liver called **angiotensinogen** and converts it to **angiotensin II** (which we will refer to as simply angiotensin). Angiotensin stimulates the adrenal cortex (see Chapter 3 for an explanation of the adrenal gland) to secrete **aldosterone**, which in turn causes the kidney to increase its reabsorption of sodium and, as a result, water (Carlson, 2010). Thus a drop in blood volume detected by the kidney or a command from the sympathetic nervous system causes an increase in the amount of water retained through reabsorption.

The ability of the kidney's collecting ducts to absorb water can also be altered by a pituitary hormone called **antidiuretic hormone (ADH)**, also known as **vasopressin (VP)**. Lack of this hormone leads to a disease known as diabetes insipidis, where an individual passes great quantities of water and must therefore drink large amounts to avoid dehydration. Although the pituitary gland releases ADH in order to increase reabsorption, ADH is actually manufactured in two groups of cells within the hypothalamus, the **supraoptic nucleus** and the **paraventricular nucleus** (Carlson, 2001). It is reasonable to expect, therefore, that the hypothalamus or regions near it are involved in the regulation of water balance.

Osmometric Thirst

Although sodium is a necessary ingredient for life, it cannot easily pass into the cell body. As a result, any buildup of sodium outside of cells creates a

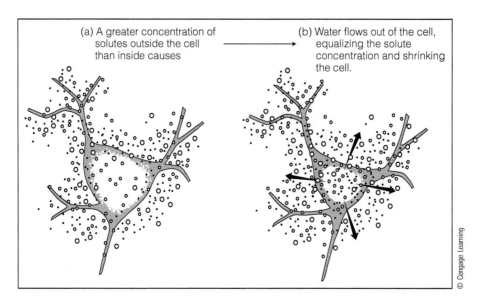

FIGURE 4.9   Osmosis.

condition in which water is pulled from the cells by a process called **osmosis** (the tendency of fluid to travel through a semipermeable membrane in order to equalize the concentrations of the fluids on either side of the membrane; see Figure 4.9). One possible mechanism of water regulation, therefore, would be specialized cells that could detect a change in their own volume as a result of cellular water loss due to osmosis. These **osmoreceptors** could trigger drinking behavior when cell volume decreased so that cell fluid balance could be returned to normal.

Indeed, indirect evidence for such a mechanism has been known for some time. For example, Verney (1947) found that injections of salt solution into the blood supply of the brain led to the secretion of ADH and, as a result, increased water retention by the kidney. Similarly, Andersson (1971) showed that salt solutions injected directly into the LH produce drinking behavior. The injections of salt solution into the brain presumably fool the osmoreceptors into functioning as if the body cells are dehydrated. Actually, the osmoreceptors alone were dehydrated by the increased concentration of sodium that drew the water from them. Normally

this would occur only if the other body cells were also dehydrated.

The research noted earlier by Blass (1968) indicated that the osmoreceptors must lie somewhere in the vicinity of the brain's frontal area, because destruction of this region leads to deficits in the control of cellular water balance. As summarized by Stricker and Sved (2000), the receptors appear to be contained in a structure known as **organum vasculosum laminae terminalis (OVLT)**, which lies along the base of the third ventricle and is outside of the blood-brain barrier (The blood-brain barrier allows some substances to pass from the blood to the brain cells, while restricting others.). This last item is important because it means that the OVLT (see Figure 4.10) can readily pick up changes in the osmolality of the blood as well as hormonal changes produced by changes in osmolality (e.g., the production of angiotensin). Changes in osmolality of as little as 1% to 2% stimulates thirst in animals (Stricker & Sved, 2000). The OVLT in turn stimulates cells in the **median preoptic area**, which in turn initiate thirst and drinking. OVLT also stimulates the supraoptic and paraventricular nuclei mentioned earlier that leads to production

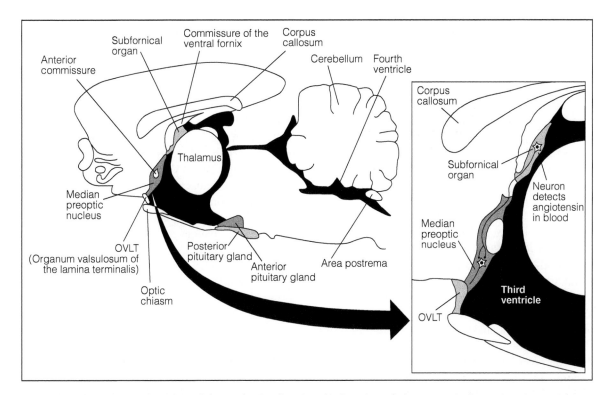

FIGURE 4.10 A sagittal section of the rat brain, showing the location of circumventricular organs. Inset: A hypothetical circuit connecting the subfornical organ with the median preoptic nucleus. From N. R. Carlson, *Physiology of Behavior*, 7th ed., figure 12.12, p. 385. Published by Allyn and Bacon, Boston, MA. Copyright © 2001 by Pearson Education. Reprinted by permission of the publisher.

of ADH and its secretion by the pituitary so that body water is conserved.

Although the OVLT controls water intake as a result of increased osmolality, animals as well as humans stop drinking well before the ingested water has had time to influence osmolality. In fact, it takes 10 to 20 minutes for ingested water to reduce osmolality (Stricker & Sved, 2000). The fact that we stop drinking before these changes have time to occur must mean that there are additional detectors that note when water has been taken in and stops the drinking process. Stricker and Sved (2000) summarize research suggesting that **sodium receptors** in the liver serve this purpose. These receptors appear to send their signals to an area of the brain known as **area postrema (AP)** (see

Figure 4.10). Additional stop signals for drinking include distension of the throat, esophagus, stomach, and duodenum (McKinley, 2009).

Volumetric Thirst

A reduction in the fluid balance of the extracellular space results in a situation known as **hypovolemia**, a condition that activates compensatory mechanisms to restore proper fluid balance (McKinley, 2009). Hypovolemia may occur for a variety of reasons. For example, loss of large amounts of blood reduces extracellular fluid and initiates thirst. Similarly, diarrhea and even vomiting can lead to hypovolemia and accompanying thirst. Loss of fluid from the extracellular body compartments does not change the osmotic balance between the cells and those compartments, so any mechanism that monitors cell volume will detect no change. Therefore a second mechanism must monitor the extracellular fluid and trigger thirst when that volume is reduced.

At least two detectors of extracellular fluid volume have been identified. "Stretch receptors located on the walls of the great veins that return blood to the heart and on the right atrium itself have been observed and presumed to mediate the increase in thirst and VP (vasopressin) secretion after blood loss. However, remarkably little data are available with which to confirm this hypothesis" (Stricker & Sved, 2000, p. 823). If this hypothesis is correct, then these receptors detect a change in blood volume and in turn stimulate the pituitary to secrete ADH (i.e., vasopressin) and the kidney to release renin. As we saw earlier, the production of renin leads to a chain of events resulting in more absorption of sodium and water.

The second system involves a hormonal response to hypovolemia (see inset Figure 4.10). The activation of thirst and subsequent water intake to compensate for reduced extracellular fluid is thought by several researchers to result from the brain's sensitivity to angiotensin. This hormone has been shown to be a powerful stimulus for drinking in several species, including monkeys, dogs, cats, goats, rabbits, and pigeons (Fitzsimons, 1973). For example, Fitzsimons and Simons (1969) found that infusion of angiotensin into the blood supply of rats with a normal water balance leads to drinking. Additionally, Epstein, Fitzsimons, and Rolls (1970) showed that injection of angiotensin directly into the brain elicits drinking, while Malvin, Mouw, and Vander (1977) found that agents that block uptake of angiotensin by the brain also block drinking.

The data just noted are consistent with the idea that angiotensin manufactured in the periphery of the body travels to the brain and stimulates cells responsible for thirst motivation. As might be expected, researchers initially looked for these detectors near or in the hypothalamus, the brain region so intimately involved with basic motivational states. Some research seemed to indicate that the medial preoptic area was the site of angiotensin detection (Epstein, Fitzsimons, & Rolls, 1970), but this site was questionable because angiotensin passes through the blood-brain barrier very slowly or perhaps not at all (Volicer & Lowe, 1971). The site of action of angiotensin was eventually determined to be a structure called the **subfornical organ** (**SFO**; see Figure 4.10) (Simpson & Routtenberg, 1973; Volicer & Lowe, 1971). The SFO is of particular interest because it lies outside the blood-brain barrier on the surface of the fluid compartments of the brain (ventricles). As a result, it can detect changes in angiotensin transported to the brain and send this information to other brain structures involved with fluid regulation (Epstein, 1982). Simpson and Routtenberg (1973) had shown that the SFO is very sensitive to angiotensin; activation of drinking occurs in less than 3 seconds when angiotensin is delivered to it. When Simpson and Routtenberg destroyed the SFO, they found that drinking in response to angiotensin was abolished. Based on these findings, they suggested that the SFO is the site of receptors sensitive to changes in extracellular body fluids. Subsequent research has confirmed the SFO to be the critical structure (see Epstein, 1982, for a review of this literature).

The neural circuitry involved with osmometric and volumetric thirst is quite complex and not yet completely understood. Several structures interact to initiate drinking when cell volume or extracellular fluid volume drops. These structures seem to be situated around the lower front area (anteroventral) of the third ventricle, as shown in Figure 4.10. In addition, water intake is also influenced by a number of hormones including relaxin, estrogen, and amylin (see McKinley, 2009, for a review).

Nonhomeostatic Drinking

As was the case with eating behavior, drinking behavior also usually occurs before homeostatic balance is disrupted. In this regard, Kraly (1984) has suggested that researchers need to study normal drinking behavior—that is, drinking that occurs before either intracellular or extracellular fluid balances are disturbed. Kraly noted, for example, that normal drinking occurs around meals for most mammals. In the rat, 70% to 90% of daily water intake occurs within a time interval ranging from 10 minutes before meals to 30 minutes after meals (Fitzsimons & LeMagnen, 1969; Kissileff, 1969) and does not appear to be a response to any homeostatic imbalance (Kraly, 1984). These data, together with other considerations noted by Kraly, suggest that drinking behavior is closely tied to eating, and, in fact, eating appears to be a potent stimulus for drinking. It would therefore seem that drinking, like eating, often occurs when no apparent homeostatic imbalance is evident. Further, because eating and drinking interact, the role of food ingestion on drinking behavior needs to be explored. As suggested by Kraly, gastrointestinal tract changes that result from food ingestion probably stimulate drinking behavior that is non-homeostatic in nature. These changes seem to involve **histamine** and angiotensin (Kraly, 1983, 1990; Kraly & Corneilson, 1990; Kraly & Specht, 1984). When food is eaten, histamine is released by stomach cells. The histamine then appears to cause production of renin by the kidney, which you recall interacts with angiotensinogen to produce angiotensin, which in turn stimulates drinking. Thus, food in the stomach triggers a cascade of events that lead to drinking. In addition, amylin, a hormone produced by the pancreas, is produced when food is eaten and if given to rats produces drinking (McKinley, 2009). Thus, amylin may also stimulate drinking under normal conditions. In opposite fashion, obestatin, produced by the stomach after food is ingested, inhibits drinking (McKinley, 2009). Thus, there is a complex interaction between eating and drinking.

Inhibitory Control of Drinking

We have examined research concerned with the initiation of drinking as a result of both intracellular and extracellular changes. But we have not yet examined mechanisms that turn off drinking. Inhibition of water intake poses a smaller problem for the body than inhibition of food intake because excess water can be controlled relatively simply by increased excretion through the kidneys. Because of this control, it would not be surprising if inhibitory mechanisms are less developed than mechanisms that initiate drinking.

As we discovered earlier, the liver appears to play a crucial role in managing hunger. There is also evidence that signals from the liver serve to shut off drinking behavior (Kobashi & Adachi, 1992; Kozlowski & Drzewiecki, 1973; Smith & Jerome, 1983). Infusions of water into the hepatic portal vein stop drinking initiated by water deprivation and by injections of saline. Furthermore, rats drink more water than normal when the vagus nerve is cut at the liver. Such a cut would prevent the receptors in the liver from signaling the brain about the arrival of water. Additional signals from the mouth, stomach, and duodenum also play a part in shutting off thirst motivation.

Regulation of Sexual Motivation

Hunger and thirst are two motivated states regulated in part by the hypothalamus. Other motivated states are also partially regulated by the hypothalamus; among them are sexual and maternal behaviors, temperature regulation, fear, and aggression. Though much remains to be understood about the mechanisms of regulation for each of these motives, we will briefly examine some of the research on regulation of sexual motivation.

Sex Hormones: Organization and Activation

The brains of males and females are set up differently as a result of the presence or absence of sex hormones (see Breedlove, 1994; Carlson, 2007;

Feder, 1984, for summaries of much of this research). Research has shown that the mammalian brain is female unless altered by the presence of male sex hormones (testosterone). Male brains are created by the presence of testosterone during a critical period in their development. According to Breedlove (1994), testosterone binds to the androgen receptor on cells that contain these receptors. The testosterone-receptor complex then binds to the cell's DNA, altering the manufacture of several proteins. These protein alterations can then change the activities of the affected cell, causing it to divide, change its shape, alter its function, and, in some cases, even die. The predominant species on which most of this research has been conducted is rodents (typically rats); however, similar processes have been found in other species and are probably involved in human brain development as well.

Sexual Dimorphism

As is probably obvious to everyone, men and women are sexually different. This **sexual dimorphism** is the result of the action of a gene found on the Y (male) chromosome. For the first six weeks of fetal development, male and female fetuses are sexually the same. In male fetuses, a gene on the Y chromosome called the **SRY gene** starts producing a protein that causes the as yet undifferentiated **gonads** (the sex organs that when mature will produce various hormones and either ova or sperm) to develop into testes. If the SRY gene is not present (as in female fetuses) the undifferentiated gonads develop into ovaries (see Carlson, 2007; or Kalat, 2009, for a clear presentation of this process). Once the prenatal ovaries or testes have developed they begin secreting hormones that differentiate both the sex organs of males and females and the organization of brain circuitry into either a male or female brain. Much of this differentiation appears to depend upon various steroid receptors present on brain neurons (see Blaustein, 2008, for a review of the role of steroid receptors). Sex hormones also have activating effects in adulthood that produce

gender specific behaviors such as intromission, thrusting, and ejaculation in males and attractivity, proceptivity, and receptivity in females (Beach, 1976; Blaustein & Erskine, 2002). **Intromission** involves penetration of the vagina by the penis, **thrusting** produces friction between the sex organs, and **ejaculation** is the introduction of sperm into the vagina. **Attractivity** concerns behaviors that attract a male to a receptive female, **proceptivity** involves species-specific behaviors that sexually arouse the male and lead to mounting, and **receptivity** involves behaviors that lead to the successful transfer of sperm to the female.

In rats, some sexual differentiation is still possible as late as 4 days after birth (human differentiation occurs prenatally). Seymour Levine (1966) conducted research on the relationship between sex hormones and male and female sexual behaviors. For example, Levine injected female rats that were less than 4 days old with the male sex hormone testosterone. The injected females did not develop normal female physiology; the ovaries were severely reduced in size, they did not produce egg cells, and the ovulation cycle was disrupted. Levine also castrated male rats at a similar age in order to reduce testosterone in them. The castrated males showed some signs of female physiology; if an ovary was surgically implanted in one of these males at maturity, the ovary produced egg cells. Similar results have been obtained with both guinea pigs and monkeys.

Levine suggested that the administration of testosterone during a critical period of an animal's life permanently alters the brain so that the female pituitary cycle is lost and the brain becomes insensitive to both estrogen and progesterone (female sex hormones), regardless of the genetic sex of the animal. This critical period appears to be the first few days after birth in rats but occurs before birth in both guinea pigs and monkeys, so injections of testosterone in these latter two species must be given before birth for masculinizing effects to be apparent. In the genetic male, minute amounts of testosterone are secreted during development in the uterus, and these minute amounts are enough to masculinize the brain. In the genetic female, or in males

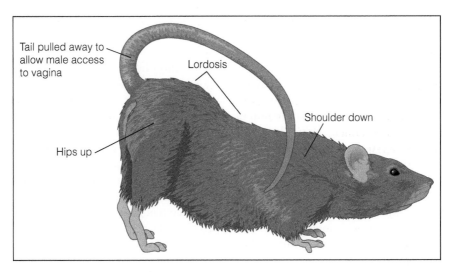

FIGURE 4.11 Lordosis behavior in the female rat. From WILSON. *Biological Foundations of Human Behavior.* (Fig. 12.9, p. 364). Copyright © 2001 Cengage Learning.

where testosterone is absent, the brain develops feminine circuitry.

More interesting from a psychological viewpoint are the long-term effects of early administration of testosterone to females. Levine injected testosterone into young female rats to masculinize them and then tested these animals in adulthood for normal female sexual behavior. Normal female rats exhibit a behavior pattern known as **lordosis**, as shown in Figure 4.11, which consists of arching the back and elevating the pelvis in order to permit mounting by the male. Lordosis behavior appears to be controlled by the presence of progesterone in VMH and the ventral tegmental area (Frye, 2001a, 2001b). In addition, progesterone may facilitate the release of dopamine from the medial preoptic area in female rats, which in turn facilitates sexual behavior (Matuszewich, Lorrain, & Hull, 2000).

These masculinized female rats did not show normal female sexual behavior even when given injections of estrogen and progesterone, hormones necessary for sexual behavior in the normal female rat. On the other hand, if these masculinized females were given additional injections of testosterone as adults, they displayed the complete copulatory pattern of male sexual behavior, including the movements associated with ejaculation. Apparently the early administration of testosterone either inhibited the development of normal female sexual behavior or blocked its expression. Similarly, when male rats castrated at an early age were given estrogen and progesterone, they behaved like normal females. The lack of early testosterone in these male rats either led to the failure of the male sexual pattern to develop or blocked the expression of the pattern. Subsequent research has consistently shown the importance of sex steroid activation in the sexual behavior of many species (see, e.g., Blaustein, 2008, for a review of the role of steroid hormones and their receptors in the sexual behavior of females).

Hypothalamic Regulation of Sexual Behavior

Much more is known about the role of the hypothalamus in the control of hunger and thirst than is known about its role in sexual behavior. Though other structures are also involved in the regulation of sexual behavior, the hypothalamus is of major importance (Sawyer, 1969).

Tumors or other pathologies of the hypothalamus can modify the development or maintenance of sexual behavior in humans. Tumors of the hypothalamus may lead to early sexual development with gonadal enlargement and the appearance of secondary sexual characteristics (pubic hair, for example) in children as young as age 8. For reasons that are still unclear, this early development seems more common in boys than in girls. Damage to the hypothalamus may also produce the opposite effect, leading to **hypogonadal conditions**, including a lack of sexual motivation, underdevelopment of the genitals, and a lack of secondary sexual characteristics.

In many animals, sexual behavior can be accomplished reflexively at the level of the spinal cord. For example, after the spinal cord has been cut to eliminate brain influence, erection, thrusting movements, and ejaculation in the male have all been shown to occur. Lordosis can also be accomplished at the spinal level (Beach, 1967; Hart, 1967). Human males with spinal cord damage have been known to accomplish erection and ejaculation, but they do not experience orgasm as a result (Carlson, 2001).

Much of the research on the physiological mechanisms of sexual behavior has been conducted on the rabbit and Japanese quail. Rabbits are particularly useful subjects because females ovulate as a result of intercourse. They therefore enable the researcher to test which brain structures are involved in sexual activity by checking for ovulation after different brain areas have been stimulated or removed. (The phenomenon of intercourse-induced ovulation also helps explain why rabbits are so numerous!)

The **medial preoptic area (POA)** of the anterior hypothalamus contains a group of cells that differ in size depending upon the sex of the individual. This group of cells, known as the **sexually dimorphic nucleus (SDN)** is bigger in males than in females (Gorski, Gordon, Shryne, & Southam, 1978; see also Carlson 2007; Kalat, 2009). Several studies (Sawyer, 1969) have shown

that lesions in the anterior hypothalamus abolish the estrous cycle in female mammals. Replacement therapy with estrogen fails to reestablish the cycle, suggesting that this part of the hypothalamus may contain cells sensitive to circulating female sex hormones. Mating behavior (e.g., vaginal-cervical stimulation) also increases activity in cells within the preoptic area of female hamsters (Ramos & DeBold, 2000). Lesions in the preoptic region, particularly the medial preoptic nucleus, abolish or reduce sexual behavior in male rats (Heimer & Larsson, 1966, 1967). This region of the male rat brain contains a large number of androgen receptors (Roselli, Handa, & Resko, 1989). Indeed, administering testosterone into the medial preoptic area will reinstate sexual behavior in castrated adult male rats (Davidson, 1980). The POA has also been shown to be involved with male sexual behavior in the quail (Balthazart, Stamatakis, Bacola, Absil, & Dermon, 2001). Additionally, a study by Dermon, Stamatakis, Tlemcani, and Balthazart (1999) found that different brain areas were activated by appetitive (viewing a receptive female) and consummatory (copulation) sexual behaviors in male quail.

In a study measuring sexual arousal in human males viewing sexually explicit film clips, Stoleru et al. (1999) found bilateral activation of the inferior temporal cortex (a visual association area), right insula, right inferior frontal areas (thought to associate sensory information with motivational states), and the left anterior cingulate cortex (controls autonomic and endocrine processes). Thus, this study identifies a series of brain activations that lead to sexual arousal in human males.

Lesions in the VMH abolish estrus in females, but estrogen replacement therapy successfully restores sexual behavior. Similar results have been obtained with males lesioned in the VMH (Buck, 1976; Sawyer, 1969). Because hormone replacement therapy successfully restores sexual behavior in VMH–lesioned animals, the role the VMH plays in sexual behavior is probably different from the roles played by the anterior hypothalamus and preoptic areas.

More recent research (see McCarthy & Becker, 2002; Baum, 2002, for extensive reviews of this literature) has implicated additional brain circuitry for male and female sexual behavior. In male rats, sensory stimulation from female pheromones and other sexual stimuli is circuited through the amygdala (A) to the bed nucleus of the stria terminalis (BNST) and from there to the POA, which integrates the information and produces sexual behavior. However, this circuit requires that sex steroid receptors be activated in the A, BNST, and POA in order for the behaviors to occur (Baum, 2002). In female rats, the POA has both inhibitory and excitatory effects on the ventromedial nucleus (VMN) of the hypothalamus which sends information to the periaquaductal gray area (PAG) where these signals are integrated with other bodily information before being sent on to the spinal cord and the production of lordosis (McCarthy & Becker, 2002). Estrogen receptors, as might be expected, are found in these structures.

The hypothalamus would seem to regulate sexual motivation, at least in part, by blocking the spinal reflex aspects of sexual behavior until conditions are appropriate for their occurrence. For example, Barfield, Wilson, and McDonald (1975) and Clark and associates (1975) found that lesions between the hypothalamus and the midbrain *increase* sexual behavior in male rats. The increased sexual behavior is the result of a decrease in the amount of time between ejaculations. Male rats normally go through a refractory period after ejaculation during which they are uninterested in sexual activity and show sleeplike EEGs. Lesions that disconnect the hypothalamus from the midbrain reduce this refractory period from approximately 5 to 2½ minutes, suggesting that the hypothalamus may normally inhibit sexual activity. Similarly, it has been shown that POA typically serves an inhibitory function on female sexual behavior; however, as noted by McCarthy and Becker (2002), some parts of the POA produce excitatory function in female rats as well.

The information reviewed in this section suggests that the hypothalamus and structures near it are sensitive to and responsible for the proper regulation of both sex hormones and sexual behavior.

The POA seems particularly important for sexual behavior in both males and females and also influences other areas, such as the VMN in females, which lead to the expression of sexual behavior. The influence of sex hormones on behavior is complex: on the one hand, they appear important for the organization of brain circuitry during fetal development; on the other, they regulate and make possible sexual behavior. Much additional research remains to be conducted before we fully understand the manner in which sexual behavior is regulated.

Regulation of Aggressive Motivation

To conclude this chapter, we will briefly consider evidence for neural circuitry underlying aggression. In particular we will examine research on animal aggression, a topic with some relevance for studies of anger and aggression in humans.

Early work by Cannon (1929) showed that the cortex of the brain is unnecessary for the expression of anger. In fact decorticate cats showed what Cannon called **sham rage**, a term used because true emotional behavior, it was assumed, could not occur without the cortex. But the rage observed included the typical behaviors seen in angry cats, such as the lashing tail and arched back, as well as snarling, clawing, and biting. The cats also showed autonomic arousal with dilation of the pupils, piloerection (erection of the fur), rapid heartbeat, and increases in adrenaline and blood sugar. The sham rage response was therefore highly similar to the normal expression of rage except that it was not directed toward the provoking stimulus (Bard & Mountcastle, 1964). Bard (1928) determined that this rage response depended on the hypothalamus being intact, particularly the posterior portion. These early studies led to the idea that the cortex of the brain acts to suppress aggressive emotional behavior directed by the hypothalamus. Although recent theory is more complex, the assumption that cortical areas serve to inhibit aggressive behavior still appears valid.

The Limbic System

As early as 1937 James Papez proposed that the hypothalamus, along with several other structures, forms part of a circuit that participates in emotional expression. Papez identified the hypothalamus, anterior thalamic nuclei, the cingulate gyrus, and the hippocampus as belonging to this circuit. Today these structures, along with the amygdala, are known as the **limbic system**, which is shown in Figure 4.12.

The involvement of the limbic system in emotion was further supported by the experiments of Kluver and Bucy (1939), who surgically removed the temporal lobes of monkeys. Bilateral (both sides) destruction of the temporal lobes resulted in a set of symptoms that included changes in emotionality. These formerly wild, aggressive monkeys became very tame after the operation and exhibited little emotionality. In some cases, anger and fear were permanently lost, while in others it returned after the operation but in much subdued form. Because these temporal lobe lesions seriously damaged the underlying amygdala and hippocampus of the limbic system, Kluver and Bucy's research provided striking confirmation of Papez's theory.

Rosvold, Mirsky, and Pribram (1954) further showed that damage to the amygdala leads to profound losses of social dominance behavior in monkeys. Because the dominance order of monkeys is maintained largely through aggression or threats of aggression, such losses indicate that the amygdala is important for the normal expression of aggressive behavior. In some monkeys, interestingly, while damage to the amygdala severely reduced

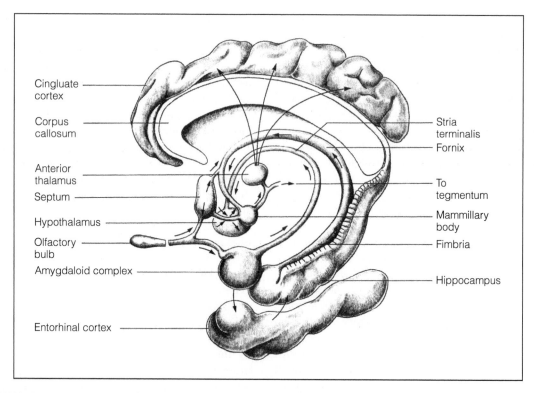

FIGURE 4.12   Structures and connections of the limbic system. From *Physiology of Behavior* N. R. Copyright © 1977 by Allyn & Bacon, Inc. Used by permission.

aggressiveness in social interactions, it increased aggression (threatening behavior toward the experimenter) if the animals were isolated. This latter result suggests that the amygdala has different effects on different kinds of aggression, a point to which we will return.

Earlier in this chapter we noted some research suggesting the importance of two areas within the hypothalamus in the regulation of hunger, thirst, and sexual behavior. Those two areas, the lateral hypothalamus (LH) and the ventromedial hypothalamus (VMH), also seem to be involved in aggressive behavior (Moyer, 1971; Smith, King, & Hoebel, 1970).

Flynn and associates (1970) have distinguished two types of aggression known as affective attack and quiet biting attack. Each is further discussed below.

Affective attack appears very similar to the rage behavior seen in the decorticate cats mentioned previously. There is significant sympathetic arousal evidenced by pupil dilation and piloerection. A cat displaying this type of aggression hisses and snarls, with its back arched, and it attacks, screaming, with claws bared and teeth ready to bite. This rather extreme set of emotionally laden behaviors can be elicited simply by electrically stimulating the VMH.

Quiet biting attack is aggression of quite a different sort. Emotionality is minimal, and no screaming or growling is observed. The cat stalks its prey and pounces upon it, biting it in the neck region. It uses its claws not to slash but to roll over the prey so that a killing bite can be made. Such behavior looks very much like the typical predatory behavior of cats and can be obtained by electrically stimulating the LH. Bandler and Flynn (1974) also found areas within the thalamus that elicited quiet biting attack when stimulated. They lesioned this area and then traced the degenerating fibers to the midbrain. When the appropriate area of the midbrain was lesioned in another group of cats, stimulation of the thalamus had no effect; however, stimulation of the LH still elicited quiet biting attack. Thus predatory aggression appears to be complexly controlled.

The **periaqueductal gray (PAG)** area of the midbrain mentioned earlier in regard to sexual motivation is also known to be involved in aggressive behavior because, even after destruction of the hypothalamus, partial aggressive responses such as spitting and snarling can still be obtained from this area (Bailey & Davis, 1969; Bard & Mountcastle, 1964). These findings suggest that the motor patterns of aggressive behavior are mediated at the level of the midbrain, while the hypothalamus may be involved in the spontaneity of aggressive behavior (Flynn et al., 1970).

The hypothalamus may in turn be regulated by the **amygdala**. Gray (1971) has proposed that the amygdala inhibits the hypothalamus, which in turn inhibits the midbrain aggressive patterns of behavior. Gray further proposed that just one neural system controls both fight (affective attack) and flight behavior. If the environment is conducive to escape, flight will occur; if escape is impossible, attack occurs. Gray argued that the decision to attack or flee is made by the VMH.

Other theorists, notably Flynn, have argued that the thalamus contains separate neural systems for attack and flight. For example, Flynn and his associates lesioned an area of the **thalamus** that resulted in the elimination of flight behavior when painfully stimulated. Although this lesion abolished flight as a response to hypothalamic stimulation, it did not eliminate hypothalamic stimulation–induced attack. The proposals of Gray and Flynn are not directly comparable, however, because Gray's concerns affective attack, while Flynn's concerns quiet biting attack. So the issue of whether attack and flight behaviors are regulated by independent neural systems or by one system cannot be definitely answered. However, it is generally agreed that the organization of aggressive behavior requires the amygdala, the hypothalamus, and the midbrain regions. Although the amygdala is often considered to exert an inhibitory influence on the hypothalamus, this is probably too simple an assumption because the amygdala is composed of several groups of nuclei (clumps of neurons) that serve different functions. For example, Miczek, Brykczynski, and Grossman (1974) showed that lesions of different parts of the amygdala produce different effects on aggressiveness: lesions in one part eliminated both attack behavior and dominance in male rats that had been dominant before surgery, while lesions in a different part had no effect on this type of aggressiveness. Similarly, aggression following footshock was only slightly reduced by some lesions, while other lesions greatly reduced it. Several types of aggression are thus apparently controlled by different systems within the amygdala.

Sensory information is also important to the expression of aggressive behavior. In fact the same electrical stimulation of hypothalamic areas that elicits attack also sets up sensory fields used during the attack (Flynn, 1969). During stimulation, for example, touching the head of a cat near the mouth causes the head to move so that the stimulus comes into contact with the lips; when the lips are touched by the stimulus, the jaw snaps open to bite. Figure 4.13 shows the sensory fields set up by electrical stimulation of the hypothalamus. Flynn's data suggest that during attack behavior, sensory fields originate and guide the attack.

Types of Aggression

The research by Flynn and his colleagues suggests that more than one type of aggression may exist and that each type may be served by its own neural system. This notion has been argued most persuasively by Kenneth Moyer (1971), who presented evidence for at least seven types of aggressive activity, as follows:

1. **Predatory aggression:** aggression elicited by a natural object of prey

2. **Intermale aggression:** aggression typically released by the presence of another male; the attack is usually without provocation

3. **Fear-induced aggression:** aggression that occurs when escape is blocked

4. **Irritable aggression:** aggression usually described as either anger or rage; attack occurs in response to a broad range of stimuli, either animate or inanimate

5. **Territorial defense:** aggression in defense of a territory; the aggression is usually against a member of the animal's own species

FIGURE 4.13 Sensory field set up by electrical stimulation of the brain. Left, shaded area indicates area that elicits head movement when touched, bringing stimulus into contact with the lips; right, sensory field along the lips that causes mouth to open when contacted by the stimulus. From "Neural Aspects of Attack Behavior in Cats," by J. P. Flynn in *Experimental Approaches to the Study of Emotional Behavior*. Copyright © 1969 by the New York Academy of Sciences. Used by permission.

6. **Maternal aggression:** aggression involving defense of the young, typically performed by the female in mammals

7. **Instrumental aggression:** aggressive behavior that is a learned response and is performed when that response is reinforced

Though little is known about the neural systems underlying most of the aggressive behaviors that Moyer has proposed, predatory aggression appears very similar to the quiet biting attack noted by Flynn, and the LH appears to be important in its regulation. Irritable aggression also seems to correspond closely with Flynn's affective attack, and the VMH has been implicated in its performance. Moyer has also provided evidence that the amygdala affects different types of aggression in more than one way. He noted, for example, that stimulation of the basal nucleus of the amygdala facilitates fear-induced aggression but inhibits predatory attack and irritable aggression, while destruction of the entire amygdala reduces all three types of aggressive behavior.

Siegel, Roeling, Gregg, and Kruk (1999) reviewed the research on the brain regions and neurotransmitters involved in aggressive behavior in cats and rats. Like the studies previously mentioned, considerable research has implicated the amygdala, the **hypothalamic aggression area (HAA)**, and periaqueductal gray (PAG) areas in the control of aggressive behavior. The HAA and PAG appear to control the expression of aggressive behavior, while limbic structures including the amygdala modulate the behavior, either facilitating it or suppressing it. Additionally, and especially in humans, the prefrontal cortex appears to play a role in the control of aggressive behavior. A disorder called **intermittent explosive disorder**, which is characterized by episodes of aggressive behavior that are out of proportion to the initiating event (American Psychiatric Association, 1994; Olvera, 2002), has been traced to areas within the prefrontal cortex as well as the amygdala (Olvera, 2002).

Researchers have also consistently found changes in the serotonin system to be related to changes in aggressive behavior in both animals (see Siegel et al., 1999, for a review) and humans (Olvera, 2002). Siegel et al. (1999, p. 373) conclude that "The overall results obtained in cat and rat indicate that **serotonin** mechanisms suppress aggression." However, they also note that many other neurotransmitter systems seem to be involved in aggressive activities including changes in **dopamine**, which appears to facilitate aggressive behaviors in the cat, and the **opioid system**, which appears to suppress aggressive behaviors. **Gamma-aminobutyric acid (GABA)**, a general inhibitory neurotransmitter, has also been implicated in modulating aggressive behavior (Seigel et al., 1999). Clearly, the control and production of aggressive behaviors are mediated by the interaction of several neurotransmitter systems.

Much remains to be worked out before we fully understand the neural systems that regulate aggressive behavior. The limbic system seems to be involved in emotionality, but how it regulates the expression of particular emotions is still largely a mystery. Of the emotions studied, anger or rage (as evidenced by aggression) has received the most attention in regard to physiological mechanisms of control (but see Calder, Lawrence, & Young, 2001, for a different view of the role of the limbic system in emotion). Models such as Moyer's are important because they point out that aggression is not a single behavior but several that are elicited by different conditions. These different types of aggression probably also depend on different neural systems.

SUMMARY

In this chapter we have analyzed theory and research concerning the physiological regulation of four motivated states. These approaches emphasize homeostasis, the view that motivation is triggered when bodily conditions move too far away from some optimal level.

Several groups of cells in or near the hypothalamus have been shown to be concerned with hunger motivation. Among the most important are LH, VMH, the arcuate nucleus, and the paraventricular nucleus. Regulation of hunger motivation is often divided into a short-term system that monitors glucose levels in the blood via specialized glucoreceptors in the liver and a long-term system that monitors leptin and insulin levels. Leptin and insulin in turn influence the production of neurotransmitters in the hypothalamus, specifically NPY and α-MSH. Obesity results from a complex interplay of genetic, regulatory, and environmental factors. These factors interact in as yet poorly understood ways.

Thirst is also conveniently divided into two systems: intracellular and extracellular mechanisms. The first system monitors the availability of water within the cells, while the second monitors the fluid surrounding the cells. Together they maintain proper hydration. Once again we find that cells in or near the hypothalamus regulate water intake. The major areas are the supraoptic nucleus, the paraventricular nucleus, the area postrema, and the subfornical organ. The hormones renin, aldosterone, and angiotensin also help regulate water balance.

Sexual behavior in animals other than humans may be the most highly regulated of the three motives discussed, because such behavior usually occurs only under appropriate hormonal conditions. Though hormonal conditions play a part in human sexual behavior, human sexuality is also controlled by learned social and cultural factors that we are presently only beginning to understand. The effect of sex hormones on human behavior, in fact, appears to be most potent during prenatal development. Prenatal testosterone has organizational effects on the developing brain. These same hormones probably influence motivation in as yet unspecified ways. In nonhuman animals, sexual behavior appears to be regulated by groups of cells in VMH and the medial preoptic region of the hypothalamus.

Limbic system structures are involved with the regulation of emotional behavior. Damage to various parts of the limbic system leads to changes in emotionality. Because anger and rage are the most easily identified emotions in animals, most physiological research on emotion has focused on the regulatory mechanisms involved in aggressive attack.

Early work showed that the cortex is not necessary for rage behavior, and subsequent research showed that the LH, VMH, HAA, PAG, amygdala, and prefrontal cortex are important. The motor patterns of attack are apparently integrated by the hypothalamus and midbrain mechanisms that are normally held in check by the amygdala and prefrontal cortex. Several types of aggressive behavior have been identified, but only a few (predatory and defensive aggression) have been associated with particular brain structures.

It is worth emphasizing that the same structures (the LH and VMH) have been implicated in several different motive states, including hunger, thirst, sex, and aggression. Many fiber tracts course through the hypothalamus, and damage to the various areas, causing changes in motivated behavior, may consist of interruption of these fiber systems. In addition, changes in behavior may result from damage to a general arousal system that is independent of the particular motive being tested. Early proposals that suggested the presence of centers within the hypothalamus for various motive states have not generally been supported by research. Clearly much work remains before we can say with any confidence how the brain regulates motivated behavior.

Considerable evidence exists for homeostatic regulation of hunger, thirst, and sexual motivation; however, these homeostatic mechanisms can be easily overridden by other factors. These overriding factors are most easily observed in the eating behavior of humans, who may become anorexic, bulimic, or obese. In each of these cases homeostasis is violated. Similarly, drinking behavior, though homeostatically regulated under some circumstances, more often occurs before such regulation is disrupted. The reasons for this "preventive drinking" result, at least in part, from an interaction between eating and drinking.

As this chapter attests, the physiological regulation of basic motives such as hunger, thirst, sex, and aggression is very complex.

KEY TERMS

SUGGESTIONS FOR FURTHER READING

Calder, A. J., Lawrence, A. D., & Young, A. W. (2001). Neuropsychology of fear and loathing. *Nature Reviews/Neuroscience, 2,* 352–363. This review looks at the evidence for and against the idea that the limbic system controls the expression of emotion.

Epel, E., Lapidus, R., McEwen, B., & Brownell, K. (2001). Stress may add bite to appetite in women: A laboratory study of stress-induced cortisol and eating behavior. *Psychoneuroendocrinology, 26,* 37–49. This article provides yet another potential trigger for eating—stress.

Siegel, A., Roeling, T. A. P., Gregg, T., & Kruk, M. R. (1999). Neuropharmacology of brain-stimulation evoked aggression. *Neuroscience and Biobehavioral Reviews, 23,* 359–389. This review provides an excellent overview of the brain systems and neurotransmitters controlling aggressive behavior in cat and rat. For the advanced student.

Taubes, G. (2001). The soft science of dietary fat. *Science, 291,* 2536–2545. This article argues that the negative effects of fat in the diet have yet to be shown. Interesting reading of a different point of view on healthy diet.

WEB RESOURCES

For direct hot links to the Internet sites listed below and other features, visit the book-specific Web site at http://psychology.wadsworth.com/petri.

Food and Nutrition Information Center: http://www.nal.usda.gov/fnic/reports/foodsec.html. This site contains a lot of useful general information about food/hunger.

The Kinsey Institute: http://www.indiana.edu/~kinsey/index.html. The site provides research and information on human sexuality.

Youth Violence: A Report of the Surgeon General—http://www.mentalhealth.org/youthviolence/surgeongeneral/SG_Site/home.asp

This site represents the conclusions reached by the Surgeon General's office on youth violence. This study was initiated as a result of the Columbine High School shootings.

PART III

THE BEHAVIORAL APPROACHES: LEARNING, INCENTIVES, AND HEDONISM

CHAPTER 5
Learned Motives: Classical, Instrumental, and Observational Learning

CHAPTER 6
Incentive Motivation

CHAPTER 7
Hedonism and Sensory Stimulation

CHAPTER 5

Learned Motives: Classical, Instrumental, and Observational Learning

CHAPTER PREVIEW

This chapter is concerned with the following questions:

1. How are motives acquired?

2. How does classical conditioning contribute to the motivation of behavior?

3. How does instrumental conditioning contribute to the motivation of behavior?

4. How is observational learning involved in the development of motives?

Johnny likes to watch television. His favorite shows involve lots of action and violence. In one show he observed a boy about his own age set a fire because the boy was angry with his parents. Johnny's observation of the firesetting sequence had no immediately observable effect on his behavior; however, about a week later, after an argument with his parents, Johnny attempted to start a fire under the coffee table.

What motivated Johnny to behave this way? Several theorists have argued that our motives can be developed and directed simply through observation of appropriate models. They have further suggested that behaviors may often be learned but not performed until sometime later when conditions are favorable for their occurrence. The example of Johnny's behavior suggests that learning can play a prominent role in the development and direction of motivation. Research has shown that several types of learning can influence both the development of motives and the way in which motives are expressed in behavior. This chapter concerns the research and theory surrounding the idea that many motivated behaviors are acquired or directed by learning.

The concept of acquired motivation is necessary for any comprehensive understanding of motivated behavior because much behavioral diversity clearly depends on motives that are acquired or altered during the life of the organism. Though motives appear to be learned in both animals and humans, most theorists believe that acquired motives account for a larger proportion of behavior in humans.

Much of the research on learned motives was conducted during the heyday of behaviorism. One of the major contributions the behaviorists made was to examine how behaviors are learned. As we shall see, several kinds of learning have been implicated in the development or modification of motivated behavior. Among them are **Pavlovian classical conditioning**, instrumental or operant conditioning, and observational learning. Although many of the studies that follow were done many years ago, they are still relevant today in showing us how new motives are acquired. More recent research has tended to look at small, specific questions rather than the more general processes that we will examine in this chapter and in Chapters 6 and 7.

Pavlovian Classical Conditioning

In the process of classical conditioning, a formerly neutral stimulus gains the ability to elicit a response from an organism because it has been associated with some other stimulus that reliably (and usually rather automatically) elicited that response in the past.

As you are probably aware, Pavlov conducted much of the early research on classical conditioning. Pavlov (1960) was originally interested in studying the digestive process, particularly the role of salivation in digestion. He chose the dog as his experimental subject because of its ability to generate copious amounts of saliva. He perfected an operation that allowed him to free the salivary gland from the inside cheek of the dog and suture it to the outside of the cheek. In this way he could connect the gland to a tube and accurately measure the amount of saliva secreted under various conditions.

Pavlov knew that a dog would begin salivating if given meat powder (or even a weak acid solution), so when he wanted his dogs to salivate, he would present meat powder to them. He noticed, however, that some of his dogs began salivating as soon as he brought them into the experimental room. Many theorists would have considered this an irritating interference to what they wanted to study. Pavlov, however, recognized that he was witnessing an interesting phenomenon, and he determined to study it in detail.

He therefore set up the situation shown in Figure 5.1. A dog was put into a harness, and the salivary gland was connected so that the amount of salivation could be measured. Then he presented meat powder and some neutral stimulus (e.g., a ringing bell) together to the dog. The meat powder of course elicited salivation in the dog; but after a few pairings of the bell and meat powder, the bell alone would elicit salivation. The bell, because of its association with the meat powder, had come to have similar effects on the dog's behavior.

Pavlov called the meat powder an **unconditioned stimulus (UCS)** to indicate that its effect on behavior was unlearned or automatic. He called the salivation response to the meat powder an **unconditioned response (UCR)**, again to indicate the unlearned nature of this response to the UCS. The bell was termed a **conditioned stimulus (CS)** because, though originally neutral, it developed (by association with the UCS) the ability to elicit a response that Pavlov called the **conditioned response (CR)**. The term *conditioned* was chosen to indicate that learning was involved in eliciting the CR by the CS.

It is important to realize that the CR and UCR are both salivation in this example, but they are considered to be different responses. This is because the UCR occurs automatically to the presentation of the UCS, while the CR develops only after several pairings of the UCS and CS. The CR is thus something new, a learned response to a formerly neutral stimulus.

If we now remove the UCS and present the CS alone, CRs will continue to occur for a while. Continued presentation of the CS without the UCS, however, eventually leads to **extinction** (a process in which the CS no longer reliably elicits a response).

From a motivational viewpoint, some of the motivating properties of the UCS (in terms of its ability to generate a response) are apparently acquired by the CS through association of the two stimuli. This means that neutral stimuli in our environment can come to have motivational influences on our behavior if they are paired with UCSs that are strongly motivational. For example, suppose that your instructor in this course announces on the first day of class that pop quizzes will constitute 50% of your final grade. Further, suppose that pop quizzes are highly anxiety producing for you,

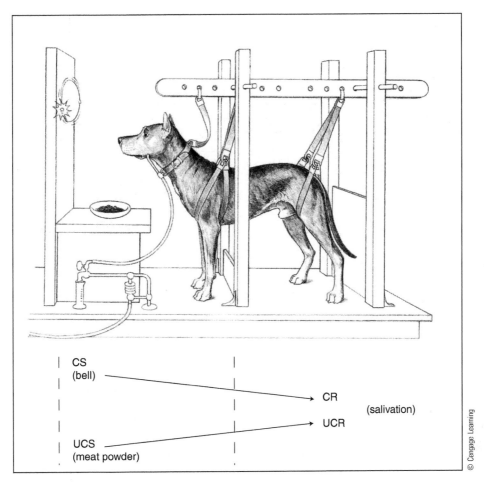

FIGURE 5.1 A typical Pavlovian setup. CS = conditioned stimulus; UCS = unconditioned stimulus; CR = conditioned response; UCR = unconditioned response.

as they are for many students. Your anxiety about whether there will be a quiz during class will lead automatically to autonomic changes associated with your aroused state—what are commonly called "butterflies in the stomach." Each day when you walk into class, you are anxious and have butterflies. The stimuli of the classroom, such as the greenish walls and cracks in the ceiling, will always be associated with your anxiety and will become capable of eliciting butterflies even on days when your instructor is absent or has announced that there will be no quiz. The formerly neutral cues of the room have now taken on motivational and

emotional properties for you and call forth the anxiety response.

Another important aspect of the classical conditioning of motivated states is that, for all practical purposes, the organism is passive in the learning process. If conditions are right, the learning will occur whether we want it to or not. This suggests that some maladaptive behaviors (e.g., phobias) may be learned via accidental pairings of neutral stimuli and negative emotional or motivational states.

There is considerable evidence that some maladaptive behaviors do result from classical conditioning situations. Pavlov was one of the first to demonstrate what is called experimental neurosis.

Experimental Neurosis

Pavlov (1960) was conducting an experiment to determine the ability of dogs to discriminate between the shapes of different objects. Projected on a screen in front of the animal was either a luminous circle or a luminous ellipse. The circle (CS) was accompanied by feeding (UCS), and salivation (CR and UCR) was measured. The dog quickly learned to salivate at the sight of the circle (Figure 5.2A). Once the conditioned response to the circle was well established, an ellipse was introduced with the axis ratio 2:1, as shown in Figure 5.2B. The

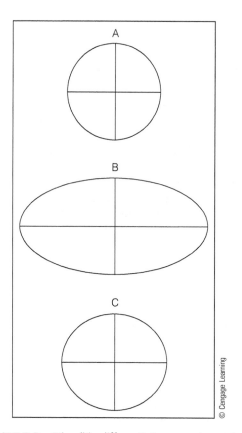

FIGURE 5.2 Stimuli in differentiation experiment that led to experimental neurosis. A = circle (axis ratio 1:1); B = ellipse (2:1); C = ellipse (9:8).

© Cengage Learning

ellipse was never paired with food, and the dog again quickly learned to salivate when the circle was presented but not when the ellipse was presented. Pavlov then began to change the axes of the ellipse so that it more closely approximated a circle. Each time the ellipse was changed, the dog showed that it could discriminate between the circle and the ellipse by salivating to the one but not the other. Eventually the axes were changed to a 9:8 ratio (Figure 5.2C), making the discrimination more difficult. After three weeks of testing the discrimination between the circle and the 9:8 ellipse, the dog's behavior began to worsen, and the conditioned response finally disappeared altogether. The dog, formerly quiet, now began moving around in the harness, bit the apparatus, and barked violently when led to the experiment room. When tested on the original discrimination between the circle and the 2:1 ellipse, there was now no evidence of discrimination. Pavlov noted that much of the behavior of the dog appeared similar to neurotic behavior seen in humans.

The **experimental neurosis** generated by Pavlov's discrimination experiment was apparently the result of the increasingly difficult discrimination. It began to interfere with behavior when the dog could no longer clearly discriminate. The task became very aversive for the dog, as evidenced by its restlessness and attack on the apparatus. The dog's reluctance to enter the discrimination room also indicated a strong motivation to avoid the frustrating situation. Of some theoretical interest is a point made by Mineka and Kihlstrom (1978). They argued that experimental neurosis is not generated by the classical conditioning procedure per se but by the organism's lack of predictability or controllability. As we shall see in Chapter 11, the ability to predict and control one's environment seems to have important motivational properties.

Classical conditioning, then, is associated with the acquisition of certain motivational states; however, it remained for Watson to show in a straightforward manner that classical conditioning can lead to the development of motivation and emotion.

John Watson and Rosalie Rayner (1920) classically conditioned a small boy to fear a white rat.

Albert, the infant in the experiment, was nine months old at the start of the experiment. Watson and Rayner tested Albert to determine what stimuli would be frightening to him. They quickly discovered that Albert was a very placid baby, showing no fear to a variety of objects (a white rat, a rabbit, a dog, a monkey, masks with and without hair, cotton wool, and even burning newspapers). The only stimulus that would reliably elicit any emotionality in Albert was the sound made when a ¾-inch-thick steel bar was struck with a hammer behind him without warning. Albert would start violently at the sound, check his breathing, raise his arms, tremble, and start to cry. The sound made by striking the bar was thus a UCS for the emotional response (UCR) of fear that Albert demonstrated.

When Albert was 11 months old, the experiment proper was begun. A white rat (CS) was presented to Albert. Just as he touched the rat, the bar was struck and he would start violently. After only two pairings of the rat and the sound, Albert became wary of the rat, no longer immediately reaching out for it. After a total of only seven pairings, Albert would begin to cry immediately upon presentation of the rat and start to crawl away so quickly that he had to be kept from falling off the examination table. It seems clear that at this point, the formerly neutral stimulus of the white rat had become an aversive stimulus that produced both emotionality and motivated behavior (as evidenced by Albert's attempts to crawl away).

Five days after the initial pairing of the rat with the sound, Watson and Rayner ran generalization tests. They were interested in determining if Albert was now only afraid of white rats or whether other similar objects might also elicit fear from him. They presented Albert with a rabbit, a dog, and a fur coat. For all three he began crying and attempted to crawl away. Albert was also wary of cotton wool (which has a furry appearance) but did not cry and eventually began to play with it. He also showed negative reactions to Watson's hair and to a Santa Claus mask. The emotionality had clearly generalized to other furry objects. A second set of generalization tests was conducted 31 days later. Albert still showed withdrawal behavior to the furry stimuli, but the reactions were much less intense than formerly. Classically conditioned emotional responses, then, can be relatively permanent. By today's standards, Watson and Rayner's generalization tests were not correctly conducted because they reconditioned little Albert several times between the initial conditioning procedure and the subsequent generalization tests (Harris, 1979). Nevertheless, their research was widely read, and subsequent research has confirmed that classically conditioned responses do generalize (Schneiderman, 1973), though the replicability of Watson and Rayner's experiment is less certain (Harris, 1979).

The search for the relationship between neurotic, maladaptive behaviors and the stimuli that trigger those behaviors was also studied by Liddell (1954). He used classical conditioning procedures to study emotionality in sheep and goats. He found that if the UCS produced an emotional UCR, then a CS paired with the UCS would also produce an emotional response. Liddell found that experimental neuroses developed in his sheep when electric shock was used to condition leg flexion, and the animal's task was made difficult. The neuroses, once developed, generalized from the experimental situation to the barn and pasture as well. Neurotic sheep displayed fast, irregular heartbeats during sleep and were very sensitive to external stimuli of any kind. When under attack by roaming dogs, the neurotic sheep were invariably the ones killed; when threatened, they ran off by themselves rather than following the flock and were thus easily attacked. Interestingly, Liddell found that young lambs could be protected from experimental neuroses simply by having their mothers present in the experiment room during the classical conditioning sessions. Under these conditions the lambs showed no neurotic behavior.

Elimination of Motivated Behaviors Through Conditioning

Just as motivation may result from the pairing of a neutral stimulus with an emotion-arousing unconditioned stimulus, so may reactions be eliminated in a similar manner. Perhaps the first person to demonstrate this was Mary Cover Jones (1924; Krasner, 1988). She was able to successfully eliminate a fear reaction to furry objects in a 3-year-old boy known as Peter by pairing the feared object with a positive (i.e., pleasant) UCS. Thus she showed that classical conditioning could be used to reduce fears as well as produce them. (Incidentally, she also showed that fears could be reduced via imitation of others who did not fear the object—presaging Bandura's Observational Learning techniques discussed later in this chapter.) Rachlin (1976) noted that maladaptive reactions may be eliminated either through extinction procedures or through a process called **counterconditioning**, in which the negative CS is paired with a strongly positive UCS (as Jones had shown). In the counterconditioning procedure, the negative CS gradually loses its aversiveness by being paired with the positive UCS and by no longer being paired with a negative UCS. Therefore, in addition to extinction of the response produced by the original CS–UCS relationship, a new positive response is generated to replace it. Counterconditioning is generally preferred over extinction procedures because it provides a specific positive response to replace the negative conditioned response.

Wolpe (1958, 1973) developed a therapeutic technique termed **systematic desensitization** that employs counterconditioning as part of its procedure. In systematic desensitization the patient is first taught to relax deeply on command (this command will eventually be used as a positive UCS for the positive UCR of relaxation). Once the person can relax on command, a list of anxiety-producing situations that involve the CS is made. The list (called an **anxiety hierarchy**) is arranged from least anxiety producing to most anxiety producing. The person is told to think about the first (least) anxiety-provoking situation on the list and is given the command to relax. Once the individual can relax at the same time that he or she is thinking about this situation, the individual is asked to think about the second situation on the list and to relax. This continues until the individual can think about the most anxiety-arousing situation and at the same time relax. When this has been achieved, the person is said to be

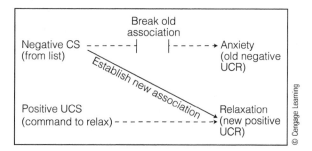

FIGURE 5.3 Wolpe's systematic desensitization technique.

desensitized. Thus, through the pairing of a negative CS (e.g., some anxiety-arousing thought) with a positive UCS (the command to relax), the negative state loses its aversiveness. The situation is diagrammed as shown in Figure 5.3.

It seems clear that motivational states can be acquired and eliminated through the process of classical conditioning. An additional line of evidence supporting the importance of classical conditioning of motivated behavior comes from Russian research on the conditioning of internal states, a procedure termed interoceptive conditioning.

Interoceptive Conditioning

Interoceptive conditioning is defined by Razran (1961) as classical conditioning in which either the CS, UCS, or both are applied directly to the internal organs or the mucosa.

Three types of interoceptive conditioning have been demonstrated. In **intero-exteroceptive conditioning** the CS is applied internally, while the UCS is applied externally. Razran reported a Russian experiment that conforms to this design. A female dog had a rubber balloon, through which cool water could be irrigated, inserted into the uterus. Paired with the CS of cool water was the presentation of food, which of course elicited salivation as the UCR. In just six to nine trials the cool water began eliciting salivation and became a stable response after only 25 pairings. That the cool water was indeed the stimulus controlling the CR was shown by the fact that the dog could learn to discriminate water temperature, salivating when cool water (8°–12°C) was irrigated through the balloon but not salivating when warm water (44°–48°C) was irrigated.

Intero-interoceptive conditioning occurs when both the CS and the UCS are applied internally. Again the Soviet literature demonstrates such conditioning (Razran, 1961). Loops were formed in the intestines of several dogs and could then be manually distended. Distensions of the intestinal loops served as a CS, which was paired with the delivery of carbon dioxide (CO_2) to the lungs (UCS). Inhalation of CO_2 leads to changes in respiration rate, described as defensive breathing. Conditioning occurred after only 3 to 6 pairings of intestinal distension and CO_2 inhalation and became stable after 5 to 16 trials. Thus intestinal distension acquired the ability to produce defensive breathing in dogs.

Extero-interoceptive conditioning occurs when an external CS is paired with an internal UCS. A human conditioning experiment reported by Razran (1961) can serve as an example of this type of conditioning. Human participants hospitalized because of urinary complications volunteered to have balloons inserted into their bladders. A series of dials was connected to the balloons so that the patient could see whether the balloon was being inflated or not. Thus the dials served as an external CS, which was paired with an internal UCS of bladder distension.

Inflation of the balloon led to reports of a strong urge to urinate, as would normally occur if the bladder were filling with urine. After several pairings of the dial readings with balloon inflation, the experimenters disconnected the dials, so that inflation of the balloons was not gauged, and manipulated the CS and UCS independently. The patients reported strong urges to urinate when the dial readings were high, even though balloon inflation was absent. This of course indicates that the dial readings had become conditioned stimuli that elicited the internal response of the urge to urinate. Low dial readings failed to produce the urge to urinate, even when the inflow of air was considerably higher than the amount that normally

produced the urge. Clearly internal changes can become associated with external stimuli.

A real-life situation that appears comparable to this experiment occurs when a physician asks you for a urine sample as part of a physical examination. The physician will usually lead you to the bathroom and turn on a water faucet before leaving you alone. The sound of running water is an external stimulus that is always associated with urination and has become a CS for urination. This sound almost always helps even the most reluctant person to provide the necessary sample.

Implications of Interoceptive Conditioning   Razran (1961) reported a total of 14 experiments involving interoceptive conditioning of one or another of the three types mentioned. These 14 experiments represent hundreds of experiments that the Soviets carried out on this type of conditioning in both animals and humans. Razran pointed out that these experiments have some important implications for our understanding of behavior.

First, we are usually *unaware of interoceptive conditioning* when it occurs. Thus some of our behavior will be unconscious to the extent that it is the result of interoceptive conditioning. Second, *interoceptive conditioning cannot really be avoided.* We carry the stimuli with us no matter where we go. It is reasonable to expect that some behaviors will result from the pairing of internal or external changes with bodily changes that happen to occur at the same time. Third, the research examined by Razran indicates that *interoceptive conditioning is more permanent* (more resistant to extinction) than typical external classical conditioning. Thus interoceptive conditioning can have long-term effects on our behavior. Finally, interoceptive conditioning has important implications for psychosomatic medicine (Buck, 1976; Tarpy & Mayer, 1978). For example, an anxiety-producing UCS that causes vasoconstriction (resulting in increased blood pressure) could become associated with tests (an external CS) so that a student becomes hypertensive in school situations. It is also important to keep in mind that conditioning may generalize to other similar situations so that test anxiety could lead to hypertension in other competitive situations.

The studies noted by Razran suggest both that motivated behavior may develop as a result of interoceptive conditioning and that we are often largely unaware of the reasons for our behavior because we are not conscious of the conditioning process when it occurs. Interoceptive conditioning can potentially play an important role in the motivation of behaviors over which we have little voluntary control; and some maladaptive behaviors might be developed in just this way.

Another area of study in which it has become apparent that classical conditioning influences motivation is taste-aversion learning. Originally it was felt that this type of learning situation was fundamentally different from classical conditioning of other behaviors (Rozin & Kalat, 1971); however, as noted by Domjan and Burkhard (1982), the learning process does appear to be one of classical conditioning. As we shall discover, however, the CS–UCS relationships in taste-aversion learning are rather different from the typical arrangements of these stimuli in standard classical conditioning.

Learned Aversions

Research associated with the topic of learned aversions has appeared under a variety of headings. Sometimes it is termed **long-delay learning** or **taste-aversion learning**, both of which describe some characteristics of the early research. **Learned aversions**, however, seems the more appropriate heading for our purposes because it emphasizes the motivational nature of the learned behaviors.

People have long known that it is very difficult to poison rats because, once poisoned, rats will avoid the bait that made them ill. Several learned-aversion studies provide some insight into why rats are so difficult to poison. A study by Garcia and Koelling (1966) provides us with our first clues. Garcia and Koelling presented one group of rats with the opportunity to drink water. At the time of drinking, an audiovisual display occurred that consisted of a flashing light and a clicking sound.

To use the researchers' terminology, the rats were exposed to "bright-noisy water." Another group of rats was also given the opportunity to drink water, but rather than an audiovisual display, the water they were given was distinctly flavored (either sweet or salty) and thus could be labeled "tasty water."

After drinking their solutions, the groups were bombarded with X-rays, which produced nausea and gastrointestinal disturbance. Two additional groups received footshock rather than the illness-inducing X-rays. The results of the study showed that the animals who had the tasty water and X-rays later avoided the flavored solution; they had formed a learned aversion to the taste of the water as a result of the illness. Of particular interest, however, was the finding that the animals with bright-noisy water did not develop an aversion to the water as a result of the X-rays. The two footshock groups showed just the opposite effects; the taste of the water did not become associated with the shock, but the audiovisual display did. Figure 5.4 shows the results of these tests.

The important point of the experiment was that the taste cues were associated very easily with illness but not with the footshock. The audiovisual cues, on the other hand, were readily associated with shock but not with illness. What the rats learned was constrained by their biological heritage. It would be adaptive to associate tastes and illness quickly, while little advantage (for rats) would occur in associating taste with some external painful agent. On the other hand, stimulation of the distance receptors (vision, hearing) would provide information about the external environment that would be useful if easily associated with externally harmful events such as pain to the foot.

In a second experiment, Garcia, Ervin, and Koelling (1966) showed that the taste-illness connection can be made even when the interval between tasting and illness is as long as 75 minutes. Thus rats are apparently programmed in such a way that they can associate illness with specific tastes, even though the illness may not occur for a considerable time after a substance has been ingested. It is not hard to see the adaptiveness of a mechanism

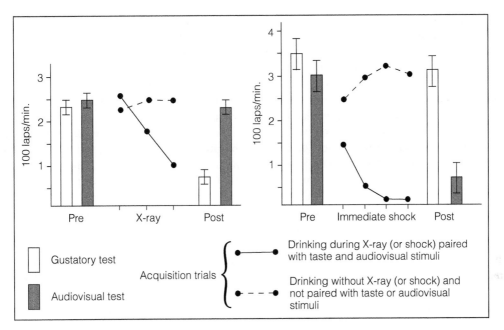

FIGURE 5.4 Water intake (measured in hundreds of laps per minute) before (Pre), during, and after (Post) learned aversion acquisition. As can be seen, nausea produced by X-rays reduced water intake associated with taste cues, both during and after acquisition, while intake was unaffected by the audiovisual display. The graph on the right shows that, although shock was not associated with the taste of water, it became associated with the audiovisual stimulation. From "Relation of Cue to Consequence in Avoidance Learning," by J. Garcia and R. A. Koelling, 1966, *Psychonomic Science, 4,* 123–124. Copyright © 1966 by the Psychonomic Society. Used by permission.

that allows associations to be made across long periods of time. This, in conjunction with the rat's sensitivity in associating illness with taste, points out why they are so difficult to poison. If the poison doesn't kill them the first time, the battle is lost, because the taste–illness association formed will strongly motivate the rats to avoid that substance in the future.

The taste aversion research just mentioned indicates that animals are predisposed to learn some associations more readily than others. This concept leads to the idea that there are **biological constraints** on what can be learned. Along these lines, Seligman (1970) proposed that the associability of events in the environment can be described as existing along a continuum. At one end of the continuum are events that can be easily and quickly

associated; these are said to be **prepared associations**. At the other extreme are associations that an organism apparently cannot learn; these are called **contraprepared associations**. Between the two extremes are said to be **unprepared associations** because, though they can be learned, numerous experiences with the events are necessary for an association to be formed. The **preparedness hypothesis** argues that different species will have evolved different prepared, unprepared, and contraprepared associations as a result of the selective pressures of evolution. Thus a species may quickly learn a response to one set of environmental circumstances but not to another set because evolution has prepared one type of association to be easily formed—while at the same time making other associations difficult or impossible. Thus biological constraints on learning exist and must be considered if we are to understand motivation.

Learned aversions with strong motivational properties for future behavior can be formed in several species in addition to rats and using stimuli other than taste. For example, quail learn to avoid water after having been made ill, and they can associate the illness to both taste and visual cues. In fact, for quail the visual cue appears to be more important (Wilcoxon, Dragoin, & Kral, 1971). Domjan, Miller, and Gemberling (1982) developed an aversion to the shape of cookies in vervet and grivet monkeys. The monkeys in this study were made ill after eating circular cookies but not bar-shaped cookies and were tested in total darkness so that visual cues could not be used. The monkeys discriminated the shapes by touch and developed an aversion to the circular cookies but continued to eat the bar-shaped cookies even when the illness-inducing injection was delayed for up to 30 minutes. It seems clear that aversion to cues associated with illness can occur with sensory modalities other than taste and is a general phenomenon seen in numerous species. Learned taste aversions have also been demonstrated in humans, as we will see in the following section.

Learned Taste Aversions in Cancer Patients

Several drugs used in the treatment of cancer produce side effects of nausea and vomiting. It is also well known that cancer patients frequently suffer loss of appetite (termed anorexia). Ilene Bernstein (1978) designed a study to determine if this loss of appetite might be a learned aversion that develops as the result of associating the taste of food eaten before the nausea-inducing chemotherapy.

Bernstein chose as participants 41 children (ages ranging from 2 to 16 years) who were receiving chemotherapy on an outpatient basis. One group of patients received a novel, unusual-tasting ice cream shortly before the drug treatment. A second control group was given no ice cream prior to the drug therapy. A third group, also serving as a control, was given ice cream but received a drug that did not produce nausea and vomiting.

The group that received the ice cream before becoming nauseated from the chemotherapy showed an aversion to the ice cream when offered it 2 to 4 weeks later. Neither of the two control groups showed any aversion to the ice cream. A retest conducted 4½ months after the first test and using a new ice cream revealed that the aversion for the initial ice cream was still present.

Of particular interest was that most of the children knew the nausea and vomiting were results of their drug therapy, not of the ice cream; yet aversion to the ice cream still developed. Humans, like rats, appear prepared to associate illness with the taste of previously ingested foods. Probably at least part of the appetite loss experienced by patients undergoing chemotherapy results from a learned aversion that develops from associating previously eaten foods with side effects of the drug treatment.

In a later study, Bernstein (1991) showed that aversions will also develop to familiar foods that have been paired with gastrointestinal toxic chemotherapy. Foods high in protein (see, e.g., Brot, Braget, & Bernstein, 1987) seemed especially vulnerable to this aversion. Of particular interest, she showed that if a novel taste is introduced between the time of the normal meal and the chemotherapy, the novel taste will interfere with the development of the aversion to the familiar meal. The novel taste is avoided, but the development of an aversion to it seems to protect the meal from becoming aversive. Such effects may be important in developing strategies to help patients on chemotherapy maintain adequate food intake.

As we have just seen, conditioned aversions may partially account for changes in the eating patterns of cancer patients undergoing chemotherapy treatments. There is also evidence that the nausea and vomiting often associated with chemotherapy can become conditioned to stimuli in the environment (Burish & Carey, 1986). Thus the stimuli of the doctor's office, smells, tastes, or even thoughts concerning the chemotherapy can come to elicit nausea and vomiting independent of the actual physical effects of the therapy.

Burish, Carey, Krozely, and Greco (1987) sought to determine whether **progressive muscle relaxation therapy (PMRT)** and **guided relaxation imagery (GI)** could be used to prevent the development of conditioned nausea and vomiting. Two groups of patients undergoing chemotherapy were used in the experiment. One group was trained in PMRT and GI prior to the first chemotherapy injection and used these techniques later to relax before scheduled injections. The second group, which received no PMRT or GI training, acted as a control group and simply rested quietly before injections were given.

The results of the study showed that PMRT and GI training reduced the feelings of nausea during the chemotherapy sessions in the trained group relative to the control group as measured by both self-reports and nurse reports. Although no significant differences between the two groups were found during the first three chemotherapy sessions, sessions four and five produced significantly more nausea in the control group. This finding is especially important because conditioned nausea and vomiting generally take three or more sessions to develop. Apparently the relaxation training reduced the severity, and perhaps prevented the development, of conditioned nausea in the trained group.

The amount of anxiety, nausea, and vomiting was also monitored at home during the 72 hours following chemotherapy. Once again, the relaxation-trained group reported lower levels of anxiety, nausea, and vomiting. As Figure 5.5 clearly shows, the relaxation-trained group was considerably below the control group on all three measures.

The nausea and vomiting produced by chemotherapy agents can be very aversive and in some cases severe enough to lead the patient to refuse treatment (Wilcox, Fetting, Nettesheim, & Abeloff, 1982). Some part of the aversiveness of chemotherapy is potentially the result of a conditioned aversion to the stimuli associated with the treatment. The relaxation procedure of Burish and associates (1987) is important because it seems to be capable

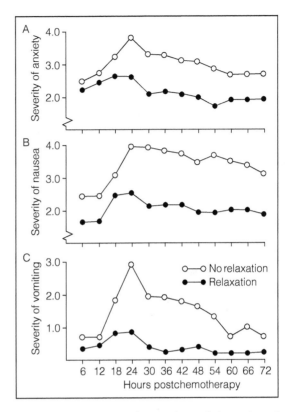

FIGURE 5.5 Mean patient ratings of A, anxiety; B, nausea; and C, vomiting; during the first 72 hours after chemotherapy. From "Conditioned Side Effects Induced by Cancer Chemotherapy: Prevention Through Behavioral Treatment," by T. G. Burish, M. P. Carey, M. G. Krozely, and F. A. Greco, 1987, *Journal of Consulting and Clinical Psychology, 55,* 42–48. Copyright © 1987 by the American Psychological Association. Used by permission.

of reducing the severity of the conditioned nausea and vomiting linked with such treatments.

Burish and his associates propose that PMRT and GI interfere with the development of conditioned nausea and vomiting by diverting attention from the chemotherapy context and thus blocking conditioning to those contextual cues. A second mechanism noted by these researchers that may limit the conditioned nausea and vomiting is the reduction of muscle contractions along the gastro-intestinal tract. PMRT and GI may reduce these contractions and thus reduce feelings of nausea and vomiting. Finally, Burish and associates suggest that PMRT and GI may interrupt conditioning of nausea and vomiting because these procedures reduce anxiety. When PMRT and GI are not used, the anxiety experienced may provide cues that can elicit nausea and vomiting through conditioning.

The work of Burish and his colleagues is an important step in reducing the strong negative motivation that often develops with chemotherapy treatment. Their work is also significant in showing how easily aversive motives can be learned through classical conditioning.

As the studies discussed in this section show, classical conditioning can lead to the development of motivated behavior in several different kinds of experimental situations. It therefore seems reasonable that some everyday behaviors are motivated by cues that originally gained the power to activate responses through the process of classical conditioning. Instrumental conditioning also seems to be a factor in the motivation of behavior. In the next section we will examine some of the variables that seem to influence the motivation of instrumentally conditioned behavior.

Instrumental Conditioning

If we are to understand the motives underlying the behaviors we observe, we must first understand how some of these motives are acquired. As we have seen, one way is through the process of classical conditioning; another way, that we will now examine, is through the reinforcement of appropriate responses, called **instrumental (or operant) conditioning**.

Whether classical and instrumental conditioning are really different processes has been the subject of considerable debate (Davis & Hurwitz, 1977), but the situations under which one or the other occurs often seem different. Classical conditioning results from the association of stimuli, while operant conditioning occurs as a consequence of a response. Whether underlying processes involved in the two situations are different or not is certainly debatable. However, we will treat them here as if they are separate processes.

Modern ideas on instrumental conditioning have evolved from the early work of Thorndike (1913), who argued that the consequences of a response strengthen the connection between that response and some stimulus in the environment. The strengthening of this connection was termed **the law of effect**, clearly the forerunner of our present concept of **reinforcement**. Skinner (1938) emphasized the idea that reinforcement serves not so much to strengthen a connection between a stimulus and a response but rather to strengthen the response itself, making its occurrence more probable. Though one can analyze the situation as one in which the response is strengthened by reinforcement, one can just as logically argue that the effect of reinforcement is to motivate behavior. (Skinner, however, preferred to analyze behavior without any reference to motivational constructs.)

The motivational properties of reinforcement have led some theorists, such as Bindra (1969), to propose that reinforcement and incentive motivation are two labels for the same phenomenon. Thus, depending on one's theoretical point of view, much of the literature on reinforcement can be interpreted as evidence of incentive motivation; similarly, much of the data on incentive motivation can be analyzed from a reinforcement point of view (incentive motivation will be examined in Chapter 6). The important point for us here is that instrumental procedures lead to the acquisition and/or strengthening of behaviors, which are motivated by the consequences of those behaviors.

Consider an hypothetical example. Suppose a school child discovers that hard work and good grades are consistently followed by strong praise from parents. If the praise is a strong reinforcer, the child will become motivated to work hard in order to obtain more praise from the parents. Now imagine another child whose parents do not particularly value good grades, and therefore do not reinforce academic performance, but do strongly reinforce their child's athletic ability. It is not hard to imagine that schoolwork for the second child will be relatively unimportant and perhaps only minimally tolerated because it allows him or her to play sports. We can generalize the example a little further and note that society rewards and punishes us for certain behaviors but not for others. Each society has different ideas of what behaviors are acceptable and will, therefore, shape our behavior. To the extent that different groups within a society also reinforce different behaviors, persons exposed to those groups will be motivated to respond in different ways. To a child growing up in the city, assertiveness and being resourceful might be strongly reinforced, while a child growing up in the farm belt may learn that hard work and patience are rewarded.

We can manipulate reinforcement in several ways that subsequently alter behavior. For example, we can alter the quantity of reinforcement and determine if large versus small rewards motivate behavior in different ways. Similarly, we can vary the quality of reinforcement and note the effect of this manipulation on behavior. We can even impose different time delays between the response and subsequent reinforcement and note behavioral changes that take place as a result. Finally, we can change a reinforcer after behavior has been established and see how contrasts between differing reinforcers influence responding. Considerable research exists on the effects of these various manipulations and can be found in any comprehensive learning textbook. Though it is beyond the scope of this text to examine this experimentation in all its complexity, we will look briefly at some general findings in each of these areas and caution the reader that many conflicting data also exist.

Quantity, Quality, and Contrasts of Reinforcement

In 1942, Crespi conducted an experiment in which different groups of rats received different amounts of reinforcement for running down an alleyway.

Rats that received larger rewards ran faster than rats that received smaller rewards; thus the amount of reward led to differing levels of performance. Crespi's experiment, as we will see in the next chapter, was used as evidence for the incentive motivational effects of reinforcement, because when he later switched the rats to a common amount of reinforcement, the behavior of all groups quickly approached the same level of performance. The initial differences in performance, however, typify the basic findings when amount of reinforcement is studied; the greater the quantity, the better the performance. This positive correlation between amount of reinforcement and performance has been dubbed the **amount of reinforcement (AOR) effect** by Bolles (1975).

The general results of Crespi's study have been replicated several times (Metzger, Cotton, & Lewis, 1957; Zeaman, 1949), and the AOR effect has been found in various situations. Based on these studies, we may conclude that increasing amounts of reinforcement usually lead to more intense or vigorous behavior. Amount of reinforcement, however, does not seem to lead to greater persistence of behavior; in fact large reinforcements lead animals to stop responding more quickly when reinforcement is withdrawn in extinction (Hulse, 1958; Wagner, 1961). This somewhat surprising finding suggests that the motivational effect of amount of reinforcement is short lived; it increases performance as long as it is present, but behavior is quickly reduced in its absence.

Like quantity of reinforcement, quality of reinforcement also has motivational effects. For example, Simmons (1924) reinforced different groups of rats with different kinds of food for finding their way through a complex maze. The group rewarded with bread and milk performed better than a second group given sunflower seeds, which in turn performed better than a third group given nothing. Likewise, Elliot (1928) found that rats perform better for wet bran than for sunflower seeds. Thus a general quality of reinforcement effect alters performance in much the same way as amount of reinforcement. This **quality of reinforcement effect (QOR)** has been found in numerous experimental situations, including complex mazes, T-mazes, runways, and runways, and operant chambers (see Bolles, 1975, for a review of this older literature).

A most interesting effect of manipulating reinforcement variables is the behavioral change one finds if the amount or quality of reinforcement is altered within an experiment. In Crespi's experiment, rats receiving both large and small amounts of reinforcement were switched to a medium amount. Before the switch to a common amount of reinforcement, the groups were performing quite differently, with the animals receiving the large reward running the fastest, followed by the medium-reward group, and finally the small-reward group. After the switch to the medium amount of reinforcement for all groups, the group that had been previously receiving the large amount

performed worse than the control group, which had been receiving this amount all along. This effect has been termed **negative contrast**. In opposite fashion, the original small-reward group performed better than the controls when switched to the medium amount of reinforcement. This effect has been called **positive contrast**.

The results of Crespi's experiment are shown in Figure 5.6. Positive and negative contrast effects have important implications for the motivation of behavior because they show that the **history of reinforcement** influences responding on current conditions of reinforcement. For rats in the small-reward group in Crespi's experiment, a switch from 1 to 16 pellets was a large change, which they reflected by overshooting the performance of the group that had received 16 pellets from the

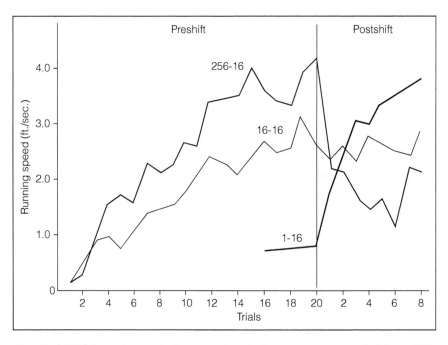

FIGURE 5.6 Crespi's (1942) incentive motivation experiment. Groups were given 1, 16, or 256 pellets of food. On trial 20 all groups were switched to 16 pellets. Note how running speed shifts rapidly when the conditions of reinforcement change. Adapted from "Quantitative Variation of Incentive and Performance in the White Rat," by L. P. Crespi, 1942, *American Journal of Psychology, 55*, 467–517. Copyright © 1942 by the University of Illinois Press. Used by permission.

beginning. On the other hand, rats in the large-reward group, switched from 256 to 16 pellets, experienced a huge change downward from what they had formerly received, and their performance dropped drastically to a level below that of the group that had continuously received 16 pellets. Because all groups were receiving the same amount of reward after the switch, the behavioral differences must have resulted from the differing histories of reinforcement that the groups had experienced.

Research conducted after Crespi's usually found negative contrast but sometimes had difficulty demonstrating positive contrast. Dunham (1968), in a review of the literature at that time, concluded that positive contrast does not exist and that when it does appear in experiments, it is due to comparisons against an inappropriate control group. Flaherty (1982), however, later reviewed contrast effects and found that positive contrast is a reliable phenomenon.

Contrast effects also occur when quality of reinforcement is changed in an experiment. Typically, shifts in the quality of reward lead to shifts in performance that are similar to those seen when amount of reinforcement is changed (Panksepp & Trowill, 1971).

One final contrast situation should be mentioned. It is particularly interesting because it involves changes in both amount and quality, although the research has not typically been analyzed from a contrast point of view. The research concerns **latent learning**—that is, learning in the absence of any reinforcement. Blodgett (1929) conducted an experiment in which one group of rats was reinforced with food for learning to traverse a maze, while a second group received nothing. The nonreinforced group appeared to learn little. When food was later provided at the end of the maze, however, the performance of the nonreinforced group quickly matched that of the group that had been rewarded throughout, indicating that the nonreinforced rats had indeed learned the maze but were not inclined to demonstrate this learning until there was some motivation to do so. The

introduction of food for the nonreinforced group represents a contrast between nothing and something. Presumably the introduction of food is an increase not only in amount but also in quality, and a strong change in performance occurs.

The importance of the latent learning experiment and others related to it (Buxton, 1940; Seward, 1949) was to argue that the effect of reinforcement is on performance (motivation) rather than on learning. Although this issue was hotly debated at the time and has never been completely resolved, it seems clear that one major effect of reinforcement is to alter the motivation of the organism. Changes in quantity, quality, and particularly contrasts between different levels of quantity and quality have large effects on motivation. Whether these variables also directly affect learning is less clear.

Primary and Conditioned Reinforcement

So far we have not distinguished between various types of reinforcement. This has been intentional because the principal characteristic of a **reinforcer** is that it increases the probability of the response that it follows. Nevertheless, we commonly make a distinction between **primary reinforcers**, which increase a response because of their very nature (unlearned reinforcers such as food, water, sex, avoidance of pain, and so on), and **secondary reinforcers** (or **conditioned reinforcers**), which come to control responding because they have been associated with primary reinforcers in the past.

Generalized Conditioned Reinforcers

Suppose a stimulus is paired with not just one primary reinforcer but several, perhaps in many different situations. What would be the effect of such multiple pairings? The stimulus would become what is called a generalized conditioned reinforcer (Reynolds, 1975). A **generalized conditioned reinforcer** gains its reinforcing properties from the several primary reinforcements with which it has been paired.

As a result, a generalized conditioned reinforcer can become somewhat independent of any individual primary reinforcer and strengthen or maintain behavior for a relatively long period of time even though not often paired with primary reinforcement. Perhaps the best example of a generalized conditioned reinforcer is money. Because money has been paired with so many reinforcers in the past it becomes a strong generalized conditioned reinforcer and will maintain behavior for long periods without recourse to primary reinforcement. Indeed some individuals appear to be so reinforced by money that increasing their supply of it becomes an end in itself.

Tokens and Token Economies

Money is not only a generalized conditioned reinforcer that can be used to maintain a variety of behaviors, it is also a **token** that serves as a reminder of the other reinforcers it will buy. Interestingly, humans are not the only animals capable of using conditioned reinforcers as tokens. For example, chimpanzees have often been used in research on token rewards. Early studies by Cowles (1937) and Wolfe (1936) showed that chimpanzees would learn a new response for token reinforcement (in these experiments poker chips could be traded for grapes) as quickly as for the grapes themselves and would learn new responses even when a delay of as much as 1 hour was instituted between the arrival of the token and its exchange for primary reinforcement. Chimps were also observed to beg and steal tokens from one another. Thus the tokens seemed to share many of the characteristics of money in human society.

Tokens other than money have also been used in several human applications. In a **token economy**, tokens are used as reinforcers for appropriate behavior and can later be exchanged for various reinforcers such as candy, cigarettes, television privileges, or other commodities and opportunities. Since the early work of Ayllon and Azrin (1968) with psychiatric patients, token economies have been used in a variety of settings such as schools (Nelson, 2010), mental institutions (Padgett,

Garcia, & Pernice, 1984), and even single individuals (Bernard, Cohen, & Moffett, 2009; Matson & Boisjoli, 2009).

Token economies have become a viable alternative to other methods of controlling unruly and inappropriate behavior and indeed, as noted later, have been used to alter a number of widely divergent behaviors. For example, Padgett et al. (1984) used tokens to help a severely retarded 25-year-old woman learn to stay on the pathways from one building to another at the institution where she lived. This woman had a 6-year history of wandering off the pathways and getting lost on the institutional grounds. The researchers paid the woman tokens for staying on the paths and charged her tokens for wandering. After only two days of this treatment, wandering was reduced to zero and remained near zero during the period in which tokens were given. A follow-up six months after treatment found that wandering was no longer a problem. Clearly the tokens were motivating enough to reduce her wandering.

A rather innovative application of token reinforcement was made by Jenson, Paoletti, and Peterson (1984). These researchers used tokens to reduce a behaviorally disturbed 10-year-old boy's chronic throat clearings. Prior to the use of tokens, the boy would clear his throat as many as 390 times in a 5-hour period. After 23 days in which he received tokens for reduced throat clearings, this behavior had dropped to as few as three throat clearings in a 5-hour period. In an educational setting, Udwin and Yule (1984) report some success with using tokens in teaching spelling words to an 11-year-old boy who had a spelling age of approximately 6 years.

One of the clearest examples of how a token economy can alter behavior is provided by Fox, Hopkins, and Anger (1987). These researchers conducted a long-term study of the effects of a token economy on accident and injury rates in two separate, dangerous, open-pit mines. As you are probably aware, mining is a hazardous occupation: in 1985, 500 people were killed in mining accidents and over 40,000 work-related injuries were reported (National Safety Council, 1986). Therefore any strategy that is useful in reducing these rates has important, and real, consequences.

Fox and his colleagues devised a token economy in which trading stamps were given to mine employees for working without accidents or injuries. These stamps could then be redeemed for various items at redemption stores. The stamps were awarded for several different categories of safety-related behavior. Employees were given stamps at the end of each month if they had not suffered a lost-time injury. Additionally, workers received extra stamps each month if all members of their work group had no lost-time injuries. Safety suggestions submitted by the workers and adopted by the mine were also rewarded with additional stamps.

Workers who missed days because of job-related accidents or injuries forfeited their monthly stamp award and monthly group award for 1 to 6 months depending on the number of days missed. Additionally, all members of an injured worker's group lost their monthly group award until the injured worker returned to work. Workers also lost the individual stamp award for one month for each $2000 worth of accident-related damage to mining equipment. Finally, failure to report an accident also resulted in loss of a month's stamp award for both the individual and the group.

The token economy thus promoted safe behavior (by awarding stamps) and punished accidents and injuries (by withholding stamps). The approach is especially ingenious for its use of social pressure to promote safety. The group stamp awards created a situation in which an accident or injury to any member of the group caused the group stamp award to be lost for all the members of that group. Thus there should have been social pressure on individuals to behave in a safe manner.

This token economy was initiated in the Shirley Basin mine in 1972 and continued for 12 years; in the Navajo mine the token economy was begun in 1975 and was still in use at the time of the article's publication (Fox, Hopkins, & Anger, 1987). When these economies were instituted, both mines had yearly averages of lost work days due to injuries that were three to eight times higher than the national average for all mines.

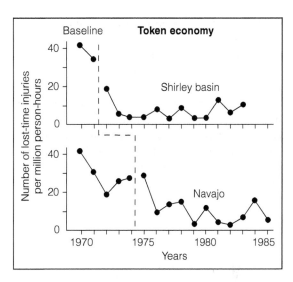

FIGURE 5.7   Number of related injuries by year (per million hours worked) that required one or more days lost from work. From "The Long-Term Effects of a Token Economy of Safety Performance in Open-Pit Mining," by D. K. Fox, B. L. Hopkins and W. K. Anger, 1987, *Journal of Applied Behavior Analysis, 20,* 215–224. Copyright © 1987 by The Johns Hopkins University Press. Used by permission.

The token economies had a dramatic effect on work-related injuries and accidents. As Figure 5.7 shows the number of lost-time injuries dropped at both mines. By the end of the second year of the economies, work-related injuries at the Shirley Basin mine had dropped to about 15% of the baseline period and for the Navajo mine to about 32% of the baseline period. Cost of injuries dropped from $294,000 a year during baseline to $29,000 a year average during the token economy at the Shirley Basin mine; at the Navajo mine they dropped from $367,696 to $38,972 a year. (The cost of the stamps during the period of the study varied between $9,288 and $12,522 a year at the Shirley Basin mine and $11,359 and $13,415 at the Navajo mine.) During the last 10 years of the token economy program the number of days lost to work injuries was about 1/4 the national average at the Shirley Basin mine and 1/12 the national average at the Navajo mine. Clearly the token economy had a large effect on behaviors associated with accidents and injuries.

Receiving the stamps appeared to be highly motivating. At one of the mines the union representative asked that the token program be written into the contract between the union and the company. Additionally, as an informal check, stamps were purposely omitted from eight workers' pay envelopes. The spouse of one of the workers called the mine demanding that the stamps be issued, and a second worker's spouse drove over 50 miles to pick up the missing stamps. If these two instances are representative of the general attitude of the workers and their families, then it seems clear that the stamps had strong motivational effects.

As these examples show, token economies can be used in a variety of settings to modify behaviors that have proven difficult to alter with more conventional techniques. Token economies may be particularly effective in situations where verbal methods are ineffective or difficult (see, e.g., the review of token economies with intellectually disabled and/or autistic children, Matson & Boisjoli, 2009). The modification and development of behaviors through the use of reinforcement provide flexibility and variability to behavior. As reinforcement is extended or withdrawn, people are motivated to behave in those ways that provide consistent reinforcement.

Many learning situations are actually composed of a combination of classical and operant conditioning. Several lines of research suggest that interactions between classical and operant conditioning have important motivational consequences too. In the next section we will examine research concerned with these interactions.

Classical-Operant Interactions in Motivation

Acquired Fear

We generally consider a stimulus motivating if an organism will learn a new operant response in order to either remain in the presence of that stimulus or to

remove itself from its vicinity. In a now-classic study, Miller (1948) showed that fear can be acquired and that its reduction will motivate new learning.

Miller used a two-compartment box like that shown in Figure 5.8. One compartment was painted white, and the other was painted black. The white side had a grid floor through which the animal could be shocked, while the black side was safe. The two compartments were separated by a door with horizontal black and white stripes. This door could either be opened by the experimenter or by the animal turning a wheel or a lever. Six-month-old male albino rats were given 10 shock trials in the white compartment after determination that the rats preferred neither the white nor black side. On each trial the experimenter dropped the door so that the rat could escape from shock in the white compartment into the safe black compartment.

Starting with the eleventh trial and continuing for five trials, each rat was placed in the white compartment and allowed to escape through the open door, though no shock was now being delivered. The rats readily performed the escape response from the white side even though shock was absent.

Following the five nonshock escape trials, 16 trials were run in which the rats had to turn the wheel slightly in order to cause the door to drop so that they could escape into the black side. Again during these trials, no shock occurred. In order to escape the white compartment, 13 of the 25 rats learned to turn the wheel. The 12 rats that failed to learn the response appeared to develop habits (e.g., freezing that interfered with learning the wheel-turning response. The 13 rats that did learn the wheel-turning response made the response more and more rapidly across the training trials, indicating that they understood the relationship between their behavior and the dropping of the door. Figure 5.9 shows the data from these animals.

After the sixteenth trial, the wheel-turning response was made inoperable, but pressing the lever would now cause the door to drop. Of the rats that had learned the wheel-turning response, 12

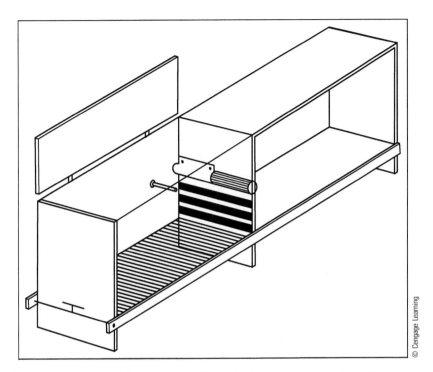

© Cengage Learning

FIGURE 5.8 Miller's 1948 acquired-drive apparatus. Shock is delivered through the grid floor on the left side of the box. Turning the wheel or pressing the lever causes the center door to drop so that the rat can enter the safe compartment on the right.

also learned to press the lever in order to drop the door, and again responding improved across trials.

Miller's experiment suggests that the cues of the white compartment became associated with the shock and developed the capability of motivating escape from the compartment. This motivation to avoid the cues of the white compartment could then be used to generate new, arbitrary responses such as wheel turning and lever pressing. These responses were presumably reinforced by the reduction of the white compartment cues that occurred when the rats succeeded in reaching the safe black compartment.

Incidentally, the motivation to avoid the white compartment was acquired through the pairing of the white compartment cues and shock, which is, of course, a classical conditioning situation. The motivation, once acquired, then generated operant behaviors that were reinforced by the reduction of

the white compartment cues that occurred when the rats reached the black side. This led some theorists (Mowrer, 1947) to argue that two factors are involved in avoidance behavior, a classically conditioned fear response and an operant response reinforced by a reduction in the acquired fear. Miller (1948) has suggested that neurotic symptoms might exemplify just this sort of situation; cues associated with fear motivate neurotic behavior, which is then reinforced by a temporary reduction in the anxiety.

The acquisition and subsequent motivating properties of aversive stimuli seem fairly well established. Brown, Kalish, and Farber (1951) showed that an acquired fear would energize other behaviors that are independent of the original fear-producing situation. For example, rats that had acquired a fear response showed a heightened startle reaction to the sound made by a toy popgun.

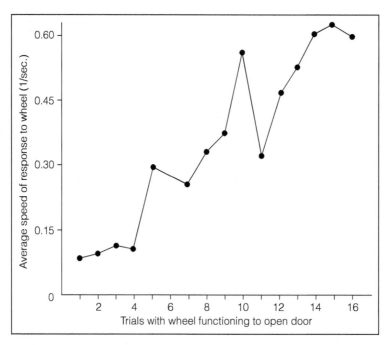

FIGURE 5.9   Average speed of wheel turning across the 16 trials in which wheel turning allowed access to the safe compartment. From Miller, 1948.

Conditioned Emotional Responses (CERs)

In a procedure termed **conditioned emotional response (CER)** training, an organism such as a rat is taught to press a lever in order to obtain food according to some schedule of reinforcement (e.g., a fixed-interval, 4-minute schedule). On such a schedule the rat can receive a pellet of food once every 4 minutes if the bar is pressed, but responses that occur prior to the scheduled interval go unreinforced. After behavior to the schedule has become consistent, the rat is subjected to pairings of a tone and shock, which are independent of the bar-pressing response using classical conditioning. If the tone is now presented alone (without shock), it will suppress the lever pressing for food. The disruption of the bar-press response is theorized to occur because the tone has become fear producing as a result of being paired with the shock. Thus, when the tone is sounded, a conditioned fear is generated in the animal that has the effect of suppressing ongoing behavior (lever pressing).

Thus, once again we see that a neutral stimulus can acquire emotional or motivational properties that lead to changes in behavior. One would expect that stimuli associated with positive emotional or motivational states ought to become conditioned motivators as well. While logically this should be true, the evidence for acquired motives based on positive states is not very convincing (Cofer & Appley, 1964). This asymmetry of effects possibly arises because of biological constraints on learning. Perhaps it is more adaptive to associate environmental stimuli with negative events, so as to avoid these events in the future, than to associate particular stimuli with positive events. Mineka (1975) has argued a similar point of view, suggesting that it would not be particularly adaptive for homeostatically controlled motives to be easily conditionable to external cues.

Learned Helplessness

We conclude this section with an examination of special learning conditions that seem to result in **demotivation** of behavior. This phenomenon has been termed *learned helplessness*.

Martin Seligman (1975, 1976) believed that learned helplessness is the laboratory analogue of reactive depression in humans. Learned helplessness can be defined as a psychological state involving a disturbance of motivation, cognitive processes, and emotionality as a result of previously experienced uncontrollability on the part of the organism. The learned helplessness phenomenon developed from studies on the interaction of Pavlovian and instrumental conditioning in avoidance learning (Maier, 1970; Overmier, 1968; Overmier & Seligman, 1967; Seligman & Maier, 1967; Weiss, Krieckhaus, & Conte, 1968). Seligman, for example, found that dogs given inescapable shock before being placed in a shuttlebox, where they can avoid the shock by jumping a hurdle, fail to learn the response. After initially struggling at the onset of shock in the shuttlebox, the dogs seem to give up and passively endure the shock.

How can we know if the results obtained in these experiments are caused by the uncontrollability of the situation or by the effects of the shock? To answer this question, researchers use what is called a **triadic design** (Seligman, 1975). In this design three groups are employed. One group is placed into a situation in which it can control its environment by making some response. For example, dogs might be trained to turn off shock by pressing a panel with their noses. A second group receives exactly the same conditions as the first group (shock), but no response they make has any effect in controlling the environment. The third group receives no treatment.

After this initial part of the experiment, all three groups are put into a new situation such as learning to jump a hurdle to escape or avoid shock. Results from experiments using the triadic design (Seligman & Maier, 1967) showed that the first group, which could control its environment, and the third group, which received no training, both learned the new response. The subjects of the second group, which had no control over their environment, initially were significantly slower to learn the new response and often did not learn it at all. Since Groups 1 and 2 both received exactly the same number of shocks, the differences in the second phase of the experiment must result from the fact that Group 1 could control its environment, while Group 2 could not. Also, the fact that Groups 1 and 3 both learned the new response showed that the aversiveness of the shock itself was not important to the effect. Thus we are forced to conclude that the helplessness effect results from the inescapability, not from the characteristics, of the shock (but see Lubow, Rosenblatt, & Weiner, 1981, for another view). Also worth noting is the point that the helplessness effect (the inability to learn to control one's environment as a result of previous experience of no control) is not the same as the theory of learned helplessness, which attempts to explain these effects.

The failure of the dogs to learn the avoidance response of jumping over the hurdle apparently resulted from the previously experienced inescapable shock. The dogs had learned that they were helpless to prevent shock earlier and therefore, when later transferred to the shuttlebox, failed to recognize that their behavior could now be effective in reducing the shock—and so they continued to be helpless. Dogs subjected to helplessness training are also different outside the experimental situation. When an experimenter attempts to remove them from their home cage, they do not resist, as normal dogs do, but sink to the bottom of the cage and adopt a submissive posture.

Although helplessness was originally demonstrated in dogs, it has also been shown in other species, including cats, fish, monkeys, rats, and even humans (Seligman, 1975). Surprisingly, rats have proven to be the most difficult organism with which to demonstrate helplessness; but if the response is difficult or unnatural (e.g., requiring three bar presses rather than one to turn off shock), helplessness also occurs in rats.

Symptoms of Helplessness

Passivity (Motivational Deficit) Seligman (1976) showed that four primary symptoms of helplessness exist: passivity, associative retardation, somatic effects, and reduction of helplessness with time. An example of passivity is provided in an experiment by Hiroto (1974). College students were put into an experimental situation in which they were subjected to inescapable noise. Later these participants were transferred to a second situation in which they could escape noise by moving their hands in a finger shuttlebox. Most of the participants sat passively, enduring the noise much as Seligman's dogs had taken shock. Participants in a control group that had initially learned to turn off the noise by pressing a button quickly learned to move their hands in order to silence the noise.

The passive aspects of learned helplessness can develop even if the situation is a positive one, such as in uncontrolled reward. Engberg and associates (1972) taught one group of pigeons to jump on a treadle to receive grain. A second group also received grain, but its delivery was unrelated to their responding. A third group received no grain. All three groups were then transferred to a situation in which they had to learn to peck a lighted key in order to obtain grain. The group that had originally learned to jump on the treadle learned the key-peck response fastest. The pigeons that had received nothing earlier were second fastest. And the group that had received "free" grain learned very slowly. Engberg and associates termed this effect **learned laziness**. Their data suggest that uncontrolled reward also makes animals less able to behave in order to receive reinforcement in the future. Seligman suggests that the passivity shown by animals in helpless situations is the result of a motivational deficit produced by the uncontrollability of events.

Retardation of Learning (Associative Retardation) Seligman noted that animals exposed to helplessness situations also develop a learning deficit. Dogs that eventually do learn to avoid shock after exposure to inescapable shock learn very slowly and often revert to their earlier behaviors of passively enduring the shock. Seligman suggested that the helpless animal has learned that the consequences of a situation cannot be altered by its behavior, which in turn makes it more difficult later for the animal to see that it can now influence what happens. Miller and Seligman (1975) also found evidence for retardation of learning in humans subjected to helplessness situations.

Somatic Effects Seligman (1976) found that helpless dogs and rats are much less aggressive in aversive or competitive situations than normal non-helpless animals. For example, if two rats are placed in a box in which the floor can be electrified and there is a safe pedestal large enough for only one rat, the rat that was earlier subjected to a learned helplessness situation invariably loses. Similarly, dogs subjected to inescapable shock as puppies always lose when competing for food with dogs that have had experience with controllable shock (Seligman, 1976). Maier, Anderson, and Lieberman (1972) obtained similar results with rats.

Reduction of Helplessness With Time Finally, Seligman noted that learned helplessness decreases with time. In the Overmier and Seligman (1967) study, dogs were helpless if tested a day after only one training session with inescapable shock. However, if a week lapsed before testing, helplessness had somewhat dissipated. Multiple training sessions with inescapable shock, however, lead to relatively permanent helplessness.

Causes and Prevention of Helplessness

The key to understanding the phenomenon of learned helplessness is the concept of control. Trauma (e.g., electric shock) by itself is not sufficient to produce learned helplessness as long as the organism can come to control the trauma in some manner. Learned helplessness results from the organism's act of learning that it cannot control what happens to it. Thus the expectation that behavior will be ineffective in changing a particular environment leads to a drastic reduction in attempts to control the environment in other situations. The helpless organism, in essence, gives up.

If control of the environment is actually the crucial component that determines the development of learned helplessness, teaching an organism that it can control its environment should reduce learned helplessness. Seligman, Maier, and Geer (1968) found that forcibly dragging helpless dogs from the shock side to the safe side of a shuttlebox eventually eliminated learned helplessness. Only by forcing the correct response from the animals could helplessness be overcome. Presumably the forced responding caused the animals to see that shock could be alleviated by responding. Other procedures (including tempting the dogs with Hebrew National Salami!) were ineffective (Seligman, 1976).

The concept of control also suggests that one might prevent the development of learned helplessness by first teaching animals to control their environments before subjecting them to helplessness situations and thus inoculate them against helplessness in this manner. Indeed, prior training in controlling shock prevents the development of learned helplessness in dogs that are later subjected to inescapable shock (Seligman & Maier, 1967).

Seligman's data on learned helplessness are very important for understanding the motivation of behavior. His analysis suggests that motivation in the present depends on experience with controlling one's environment. Lack of success in the past will tend to have a demotivating effect upon future behavior. When the lack of success (control) is extreme, the organism may stop responding altogether.

Seligman (1975, 1976) pointed out the similarity between the laboratory phenomenon of learned helplessness and the real-world phenomenon of depression. He believed that learned helplessness is an animal model for certain types of depression in humans. He proposed in particular that the symptoms of learned helplessness are similar to those of reactive depression, which seems to be triggered by some external event such as the loss of a job, death of a loved one, rejection, financial problems, physical disability, or even old age. For example,

depressed individuals tend to be passive, tend to have a negative cognitive set (i.e., they believe that their behavior will be ineffective), are usually less aggressive and less competitive than nondepressed persons, and usually improve with time. Depression, like learned helplessness, may be caused by the belief that responding will be useless in providing relief from aversive situations. Work on learned helplessness suggests that individuals suffering from reactive depressions might be helped by therapies that show them how their behavior can be effective in changing their environment.

The proposed similarity between learned helplessness in animals and depression in humans has generated great debate among theorists. Several criticisms of Seligman's approach include those of Costello (1978) and Wortman and Brehm (1975). Costello, for example, argued that data collected on depressed individuals by Seligman and his colleagues (Miller & Seligman, 1975) do not necessarily support the idea that the depressed individual believes that his or her behavior is ineffective but may indicate a general lowering of motivation in depressed persons.

A second, more damaging criticism of the learned helplessness model of depression is the fact that depressed persons usually feel guilty and blame their failures on their own inadequacies. It is hard to see how belief in a lack of control would lead to self-blame; rather the self-blame and guilt manifested by depressed individuals suggest that depressed persons believe that they do have control but that events still turn out wrong (Costello, 1978). The learned helplessness model of depression, then, does not predict the loss of self-esteem that is prevalent in cases of depression.

Criticisms leveled against the theory caused Seligman and his colleagues to reevaluate and reformulate the learned helplessness model of depression (Abramson, Seligman, & Teasdale, 1978). The reformulated theory emphasizes the importance of the individual's attribution of the reasons for lack of control. For example, the lack of control might result from some personal inability or simply uncontrollable factors. The amount of helplessness shown and its time course should be influenced by the attributions that one makes about why one has no control over events. The reformulated theory applies to human behavior, particularly to depression; however, an attributional analysis of helplessness does not appear necessary to explain the animal research. We will examine Seligman's reformulated theory in detail in Chapter 10, along with other attribution models of motivation.

The importance of Seligman's research as it relates to this chapter is that it points out, once again, the interaction of classical and operant conditioning in the motivation of behavior. Learned helplessness situations can lead to deficits in motivation, which then influence later behaviors in various situations. The results of helplessness studies point out the importance of past experience, formed in classical and operant conditioning situations, to alter the motivation for future behavior.

Observational Learning (Modeling)

We will continue this discussion by examining a third type of learning that has also been implicated in the acquisition and direction of motivated behavior.

Studies of observational learning are based on the idea that a large part of human behavior results from **vicarious learning**; that is, we all learn a great deal simply by observing others. This approach, called **social learning theory**, emphasizes the idea that social conditions are important determiners of behavior (Bandura, 1971; Rotter, 1954). Social learning theory was first recognized as an important contributor to behavior by Miller and Dollard (1941); however, Albert Bandura and his associates were influential in the development of several concepts of social learning theory that apply especially to motivation (Bandura, 1969, 1971, 1977).

Bandura argued that humans are neither compelled by inner forces, such as the Freudian model suggests, nor totally controlled by the environment, as held by the strict behaviorist model. Rather,

human functioning is best understood as the result of interactions between particular behaviors and the conditions that control them. Considerable emphasis is placed on vicarious, symbolic, and self-regulatory processes as determiners of behavior.

The social learning analysis of behavior argues that our ability to learn through observation (termed **modeling**) is large and allows us to build patterns of behavior without having to resort to trial and error. We learn to be motivated by particular objects in our environment, and we learn emotional responses to particular situations through modeling. These observed behaviors are stored symbolically and then retrieved at some later time to guide behavior. Our ability to represent events symbolically also allows us to foresee the probable consequences of a behavior and thus alter our behavior accordingly.

Finally, humans can regulate their own behaviors internally. We can reinforce ourselves for appropriate behavior and punish ourselves for inappropriate behavior. This **self-reinforcement** increases performance primarily through its motivational effects. In determining whether to reinforce ourselves, we compare our present behavior against that of others and our own past performances. We also evaluate our behaviors by noting how other people react to them. Finally, we will tend to adopt as standards of performance the standards that we observe in others (Bandura, 1977). As seen by social learning theory, then, we are active, observing organisms who profit from the experiences of others and can store these observations symbolically for future use and regulate our behavior through self-administered rewards and punishment.

An important point is that observational learning occurs without either the practicing of a response or reinforcement. Consider the various ways in which we could murder someone, as modeled for us by television. Most people can think of at least several ways in which the deed could be done, though few of these behaviors (one hopes) have actually been performed or rewarded. The point is that the potential behaviors have been learned, even though they have not been performed.

The primary **functions of reinforcement**, according to Bandura, are **informational** (telling us what effects our behavior has on the environment) and **motivational**. Rewards and punishers serve as motivators because they lead to the development of expectancies that particular responses will cause particular outcomes. Bandura argued that our cognitive abilities allow us to convert these expectancies into current motivators.

Modeling Processes: Attention, Retention, Reproduction

Attention   Before we can profit from the modeled behavior of others, we must first attend to their behavior. Accordingly, we will observe and imitate models with whom we are in frequent contact more than those we see less frequently. The characteristics of the model also influence our attention processes. Some models attract us so strongly that we cannot seem to avoid being influenced by the behaviors they depict. Television can sometimes serve as this sort of model.

Retention   Once we have observed a behavior, we must still incorporate it into memory in some form. Bandura argued that modeled behavior is stored in both a verbal code and an imaginal code. When trying to remember an observed behavior, we remember both a series of verbal instructions (turn the nut to the left) and an image of the behavior (imagining a wrench turning the nut to the left). The verbal and imaginal memory codes serve as a guide for reproducing the observed behavior (we pick up the wrench and turn the nut to the left). Rehearsal of the behavior, either actual or mental, improves the performance of the behavior. Interestingly, Bandura sees rehearsal as primarily aiding in the recall of the observed behaviors rather than in the strengthening of correct responses.

Reproduction   Even though we have observed and symbolically stored a behavior, we can imitate it only if we can string together the correct pattern of responses. Normally our responses are rough approximations of the observed behavior. We then refine these approximations as a result of the information feedback we receive about the consequences of the behavior. Thus, in teaching someone to serve in tennis, one first demonstrates the motions required to get the serve into the opposite court. The observer then approximates the serve (usually very roughly) and alters the next attempt based on the results of the first (e.g., hitting the ball in a more downward fashion if the first attempt was long).

Modeling Processes: Vicarious Reinforcement

While behavior is influenced by the direct reinforcement of responses, it is also influenced through observing the effects of a model's behavior. If we see a model being reinforced for a particular behavior, we too are likely to perform that behavior. On the other hand, if we observe the model being punished for a particular behavior, we will be less likely to perform that response ourselves. Such patterns are called **vicarious reinforcement** situations because we alter our behavior as a result of observing the consequences of others' behaviors.

Vicarious reinforcement can be distinguished from observational learning by noting that we may learn particular behaviors simply by observation without necessarily noting the consequences of those behaviors. However, observing the effects (reward or punishment) of a particular behavior performed by a model will alter the probability that we will perform the modeled behavior. Thus observation of reinforcement or punishment, though unnecessary for the occurrence of observational learning, does alter the likelihood that we will engage in the behaviors we have observed.

Vicarious reinforcement is important for our understanding of motivated behavior. If, for example, we observe someone cheating on a test and, as a result, getting a good grade, we may be less reluctant (more motivated) to cheat also. Bandura (1971, 1977) pointed out that one main effect of observing modeled behavior is to strengthen or weaken inhibitions related to particular behaviors. Thus vicarious reinforcement is important because it may disinhibit motivated behaviors normally kept in check. In a similar fashion, observation of modeled behavior may also serve to check behaviors that an individual would be inclined to perform otherwise. In this regard it seems likely that one aspect of socialization involves learning to inhibit impulses (via observation) that are not for the common good or accepted in the culture in which one lives.

Bandura (1977) also pointed out that vicarious reinforcement serves as a reference standard against which we compare the rewards that we receive. The observation of another person being highly rewarded for performing a behavior for which we have received only a little reduces the effectiveness of our reward. Vicarious reinforcement, then, can obviously work either to motivate or demotivate behavior, depending on what we observe.

Learning and Aggression

Consider the following. On December 13, 1966, NBC aired a drama written by Rod Serling titled *The Doomsday Flight* (R. N. Johnson, 1972). The story line concerned a bomb threat to an airline that was designed to extort a large sum of money. The airline is led to believe that a barometric bomb had been placed on the plane before takeoff. If the airline did not meet the extortionist's demands, the bomb would go off automatically when the plane descended below an altitude of 5,000 feet. Of course, if the airline paid the ransom, then the caller promised to tell them where the bomb was hidden and everyone would be safe.

Before the show had even concluded, a bomb threat was made against an airline that was very similar to the particulars of the television show. Within 24 hours of the broadcast, four more extortion demands were made to various airlines.

On July 26, 1971, *The Doomsday Flight* was rerun by a television station in Montreal. A few days later a caller threatened a 747 with 379 persons aboard shortly after the plane had taken off. The caller insisted that a barometric bomb had been placed on the plane and would go off if the plane descended below an altitude of 5,000 feet (not even the altitude was changed!). The airline, by now aware of the scriptwriter's solution, diverted the plane to Denver, whose airport's altitude is 5,339 feet. It would seem that both extortionists and airline officials are capable of modeling their behavior after that observed on television.

The modeling of potentially violent and aggressive behavior after the scripts of television shows occurs from time to time; the aggressive behaviors seen after *The Doomsday Flight* are not peculiar to that particular script (see Geen, 1972, and the *Baltimore Sun,* 1990, for other examples). The point of this example, and others that could be mentioned, is that they suggest some aggressive behaviors may be learned.

As we have seen earlier in this chapter, motives can be learned as a result of classical conditioning, operant conditioning, and observational learning. Let us see how these three types of learning may also contribute to aggressive motivation.

Classical Conditioning and Aggression

Ulrich and Azrin (1962) developed what they termed a **pain-aggression model** of some types of agonistic behavior. For instance, if two rats are placed in a cage with a grid floor through which electric shock can be administered, the rats will rear up on their hind feet and box at each other. If an animal has only inanimate objects against which it may aggress, it may nevertheless attack such objects (Azrin, Hutchinson, & Sallery, 1964). If painful stimulation elicits aggressive behavior reflexively, as they suggest, then it ought to be possible, using classical conditioning, to pair a neutral stimulus with pain so that the conditioned stimulus also elicits aggression. Vernon and Ulrich (1966) demonstrated the classical conditioning of aggressive behavior, although in their study the conditioned response was not very strong and took many trials to develop. Additionally, Adler and Hogan (1963) were able to cause Siamese fighting fish to emit threat displays to a formerly neutral stimulus by using classical conditioning procedures.

Some evidence also exists for classical conditioning of aggressive behavior in humans. Berkowitz and LePage (1967) conducted an experiment in which participants were directed to deliver electric shock to another person when that person made mistakes on a learning task. In one condition, a gun was present in the same room as the participant; in a second condition it was absent. Berkowitz and LePage found that more intense shocks were given in the presence of the gun than in its absence. They argue that the gun served as a situational cue that elicited more aggression because guns have been paired with aggression in the past. Although not a direct test of the classical conditioning of aggression, their results can be interpreted as deriving from the former pairing of guns and stimuli that elicit aggression.

Apparently aggression-eliciting stimuli can be quickly learned. Berkowitz and Geen (1966) conducted an experiment in which individuals were subjected to shock by a person who was supposedly evaluating their performance on a task. Following this part of the experiment, some participants saw parts of the film *Champion* in which Kirk Douglas takes a terrible beating during a boxing match. Others saw a film of a footrace. After viewing the films, the participants were given the opportunity to evaluate the performance of the individual who had shocked them earlier by now shocking him. Some participants were told that the name of the person they were evaluating was Bob, while others were told his name was Kirk (as in the boxing movie). Participants who had been shocked, seen the boxing movie, and were shocking a person named Kirk were more punitive than those who had been shocked, seen the boxing movie, but were shocking a person named Bob. Apparently the association of the name Kirk with aggression in the movie led to the name's eliciting more aggression later.

Such seemingly simple and subtle associations may have an influence on how we behave toward other people. Changes in aggressive behavior may then occur as a result of prior associations formed through the process of classical conditioning. In 1974, Berkowitz reviewed the available literature on the learning of aggressive behavior and concluded that some human aggression could be understood as resulting from classical conditioning. **Impulsive aggression**, where an individual may react aggressively almost without thinking, seemed especially open to classical conditioning procedures. Berkowitz concluded, however, that classical conditioning could not account for all types of violence that humans commit.

Instrumental Conditioning and Aggression

As we have seen earlier, operant conditioning procedures can also lead to learned motives. It seems likely, therefore, that operant conditioning principles would be involved with learned aggressive behaviors. As you will recall, in this type of learning a response leads to some consequence. If the consequence is reinforcing, the probability of the behavior that produced it will increase in the future. Thus, if a young child hits a playmate and as a result gains access to a desired toy, it is reasonable to expect that the child will resort to hitting playmates in the future when desiring something they have.

Laboratory studies of operant aggression have sometimes used verbal reinforcement such as praise to alter aggressive behavior in humans. For example, Geen and Pigg (1970) conducted an experiment in which college students were told to deliver shock to another person when that person made mistakes in a learning task. The experimental group of participants was praised for its aggressive behavior; the control group was not. The praised group delivered more shocks than the control group and, in addition, also used higher intensities. Later both groups were also given a word association test; the praised group emitted more aggressive words, suggesting that the verbal reinforcement increased not only the aggressive behavior of delivering shocks but other aggressive responses as well.

The act of aggression may itself be reinforcing. Myer (1964) found, for example, that some rats will attack and kill mice even though given no conventional reward for doing so. These killer rats were not hungry, nor were they allowed to eat the mice they killed. Nevertheless, killer rats would reliably kill again and again when given the opportunity. Not all rats are killers; however, Myer and White (1965) found that rats that did kill mice would learn to choose the arm of a T-maze where they could attack and kill a mouse, whereas nonkillers would choose the arm containing a rat pup (which they do not kill). Killer rats have also been taught to press a lever in order to be given the opportunity to kill (Van Hemel, 1972).

Whether humans find aggression rewarding is not clear, but aggressive behavior in humans may be reinforced and maintained by secondary reinforcement: social approval by peers, increased attention, and so forth. Brownmiller (1975), for example, notes that social approval can become a powerful reinforcer of aggressive behavior in gangs.

In summary, it seems evident that aggressive responses are subject to the same rules of reinforcement as other behaviors. If aggressive behavior is followed by consequences that are positive for the individual, those aggressive responses will become more probable.

Modeled Aggression

We began this discussion of aggression with the example of individuals using behaviors they had seen demonstrated on television to attempt to extort money from airlines. Such behavior is termed observational learning or modeling. The classic experiment of modeling of aggressive behavior was conducted by Bandura, Ross, and Ross (1961, 1963) and has been briefly mentioned at several points earlier in this book. Let us now look more closely at how these researchers demonstrated observational learning of aggressive behavior.

In their experiment they matched nursery school children on aggressiveness before the experiment began and assigned them to one of five groups. Group 1 observed adult models behaving in an aggressive way against a Bobo doll. Group 2 saw a filmed version of the same behavior. A third group watched a model in a cat suit performing the aggressive behaviors on a television. Two control groups were also included. The first control group (group 4) was not exposed to any modeled aggressive behavior; the second control group (group 5) saw an adult model behave in a calm, nonaggressive manner. Children in all five groups were then mildly frustrated and put into a new situation with a room containing toys, some of which were the same toys that the aggressive groups had seen used earlier by the models.

The models in this experiment had been instructed to use nontypical kinds of aggressive responses. In addition, the models used particular words such as *socko*, *pow*, and so forth, while behaving aggressively. These nonstandard aggressive behaviors and the verbalizations were used to more easily determine when the children were modeling the behavior they had seen earlier. The results were clear. In all three of the groups that saw a model behave aggressively, imitative aggression was initiated. The children tended to use the same novel aggressive behaviors they had seen and also tended to use the verbalizations they had heard. These same responses were almost nonexistent in the two control groups, so it seems clear that these behaviors were modeled on the behavior the children had observed. Although the greatest degree of modeling occurred with the live model, statistical analyses showed that the filmed model was just as effective in producing the modeled aggressive behaviors. The children were less inclined to imitate the cartoon character, although the imitative behavior of this group was still considerably above that of the two control groups.

Of some theoretical interest was the additional finding that total aggressive responses of the three groups of children who had seen modeled aggression were also increased. That is, observing someone else behaving aggressively seemed to not only provide a model for novel aggressive responses but also had the effect of disinhibiting the typical aggressive behaviors of these children.

Although the studies of Bandura and his associates have been criticized as being unrealistic and perhaps biased toward the production of aggressive behavior (Bobo dolls are designed to be hit), the number of studies that have now accumulated (Bandura, 1973; Eron & Huesmann, 1984) makes it difficult to deny that aggressive behaviors can be learned through modeling.

From the brief summary of studies noted in this section, it is apparent that aggressive behavior can be learned. This learning may sometimes result from association of stimuli that are present at the time aggressive responses are triggered (classical conditioning). It may also occur because aggressive behavior is rewarded (operant conditioning). Finally, aggressive behavior may occur because it is observed in others, seen on television, or read about in the media (modeling). Although our nervous systems are surely programmed to allow aggressive behaviors to occur, many, if not most, of the circumstances in which these aggressive behaviors occur are learned. And just as we can learn when to aggress, we just as surely can learn to inhibit aggressive behaviors through these same learning processes.

Sexual Motivation and Learning

Research with animals points out the importance of learning in the production of sexual behaviors. For example, Fillion and Blass (1986) exposed male rat pups to a specific odor (citral, a lemon-like scent) during suckling. When exposed in adulthood to receptive females scented with citral, these male rats ejaculated more quickly than when exposed to females not scented. Thus the early odor experience had an effect on later adult sexual behavior. Lorenz (1970) has argued that the early experience of imprinting (see Chapter 2) can create an irreversible bond that influences sexual behavior at maturity. As we saw in Chapter 2, however, the lasting effects of imprinting on later sexual

behavior do not occur for all species (Mortenson, 1975).

A second example of learning on sexual behavior is the finding that castrated male animals with prior sexual experience maintain their sexual behavior longer when compared to sexually inexperienced males who have been castrated (Hart, 1974). This maintenance must be the result of learning. Additionally, Harlow and Harlow (1962, 1966) have shown that social isolation impairs the development of skills necessary for normal sexual behavior in monkeys. Although their monkeys appeared to have adequate sexual motivation, the monkeys had apparently not learned how to behave appropriately. The Harlows' results support the notion that learning is a crucial component in the expression of normal sexual behavior. Domjan, Blesbois, and Williams (1998) have shown that male quail that were classically conditioned to a place paired with the chance to copulate released more semen and more spermatozoa than nonconditioned subjects. Similarly, Agmo (1999) has shown that the execution of sexual reflexes functions as a reinforcer in rats. The Domjan et al. finding suggests that learned components of sexual behavior could influence reproductive fitness, while Agmo's results show that engaging in sexual behavior supports learning.

Pfaus, Kippin, and Centeno (2001) have done an extensive review of the literature regarding animals' learned sexual behaviors. They provide numerous examples of the role of learning in the sexual behavior of many different species. They note: "Sexual behavior is directed by a sophisticated interplay between steroid hormone actions in the brain that give rise to sexual arousability and experience with sexual reward that gives rise to expectations of competent sexual activity, sexual desire, arousal, and performance. Sexual experience allows animals to form instrumental associations between internal or external stimuli and behaviors that lead to different sexual rewards. Furthermore, Pavlovian associations between internal and external stimuli allow animals to predict sexual outcomes" (Pfaus, Kippin, & Centeno, 2001, p. 291).

Pfaus et al. (2001) summarize many different studies of learned sexual behaviors in animals. They note, for example, that:

1. Stimuli that are reliably present before copulation elicit sexual excitement in male rats and male quail.

2. Male rats prefer a location that has been previously paired with a mate (called a **conditional place preference, or CPP**), as do female rats if they have control over the pace of copulation.

3. Both male and female rats and monkeys will learn a bar-press response to gain access to a mate.

4. In rats, vocalizations that occur during copulation depend on prior sexual experience (i.e., learning).

5. Classical conditioning has been shown to elicit courtship behaviors in mice, gouramis, sticklebacks, pigeons, and Japanese quail.

6. Previous sexual experience in animals influences the speed of copulation (i.e., they learn to become more efficient).

7. Mate preferences in some species appear to be learned early in life.

8. Prior sexual experience has a strong disinhibitory effect on sexual behavior.

9. Humans habituate to erotic stimuli that are repeated.

10. Humans show classical conditioning of sexual arousal (see, e.g., Lalumiere & Quinsey, 1998, following).

Clearly, in animals as well as humans, much of sexual behavior is learned or modified by learning.

Many researchers believe that most variations in human sexual behavior (fetishes, sadism, voyeurism, exhibitionism, and so forth) are also the result of learning processes. What is not clear, however, is how these particular sexual variations are learned. One example of a learned sexual variation is an experiment by Rachman (1966; see also Rachman & Hodgson, 1968), who was able to produce a boot fetish in three male participants by pairing slides of boots with slides of nude women. For the three participants, who were young, unmarried psychologists, penis volume changes were obtained with the boots after 24 to 65 pairings of the boot-nude slides. The artificial fetish was extinguished at the conclusion of the experiment. This particular learned sexual behavior can be understood as an example of classical conditioning. Lalumiere and Quinsey (1998) also found evidence for the classical conditioning of sexual arousal in male college students. Although it seems evident that learning plays a major role in the sexual behavior of humans, the conditions that exist at the time sexual behaviors are learned are usually not known. Future research may provide some insight into how various sexual behaviors are learned.

Learned Sexual Values

Our culture teaches us rules of sexual conduct that are called **sexual values** (Luria et al., 1987). For example, societies decree what sexual behaviors are normal and under what conditions these behaviors should occur. They also teach us with whom we may have sex and with whom we may not.

We learn how to behave sexually by learning the rules of the society in which we live. The agents of this learning are parents and other relatives, religious and political leaders, books, movies, television programs, sex education classes in schools, and even advertising. Although the learning is often incidental, we learn nevertheless.

Although we tend to think that the rules of our society are correct, cultures differ widely in what is acceptable. Extreme obesity was considered erotic in early Hawaiian society. In Polynesia, the exchange of betel nuts and pepper was considered a sexual act between an unrelated man and a woman; eating together was forbidden of an adult brother and sister in one society because it was considered incestuous (Davenport, 1976). It is useful to remember that sexual values and behaviors considered appropriate or inappropriate can vary widely across cultures and thus must result from learning.

According to Luria and associates (1987), most people learn the rules of sexual behavior during adolescence. These writers indicate that in the United States sexual intercourse is approached through a series of increasingly intimate interactions, beginning with the most public parts of the body and progressing to the most private. Obviously, adolescents have learned what behaviors to engage in and in what order. It seems likely that much of this learning is a combination of information gained from same-sex friends, sexual exploration with a partner, and masturbation (Luria et al., 1987).

SUMMARY

In this chapter we have examined the role of learning in the development and direction of motivation. As we have seen, three separate learning processes—classical conditioning, operant conditioning, and modeling—are capable of developing motivational states. Classical conditioning has been shown to be involved in the generation of experimental neuroses, the development and elimination of emotionally motivated states, and learned aversions. Additionally, appropriate situations can lead to the classical conditioning of interoceptive states, which can in turn contribute to psychosomatic illness.

Instrumental conditioning techniques can also generate motivation. Parameters of reinforcement such as quantity and quality of reward influence motivation; in general, more and better-quality rewards generate more motivation. Contrasts between differing amounts of reinforcement are also important for motivation; the past history of reinforcement influences the motivational value of current reinforcers. Operant conditioning also interacts with classical conditioning to produce motivated states.

The interaction of classical and operant conditioning is an important factor in learned motives. Acquired fears, conditioned emotional responses, and learned helplessness are all examples of motivation generated as the result of this interaction. Learned helplessness has been proposed as a potential explanation for some depressed behaviors seen in humans. Although the original model of learned helplessness was too simple to explain all aspects of depressed human behavior, later modifications of the model (covered in more detail in Chapter 10 of this text) come closer to doing so.

Human motivation can also be generated through the simple observation of others. When we see others rewarded for behaving in particular ways, we not only learn those behaviors through observation but are also motivated by their successes or failures to modify our behavior. According to Bandura, reinforcement informs us of the effects of our behavior as well as motivates us to behave. Vicarious reinforcement from the observation of others influences us, as does self-reinforcement.

Learning also plays a prominent role in two important motives, sexual behavior and aggressive behavior. We learn which sexual behaviors are appropriate in our culture and how to engage in those behaviors via learning. The initiation of aggressive behaviors is also learned in many circumstances, although the ability to behave aggressively surely has some innate components.

The focus of this chapter then has been on the importance of learning processes in the development and initiation of motivated behaviors. As we have seen, learning has a large influence across many species and many behaviors. If we wish to understand the full range of motivated behavior, we clearly must examine how learning contributes to its development.

KEY TERMS

Pavlovian classical conditioning, *149*

unconditioned stimulus (UCS)/ unconditioned response (UCR)/conditioned stimulus (CS)/conditioned response (CR)/extinction, *150*

experimental neurosis, *152*

counterconditioning/systematic desensitization/anxiety hierarchy/desensitized/ interoceptive conditioning/ intero-exteroceptive conditioning, *154*

intero-interoceptive conditioning/ extero-interoceptive conditioning/implications of interoceptive conditioning, *155*

long-delay learning/ taste-aversion learning/ learned aversions, *156*

biological constraints/prepared associations/contraprepared associations/unprepared associations/preparedness hypothesis, *157*

progressive muscle relaxation therapy (PMRT)/guided relaxation imagery (GI), *159*

instrumental (or operant) conditioning/the law of effect/reinforcement, *160*

amount of reinforcement (AOR) effect/quality of reinforcement effect (QOR), *161*

negative contrast/positive contrast/history of reinforcement, *162*

latent learning/reinforcer/ primary reinforcers/secondary reinforcers/conditioned reinforcers/generalized conditioned reinforcer, *163*

token/token economy, *164*

conditioned emotional response (CER), *168*

demotivation/triadic design, *169*

passivity (motivational deficit)/ symptoms of helplessness/ learned laziness/retardation of learning (associative retardation)/somatic effects/ reduction of helpness with time, *170*

vicarious learning/social learning theory/modeling/self-reinforcement, *172*

functions of reinforcement/ informational/motivational/ attention/retention/ reproduction/vicarious reinforcement, *173*

pain-aggression model, *174*

Impulsive aggression, *175*

conditional place preference, or CPP)/sexual values, *178*

SUGGESTIONS FOR FURTHER READING

Bernstein, I. L. (1991). Aversion conditioning in response to cancer and cancer treatment. *Clinical Psychology Review, 11*, 18–191. This article shows how learned aversions can develop during the course of chemotherapy treatment.

Lopez, H. H., & Ettenberg, A. (2002). Sexually conditioned incentives: Attenuation of motivational impact during dopamine receptor antagonism. *Pharmacology, Biochemistry and Behavior, 72*, 65–72. This article shows how a neutral cue can become a conditioned incentive (motivator) for sexual behavior in rats. It also suggests that the neurotransmitter dopamine plays a role in this learning. For the advanced student.

Pfaus, J. G., Kippin, T. E., & Centeno, S. (2001). Conditioning and sexual behavior: A review. *Hormones and Behavior, 40*, 291–321. These authors provide an excellent review of animal research on the learned components of sexual behavior.

WEB RESOURCE

For direct hot links to the Internet sites listed below and other features, visit the book-specific Web site at http://psychology.wadsworth.com/petri.

CHAPTER 6

Incentive Motivation

Bob inched along in highway traffic, looking both right and left at the restaurant signs. It was almost noon and he had not had anything except coffee since lunch yesterday. He had worked all night on a new advertising promotion for the bank and, just moments before, had finished it. The position of senior advertising analyst recently opened up, and he thought he had a good chance for the position if his current campaign were successful. He had worked toward this for the past three years, and his promotion now hinged on this one project.

As Bob drove along, stopping frequently because of red lights, he mused about where to eat. The familiar fast-food places crossed his vision, but he was unmoved by them. What he really wanted was a big steak and a baked potato and salad, not a greasy hamburger and cold French fries. The thought of the steak made his mouth water, and he increased the speed of his car.

This short vignette of a few moments in the life of a fictitious individual illustrates several ideas concerning the concept of incentive motivation. Just what do we mean by incentives and incentive motivation? First, it is important to note that the term *incentive* usually describes some **goal object** that motivates us (a big steak was an incentive for Bob). Incentives, then, are generally important for us to either reach or avoid a goal. Like Bob, we may value the sensations associated with a good meal (a positive incentive) and avoid tasteless ones (a negative incentive). Incentives differ in **value** for us from moment to moment and from one time to another. While Bob was working on his project, steak was not an incentive and did not influence his behavior; but after the project was completed, a good meal was an incentive that caused him to drive down a crowded highway in order to obtain it. We may also assume that after he eats the meal, another similar meal would hold little value for him, although other incentives might then influence his behavior.

Incentives motivate behavior. This can be seen in yet another way in the story of Bob. A strong motivation existed in him to gain the promotion to senior advertising analyst and had in fact influenced his behavior for three years. The incentive of promotion was strong enough to override temporarily his physiological needs for food and sleep. Another point to observe in the episode is that incentives are not "wired in" but learned. Bob was not born with a need to become senior advertising analyst; somewhere along the way he learned something that made this an important goal for him. Finally, Bob's story illustrates the idea that **thoughts** can serve as incentive motivators. We will explore this approach later in the chapter and more fully in Part IV of this book.

The concept of incentives as motivators of behavior has been a useful tool in attempting to explain why people (and animals) do the things they do. Its use in theory recognizes that objects or events can modify and influence our behavior over and above physical needs.

Incentive motivation may be thought of as a **mediator** (**M**) that comes between the stimulus characteristics (S) of some goal object and the responses (R) that are directed toward that object. We can view this relationship between stimulus, mediator, and response as S→M→R. Further, Overmier and Lawry (1979) have provided considerable evidence that this linkage actually consists of two separate links, one between the stimulus and the mediator (S→M) and a second between the mediator and the response (M→R), so that the relationship should be analyzed as S→M, M→R. Each link may be separately influenced by the conditions in situations where incentives are present, so the possible outcomes of manipulating incentive motivation can be complex.

Incentive theorists have been concerned with how M is established and what properties of M cause it to alter behavior. As we shall discover, many theorists have emphasized **classical conditioning** as the way in which M is established, but they disagree on its properties. One approach has emphasized the energizing properties of M, a second has suggested that emotionality is important, while a third has emphasized the informational aspects of the mediator. We shall examine each of these approaches in the following sections.

Incentives as Energizers

The concept of internal drives was once the primary device used to account for the motivation of behavior. Several experiments, however, showed that external objects (goals) also motivate behavior, thus forcing a modification of this system. As representative of this work, we will reexamine the classic experiment of Crespi (1942) previously discussed in Chapter 5.

Recall that Crespi trained rats to run down an alleyway to get pellets of food. One group of rats got a large reward (256 pellets), while a second group got a small reward (1 pellet) for the same behavior. A third group served as a control, receiving 16 pellets throughout the experiment. On the 20th trial, Crespi switched the large- and small-reward groups to 16 pellets so that all three groups received the same number of pellets per trial. The large-reward group, now getting smaller rewards, abruptly slowed down in relation to the control group; the small-reward group, now receiving a larger reward, quickly began running much faster in relation to the controls. Figure 6.1 shows the results of his study. Zeaman (1949) obtained similar results under similar conditions.

The important point for our present discussion of Crespi's experiment is that the behavior (of running down the alleyway) changed drastically and quickly when the incentives were changed. Up to the time of Crespi's experiment, theorists such as Hull (1943) had assumed that different amounts or sizes of reward influence the rate of learning but do not alter the motivation of the organism. Crespi's study showed that just the opposite is true; different

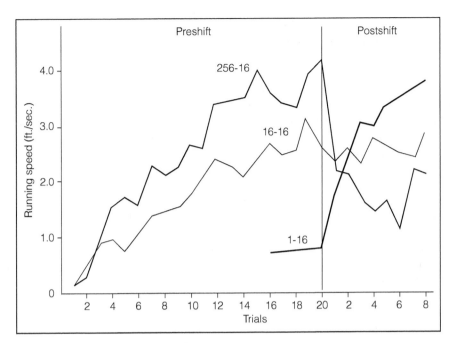

FIGURE 6.1 Crespi's (1942) incentive motivation experiment. Groups were given 1, 16, or 256 pellets of food. On trial 20 all groups were switched to 16 pellets. Note how running speed shifts rapidly when the conditions of reinforcement change. Adapted from "Quantitative Variation of Incentive and Performance in the White Rat," by L. P. Crespi, 1942, *American Journal of Psychology*, 55, 467–517. Copyright © 1942 by the University of Illinois Press. Used by permission.

incentive objects influence how hard the organism is willing to perform but not what is learned. The term *incentive* was chosen to represent this type of motivation.

Incentive Motivation (K)

In the early 1950s theorists began to incorporate the concept of **incentive motivation (K)** into their explanations of behavior (Hull, 1951, 1952; Spence, 1956). If a goal can influence behavior even before that goal is reached, then organisms must in some way come to anticipate the availability of the goal. This anticipation must then motivate them to behave in ways that will get them to the goal. The next question then becomes, how does this anticipatory motivation that we call incentive develop?

Hull–Spence and r_g–s_g   Because of the general similarity of their approaches, we will consider Hull and Spence together. Both used the symbol K for incentive motivation in their formulas for behavior, and both assumed that the incentive value of a goal object could be indexed by the vigor of the consummatory response it elicited. Thus in the case of food, a large reward should lead to more vigorous chewing and swallowing than a small reward. The **consummatory response** (R_G), however, does not occur in a vacuum; for rats, the stimuli of the goal box are present during its occurrence (visual sensations of the food cup, texture of the floor, brightness of the walls, etc.). Stimuli present when R_G occurs will become associated with it (via classical conditioning) and will tend, after a few trials, to elicit R_G directly. To the extent that these stimuli (the same floor texture and wall brightness in the start box of a maze) also occur before the organism reaches the goal box, they will tend to elicit R_G before the goal. It would be rather disruptive (and maladaptive) if a rat sitting in the start box of a maze responded with a full-blown R_G, chewing and swallowing nonexistent food. At the very least it would interfere with the necessary responses of getting from the start box to the goal box, where the food could actually be obtained. For this reason it was assumed that stimuli similar to those present in the goal box would elicit only a **partial consummatory response** (or **fractional anticipatory response** [r_g]), which would not interfere with the instrumental responses (running) required in order to reach the food. Thus a rat might salivate or make small chewing movements in the start box but would not express the full-blown R_G.

This approach further assumed that the organism could sense that it was making these r_g's. For example, close your eyes and hold your right arm out straight. Now, with your eyes still closed, bend your elbow 90 degrees. Even with your eyes closed, you know that your arm is bent because of sensory feedback from your arm muscles and joints. The logic for sensing the r_g's is the same; sensory feedback in the form of stimuli (**partial response stimulus feedback** [s_g]) inform the organism that it is making r_g's.

The occurrence of these partial responses and their stimuli (**fractional anticipatory response mechanism**, commonly called the **r_g-s_g mechanism**) serves to motivate the instrumental responses that must be made in order to get to the goal box and engage in the R_G. This explanation, we should emphasize, is entirely a mechanical one. Through the process of classical conditioning, the stimuli in the environment come to elicit small parts of the final R_G, and the feedback from these responses serves to motivate ongoing behavior. Though the sight of a rat frantically pushing at the door of the start box might appear to express the rat's anticipation of an expected reward at the end of the maze, the model assumes no thinking on the part of the rat. We could in fact program a computer to behave similarly. Hull (1930, 1931) originally

proposed the r_g-s_g mechanism to explain the apparent purposiveness of behavior and the anticipation of goals. Spence (1956) applied the mechanism to incentive motivation, proposing that incentive motivation is the result of these r_g's and their feedback s_g.

Incidentally, r_g-s_g occurs throughout the path from start box to goal box, to the extent that stimuli are similar along the way. As the organism approaches the goal area, more and more stimuli should occur that have been associated with R_G; thus r_g-s_g should increase and increasingly motivate ongoing behavior. This accounts for the often observed phenomenon that organisms appear more motivated (e.g., by running faster) near the goal. Figure 6.2 provides a schematic representation of the process.

But what if the stimuli are different in the beginning than at the goal? According to Hull and Spence, the answer is that the stimuli that become associated with R_g and thus develop r_g-s_g do not have to be external to the organism. The sensations we feel when hungry, for example, are with us all the way from start to goal; and because they are present when R_g occurs, they should also elicit a fractional anticipatory response (r_g).

One final point should be mentioned concerning the fractional anticipatory response mechanism,

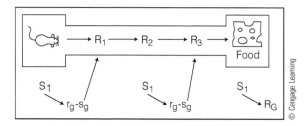

FIGURE 6.2   The r_g-s_g mechanism. Food at the end of the runway leads to the consummatory response R_G. Any stimuli present at the time RG occurs will tend to elicit a fraction of that response (r_g). When these stimuli (S_1) appear earlier in the maze, they will call forth r_g and its feedback stimulus s_g. The r_g-s_g complex then serves to energize the instrumental responses (R_1, R_2, and so on) that lead to the goal.

as r_g-s_g has come to be called. As originally formulated, it was a peripheral explanation of incentive motivation, and r_g was thought to consist of minute muscular responses and the associated sensory feedback from these muscle contractions. Attempts to locate and measure r_g's did not prove to be very successful (see Bolles, 1975, for a thorough review; also Beck, 1978; Black, 1969; Logan, 1968).

The Persistence of Behavior

Surely one of the most fundamental aspects of people's behavior is that it persists even in the face of difficulty. For example, a student studies for a test but nevertheless does not do well. What does the student do for the next test? Many times he or she studies even harder. The question is, why? Amsel, using rats as a model, has studied this question for many years (Amsel, 1972; Amsel & Roussel, 1952), and suggests that a mechanism very much like rg-sg may be involved.

Amsel and r_f-s_f Amsel was primarily interested in the question of what happens when a rat reaches a goal where it has been rewarded in the past and now finds nothing. If the rat has been in the situation several times and has been rewarded, incentive motivation will have developed (following the Hull-Spence approach) via r_g-s_g. But if the rat now discovers that its efforts are for naught, according to Amsel, an **unlearned frustration response** occurs (symbolized as R_F). Any stimuli present at the time R_F occurs will tend to become associated with it; and if these stimuli also occur earlier in the sequence of events, they will tend to elicit **partial** or **anticipatory frustration responses** (r_f). As with r_g-s_g, the organism knows it is making these responses because of feedback stimuli (**frustration response stimulus feedback** [s_f]). These partial frustration responses typically cause the animal to stop its present behavior and engage in some other behavior. Frustration from nonreward, then, normally leads to **competing responses** that take the organism off in new and perhaps more adaptive directions.

Suppose, however, that we design our situation so that competing responses are difficult to make and also arrange that whatever original responses can be made have been followed by reward in the past. What would happen?

Amsel proposed that the partial frustration responses (r_f) and their associated stimulus feedback (s_f) become counterconditioned to the responses the organism is making. By using the term **counterconditioning**, Amsel is saying that the motivation generated by the frustration of nonreward gets channeled into the very response that causes the frustration. The competing responses that would normally develop as a result of this frustration are countered by the situation, and the motivation becomes conditioned to the only responses that can easily occur: the responses leading to the sometimes reward-filled goal box. In other words, the **r_f-s_f mechanism** serves as a motivator for ongoing behavior, just as r_g-s_g would under other circumstances.

When might such circumstances as just described occur? They occur when an animal or a person is put on a **partial reinforcement schedule** (**PRF**). On such a schedule, at times some of a rat's responses are rewarded with a bit of food or a lick of water, while at other times the same responses go unrewarded. To return to the example of the student studying for a test, if studying has been reinforced in the past, but studying this time didn't work, then frustration should develop.

One of the best-established phenomena in psychology is that rats reinforced on a partial reinforcement schedule persist in responding longer when the reinforcer is taken away (extinction) than when they have been reinforced for every response (a **continuous reinforcement schedule**, or **CRF**).

How might frustration theory account for this persistence? During training the continuous reinforcement group is rewarded on every trial. Thus r_g-s_g should build up and motivate the necessary responses for reaching the goal.

For the partial reinforcement group, r_g-s_g would build up too, although more slowly, on those training trials that are rewarded. In addition, r_f-s_f would build up on trials that went unrewarded. Initially this would lead to competing responses (resulting in less or slower behavior). These competing responses would eventually die out because they always went unreinforced (extinguish), and r_f-s_f would become counterconditioned to the same response that r_g-s_g is activating. For the partial reinforcement group, then, we have two sources of incentive motivation on every trial, r_g-s_g (built up on rewarded trials) and r_f-s_f (built up on non-rewarded trials). Because the competing responses generated by r_f-s_f have extinguished, the incentive motivation generated by r_f-s_f will become channeled into whatever responses can occur (the responses leading to the goal because they are sustained by r_g-s_g).

Now for the crucial part. In extinction the CRF group responds and goes unrewarded. This leads to R_F and thus to r_f-s_f and the development of competing responses. If the reward has been permanently removed, the incentive effects of r_g-s_g will die out rather quickly and become replaced by r_f-s_f and competing responses. Because r_f-s_f has never been counterconditioned in CRF animals, its occurrence will not cause the running responses to continue but will lead to a quick cessation of responding—because r_g-s_g is no longer present to sustain the correct responses—and r_f-s_f will elicit competing responses. Continuously reinforced animals consequently stop responding rather quickly. The partially reinforced group, on the other hand, has two sources of motivation that have been connected to the responses no longer being rewarded. The r_g-s_g part will die out, but the responding will continue longer in this group because it is sustained by the motivation generated by r_f-s_f. Amsel's approach therefore provides a neat explanation of the well-known fact that partially reinforced responses are more persistent than continuously reinforced responses. This effect is called the **partial reinforcement extinction effect** (**PREE**) and is quite reliable. A student, having been reinforced with a good grade on some occasions by studying and not on others, will act similar to the rat; in other words, the frustration of receiving a low grade will channel into the only behavior that sometimes pays off—studying.

If you stop to consider the real world, you soon discover that partial reinforcement is the rule rather than the exception. Perhaps only in the laboratory can we constrain the environment in such a way as to make continuous reinforcement possible. We make many hundreds of responses every day, most of which are not immediately, if ever, rewarded; yet we persist. Why? Perhaps for the same reason the rat does—because sometimes it pays off, and nothing else seems to work.

The frustration of doing badly on a test may motivate us to study harder for the next one (if we have been rewarded in the past by studying hard). On the other hand, doing poorly on a test may lead to competing behavior (if we have not been previously rewarded for studying), such as listening to our favorite CDs. The important point is that frustration will channel into ongoing behavior and make it more persistent if that behavior has been rewarded at some time in the past; otherwise it will lead to competing behavior that will reduce persistence. Thus the type of behavior activated depends on earlier experiences with reward and nonreward. What sort of evidence did Amsel provide in support of his ideas? Actually quite a bit.

In a now-classic experiment, Amsel and Roussel (1952) ran rats in the situation depicted in Figure 6.3. Rats ran from the start box to goal box 1, where they were fed; then they ran alley 2 to goal box 2 to get additional food. After the rats were trained on this procedure, food was sometimes withdrawn from goal box 1. Amsel surmised that this should lead to R_F, which would show up as faster running in alley 2 on nonreinforced trials.

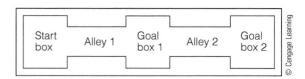

FIGURE 6.3   Diagram of the experimental situation in Amsel and Roussel's 1952 frustration experiment. See text for explanation.

He compared the speed of traversing alley 2 on reinforced versus nonreinforced trials and found that, indeed, rats ran faster after nonreinforced trials. While the results of this experiment were open to several alternative explanations, further research has supported Amsel's approach. Nonreward following a response that has been regularly reinforced in the past does energize behavior, as Amsel claimed it should.

Does frustrative nonreward lead to competing behavior? Again research seems to bear Amsel out. In a study by Adelman and Maatsch (1955), two groups of rats were taught to run to a goal box to obtain food. Later the food was withheld (extinction was introduced). One group of rats was allowed to retrace its path from the goal box to the start box, while the second group was allowed to escape from the situation by jumping completely out of the goal box. The rats allowed to retrace their path quickly extinguished, while the rats allowed to jump out of the goal box continued to run to the goal box for many trials. For both groups the frustration of nonreward led to new responses, as Amsel predicted. The rats allowed to retrace developed a new response that competed with the old running response, and they extinguished quickly. For the rats allowed to jump out, competition between this response and the running response did not occur, and they extinguished much more slowly. Thus frustrative nonreward does seem to produce new responses that can compete with previously learned responses.

A study by Ross (1964) provides strong support for both the energizing effects of frustration and the incorporation of this energy into behaviors present at the time frustration occurs. In the first phase of the experiment, six groups of rats were trained to make one of three responses in order to get food. Three of the groups received continuous (100%) reinforcement and served as controls against which the others, receiving partial (50%) reinforcement, could be compared. For two of the groups, the required response was to run to the food well; for two other groups, the correct response was to jump a gap in the floor to get to the food; and for the last two groups, the correct response was to climb a wire mesh wall in order to reach the food. (One group in each pair was continuously reinforced for making the correct response, while the other group was partially reinforced.) All three responses were about equal in difficulty and were in fact learned at approximately the same rate. Amsel's frustration theory predicts that the animals in the three partially reinforced groups should experience frustration on the nonreinforced trials and that the resulting r_f-s_f should become conditioned to whatever response the rats had to learn to get to the goal (running, jumping, or climbing).

In a second phase of the experiment, all six groups were taught to run for water in an experimental chamber different from that used in phase 1 and were reinforced 100% of the time. In the crucial final phase of the experiment, the running response to water was extinguished. The extinction process should reinstate frustration, and Amsel's theory predicts that the responses conditioned to frustration during phase 1 should lead to differing rates of extinction in the final phase of the experiment as a function of whether the response initially associated with r_f-s_f facilitated or hindered the running response learned in phase 2. For the animals taught to run in phase 1, the frustration reinstated during extinction should lead to increased persistence, because running was the correct response in phase 2, and r_f-s_f should channel into the ongoing response. For rats taught to jump in phase 1, reinstitution of frustration by extinction should interfere somewhat with running and reduce resistance to extinction. For the climbing group, reinstitution of frustration should call up the climbing response, which should seriously interfere with the running response, and extinction should occur quickly. The three partial reinforcement groups, when compared against their respective continuous reinforcement controls, behaved as predicted by frustration theory.

Ross's data provide confirmation of both the energizing effects of frustration and the channeling of this energy into ongoing behavior. Further, the effects of this channeling on behavioral persistence were shown to depend upon the relationship of the energized response to the response being extinguished. The energized response may lead to either greater or reduced resistance depending on whether it facilitates or hinders the response undergoing extinction.

Amsel's frustration theory appears able to handle many of the phenomena known in learning and motivation research. It is an incentive theory because the presence or absence of the goal influences the motivation of the organism. Anticipatory frustration responses and their stimulus feedback (r_f-s_f) may lead to the energizing of competing behavior or to the activation of instrumental behavior, depending on the circumstances. The persistence of behavior, then, is established according to the organism's past history with the incentive.

Amsel (1972) saw frustration theory as part of a more general theory of persistence. Persistence develops whenever organisms learn to approach or to continue responding despite stimuli that would normally disrupt that behavior. This occurs because the disruptive stimuli become counterconditioned to the ongoing responses in the situation. Amsel noted that emotional responses and their consequent feedback stimuli are sometimes disruptive, but they can also eventually become counterconditioned to ongoing behavior.

Consider the initial frustration you feel when the deadline for a paper approaches. This unpleasant state may initially lead to all sorts of competing behaviors that put off the work necessary for completion of the paper. However, when you finally begin to work on the paper as a result of the approaching deadline, you may discover that the pressure (frustration) will generate the responses needed to complete the task. One might argue that one aspect of a good student's behavior is having learned to channel (countercondition) the frustrations of college life into constructive behavior.

Amsel's frustration theory has proved enormously successful; however, it is only one of several theories that attempt to describe how incentive motivation may alter behavior. And it has been criticized on a number of points (Bolles & Moot, 1972; Staddon, 1970). Also, Amsel's theory describes the motivating properties of the removal of an expected incentive; it does not deal directly with the positively motivating properties of incentive availability, which it assumes is covered by the r_g-s_g mechanism.

Incentives as Generators of Emotion

The research of Amsel and his colleagues provides support for the notion that the mediating effect of an incentive is motivational; other theorists, such as Neal Miller, Frank Logan, and O. Hobart Mowrer, have taken somewhat different approaches. We will examine Mowrer's theory as one alternative to the r_g-s_g approach because he proposes that incentive motivation mediates between stimulus and response by creating emotional states.

Mowrer: Fear, Hope, Relief, and Disappointment

Mowrer (1960) argued that incentive motivation is the primary instigator of behavior. For Mowrer incentive motivation is closely tied to the learning of emotional responses. He proposed four primary emotions were involved: **fear**, **hope**, **relief**, and **disappointment**.

According to Mowrer, any increase in drive (i.e., motivation, e.g., from electric shock or food deprivation) leads to the emotion of fear. The emotional responses associated with the state of fear will become connected to any stimuli that are also present at the time the emotion occurs. After several such pairings, the stimuli become cues that signal the approach of an increase in drive and create a state of fear before the actual arrival of the increased drive state. This conditioned fear then motivates the organism to make whatever responses it can to remove itself from the situation containing the fear cues. The role of reinforcement in Mowrer's system is to activate one of the four emotions rather than to influence instrumental responses directly. For Mowrer, then, learning alters what the organism *wants* to do rather than what the organism *can* do.

In an analysis similar to that of fear, Mowrer proposed that a decrease in drive (e.g., a full stomach) is accompanied by the emotion of hope. Any cues present at the time hope occurs will become associated with the emotion and eventually begin to serve as signals that a decrease in drive (and thus hope) is imminent. Thus Mowrer again saw behavior as being activated by an emotional incentive. Stimuli that produce the emotion of hope will activate behaviors that keep the organism in their presence, while stimuli associated with fear will activate avoidance behaviors.

Mowrer proceeded a step further to analyze the situation in which hope is expected (because the cues for it are present) but not forthcoming. Such a situation leads to the third emotional construct of incentive motivation—disappointment. Disappointment occurs when hope cues that predict a decrease in drive do not lead to an actual reduction in drive. Disappointment, like fear, is a negative state for the organism and motivates behavior that will have the effect of removing the cues that signal disappointment.

Finally, in a symmetrical fashion to his analysis of disappointment, Mowrer proposed the emotion of relief. Relief occurs when cues that signal an increase in drive are taken away. Stimuli present at the time the fear cues are removed will become relief signals. Thus a bell ending a difficult laboratory class could become a relief cue if the stimuli associated with the class have become fear cues. As with hope, organisms attempt to maintain situations that predict relief.

Let's look at an example. A rat is taught to press a lever in order to obtain pellets of food. Food in the stomach reduces drive and thus produces hope. A light above the bar is always on when food arrives. After several trials in which the rat obtains food in the presence of the light, the light becomes a cue that food (and therefore a decrease in drive) is about to occur. At this point the light will activate behaviors that keep the rat in its presence, and it becomes an activator of hope even before the food

arrives. If we carry our imaginary experiment a step further, we can see how Mowrer's concept of disappointment might work. Suppose we sound a tone for 5 seconds, after which we turn off the light and remove the lever from the chamber. After a few pairings of tone and light, the tone will become a cue signaling the removal of hope. The tone will activate the emotion of disappointment as well as behaviors designed to remove the rat from this aversive situation.

Mowrer's approach to incentive motivation emphasized the importance of emotion as a mediator between the stimulus characteristics of incentive objects and instrumental behavior; thus, rewards and punishers generate emotion. Cues associated with the triggering of emotion eventually become capable of triggering the emotion before the emotion-producing event. The activation of this anticipatory emotion then directs instrumental behavior toward or away from objects in the environment.

Bolles (1967) and Miller (1963) have pointed out several conceptual difficulties with Mowrer's approach. Miller noted that although the system can account for much behavior once behaviors start occurring, it does not explain how behavior is triggered the first time. For example, once a rat has learned that cues in the start box of a maze are associated with hope because food is in the goal box, behavior will continue; but what causes the rat to traverse the maze the first time? Mowrer provided no ready answer, and Miller considered this problem a fatal flaw in the theory.

Incentives as Carriers of Information

Mowrer's approach suggests that informational stimuli generate emotions that in turn lead to approach or withdrawal behavior in the situation. Other theorists have also emphasized the importance of the informational aspects of cues for incentive motivation without necessarily invoking the notion of emotionality. Their theories emphasize the idea that incentive motivation serves to mediate between stimulus and response because predictive stimuli generate incentive motivation, which in turn directs appropriate responding. Although these approaches are in many respects similar to Mowrer's, they differ in emphasis; emotions are seen not as the instigators of behavior but as cues that predict (provide information about) the goal and direct behaviors toward that goal. The concept of predictability as an explanation for incentive effects owes much to the theoretical concepts of Tolman. We turn next to Tolman's ideas before examining the concept of predictability.

Tolman: Cognitive Formulations

The approaches examined so far have emphasized mechanical explanations of incentive effects on behavior, but not all theorists have chosen to view incentives in that way. Most notable among this latter group was Tolman, who argued that incentive motivation results from the development of **expectancies**. Let us briefly examine his point of view.

Edward Chase Tolman (1959, 1967) provides a good counterpoint to the incentive theory of Hull and Spence. While those researchers attempted to reduce behavior to the smallest possible unit (an approach termed **reductionism**), Tolman took a much more **holistic** view. Tolman was much less concerned with the particular muscular responses made on the way to the goal than with the fact that organisms worked to obtain goals. He viewed behavior as **purposive**; rats as well as humans, he thought, develop expectations that particular behaviors will lead to particular goals, a theory which, incidentally, was a precursor of modern cognitive approaches to behavior.

Tolman (1967) pointed out that different goals have different values for an organism. For example, Simmons (1924) trained rats to find their way through a complex maze, and different groups received different rewards at the end. She found that a group given bread and milk performed better than a second group given sunflower seeds as a reward, and the second group, in turn, performed

better than a group given nothing. In a similar experiment, Elliott (1928) found that wet bran led to better performance in a complex maze than sunflower seeds.

Following the earlier work of Blodgett (1929), Tolman and his students continued work on a concept called **latent learning**. These studies attempted to show that reinforcement is not necessary for learning to occur. Additionally, they showed the importance of appropriate incentives for the performance of learning. In these experiments groups of rats were trained to traverse a complex maze. One group received food at the end of the maze and learned to run quickly and reduce errors to receive the reward. A second group received nothing at the end of the maze; its performance showed little indication of having learned how to get through the maze efficiently. A third group received nothing in the maze until the 11th trial, when it began to receive food rewards. During the first 10 trials, this third group, like group 2, showed little evidence of any learning. When reward was introduced, however, the third group's performance rapidly improved to the level of group 1. This rapid change in performance indicated to Tolman that learning had occurred during the first 10 trials, but was not apparent in performance until the food incentive was introduced (Tolman & Honzik, 1930a).

These experiments led Tolman to conclude that goal objects exert different amounts of demand on performance, or, in simpler terms, that **incentives differ in value**. Incentives thus come to have control over behavior, their effects depending on the value of the particular incentive for the organism.

Expectancy   An important aspect of Tolman's view was that incentive objects influence behavior only if they are experienced enough times so that a cognitive expectation is built up. By cognitive expectation, Tolman meant that the organism, after several experiences with a goal, comes to expect that particular behaviors will lead to that goal in the future. Thus the rat that has received wet bran mash 10 times in a row for traversing a maze will come to expect that traversing the maze this time will lead to wet bran mash.

What would happen if, as devious experimenters, we changed the rules of the game? Tolman said that changing incentives after an expectation has been acquired leads to a disruption of behavior, particularly if the change is from a more demanded to a less demanded incentive. Tolman noted in fact that just such a change provides evidence for the existence of cognitive expectancies. As an example of such an experiment, he cited a classic study by Tinklepaugh (1928) in which monkeys observed an experimenter place food under one of two containers; then after a short delay they were required to choose the correct container to obtain the reward. On some trials Tinklepaugh changed the reward during the delay (and out of sight of the monkey) from a more preferred substance, such as banana, to a less preferred substance, such as lettuce. The monkeys, on discovering the lettuce, did not eat it but searched for the lost banana and sometimes shrieked at the experimenter as if angry (apparently the monkeys also had some expectation of where the devious change originated). For Tolman, disruption of the normal, learned behavior of choosing the container under which the monkey had seen food placed indicated that a cognitive expectation of obtaining a bit of banana had developed.

Tolman also recognized the interaction of the physiological state with the incentive value of the goal. Tolman cited an experiment by Szymanski in which a female rat was taught to run a maze in order to get to her litter. As the litter became older and no longer nursed, the speed and accuracy of the female rat declined, presumably because the litter was no longer a strongly valued incentive. Thus the changed physiological state (of the mother rat) reduced the incentive value of the litter.

Tolman presented a model of incentive motivation that emphasized the buildup of expectancies concerning the behaviors that will lead to certain goals. These expectancies both energize and guide behavior. Positive incentives are approached and negative incentives are avoided; more highly valued incentives energize behavior more than less-valued incentives. When an expectancy is disconfirmed, as

in the Tinklepaugh experiment, behavior is disrupted. Unlike the Hull-Spence approach, which explains incentives in terms of minute, partial, consummatory responses, Tolman conceived incentives to be **central representations** (**thoughts**) of the relationship between particular behaviors and the goals to which they led.

The theories of both Mowrer and Tolman are similar in that they emphasize that cues (expectancies) are important in the development of incentive motivation. Perhaps the mediating effect of an incentive depends on its ability to predict goals in just this way. Several theories that stress the importance of predictability in the development of incentive motivation have been proposed; we will examine only two, the ideas of Overmier and Lawry and those of Bindra.

Predictability

Bolles and Moot (1972) proposed that cues become incentive motivators to the extent that they predict the arrival or withdrawal of some goal object. In their view, whether a cue takes on motivational control (becomes an incentive motivator) depends on whether it predicts some future event. **Predictive cues** are thought to motivate ongoing behavior and reinforce completed responses (i.e., act as secondary reinforcers).

One way to make a cue predictive is to pair it with a reinforcer such as food in a classical conditioning procedure. Each time the stimulus is presented, so is the food. Once the stimulus has been paired with a reinforcer for several trials, we can change the situation so that a bar-press response is required in order to obtain food. The question of interest is whether presentation of the cue associated with food in the classical conditioning situation will influence the learning of the bar-press response. If bar-pressing is facilitated by the presence of the cue, we have evidence for an incentive effect of the cue (appropriate control groups are necessary, however, in order to say that the cue previously associated with food facilitates the instrumental response). Experiments involving this transfer-of-control design have often obtained facilitation (Bolles & Moot, 1972; Trapold & Overmier, 1972) as the theory predicts.

Bolles and Moot noted, for example, that cues associated with food facilitate performance of an operant response, while cues predicting the withdrawal of food have a demotivating effect. This suggests the interesting possibility that we may find ourselves unmotivated to perform certain behaviors because the cues associated with the task predict lack of success. Perhaps the child who has little motivation for schoolwork is immersed in a school or home environment that contains cues paired with a lack of success in the past. These cues would have a demotivating effect on the child's performance, and because the pairing process requires nothing of the child other than exposure to the cues, the child will probably not even be aware of why school is a bore. Clearly it is important, both theoretically and practically, to understand how predictive cues may influence the motivation of organisms.

The Overmier and Lowry Model

As noted at the beginning of this chapter, incentive motivation can be conceptualized as acting like a mediator between environmental stimuli and responses to those stimuli. Further, as noted earlier, Overmier and Lawry (1979) regard the mediational aspect of incentives as composed of two separate links: there is one link between the stimulus and mediator (S→M) and a second independent link between the mediator and response (M→R). Considerable evidence has been accumulated (see Overmier & Lawry, 1979, for an extensive review) that one way in which incentives mediate behavior is through their informational properties; incentives, according to this point of view, serve as cues that aid in response selection. Overmier and Lawry have noted, however, that an informational explanation cannot account for all that is known about mediation effects in transfer-of-control experiments, and they have further suggested that incentives have both an energizing and a cueing function. Thus when cues associated with a goal

reappear at a later time or in a different situation, they are thought to both energize behavior and direct responding according to associations they have gained earlier.

Though both energizing and informational aspects of mediators play a role in altering learning and performance, Overmier and Lawry have provided evidence that the informational aspects are the more important, at least in situations in which these two aspects of an incentive compete for the control of behavior. The data presented by Overmier and Lawry (1979) for their dual-link, mediation explanation of incentive effects are based on a series of complex and subtle experiments that are beyond the scope of this discussion; however, the studies reported by them support the view that incentives alter performance because they provide information about goals.

Stimuli that are consistently associated with reinforcement become reinforcers in their own right and are called **secondary** (**conditioned**) **reinforcers** as we have already noted in Chapter 5. Many theorists believe that reinforcement serves to develop incentive motivation rather than to strengthen stimulus-response connections (Bindra, 1969; Klinger, 1977; Trapold & Overmier, 1972). This means that secondary reinforcers are also incentive motivators and should have both energizing and response selection properties.

Most of us have probably never considered why money is worth working to obtain, we just do it. However, when you consider it more carefully you realize that it is, after all, just paper and ink or small circular globs of metal. Why do we value it? We value money because we associate it with rewards that have value for us. These may be either physiological (money buys food, water, sex, avoidance of pain) or learned (money buys status, a new car, a house in the suburbs, etc.). For humans, money serves as a strong secondary reinforcer. Because secondary reinforcers are also incentive motivators, money activates and directs our behavior because it predicts the availability of items of importance to us; if we could not buy items with money, having it would not be motivating. In periods of high economic inflation, any given amount of money (e.g., a dollar) does become less motivating. Many years ago a dollar would get us into a movie and buy a bag of popcorn too. Today parking in the lot next to the movie theater in most large cities will cost several dollars. A dollar obviously does not have the same incentive value it once had because it predicts less (in terms of what it represents or can be exchanged for) than it did formerly.

It is important to recognize that incentives are relative rather than absolute. How motivating a particular incentive will be depends on the background of events against which it is compared. Because the background changes over time, so will the value of incentives.

The work of Trapold and Overmier (1972), Bolles and Moot (1972), and Overmier and Lawry (1979), as well as others, has contributed a great deal to our understanding of the manner in which a stimulus associated with a goal can become an incentive motivator. Dalbir Bindra at McGill University developed a motivational model that incorporates not only predictive cues but also organismic states (drive) and goals. We turn now to a brief overview of his thinking. (For a more complete understanding of Bindra's approach, see Bindra, 1968, 1969, 1972, 1974.)

The Bindra Model   Bindra proposed a model of behavior that emphasized the production of a **central motive state** (first proposed by Morgan, 1943) that activates goal-directed behaviors toward incentive objects. According to Bindra, motivational state and emotional states are identical, so his model is also a model of emotional behavior.

Bindra argued that a central motive state is generated whenever certain organismic conditions exist (such as changes in hormonal conditions or blood sugar) and the organism is stimulated by the properties of an incentive object (odor, taste, visual or auditory stimuli). Thus the organismic state (drive) and the stimuli from the goal object (incentive) combine to produce a central motive state.

The activation of this central motive state triggers innate sensory-motor coordinations (generally autonomic) such as salivation or heart rate changes that prepare the organism for contact with (or escape from) the incentive object. In addition, activation of the central motive state triggers sensory-motor coordinations previously established by either learning or maturation. For example, the central representation (memory) of the stimulus properties of food activates instrumental approach behaviors and, on contact with food, consummatory behaviors such as chewing and swallowing.

Bindra's system assumes that incentive stimuli serve both energizing and directional functions. The steering of behavior is accomplished by the stimuli associated with the goal object (food) and serves to select the proper behaviors (approach, chewing, swallowing) rather than other possible responses. Neutral stimuli can become incentives through simple pairing with other incentives that already arouse the central motive state. Through this contingency learning process, a stimulus (the sound of a can being opened heard by your dog) can become a predictor of future stimuli (the odor, taste, and texture of the dog food) and serve to motivate behavior.

Our previous example illustrates how a stimulus can gain motivational properties, but let's also see how a stimulus can demotivate behavior. Suppose that a certain stimulus (S_1) always predicts the absence of a second stimulus (S_2). Suppose further that S_2 is a stimulus characteristic of some highly preferred goal object. Because S_1 predicts the absence of S_2, S_1 will suppress the central motive state. Unless the central motive state is present, behavior will not occur.

This brings us to a point that is probably obvious but still worth mentioning. Incentive objects may be either positive or negative. **Positive incentives** generate approach behavior, while **negative incentives** generate withdrawal. Because neutral cues can become attached to incentives, such formerly neutral cues can come to predict three possible relationships. A positive relationship (in which S_1 leads to S_2) predicts the imminent presentation of an incentive object. A negative relationship (in which presentation of S_1 is followed by the absence of S_2) predicts that the incentive, either good or bad, will not be forthcoming. Finally, a neutral relationship exists when a stimulus has no consistent relationship with the incentive and thus provides no information about its occurrence (S_1 predicts nothing about the occurrence of S_2). The particular behavior that one observes, then, will depend on whether the incentive itself is positive or negative (food versus shock) plus the relationship between the stimuli that provide information about the incentive object. For example, a stimulus always associated with the absence of shock (and where other stimuli predict shock) would be expected to elicit approach, while another stimulus associated with the absence of food (and where other stimuli predict food) would elicit withdrawal.

Bindra's system is particularly interesting because it attempts to provide in one coherent framework a model that includes the state of the organism (drive), the influence of the goal properties (incentive), and the association of cues with the incentive (predictability). Bindra's model still draws interest. For example, Agmo (1999) has proposed a model of sexual motivation based on Bindra's original model.

Before ending our discussion of incentive motivation, we must examine one more theoretical approach. The approach proposed by Eric Klinger (1975, 1977) is important because it stresses cognitive factors (in a fashion similar to Tolman) and because it is an incentive theory derived from work with humans. As we will see, incentives in Klinger's system serve as mediators between stimulus and response to the extent that they are emotionally meaningful.

Klinger: Meaningfulness

The events of 9/11 have reminded many of us what is really important—family, friends, relationships. Few other things mattered on that day as we all watched in horror at what people are capable of doing to one another. That day began a reassessment for many people of their own priorities. Interestingly, Eric Klinger many years ago proposed that relationships with family, spouse, and friends are the basis for much of human motivation. Specifically, his research indicated

to him that incentive motivation in the form of relationships was crucial.

Klinger's basic idea is the importance of meaningfulness for people's lives. **Meaningfulness**, in turn, is provided by incentives toward which people work. He believed that people pursue those objects, events, and experiences that are emotionally important for them. Thus emotionality is incorporated into the incentive concept for Klinger as it was for Mowrer. If a person is deprived of the incentives important to him or her, life becomes less meaningful. People therefore are motivated to work (behave) in order to obtain those incentives that are prized.

One interesting aspect of Klinger's approach is his demonstration that those incentives that provide meaningfulness are not extraordinary. In fact family, children, and personal relationships seem to be the most common sources of meaning for most people (Klinger, 1977). Klinger also noted that those people who are most certain their lives are meaningful mention very concrete categories when describing what is meaningful for them.

Incentives and Goals   Klinger makes a distinction between incentives and goals in human behavior. Incentives are objects or events that are valued. However, people will not necessarily be willing to work to obtain everything that has incentive value. For example, a person might value owning a 50-foot yacht but be unwilling to behave in such a way as to obtain one (such as taking on a second job). While a yacht is an incentive because it is valued, it is not a goal unless the individual is willing to expend effort in order to obtain it. Thus goals are always incentives, but incentives may or may not also be goals. Ultimately, goals are the more important because they are what we are motivated to obtain.

Klinger noted that, in a very real sense, no organism really exists separate from its goals (because goals such as food, water, and avoidance of pain are necessary for survival), although, at the human level, goals may include items unnecessary for survival (intimacy, understanding, religious belief, etc.). Thus goals (and therefore incentive motivation) are a part of the very fabric of life and influence behavior continually.

When a person decides to pursue a particular incentive (so that it becomes a goal), that person is said to be committed to that particular goal. Klinger chose the term *committed* to emphasize the idea that working toward a goal requires a dedication to obtaining that goal, and as we shall see shortly, goals are not easy to give up. Such a goal is termed a **current concern** by Klinger. An individual is usually committed to several current concerns at any one time, and his or her behavior will therefore be a compromise among these various goals.

Disengagement Phases   A current concern continues to influence behavior until either the goal is reached or the individual goes through the process of disengagement. Disengagement occurs when a goal is made unreachable. Klinger believed that available evidence from various sources suggests that disengagement from a goal involves a shifting of behavior through a series of phases.

1. **Invigoration.** If blocked from reaching a goal, the behavior of an individual at first becomes stronger. Klinger in fact considered Amsel's frustration effect (mentioned earlier in this chapter) as an example of invigoration. Klinger also suggested that one consequence of invigoration is that the blocked incentive becomes more attractive and other incentives become temporarily reduced in attractiveness (see Klinger, 1975, for a review of experiments leading to this conclusion). Thus the individual in the invigoration phase becomes rather single-minded in his or her attempt to reach the blocked goal.

2. **Primitivization.** If stronger, more concerted efforts do not succeed in making a goal obtainable, behavior is seen as becoming more stereotyped and primitive until it becomes destructive. For example, Barker, Dembo, and Lewin (1941) showed that children's play behavior becomes more primitive after frustration. Similarly, Hinton (1968) showed that adults respond more primitively on tests of

originality and divergent thinking after frustration.

3. **Aggression.** As blocking of goal attainment continues, responding becomes more and more primitive until it becomes aggressive. Aggressive behavior as a response to blocking of goal attainments is well documented (Dollard et al., 1939; Johnson, 1972) and may be the individual's last attempt to obtain a goal before giving up (Klinger, 1975).

4. **Depression.** According to Klinger, when all attempts at reaching a goal fail, depression sets in. The depressive state may vary from mild disappointment to extreme depression. Typically, instrumental striving for the goal stops, and the individual expresses feelings of helplessness and hopelessness. Depressed individuals also become uninterested in the incentives that usually influence them and appear unmotivated in social interactions (Libet & Lewisohn, 1973). Klinger believed that depression is a normal part of disengaging from an unobtainable goal and that the depressive state may serve gradually to reduce the emotional value of the incentive so that other incentives may again be pursued.

5. **Recovery.** The final phase of the disengagement process is recovery. As Klinger noted, not much is known about what triggers recovery in the natural situation, but recovery usually does occur. Klinger suggested that successes in obtaining other goals may serve to stimulate recovery from depression. For example, Beck (1967) has shown that depressed patients are particularly sensitive to success in minor tasks.

Grief as Disengagement   Anyone who has lost a close personal friend or relative through death knows the feelings associated with what is commonly called grief. Bowlby and Parkes (1970) suggest that working through the grief process involves four separate dimensions. First, there is **shock or numbness**, during which decision making may be difficult. During this stage the grieving individual may show panic, distress, and even anger. Phrases such as *this can't be* indicate difficulty in accepting the loss.

The second dimension of mourning (the working through of the grief) involves a **yearning and searching** for the lost person. Stimuli associated with the departed individual bring reactions of restlessness, anger, or ambiguity, and the grieving individual asks questions such as "What does it mean?" or "How can this be?"

The third dimension noted by Bowlby and Parkes involves **disorientation and disorganization**. This dimension often involves depression and feelings of guilt, as expressed by such thoughts as "Did I do all that I could?" Finally, the fourth dimension involves **resolution and reorganization**. Gradually the individual begins to put the death of the loved one into perspective and begins to behave more competently. New roles may be assumed, and one's thoughts become congruent with the reality of the situation.

Bowlby and Parkes's dimensions of the mourning process bear striking resemblance to the disengagement phases proposed by Klinger (1977). From Klinger's perspective the mourning process can be viewed as an example of disengaging from an important lost incentive (the loved one). Outbursts of panic and distress and feelings of restlessness represent the invigoration phase of the cycle, while anger and disbelief constitute the cycle's frustration-aggression aspect. Bowlby and Parkes's disorientation and disorganization dimension corresponds closely with Klinger's depression phase, which generally precedes the final disengagement from the incentive and leads to behavior directed toward new incentives (or toward old ones temporarily overshadowed by the loss). Thus the resolution and reorganization dimension of Bowlby and Parkes corresponds well with Klinger's recovery phase.

A point suggested by the analysis of grief is that an individual with several important incentives might be expected to deal with the loss of a loved one better than another who has few incentives other than the deceased. Perhaps with these latter individuals, we need to develop new incentives or

help them redirect their behavior toward existing incentives. We often seem to do this intuitively; at funerals people often express such advice as "You've got to live for your children now."

Incentive Aspects of Sexual Motivation

In this chapter we have examined research showing that many behaviors are motivated by the characteristics of their goal objects. We have used the term *incentive motivation* to describe such situations. Does sexual motivation also have some of the characteristics of incentive motivation? Incentive motivation theories tell us that the characteristics of goals are often quite important in motivating behavior. If the goal is copulation, then the question becomes, what sort of stimuli possessed by an animal would reliably produce sexual arousal and sexual behavior in a potential partner? For many animals, chemicals associated with sexual readiness are important stimuli for attracting a mate. Female rats in estrus (sexually receptive) produce a urinary chemical that attracts male rats (Pfaff & Pfaffmann, 1969). According to Money and Ehrhardt (1972), male rhesus monkeys are aroused, at least in part, by the vaginal odor of sexually receptive rhesus females.

Pheromones

Chemical signals (in this example the chemical signaling sexual readiness) are called pheromones and appear to be innately recognized by the nervous system. "**Pheromones** are … chemical messengers that are emitted into the environment from the body where they can then activate specific physiological or behavioral responses in other individuals of the same species" (Grammer, Fink, & Neave, 2005, p.136). In animals, pheromones have been shown to influence estrous cycles and age of reproductive maturation, prevent implantation of fertilized embryos, and indicate the sexual readiness of females (Bartoshuk & Beauchamp, 1994).

Chemicals providing information to one animal about another's sexual readiness appear to be detected by a group of receptors that are separate from the primary olfactory system. This secondary system is called the **vomeronasal organ (VNO)** and it sends its information to the accessory olfactory bulb, a different brain location than that to which normal odors are sent (Bartoshuk & Beauchamp, 1994; Carlson, 1994). The vomeronasal organ, and especially the accessory olfactory bulb, appear to be responsible for many of the effects of pheromones on behavior since damage to this system disrupts the effects of the pheromones but not other behaviors (Bartoshuk & Beauchamp, 1994).

Although there is no direct evidence that humans are sexually aroused by specific chemicals produced by a potential sexual partner (Luria et al., 1987), it is possible that human sexual behavior may be determined in part by pheromones. The role of pheromones in human sexual behavior appears more likely since it has been shown that the human nose has a vomeronasal organ (Garcia-Velasco & Mondragon, 1991), although it is also likely that one would not be consciously aware of sensations detected by this receptor system (Bartoshuk & Beauchamp, 1994). There has been considerable debate over the functionality of the VNO in humans. It had long been regarded as vestigial; however, at least three separate studies have found evidence for its functionality in detecting pheromones, even in minute amounts. Thus it would appear that humans do have a working pheromonal detection system. Moreover, additional studies have reported evidence for pheromonal detection within the main olfactory system of mice (Wang, Nudelman, & Storm, 2007). Wang et al. suggest that a similar system may exist in humans.

Grammer et al. (2005) note evidence for at least four different functions of pheromones in general: opposite sex attractants, same sex repellents, mother–infant bonding attractants, and menstrual cycle modulators. As we shall see, there is experimental evidence for human pheromone activity in at least three of these behaviors.

Menstrual Cycle Modulators   In an ingenuous study, Stern and McClintock (1998) showed for the first time that humans do communicate using pheromones. Their research confirmed that exposure to odorless axillary (armpit) compounds from women could both accelerate and retard the menstrual cycle of other women exposed to these compounds. Whether exposure accelerated or retarded the cycle was dependent on where the "donor" was in her own menstrual cycle. The effect of the acceleration or retardation was to synchronize the menstrual cycles of women living close together. Although the synchronizing of menstrual cycles of women living together has been known for some time (see, e.g., McClintock, 1971), this is the first demonstration that a human pheromone provides the cue for such synchronization. The research also opens the possibility that other behaviors may be controlled by pheromones, as is known to be the case with other animals.

Opposite Sex Attraction Signals   Cornwell and associates (Cornwell et al., 2004) found a significant correlation between the attractiveness of male faces and a particular male pheromone they called MP2 (4,16-androstadien-3-one). Perhaps not coincidentally, this same substance produces the strongest reaction from cells in the female VNO (Jennings-White, 1995). For women, there was a significant positive correlation between masculine faces and mp2 when asked to judge the faces for a long-term relationship. It would seem that facial masculinity and the androstene steroid mp2 provide signals about the quality of a male mate. Similarly, Cornwell et al. found a correlation between female facial preferences in men and FP (the female pheromone [1,3,5(10),16-estratetrael-3-ol]). As with the female sample, this correlation only occurred when the men were asked to make judgements of females faces for a long-term relationship. There is a large number of studies showing that feminine faces provide strong signals of female fertility (see, e.g., Buss, 2008). Cornwell et al. (2004) suggest that humans use a variety of signals when selecting a mate and that both facial characteristics (indicating masculinity or feminity) and the presence of masculine or feminine odors provide such cues. Additionally, Cutler, Friedmann, and McCoy (1998) found in a double blind study that men who used a cologne diluted with a synthetic male hormone engaged significantly more often in sexual intercourse and sleeping with a woman in comparison to a placebo control group. One possible explanation for these findings is that the pheromone in the aftershave increased sexual interest in the women exposed to these men. A similar study using women (McCoy & Pitino, 2002) obtained a similar result for women. In a double blind placebo-controlled study, women who wore a perfume containing a synthetic female pheromone had a significantly greater frequency of sexual intercourse, sleeping next to a partner, formal dates, and petting/affection/kissing compared to the placebo control group. McCoy and Pitino suggest that the pheromone acted as a sex attractant to men. Together, these studies imply that male and female pheromones do influence the sociosexual behavior of both men and women. Other studies have found that during ovulation women find the smell of men more attractive (or perhaps less disgusting?). Human pheromones, do thus, appear to have an incentive motivational effect on sexual behavior in humans.

Vaglio, Minicozzi, Bonometti, Mello, and Chiarelli (2009) also provide evidence for a pheromonal recognition system between mother and infant. Their evidence suggests that axillary and nipple-aerola regions produce volatile substances that aid in mother–infant recognition.

Learned Sexual Stimuli

It is also clear that neutral stimuli associated with the chance to engage in sexual behavior can become incentive motivators through learning processes. For example, Lopez and Ettenberg (2002) allowed male rats to copulate with female rats in the presence of a distinctive odor (either orange or almond extract) five separate times. Between each of these copulations the male rats were exposed an equal number of times to the nonused scent while in isolation. After this initial training the rats were then allowed to run down a runway to a scented or unscented goal box. In the scented condition the scent was either the scent associated with the sexual activity, or the scent associated with the isolation. As shown in Figure 6.4, the rats ran most quickly to the scent previously paired with sexual activity, even though no sexual activity occurred in this apparatus when compared to both the scent-isolation condition and the unscented condition. Thus, the scent associated previously with sexual activity became a conditioned (learned) incentive motivator.

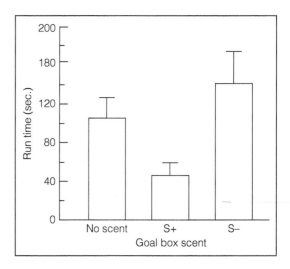

FIGURE 6.4   Mean (+S.E.M.) run times for 16 male subjects tested for their motivation to approach an unscented goal box (two trials), an S+ scented (one trial), and an S− scented goal box (one trial). Subjects took significantly less time to enter an S+ scented goal box versus an S− scented or unscented goal box.
From H. H. Lopez and A. Ettenberg (2002), Sexually Conditioned Incentives: Attenuation of Motivational Impact during Dopamine Receptor Antagonism. *Pharmacology, Biochemistry and behavior, 72,* 65–72, p. 68, © 2002 Elsevier. Used with permission.

Humans, however, are predominantly visual animals and so we might expect that visual stimuli provided by a potential sexual partner would have strong incentive value.

Money and Ehrhardt (1972) argue that humans have a sexual signaling system, which at a distance is visual and on close-up involves touch. Given our previous discussion of pheromones, we should probably also include them in the "close-up" category. Both men and women find some potential partners more sexually arousing than others. What sort of visual signals might prove attractive? One way to try to answer this question is to ask what sorts of attributes an individual finds alluring in a member of the opposite sex. The answer seems to be **physical attractiveness** (Harmatz & Novak, 1983; Luria et al., 1987; Symons, 1979; see also Cunningham, 1986, for an interesting analysis of the facial attributes that men find attractive in women).

Research is consistent in showing that physical attractiveness is a major component of sexual attractiveness (Harmatz & Novak, 1983). Berscheid and Walster (1974), for example, found that participants rated as attractive by trained observers reported having more dates than participants rated as less attractive by these observers. Furthermore, Berscheid and Walster report that people generally agree very closely on ratings of physical attractiveness and that physical attractiveness has a large influence on the formation of heterosexual relationships. Cunningham (1986) has found that the physical characteristics of the female face that are rated as attractive by males include large eyes, small nose, small chin, prominent cheekbones, narrow cheeks, high eyebrows, large pupils, and a large smile. More recent research by evolutionary psychologists confirm these traits and add large lips, rounded face, and facial symmetry as important cues (see, e.g., Buss, 2008, for an overview). A nonfacial cue that has received a lot of recent attention is waist-to-hip ratio as an important attractiveness cue (see, e.g., Singh, 1993). A woman's waist-to-hip ratio around 0.7 is judged as most attractive by men.

It also has been noted that members of heterosexual pairs tend to be approximately equal in attractiveness (Symons, 1979). This effect is often known as **assortative mating** (Thiessen & Gregg, 1980); that is, people tend to sort themselves out in such a way that mating couples are approximately equal in attractiveness as well as other characteristics, including similarities in their genetic make-up (Russell, Wells, & Rushton, 1985).

Kampe, Frith, Dolan, and Frith (2001) have found that direct gaze of attractive faces activates dopaminergic regions within the brain that are associated with reward prediction. These researchers suggest that direct gaze by an attractive person (of either sex) is rewarding in social situations. So it would appear that attractiveness is a very basic component of social interactions.

Symons (1979) provided a thoughtful and thought-provoking review of the characteristics that constitute physical attractiveness that is still relevant today (see also Buss, 1994; 2008; Cunningham, 1986). He argues that physical attractiveness is an indicator of likely reproductive success and, therefore, evolutionary pressure has been brought to bear on attractiveness and its recognition. This evolutionary pressure has led to the innate recognition of, and preference for, certain (and different) physical traits in men and women.

Female Attractiveness

According to Symons (1979), the two major attributes of female attractiveness are health and age. A healthy, young woman is more likely to successfully reproduce and raise offspring. Symons's analysis suggests that men should find attractive any characteristics that are indicators of health. He notes that Ford and Beach (1951) found that a good complexion and cleanliness were considered attractive by all the groups they studied. In primitive cultures, complexion and cleanliness ought to provide some indication of health and, as a result, ought to be seen as attractive. Symons suggests that other physical characteristics such as clear eyes, firm muscle tone, good teeth, beautiful hair, and so forth might also be indicators of health and thus seen as attractive (see also Cunningham's list of facial attributes previously noted). Although there are few good data on the subject, it is interesting that many of the products advertised for women do attend to these physical characteristics (contact lenses for the eyes, health clubs to increase muscle tone, toothpaste that whitens teeth, hair dyes, perms, make-up and so on). Symons proposes that paying close attention to the skin and being attracted by a clear complexion are probably innate.

Youth is the second physical characteristic that Symons says is important to attracting a man to a woman. Indeed G. C. Williams (1975) has argued that youth is the most important determinant of human female attractiveness. The age of the female is important because it is closely linked to her reproductive value. A woman of 20, for example, has almost all of her reproductive years in front of her, while a woman of 35 has most of her reproductive years behind her. As Figure 6.5 (from Buss, 2008, p. 141) shows, the peak reproductive value of a woman is approximately 20 years old. According to this analysis, then, men ought to be strongly attracted to younger women because of their greater reproductive value. Symons (1979) provides cross-cultural data to support the idea that youth in women is a strong sexual attractor to men. He also believes that youth as a factor in sexual attractiveness is relatively innate. In other words, men are genetically programmed to find younger women sexually attractive.

Neither health nor age has been seen as an important variable by most researchers of attractiveness, however. It is somewhat ironic that most studies have been conducted in Western countries, where health is relatively good, and where most of the participants have been of college age (young); it is no wonder, then, that health and age have been largely overlooked as major contributors to female attractiveness. Further studies of

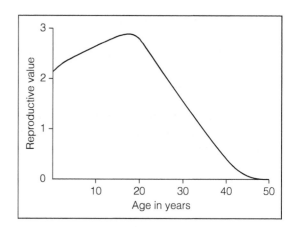

FIGURE 6.5 Typical Reproductive Value Curve for Women. The figure shows the number of children a woman of a given age is likely to have, on average, in the future. Data extrapolated from Symons (1979); Williams (1975). Figure produced by Buss (2004). Reprinted with permission.

these two variables could provide important insights into physical attractiveness.

The third characteristic that Symons proposes as sexually attractive in women is novelty. According to Symons, in a primitive hunter-gatherer society a man could expect to produce four or five offspring with one wife during her reproductive years. If, however, he had a second wife he could double his reproductive success. Where multiple wives were not possible, an extramarital affair that led to just one additional offspring would have increased his reproductive success by 20% to 25%. Since behavioral strategies that lead to the greatest number of offspring will tend to be selected, one can understand why men should be attracted to, and desire to mate with, numerous females. Thus one strong characteristic that should be attractive in women is novelty.

In herd animals the female novelty effect can be quite strong. For example, after a bull has ceased to copulate with a cow the introduction of a new cow will lead to copulation anew, and the response of the bull to the seventh cow will be almost as strong as to the first (Schein & Hale, 1965). Rams show a similar effect to the introduction of new ewes, and male rats also show this phenomenon. Even roosters copulate more when multiple partners are available (Symons, 1979).

The stimulatory effect of the introduction of a new female on male sexual behavior has been dubbed the **Coolidge effect** after a purported conversation between President Calvin Coolidge and his wife. Supposedly the president and first lady were visiting a government farm. In passing by the chicken coops, Mrs. Coolidge asked her guide whether the rooster copulated more than once a day. Her guide assured her that the rooster copulated with the hens dozens of times per day. Mrs. Coolidge asked that this fact be told to the president. Later the president passed by the chicken coops and was given the information about the rooster that Mrs. Coolidge had requested. The president, on hearing the information, asked whether the copulations were with the same hen every time. The answer was that the copulations were with a different hen each time. The president asked that that information be conveyed to Mrs. Coolidge (Bermant, 1976).

Finally, Symons argues that there is no convincing evidence for specific physical characteristics of the female that are capable of stimulating the male visually (in this regard he disagrees with Morris, 1967). The most consistent sexually arousing stimulus for males is the sight of the female's genitals; however, unlike some other primates, in which estrus produces highly visible changes in coloration or size of the female's genitals, human females experience no such obvious changes.

Research has shown that there are consistent differences in male preference (some men consistently prefer long legs, others large breasts, and so forth; Wiggins, Wiggins, & Conger, 1968); however, it is likely that these preferences are learned. Luria and associates (1987) have argued that the only innate sexually arousing stimulus is light touch, especially of the genitals, and that preferences for large breasts, long legs, or firm buttocks are learned erotic stimuli.

Male Attractiveness

If men are attracted to healthy, young women who are novel, what characteristics do women find sexually attractive in men? Compared to the male, the human female has fewer potential offspring and a much higher parental investment in those she does produce. As a result, evolutionary pressures ought to have selected for conservatism in female sexual behavior. That is, in a society where males compete for status, the female is likely to have greater reproductive success by remaining with one high-status male who can provide her and her offspring with the essentials for survival. Thus, one would predict that social dominance and status would be especially attractive to the female.

Symons suggests that in the female what is innate is a selection rule (attraction to high status males) rather than recognition of specific traits such as health and age. Thus, according to this analysis, the physical attributes of the male should be less important than characteristics indicative of status. Ford and Beach (1951) report that, cross-culturally, male attractiveness is typically based on skills and abilities rather than appearance. Skills and abilities ought to be related to status in that men with high levels of skills or abilities ought to be more likely to achieve high status. It is of some interest in this regard that Berscheid and Walster (1974) found that the only male physical trait that was consistently considered sexually attractive to women was height. Taller males might be expected to have some advantage in male-male competition, and thus attraction to taller males, on average, could be expected to confer some reproductive advantage to the female.

Symons (1979) too suggests that male sexual attractiveness depends less on handsomeness than on skills and abilities. Buss (1994, 2008) has suggested a similar idea—that women will prefer men who can provide adequate resources for her offspring. Since skills, abilities, status, and the accumulation of resources generally take some time to develop, one could also argue that women will often prefer older males to younger males. Certainly in some primitive cultures younger men have had to compete against older, dominant men for young women (Symons, 1979).

More recent studies have shown, however, that certain male characteristics (that indicate high testosterone levels) are viewed as attractive by women, they just do not seem to be as important in choosing a mate as attraction cues are for men (see Buss, 2008, for a review of much of this research).

To summarize, it would appear that characteristics of the goal object (the potential sexual partner) for heterosexually motivated behavior do act as incentive motivators for sexual attraction. For the male, physical attributes associated with health and youth are sexually stimulating, as is novelty. For the female, sexual attractiveness would appear to be based less on physical characteristics such as handsomeness than on dominance, status, and resources. These differences in sexual attraction appear to be understandable in terms of the differing needs of the male and the female in assuring the survival of their genes (however, see Miller, Putcha-Bhagavatula, & Pedersen, 2002, for research suggesting a different point of view).

Incentive Motivation and Physical Addictions

One of the more recent developments of addiction research is the realization that addictions are perhaps best understood as resulting from incentive motivation. Typically incentive motivation has been analyzed as resulting from the **hedonic** (i.e., pleasure or pain) **value** of the incentive object. However, research on drug addiction suggests that this may be too simple an approach. The incentive motivational properties of an object appear to be composed of both a hedonic value and a **craving** for that object (Robinson & Berridge, 2000, 2001). As reviewed by Robinson and Berridge (2000, 2001) it appears that addiction can be understood as being generated by a craving for the drug rather than the pleasure produced by the drug or the pain caused by its withdrawal. Although the reward value of a particular drug like cocaine may initially be due to the

high experienced by using the drug, the addiction appears to be due to a change in circuitry of the brain underlying incentive motivation effects. These changes then are thought to produce the craving for the drug even when the experienced high is no longer very strong, and even when withdrawal symptoms are not pronounced. Let us examine this idea in a little more detail.

Based on a review of the available literature, Robinson and Berridge (2000, 2001) argue that traditional explanations of drug addiction, such as the positive reinforcement from the drug high or negative reinforcement from withdrawal or hedonic (pleasure and pain) explanations, cannot account for the compulsive nature of drug-seeking and drug-taking behavior. Instead, they propose that, in the addict:

1. Potentially addictive drugs share the ability to produce long-lasting adaptations in neural systems.

2. The brain systems that are changed include those normally involved in the process of incentive motivation and reward.

3. The critical neuroadaptations for addiction render these brain reward systems hypersensitive ("sensitized") to drugs and drug-associated stimuli.

4. The brain systems that are sensitized do not mediate the pleasurable or euphoric effects of drugs (drug "liking"), but instead they mediate a subcomponent of reward we have termed *incentive salience* (drug "wanting"). (Robinson & Berridge, 2001, p. 103)

Further, they propose that when this incentive salience system becomes sensitized it generates compulsive drug-seeking behavior.

They also note that individuals vary greatly in the likelihood that they will become sensitized by particular drugs. Thus, one person might take drugs recreationally and develop little or no addictive behavior, while another person may become sensitized and develop compulsive drug-taking behavior. Furthermore, once sensitized, the drug craving that results is long lasting (presumably because of the adaptations to the underlying neural systems), which might help explain why drug addiction can be so hard to overcome.

A second reason why sensitized persons may find it hard to quit is that the stimuli associated with drug taking (e.g., drug paraphernalia, the environment in which the drug taking occurs, etc.) become classically conditioned to drug taking and therefore become capable of eliciting the drug craving too. Robinson and Berridge propose that some aspects of the drug craving are mediated by implicit memory processes and are, therefore, outside of awareness by the individual. Such an explanation could help one understand why many addicts do not seem to comprehend their own cravings for drugs. Finally, Robinson and Berridge review evidence implicating the role of the neurotransmitter **dopamine** in the drug craving aspects of addiction.

Behavioral Addictions

The research on incentive motivation clearly shows that goal objects in the environment have motivational effects on our behavior. Because of these motivational effects, it is reasonable to ask if some **behavioral addictions** might also be understood as resulting from incentive motivation processes.

The term *addiction* has typically been used to describe a need for substances that produce a physical dependence (Holden, 2001); however, as noted by Holden (2001, p. 980), "as far as the brain's concerned, a reward's a reward, regardless of whether it comes from a chemical or an experience." Thus, if a person were to find a particular behavior especially rewarding, it might be because that behavior triggers reward circuits in the brain that are usually triggered by more basic behaviors such as obtaining food or sex with a mate

or by various drugs of abuse such as cocaine. Indeed, it has been shown that people addicted to cocaine show brain activity changes similar to those produced by cocaine when viewing a videotape of cocaine paraphernalia or of a person getting high on cocaine (see, e.g., Wexler et al., 2001). Other research, summarized by Helmuth (2001), suggests that addictions compromise the memory and motivational systems in addition to triggering the reward circuitry. Thus, cues associated with an addiction can induce the cravings for the addicted object.

If experiences can be rewarding, then for some people certain behaviors may become as addictive as drugs. For example, some people find jogging rewarding to the point that it appears similar to an addiction. Other people can become so motivated by gambling that it costs them not only money, but their jobs, homes, and relationships. Still others appear to have a compulsive need to shop, so much so that it takes on many of the properties of an addiction. There has even been talk of Internet addiction (see Chakraborty, Basu, & Kumar, 2010, for an overview). Holden (2001) summarizes research indicating that gambling, sex, compulsive overeating, compulsive shopping, and running can exhibit the properties of an addiction in some people. It is thought that these behavioral addictions occur because the behaviors stimulate the same reward circuitry as more basic motives. Further, cues associated with these behaviors become incentive motivators by inducing a craving for those behaviors.

It would be interesting to see if the incentive-sensitization model of drug addiction would also apply to behavioral addictions. Perhaps future research will make such a connection.

SUMMARY

In this chapter we examined the concept of incentive motivation. The basic idea underlying the concept of incentive motivation is that the characteristics of the goals we work to obtain influence our behavior. Explanations of incentive motivation have

ranged from highly mechanical stimulus-response theories, such as the Hull-Spence and r_g-s_g mechanism, to the more cognitive theories of Tolman and Klinger. Amsel's analysis of the persistence of behavior as resulting from the counterconditioning of fractional frustration responses is an extension of the Hull-Spence model.

Mowrer's emphasis on the idea that incentives generate emotion has provided an alternative proposal for how goals may generate behavior and is related to the currently popular explanations that emphasize the informational property of incentives. Tolman's emphasis on the importance of expectancies as generators of behavior was also a significant contribution to our understanding of incentive motivation and, like Mowrer's theory, pointed out the importance of informational cues.

Theories stressing the importance of the informational properties of cues associated with goals and the effects of these cues on behavior have emphasized the concept of predictability. Perhaps the most extensive analysis of incentives from this point of view has been conducted by Overmier and Lawry, who regarded incentives as mediators between stimuli in the environment and the responses of the organism. Others, such as Bolles and Moot, and Trapold and Overmier, have also stressed the importance of predictability in incentive motivational situations, while Bindra has attempted to gather together the concepts of drive, incentive, and predictability in the concept of central motive state.

Klinger has analyzed human behavior from the perspective of incentive motivation and concluded that incentives are the major force underlying what we do. Klinger argued that we work to obtain the goals that are emotionally meaningful to us. In addition, incentives influence not only our actions but also our thoughts and even which environmental events influence us. Further, disengaging from a sought-after goal is difficult and involves a series of predictable phases.

Incentive motivation continues to be an important theoretical approach to understanding the motivation of behavior. As we have just seen, some aspects of sexual attractiveness appear to fit an incentive motivation approach. The goals toward which we work clearly provide a strong source of motivation. For human behavior, this source of motivation often seems to outweigh other sources, including, at times, homeostatic regulation.

Finally, research on physical addictions has shown that drug addiction may result from changes in the brain-reward circuitry underlying incentive motivation—in particular, those circuits responsible for drug cravings. Behavioral addictions share many characteristics with drug addictions, including the importance of cues in our environment. Cues that have been associated with particular behaviors seem to induce cravings for those behaviors in much the same way that cravings are produced in substance abuse.

KEY TERMS

goal object/value, *181*
thoughts/mediator (M)/classical conditioning, *182*
incentive motivation (K)/ consummatory response (R$_G$), *183*
partial consummatory response/ fractional anticipatory response/partial response stimulus feedback [sg]/ fractional anticipatory response mechanism (rg-sg mechanism), *184*

unlearned frustration response/ R$_F$/partial or anticipatory frustration responses (r$_f$)/ frustration response stimulus feedback (s$_f$)/competing responses/ counterconditioning/r$_f$-s$_f$ mechanism/partial reinforcement schedule (PRF)/continuous reinforcement schedule (CRF), *185*

partial reinforcement extinction effect (PREE), *186*
fear/hope/relief/ disappointment, *188*
expectancies/reductionism/ holistic/purposive/latent learning/incentives differ in value, *190*
central representations (thoughts)/predictive cues, *191*
secondary (conditioned) reinforcers, *192*

SUGGESTIONS FOR FURTHER READING

Miller, L. C., Putcha-Bhagavatula, A., & Pedersen, W. C. (2002). Men's and women's mating preferences: Distinct evolutionary mechanisms? *Current Directions in Psychological Science, 11,* 88–93. This article questions the evolutionary differences in male and female mating preferences noted by Buss and others.

Morrone, J. V., Depue, R. A., Scherer, A. J., & White, T. L. (2000). Film-induced incentive motivation and positive activation in relation to agentic and affiliative components of extraversion. *Personality and Individual Differences, 29,* 199–216. For a somewhat different view, this article provides evidence for a relationship between extraversion and incentive motivation.

Powell, J., Dawkins, L., & Davis, R. E. (2002). Smoking, reward responsiveness, and response inhibition: Tests of an incentive motivational model. *Biological Psychiatry, 51,* 151–163. This article extends the incentive motivation model to smoking and suggests that abstinence from smoking may impair motivation.

Robinson, T. E., & Berridge, K. C. (2003). Addiction. *Annual Review of Psychology, 54,* 25–53. This article provides a good overview of the major theories of how addiction develops.

WEB RESOURCES

For direct hot links to the Internet sites listed below and other features, visit the book-specific Web site at http://psychology.wadsworth.com/petri.

http://www.pbs.org/wnet/closetohome/science/html/animations.html

Excellent animations showing how neurotransmission is altered by cocaine, alcohol, and opiates, from the Bill Moyers PBS show Moyers on Addiction: Close to Home.

CHAPTER 7

Hedonism and Sensory Stimulation

"If it feels good, do it." I noticed this quotation on a bumper sticker as I drove to my office some years ago. The saying is an explanation of motivated behavior (though a modern version) that has been with us for as long as recorded history. Democritus, a contemporary of Plato in ancient Greece, argued that we behave in order to obtain the greatest amount of pleasure (Bolles, 1975). Epicurus, whose name is more commonly associated with this approach, also believed that we are motivated to obtain pleasure. Such an approach is termed **hedonism** and can be defined as the seeking of pleasure and avoidance of pain.

Hedonic theories emphasize the idea that cues or stimuli have motivational properties because they have become associated with positive or negative experiences. In many respects, this is similar to arguments concerning incentive motivation. One might argue that incentives motivate behavior because they arouse hedonic effect; that is, perhaps goal objects become incentives because they arouse pleasure or pain.

Hedonism

Various philosophers throughout the ages have argued for hedonic explanations of behavior. Hobbes, for example, believed that all actions are motivated by the desire to obtain pleasure and avoid pain (Bolles, 1975; Woodbridge, 1958). Spencer proposed that pleasurable behaviors have survival value for an organism; that is, those behaviors perceived as pleasurable were adaptive over the history of the species. He believed that random responses that led to pain were reduced in probability. Thus, for Spencer, pleasure and pain became important modifiers of behavior. Spencer's approach was clearly a forerunner of

CHAPTER PREVIEW

This chapter is concerned with the following questions:

1. Can the concept of hedonism (seeking pleasure and avoiding pain) explain some motivated behaviors?

2. Does sensory stimulation motivate behavior?

3. What effects does sensory restriction have on motivated behavior?

4. Can some behaviors be explained in terms of opponent processes in the nervous system?

Thorndike's law of effect, which was itself a fore-runner of modern reinforcement theory (Young, 1961).

Troland (1932) believed that the nervous system is especially tuned to pleasurable and aversive events. He divided stimulation into three categories: beneception, nociception, and neutroception. **Beneception** occurs when pleasant feelings are aroused by stimuli, while **nociception** occurs as the result of stimuli that arouse unpleasant feelings. The third category, **neutroception**, exists when stimuli cause neither pleasant nor unpleasant feelings. Troland believed that sensations can be classified in one of these three categories. Vision, audition, cutaneous touch, and kinesthesis were considered neutroceptive. Pain, bitter taste, intense salt, intense sour, nauseating or repugnant smells, cold, excessive heat, hunger, thirst, and some visceral responses were considered nociceptive. Beneceptive stimuli included erotic stimuli, sweet tastes, some pleasant smells, low intensities of salt and sour, and some visceral responses. Thus, according to Troland, the hedonic value of an object in the environment is closely tied to the sensory qualities it possesses and the effect those stimuli have on the nervous system in terms of beneception, nociception, or neutroception.

Beebe-Center (1932) suggested that pleasantness and unpleasantness exist as opposite extremes on a **hedonic continuum** (Troland, 1932, also suggested this). Somewhere between the extremes of pleasant and unpleasant feelings lies a neutral zone where stimuli are neither pleasant nor unpleasant. Beebe-Center maintained that pleasant and unpleasant sensations depend on the way in which the sense organs react to stimulation. Reactions of the sense organs in one manner (which he called **bright pressure**) produce pleasant feelings, while reactions of a different type (which he termed **dull pressure**) produce unpleasant feelings. Thus, Beebe-Center believed that pleasant and unpleasant feelings result from different types of activity in the sensory systems. Beebe-Center was also one of the first theorists to acknowledge that instructions can change the perceived pleasantness or unpleasantness of stimuli. This influence of instructional set indicates that pleasantness and unpleasantness are relative to whatever else is happening to us. Beebe-Center believed that instructions alter the pleasantness of stimuli by changing the actions of the sense organs rather than by altering perception of the stimulation at some more central (brain) level. Today we would be inclined to argue that the effects of instructions are more central in nature.

P. T. Young: Sign, Intensity, and Duration

Paul Thomas Young is perhaps the best known hedonic theorist. Young's extensive research on food preferences led him to agree with Beebe-Center that there exists a continuum with maximum negative affect (unpleasant or aversive stimuli) at one end and maximum positive affect (pleasant stimuli) at the other end. According to Young, the affective processes represented by this continuum have three properties: sign, intensity, and duration.

Positive affect is associated with approach behavior, while negative affect is associated with avoidance. Thus we can determine the **sign** of a particular affective situation by observing whether the organism approaches (+) or avoids (−) the situation. For example, rats will approach and drink a sweet-tasting fluid but will avoid (after initial contact) a bitter-tasting solution.

Affective processes also differ in intensity. To observe affective **intensity** differences of various substances, researchers usually employ **preference tests**. In a two-choice situation, the chosen substance is considered to be hedonically more intense than the nonchosen one. One might, for example, compare different solutions of sugar water. If the concentration of sugar in the water is different in the two bottles, a rat will prefer the more highly concentrated solution. Through the use of preference tests, we can chart hedonic intensity differences.

The third property of the hedonic continuum is **duration**. Some hedonic processes may last only

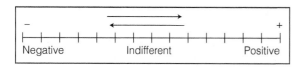

FIGURE 7.1   Young's hedonic continuum. From P. T. Young, "The Role of Affective Processes in Learning and Motivation," *Psychological Review*, 66, 104–125. Copyright © 1959 by The American Psychological Association. Used with permission.

as long as sensory stimulation lasts, while others presumably outlast the stimulation.

Young graphically represents the hedonic continuum as shown in Figure 7.1, which exhibits the range of the hedonic continuum from the maximum negative end (distress), through a neutral indifferent zone, to the extreme positive end (delight). Differences in intensities are represented by the arbitrary units marked off along the continuum. The arrows represent the ways in which hedonic affect can change. The arrow pointing toward the positive end represents the direction of hedonic change that organisms attempt to maintain. Young believed that the nervous system is constructed in such a way that organisms attempt to maximize positive affect and minimize negative affect. In addition, organisms will learn behaviors that lead to positive affective change and away from negative affective change.

Though the arrow pointing toward the positive end of the continuum is the preferred situation for an organism, changes also occur in the opposite direction, indicated by the arrow pointing toward the negative end of the continuum. When such negative changes occur, an organism will be motivated to reduce the negative affect situation (i.e., to behave in some way that will again minimize negative affect and maximize positive affect).

Sensory Stimulation and the Hedonic Continuum

Sensory stimuli provide information to an organism about the conditions of its external and internal environment. Affective processes, as represented

by the hedonic continuum, convey little information other than whether something is "good" (pleasant) or "bad" (unpleasant) and, in choice situations, "better than" or "worse than." Young saw this affective information as biologically primitive and of a different order from the more sophisticated discriminations we are capable of making from sensory information. This means that the hedonic continuum is not equivalent to sensory stimulation. This difference is most apparent when one compares the relationship of changes in hedonic intensity.

If we compare increases in the concentration of sugar with increases in hedonic intensity (as measured by a choice situation with laboratory animals), we discover that as a sugar solution becomes more concentrated, it is preferred over less concentrated sugar solutions as far up the concentration scale as we care to go (Young & Greene, 1953). Based on these data alone, we might be inclined to conclude that sensory and hedonic intensity are closely correlated; it is quite clear, however, that this is not true. Young and Falk (1956), for example, showed that for choices between distilled water and salty water, initial preferences were for the salt solution. As concentration of the salt solution was increased, however, the distilled water was preferred. Thus, preference for salt solutions increases with intensity of the solution only up to a point, after which it decreases again. For salt solutions, obviously, as sensory intensity increases, positive affect initially occurs but later turns to negative affect as the salt concentration continues to rise. Thus, we cannot assume that changes in sensory intensity will initiate similar changes in hedonic affect.

The hedonic processes represented by the hedonic continuum have motivational influences on behavior. First, positive affect is closely associated with approach behavior and negative affect with withdrawal. Second, Young believed that affective processes both activate and direct behavior so that maximum positive affect and minimum negative affect are maintained. Third, affective processes lead to the development of stable motives and dispositions. For example, the sweet taste of ice cream may lead to the development of choosing ice cream over other foods.

Changes in motivation are also seen as dependent on changes in hedonic value. If, for example, a rat is given a choice between two substances such as flour and sugar, it will prefer the sugar (Young, 1973). If, however, one of the test foods is replaced by a new food, an abrupt change may occur in the behavior exhibited toward the old substance in the choice situation. This suggests that introduction of the new substance has altered the motivation of the organism.

Young believed that the changes in motivation observed when a novel food is introduced occur because the organism has developed an expectancy of choice between two substances of different hedonic value. This expectancy is the result of hedonic feedback from the previous sampling of the substances; that is, the organism samples the substances it may choose between and develops a preference for one of them based on the hedonic value of each. On the first trial after a novel substance has been introduced, the expectancy that has developed is disconfirmed, and the motivation of the organism changes accordingly. Thus, changes in goal objects lead to changes in expectancy, which in turn alter performance.

The Motivational Influence of Sensations

Carl Pfaffmann (1960) conducted much research on the physiological mechanisms of taste, and his work seemed to agree with Young's ideas. Pfaffmann suggested that sensory stimulation by itself is motivating and leads to approach or withdrawal behavior. He noted, for example, work done by Stellar, Hyman, and Samet (1954), which showed that animals display the typical preference-aversion function for salt (NaCl) even if the fluid passing through the mouth—and thus over the sensory receptors for taste—never reaches the stomach (because of an esophageal fistula). This research indicated that the taste sensations are sufficient to trigger approach or avoidance behavior

without having to be tied to any physiological change.

In agreement with Young, Pfaffmann noted that hedonic intensity and sensory intensity are not equivalent. Recording the electrical activity of the chorda tympani (a cranial nerve sending taste information to the brain), he showed that as salt concentration in a fluid increases so does the electrical activity of the nerve. However, hedonic value (as evidenced by choices) at first increases and then decreases as the salt concentration becomes greater. The relationship between the electrical activity of the chorda tympani and hedonic value can be seen in Figure 7.2. Additional evidence for the importance of sensory information in motivating behavior can be seen in the fact that nonnutritive substances such as saccharin are rewarding (and thus motivate behavior designed to obtain them) because of their sweet taste (Sheffield & Roby, 1950; Sheffield, Roby, & Campbell, 1954). Pfaffmann believed that the stimulus properties of a tasted substance directly determine the hedonic value of the substance.

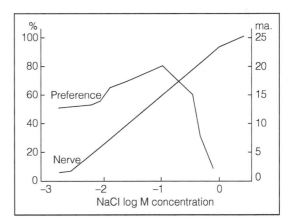

FIGURE 7.2 Preference for increasing concentrations of salt and chorda tympani nerve firing in rats. From "The Pleasures of Sensation," by C. Pfaffmann, 1960, *Psychological Review, 67,* 253–268. Copyright © 1960 by the American Psychological Association. Used with permission.

Hedonic Value and Contact Receptors

The stimulation of contact receptors (such as taste) seems much more often associated with strong emotion than is the stimulation of distance receptors (e.g., vision). Contact receptors are also much more often associated with consummatory activity (taste—eating, genital contact—intercourse, etc.).

The hedonic tone provided directly by contact receptors may be an evolutionary adaptation. For example, distance receptors (vision) give some lead time for one to make a judgment and react, but contact receptors often involve stimuli (such as pain) that require a quick reaction if the organism is to survive. Hedonic value (pleasure or pain) may therefore have evolved in conjunction with stimulation of the contact receptors to quickly direct behavior. Though the relationship between stimulation of the contact receptors and hedonic value should be considered speculative, Sherrington (1947), as early as 1906, noted the existence of a relationship between contact receptors, emotion, and consummatory behavior. Additionally, those theorists who have argued most persuasively for hedonic theories of motivation have usually studied behaviors associated with the stimulation of contact receptors. Hedonic explanations of motivation may prove to be less useful when applied to behaviors associated with the stimulation of distance receptors.

We will now examine research on pain as one example of hedonistic explanations of motivation.

Pain

Pain normally occurs when the body is injured. Pain is useful because it tells us we have been injured and often causes us to alter our behavior so that the injured part of our body has time to heal. On the other hand, pain can often seem out of proportion to the size of the injury. Small injuries can sometimes be terribly painful. Anyone who has broken a tooth can attest to the terrible pain that accompanies such a seemingly trivial injury. Or consider the phenomenon of phantom limb pain, where excruciating pain may be experienced even though the involved body part has been amputated. In these cases, pain does not seem very adaptive and may, in fact, interfere with more adaptive behaviors.

One of the foremost researchers in the study of pain is Ronald Melzack, who, with Patrick Wall in 1965, proposed a theory of pain that is still influential today (see, e.g., Kalat, 2001). Prior to their model, pain was thought to result from pain receptors sending their messages along specific pain fibers to the brain, where pain was then experienced. Melzack (1961; Melzack & Wall, 1965) realized that the perception of pain was much more variable and much more modifiable than people thought. For example, about 65% of men wounded in battle feel no pain when brought to the combat hospital (Beecher, 1959; Melzack, 1961; Warga, 1987), yet approximately 80% of civilians with similar injuries typically report severe pain and ask for pain medication. Similarly, it is well known that football players, boxers, and other athletes often continue to play even though hurt, because they are unaware of the injury. Such examples led Melzack to realize that no simple and direct relationship existed between the severity of an injury and the amount of pain experienced.

Furthermore, pathological pain states such as **causalgia** (a severe burning pain that is sometimes caused by a partial lesion of a peripheral nerve), **peripheral neuralgia** (which can occur following peripheral nerve infection), and the previously mentioned **phantom limb pain** are often *unsuccessfully* treated by surgical lesions of either the peripheral or central nervous system. If the experience of pain was simply the result of the stimulation of pain receptors and the perception of those signals by the brain, then "disconnection" surgery ought to abolish the pain of causalgia, neuralgia, and phantom limbs. The fact that such surgeries are often unsuccessful suggests that the experience of pain is more than just simple perception of painful stimulation.

Additionally, Melzack (1961) pointed out that if a person's attention is focused on the painful aspects of a procedure, pain is often experienced more intensely. Hall and Stride (as noted by Melzack, 1961), for example, showed that the word *pain* in a set of instructions caused anxious participants to report electric shock as painful, even though this shock level was not considered painful by the participants if the word *pain* was absent. This and other experiments on the psychological aspects of pain indicate that higher brain processes can alter the experience of pain.

Based on the evidence previously noted and information concerning the physiology of the peripheral nervous system, Melzack and Wall proposed a model of pain that emphasized the role of higher brain processes in controlling the experience of pain and a modulating system within the spinal cord that influenced how much pain information reached the brain. This model was called the **gate control theory** of pain. Melzack and Wall's theory proved to be very influential and generated much research.

Research since the original publication of the gate control theory has shown that the pain control gates are modulated by neurotransmitter changes involving the **endogenous opiates** and perhaps other factors as well. For example, Pomeranz, Cheng, and Law (1977) showed that removing the pituitary of mice drastically reduced the analgesic effects of electroacupuncture. Since the pituitary was known to produce pain-killing endorphins, it seemed possible that the analgesic effects of acupuncture might result from the stimulation of sensory nerves, which in turn triggered the pituitary to secrete endorphins.

In a further study, Peets and Pomeranz (1978) examined the analgesic effects of electroacupuncture on a strain of mice known to be deficient in opiate receptors (CXBK strain). When the analgesic effects of electroacupuncture on the opiate-deficient and normal mice were compared, the opiate-deficient mice showed little analgesic effect of the acupuncture, while the normal mice showed the standard analgesic effect. Further evidence for the role of an opioid system in the gating of pain is suggested by studies that show that **naloxone**, which blocks the effects of opiates, also blocks the analgesic effects of acupuncture (Peets & Pomeranz, 1978; Pomeranz, 1981).

Fillingim, King, Ribeiro-Dasilva, Rahim-Williams, and Riley (2009, p. 447) reviewed both clinical and experimental research on gender and pain. The research is consistent in showing that there are gender differences. For example, "epidemiologic studies clearly demonstrates that women are at substantially greater risk for many clinical pain conditions and there is some suggestion that postoperative and procedural pain may be more severe among women than men." Additionally, experimental studies show that women have greater pain sensitivity than men. As Fillingham et al. note, gender differences in pain probably result from a number of factors, including genetics, hormonal differences, differing gender roles, and other psychosocial factors. Additionally, learning and emotional reactions (see, e.g., Butler, Nilsson-Todd, Cleren, Lena, Garcia, & Finn, 2011) and even placebos (Price, Finniss, & Benedetti, 2008) can modulate pain as well. It is, thus, abundantly clear that experienced pain is not just a straightforward signal of damage to a specific part of the body but involves many complex interactions among brain systems.

Other areas of the brain also contribute to the modulation of pain. In particular, portions of the thalamus, limbic system, prefrontal cortex, somatosensory cortex (both primary and secondary), and cingulate cortex are involved with the perception of pain (Carlson, 2010). Recently, the basal ganglia have been shown to play a role in pain too (Borsook, Upadhyay, Chudler, & Becerra, 2010). In addition, the periaqueductal gray matter in the brain stem appears to be important in the reduction of pain produced by the endogenous opiates. This area, through connections to the nucleus raphe magnus in the medulla and from there to the dorsal horn of the spinal cord, may also influence the perception of pain at the level of the spinal cord (see Carlson, 2010). The endogenous opiates appear to produce analgesia by blocking the production of a transmitter known as **substance P** as shown in Figure 7.3 (see Kalat, 2009, for a brief summary of this work).

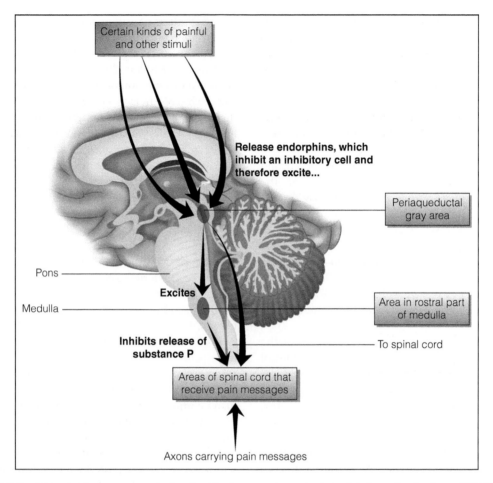

FIGURE 7.3   Major brainstem structures involved in the experience and modulation of pain. From KALAT. *Biological Psychology*, 10e. Copyright © 2009 Cengage Learning.

Thus the central modulation of pain, first noticed by Melzack, seems to be mediated, at least in part, by the action of endogenous opiates. Indeed Bandura, O'Leary, Taylor, Gauthier, and Gossard (1987) have shown that cognitive control of painful stimulation results, in part, from activation of the opioid system.

Whether the hedonic value of objects is limited to the stimulation of contact receptors or not, the importance of sensory stimulation per se to motivation has been extensively studied. Research has ranged from an examination of curiosity and exploratory behavior to studying the effects of depriving organisms of sensory stimulation. As we will see, the importance of sensory stimulation to normal behavior has been shown in many different experimental situations.

Novelty, Curiosity, and Exploratory Behavior

A group of studies performed primarily in the 1950s indicated that external stimuli can serve to motivate behavior directly. Terms commonly used to describe the motive state generated by external stimuli included curiosity, exploratory drive, manipulation motives, stimulus hunger, and need for stimulation (Cofer & Appley, 1964). Although the information gained from these experiments was often used as evidence against the then currently popular need reduction or drive reduction theories of motivation, the information is of interest in itself because it indicates that changes in the sensory qualities of the environment lead to changes in motivated behavior.

In an early review of this literature, Cofer and Appley (1964) noted that studies on sensory stimulation and motivation could be grouped into studies indicating that behaviors are released by stimulation and studies indicating a need for stimulation. We will examine each in turn.

Behaviors Released by Stimulation

Harry Harlow at the University of Wisconsin studied primate behavior extensively. He pointed out that external stimuli are important in motivating behavior and also argued that much of human behavior is motivated by such nonhomeostatic mechanisms. For example, humans learn even though they are not hungry or thirsty, and they solve problems that have no utility, such as playing chess or bridge. These behaviors often seem motivated simply by the sensory stimulation they provide (Harlow, 1953).

In one experiment, Harlow, Harlow, and Meyer (1950) gave monkeys mechanical puzzles that could be disassembled. One group was given no food reward for solving the puzzle, while another group was given food. Delivery of food actually tended to disrupt performance on the puzzles, and the rewarded group lost interest in the puzzles sooner than the nonrewarded group. For the nonrewarded group, the behavior was apparently maintained by a motive to manipulate or explore the puzzle. Though Harlow approached these studies as examples of drives, these new drives

were nonhomeostatic and sensory in nature (Levine, 1975).

Berlyne (1960, 1963) conducted considerable research on the conditions that motivate us to attend to our environment. He argued that exploratory activity has the function of altering the stimulus field in which we are immersed. Exploratory activity seems primarily involved in altering the stimulus input that we receive rather than causing any changes in body tissues. Exploratory behavior was also thought to be a function both of the state of the organism and of external stimuli such as surprise, change, ambiguity, incongruity, and uncertainty.

Berlyne suggested that factors such as novelty and uncertainty have motivational properties because they increase the arousal level of the organism. He argued that we attempt to maintain an optimal level of arousal. If stimulation drops too low (as in boredom), we become motivated to increase our arousal level. On the other hand, if our arousal level becomes too high, we will be motivated to lower it. Thus novel or surprising stimuli will motivate behavior directed toward themselves if they provide a small change in arousal, because small changes in arousal are pleasant. As supportive evidence, Berlyne (1951, 1958a, 1958b) found that novel stimuli, as compared to familiar stimuli, cause one to orient toward them. Human infants 3 to 9 months old, for example, looked at figures that had the greatest amount of contour, and adults were attracted to complex or incongruous pictures presented to them. All of these situations would be expected to cause small changes in arousal and thus would be pleasant.

Montgomery (1953) also studied exploratory behavior. He allowed rats to explore one of three mazes that were painted black, white, and gray, respectively. Each rat was allowed to explore twice, and the amount of time spent in exploring the second time was related to the color (rats are color blind, so their responding must have been based on grayscale differences between the three mazes) of the first maze explored. Montgomery found that maximum exploration occurred when the second maze was maximally different from the first (black first, white second; white first, black second) and that least exploration occurred when the second maze was identical to the first (white first, white second; black first, black second). Intermediate amounts of exploration occurred when the stimulus change from first to second maze was intermediate (white to gray; black to gray). Thus the amount of exploratory behavior shown by Montgomery's rats seemed controlled by the degree of stimulus change involved. Montgomery's data fit nicely with Berlyne's in suggesting that stimulus change (novelty) motivates behaviors such as exploration.

Donald Hebb (1966) believed that moderate changes in arousal are reinforcing. Because we become habituated to the familiar, we will approach new stimulus situations; if the new stimulation is too arousing, however, we will withdraw from the situation. Hebb assumed that the brain as well as the body needed to be active. According to Hebb, play behavior, seen in many organisms, occurs when other needs are not active. Though often muscular, play behavior also has a neural component because many of the games that organisms play depend on memory of earlier experiences (e.g., otters sliding down a mudbank into the water or a child playing patty-cake). Play behavior often seems to occur as the result of boredom and serves to provide a higher level of arousal.

Studies of exploratory behavior, play, novelty, and uncertainty showed that motivation can be triggered by situations that lead to increases in stimulation. Berlyne and Hebb proposed that motivation is activated when stimulus conditions are either too high or too low. In essence, the theories of Berlyne and Hebb are also arousal theories (see Chapter 3 for other views of arousal); deviations away from optimal arousal in either direction—too much or too little—trigger motivation in organisms to behave in ways that bring arousal back to the optimal level. Thus, exploration, play, and reactions to novelty or uncertainty can be seen as behaviors that alleviate the deprivation that occurs from too little stimulus change (Fowler, 1967). Such an analysis suggests that depriving an organism of changing stimulus input (either by

eliminating it or by making stimulation unchanging) should lead to motivated behavior. As we shall see in the next section, that is precisely what happens.

The Need for Stimulation

Many different studies suggest that a need for stimulation exists. Some studies have attempted to reduce the absolute level of stimulation to very low levels, while others have examined the effects of reduction in the patterning of stimulation (usually of a visual nature). Finally, some studies have examined the roles of monotonous or unchanging environments (Kubzansky & Leiderman, 1961). These studies are collectively called sensory deprivation experiments.

The effects of **sensory deprivation** have been researched in developing organisms as well as in adults. Results of both types of studies generally indicate a disruption of normal behavior (but see Suedfeld, 1975). We will first examine research on deprivation that occurs early in development and its relationship to motivational processes; then we will analyze behavioral changes that occur in adult animals as a result of sensory deprivation.

Early Sensory Restriction   Thompson and Melzack (1956) studied the effects of sensory restriction on the development of Scottish terriers. A 4-week-old group of Scotties was divided into two subgroups. One subgroup was raised normally and served as a control for the second subgroup. The members of the second subgroup were each raised in individual cages. This experimental group was maintained in relative isolation for 7 to 10 months.

When the experimental Scotties were let out of their isolation condition they were extremely active and playful (much like puppies), quite different in this regard from the normally raised controls. The isolated dogs continued to explore their new environment long after the control subjects had grown bored with their new surroundings. Also, the isolated Scotties explored more in maze tests than the controls, even several years after release from isolation, and exhibited higher activity levels. Thus, sensory restriction apparently altered the normal motivational behavior of the dogs.

In another part of the experiment, the two groups of Scotties were tested for their reactions to both strange and painful objects (such as an electrified toy car that delivered a shock when touched). Normal Scotties quickly learned to avoid the car by running away. The isolated Scotties became highly agitated by the strange object but did not avoid it, behaving as if uncertain what to do about this strange, painful object. Most of them seemed unaware that the pain they experienced was induced by an external object in their environment.

Several tests of problem-solving ability were also conducted, and the experimental Scotties were always deficient compared to the normals in ability. For example, the experimental Scotties were unable to correctly choose the box under which they had just seen a piece of food hidden, while those in the control group could choose correctly even after a delay of 4 minutes. On maze tasks, the isolates made approximately 50% more errors than the normals. Finally, when normal and isolated Scotties were put together, the normals were always dominant, even when considerably younger than the restricted dogs.

Sensory restriction, then, had long-lasting (and apparently permanent) effects on the behavior of the isolated Scotties. Though not appearing unmotivated, the isolates seemed hyperexcitable and unable to direct their behavior in an efficient, adaptive manner. Thompson and Melzack's research suggests that sensory restriction may alter the ways in which motivated behavior is directed (such as nonescape from painful objects) and opens the question of whether sensory restriction may induce emotionality (hyperexcitability) when normal levels of stimulation are provided.

In studies of cats, monkeys, and chimpanzees, Riesen (1961) reported very similar effects. For example, he restricted the visual sensory input of kittens by raising them in dark cages. He noted that exposure of these cats to a normal-lighted environment revealed perceptual deficits and violent emotionality. Riesen found that his dark-reared animals showed (a) hyperexcitability, (b) increased incidences of convulsive disorders, and (c) localized motor impairment.

In regard to hyperexcitability, Riesen found that normal levels of illumination produced extreme fear in animals that had been dark-reared. Also, when normal patterned vision was allowed, many of the cats went into convulsions. Susceptibility to convulsions seemed to relate to the absence of patterned vision during development rather than to the absence of light per se, because cats that were dark-reared but handled and tested daily (thus allowing some patterned visual experience) did not develop the seizures. In regard to the motor dysfunction, Riesen found that visual nystagamus (involuntary rapid movement of the eyeball) was common in both cats and monkeys deprived of patterned light.

Riesen concluded that the increases in stimulation were emotion producing for his dark-reared subjects. In this respect, his work seemed to agree with that of Hebb (1949), who argued that emotional disturbance may sometimes result as a consequence of incongruent sensory input. In Riesen's experiment the lighted environment was incongruent with the rearing histories of the animals.

Like the Scotties in the Thompson and Melzack study, Riesen's animals were hyperexcitable and emotional. Also as in Thompson and Melzack's study, Riesen's animals did not cope well with new and strange stimulus situations. Riesen's study further seemed to suggest that early sensory restriction may alter the normal functioning of the brain, as evidenced by the increased susceptibility to seizure and motor dysfunction. Other evidence (Hirsch & Spinelli, 1970, 1971) has supported this conclusion, showing that the visual patterning experienced early in development influences development of the visual processing circuits.

Research on sensory restriction indicates that adequate stimulation is necessary for normal development. Though much of the effect of sensory restriction probably results from physiological and perceptual changes, the research also suggests that motivational and emotional changes occur. New sensations, to a deprived animal, lead to fear and withdrawal.

Attachment

Maternal Deprivation The parents of young animals provide a rich source of stimuli to the developing organism (sight, smell, touch, sound, temperature). Studies of maternal deprivation have shown that the lack of adequate parent-infant interactions also produces long-lasting effects. These effects may be due in part to reduced sensory stimulation from both environment and parent.

The term *maternal deprivation* does not always mean the loss of the mother exclusively. Maternal deprivation also refers to situations in which the developing organism receives little or no consistent care from whomever is responsible for it. In most mammals this is the mother, but in humans "mothering" can be provided by any number of people, including the mother, father, siblings, other relatives, or even caretakers of various sorts.

Additional work by Harlow shed much light on the importance of maternal stimuli for the adequate development of young organisms. He used rhesus monkeys to examine attachment processes that occur between the infant and its mother. Harlow (1958) pointed out that the view of the mother–infant attachment process (what we would commonly call love) argued that the process is a derived (that is learned) motive and is based on the fact that the mother is closely associated with reduction of the infant's needs (hunger, thirst, warmth, and so on). Derived motives, however, usually extinguish quickly when association with the primary motive is cut, but the mother–infant attachment seems lifelong.

In observing infant monkeys that for various reasons had been separated from their mothers, Harlow noted that the infants developed a strong attachment to cloth pads placed in their cages and became emotional when the pads were removed for cleaning (reminding us of Linus from the "Peanuts" cartoon, who feels insecure without his blanket).

In an initial experiment, baby monkeys were taken from their mothers at birth and put into individual cages. Attached to each cage was a second cage containing surrogate (substitute) mothers made either of wire or soft terrycloth. These surrogate mothers are shown in Figure 7.4. For half of the baby monkeys, the wire mother provided the nourishment. As can be seen in Figure 7.5, the monkeys spent the largest amount of time with the terrycloth mother, regardless of which mother nourished it.

The cloth mother was more than just a soft place to sit, as became evident when these baby monkeys were made anxious; they ran to the cloth mother, who served as a source of security. In a strange environment (such as a new room), the cloth mother served as a secure base from which exploratory forays were made by the infant monkeys. If the cloth mother was absent (or only the wire mother was present), the infant monkeys exhibited freezing behavior, vocalizing and rocking back and forth. Clearly, then, the baby monkeys developed a strong attachment to the cloth mother as a result of the **contact comfort** (body contact) provided.

Harlow and Suomi (1970) examined a number of different stimuli of the surrogate mother that might have provided sensations leading to attachment behavior. They found that while contact comfort was the most important of these stimuli when held constant, lactation, temperature, and rocking movement were also involved in the attachment process. Facial design was not important; as Harlow and Suomi noted, to a baby the maternal face is beautiful regardless of how others might judge it. Sensory stimulation involving contact comfort, feeding, temperature, and movement are apparently important sources of attachment for infant monkeys. The infant monkey is motivated to remain near its mother (whether real or surrogate), and the mother serves as a source of security from which the infant explores and learns about its world.

While the infant monkeys in the experiments just described became attached to their surrogate mothers, they also showed many bizarre behaviors and were socially abnormal. Harlow and Harlow (1962) investigated the importance of both the

FIGURE 7.4 Surrogate mothers provided by Harlow to his infant rhesus monkeys. From "Nature of Love— Simplified," by H. R. Harlow and S. J. Suomi, 1970, *American Psychologist, 25*, 161–168. Copyright © 1970 by the American Psychological Association. Used with permission.

mother and peers on normal social development of the infant. They separated infant monkeys from their mothers at birth and raised them in wire cages for varying amounts of time. Semi-isolated, the monkeys could still see and hear other monkeys but could not interact with them. Isolation from birth to 3 months produced effects that were later reversible, and the effects of isolation appeared minimal, but monkeys isolated from birth to 6 months developed strange behaviors that appeared more permanent. Monkeys isolated for longer (some from birth to 2 years) were extremely abnormal. They stared fixedly into space, paced their cages, rocked and clasped themselves, and developed compulsive habits such as chewing or tearing at their own bodies until they bled. They also showed abnormal fear of other monkeys and were socially unable to cope. For example, female isolates would fight viciously when approached by a male, and none were mated naturally. When some of these isolated females were artificially inseminated, their behavior toward their own infants ranged from indifference to outright abuse. These motherless mothers were totally inadequate.

One might be tempted to conclude that adequate maternal care is all that is necessary for normal social adjustment, but at least for monkeys we are not justified in drawing that conclusion. Monkeys raised with their mothers but not allowed social interaction with peers do not develop normally either, nor do monkeys raised with peers but without a mother. Experience with both mother and peers is apparently necessary for normal development (Harlow & Harlow, 1966; Sackett, 1967).

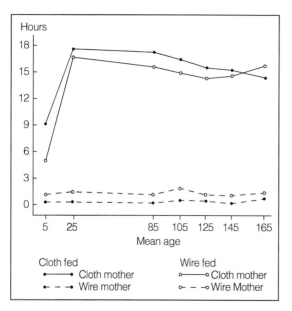

FIGURE 7.5 Contact time (in hours) for cloth and wire mothers. Note that regardless of which surrogate fed the infant, most time was spent with the cloth mother. From "Nature of Love—Simplified," by H. R. Harlow and S. J. Suomi, 1970, *American Psychologist*, 25, 161–168. Copyright © 1970 by the American Psychological Association. Used by permission.

The indifference and abuse of the motherless monkey mothers bear a striking resemblance to incidents of human child abuse. Frequently in cases of child abuse, the abusing parent was also abused as a child. This suggests that proper parenting behavior depends at least partly on having observed how parents behave. If learning about parenting while growing up is important, it is not at all surprising that Harlow's motherless mothers were inadequate. Parenting can be understood as a motivated behavior that results in part from a learning process termed *modeling*. As we saw in Chapter 5, many human motives appear to result from modeling.

Protest, Despair, Detachment, and Ambivalence Harlow's studies provide a backdrop against which human infant behavior can be better understood. We have known for

some time that children separated from their parents go through a series of behavioral changes that include **protest, despair, detachment,** and **ambivalence**. Protest and despair following separation have also been extensively studied in monkeys (Mineka & Suomi, 1978).

Bowlby (1973) reported several studies conducted during World War II that are relevant to the discussion of parent–child separation. These studies indicated that a child separated from its parents goes through a series of predictable behaviors. When a child was initially separated from his or her parents, there was considerable protest in the form of crying. The crying continued for several days and occurred sporadically for up to 9 days, most commonly at bedtime and during the night. At the same time these children became uncooperative with their attendants.

Following this protest stage, despair set in. The children now began to accept some comfort from the attendants and sometimes became very possessive of their attendant. Hostility directed toward other children in the situation increased, and toilet training regressed.

When the children were returned to their parents, varying degrees of detachment were shown. The degree of detachment appeared to depend on the length of time the child had been separated from the parents. In some cases the detached behavior persisted for several days following reunion with the parents.

The detachment phase was followed by a phase of ambivalence in which the child showed hostility, rejection, and defiance of the parents on the one hand, and clinging, crying, and demanding behavior of the parents on the other. The ambivalence phase sometimes lasted as long as 12 weeks.

As a general rule, familiar people (grandparents or siblings) and familiar objects (favorite toys) reduced the intensity of the separation effects. A second important factor was the mothering available from the parental substitute; the more mothering that was available, the less intense was the separation experience. Let us now examine research concerning the lack of adequate mothering in which the effects, much as in Harlow's monkeys, seem permanent.

A 1915 survey by Knox (cited by Patton & Gardner, 1963) found that 90% of institutionalized infants died within a year of admission even though they received adequate physical care. Such startling statistics imply that something important for survival was missing in these infants' lives. Spitz (1946), in describing a syndrome he called anaclitic depression, noted that some institutionalized children show depression, a failure to respond to stimulation, and a loss of appetite and weight. A clue to the possible source of this depressed state was provided by a study of an institution where infants received more individual attention and did not develop depressive symptoms. Infants apparently need close interaction with an individual responsible for their care if they are to develop normally.

Deprivation Dwarfism (Psychosocial Dwarfism) Gardner (1972) and Patton and Gardner (1963) have shown that lack of appropriate home conditions may result in a condition called *deprivation dwarfism*. (See also Money, 1977; Money & Wolff, 1974; Wolff & Money, 1973.) Deprivation dwarfism is a reduction of bone maturation and growth to the point that the child's physical maturation is much less than normal for its age, and these researchers found that children suffering from deprivation dwarfism were retarded in growth. Heights for age ranged from 20% to 65% of normal. The children appeared malnourished, though in most cases their diets seemed adequate. Emotionally, these children were lethargic, apathetic, and withdrawn. Their faces were sad, rarely smiling, and they typically avoided contact with other people.

This reduction in growth does not result from neural-endocrine problems or from disease but from the social environment in which these children are forced to live. Robert Patton and Lytt Gardner (1963) studied six cases of thin dwarfs. These children were stunted both physically and psychologically. All came from disordered families in which one or both parents were emotionally disturbed and unable to cope with parenthood. Fathers were often absent from the home, and none were able to maintain steady jobs. Mothers

had often come from similar family situations. The relationship between the parents was typically discordant and often violent. Maternal attitude toward the children ranged from outright hostility to indifference and annoyance. Parental care of the children could be described, at best, as passively neglectful.

When these children were removed from their hostile and deprived environment (e.g., to a hospital), they began to improve both physically and psychologically. Most of the children immediately started growing again. That these children improved in a hospital situation is in marked contrast to normal children, who often react to hospitalization with many of the symptoms of children separated from their parents.

Patton and Gardner were able to follow up with two of the six children through late childhood. These children remained below average in height and weight, and skeletal growth was still behind chronological age. Residual effects of the early deprivation experience on both personality structure and intelligence also existed. Furthermore, although hospitalization produced a catch-up phenomenon in these children, return to the disordered environment reinstated the dwarfism symptoms (Gardner, 1972; Goodwin, 1978).

How can maternal deprivation and emotional and social disorder reduce physical development? Patton and Gardner have proposed that environmental deprivation and emotional disturbance can influence endocrine functioning. The pituitary gland seems to be particularly affected.

The pituitary gland secretes a substance called **growth hormone (somatotrophin)**, which stimulates growth. Quantity of growth hormone is known to be subnormal in children suffering from deprivation dwarfism, even though no pituitary malfunction is present. (The fact that these children start growing again when conditions improve also indicates that the pituitary is not malfunctioning but is being shut down by other factors.) It appears that the mechanism suppressing growth hormone is a disruption of the normal sleep pattern.

Children classified as deprivation dwarfs show abnormal sleep patterns. It is known that more growth hormone is secreted during the first 2 hours of sleep than at any other time, and if the person doesn't sleep, the hormone isn't secreted. Thus the poor social environment apparently leads to a disruption of the normal sleep patterns in these children, and the abnormal sleep pattern then alters the secretion of growth hormone, which leads to the reduction in growth.

Maternal deprivation, then, can have far-reaching effects on both physical and psychological growth. Such effects emphasize the importance of an adequate sensory environment for proper development.

Patton and Gardner (1963) have argued that a critical period exists during which external stimulation is necessary for optimal development. Without adequate stimulation, permanent deficiencies result. The disordered social environment in which these children are forced to live is nonoptimal. They are neglected, ignored, and abused by the parents. As a result they are stunted physically, emotionally, and psychologically. Harlow, too, from his work on monkeys concluded that a critical period for normal development exists. The data from both animal and human research are consistent in showing that stimulation is necessary for normal development and that lack of stimulation leads to behaviors indicating motivational deficiencies such as lethargy, apathy, and withdrawal.

Mother–infant and peer–peer interactions are apparently important sources of the stimulation necessary for the normal development of an organism. Indeed, one researcher who observed mother–infant interactions in free-ranging baboons (Nash, 1978) has suggested that differences in mother–infant interactions may partly account for personality differences observed in adulthood. The research on maternal deprivation and infant interaction is generally consistent in showing that deficiencies in mother–infant and peer–peer relationships lead to motivational deficiencies. The motivation of deprived organisms often is not only lowered but also may be inappropriate or bizarre. Changes in emotionality are also evident.

Because stimulation is apparently so important for the normal development of organisms, one

might also expect that continued stimulation is a necessary condition for normal adult functioning. This does, in fact, appear to be true.

Sensory Deprivation in Adults Sensory deprivation studies usually deprive participants of several sensory inputs simultaneously. Most often, visual and auditory inputs are reduced or eliminated; however, tactile and other senses may also be reduced. Sensory deprivation studies may attempt an absolute reduction of sensory stimulation, a reduced patterning of sensory stimulation, or an imposed structuring (usually monotonous) of the sensory environment without any reduction in stimulation (Kubzansky & Leiderman, 1961). Most of the studies on sensory deprivation are of the reduced patterning type, because absolute reductions in stimulation are difficult to achieve.

Much of the early work on sensory deprivation was carried out at McGill University during the period 1951–1954 (Heron, 1961). In the classic sensory deprivation situation, a male college student was asked to lie on a bed for 24 hours in a lighted, semi-soundproofed room. Patterned vision was eliminated by the use of translucent goggles that admitted only diffused light. Cotton gloves were attached to long, cardboard cuffs that extended from beyond the fingertips to the elbow to reduce tactile stimulation. The participant's head rested on a U-shaped pillow, which reduced auditory stimulation, and an air conditioner provided monotonous background noise that masked extraneous sounds (Heron, 1957, 1961). Figure 7.6 shows the deprivation chamber and basic apparatus used.

Several behavioral tests were conducted both during and after the isolation period (IQ tests, digit span tests, associative learning tasks, etc.). A propaganda talk on the existence of psychic phenomena (telepathy, ghosts, etc.) was also given, periodically interrupting the isolation period.

Perhaps the most striking result of the experiment was that participants could not long tolerate the isolation conditions. In the first experiment (Bexton, Heron, & Scott, 1954) participants usually quit the experiment after 2 or 3 days. In a later experiment, the researchers used themselves as

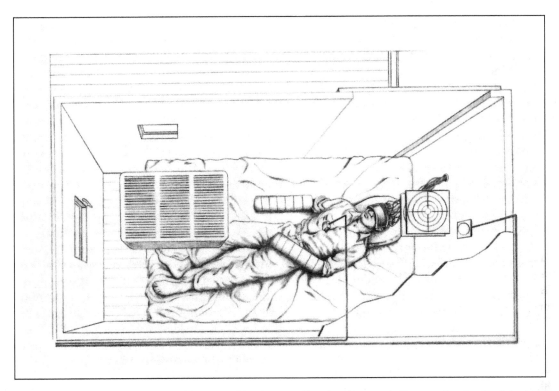

FIGURE 7.6 Sensory deprivation chamber used by the McGill University group. See text for details. Adapted from "The Pathology of Boredom," by Woodburn Heron. Copyright © 1957 by Scientific American, Inc. All rights reserved. Used by permission.

participants and were able to tolerate the conditions for only 6 days (Heron, Doane, & Scott, 1956). Sensory-deprived participants experienced boredom, restlessness, irritability, and a strong desire to terminate the experiment. Additionally, the participants showed impaired thinking, disturbed visual perceptions (hallucinations), and changes in emotionality, as well as changes in the electrical activity of the brain as measured by the EEG. Isolated participants were inferior to controls in 6 out of 7 intellectual tests and also did less well than controls on tests of perceptual ability. The isolated participants also showed a greater change in attitude than the controls after the talk on psychic phenomena, though both groups showed a change toward belief in such events.

Visual perception was influenced by the loss of patterned vision. When the goggles were removed,

plane surfaces appeared warped, and objects in the environment seemed to move when the participant moved. Surfaces such as walls often appeared to shimmer or undulate, and participants in the experiments reported very strong afterimages. Spatial orientation was also disrupted by the sensory isolation. For example, toward the end of the isolation period, some participants became so disoriented that they had to call for help because they got lost in the bathroom.

What are we to make of these results? From the point of view of motivation, sensory deprivation conditions for most people are clearly aversive. The results suggest that people need to maintain a certain level of stimulation and that they become motivated to increase it if deprived of adequate stimulation levels. Adequate stimulation also seems necessary for efficient functioning, because reduced stimulation led to decreased performance on most of the experimental tasks. Although the hallucinations reported by Heron and associates have proven more elusive to other researchers, both perceptual and intellectual functioning were clearly altered by reduced sensory input. Sensory restriction and deprivation in the form of inadequate maternal care, as previously noted, leads to permanent deficiencies. And sensory deprivation in adults apparently leads to temporary disruptions of behavior.

Jerome Bruner (1961) believed that the effects of isolation can be understood in relation to the development of adequate models or strategies for evaluating information. The deprived child lacks the rich, varied environment that will allow the proper development of these models. In this regard, Bruner noted that social contact may be important because it provides a complex sensory environment. He suggested that the adult who has already developed adequate processes for dealing with incoming sensory information is constantly monitoring and correcting strategies as conditions change. The effects of sensory deprivation in the adult may be to disrupt this evaluation process, which in turn may lead to a reduction in cognitive abilities and distortion in the perception of events.

A study by Bennett (1961) of jet pilots supports the idea that sensory deprivation in the adult disrupts the evaluation process. Bennett examined five cases of disorientation in fliers. In all five cases the fliers were either pilots or navigators who became disoriented when flying a straight, level course at high altitude.

Symptoms of disorientation included feelings of confusion and a loss of contact with their surroundings. In three of the five cases, the illusion of turning was reported. In all five cases, the disorientation occurred at altitudes above 20,000 feet when the fliers had been on a straight, level course for periods ranging from 45 minutes to 2 hours and 20 minutes. The person suffering the disorientation was in all cases isolated from the rest of the crew.

Clark and Graybiel (cited by Bennett, 1961) have reported similar findings from navy and marine pilots. These pilots reported feelings of spatial disorientation, isolation, and detachment from

the earth. Three conditions were associated with the disorientation: flying alone, flying at high altitude, and a minimum of activity.

The symptoms reported by the fliers are remarkably similar to the symptoms seen in sensory deprivation experiments. Bennett noted that the lone pilot, flying at high altitude on a straight and level course, is actually quite sensory deprived, for little movement is detectable at that altitude and there is little to do. It seems reasonable to suppose, then, that the disorientation seen in these fliers resulted from the restricted sensory environment that high altitude imposes (no equipment malfunctions were found in any of these cases).

As further support for the sensory deprivation hypothesis, Bennett noted that all the disorientation symptoms were reduced or eliminated if activity was required or other people to talk with were present. Bennett's work with pilots in real-life situations also supports the idea that changing stimulation is necessary for effective behavior and that without adequate stimulation, adaptive behaviors are reduced.

Sensory deprivation effects are probably not confined to high-altitude flying. Any situation that provides reduced or monotonous stimulation and little activity may be a candidate for disorientation effects. For example, driving alone at night on an arrow-straight interstate highway might produce effects similar to those produced by high-altitude flying.

Goldberger and Holt (1961) pointed out that some people tolerate sensory deprivation better than others. In one study, these researchers divided individuals into two groups based on their ability to deal with primary process thought (as measured by the Rorschach test). Results showed that participants who scored as mature handlers of primary process thought (with a minimum of anxiety) tolerated sensory deprivation better and showed less negative emotionality and more pleasant emotionality during the deprivation period.

The Goldberger and Holt study suggests that some people (those who are emotionally secure) can profit from isolation experiences if the isolation is not too protracted or severe. Suedfeld (1975) has also suggested that sensory deprivation may have beneficial effects. Suedfeld noted that some of the early studies of sensory deprivation may have been very anxiety provoking because of the experimental situation. For example, some researchers provided panic buttons, while others used anxiety-arousing instructions or release-from-liability forms. Orne and Scheibe (cited by Suedfeld, 1975) obtained some of the typical results of deprivation studies, in fact, by using only these peripheral, anxiety-arousing conditions without any subsequent sensory deprivation.

Suedfeld noted that beneficial effects of isolation, though reported, have not been emphasized. Some participants have reported enjoying the deprivation experience. In a series of studies (Suedfeld & Ikard, 1974; Suedfeld & Kristeller, 1982; Suedfeld, 1977, 1980) Suedfeld has shown that reduction of stimulation can be therapeutically helpful. In an environment that he calls **REST (Restricted Environmental Stimulation Technique)**, participants have shown improvement in controlling such habits as smoking and overeating and such stress-related problems as hypertension (Suedfeld & Kristeller, 1982). The participants of these studies are usually asked to remain in a darkened and quiet room for 24 hours; depending on the focus of the study, they may hear antismoking or weight-control messages. Follow-up reports have indicated that the combination of REST and messages leads to significant reductions in smoking and greater weight loss in the participants of these studies. Of particular interest, foods taken into the REST situation by participants were later reported to be less preferred and to be consumed less. Although the reasons for changes in food preference associated with REST are presently unclear, the results suggest that some individuals might improve weight control by using procedures (like REST) that reduce the attractiveness of preferred foods (Suedfeld & Kristeller, 1982).

The consequences of restricted sensory input, therefore, may not always be negative; Suedfeld's research seems to indicate that restriction of the sensory environment may be used to modify behaviors that have proven difficult to change using other behavioral techniques. The motivational changes caused by REST are not well understood; perhaps, future research will lead to the development of a theoretical framework within which changes in motivation as a result of sensory restriction, whether positive or negative, can be explained.

Sensation Seeking

The research noted previously on sensory deprivation suggests that some minimal amount of sensory stimulation is necessary for normal functioning and that when sensory restriction occurs, people seek out stimulation and can become more susceptible to persuasion. Although the research indicates that everyone needs some minimal level of stimulation, the optimal level for any given individual may differ from the optimal level for someone else. That is, some people may require higher levels of stimulation while others seek out lower levels. Marvin Zuckerman (1979b; 1994; Zuckerman, Kolin, Price, & Zoob, 1964) sought to determine these levels by developing a scale that measured **sensation seeking**. "Sensation seeking is a trait describing the tendency to seek novel, varied, complex, and intense sensation and experiences and the willingness to take risks for the sake of such experience" (Zuckerman, 1994, facing title page). The **Sensation Seeking Scale (SSS)** has gone through several modifications over the years and has proven to be a reliable measure of the differences in the level of stimulation that people seek out. Several different formats of the SSS have been developed as well as translations into 15 other languages (see Zuckerman, 1994, Chapter 2, for a good overview of the development of the device and its evolution to the present forms). There are also children's forms of the SSS for the United States, Spain, and Sweden.

From a person's responses, one can derive a total SSS score and scores on four subscales: thrill and adventure seeking (TAS), experience seeking (ES), disinhibition (DIS), and boredom susceptibility (BS). From the initial publication of the SSS in 1964 through 2011 there were more than 900 articles published looking at various relationships between SSS and other traits and behaviors. Sensation seeking and its various relationships continue to interest researchers (see, e.g., Amico, 2010; Breslin, Sobell, Cappell, Vakili, & Poulos, 1999; Deery & Fildes, 1999; Donohew, Zimmerman, Cupp, Novak, Colon, & Abell, 2000; Egan, Charlesworth, Richardson, Blair, & McMurran, 2001; Forthun, Bell, Peek, & Sun, 1999; Lalasz & Weigel, 2011; Leone & D'Arienzo, 2000; Lopez-Bonilla & Lopez-Bonilla, 2010; Morrongiello, Sandomierki, & Valla, 2010; Slanger & Rudestam, 1997; Neria, Solomon, Ginzburg, & Dekel, 2000; Tonetti, Adan, Caci, De Pascalis, Fabbri, & Natale, 2010; Vanwesen-beeck, 2001; Zacny, 2010).

Age and **sex** are two of the most influential factors observed in sensation seeking (Zuckerman, 1994). Men are consistently higher in sensation seeking than women, and for both men and women sensation seeking declines with age. Sensation seeking typically peaks during late adolescence or the early 20s (Zuckerman, 1994). As you might expect, engaging in **risky behaviors** is also associated with higher scores on sensation seeking. High sensation seekers, in fact, rate situations as less risky than do low-sensation seekers (Zuckerman, 1994). Zuckerman suggests that the lower appraised risk shown by high sensation seekers is due to their having successfully experienced more risky situations in the past. Low sensation seekers seem to have higher levels of anxiety when confronted with typical phobic situations such as snakes, heights, darkness, or blood (Zuckerman, 1994).

Sports is another arena where people differ in regard to sensation seeking. In general, persons who participate in sports tend to score higher on sensation seeking. This is especially true for high- and medium-risk sports such as skiing and football (Zuckerman, 1994). Interestingly, the attraction to these sports does not appear to be the risk involved, as people who engage in these sports attempt to reduce the risk as much as possible by developing their skills, careful planning, and intense concentration (Zuckerman, 1994). **Risky vocations** (e.g., piloting airplanes, police work, fighting fires) also tend to attract more high than low sensation

seekers, and high-sensation seekers engaged in risky jobs often engage in additional risky behaviors outside of their jobs as well (Zuckerman, 1994).

High- and low-sensation seekers differ from each other in yet another way: they differ in how they react to social interactions. High-sensation seekers find **social interactions** a positive experience while low-sensation seekers find them stressing (Zuckerman, 1994). High-sensation seekers are also more likely to be dominant in social interactions and are more demonstrative in their nonverbal behaviors, such as eye gaze and posture, than low-sensation seekers. They are more **emotionally expressive** in social situations than low-sensation seekers as well (Zuckerman, 1994). According to Zuckerman, high sensation seekers are more likely to see love as a game and have trouble with commitment. Low-sensation seekers, on the other hand, are more likely to be looking for a long-term partner. High-sensation seekers' attitudes are more **sexually permissive** than low-sensation seekers' and they have engaged in a greater variety of sexual behaviors with more partners than low-sensation seekers (Zuckerman, 1994). High-sensation seekers are also more likely to **divorce** than low sensation seekers.

There is also a good deal of information relating sensation seeking to **drug use**. For example, smokers of both sexes score higher on sensation seeking than nonsmokers. Higher sensation seeking is also related to alcohol and drug use in preadolescence and adolescence (Zuckerman, 1994), with illegal drug use and polydrug use, rather than the type of drugs used, being related to higher sensation seeking. Zuckerman suggests that high-sensation seekers are initially driven to try illegal drugs by the need for novelty and curiosity, but once tolerance to a drug develops, sensation seeking is no longer important.

Zuckerman (1994, p. 155) sums up the differences in risk taking between high- and low-sensation seekers in the following way:

> Sensation seekers are attracted to activities and situations offering novel or intense experiences, and they are willing to accept the risks involved, although they do not seek to

maximize them. Low-sensation seekers are less attracted to these kinds of experiences, regard them as more risky, and anticipate more unpleasant, anxious reactions if they engaged in such activities. Even though low-sensation seekers anticipate anxiety inn what they regard as risky situations or activities, they are not generally anxious or neurotic people. They are just cautious and conservative with a preference for a world that is predictable and safe.

Thus it would seem that the optimal level of stimulation can vary widely from one person to another and that people are motivated to engage in activities (or to avoid them) in order to maintain the level of stimulation that they prefer.

As mentioned earlier, the relationship of sensation seeking to many different behaviors continues to be examined. For example, Breslin et al. (1999) looked at the effects of alcohol, gender, and sensation seeking on gambling choices. They found that alcohol use did not affect gambling choices, but sensation seeking did. Deery and Fildes (1999) in a study of young novice drivers in Australia were able to identify five separate subtypes of drivers. The two most deviant groups reported high levels of driving-related aggression, competitive speeding, driving to reduce tension, and sensation seeking. These two groups also showed the least skill in a second study using a driving simulator. Donohew et al. (2000) in a study of 2,949 ninth-grade students found that risky sex was most strongly associated with high-sensation seeking and impulsive decision making in sexually active teens.

Lest one thinks that high-sensation seeking is always a negative trait, Neria et al. (2000) report research showing that decorated Israeli **war** veterans scored higher in sensation seeking and were less influenced by war-related problems (such as posttraumatic stress disorder, or PTSD) than either a group suffering from combat stress reaction (CSR) or a control group of soldiers neither decorated nor suffering from combat stress. They suggest that high-sensation seeking has a stress-buffering effect that helps both in a presently dangerous situation and in long-term adjustment to the stress of war.

Opponent-Process Theory: Hedonism Revisited

The concept of hedonism is intimately tied to sensory input because we tend to experience sensory information as pleasant, unpleasant, or neutral. To conclude this chapter, we will consider a homeostatic model of hedonic quality proposed by Solomon and Corbit in the 1970's (Solomon, 1977, 1980; Solomon & Corbit, 1974). Solomon and Corbit proposed that both pleasant and aversive hedonic states are opposed by a central nervous system process that reduces their intensity. The process reduces these primary hedonic sensations by producing a hedonic state that is opposite in quality to that of the initial stimulus. Thus, stimuli that give rise to pleasurable feelings will be opposed by aversive feelings generated by the process; conversely, stimuli that initially give rise to aversive feelings will be opposed by pleasant feelings generated by the process. Let's look at how this opponent-process mechanism is presumed to work.

The model proposes that every affectively important situation has five characteristics. When a stimulus is detected, it produces a hedonic reaction that (a) quickly peaks; after the hedonic peak, there occurs (b) an adaptation phase during which the intensity of the hedonic experience declines and eventually reaches (c) a steady level; if the stimulus that started this chain of events now disappears, there occurs (d) a peak affective after-reaction with characteristics opposite to the original hedonic state; this after-reaction slowly (e) decays until the intensity of the affective after-reaction returns to zero. Figure 7.7 charts these five characteristic features of an emotional reaction to a stimulus.

The opponent-process model assumes that the physiological process that triggers the initial hedonic reaction (call it **state A**) will be opposed by a second physiological state, which will trigger an opposite hedonic reaction (**state B**). The decline in hedonic value from the peak of state A to the steady level results from state B's effect of reducing state A. Thus the steady level of hedonic intensity in

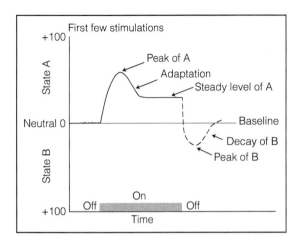

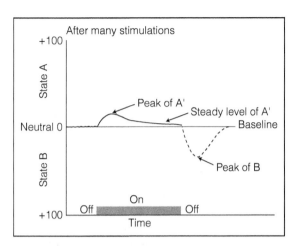

FIGURE 7.7 The five phases of an affective reaction to a stimulus. Adapted from "An Opponent-Process Theory of Motivation," by R. L. Solomon and J. D. Corbit, 1974, *Psychological Review, 81,* 119–145. Copyright © 1974 by the American Psychological Association. Used by permission.

FIGURE 7.8 Characteristics of the opponent process after many stimulations. Note the increase in the size of state B in comparison to state A. Adapted from "An Opponent-Process Theory of Motivation," by R. L. Solomon and J. D. Corbit, 1974, *Psychological Review, 81,* 119–145. Copyright © 1974 by the American Psychological Association. Used by permission.

Figure 7.7 is state A minus state B. When the stimulus creating state A is no longer present, the full force of state B (the opposite hedonic reaction to state A) is felt. The state B experience then slowly decays until hedonic intensity returns to zero.

States A and B differ from each other in several ways in addition to their being of opposite hedonic quality. For example, state A develops very quickly and is closely associated with the intensity of the stimulus that produced it; when the stimulus triggering state A is removed, the hedonic state A ceases. State B, however, develops slowly, and rather than being generated by a stimulus, it is produced as a reaction to state A. Further, state B is slow to decrease; when state A is removed, state B continues for some time because it decays slowly. State A differs from state B in yet another way. Repeated presentations of the stimulus that produced state A have no effect on the intensity of state A; however, repeated elicitation of state B leads to a strengthening of state B. Because activation of state B has the effect of reducing the intensity of state A, as noted previously, repeated

presentations of the stimulus that triggered state A will actually lead to a reduction in the hedonic intensity of state A, because state B will increase in intensity, as shown in Figure 7.8.

Drug Addiction: An Alternative to the Incentive-Sensitization View

Opponent-process theory appears capable of explaining some of the behaviors associated with drug addiction. An addicting substance will initially give rise to pleasurable feelings (state A). The opponent-process, however, will gain in strength as the person continues to use the drug, so that a strongly aversive state B develops. Because the pleasurable experiences of state A are reduced by the growing aversive state B, a point will be reached where the addicted individual will maintain drug use not for the pleasure it brings but rather to avoid the aversiveness of state B (withdrawal symptoms) that occurs when the drug-maintained state A is absent.

Furthermore, neutral stimuli that reliably precede states A and B can become conditioned to these states. Thus, any cue that consistently occurs before the high of a drug state A will begin to act as a secondary reinforcer for continued drug use. Similarly, neutral stimuli reliably associated with the aversive state B of drug withdrawal will negatively reinforce behaviors that reduce or eliminate these stimuli. The obvious way to avoid these negative stimuli is to use the drug again. The addict, then, is caught in a double bind; stimuli associated with both the pleasurable state A and the aversive state B tend to maintain drug use. Both sets of stimuli reinforce the same behavior—taking drugs. The associative (learned) effects of these stimuli are of course added to the behavioral effects of the pleasurable state A and the aversive state B, which also promote continued drug use.

Additionally, it appears that the tolerance that develops to a continually used drug can be at least partly explained as the result of conditioned A and B states. For example, Siegel (1975, 1977; Siegel, Sherman, & Mitchell, 1980) has shown that rats develop a conditioned tolerance of morphine in environmental situations that signal impending drug administration. Siegel has proposed that cues signaling drug injection have become conditioned to a compensatory process, a process that, according to Solomon (1980), apparently has many of the same characteristics as the opponent-process state B aroused by drug injection.

Researchers and physicians have known for many years the extreme difficulty involved with breaking a drug habit. The opponent-process model provides a potential theoretical basis for understanding why drug habits are so difficult to break. A model we discussed in Chapter 6 (incentive-sensitization model see Robinson and Berridge 2000, 2001, pg. 202.) can also account for many of these effects. Perhaps one or the other of the these two models will help us develop new approaches to drug abuse that will be more effective than those currently in use.

Thrill Seeking

The previous section on sensation seeking examined reasons for differing levels of stimulation. But

could the opponent-process model play a role as well? Opponent-process theory suggests that one reason people engage in behaviors such as riding roller coasters, skydiving, racing automobiles, and playing dangerous sports is the strong state B that occurs after the initial fear-producing (or painful) state A.

One such example is parachuting. Epstein (1967; as cited by Solomon, 1980) has studied the emotional reactions of military parachutists. Prior to their first jump, chutists appear anxious. During the first freefall (before the chute opens), signs of terror are often present: eyes bulge, lips are pulled back tight against the teeth, bodies curl forward, and involuntary urination sometimes occurs. Clearly an aversive state A seems to occur during the initial jump. Upon landing safely, the chutists initially appear stunned for several minutes and then begin to interact socially, often in quite animated ways. Solomon has suggested that this after-reaction to the jump, which may last for up to 10 minutes, is a highly positive state B that is opposite in emotional quality to the fear-producing state A.

For an experienced chutist, however, the picture is quite different. With repeated jumps, the fearful state A is reduced to the point that the chutist appears not frightened but eager. According to opponent-process theory, the reduction in fear occurs because the positive state B, building up over many jumps, reduces state A. Experienced parachutists look tense or excited prior to the jump and report a thrill rather than terror during freefall. After landing, the returned chutists are very physically active, and they may jump, shout, and talk excitedly. This period of euphoria, which may last as long as 2 or 3 hours, is often described as exhilarating.

According to the opponent-process model, then, people may engage in frightening or dangerous behaviors because of the reduction in the initially aversive state A and the highly positive opposite reaction that occurs when the behavior ceases. The model presented by Solomon has potential applications for a wide variety of frightening, dangerous, or stressing situations into which people put themselves. Running marathons, skydiving, hang gliding, riding roller coasters, and watching horror movies may all have in common a strongly positive state B that follows the initial aversive state A. Further, many of these activities, in a manner similar to drug use, seem to have an addictive quality—precisely as opponent-process theory predicts.

Social Attachment

Opponent-process theory has also been applied to the attachment process (Hoffman et al., 1974; Hoffman & Solomon, 1974; Mineka, Suomi, & Delizio, 1981; Starr, 1978). Starr (1978), for example, imprinted young ducklings on a moving model of a female mallard duck. (Recall that in Chapter 2 we examined the imprinting process from the point of view of instinctively motivated behavior and that imprinting appears to lead to social attachment in many species of birds.) Starr assumed that some aspect of the imprinting stimulus triggers a positive state A, because numerous studies have shown that young birds are highly motivated to approach and follow an imprinting stimulus and that such a stimulus can serve as a positive reinforcer (Hoffman & Ratner, 1973). Further, removal of an imprinted stimulus typically leads to distress calling (a characteristic vocalization with a frequency that ranges between 2000 and 5000 Hz), which Starr used as a measure of the negative state B. Starr's assumptions were based in part on a study by Hoffman and associates (1974), which showed that distress calling to the withdrawal of an imprinted stimulus increased with increasing exposure to that stimulus. Thus, in the study by Hoffman and associates, distress calling appeared to index the growth of the negative state B opposing the positive state A that occurs when the imprinted stimulus is presented.

Starr not only replicated the basic findings of Hoffman and associates but found that an important factor in the development of the negative state B is the time interval between successive presentations of the imprinting stimulus. Thus, if the interval between presentations is short—say, 1 minute—then the negative state B grows as predicted by opponent-process theory. On the other hand, if

sufficient time is allowed to elapse between presentations so that the negative state B has time to decay (5 minutes in Starr's study), then state B doesn't grow stronger. This important finding, termed the critical decay duration by Starr, demonstrates that growth of state B (and thus subsequent reduction of state A) depends on the time interval between activations of state A: if the time interval is short, state B will grow and reduce the emotional quality of state A; however, if the time interval is large enough so that state B decays, no reduction in the quality of state A will occur. Based on this finding, we might predict that jumping out of an airplane only once a year would lead not to exhilaration but to continued terror.

Additionally, Starr found that changes in the intensity of the imprinting stimulus (e.g., adding sound) and changes in duration (decreasing the amount of time the stimulus is present) also influence the critical decay duration. Thus a stimulus that triggers a more intense state A creates a state B that takes longer to decay; conversely, a stimulus that triggers a weak state A will lead to a state B that decays faster. Starr's work suggests that the emotional impact a stimulus will have depends on the intensity, duration, and frequency with which we encounter that stimulus: strong stimuli of long duration or repeated frequency will generate a large state B that will oppose state A. If state A is positive, then its emotional impact will be reduced (i.e., there are negative consequences of often-repeated positive experiences), while a negative state A will become less aversive and perhaps even enjoyed (i.e., there are positive consequences of often repeated negative experiences).

The use of opponent-process theory to explain attachment processes has generality beyond the study of imprinting in birds. Mineka and associates (1981) have found that the model also works well in describing behavioral changes in adolescent monkeys that experience multiple separation experiences. In a series of experiments, these researchers found that multiple separations lead to increased social contact on reunion, that this contact declines across days, and that multiple separation experiences increase depressed and agitated behaviors. Their data suggest that for a socially attached monkey some aspect of its source of attachment (mother, peers) produces a positive state A, which is opposed by a negative state B. Under normal conditions, state B leads to reduced social contact; however, when the source of attachment is removed, the negative state B leads to self-directed behaviors such as clasping or agitated, stereotypic movements. When the monkey is reunited with its source of attachment, increased social contact occurs, presumably because state B has decayed somewhat and thus state A is heightened. More importantly, however, the researchers found that additional separations lead to a growth in state B so that self-directed maladaptive behaviors become more pronounced and socially directed behaviors decrease. As noted by Mineka et al. (1981), the agitated, stereotypic behaviors of these monkeys appear similar to the ceaseless activity often seen in patients with agitated depressions (Beck, 1967, p. 42).

As we have seen, opponent-process theory has been expanded to cover a host of behaviors that have often seemed quite dissimilar. Indeed, opponent-process theory has been applied to behaviors as disparate as breastfeeding (Myers & Siegel, 1985), habitual blood donation (Piliavin, Callero, & Evans, 1982), self-injurious behavior (Franklin, Hessel, Aaron, Arthur, Heilbron, & Prinstein, 2010), suicide (Van Orden, Witte, Cukrowicz, Braithwaite, Selby, & Joiner, 2010), exercise and emotion (Markowitz & Arent, 2010), pain relief (Leknes, Brooks, Wiech, & Tracey, 2008), prejudice and helping behavior (Graziano & Habashi, 2010), frontal lobe EEG activity (Kline, Blackhart, & Williams, 2007), and brain lesions blocking morphine reward (Vargas-perez, Ting-A-kee, Heinmiller, Sturgess, & van der Kooy, 2007). The concept of opponent processes that are of opposite hedonic quality and that interact to produce an affective state has proven to be a productive model in various fields of psychological research.

SUMMARY

In this chapter we have explored the related ideas of sensory stimulation and hedonism, and we have seen that the concept of pleasure and pain as behavior motivators has a long history. Young has suggested that there exists a hedonic continuum along which pleasurable and painful stimuli vary. Because we can move back and forth along this continuum, what is pleasurable at one time may be neutral or even painful at another time.

Considerable evidence suggests that sensory stimulation is important to the development and maintenance of normal motivated behavior. As a result, behaviors such as curiosity and exploration may have developed, in part, to maintain adequate levels of stimulation. Research on sensory restriction, in both young organisms and adults, also supports the notion that stimulation has motivating properties. Thus, maternal deprivation leads to various abnormalities in young monkeys, and, given

the opportunity, sensory-deprived organisms will work to maintain stimulation.

Sensory isolation and abuse in children can lead to deprivation dwarfism, and sensory restriction in the adult leads to a variety of reported problems ranging from difficulties in concentration to hallucinations. Furthermore, there is abundant evidence that individuals differ in their need for stimulation as measured by the sensation-seeking scale, and consistent behavioral differences in motivation exist between persons scoring high and low on sensation seeking. Thus, sensory stimulation has been shown to have important motivational properties, and adequate stimulation seems necessary for normal functioning.

The effect of stimuli on an individual may result from processes that occur in the brain itself. The opponent-process theory of Solomon and his associates proposes that the initial emotional state created by a stimulus will be opposed by a second emotional state that is its opposite. The reoccurrence of a stimulus leads to a growth of the second state, which reduces the emotional quality of the first state. As a result, highly positive stimuli can become less motivating over time, and, conversely, highly negative stimuli can lose much of their aversive properties with repeated exposures.

Various behaviors, including drug addiction, risk taking, attachment, and suicide, as well as many others, have been analyzed using opponent-process theory. At this point in our understanding, opponent-process theory can be seen as a modified version of hedonism that helps us better understand how the stimuli we encounter in our everyday lives motivate us.

KEY TERMS

hedonism, *206*
beneception/nociception/ neutroception/hedonic continuum/bright pressure/ dull pressure/sign/intensity/ preference tests/duration, *207*
causalgia/peripheral neuralgia/ phantom limb pain, *210*
gate control theory/endogenous opiates/naloxone/ substance P, *211*

sensory deprivation, *214*
contact comfort, *216*
protest, despair, detachment/ ambivalence, *218*
growth hormone (somatotrophin), *219*
REST (Restricted Environmental Stimulation Technique)/sensation seeking/Sensation Seeking Scale (SSS), *223*

age/sex/risky behaviors/sports/ risky vocations/social interactions/emotionally expressive/sexually permissive/divorce/ drug use, *224*
war/state A/state B, *225*

SUGGESTIONS FOR FURTHER READING

Iwata, K., Yamamoto, M., Nakao, M., & Kimura, M. (1999). A study on polysomnographic observations and subjective experiences under sensory deprivation. *Psychiatry and Clinical Neurosciences,* *53*, 129–131. This short article examines the occurrence of visual images and EEG data during sensory deprivation. The authors suggest that sensory deprivation may produce a level of consciousness that differs from either wakefulness or sleep.

Lewis, M. H., Gluck, J. P., Petitto, J. M., Hensley, L., & Ozer, H. (2000). Early social deprivation in nonhuman primates: Long-term effects on survival and cell-mediated immunity. *Biological Psychiatry,* *47*, 119–126. This study found long-term effects of social deprivation during the first year of life. Mortality and immunity were especially altered. Males were particularly likely to die as a result of the early social deprivation.

WEB RESOURCES

For direct hot links to the Internet sites listed below and other features, visit the book-specific Web site at http://psychology.wadsworth.com/petri

http://www.emedicine.com/PED/topic566.htm
This Web page provides a thorough exploration of factors involved with deprivation dwarfism (also called *psychosocial dwarfism*).

http://www.iasp-pain.org/
This site provides information from the International Association for the Study of Pain.

http://plato.stanford.edu/entries/hedonism/
This Web site at the Stanford Encyclopedia of Philosophy provides information on philosophers' thoughts on hedonism.

PART IV

COGNITIVE APPROACHES TO MOTIVATION

CHAPTER 8

Cognitive Motivation: Expectancy-Value Approaches

CHAPTER PREVIEW

This chapter is concerned with the following questions:

1. Which early cognitive theorists helped to develop the concept of expectancy-value?

2. How do expectancy-value theories explain the motivation of behavior?

3. How does the expectancy-value concept add to our understanding of social learning, achievement motivation, the relationship between attitudes and behavior, and social loafing?

Sarah was hungry again. As a matter of fact, Sarah was always hungry. Since her heart attack, the doctor had insisted that she lose 50 pounds, and her daughter, with whom she lived, was watching her like a hawk. Still the hunger nagged at her. She pondered the problem. If she went into the kitchen and opened the refrigerator door, her daughter Doris would certainly come running. The candy in the dish on the coffee table was also off limits; Doris would notice immediately if she reached for one.

Then Sarah was struck by an idea. Doris had bought some candy for Halloween and had stored it away in the basement cupboard. If Sarah went downstairs, Doris would assume that she was going to do some washing or ironing. She could take a small candy bar and Doris would never be the wiser. Sarah hefted herself slowly from the chair and headed for the basement—not for the last time that week. And Doris was surprised when Halloween came.

Sarah's behavior demonstrates the idea that our actions are determined by a field of forces working together. The heart attack, the doctor's orders, and her ever-present daughter limited the ways in which Sarah could deal with her perceived hunger. All these forces working together led to her devious solution of eating the Halloween candy a little at a time. Her solution exemplifies a way of analyzing human motivation suggested by Kurt Lewin. We will examine his theory later in this chapter.

The previous sections of this book have concentrated on explanations of behavior motivation that usually do not require a thinking, purposeful organism. Certainly, some types of motivated behavior are relatively fixed and mechanical in nature, but other motive states seem best explained in terms of rational thought processes. Such approaches are generally termed **cognitive theories**, and they will be the focus of Chapters 8 through 11. Furthermore, because humans are social animals, our thoughts, behaviors, and motives are often influenced by those around us. Thus many of the theories in Chapters 8 through 11 will examine the role that our social world plays in motivation. This is known as the social-cognitive perspective. In the remainder of this chapter, we present the historical development and the unique features of some important cognitive theories of motivation. In this discussion, we emphasize two important concepts: expectancies that a behavior will lead to a certain outcome and the value associated with that outcome. We then present a general cognitive approach known as expectancy-value theory, which is based on these two concepts.

As Bolles (1974) pointed out, cognitive explanations of behavior are nothing new. Some of the early Greek philosophers were cognitive in their approach to understanding the world about them. Plato, for example, argued that we do what we perceive to be right based on our ideas of what is right. Motivationally, Plato thought that we attempt to maximize virtue, which we determine by our thoughts. Psychologists have defined cognition a little more narrowly than these early Greek philosophers. Although definitions vary somewhat, the term **cognition** is generally used to describe those intellectual or perceptual processes occurring within us when we analyze and interpret both the world around us and our own thoughts and actions. Because of the active, interpretative nature of these processes, the term **information processing** is often used in connection with the concept of cognition. One of the early proponents of the study of cognition was, ironically, the behaviorist E. C. Tolman.

Tolman's Purposive Behavior

Tolman (1932) argued that in order to understand behavior we must study it as a phenomenon in its own right. He argued that behavior has both descriptive and defining properties and is more than just sequences of muscle twitches. Thus, Tolman advocated a holistic study of behavior, in contrast to reductionistic approaches (e.g., those of Clark Hull, 1943) that attempted to understand behavior by reducing it to its smallest individual

elements. According to Tolman, behavior is **molar**—something to be studied as a whole and not reduced to its component parts.

Characteristics of Molar Behavior

Tolman believed that molar behavior has certain defining properties. First, behavior is always directed toward or away from some specific goal. Thus, the behavior of a hungry rat running through a maze can be characterized as an attempt to reach the goal of food at the end of the maze. Behaviors are heavily influenced by the various characteristics of the goal toward which they are directed. Behavior directed toward a goal is also **persistent**, tending to continue until the goal is obtained.

A second major characteristic of molar behavior is that behaviors leading to a goal form a **consistent pattern** of responses. Behavior is not random, but represents ways in which the organism attempts to reach the goal. For example, in driving to work I make a specific pattern of responses that succeed in getting me from my doorstep to my office. This pattern of responses is relatively constant and is quite different from the pattern of responses I make when working toward other goals such as going to a movie.

The third major characteristic of molar behavior is a **selectivity** to behavior, so that the shortest or easiest path to the goal will be the one taken. Several different roads will take me from my home to my office, but I usually choose the most direct one.

According to Tolman, then, we must know the goal toward which behavior is directed, the ways in which the organism behaves in order to reach the goal, and the possible routes that may be taken to reach the goal. Unless we know these three things, our understanding of the observed behavior will be incomplete.

Purpose and Cognition

The three characteristics of molar behavior imply that an organism has some knowledge about the goals toward which its behavior is leading. Thus, behavior was seen by Tolman to be purposive. For Tolman, whether the behavior in question is that of a rat or a human, it is characterized by cognition and purpose.

Tolman was careful to define what he meant by purposiveness. First, the purposiveness of behavior is objectively defined by the behaviors observed and not by inference to anything subjective. That an organism will learn a series of behaviors in order to reach some goal is evidence, Tolman argued, for the purposiveness of behavior. As an example, consider my cat. As a kitten it would sometimes claw the furniture. In typical psychological fashion, I thought to break this habit by quickly following the clawing response with a period of nonreinforcement (putting the cat outside whenever it clawed the furniture). The furniture clawing decreased but did not disappear. When the cat, now an adult, desires to go outside, as you can probably guess, it gets me to let it out by perfunctorily clawing the couch, then running to the door. It seems hard to deny, at least from Tolman's point of view, that the behavior of clawing the couch has the purpose of reaching the goal of getting outside (it may also be instructive in pointing out that when we try to modify behavior, we don't always get what we expect!).

The example of my "cognitive" cat is perhaps an appropriate place to mention another point made by Tolman, which is often called the **learning-performance distinction**. My cat did not initially learn to claw the furniture in order to be let out. Clawing things is a behavior most cats seem to do; however, because I created a contingency between this behavior and being put outside, the cat learned and, from Tolman's point of view, came to expect that this particular behavior in the future would lead to the goal of being put out. At times when the cat does not want to be outside, no evidence exists that it knows this particular relationship; it must be motivated to go out before this particular behavior is performed.

Consider another example of the learning-performance distinction. Suppose you have just arrived for a visit in an unfamiliar city and are trying to find your hotel, which you ultimately succeed in doing after making several wrong turns. After checking in and unpacking, you realize that you are hungry. You immediately remember that you passed several restaurants during your search. At the time you passed the restaurants, you did not stop to eat because the motive to find your hotel was more salient to you than was your hunger. But you did learn something about the neighborhood that you could use when your hunger motive became dominant. You may recognize that this example is conceptually similar to the study of latent learning discussed in Chapter 6 (Tolman & Honzik, 1930a) in which one group of rats ran through a maze without receiving a reward until their eleventh trial. During the first 10 trials, they demonstrated very little learning, but as soon as the food reward was introduced, their performance improved substantially. Thus, as Tolman argued, learning can occur in the absence of any behavioral change; motivation is necessary for learning to be translated into performance.

In the process of learning that particular behaviors lead to particular goals, Tolman asserted, **expectancies** are established. These involve both the expectancy that a particular set of behaviors will lead to a specific goal and the expectancy that specific goals can be found in particular locations (Cofer & Appley, 1964). The Tinklepaugh (1928) experiment, also discussed in Chapter 6, is another good example of Tolman's view of cognitive expectancy. Recall that in this study monkeys became agitated when the banana that they expected to find under a container had been replaced with less desirable lettuce. Thus, for Tolman, organisms do not learn specific stimulus–response connections; they learn which behaviors lead to which goals.

Tolman's approach emphasized the idea that organisms develop a **cognitive map** of their environment. This map indicates the places in which particular goals may be found. Tolman's ideas were in sharp contrast to the strict stimulus–response approaches emphasizing the idea that learning consists of chains of responses (e.g., turn left, then right, then right again). Thus, for Tolman, an organism learns a general concept about the place where reinforcement can be found, not a series of responses to reach a goal. The study described in the next paragraph illustrates the difference between Tolman's idea of place learning and the traditional behaviorist idea of response learning. You might find it helpful to keep the following analogy in mind as you read. Suppose you have two friends, George and Tom, and they both need directions to a party you are having. You know that George navigates by landmarks, so you tell him to go up the street and make a right at the gas station and then another right at the first traffic light and that he'll find your house at the end of the block. George is a response learner—he learns the response (left or right) necessary to reach his goal. Tom, on the other hand, navigates by a cognitive map of his environment, so you tell him to head north for three blocks, east for two, and then south for one block. Tom exhibits place learning because his cognitive map tells him where he is relative to the places around him.

The concept of a cognitive map suggests that organisms acquire expectations both that behavior will be rewarded and that the reward can be found in specific locations. Tolman in fact argued that place learning is the more usual way in which animals learn. Experiments by Tolman, Ritchie, and Kalish (1946, 1947) revealed the ease with which place learning can occur. An elevated maze in the shape of a cross was used to run two groups of rats (Figure 8.1). One group, the response-learning group, was sometimes started from start box 1 and sometimes from start box 2, but in either case the correct response was to turn right to obtain food. Thus, if the rats started from

box 1, they found food in goal box 1, but if they started from start box 2, they found food in goal box 2. These rats are using the same approach as George in the analogy previously mentioned. A second group, the place-learning group, was also randomly started from either start box 1 or start box 2, but regardless of where these rats started, they always found food in the same place. If, for example, the food was in goal box 1, the correct response from start box 1 was a right turn, but if the rats started from start box 2, the correct response was a left turn. To efficiently solve the problem, the rats in group 2 had to learn the place where the food was to be found relative to their current position (just like Tom did), rather than learning a simple turning response.

As you can see in Figure 8.2, the place-learning group learned much more quickly than the response-learning group. This finding seems to indicate that learning where rewards can be found is easier than learning a specific set of responses;

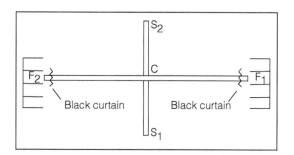

FIGURE 8.1   Elevated maze used by Tolman, Ritchie, and Kalish in their studies of place learning. S_1 and S_2 are starting points, while F_1 and F_2 are food boxes; C is the center choice point of the maze. From Tolman, E. C., Ritchie, B. F., & Kalish, D., "Studies in spatial learning," *Journal of Experimental Psychology, 36,* 13–24. Copyright © 1946 American Psychological Association. Reprinted with permission.

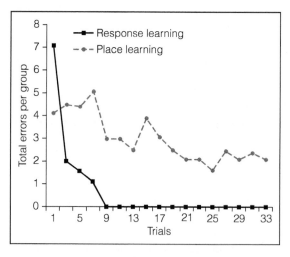

FIGURE 8.2   Number of errors (vertical axis) as a function of number of trials (horizontal axis) in the maze learning study conducted by Tolman, Ritchie, and Kalish. Note that the rats in the response learning condition never eliminated their errors whereas the rats in the place learning condition did so by the ninth trial. From Tolman, E. C., Ritchie, B. F., & Kalish, D., "Studies in spatial learning," *Journal of Experimental Psychology, 36,* 13–24. Copyright © 1946 American Psychological Association. Reprinted with permission.

additionally, it supports the notion that animals develop expectations about the environment that have the characteristics of a cognitive map.

As is often the case in psychology, these results did not go unchallenged, and other experiments sometimes found that response learning was easier than place learning (see Hilgard & Bower, 1975, for a review of this work). Restle (1957) provided a potential solution to the conflicting studies by suggesting that both response and place learning are possible, and which type of learning occurs depends upon the salience of the cues in the situation. In the original study by Tolman and associates, for example, many extra-maze cues were available that made place learning easy; when place cues are reduced, response learning becomes more dominant. It seems clear at this point that both response learning and place learning can occur. Petri and Mishkin (1994; Mishkin and Petri, 1984; see also Squire, 1992) have suggested that different circuits within the brain mediate cognitive learning on the one hand and stimulus–response learning on the other. They also suggest where these circuits might be and how they might work. The important point for our purposes is that when it occurs, place learning suggests that expectations do develop concerning where rewards can be found.

Tolman's theory has had its detractors. Most of the strict stimulus–response theorists of his time took issue with his emphasis on the cognitive aspects of behaviors. The major criticism of Tolman's theory centers on its lack of detail (Hilgard & Bower, 1975); because of the theory's imprecise nature, definite predictions could not always be made. Nevertheless, Tolman's research proved to be particularly difficult for stimulus–response theories to explain. Perhaps more than anyone else, he brought about a reevaluation of the strict stimulus–response approach that has, in turn, led to a greatly increased emphasis on cognitive processes such as expectancies as explanations for behavior.

Kurt Lewin's Force Field Theory

Another early psychologist who recognized the value of a molar approach to understanding motivation was Kurt Lewin. Lewin (1936, 1938) described a homeostatic cognitive model of behavior motivation. His approach was a dynamic one, emphasizing that the forces acting to initiate behavior are constantly changing. Instead of postulating a single motive to explain behavior, Lewin pointed out that several forces may simultaneously exert influence on an organism; thus, the behavior observed is the result of the total forces acting upon the individual.

Lewin's approach is considered here with other cognitive approaches for at least three reasons. First, his thinking was heavily influenced by the Gestalt school of psychology, with which he was closely associated. The Gestalt approach emphasized the active problem-solving and insightful nature of behavior, rather than the mechanical connections of stimulus–response approaches. Second, Lewin's motivational constructs included psychological needs (which he termed *quasi-needs*) that often seem to be cognitive in nature. Finally, Lewin included the concept of *valence* or *value* as a means of explaining why one behavior might be chosen over another when trying to satisfy a need. Lewin's idea of value and Tolman's notion of expectancies are both components of the expectancy-value approach to motivation, which is the primary focus of this chapter.

To emphasize his belief that behavior can be understood only as the result of all the forces acting on an individual, Lewin described behavior in terms of **field theory**. Field theory emphasizes the idea that the reaction of an object is the result of all the forces acting upon that object within the field containing it. The *field* in field theory is actually a field of conflicting forces. For example, the reaction of a kite depends upon the field of forces acting upon it. Changing wind conditions, gravity, and counter-force applied by the kite flyer all serve to define the ultimate behavior of the kite.

Lewin argued that human behavior can be similarly understood to result from all the forces acting upon an individual at the time the behavior occurs. Lewin therefore described behavior (B) as a function (f) of two major components, the person (P) and the psychological environment (E):

$$B = f(P + E)$$

Lewin's theory is thus a variation of a familiar theme in psychology—the interaction between the individual and the situation in the determination of behavior. In order to more fully appreciate Lewin's system, we must examine the constructs of the person and the psychological environment. We begin with the person.

The Person

Figure 8.3 depicts the regions of the person. The outside ring labeled S–M represents the portion of the individual that interacts with the psychological environment. Sensory information (S) comes into the person via this region, and motor output (M) proceeds out through this region. The center portion of the individual (the inner-personal region, labeled I–P in Figure 8.3) is divided into many separate regions, each of which represents a potential need of the individual. Needs create a state of tension that we are motivated to reduce. Lewin postulated two types of needs that lead to the production of **tension: physiological needs** and **psychological needs** (also termed **quasi-needs**). Physiological needs include factors such as hunger and thirst, while psychological needs can be as diverse as the

need to find a life partner or the need to finish an uncompleted task.

The regions in Figure 8.3 nearest the S–M area labeled p (for peripheral) are less crucial needs; that is, they are less central to the person's well-being. The interior regions represent the more important central (c) needs of the individual. As an example, one might think of the need for food or water as a central need and the need to cut the grass as more peripheral. The central core of the inner-personal region was seen by Lewin as having a greater influence on behavior because the core regions are in contact with many other regions. In Lewin's model this is shown by the central region's common boundaries with many other regions.

Motivational Properties of the Inner-Personal Region (Tension)

Tension is the motivational construct that Lewin used for internal motivation of the person. For example, some region within the inner-personal area may represent the potential need for water; when the body becomes dehydrated, this particular region will be in a state of tension (indicated in Figure 8.3 by the plus signs).

When tension exists, the individual becomes motivated to reduce it; thus, Lewin's model was homeostatic in character. The reduction of tension can be accomplished in one of two ways: it can be spread evenly throughout the entire inner-personal region, or it can be alleviated through a process termed **locomotion**, in which some particular region of the psychological environment dissipates the tension. Suppose that within my inner-personal region a region of tension exists because I "need" (want) a soft drink. If I am on a diet and I decide to deny myself the calories, the tension that results from this need may have to be spread evenly through my inner-personal region, raising my overall tension slightly but restoring the total region to balance. On the other hand, I might eliminate the tension by searching through my memories to find that (a) there is a soft-drink machine on the third floor, and (b) I have money with which to buy a drink. In this second instance, locomotion has

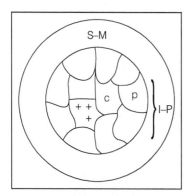

FIGURE 8.3 The person. S–M = sensory-motor region; I–P = inner-personal region; p = peripheral region or need; c = central region or need. Pluses symbolize an inner-personal region in a state of tension. From *Principles of Topological Psychology*, by K. Lewin. Copyright © 1936 by McGraw-Hill Book Company. Used by permission.

occurred if I use this information to reduce the tension. Notice how my behavior is the product of needs, memories, knowledge of my diet, and many other forces in my psychological field.

If I choose not to get the soda, the overall tension of the inner-personal region will increase slightly, but each region within the inner-personal region will be equal. It is at this point that the boundary conditions become important. If some boundaries are impermeable (do not allow passage of the tension), the increased tension cannot be spread evenly across the entire inner-personal region, and motivation will continue to exert an influence in order to equalize the tension. Also, if the region in which the tension exists has an impermeable boundary, the tension cannot be reduced either by spreading it out or by locomotion to some appropriate region in the psychological environment. This latter case appears conceptually similar to Freud's concept of repression.

The Psychological Environment

The psychological environment, which consists of regions and boundaries, is not identical to the real world but is comprised of all the **psychological facts** of which one is aware. Thus, psychological facts form the total of our knowledge as it exists in memory. For example, a fact might consist of the knowledge that food is in the refrigerator or the knowledge of a series of movements that will get us to the kitchen.

Lewin conceptualized the satisfaction of a tension state to be the result of a locomotion from the inner-personal area, in a state of tension, to the appropriate psychological fact that satisfies the need. The border of the regions in the psychological environment, like those of the inner-personal region, have differing permeabilities so that movement is easier through some regions than others. This means that, although several possible routes to a psychological fact may exist, one path will be easier because of the boundary conditions of the intervening regions (Figure 8.4). In addition, when a need state exists in the inner-personal region, those areas of the environment that can satisfy a need acquire a value, which he termed **valence**. This valence can be positive or negative, and it determines which psychological facts are most attractive as a way of satisfying the need. For example, two foods may be available to satisfy your hunger but one may be unattractive to you (negative valence) and the other may be one of your

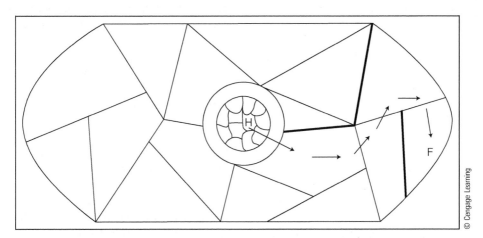

FIGURE 8.4 The person in the psychological environment. H = a core region in a state of tension due to hunger. The arrows indicate the direction of locomotion. Heavy black lines indicate impermeable barriers. F = food.

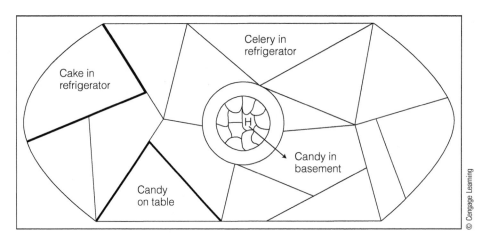

FIGURE 8.5   Sarah's life space.

favorites (positive valence). Thus, valence is yet another force that determines our behavior according to Lewin's field theory.

Let's return to our example of Sarah and Doris at the beginning of this chapter. Figure 8.5 diagrams the situation. Sarah's hunger creates a tension in her inner-personal region that motivates her to get something to eat. Her recent heart attack, her daughter Doris, and the doctor's orders to reduce weight place barriers on her desire to eat. The impermeable boundaries (represented by thick lines) in the figure indicate the psychological facts that she cannot eat the cake in the refrigerator or the candy on the table, even though they have a positive valence. Further searching through her psychological facts indicates to her that she is allowed to eat the celery in the refrigerator as indicted by the permeable boundary (represented by thin lines), but she does not like it (i.e., it has a negative valence). She solves the problem by eating the Halloween candy (positive valence) hidden in the basement because her daughter will not suspect that she is going there to eat (permeable boundary). Sarah's behavior can be seen as a result of all the forces acting upon her, and it fits Lewin's concept of motivation.

One way of summarizing Lewin's approach is to note that to understand behavior one must understand all the forces that are related to that

behavior (Korman, 1974). For Lewin, as for Tolman, this meant that behavior must be understood as a whole rather than from small behavioral components. Though Lewin's analysis of behavior is compelling, it is far from satisfactory. First, many of his terms are not clearly defined and are therefore open to differing interpretations. For example, psychological facts are in some cases voluntary behavior (e.g., opening a door), while at other times they are subjective thoughts (e.g., remembering your fifth birthday). The differing types of psychological facts are not well delineated so the concept remains unclear. Second, psychological facts can change from moment to moment, but Lewin does not inform us of the conditions that cause their change. Third, several theorists have pointed out that Lewin's analyses are post hoc (after the fact). He inferred what the conditions were *after* the behavior had occurred (Arkes & Garske, 1977; Weiner, 1972). In psychology as in all science, theories that predict behavior are much more valuable than those that attempt to explain it after it has occurred. Finally, although he conducted experiments in order to test his ideas, Lewin's experiments often lacked proper control groups, thus making the database for his ideas rather weak (Arkes & Garske, 1977; Weiner, 1972).

Although both Tolman's and Lewin's theories suffer from some serious flaws, they are important because they emphasized the cognitive nature of motivation. They also stressed the importance of looking at behavior from a molar perspective, which was very much in contrast to the reductionist approach favored by most traditional behaviorist researchers. Finally, Tolman's concept of expectancies and Lewin's idea of valence or value are still with us today in the form of the expectancy-value approach to motivation.

Expectancy-Value Theory

We turn now to an examination of more modern cognitive approaches to the understanding of motivation, known collectively as **expectancy-value theory**. The basic idea underlying expectancy-value theory is that motivated behavior results from the combination of individual needs and the value of goals available in the environment. Expectancy-value theories also stress the idea that the probability of behavior depends not only upon the *value* of the goal for the individual but also upon the person's *expectancy* of obtaining the goal. For example, almost everyone would place a high value on winning the lottery, but a much smaller number of people truly expect that it will happen.

The general expectancy-value model assumes that motivation is best understood from a molar perspective. This idea is, once again, congruent with the perspective of Tolman and Lewin, but not with the stimulus–response explanations of incentive motivation proposed by Hull and Spence (as noted in Chapter 6). Instead of analyzing the effects of goal objects in terms of fractional consummatory responses and their feedback, expectancy-value theory argues for a cognitive representation of goal objects. This cognitive representation includes both an expectation that certain behaviors will lead to certain goals and the value of those goals for the organism.

The concept of expectancy is important because it assumes that behavior is a function of one's estimation of obtaining the valued goal. Thus, even a highly valued goal such as winning the lottery may not generate much behavior if the

expectancy of successfully reaching the goal is very small. Expectancies are generally regarded as being built up through experience, and the motives that expectancy-value theories generally attempt to explain are usually psychological in nature rather than physiological (Korman, 1974). Moreover, expectancy-value approaches emphasize an active organism that is shaped by its own unique experiences. Unlike the one-size-fits-all approach of Hull, expectancy value theorists take a more idiographic approach, meaning that they often include individual differences as part of their explanation of motivation (Graham & Weiner, 1996). Expectancy-value theory has been applied to a number of psychological fields, including social learning theory, achievement motivation, the relationship between attitudes and behaviors, and an intriguing phenomenon known as social loafing. In the remainder of this chapter, we will examine expectancy-value theory in the context of each of these topics.

Social Learning Theory

Social learning theory attempts to explain the internal and external (social) factors that influence the acquisition and regulation of behavior. Internal factors of importance include expectancies and subjective values that we place on goals, while external factors include the particular social situations that we experience. Both internal and external factors contribute to how we behave.

One of the originators of social learning theory was Julian Rotter, who was a student of Kurt Lewin at the University of Iowa. Rotter (1954) noted four basic concepts of expectancy-value theory present in his social learning analysis of behavior. First, according to Rotter, our preference for an event is determined by that event's **reinforcement value**, which is its desirability to us. The reinforcement value of an event, however, is relative; we compare one situation against another to arrive at the value for any particular one. For example, earning a high grade in this course probably has higher reinforcement value to you than doing laundry, but lower reinforcement value than finding a well-paying career. Second, we make **subjective estimates** of our chances of obtaining particular reinforcers, or, to put it in expectancy-value terms, we develop expectations about obtaining goals (e.g., most people realize that winning the lottery is unlikely). Third, our expectations are determined by **situational factors**. Our expectations about a particular situation will be based on similar situations that we have encountered in the past. For example, if you have done well in other psychology courses, you probably will expect to do well in this one. Fourth, our reactions in new situations will be based on **generalized expectations** from the past. Even though we may never have been in such a situation before, these generalized expectations will guide behavior. Thus, even if you have never taken an essay exam before, you may expect to do well if you have consistently done well on other types of tests. Finally, Rotter has suggested that behavior depends upon the multiplication of expectancy and value, so that we may write the following formula:

$$B = E \times V$$

where B stands for behavior, E stands for expectancy, and V stands for value. Thus, according to Rotter, behavior occurs as the result of our expectations of achieving goals and the value those goals have for us.

In situations where more than one behavior is possible, we should choose the behavior with the largest combination of expected success and value. Suppose, for example, that you are trying to decide whether you should go hiking or bowling on a particular Saturday. Suppose that hiking's value to you, on a scale of 1 to 10, is about a 7. The value of bowling is only a 5. However, you have heard conflicting weather forecasts for the day, and in the past you have found hiking in the rain to be intolerable. If the chance of rain is 50% (or 0.50), then the behavior potential of hiking is 7 (its reinforcement value) times 0.50 (your expectation of a successful, rain free hike), or 3.5. On the other hand, you are sure that you would be able to go bowling (i.e., an expectation of 100%, or 1.0) so the behavior potential of bowling would be 5 times 1.0 or 5.0. Thus, in this case, Rotter's expectancy-value model

predicts that you would choose to go bowling because it provides you with the largest combination of expected success and value.

We face such choices daily, and the expectancy-value perspective predicts that we attempt to maximize their expected value. However, the sheer number of decisions that we must make limits the practical utility of this approach. Each day, we have to decide what to wear, what to eat, how to behave in interactions with others, to name just a few of the countless choices that we must make. We simply do not have the ability to weigh the alternatives of every decision—if we did we would not get very much accomplished! In many cases we use **heuristics**, or mental shortcuts to guide us in our decision making process (see Gigerenzer & Selten, 2001, for a complete discussion of this concept, which is known as "bounded rationality"). Furthermore, though we sometimes weigh the pros and cons of making particular choices, we also often behave impulsively, without considering the potential costs and chances of success that our behavior entails. Store managers use this human behavioral trait to their advantage by running sales on items that may actually lose them money in order to get us into the store, where we then buy other prominently displayed items at higher prices.

Rotter has taken the concept of expectation a step beyond that discussed so far. He has argued that there are important individual differences in expectations about the control of reinforcement. Some people feel that their behavior is responsible for the reinforcements they receive, while others believe that the reinforcements are controlled by forces outside themselves.

Rotter (1966, 1975) argued that individuals can be placed along a **continuum of internality-externality** in regard to how they perceive behavior as being reinforced. **Internal individuals** perceive rewards and punishments as resulting from their own actions; that is, they believe themselves to be in control of their own behavior. **External individuals** perceive the rewards or punishments they receive as being beyond their control. For external individuals, both good and bad events are attributed to

TABLE 8.1 Three questions from Rotter's Internal-External Locus of Control Scale. Respondents are asked to choose one of the two possible for each question. Responses 5a, 6b and 11b indicate an external locus of control. Rotter, 1996.

5a. The idea that teachers are unfair to students is nonsense.
5b. Most students don't realize the extent to which their grades are influenced by accidental happenings.
6a. Without the right breaks, one cannot be an effective leader.
6b. Capable people who fail to become leaders have not taken advantage of their opportunities.
11a. Becoming a success is a matter of hard work; luck has little to do with it.
11b. Getting a good job depends mainly on being at the right place at the right time.

© Cengage Learning

luck, fate, powerful others, or conditions over which they have no power.

Rotter developed a 29-item, forced-choice test that assessed a person's internality–externality called the **locus of control scale** (see Table 8.1). The questionnaire has been widely used and has been translated into at least 13 languages (Beretvas, Suizzo, Durham, & Yarnell, 2008). Other measures of locus of control have also been developed, some for specialized populations such as children (Nowicki & Strickland, 1973) and the elderly (Duke, Shaheen, & Nowicki, 1974). In general, participants who score high in the external direction do not function as well as internals. Externals are more likely to be disruptive (Tony, 2003); to have lower grades in school (Shepherd, Fitch, Owen, & Marshall, 2006); to have trouble staying on a diet (Adolfsson, Andersson, Elofsson, Rossner, & Unden, 2005); and to fail to comply with medical advice (Hong, Oddone, Dudley, & Bosworth, 2006).

Rotter's internal-external locus-of-control construct is not strictly motivational (Lefcourt, 1966). Although, locus of control was initially conceived to be a generalized expectancy concerning the ability to control the reinforcements one receives, researchers have found that there are some situations in which an internal person may attribute rewards and punishments to external causes, and vice versa. In other words, labeling someone as an *internal* or an *external* based on their score on a general locus of control scale appears to be too simplistic to account for the complexity of human motivation. Thus, researchers have begun to apply locus of control in a more domain-specific manner. Individual scales have been developed to assess locus of control specific to health (Wallston, Wallston, & DeVellis, 1978), work (Spector, 1988; Oliver, Jose, & Brough, 2006), sleep (Vincent, Sande, Read, & Giannuzzi, 2004), driving (Ozkan & Lajunen, 2005), and alcohol consumption (Goggin, Murray, Malcarne, Brown, & Wallston, 2007).

Rotter's social learning theory in general, and his concept of locus of control in particular, has spawned a great deal of research. However, he was not the only theorist who studied social learning. In reality, social learning theory is a group of theories that share common core assumptions, but differ in subtle, but important, ways (e.g., Bandura, 1977; Mischel, 1973). Indeed, one of the most famous theories within the social learning tradition was developed by Albert Bandura. However, Bandura's social learning theory has evolved into a much broader framework that includes control over the quality of one's life, or what Bandura calls human agency. We will discuss it and other theories of competence and control in Chapter 11.

Social learning theory currently has many practical applications. For example, Bushwick (2001) has argued that poor social learning may contribute to the development of autism. Other researchers have applied a social learning analysis to alcohol use (LaBrie, Huchting, Pedersen, Hummer, Shelesky,

& Tawalbeh, 2007), violence (Mialon & Mialon, 2006), academic achievement (Lan & Repman, 1995), leadership (Brown, Trevino, & Harrison, 2005), and both positive (e.g., safe sex practices) and negative (e.g., coercive sexuality) sexual behaviors (Hogben & Byrne, 1998).

The expectancy of reaching valued goals, then, is an important aspect of social learning theory. Expectancies and valued goals have also played an important role in the development of theories of achievement motivation. We will examine this role in the next section.

Expectancy-Value Theory and the Need for Achievement

Much of the early work on psychological motives was conducted by Henry Murray (1938), who believed that motivational processes result from individual needs that can best be observed in natural settings or clinical situations. Further, Murray argued that people can be classified according to the strengths of the various needs he identified (Steers & Porter, 1983). Murray defined **needs** to be a recurrent concern for a goal state and believed that a need consists of two components. The first component is directional in nature and includes the object that will satisfy the need. The second component consists of the energy that drives the behavior and can be thought of as the intensity of the need.

Murray and his colleagues at Harvard studied the needs of a group of college-age men and developed a list of approximately 20 major needs (**manifest needs**) as well as several latent needs, inner states and general traits. A few of Murray's manifest needs are the need for achievement, autonomy, dominance, understanding, and the need to be nurturant. Any given individual could be regarded as possessing several needs that direct and energize his or her behavior. These needs were considered to be learned and were thought to be activated by environmental cues.

Of all the needs outlined by Murray, most research has been devoted to understanding the need to achieve. Murray (1938, p. 164) defined the **need for achievement** as follows: "To

accomplish something difficult. To master, manipulate or organize physical objects, human beings, or ideas. To do this as rapidly and as independently as possible. To overcome obstacles and attain a high standard. To excel one's self. To rival and surpass others. To increase self-regard by the successful exercise of talent." As you can no doubt see, Murray considered achievement motivation a rather complex need that can be fulfilled in different ways by different persons; however, as is also evident in the quote, the need for achievement concerns doing difficult tasks quickly and doing them well.

The measurement of achievement motivation began with two researchers at Wesleyan University, David McClelland and John Atkinson. McClelland adapted a technique first used by Murray (1936) that asked participants to make up a story or describe a situation depicted in an ambiguous picture (see Figure 8.6). The technique, known as the **Thematic Apperception Test (TAT)**, is used clinically, but McClelland and his associates felt that it could also be used to determine an individual's motives. They felt that important motives of an individual could be assessed by analyzing the TAT story for certain themes. Such an approach is called **content analysis**.

SKETCH IN THE DORMITORY.

FIGURE 8.6 An example of the type of picture used in the Thematic Apperception Test. Picture Collection, The Branch Libraries, The New York Public Library, Astor, Lenox and Tilden Foundations.

To test the validity of their assumption, McClelland and Atkinson (1948) arranged to have men at a submarine base go without food for varying lengths of time up to 16 hours. None of the participants knew that they were participating in a study on the effects of hunger. Participants were led to believe that they were being tested for visual acuity. The men were asked to look at slides of various scenes that might suggest food seeking or eating and then write stories that answered questions such as: "What is happening?" "What led up to the situation?" "What is wanted?" "What will happen?" A scoring system was devised that allowed classification of stories from food-deprived and nondeprived individuals in terms of the story contents. The results clearly showed that amount of food deprivation (1, 4, or 16 hours) was related to the food imagery found in the stories. This study provided evidence that motive states were reflected in the interpretations that individuals gave to the TAT pictures.

McClelland and associates (1949) then developed an experimental situation in which need for achievement could be aroused and, in a fashion similar to the food deprivation study, developed a scoring system based on achievement-related images in the TAT as a measure of need for achievement. In this experiment, one group of students was given several tasks to perform under relaxed conditions. Specifically, these students were told that the tasks had been recently devised by some graduate students and that the group was being asked to participate in order to evaluate these tasks. The instructions were designed to lead to minimal ego involvement on the part of the participants because the emphasis was on testing the tasks themselves rather than the students. A second group of participants was termed the *failure condition*. Participants in this group were given the first task to perform and, after scoring their own tasks, were given a questionnaire asking for such personal information as estimated class standing, IQ, and so on. The purpose of the questionnaire was to get the participants ego-involved by making the test scores known to each participant in relation to other achievement-related facts asked by the questionnaire. The experimenters then led the

participants to believe that the tasks they had just undertaken were actually intelligence tests, and the experimenters quoted norms that were so high that practically everyone in the group failed (scored in the lowest quarter of the norms). The rest of the tasks were then administered.

The instructions for the ego-involved failure group apparently had the desired effect, because the participants were dismayed when the unrealistically high norms were announced. Finally, the participants in both groups were given what they thought was a test of creative imagination but was actually the TAT pictures used to score achievement imagery (several other conditions were also run, but for our purposes we note only the results of these two groups). A scoring system for analyzing the content of the TAT stories was developed, and the results showed that need-for-achievement scores were higher for the failure condition than for the relaxed condition. For example, the failure condition produced imagery that significantly more often involved a concern for performing a task well in relation to a stated standard of excellence. Results indicating an increase in achievement imagery as a function of ego-involving or achievement-orienting conditions have been replicated many times (Veroff, Wilcox, & Atkinson, 1953).

Motive for Success, Probability of Success, and Incentive Value Achievement motivation theory for Atkinson was an expectancy-value theory because he assumed that the tendency to engage in a particular activity is related to the strength of an expectation (belief) that the behavior will lead to a particular consequence. In addition, the value of that consequence for the person is important (Atkinson & Birch, 1978). Thus, people are assumed to engage in achievement-related situations as a result of their belief that doing so will lead to particular valued goals.

In achievement theory, T_a is used to symbolize the **tendency to approach (or to avoid) an achievement-related situation**. Although this tendency is influenced by external rewards (money, approval), most research emphasis has focused on intrinsic (internal) variables such as the pride associated with achievement or the shame associated with failure.

The tendency to approach or avoid achievement situations is thought to result from four variables: the **motive for success** (M_s), the **motive to avoid failure** (M_{af}), the estimated **probability of success** (P_s), and the **incentive value** (I_s) of achieving success. M_s and M_{af} are regarded as stable personality characteristics that will vary in strength from one individual to another, but will be relatively permanent within individuals across different situations. Both M_s and M_{af} are thought to be learned early in life through association with parental rewards where achievement-related cues were present at the time reward was received. M_s will be high in those individuals for whom achievement cues have been paired with positive emotions in the past. However, a strong M_{af} will develop if a person's attempts at achievement have been associated with negative emotional consequences.

Expectancy-value theory conceptualizes all individuals as possessing both M_s and M_{af}. However, the two motives will possess different strengths in different people because of varied past experiences (good and bad) in achievement-related situations. Thus, people whose $M_s > M_{af}$ (the symbol > is to be read "greater than") will tend to approach achievement situations, while people whose $M_{af} > M_s$ will generally avoid them. The intensity of this motive to approach or avoid a situation is determined by the remaining two variables: P_s and I_s.

In contrast to the relatively stable M_s and M_{af}, P_s and I_s are assumed to vary from situation to situation. Recall that P_s is the person's *subjective estimate* of succeeding (obtaining the desired goal) in the particular situation. The incentive value of success (I_s) is the value of actually achieving the goal and represents the fact that some goals are worth more than others. For intrinsic goals, it is believed that P_s and I_s are inversely related to each other. In other words, the easier the task, the less value obtaining of the goal will have; the harder the task, the greater the value of success. For example, suppose that you are a research participant in a study on achievement. You are given a puzzle to solve, which you do

successfully. You will probably take more pride in your achievement if you are told by the experimenter that the puzzle is very difficult and that very few people can do it (low P_s; high I_s) than you would if you were told that almost everyone solves the puzzle correctly (high P_s; low I_s).

If we further examine the relationship between P_s and I_s for tasks of varying difficulty, an interesting pattern emerges. It turns out that tasks of moderate difficulty are stronger motivators (to approach or to avoid an achievement situation) than tasks that are either very easy or very hard. Easy tasks maximize P_s, but their completion does not give us a sense of achievement because they are so effortless (low I_s). As a matter of fact, if we should happen to fail at an easy task, we would probably experience some degree of shame. On the other hand, extremely difficult tasks have high I_s, but we may avoid them because P_s is so low. However, we are less likely to feel shame if we fail at a difficult task. It is the moderately difficult task that provides us with a fair challenge (moderate P_s and I_s) that, if met, will result in a feeling of accomplishment. But, moderately difficult tasks also provide us with a real possibility of failure. How does expectancy-value theory help us to predict whether a person will choose to approach or avoid a task of moderate difficulty? It depends on one's level of M_s and M_{af}. Consider the contrasting examples of Terrence and Denise.

Terrence is a high school senior who is applying to college. He has the choice of applying to a highly prestigious university with a very low acceptance rate (low P_s, high I_s); a well-regarded state university with a moderate acceptance rate (moderate P_s, moderate I_s), or to a less prestigious safety school, which has a very high acceptance rate (high P_s, low I_s). To which will he apply? According to expectancy-value theory, it depends on his M_s and M_{af}.

Suppose that, in the past, Terrence has often had his attempts at achievement associated with negative emotional consequences. In short, Terrence has a strong M_{af} and a weaker M_s. Because his $M_{af} > M_s$, Terrence will generally attempt to avoid all achievement situations.

However, achievement situations of moderate difficulty (e.g., applying to the state university) should be the most aversive to Terrence. If Terrence were to apply to the safety school, he would maximize his P_s, which is very important to someone with a strong M_{af}. If he were to apply to the highly prestigious school, the odds are that he would fail to gain admission, but he could attribute the failure to the very low P_s inherent in the task. Either of these two options would be preferable to applying to the state university, where he has a moderate chance of failing at a task that many people can accomplish (something that is very aversive to an individual with a strong M_{af}). The lower half of Figure 8.7 depicts the relative likelihood of Terrence's application decision based on expectancy-value theory.

Denise is also a high school senior who must make the same decision as Terrence. The difference is that Denise's past experiences in achievement situations have met with positive emotional consequences. Thus, Denise's $M_s > M_{af}$. If Denise were to apply to the safety school she would likely be accepted, but this would not provide much sense

of accomplishment for someone with a strong M_s. Conversely, applying to the highly prestigious school provides her with a low P_s, which is also unappealing to someone who is motivated to succeed. Expectancy-value theory predicts that Denise would be most likely to apply to the state university, because she has a moderate chance at accomplishing a goal that has value for her. The upper half of Figure 8.7 depicts the relative likelihood of Denise's application decision, which you will notice is the mirror image of that of Terrence.

Research on Achievement Motivation
The theory of achievement motivation developed by Atkinson and his associates has generated a tremendous amount of research. We will not attempt to survey this vast literature but will examine a few studies that have tried to test some of the basic predictions of the theory.

In early experiments on achievement motivation, researchers typically measured M_s and M_{af}, then artificially set P_s by telling the participants what they could expect in regard to the probability of success. Because the incentive values of success is

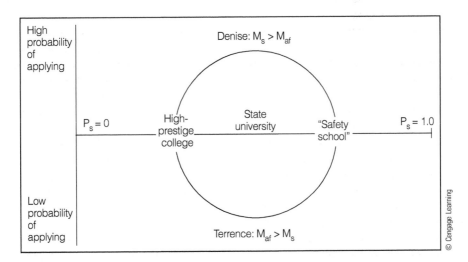

FIGURE 8.7 Schematic of the predicted behavior of Terrence and Denise based on expectancy-value theory. The horizontal axis represents probability of success (P_s) and the vertical axis represents probability of engaging in the behavior, from lowest (bottom) to highest (top). Terrence, whose $M_{af} > M_s$, should tend to avoid situations in which P_s is moderate. Conversely, Denise should seek out such situations because her $M_s > M_{af}$.

inversely related to P_s, the experimenters were, in essence, setting this also.

Achievement theory predicts that the tendency to approach achievement situations will be maximal for people high in M_s for tasks they perceive as being intermediate in difficulty. Intuitively, we might expect that an achievement-oriented person such as Denise would attempt tasks that are hard enough to award a sense of accomplishment when successful but not so difficult as to eliminate success nor so easy as to make success worthless. On the other hand, a person like Terrence who is high in M_{af} will tend to choose tasks that are either very easy or very difficult.

Atkinson and Litwin (1960) tested these predictions by assessing M_s and M_{af} in college men. These men were then asked to participate in a ring-toss game and could select the distance to the peg anywhere from 1 to 15 feet. As expected, men whose $M_s > M_{af}$ chose distances that were intermediate. However, men with $M_{af} > M_s$ did not choose extreme distances (1 or 15 feet) more often than intermediate distances, though there was a secondary preference at 1 to 2 feet. Clearer evidence was obtained by Isaacson (1964), who found that men higher in M_s than M_{af} chose college majors of intermediate difficulty more often than men who were higher in M_{af} than M_s.

Criticisms of Need-Achievement Theory

Need-achievement theory has been criticized on a number of methodological and theoretical counts. There have been failures to replicate some important findings, including several experiments that call into question the finding that persons high in M_s prefer tasks of intermediate difficulty. Weinstein (1969), for example, found no consistent relationship between several measures of achievement motivation and risk taking. Ray (1982), using somewhat different measures than those examined by Weinstein, also found no relationship between achievement motivation and preferred task difficulty. Blankenship (1992) found that achievement motivation and task difficulty were unrelated to latency to engage in an achievement task. Cooper (1983), in a complex study examining seven predictions of achievement theory, found that level of task difficulty was one of two predictions not supported by his data. So the basic prediction that persons high in M_s will choose tasks of intermediate difficulty should apparently be viewed with some caution. However, as Cooper also noted, five of the seven predictions made by achievement theory were supported, and we can thus place some confidence in the theory as a whole.

From a theoretical standpoint, Carver and Scheier (2000) have pointed out that the dual constructs of motive for success (M_s) and motive to avoid failure (M_{af}) make interpreting research on achievement motivation difficult. For example, if individuals high in need for achievement behave differently than individuals low in this need, this effect could be due to differences in M_s, or M_{af}, or a combination of the two motives. Some researchers have even questioned whether the need for achievement is motivational. For example, Entwisle (1972) noted that for ninth-grade participants the number of words in a TAT story correlated better with their grades than the need-achievement scores! This is difficult to understand if need for achievement is an activator of achievement behavior that would presumably be reflected in grades. Similarly, Klinger (1966) has suggested that need-achievement scores are largely situational. Thus, specific situations may lead to increased achievement imagery (as measured by the TAT) and to increased achievement behavior; that is, although achievement imagery is related to achievement performance, it may not be a causal relationship.

Perhaps the most serious criticism is that achievement motivation is multidimensional and is thus more complicated than need-achievement theory suggests. Recall that Rotter's concept of locus of control was found to be too general to account for the variability in one's behavior—a person could be an internal in some situations and an external in others. It appears that achievement motivation is also too complex to be explained by the relationship between a general approach motive (M_s) and a general avoidance motive (M_{af}), and this has led researchers to revise the theory.

Revisions to Need-Achievement Theory

In order to more fully explain achievement motivation, many researchers turned their attention to more specific achievement goals rather than to general achievement motives. For example, Raynor (1969, 1974) has pointed out that not all achievement situations are of equal importance; some have future implications, while others do not. These future goals may have intrinsic or extrinsic aspects, or both, and their effect will be an intensification of present achievement behavior. For example, doing well as an undergraduate may determine whether or not an individual gets into medical school. The future possibility of getting into medical school should influence his motivation on a current task (e.g., doing well on a crucial chemistry exam). This same person might also be motivated to win the game of darts that he is currently playing. But because the dart game has few future implications, the intensity of this behavior will be much lower.

Raynor's extension of achievement theory suggests that the value of a present activity toward obtaining some future goal is an important variable in determining achievement behavior. Data supportive of Raynor's approach have shown that persons high in M_s and low in M_{af} received significantly higher grades in a course when the perceived importance of that course for some future goal was high than they did when it was low (Raynor, 1970). More recently, Turner and Schallert (2001) studied students who had gotten poor midterm grades in a difficult college course. Those students who had career goals that were linked to success in the course (i.e., graduate school admission) were more likely to use poor midterm grades as a motivator, and to improve their subsequent performance in the course. Those students who did not view the course as important for their future goals were not as resilient to poor performance feedback. Clearly, goals must be taken into account when we try to understand achievement behavior, and we will now briefly review some models of achievement motivation that do just that.

Dweck (1986) and Dweck & Elliott (1983) identified two specific types of goals, which they termed **learning** (often called **mastery**) goals and **performance** goals. Someone motivated by a learning goal will seek to master a task for the sake of increasing *personal* competence. With performance goals, on the other hand, how one's level of competence compares to others is the primary motivator. For example, consider John and Marilyn, two college students who are taking a course in public speaking. John is motivated to master the ability to speak before a group due to a desire to become competent at the task—his is a learning or mastery goal. However, Marilyn is less concerned with task mastery and more concerned with how her competence will be judged in comparison to others. Because her goal is performance, she will behave in a manner that maximizes positive evaluation and minimizes negative evaluation.

In theory, learning goals should be associated with positive outcomes such as increased enjoyment of the task and greater persistence if the task is difficult. Conversely, performance goals should result in negative outcomes such as less intrinsic enjoyment of the activity and a greater likelihood of giving up in the face of adversity (Dweck, 1986; Elliot, 1999). Research on these topics generally bears out the predictions for mastery goals, but is equivocal in its support of performance goals. For example, Hulleman, Durik, Schweigert, and Harackiewicz (2008) report that mastery goals are positively related to a student's interest in a college course (intrinsic value) and perception of the usefulness of the course material in their careers (utility value). Mastery goals are also related to increased effort expended in an academic setting (Fenollar, Roman, & Cuestes, 2007). Some researchers have found that performance goals are related to negative outcomes such as lower academic achievement and lower intrinsic interest in learning (Meece, Blumenfeld, & Hoyle, 1988). However, others have found that performance goals are related to positive outcomes, such as the perceived value of education (Midgley, Arunkumar, & Urdan, 1996). Moreover, as you may have already surmised, learning and performance goals are not necessarily mutually exclusive—they can both motivate our behavior. Perhaps Marilyn, our student of public speaking, is motivated to both master the task and to be judged as a competent public speaker.

Elliot and colleagues (Elliot & Church, 1997; Elliot & McGregor, 2001) proposed a revised model to account for the inconsistencies in the literature on performance goals. This hierarchal framework is a synthesis of the learning/mastery-performance goals of Dweck and the motives to approach success and avoid failure of Atkinson. In this model, the motive for success and motive to avoid failure are viewed as general needs that do not energize behavior directly. Instead, these general motives interact with the two types of achievement goals (i.e., mastery and performance) to produce the 2×2 matrix depicted in Figure 8.8. Thus, one can be intrinsically motivated to succeed (mastery-approach goal) or intrinsically motivated to avoid failure (mastery-avoidance goal). Similarly, one may be motivated to perform better (performance-approach goal) or to avoid performing worse (performance-avoidance goal) in comparison to others.

As the research on achievement motivation evolves, so must the techniques to measure concepts of interest. Because early instruments such as the TAT do not take into consideration the complexity of Elliot's model, Elliot and Murayama (2008) have developed a scale to measure each of the four goals depicted in Figure 8.8. Their **Achievement Goal Questionnaire–Revised (AGQ–R)** is a 12-item instrument that uses a 5-point agree–disagree answer format to assess mastery-approach goals (e.g., "My aim is to completely master the material presented in this class."), mastery-avoidance goals (e.g., "I am striving to avoid an incomplete understanding of the course material."), performance-approach goals (e.g., "My goal is to perform better than the other students."), and performance-avoidance goals (e.g., "My aim is to avoid doing worse than other students."). Elliot and Murayama (2008) present evidence that the AGQ–R is both valid and useful in predicting achievement-related motives and behavior. Specifically, the researchers distributed the AGQ–R as well as a measure of intrinsic motivation (which included measures such as "I think this class is interesting") and a measure of exam performance to a sample of 229 undergraduates. They predicted that exam performance would be positively related to performance-approach goals and negatively related to performance-avoidance goals. They also predicted that intrinsic motivation would be positively related to mastery-approach goals and negatively related to mastery-avoidance goals. They found support for each of their predictions except the last one.

This 2×2 matrix has been the subject of considerable research. Although the model is generally confirmed by the data, some concepts such as the mastery-avoidance component need more empirical support. In addition, some researchers argue that goals other than mastery and performance should be considered as well (e.g., Ryan & Pintrich, 1997; Urdan & Maehr, 1995). Many researchers also note the difficulty in achieving consensus regarding the use of terms (e.g., "learning" and "mastery" are often used interchangeably). Conversely, it has also been argued that researchers sometimes use the same term to describe different concepts (Hulleman, Schrager, Bodmann, & Harackiewicz, 2010). Finally, the instruments used to measure goals and motives vary considerably from study to study. In all research, the conclusions that can be drawn from research results

	Goal is to develop competence	Goal is to demonstrate competence
Motivation to succeed	Mastery-approach goal	Performance-approach goal
Motivation to avoid failure	Mastery-avoidance goal	Performance-avoidance goal

FIGURE 8.8 The 2×2 Achievement Goal × Motivation matrix developed by Elliot and McGregor. From Elliot, A. J. & McGregor, H. A. (2001). "A 2×2 achievement goal framework," *Journal of Personality and Social Psychology*, 80, 501–519. Copyright © 2001 American Psychological Association. Reprinted with permission.

are limited by the accuracy of the measuring instruments used in the study. Thus, the lack of agreement among researchers on how to accurately define and measure achievement motivation remains a serious issue that the field must address.

Despite, or perhaps because of, the theoretical complexity and methodological challenges inherent in studying achievement motivation, it remains the subject of a great deal of research, much of which is conducted in environments where achievement has traditionally been evaluated, such as educational settings, the workplace, and athletic events. Achievement motivation, as we have discussed it to this point, relates primarily to intrinsic motivational factors; that is, the achievement motive and the motive to avoid failure are seen as internal spurs to behavior. But people sometimes behave in achievement situations because of external factors such as money, obtaining a scholarship, and so on (Feather, 1961). Such factors are grouped under the general heading **extrinsic motivation** and include the kinds of variables usually labeled as *reinforcement* or *reward* (e.g., Lepper & Greene, 1978; Turner & Schallert, 2001; Pintrich & DeGroot, 1990; Sansone & Harackiewicz, 2000). Thus, some researchers have argued that achievement motivation is perhaps best viewed as one component of more global motives such as self-efficacy or competence. We will return to these topics in Chapter 11. We now turn to two areas of social cognition that can also be understood from an expectancy-value perspective: the relationship between attitudes and behaviors and the phenomenon of social loafing.

Attitudes, Behaviors, and Expectancy-Value

Have you ever wondered why so many organizations want to know your attitude or opinion on something? Election pollsters inquire about approval ratings of politicians, restaurants and hotels ask us to fill out customer satisfaction surveys, pop-up ads appear on Web sites asking us to tell them what we think about a product or service. Why?

Generally, these organizations are not as interested in our attitudes as they are in our behavior—they want to use our attitude to predict future behavior such as whether we will vote for a particular candidate, eat at the restaurant again, or buy a certain product. Thus, **attitudes**, which are positive or negative evaluations of an object, event or idea, are often used to predict behavior.

Unfortunately, the relationship between attitudes and behavior is not a simple one. In a classic study, Bickman (1972) and his students individually interviewed 506 people who were walking in front of either a college library or a storefront nearby the college. Each person was asked: "Should it be everyone's responsibility to pick up litter when they see it, or should it be left for the people whose job it is to pick up?" Not surprisingly, 94% of the participants said that everyone is responsible for picking up litter. The interview was conducted on a sidewalk about 10 feet in front of a page of crumpled newspaper that the experimenter had placed next to a small trash can. The participants (409 college students and 97 nonstudents) could not avoid seeing the litter and trashcan because they had to either change their path to walk around them or step over them. Given that almost everyone held the attitude that picking up litter is everyone's responsibility, one might expect that most people would pick up the paper and put it in the trashcan. However, only 8 people did (1.4% of the total).

There are several reasons why attitudes often do not predict behaviors very well, as indicated by Bickman's research and many other studies. First, attitudes are more strongly correlated with patterns of behavior than they are with individual behaviors. For example, consider someone who has a positive attitude toward energy conservation. One day we see her leave a room without turning off the lights—a behavior inconsistent with her attitude. However, if we observe her behavior over a longer period of time such as a full day or a week, we may see that she takes the stairs instead of the elevator, drives a hybrid car, and buys products made from recycled materials. Thus, her overall pattern of behavior is consistent with her attitude, even though certain

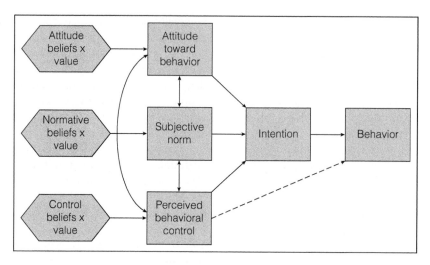

FIGURE 8.9   Schematic diagram of the Theory of Planned Behavior. Copyright © 2006 Icek Ajzen. Reprinted with permission.

individual behaviors may be contradictory. Another reason for the inconsistency between attitudes and behavior is that some attitudes are more important to us (i.e., hold more value) than others. For example, a person may hold a positive attitude toward energy conservation, but this attitude may not be strong enough to motivate behavior. Finally, our behavior is determined by several factors in addition to attitudes. A person may be in a hurry and not have the time to drive to the recycling center or may be worried about the health of a friend and may not notice that the light is on when they leave an empty room, etc. Thus, behavior can best be understood as being the result of the interaction between attitudes and other important factors. This is the approach taken by Icek Ajzen (1988, 1991) in his theory of planned behavior, which is grounded in expectancy-value theory.

The Theory of Planned Behavior

According to Ajzen[1] (1991), a strong predictor of behavior is one's **intention** to perform or not to perform a given action, because intentions provide us with a measure of how much effort someone is

willing to expend. Election pollsters understand this concept—they know that the results of a poll of registered voters are generally not as accurate as those of a poll of likely voters (i.e., people who *intend* to vote in the next election). Thus, intentions are a major motivational concept in the theory of planned behavior (see Figure 8.9). Note that our discussion begins on the right side of Figure 8.9 and proceeds from right to left. Intentions, however are not enough; a person must have resources such as the time and the ability to perform the behavior. Ajzen used the term **actual behavioral control** to denote factors such as time and ability. Thus, a person with the actual behavioral control and the intention to perform a behavior is likely to do so. Note that actual behavioral control does not appear in the model depicted in Figure 8.9. Rather, it is assumed to be a necessary condition for the behavior to occur. For example, someone who cannot fly a plane is unlikely to successfully perform that behavior no matter how hard he or she tries.

Ajzen does include **perceived behavioral control** as one of the precursors of intentions (represented by a solid line in Figure 8.9) and as a direct predictor of behavior (dotted line). Perceived behavioral control is one's level of belief in one's ability to successfully perform a given

---

[1]Ajzen's theory of planned behavior is an extension of an earlier Theory of Reasoned Action developed by Fishbein & Ajzen, 1975.

behavior and, when one's perception is accurate, provides a very close approximation of actual behavioral control (Ajzen, 1991). The other two major components of the model are one's attitude toward the behavior and one's perception of the way important others view the behavior, or what Ajzen calls **subjective norm**.

To illustrate the model, suppose a friend of yours whom we'll call Clare is trying to decide whether to take a course in motivation next semester. Measuring Clare's intention to take the course should be a good predictor of her behavior assuming that actual behavioral control is present (e.g., if the course isn't offered next semester, she can't take it). In order to discern her intention, we should determine whether she has a positive or negative evaluation of the course (i.e., her attitude). In addition, we should find out whether her friends have taken or plan to take the course (i.e., subjective norm). Finally, we should determine whether or not she thinks she can fit the course into her schedule (i.e., perceived behavioral control). Note in Figure 8.9 that these three factors combine to determine Clare's intention. Also note that the double arrows connecting these factors mean that each factor can reciprocally influence the others. For example, being a friend of Clare's who is currently taking the course, your behavior will be part of the subjective norm component. However, your evaluation of the course is likely to influence Clare's attitude toward taking the course as well.

Another nuance to the model is the dotted line that goes from perceived behavioral control directly to behavior. According to Ajzen, perceived behavioral control can influence behavior directly in cases where the behavior is not fully under the person's control. Thus, when one has total control over one's behavior, measuring intention should be a good predictor of behavior. However, when the ability to perform the behavior is not under our complete control, perceived behavioral control becomes more important in the prediction of behavior. For example, consider two scenarios where we hold constant Clare's intention to take the course and we vary her perceived behavioral

control. Assume that there is only one section of the course being offered and that the class meeting time conflicts with Clare's work schedule. If in the past Clare has not been able to readjust her work schedule around her classes, her perceived behavioral control is likely to be low. In this case, she is unlikely to expend much effort to take the course. If on the other hand, Clare has usually had success at juggling work and school, she is likely to be confident that she can do it again (because of her high perceived behavioral control) and will probably persevere in her effort to take the course.

In an attempt to further explain why behavior occurs, Ajzen has proposed that each of three major components of intention is formed via an expectancy-value process, as indicated in the far left of Figure 8.9. According to Ajzen, attitudes, subjective norms, and perceived behavioral control are all a product of our **salient beliefs** about a behavior combined with our **evaluation** or value of the outcome. Before discussing this aspect of the theory, it is important to note the distinction between a belief and an attitude. A *belief* is what a person thinks to be true; an *attitude* is a positive or negative evaluation of something. Thus, beliefs are cognitive whereas attitudes include both a cognitive and an affective (i.e., emotional) component. For example, suppose two people share the same belief that there is likely to be some form of life on other planets. One person is fascinated by this prospect and would like to study it further, but the other finds it unpleasant because it conflicts with his or her religious beliefs. These people have different attitudes toward the same belief or, put another way, have made a different evaluation of the same object. Note that objects or ideas that are important to us often quickly acquire a positive or negative evaluation. Ajzen further states that, although we all have formed many beliefs during our lifetimes, the ones that have the greatest impact are those that are the most salient, or readily accessible in memory.

Consider how your friend Clare may have formed her attitude toward the behavior of taking a course in motivation. According to the theory of planned behavior, Clare likely has several salient beliefs toward this behavior, each of which is associated with an outcome to which she assigns a value (depicted in the upper left of Figure 8.9). Suppose Clare believes (i.e., expects) that the course will likely be offered early in the morning on Tuesdays and Thursdays and by a particular instructor, with whom Clare has taken a course in the past. Each of these salient beliefs will quickly be associated with an evaluation (i.e., value). The time of day may be desirable if it fits her work schedule or undesirable if she prefers to sleep in; the instructor will be evaluated based on her experience in the previous course, etc. In this expectancy-value model, Clare's attitude will be formed by the sum of her salient beliefs or expectancies about the behavior multiplied by the value of each. According to Ajzen, the other two predictors of Clare's intention will be formed in a similar way—her salient beliefs/expectancies related to the subjective norm and perceived behavioral control will be weighted by their value and summed to produce her perception of each.

If we look at our example in its entirety, the theory of planned behavior holds that Clare's salient beliefs and her value of each combine to form her attitude, perception of subjective norm, and perceived behavioral control related to taking the motivation course. She then uses each of these components to determine whether or not she intends to take the course. Assuming that actual behavioral control is present (e.g., the course is being offered), and perceived behavioral control is high, her intention should be a good predictor of her behavior, which in this case is whether or not she registers for the course.

The Theory of Planned Behavior: Research and Applications   The theory of planned behavior has been the subject of over 1,000 research studies, many of which focus on predicting behaviors related to health and safety. In general, the theory of planned behavior increases accuracy in predicting behaviors as diverse as texting while driving (Nemme & White, 2010), gambling (Martin et al., 2010), exercising (Kwan & Bryan, 2010), academic cheating (Stone, Jawahar, & Kisamore, 2010), using public transportation instead of driving (Gardner & Abraham, 2010),

engaging in safe sex (Albarracin, Johnson, Fishbein, & Muellerleile, 2001), drinking alcohol (Glassman, Braun, Dodd, Miller, & Miller, 2010), and taking medication (Williams, Povey, & White, 2008) to name just a few.

Studies that test predictive models such as those noted above are useful in understanding relationships between variables. However, just because the variables in the model are correlated does not necessarily mean that one causes the other (e.g., Does a change in attitude cause a change in intention and subsequent behavior?). Unfortunately, comparatively few studies have been conducted in which researchers *manipulate rather than simply measure* attitudes, norms, or perceived behavioral control and then determine if these manipulations cause changes in intentions and/or behaviors. Moreover, many of the studies that do test for causal relationships suffer one or more of the methodological flaws discussed below. Thus, although there is a large body of evidence supporting the predictive utility of the theory of planned behavior, there is much less data on whether or not the theory can be useful in designing intervention strategies to effect desired changes in behavior such as reducing cheating or increasing exercise compliance.

Criticisms of The Theory of Planned Behavior   As you have probably surmised, the theory of planned behavior is multifaceted. This means many variables need to be measured in order to test the theory properly (see Figure 8.9). Unfortunately, some variables are difficult to quantify accurately, and this means that the methodology of many studies has been called into question. We will use the attitude component of the theory as an example, but the situation is the same for subjective norms and perceived behavioral control. In order to measure attitude, participants are often asked to provide numerical ratings of their expectation for each salient belief as well as the value of each. These numbers are then multiplied together and summed to form an overall attitude measure, as is standard in expectancy-value theories. One criticism of this approach (French & Hankins, 2003) is that the scales on which these variables are measured (often 7 point interval scales with no true 0 point) do not provide data that are suitable to compute ratios (e.g., Does someone who provides a rating of 6 really value an outcome twice as much as someone who provides a rating of 3?; Does a rating of 7 indicate seven times the value of a rating of 1?; etc.). Furthermore, because the ratings for each belief are summed to form one overall attitude measure, it is often difficult to assess the relative importance of each individual belief in the determination of the attitude score. Because some beliefs are likely more important than others, this may contribute to the difficulty in determining which beliefs to target with intervention strategies when testing causal relationships (Elliott, Armitage, & Baughan, 2005).

Finally, the utility of the theory is often assessed by calculating the percent of variance in the intention or behavior variables that is accounted for by using the three predictor variables (i.e., attitude, norms, and perceived behavioral control). A value of 100% indicates that we could make a perfect prediction of a person's intention or behavior; a value of 0% indicates that the model is of no predictive utility at all. This value varies from study to study, but it is typically between 30% and 40%, indicating that the theory of planned behavior is of use but that there is still a large amount of variance unaccounted for (e.g., Armitage & Conner, 2001). This has led researchers to include additional variables such as personality traits or other aspects of one's perception of one's self in their studies to increase the predictive power of the model (e.g., Hagger & Chatzisarantis, 2009; Picazo-Vela, Chou, Melcher, & Pearson, 2010; Rise, Sheeran, & Hukkelberg, 2010). Generally, these additional predictors increase the variance accounted for by a few percentage points. However, they further complicate the model and make interpretation of the relationship among the variables even more difficult.

Comparing and Contrasting Three Expectancy-Value Theories

You may have noticed the structural similarity between the theory of planned behavior and the theories of Rotter and Atkinson. Rotter's locus of control is analogous to Ajzen's idea of perceived behavioral control. However, locus of control is assumed to be a generalized expectancy that is stable across situations, whereas perceived behavioral control varies from situation to situation. Atkinson's probability of success (P_s) changes based on the situation, but his motives to succeed and to avoid failure are stable personality traits. Thus, the three theories vary in the relative importance of situational factors as compared to personality traits in the determination of behavior. As we move from Rotter to Atkinson to Ajzen, situational factors become comparatively more important. We continue this trend with our final topic in this chapter: social loafing.

Social Loafing

Humans spend a great deal of time working together in social groups. Sports teams, clubs, civic organizations, work groups, committees, neighborhood associations, and the military are just a few examples of groups of people working in concert to achieve a goal. Logically, working in groups often makes sense: difficult tasks can be divided into more manageable ones, people can concentrate on assignments that match their areas of expertise, and problems can often be solved more easily if looked at from a number of perspectives. In short, "two heads are (often) better than one." However, working collectively also provides individual group members with an opportunity to slack off based on the expectancy that the rest of the group will work hard enough to accomplish the valued goal. This phenomenon is known as **social loafing**, and it has been the subject of much empirical research. We will now briefly review the history and current status of the social loafing phenomenon, with an emphasis on understanding social loafing within an expectancy-value framework.

In the late 1800s, a French agricultural engineer named Max Ringelmann was interested in quantifying the work efficiency of humans and draft animals such as horses and oxen (see Kravitz

& Martin, 1986, for a description of Ringelmann's work, which was originally published in French). Ringelmann's primary interest was in determining the most efficient method to perform a task (e.g., Can a weight be moved more easily by pushing or pulling it?). To this end he asked human research participants, both individually and in groups, to pull on a rope as one would do when playing tug-of-war. He then measured the force applied to the rope with a dynamometer, to which the other end of the rope was attached. The results were intriguing. When participants pulled on the rope alone, the average amount of force per individual was 83.5 kilograms (about 184 pounds). When they pulled in groups of seven, obviously the total amount of force applied to the rope was much greater; however, the average amount of force per individual was only 65.0 kilograms (143 pounds). In comparison, if seven people pulled on the rope individually and their output summed, they would be expected to produce a total of 584.5 kilograms of force (7×83.5). However, groups of seven pulling together only produced a total of 455 kilograms of force (7×65). Groups of 14 produced even less force per individual than did groups of seven. Thus, Ringelmann was the first to find empirical evidence that individual performance within a group decreased as group size increased. Ringelmann noted that the effect could be due to a loss of motivation among individuals in the groups, but he believed that the more likely explanation was a lack of coordination of effort.

Strangely, although Ringelmann's results were periodically cited in the literature on group performance, no experiments were done to replicate his findings until almost 100 years after his original work. The phenomenon was not studied again until Ingham, Levenger, Graves, and Peckham (1974) conducted two studies to investigate what they called the **Ringelmann effect**. In the first study, they used a rope-pulling mechanism similar to Ringelmann's and found that mean individual pulling effort did indeed decrease as group size increased from one to six people. In the second study, they sought to determine whether this effect was due to poor group coordination or to

a loss of motivation among group members. In this study, all participants pulled on the rope alone. However, some believed that they were pulling on the rope as part of a group that ranged from two to six people. Ingham et al. employed one to five confederates who, always occupying positions behind the real participant, pretended to pull on the rope without actually doing so. Thus, there could be no loss of force due to lack coordination of effort because only one person was actually pulling on the rope in each trial. If there was a difference in performance, it would be due to a loss of motivation due to the participant's perception that others were pulling along with him. The results indicated that mean individual pull scores once again decreased as a function of (perceived) group size, although performance did not decrease very much beyond a perceived group size of three. Thus, Ingham et al. (1974) replicated Ringelmann's original results and also provided evidence that the effect is due, at least in part, to a decrease in motivation due to increased group size.

Another important early study of the Ringelmann effect was conducted by Latané, Williams, and Harkins (1979). Latané et al. tested their research participants in groups of one to six. Instead of pulling on a rope, however, the participants were asked to clap or cheer as loud as possible. Participants' output was quantified in dynes/cm^2, which is a measure of the amount of effort involved in producing sound pressure. Latané et al. found what Ringelmann and Ingham et al. (1974) had found—that effort decreased as group size increased —or, as they put it, that "the sound of 12 hands clapping is not even three times as intense as the sound of 2" (Latané, et al. 1979, p. 825). In an attempt to quantify the degree to which the effect is due to reduced motivation, a second study was conducted in which the participants shouted and clapped in groups of one, two and six while wearing headphones and blindfolds. This sensory deprivation apparatus allowed Latané et al. to include another variable in the study, which they termed *actual groups* versus *pseudogroups*. In the actual groups, the participants were actually shouting and clapping with one or five other participants. In the pseudogroups, the

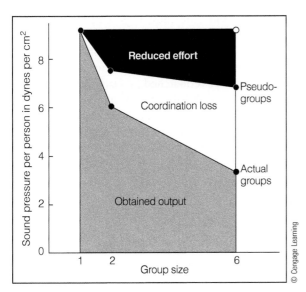

FIGURE 8.10 Average amount of sound pressure generated per person (vertical axis) as a function of group size (horizontal axis). The difference between the output of the actual groups and pseudogroups can be attributed to coordination loss. The difference between the pseudogroups and the horizontal dotted line on top of the graph can be attributed to social loafing. Latane, Williams, and Harkins, 1979, Study 2.

participants were really shouting and clapping alone while the confederates around them sat quietly.

The results of the second study are presented in Figure 8.10. Group size is listed on the horizontal axis and sound pressure on the vertical axis. The dotted line across the top of the graph indicates the amount of output that would be expected if participants' individual output was unaffected by group size. As you can see, both the actual groups and the pseudogroups exhibited a decrease in output as group size increased, with the actual groups producing at the lowest level. Because the actual and pseudogroups both *believed* that they were participating as part of a group, the difference between these groups (represented by the white area in the graph) is probably due to a lack of coordination among group members. This could be the result of participants failing to shout or clap in unison, or to the sound waves from one person canceling those of another

person, etc. However, there was no loss of coordination in the pseudogroups because only one person was yelling or clapping at a time. Thus, the loss of productivity labeled *reduced effort* in the graph is due to the expectancy that participants had that they were part of a larger group.

The two studies by Latané et al. (1979) are important for several reasons. First, they provide evidence that the Ringelmann effect occurs in tasks other than rope pulling. Second, they represent an attempt to quantify the degree to which the effect is due to loss of motivation. Finally, the authors coined the term *social loafing* which they defined as "a decrease in individual effort due to the social presence of other persons" (Latané, et al. 1979, p. 823).

The phenomenon of social loafing, which has replaced the term Ringelmann effect in the literature, has been studied extensively and found to be robust. In addition to physical tasks such as rope pulling, shouting, and clapping, it occurs in a variety of cognitive tasks, including brainstorming (van Dick, Stellmacher, Wagner, Lemmer, & Tissington, 2009) and problem solving (Arterberry, Cain, & Chopko, 2007). Although most social loafing research is conducted in the laboratory, it has also been documented in field studies of intact work groups (e.g., Liden, Wayne, Jaworski, & Bennett, 2004), online communities (e.g., Shiue, Chiu, & Chang, 2010), and, perhaps not surprisingly to you, college students completing group assignments (e.g., Aggarwal & O'Brien, 2008). Finally, it develops early in life; social loafing has been reported in children as young as 4 years of age (Thompson & Thornton, 2007). Given the pervasiveness of social loafing, it is important that we develop a deeper understanding of it. For that, we turn once again to expectancy-value theory.

Expectancy-Value Theory and Social Loafing

Recall that expectancy-value theory predicts that individuals will be motivated to engage in a behavior if they value the outcome and expect that their effort to achieve the outcome has a reasonable chance of success. Consider the following example of expectancy-value theory and individual behavior. Earl is competing against another person in a tug-of-war event at a fair. Expectancy-value theory predicts that he would exert the greatest effort if he *valued* the prize to be won and *expected* that his effort would give him a reasonable chance of winning. Now suppose that Earl is competing as part of a tug-of-war team. His individual expectancy and value perceptions are still important in predicting his individual effort. However, there are other factors unique to a group setting that also have an effect on individual performance. For example, Earl might now also consider whether it is really necessary for him to exert maximum effort for the team to win, whether his individual effort will be rewarded, whether others on the team are likely to slack off or exert their maximum effort, etc. Thus, expectancy-value theory can be applied to the behavior of individuals in complex group settings as well.

Several researchers have attempted to explain social loafing from an expectancy-value perspective (e.g., Karau & Williams, 1993; Kerr, 1983; Shepperd, 1993) and these approaches have much in common. We present one of them below—the **Collective Effort Model** (**CEM**) developed by Karau and Williams (1993). Grounded in expectancy-value theory, the CEM predicts that individuals will be motivated to perform well in tasks if they expect that their effort will lead to obtaining a valued goal. Thus, an important part of the CEM is the basic relationship between expectancy and value:

$$\begin{array}{c} \text{Individual Effort/} \\ \text{Performance} \end{array} \rightarrow \begin{array}{c} \text{Individual} \\ \text{Outcomes} \end{array}$$

However, the CEM also takes into account the complexity of collective effort by specifying three requisite conditions for maximal individual effort. First, one must expect that one's individual effort (and subsequent performance) will lead to improved group performance. In our tug-of-war example above, Earl must expect that his effort will improve the performance of the group as whole. Second, one must expect that the group's performance will lead to a valued group outcome. Earl and the members of his team must expect that they have a reasonable chance to win. If they appear to be overmatched, social loafing is more likely to occur. Finally, the group outcome must result in a valued individual outcome. Winning should result in a reward for Earl, either intrinsic (e.g., positive self-evaluation, feeling of belonging) or extrinsic (e.g., a share of the prize). Thus, the CEM predicts:

$$\begin{array}{c}\text{Individual}\\\text{Effort/}\\\text{Individual}\\\text{Perfor-}\\\text{mance}\end{array} \rightarrow \begin{array}{c}\text{Group}\\\text{Perfor-}\\\text{mance}\end{array} \rightarrow \begin{array}{c}\text{Group}\\\text{Out-}\\\text{comes}\end{array} \rightarrow \begin{array}{c}\text{Individual}\\\text{Out-}\\\text{comes}\end{array}$$

Why then does social loafing occur? In short, because individual effort/performance does not lead *directly* to individual outcomes. Instead, the link between individual effort and individual outcomes is mediated by group performance and group outcomes, which are factors that are largely out of the individual's control. According to the CEM, if any one of the links above is broken, social loafing is likely to occur. Thus, an intense effort from one individual may not result in a positive individual outcome because the group outcome may not be achieved. Conversely, individuals may loaf because they expect that the group (and, thus, the individual) outcome will be achieved even without their maximum individual effort. From an evolutionary standpoint, this strategy makes sense. As long as the goal can be achieved, why exert more effort than necessary?

The CEM has received empirical support from many studies, including two conducted by Shepperd and Taylor (1999). In the first study, the importance of the link between individual performance and group performance was tested. Participants, working in groups of 3–5, were asked to brainstorm and to list as many uses for common objects (e.g., knife, comb, etc.) as possible. The brainstorming task was set up so that each participant wrote answers individually on slips of paper and then put them into a common box. Each participant's paper was slightly different in size, making it possible for the experimenters to determine the input of each individual in the group.

Shepperd and Taylor included six different conditions in this study. In three of the conditions, participants were told that their individual performance (i.e., number of uses generated) would be evaluated. Evaluation of individual performance in a group tasks has been found to reduce social loafing, presumably because people do not want to be associated with a substandard performance (e.g., Harkins, 1987). In the other three conditions, participants were led to believe that their individual performance would not be evaluated. Shepperd and Taylor also included another variable, instrumentality, which had three levels. In the instrumentality control conditions, participants were not told that there was a prize for good group performance. In the other instrumentality conditions, participants were told that there were 40 groups participating in the study and that the groups who scored in the top 10% would receive a prize. The difference between the instrumentality conditions was the false feedback that they were given on practice trials. In the high instrumentality conditions, participants were told that they were very close to being in the top 10% after the practice trials. They were led to expect that they could probably earn the prize with a little extra group effort. In the low instrumentality conditions, participants were told that they were not very close to earning the prize in an effort to create the expectation that they probably could not win the prize, even with an increase in group effort. Thus, the study had two independent variables: individual evaluation (yes or no) and instrumentality (control, low or high).

The results of this study, which are presented in Figure 8.11, support the importance of the link between individual performance and group performance in reducing social loafing. Looking at the left side of the Figure 8.11, we see that participants in the no-evaluation control condition performed worse than participants in the evaluation control condition. This same pattern is evident in the two low-instrumentality conditions. Put another way,

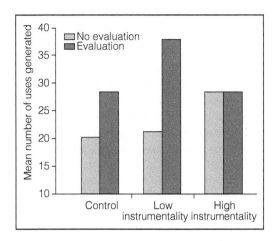

FIGURE 8.11 Performance on a brainstorming task (vertical axis) as a function of evaluation condition and level of instrumentality (horizontal axis). Social loafing, as indicated by a difference between evaluation and no evaluation conditions, was eliminated when the link between individual performance and group performance (i.e., the high instrumentality conditions) was salient. Shepperd and Taylor, 1999, Study 1.
From Sheppard, J. & Taylor, K., "Social loafing and expectancy-value theory," *Personality & Social Psychology Bulletin, 25*, 1147–1163. Copyright © 1999 Sage Publications. Reprinted by permission.

the participants in the two no-evaluation conditions loafed. Why? Recall that the control groups were not told that there was a prize for good performance; the low-instrumentality groups were told about the prize, but were led to expect that they had very little chance of winning it. Thus, in both cases, there was little incentive to perform well, unless one's individual performance was being evaluated. If we now look at the high-instrumentality conditions, we see that there is no difference between the evaluation and no-evaluation conditions. Both performed at a high level. It seems that when increased individual performance carries with it the expectation of increased group performance (i.e., the first phase of the CEM), social loafing does not occur.

Shepperd and Taylor conducted a second study to examine the link between group performance and group outcomes, which is the second phase of the CEM. The second study was very similar to the first, but there were a few important differences. First, there were no practice trials on which false feedback was given. In addition, the instrumentality manipulation was changed such that participants in the high instrumentality conditions were led to believe that the top 70% of groups would win a prize. These participants expected that good group performance would probably lead to a valued outcome. Participants in the low-instrumentality conditions were informed that they had a 1 in 200 chance of winning a prize, but that they could improve the odds to 1 in 20 if they were in the top 10% of all the groups in the study. Thus, these participants expected that even good group performance was not likely to yield the valued outcome. The results of the second study are presented in Figure 8.12. As you can see, the pattern of results is very similar to that of the first study. Participants in the no-evaluation control and

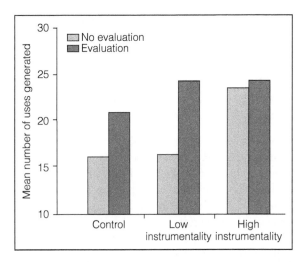

FIGURE 8.12 Performance on a brainstorming task (vertical axis) as a function of evaluation condition and level of instrumentality (horizontal axis). Social loafing, as indicated by a difference between evaluation and no evaluation conditions, was eliminated when the link between group performance and group outcomes (i.e., the high instrumentality conditions) was salient. Shepperd and Taylor, 1999, Study 2. From Sheppard, J. & Taylor, K., "Social loafing and expectancy-value theory," *Personality & Social Psychology Bulletin, 25,* 1147–1163. Copyright © 1999 Sage Publications. Reprinted by permission.

low-instrumentality conditions loafed relative to their counterparts in the evaluation conditions. However, the participants in the no-evaluation high-instrumentality condition did not loaf because they expected that good group performance would result in earning a valued group outcome. Thus, it appears that the CEM is useful in predicting under what circumstances social loafing is likely to take place. To the extent that these conditions can be manipulated, social loafing can be reduced.

Predicting and Reducing Social Loafing Karau and Williams (1993) gathered the results of 78 studies, calculated the magnitude of social loafing effects, and performed a quantitative review known as a meta-analysis to determine the overall impact that different variables have on social loafing. The results support many of the predictions they made based on the CEM. Some of these include the findings that loafing can be reduced if participants: a) *expect* their individual contributions are identifiable; b) *expect* that their contributions are unique and necessary for group success (i.e., no one else can "pick up the slack" if they do not perform well); and c) *value* the task they are performing as being meaningful. They also found that loafing decreases along with group size (i.e., people loaf less in small groups) and task complexity (i.e., people do not loaf as much on simple tasks as they do on complex ones).

Another variable that can be manipulated to reduce social loafing is reward structure. Recall that the CEM distinguishes between situations where individual effort/performance leads directly to individual outcomes and when this relationship is mediated by group effort/performance and group outcome. Thus, whether the reward is based solely on individual performance or on group performance will have an impact on motivation. Consider a group of people working as a team to achieve a goal. Rewarding them based solely on individual performance means that each person's contribution must be identifiable, and this should reduce social loafing. However, individuals will not be motivated to help their teammates because there is no incentive to do so. On the other hand, if the reward is based solely on group performance, people will be more motivated to help one another to achieve the group goal, but also more likely to loaf. One solution to this dilemma is to combine the advantages of each approach into a hybrid reward structure where individual performance is rewarded, but only if group goals are met.

In 2010, Pearsall, Christian, and Ellis found that hybrid reward structures increase group performance and reduce social loafing. They randomly assigned 360 undergraduates into 90 4-person teams who competed with each other at both the team and individual level on a combat simulation computer game. Each team member had specific responsibilities that no other member of the team could duplicate (e.g., one team member controlled the team's tanks and another flew the team's jets). Thus, cooperation among team members would be necessary for the group as a whole to perform well. There were individual competitions between, but not within, teams as well. For example, the performance of the tank driver from one team was compared to the tank drivers from other teams so that individual rewards could be given.

The 90 teams were randomly assigned to one of three reward structures. Members of teams in the individual reward condition were told that they could win $40 if they were one of the top individual performers in the contest (e.g., top scoring tank driver). This individual reward would be given regardless of how well the team did as a whole. Teams in the cooperative reward condition were told that the top-scoring teams would each receive $40 per team member and that individual scores would not be rewarded. Teams in the hybrid reward condition were told that each individual team member's score could win $40 but only if the team's score reached a certain level. Thus the hybrid groups were operating under a reward structure that required good individual and team performance while the other two conditions rewarded one or the other. Three outcome variables were measured: team performance, perceived level of social loafing on each team, and cooperation (as measured by amount of information shared among team members).

Recall that only the team score is of value to the cooperative teams, so one might expect that

they would have a high level of information exchange among team members, but also a high level of social loafing. Conversely, because the team score has no value to the individual teams, they would be expected to have low levels of both of these variables. This is exactly what happened. Because the hybrid teams were motivated by both individual and team goals, they shared information as much as the cooperative teams (see Figure 8.13) but loafed at a low level that was comparable to the individual teams (see Figure 8.14). Furthermore, the teams in the hybrid condition had the highest overall team performance, followed by teams in the cooperative and individual conditions, respectively.

Thus it appears that expectancy value theory in general, and the CEM in particular, is useful in understanding, predicting, and controlling social loafing.

Alternatives to the Expectancy-Value Approach to Social Loafing Although expectancy-value/CEM can explain social loafing, it is not the only theory that has been proposed.

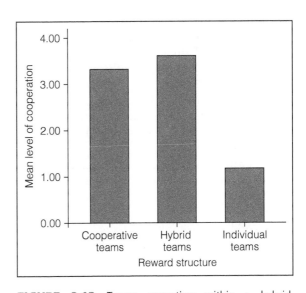

FIGURE 8.13 Teams operating within a hybrid reward structure cooperate by sharing information as much as teams operating within a purely cooperative reward structure. Adapted from Pearsall, Christian and Ellis, 2010.

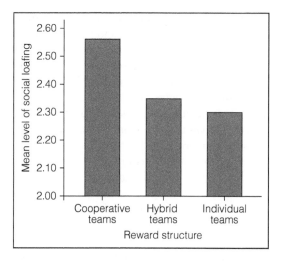

FIGURE 8.14 Teams operating within a hybrid reward structure were no more likely to loaf than were teams operating within a purely individual reward structure. Adapted from Pearsall, Christian and Ellis, 2010.

For example, Latané, Williams, and Harkins (1979) argue that **social impact theory** explains the social loafing phenomenon. According to this theory, performance in a group decreases because the pressure to work is dispersed among the members of the group. The larger the group, the less pressure each member of the group feels to perform. Other researchers have proposed explanations of social loafing based on self-attention (Mullen, 1983) and arousal reduction (Jackson & Williams, 1985). Despite the alternative explanations, the expectancy-value based CEM is the most comprehensive and has considerable empirical support.

Although social loafing is quite common, the presence of others does not always decrease an individual's level of performance. In Chapter 9, we will discuss an effect known as *social facilitation*, which is an increase in performance as the result of the presence of others. Thus, in many ways, it is the opposite of social loafing.

SUMMARY

The work of Tolman and Lewin laid the groundwork for the modern cognitive theories of motivation. Both emphasized the cognitive nature of many motives and the importance of the goals toward which the behavior was directed. In addition, both advocated the use of a molar approach to understanding motivation.

Tolman stressed the concept of the purposiveness of behavior. He pointed out that goals direct our behavior and that organisms develop cognitive representations, which he termed *cognitive maps*, of their world. His research emphasized the development of expectancies and the control of behavior by those expectancies. He also believed that learning can occur in the absence of behavioral change and that motivation was necessary for an organism to demonstrate that it had learned a behavior. His ideas contrasted sharply with the more mechanical stimulus–response formulations that were current at the time he wrote.

Lewin was influenced by the Gestalt school of psychology. His field theory stressed the dynamic nature of behavior and suggested that observed behavior results from all the forces acting on an individual at any given moment. Thus, behavior is a function of the interaction between forces that reside within the person as well as those in the environment. Many of the motives that generate behavior, according to Lewin, are cognitive in nature. These cognitive motives influence behavior in the same way as do physiological needs. Lewin also proposed the concept of valence, or value, to explain why one behavior is chosen over another when an organism has a choice of which to engage in.

The concepts of expectancies (Tolman) and value (Lewin) have been used by other theorists who employ an expectancy-value approach, which regards motivation as the result of the combination of the expectation that one can obtain particular goals and the value or incentive provided by those goals. Expectancy-value theory has been applied to a number of areas including social learning theory, achievement motivation, the relationship between attitudes and behavior, and social loafing. The social learning theory of Julian Rotter includes the expectancy-value concepts of reinforcement value, subjective estimates of success, situational factors, and generalized expectancies. Rotter believed that when we have a choice between two or more behaviors, we will choose the one with the largest combination of expectation of success and value of the outcome. Furthermore, Rotter noted that our expectations can be internalized and become part of our personality. He argued that people with an internal locus of control have a generalized expectancy that they control the reinforcements that they receive; people with an external locus of control expect that these events are governed by outside forces such as fate or luck.

Henry Murray believed that individuals can be classified according to how strong their needs are in various domains, one of which is their need to achieve goals that they set for themselves. Murray's idea spawned a large body of research on achievement motivation, much of which is grounded in expectancy-value theory. Atkinson and his associates developed a model for achievement behavior that emphasized the stable personality characteristics of need for achievement, which are the motive for success and the motive to avoid failure. In addition to these stable characteristics, achievement behavior was regarded as depending upon one's expectancy of succeeding in a particular situation, indexed by the individual's subjective probability of success. Finally, the value of reaching the goal in terms of pride of accomplishment or shame of failure was also regarded as important in determining achievement behavior. Atkinson presented some evidence for the prediction that tasks of intermediate difficulty would have greater motivational strength than tasks that are either very easy or very difficult.

Moreover, individuals high in a motive for success should be motivated to engage in these moderately difficult tasks, whereas individuals high in a motive to avoid failure should avoid them. Subsequent research has called these findings into question, and revisions to achievement theory have been made to make it more sensitive to the influence exerted by goals that are salient to an individual in a particular situation.

Expectancy-value theory has also been applied to the study of the relationship between attitudes and behavior. Unfortunately, much research indicates that attitudes alone are not very good predictors of behavior. The theory of planned behavior, which was developed by Ajzen, was an attempt to include factors in addition to attitudes that would be predictive of whether or not a person would choose to engage in a particular behavior. According to the theory, a person's intention is a better predictor of behavior than is his or her attitude. Intentions are determined by attitudes, subjective norms, and perceived behavioral control. Each of these factors is formed via an expectancy-value process by which salient beliefs/expectations are weighted according to their value to the individual. Empirical tests of the theory of planned behavior generally support its predictive utility. However, whether the model represents a causal relationship rather than a correlational one still needs to be determined.

The intriguing phenomenon of social loafing has also been approached from an expectancy-value perspective. The CEM of social loafing holds that individuals sometimes loaf when working in groups because individual rewards are not directly tied to individual performance. Instead, individual performance must lead to group performance, which leads to a group outcome, which leads to an individual outcome. According to the CEM, if any of the links in this chain is broken, individuals are likely to loaf.

The underlying theme in this chapter is that theorists are again coming back to the notion that we are thinking, rational, decision-making organisms. To understand the complex behavioral patterns of the human, we must take into account the individual's expectations, past experiences, values, attitudes, and beliefs. We must also understand how these various cognitive structures interact and the processes through which they guide behavior.

Ignoring the cognitive component of motivated behavior can only lead to an incomplete understanding of the forces that shape our lives.

KEY TERMS

cognitive theories, *235*

cognition/information processing/molar/persistent/consistent pattern/selectivity, *236*

learning-performance distinction/expectancies/cognitive map, *237*

field theory, *239*

tension/physiological needs/psychological needs (quasi-needs)/locomotion, *240*

psychological facts/valence, *241*

expectancy-value theory/social learning theory/reinforcement value, *243*

subjective estimates/situational factors/generalized expectations/

heuristics/continuum of internality-externality/internal individuals/external individuals, *244*

locus of control scale, *245*

needs/manifest needs/need for achievement/Thematic Apperception Test (TAT)/content analysis, *246*

tendency to approach (or to avoid) an achievement-related situation (T_a), *247*

motive for success (M_s)/motive to avoid failure (M_{af})/probability of success (P_s)/incentive value (I_s), *248*

learning (mastery) goals/performance goals, *251*

achievement goal questionnaire–revised (AGQ–R), *252*

extrinsic motivation, *253*

attitudes, *253*

intention/actual behavioral control/perceived behavioral control, *254*

subjective norm/salient beliefs/evaluation, *255*

social loafing, *257*

Ringelmann effect, *258*

collective effort model (CEM), *260*

social impact theory, *264*

SUGGESTIONS FOR FURTHER READING

Gigerenzer, G., & Selten, R. (Eds.). (2001). *Bounded Rationality: The Adaptive Toolbox*. Cambridge, MA: The MIT Press. This book discusses bounded rationality, or the use of heuristics in decision-making when it is impractical or impossible to evaluate all decision-relevant information.

McClelland, D. C. (1961). *The Achieving Society*. New York: Van Nostrand. This book provides a good overview of much of the early work on achievement as well as the cross-cultural research.

Karau, S., & Williams, K. (1993). Social Loafing: A meta-analytic review and theoretical integration. *Journal of Personality and Social Psychology*, *65*, 681–706. This article reviews the literature on social loafing and describes the CEM.

Lewin, K. (1936). *Principles of Topological Psychology*. New York: McGraw-Hill. Lewin outlines his field theory.

Tolman, E. (1932). *Purposive Behavior in Animals and Men*. New York: Appelton-Century. Tolman presents his purposive behaviorism.

WEB RESOURCES

http://people.clemson.edu/~switzed/teaching/
edf955/VIE.doc
This link provides an annotated bibliography of
resources related to expectancy-value theory.

http://www.westga.edu/~distance/ojdla/winter84/
piezon84.htm
This paper presents an overview of social loafing,
including loafing that occurs in online groups.

http://people.umass.edu/aizen/background.html
Ajzen's homepage, with links to information on the
Theory of Planned Behavior.

CHAPTER 9

Cognitive Consistency and Social Motivation

Tim was walking down the stairs from the fifth floor when he heard someone fall on the stairs several floors below. The woman screamed as she stumbled on a step, and there was a great clatter as books, pencils, notebooks, and a purse careened down the stairs. Leaning over the railing, Tim could see her lying at the foot of the stairs and could also hear her moaning softly for help.

Tim was planning on stopping on the third floor, which is where his next class was to be held. But the woman was on the second floor landing. After considering his options as he descended, he decided to head straight to class. After all, he thought, there are lots of other people on the stairs. By the time I get down there, others will have helped her. Besides, he reasoned, I don't know anything about first aid, so I couldn't be of much help anyway. At that thought, he turned from the stairs and entered the third floor, relieved to flee the emergency that existed just below. As he continued on his way, he had second thoughts. Like most people, Tim thinks of himself as a good person. But he also knows that "good people" should provide help when it is needed. This inconsistency bothered him.

Tim's experience illustrates the two main themes of this chapter. First, we will see how some situations, such as the one in which Tim found himself, can create a state of inconsistency in the thoughts or behaviors of a person, which in turn generates motivational states that lead the person to resolve the inconsistency. Next, we will explore the impact that social situations have on our motives and behavior. Tim's behavior was shaped by the woman who needed help as well as by the other people on the stairs. As we will see, we can be influenced by observing the behavior of others, by deciding how to respond to their requests or orders, or even by the mere presence of other people. Much of what we will study in this chapter falls within the

CHAPTER PREVIEW

This chapter is concerned with the following questions:

1. What is cognitive consistency, and how does a lack of it generate motivation?

2. How does the presence of others motivate our behavior?

3. What has been found concerning motives to conform, comply, or obey?

4. How do situational factors influence whether or not we come to someone's aid in an emergency?

domain of social psychology; however, we will only discuss research that examines the role of social situations in the activation and direction of behavior. Although many additional topics might be included here, those presented should help the reader understand the importance of cognitive consistency and social motivation.

Cognitive Consistency Theory

In Chapter 8, we discussed the influence that attitudes can have on behavior. In this chapter we will again examine this relationship, but from the opposite direction. That is, a change in behavior can motivate a change in attitude, especially when the behavior and the attitude are inconsistent with each other. Cognitive consistency theory is really a group of theories that share the same assumption that humans have a preference for consistency in their cognitions, attitudes, and behaviors.

Cognitive consistency theories of motivation begin with the idea that inconsistencies between thoughts, beliefs, attitudes, and behavior can generate motivation. This motivation is often conceived as similar to a state of tension; it is aversive and activates behaviors that are designed to reduce tension. Consistency theories are thus homeostatic theories; the optimal state for an individual is one in which one's thoughts, beliefs, attitudes, and behaviors are consistent with one another. According to the cognitive consistency model, the fact that Tim felt tension due to the inconsistency between his belief that he is a good person and his failure to help the woman who fell should motivate him to reduce this inconsistency. Researchers have developed several specific theories that share the cognitive consistency approach, and we will cover two of the most influential ones, the first being balance theory.

Balance Theory

The first formal cognitive consistency theory was proposed by Fritz Heider (1946). Heider believed that a tendency exists for relationships between people, objects, or both to be balanced, and for this reason his approach is often termed **balance theory**. In balance theory, relationships between people and objects may be positive or negative. For example, a positive relationship might involve liking (Craig likes Caroline) or belonging (Charles is a member of the Democratic party). Negative relationships can be similarly understood (Patricia dislikes milk; Bill, a Republican, doesn't belong to the Democratic Party). Although Heider recognized that balanced or unbalanced relationships can be much more complex than those we are about to describe, the basic principles of balance theory are often illustrated using triadic (three) situations which involve two people and a third object/event/person/idea. Figure 9.1 presents four balanced and four unbalanced relationships which are explained below.

The easiest way to determine if a relationship is balanced is to multiply the three signs together. If the result is positive, the relationships are balanced; if negative, an imbalance exists (Morrissette, 1958). Suppose, for example, that a newlywed couple is looking for a house to buy together. In the first triangle in Row A, Jesse (obviously) feels positively about Denise (+). If they find a house that Jesse likes (+) and that Denise likes (+), the product of the three signs is positive (i.e., three positive signs multiplied together yields a positive value), and the relationship is balanced because everyone is in agreement. Similarly, the second triangle depicts a situation where they find a house that Jesse dislikes (−) and Denise dislikes (−), so the relationship is also balanced (i.e., two negatives and a positive multiplied together yields a positive value).

However, suppose they find a house that Jesse likes (+) but Denise dislikes (−) as shown in the first triangle in row B. Now the product of the three signs is negative, and the relationship is not balanced, at least from Jesse's point of view. When an imbalance occurs, motivation is triggered to return the relationship to a balanced state. Jesse may try to restore the balance in one of several ways. For example, he might try to convince Denise to like the house, or he might decide that Denise is right and dislike the house too. Or, finally, he might end up disliking Denise as a result.

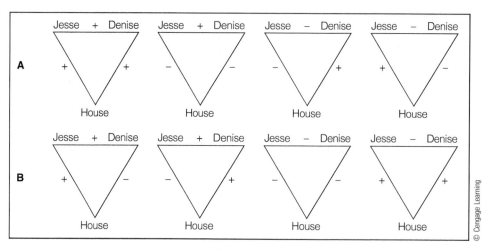

FIGURE 9.1 Balanced and unbalanced relationships between triads. Row A: balanced relationships from the point of view of Jesse; Row B: unbalanced relationships from the point of view of Jesse.

Any one of these methods could be used by Jesse to restore balance to the situation.

The positive and negative relationships discussed by balance theory are all inside the head of the person making the judgments. This suggests that balance may sometimes occur as a result of the perceptual distortion of the participant. For example, Levinger and Breedlove (1966) found that married partners assumed that their attitudes were much more similar than in fact they were. Thus, spouses may distort their perceptions of each other's attitudes in order to maintain a balanced relationship.

Research on balance theory has generally supported the concept that imbalanced relationships are motivational. For example, Jordan (1953) found that people judged hypothetical imbalanced relationships to be more unpleasant than hypothetical balanced relationships. Similarly, in 2006, Basil and Herr found that balanced relationships were judged to be more appropriate than imbalanced ones. However, as is the case with all theories, balance theory has its detractors.

Problems With Balance Theory

In our example of Jesse and Denise and the new house, we noted several ways in which Jesse

might restore balance to the situation. First, it is undoubtedly true that people resolve cognitive inconsistencies in various ways, but balance theory has little to say about *how* a person will resolve the imbalance. We cannot predict from balance theory how a specific situation is likely to be resolved.

Second, balance theory does not take into account the importance of the items that are out of balance. The relationship between Jesse and Denise could probably survive a dispute about what color to paint the dining room; a disagreement about whether or not to have children would be much more serious. Clearly some relationships are more important than others, yet balance theory has little to say about how these differences influence the behaviors that occur.

A third problem involves the question of how much imbalance must occur before behavior is triggered. Balance theory dichotomizes relationships as either balanced or out of balance. In reality, there is a continuum along which this classification can be made. Suppose Jesse and Denise belong to different but closely related religions. They will disagree on a few points, so the relationship is technically out of balance. However it will not be as out of balance as would be the case if one is staunchly religious and the other an atheist. Unfortunately, balance theory does not give us any direct way to gauge the degree or amount of the imbalance and remains unclear as to how much imbalance is required before behavior is triggered.

The three problems noted are all part of a more general weakness—balance theory's lack of specificity. Balance theory, though useful in pointing out the general motivating property of imbalanced states, has not been specified in enough detail so that accurate predictions can be made. Nonetheless, balance theory is still influential (see Crandall, Silvia, N'Gbala, Tsang, & Dawson, 2007, for a discussion). Some of the difficulties of balance theory were addressed by Leon Festinger (1957), who proposed a far-reaching theory of cognitive dissonance that has dominated research on cognitive consistency motivation.

Cognitive Dissonance

Cognitive dissonance as a concept stresses the idea that we attempt to maintain consistency of our beliefs, attitudes, and opinions with our overt behavior (Abelson et al., 1968). As long as consistency is maintained, no motivation is triggered.

Our cognitions about ourselves and the world around us can be related to each other in one of three ways. Cognitions can be consonant (consistent), irrelevant, or dissonant. According to dissonance theory, only when cognitions are dissonant is motivation activated to resolve the dissonance. Two cognitions are considered to be dissonant if, considered together, they represent an inconsistency. For example, suppose that you smoke but you also know that smoking can cause cancer and other serious health problems. According to Festinger (1957), these elements are dissonant and produce an aversive, negative motivational state, which in turn triggers specific mechanisms to reduce the dissonance. In this regard, dissonance is often conceived to resemble a state of tension and seems to have many properties of a drive.

How can we reduce cognitive dissonance? As with balance theory, there are several ways in which we can reduce dissonance. We will discuss three of them. First, one may change one of the cognitions in order to reduce the dissonance. For example, the dissonance created by smoking could be reduced if we change our cognition about the effects of smoking: "Smoking can't be that bad; after all cigarettes are not illegal." A second way in which we can reduce dissonance is to alter behavior in order to reduce inconsistency between cognitions. One can quit smoking to reduce dissonance, but this is much more easily said than done. A third way in which we can reduce dissonance is by adding consonant cognitions, which effectively reduce the dissonance without changing any of the conflicting elements. Even though you know that you smoke and you know that smoking is bad for you, you could reduce dissonance by adding cognitions such as "smoking relaxes me" or "by the time I get cancer, science will have a cure for it." Adding consonant cognitions is conceptually similar (if not identical) to the defense mechanism of **rationalization**. In rationalization we reduce anxiety by devaluing the original situation that led to the anxiety or by finding additional rewards in the situation different from those obtained.

How will an individual reduce dissonance? Dissonance theorists suggest that the method chosen will be whichever is easiest. In our smoking example, it is tough to deny that one smokes or that smoking causes health problems, so changing one of the cognitions is difficult. Changing behavior (i.e., quitting smoking) is straightforward but also very demanding. In this case, many smokers choose the third option—adding consonant cognitions (e.g., "I can quit anytime I want.")

Dissonance, then, is believed to occur when inconsistency or conflict exists between cognitions. In this respect dissonance is similar to balance theory. However, one major advantage of dissonance theory over balance theory is that the magnitude of dissonance can presumably be quantified. The total dissonance that an individual experiences depends upon the number of conflicting elements in relation to the number of consonant elements. Thus, total dissonance equals dissonant elements (D) divided by the sum of the dissonant and consonant (D + C) elements: $(D_{total} = D/D + C)$. The more elements that are dissonant, the greater the overall dissonance. Another advantage that dissonance theory has over balance theory is that the strength of the dissonance created is also thought to depend upon the importance of the cognitive elements in conflict. The more important the elements are to the person, the more dissonance one will experience. Thus, Jesse and Denise should experience much more dissonance about whether or not to have children than about what color to paint the dining room.

Research on Dissonance

Cognitive dissonance has generated more research (and controversy) than any other cognitive consistency theory. We will not attempt to cover all of this research but will focus on a few research areas most often cited as evidence of cognitive dissonance.

Induced Compliance One of the most cited examples of cognitive dissonance is the situation in which one publicly behaves in a manner contrary to one's privately held opinions (Festinger, 1957). Such a situation will lead to the production of dissonance if one is engaging in such behavior without sufficient justification for doing so. For example, consider two people, Stan and Dianne, who both strongly believe that people should be allowed to drive as fast as they want on interstate highways. However, they both drive at or slightly over the speed limit in order to avoid getting stopped by the police. Under these conditions little dissonance should occur because there is sufficient justification for their behavior—they don't want to get a speeding ticket. But now suppose the law is changed and the speed limit is eliminated. Dianne increases her driving speed to make her behavior consistent with her attitude, so she experiences no dissonance. But Stan notices that his driving speed has not changed and concludes that his current driving speed is the safest way to travel. This inconsistency between his current behavior and his initial attitude caused Stan to change his attitude about driving. Thus, if one behaves in a particular way but cannot justify the conflict of the behavior with one's attitude, dissonance should occur, and attitude change should follow. Such a situation is called induced compliance.

Festinger and Carlsmith (1959) tested the induced-compliance phenomenon by having three groups of participants perform repetitive, unproductive, and highly boring tasks (packing and unpacking spools and turning pegs in a pegboard). After an excruciating hour of performing such tasks, the participants of two such groups were asked by the experimenter to convince waiting participants that the experiment was interesting! They were told that the study was about the effect of expectations on performance and that the next participant was in the group that was supposed to believe the task was enjoyable. Furthermore, the participants were told that the experimenter usually had an assistant to do this task, but that the assistant was unavailable on that day. Participants in one group were paid $20 for lying to the waiting individuals ($20 was a considerable amount of money in the 1950s), while participants in the second group were paid only $1. A third group served as a control; its members were not asked to convince anyone that the experiment was interesting.

The persons that the participants were asked to convince, however, were confederates of the experimenter, and their purpose was to make sure that the participant actually tried to convince them that the experiment was indeed interesting. After the participants had completed their own bit of deception, they were asked to rate how interesting the experiment actually was to them. Ratings were provided on a scale of −5 to +5 where −5 represented "extremely dull and boring," +5 represented "extremely interesting and enjoyable," and 0 represented "neutral, neither interesting nor uninteresting."

The control group, as expected, rated the experimental task as boring. The participants who were paid $20 also rated the experiment as boring, while the participants who were paid only $1 rated the task as significantly more enjoyable than either of the other two groups (see Figure 9.2).

According to dissonance theory, the $1 group should have had insufficient justification for engaging in behavior contrary to their attitudes about the experiment; that is, they believed that the experiment was dull but had just tried to convince someone that it was interesting. The insufficient

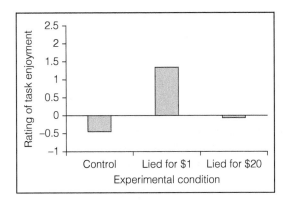

FIGURE 9.2 Level of task enjoyment as a function of dissonance condition. Adapted from Festinger and Carlsmith, 1959.

justification for their behavior (e.g., "I wouldn't lie to someone for $1") led them to alter their attitudes about the experiment so that they came to believe the experiment was more interesting and enjoyable than they initially believed. The participants who were paid $20, on the other hand, could easily justify their counterattitudinal behavior on the basis of the money (e.g., "I lied because they gave me 20 bucks"); therefore their attitudes about the tasks did not change.

The generality of the induced-compliance type of experiment can be observed in punishment situations as well. For example, Aronson and Carlsmith (1963) found that the threat of mild punishment was more effective than the threat of strong punishment at reducing children's desire to misbehave. It is both important and interesting to note that, contrary to learning theory, dissonance theory predicts that small rewards and punishments are more influential in changing motivation than are large rewards and punishments. Furthermore, the behavior change produced by dissonance is likely to be more permanent because the individuals have, in essence, convinced themselves that their behavior is correct.

Justification of Effort Dissonance theory also predicts that the more effort we expend in order to reach a goal, the more we will value the object of our effort (note once again, it is the behavior that influences the attitude). In 1959, Aronson and Mills tested this prediction by manipulating severity of initiation to a group and measuring favorability ratings toward that group. They asked college women to volunteer for a study in which they believed that they would be participating in a group discussion about sex. Before they were allowed to join the discussion group, however, they first had to pass a test to determine if they were mature enough to handle the discussion material. In the severe initiation condition, participants were required to read aloud a list of obscene words, many of which are still considered obscene today, and some very graphic descriptions of sexual activity in the presence of a male experimenter. Participants in the mild initiation condition were required to read aloud only mildly sexual material. Both groups of participants were then allowed to listen to a tape of what they thought was an actual group discussion—but was actually a rather boring description of animal sexual behavior. Finally, the participants in the two groups were asked to rate the discussion they had heard and their own interest in participating in future discussions. The group subjected to the severe initiation of reading lurid passages and four-letter words aloud rated the taped discussion as more interesting than did the mild initiation group. They also indicated more interest in future participation than did participants in the mild initiation group. Dissonance theory suggests that the severe initiation group experienced dissonance at the discrepancy between what they were required to do and the uninteresting nature of the supposed discussion. In order to reduce their dissonance, they came to believe that the discussion was interesting, and they indicated their desire for further participation.

One is reminded of the hell week activities of some fraternities and sororities and the secret initiations required of membership in some groups. All these activities should serve to create dissonance later if the individual's expectations are not met—and, as a result, lead the individual to value the membership more. Similarly, people who remain in what seem to be unhappy marriages or long-term relationships may do so to reduce dissonance; they have already invested so much effort in the endeavor that they convince themselves that the relationship is better than it really is. Apparently one reason why we value things for which we have expended a lot of effort is to reduce the dissonance we experience when these things turn out to be less than we had hoped.

Postdecisional Dissonance and Selective Exposure to Information

A third area of research on dissonance concerns the behaviors in which people engage after choosing among several alternatives. Suppose, for example, that you are trying to decide which of two highly desirable cars to buy. You like both cars for somewhat different reasons but can only buy one. The choice you eventually make between these two positive alternatives should create dissonance, which in turn should lead you to subsequently revalue the two cars. You may revalue the chosen car upward to reduce the dissonance the choice created, and you may revalue downward the car not chosen. In other words, after having made your choice, you will like your chosen car more and the unchosen one less. Additionally, dissonance theory predicts that you will selectively expose yourself to new information that reinforces your choice; that is, you will be sensitive to advertisements or information that supports your choice and will attempt to avoid information indicating that your choice was wrong. All these behaviors help reduce the dissonance created by your choice of one desirable car over the other.

Research on postdecisional behavior has generally supported dissonance theory when certain additional factors are taken into account (Wicklund & Brehm, 1976). In a study by Brehm (1956), women were told they could keep one of two products that they had rated as equally desirable *before* they made their choice. They were then asked to rate the product again after they had made their decision. As predicted by dissonance theory, the rating for the chosen object increased, while the rating for item that was not selected decreased. Thus in this study, choosing between two products of similar value created dissonance, which in turn led to a

change in attitude about the products, with the chosen one becoming more highly valued. In Brehm's study a second group of women was asked to choose between two products of very different value. Because the alternatives were quite different in value and the choice was therefore easy, little dissonance was generated and, as a result, postdecisional attitudinal changes were small, as predicted by dissonance theory.

Unless a choice requires surrendering a valued alternative, however, no dissonance occurs to trigger postdecisional changes. The decision needs to be final; if you can still change your mind, you should not experience any dissonance. This was illustrated by a pair of clever field experiments (Knox & Inkster, 1968) in which bettors were interviewed at a horse racing track either a few seconds before or a few seconds after they placed their bet. All bettors were placing $2 bets on which horse would win the race and all were asked for their level of certainty or confidence in their choice. As anyone who has ever placed a bet at race track knows, once you buy your ticket, you have made a decision that cannot be changed. Thus, the post-bet interviewees should have experienced more dissonance because they likely had to choose between two or more attractive alternatives. The pre-bet interviewees likely had this same dilemma, but they could still have changed their mind at the time they were interviewed. Which group should have reported higher confidence ratings? If you said the post-bet group, you are correct. Because they felt dissonance about their (now final) decision, they could reduce this dissonance by changing their cognition about the choice. In effect, they convinced themselves that they were correct.

In a conceptually similar set of studies, Brownstein, Read, and Simon (2004) found evidence that the reevaluation of alternatives may begin to occur even *before* the choice is made and continue through the post-choice phase. They asked bettors to rate their chances of winning on four occasions, three times before they bet and once afterward. They found evidence for what they called **prebet bolstering**, or a tendency of bettors to become more convinced about their (ultimately) chosen alternative on each successive evaluation, even though the first three ratings were made before their bet was placed. Another interesting finding was that the bettors did not change their evaluation of the other horses (i.e., they did not devalue their unchosen alternatives as would be expected by dissonance theory). Because of this and other inconsistencies in the literature, it appears that more research is needed in the area of dissonance and decisions (see Chen & Risen, 2010, for a discussion).

When Prophecy Fails

One of the most interesting aspects of dissonance theory is that it often makes nonobvious predictions. One such case involved a field study of a group of people who believed that their city was going to be destroyed by a great flood. Mrs. Keech, the leader of the group, had received a message from outer space telling her that the city would be destroyed on December 21. Festinger and his colleagues became aware of the group as a result of newspaper reports. Based on the cognitive dissonance formulation, they predicted that when the prophecy was disconfirmed, the group of believers would not forsake their beliefs but would try to win additional people to their cause in order to provide additional support for their initial beliefs. Festinger and his colleagues infiltrated the group so that they could study what happened when the predicted disaster did not occur. Their results are reported in the book *When Prophecy Fails* (Festinger, Riecken, & Schachter, 1956).

On the designated night, the small band of followers gathered at the prophet's home to await the disaster. Before their meeting, Mrs. Keech had received a message telling the group that they would be saved by a flying saucer that would pick them up at midnight. As the clock struck midnight, everyone waited expectantly, but after several minutes nothing had happened. Determining that the time was correct, everyone sat somewhat dazed. Then with despair they began to look for some explanation. One could expect that at this point, considerable dissonance

would be present in all the believers, because many had committed themselves wholeheartedly to their belief in the disaster by quitting their jobs and spending their money in expectation of the End. In addition to considerable dissonance, there should also have been a reluctance to admit the disconfirmation. Given the degree of commitment and the social support provided by the other believers present, the dissonance should have been more easily reduced by some method other than admitting that the whole experience was not real.

The group's behavior provided striking support of Festinger's prediction (but not of their own). At 4:45 a.m. Mrs. Keech informed the group that she had received another message. The message indicated that the strength of the group's belief had in fact saved the city from the flood. With this explanation, the dissonance could be reduced and the original beliefs kept intact. And the group became much more active in proselytizing people to its own beliefs.

Festinger's field study points out both how dissonance may be created by disconfirmation of our beliefs and how we often seek the easiest solution for reducing the dissonance. For the group of believers, rejecting its belief in the disaster was not easy, given their involvement in terms of time, money, and so on. For Mrs. Keech's group it was easier to discover a new reason for the disconfirmation than to give up the old beliefs. As I write these words in 2011, I am reminded of the small but vocal groups of people who claim that the Mayan calendar foretells the end of the world in 2012. By the time you read these words, it is likely that the prophecy will have been proven incorrect. You might find it of interest to look at the groups' Web sites to see if you can identify their means of dissonance reduction.

Dissonance theory continues to inspire research with important practical applications. For example, inducing cognitive dissonance has been used to encourage safe sex practices (Stone, Aronson, Crain, Winslow, & Fried, 1994), reduce prejudice (e.g., Heitland & Bohner, 2010), and reduce the risk of eating disorders in women (e.g., Stice,

Chase, Stormer, & Appel, 2001) to name just a few of the domains in which dissonance interventions have been employed.

Challenges to Dissonance Theory

While dissonance theory has generated much research, it has also created large controversy. Perhaps the most important criticism of dissonance theory aims at its vagueness (McGuire, 1966). For example, Aronson (1968) pointed out that the theory is primitive and lacks precision, which makes the prediction of whether any two cognitions will conflict in a given individual virtually impossible. A second problem is one we have seen before: dissonance (like an imbalanced triad in balance theory) may be remedied in several different ways. The theory itself, however, does not provide any definitive statement about which particular way will be chosen in a given situation or by a given individual. A third criticism of dissonance theory is that alternative explanations have not always been ruled out (e.g., Zentall, 2010). One of the most compelling of these rival theories is self-perception theory.

Self-Perception Theory

Suppose you observe a classmate, whom you don't know particularly well, playing a newly released video game on his cell phone before class one day. The next day you see him playing the same game. The scenario repeats itself for a third day. You would probably conclude that this person "must like that game." Now suppose that everything is the same about the situation, except that it is you who have been playing the game on three successive days. After the third day, you might notice your behavior and conclude "I guess I like this game." Daryl Bem (1967) has proposed an alternative to dissonance theory emphasizing the idea that we observe our own behavior much as an outsider might do, then make judgments based on these observations. These self-descriptive statements, then, are reported as our attitudes. Bem's alternative is called **self-perception theory**.

Bem argued that many of the experimental results quoted as supportive of a dissonance approach can in fact be explained through the concept of self-perception. He noted that the behavior measured in almost all dissonance studies is self-description of an attitude or a belief. As just one example of how this might work, let's analyze the already mentioned Festinger and Carlsmith's (1959) induced-compliance study. Recall that one group of participants was given $20 in return for telling a waiting participant that the boring experiment was interesting, while a second group of participants was paid only $1.

Bem noted that an outside observer who watched the experiment and behavior of the two groups would predict that the participants paid $1 must have enjoyed the experiment because they weren't paid enough to lie about it; on the other hand, the observer would also predict that the participants paid $20 behaved as they did because the amount of money was sufficient to justify their behavior. In other words, an observer of the total situation would attribute the $20 participants' behavior to the money but would attribute the $1 participants' behavior to enjoyment of the experiment. Because an observer, who is not experiencing dissonance, reaches the same conclusion as the participants who, according to Festinger, are experiencing dissonance, Bem argues that dissonance is not necessary for the effect to occur.

Carrying the analysis one step further, Bem argued that we are that outside observer of our own behavior; that is, we analyze our own behavior in the same fashion as we would analyze someone else's behavior. Thus a $20 participant, observing that he or she has just told the waiting participant that the boring experiment was interesting, decides that he or she behaved that way because of the money involved. The $1 participant, who observed the self-behavior concludes that the experiment was enjoyed because the money involved was not sufficient justification for lying about the experiment.

To test his hypothesis, Bem conducted what he called an *interpersonal replication* of the Festinger and Carlsmith experiment. In this study he divided participants into one of three conditions (i.e., control,

$1, or $20) and had each listen to an exact description of what a participant in the corresponding condition in the Festinger and Carlsmith study would have done. Observers in the $1 and $20 conditions then listened to communications between the participant who had just completed the task and the participant being convinced that the tasks were interesting. Then the observers were asked to predict how enjoyable the participant would have rated the tasks. Thus, the observers in Bem's study had the same information as the participants in Festinger and Carlsmith's study. The important difference is that Bem's observers did not participate in the experiment, so they were not experiencing any dissonance. The results of Bem's study (Figure 9.3) replicated those of Festinger and Carlsmith (Figure 9.2), with $1 participants being expected to be more favorable toward the experiment than $20 or control participants.

Bem argued that the results of the induced-compliance type of experiment and his replications of it suggest that participants simply make self-judgments based on the kinds of evidence publicly available to anyone, not as a result of aversive motivation generated by an inconsistency between attitude (The experiment was boring.) and behavior (I've just told the new participant it was really interesting.). Bem (1967) also noted that the interpersonal replication technique successfully reproduced the results of a wide range of dissonance studies, including several that we have discussed previously.

Bem's analysis does not require the development of a motivational state of tension that leads to changes in attitude or behavior but requires only that one analyze his or her own behaviors in the same way that one analyzes the behavior of others. Such an approach is called attribution theory, and we will look more closely at such approaches in Chapter 10. In addition, self-perception theory has been used to explain other phenomena such as the foot-in-the-door effect, which we discuss later in this chapter.

Dissonance or Self-Perception?

Despite the weaknesses of cognitive dissonance theory, it has weathered much of the criticism leveled against it. Although self-perception theory can account for some dissonance effects, the results of many studies cannot be adequately explained without postulating the existence of a motivational state of dissonance (e.g., Fazio, Zanna, & Cooper, 1977; Harmon-Jones, Brehm, Greenberg, Simon, & Nelson, 1996). There is also evidence that participants who undergo dissonance manipulations exhibit changes in brain activity that are not seen in control participants (e.g., van Veen, Krug, Schooler, & Carter, 2009).

Researchers have proposed revisions to dissonance theory that improve its specificity and its utility in making predictions (e.g., Aronson, 1992; Cooper & Fazio, 1984; Stone & Cooper, 2001). Nonetheless, there is substantial evidence for self-perception theory as well. As is often the case, it appears that each theory has advantages over the other, depending on which other variables are present in the situation. For example, self-perception theory best explains changes in attitudes that are not well-formed or strongly held. However, when our behavior is inconsistent with pre-existing, important attitudes, dissonance theory provides the more compelling explanation.

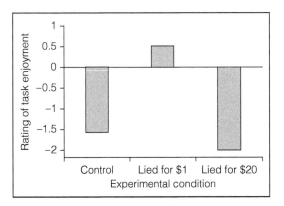

FIGURE 9.3 Level of task enjoyment in an interpersonal replication of Festinger and Carlsmith's (1959) induced-compliance study. Adapted from Bem, 1967.

A Problem for Consistency Theories

In general then, cognitive dissonance theory has generated a large body of research and has led to the examination of questions that might not have been asked otherwise. It is also a very appealing theory because of its simplicity and its ability to account for sometimes counterintuitive types of behavior. However, there is one nagging problem that confronts dissonance theory, balance theory, and other consistency models of motivation. Simply put, there are too many cases in which people do not seem to be troubled by, or motivated to reduce, a state of cognitive inconsistency.

Recall that the basic premise of consistency theories is that people strive for cognitive consistency over inconsistency. However, some people under some conditions seem to be inconsistency seeking rather than inconsistency reducing. Pepitone (1966) has noted several reasons why an individual might seek out inconsistency. For example, we might increase inconsistency so as to maximize our pleasure when the inconsistency is finally reduced. Sexual foreplay is sometimes used as an example of such a situation (Pepitone, 1966). Also, we may seek inconsistency in order to mask more serious or painful inconsistencies. Pepitone suggested that hypochondriacs who mistakenly believe they are ill may be masking more serious inconsistencies that create anxiety. He also noted that we may seek inconsistency because the optimal level of stimulation may be higher than we often assume; that is, a certain amount of inconsistency may actually be beneficial in keeping motivational tension at some nonzero optimal level.

Furthermore, Singer (1966) has pointed out that motivation generated from inconsistency of cognitions is not so strong that it overrules normal behavior. We do not, for example, stop eating until we have resolved the inconsistency between our attitude about our tennis game and the fact that we have just lost three straight sets. Similarly, if consistency motivation is important, why aren't our thoughts highly consistent? (see Korman, 1974). Bem (1970) has in fact suggested that inconsistency may not be very important for some persons. Support for Bem's idea was provided by Cialdini, Trost, and Newsome (1995) who developed a scale to measure one's preference for consistency (PFC). People who have a high PFC prefer consistency and are likely to experience dissonance and be motivated to reduce it. However, individuals with a low PFC may actually prefer unpredictability and do not seem to be motivated to restore balance or reduce dissonance (Cialdini et al., 1995). In fact, Bator and Cialdini (2006) found that low PFC individuals displayed effects *opposite* of what would be expected under conditions that should produce dissonance. There is also evidence that culture has an impact on the applicability of cognitive consistency theories. People from collectivist cultures such as Japan and Korea are less driven to maintain cognitive consistency than are people from individualist cultures, which include Australia and the US (e.g., Heine & Lehman, 1997; Kashima, Siegel, Tanaka, & Kashima, 1992).

Motivation generated by cognitive inconsistency may be more limited in scope than was once believed. In all fairness to the consistency theorists, we should note that the complexity of consistency motivation is certainly part of the reason that the theories have not worked as well as hoped. Probably we must consider the links between several cognitions in most situations in order to understand the changes in behavior that occur. It is also reasonable to suppose that changing one relationship between two cognitions may change the relationship of those cognitions to other elements as well; one changed relationship may change a whole host of other relationships. Analyzing the relationships of cognitions to each other and to behavior is obviously extremely complex and deserves continued study, and one fertile area for doing this is the study of social motivation.

Social Motivation

A moment's reflection should convince you that we behave differently when alone than when in the presence of others. The phenomenon of social loafing, which we discussed in Chapter 8, is one example of the negative influence that the presence of others can have on our behavior. In contrast, having others around can also enhance the manner in which we perform many tasks. In this section, we will look briefly at the energizing effects of the presence of others, then proceed to examine how social situations can lead to conformity, compliance, and obedience to authority. We then turn to the effect that the presence of others has on helping behavior.

Social Facilitation and Inhibition: Coaction and Audience Effects

In the late 19th century, it was discovered that the presence of others sometimes has strong effects on the behavior of individuals (Triplett, 1898). Triplett examined records from cycling contests and found that racers perform better when competing against each other than when riding alone against the clock. This was a correlational study, so Triplett could not infer a cause–effect relationship because other factors, such as reduced air resistance from following another rider, could have been responsible for the results. He then conducted a laboratory experiment in which he asked children to wind fishing reels as fast as possible either alone or while competing with another child. Once again, the participants in competition with one another performed better than those working alone. This social facilitation of behavior is probably one reason why new records are set in Olympic games or, for that matter, in any competitive situation. In some sports this effect is even factored into the competition. In track and field for example, distance races will often include a rabbit or a runner who is only in the race to pace the other runners for the first part of the contest. Thus, the presence of others energizes the behavior of the contestants to higher levels.

Humans also show a social facilitation effect in noncompetitive situations. Redd and deCastro (1992) found that college students consumed more food, water, sodium, and alcohol when other people were present. Food intake was 60% higher in these college students when eating with others. In another study, deCastro and Brewer (1992) found that large groups increased the meal size of individuals by as much as 75%. Social facilitation has also been shown to occur in shopping situations (Sommer, Wynes, & Brinkley, 1992) and in the expression of emotion (Buck, Losow, Murphy, & Constanzo, 1992).

The energizing of behavior as a result of the presence of others is called the **coaction effect** and is well documented not only in humans but also in other animals. We know, for example, that satiated chickens will begin to eat if put into a cage with other chickens that are feeding. A chicken will in fact consume as much as 60% more grain when raised with another chicken as compared to its consumption when raised alone (Zajonc, 1972). Chickens will even eat more when exposed to a videotape of another chicken eating (Keeling & Hurnik, 1993) and monkeys will drink more orange juice when presented with a mirror image of themselves (Straumann & Anderson, 1991). This facilitation of behavior has also been observed in other animals including dogs and armadillos and occurs not only in feeding behavior but also in drinking, running, and sexual behavior. Even the lowly cockroach is not immune to coaction effects! Zajonc, Heingartner, and Herman (1969) built a roach runway and measured the speed with which roaches would run to escape light (roaches are negatively phototaxic, as anyone knows who has cockroaches and has turned on the kitchen light in the middle of the night). Roaches paired in the runway ran faster than those who had to go it alone.

Interestingly, most of the effects observed in coacting individuals also occur if one member is behaving and others serve as an audience. This **audience effect** also occurs in the cockroach. In an experiment like the light escape runway just mentioned, Zajonc, Heingartner, and Herman (1969) ran roaches either with or without a roach audience observing the performing roach. Roaches that had an audience ran significantly faster in a simple maze than those that did not.

As is true of most aspects of motivation however, understanding coaction and audience effects is not as simple as these examples might imply. The effect of others on our behavior is not always facilitative. Sometimes the presence of others causes our behavior to deteriorate and we do worse than we might have done if left alone. This often seems to happen in professional sports. The presence of a large crowd often causes the old pros to play over their heads, while the rookie challenger's behavior worsens. In some cases, the audience may want us to succeed, yet their presence might still hinder our performance. For example, Baumeister and Steinhilber (1984) have found evidence of a home field disadvantage in professional sports playoff series; the visiting teams win more series-deciding playoff games than do the home teams.

The psychological explanation usually given for these seemingly contradictory effects of the presence of others is that coactors and audiences will facilitate performance if the performer's correct response is highly likely (a **dominant response**, in psychological terminology), whereas the presence of others will lead to a worsening of behavior if the performer's correct response is low in probability (Zajonc, 1965). This is apparently because the presence of others arouses us, and this arousal or drive tends to trigger whatever response is dominant (e.g., Platania & Moran, 2001). If the dominant response is correct, because of practice or overlearning, the behavior is facilitated; if the dominant response is incorrect, the behavior is degraded. Thus, to return to our old pros and rookie challengers example, the old pros could be expected to have the correct responses more available because of greater experience and so will show social facilitation, while the rookie will tend to show a deterioration of behavior as a result of the presence of others. The presence of others, then, arouses us to action. As a result, our behavior may be either improved or worsened by the presence of others, depending upon how likely it is that the correct response for that situation is available to us.

One problem with the arousal or drive explanation for social facilitation is that the term *arousal* is vague (e.g., Sanders, 1981); researchers have not defined exactly what arousal means in this context. Moreover, it has been difficult to articulate how arousal is distinct from other possible negative

effects that the presence of an audience can have on an individual, such as evaluation apprehension (e.g., Cottrel, 1968) or distraction (e.g., Sanders & Baron, 1975). There is also evidence that all research participants in social facilitation studies, even those who perform a task in a no-audience control condition, may feel as though they are being monitored (by the experimenter) and thus feel some form of arousal as well (Griffin, 2001; Griffin & Kent, 1998).

In an attempt to clarify the role of arousal in social facilitation, Blascovich, Mendes, Hunter, and Salomon (1999) have developed a model that explains social facilitation effects in terms of challenge and threat motivation. According to this model, performing a well-learned task in front of an audience produces a distinct physiological **challenge response** that includes increased heart rate and **vasodilation** (i.e., widening of the blood vessels) but no significant increase in blood pressure. This response is conducive to skilled performance. On the other hand, when a novel task is performed in the presence of an audience, a physiological **threat response** occurs. The threat response includes increased heart rate but no vasodilation, which results in an increase in blood pressure. The threat response is associated with impaired performance.

To test their model, Blascovich et al. conducted a study in which participants performed either a novel or well-learned task in front of an audience or alone. They measured both performance on the task and physiological responses to the situation. The results supported their hypotheses. Participants who performed the well-learned task in front of an audience exhibited the physiological challenge response and scored very well on the task. Conversely, participants who performed the novel task in front of an audience did not perform as well and exhibited the predicted threat response. It is important to note that it is the interaction of the audience and the type of task (i.e., well-learned vs. novel) that produces the distinct physiological responses of challenge or threat. Thus, our behavior may be facilitated in some situations and worsened in other situations. We may perform brilliantly on the court and miserably on a test; in both cases, our performance may result from the presence of others.

Social Influence

We turn now to an examination of the powerful influence that the presence of others can have on our individuality and ethical behavior. The studies within this general category involve examination of a continuum of social influence, which includes conformity, compliance, and obedience to authority. As you will see, the primary difference between these phenomena involves the manner in which the social influence manifests itself. Social influence can occur implicitly (i.e., conformity), explicitly in response to a request (i.e., compliance), or to an order from an authority figure (i.e., obedience).

Conformity

Most of us have found ourselves in situations where our motivation to act in a particular way has come under group pressure. For example, we might find ourselves drinking alcohol or experimenting with drugs as a result of group pressure, even though we personally do not wish to drink or take drugs. As anyone who has ever been in this situation knows, the motivation to "go along" with the group can be terribly strong. Brown (1965) noted that the mere existence of a group seems to trigger a motivation to agree or conform to the group's wishes. Even exposing research participants to subtle nonconscious cues related to conformity has been found to increase conformity behavior (e.g., Epley & Gilovich, 1999).

All of us, whether we admit it or not, are conformists. Of course we do not all conform to the same rules, but in group situations we are very likely to agree with the group when decisions must be made. **Conformity**, then, is a change in one's beliefs or behaviors as a result of real or imagined pressure from a group or individual.

The strength of our conformity to group pressure has been shown in a number of studies. Sherif (1947), for example, had participants individually judge the amount of movement they perceived of

a point of light in a dark room. In fact there was no movement, but the perception of such movement in a dark room, called the **autokinetic effect**, is a very strong illusion. The participants differed widely in their individual estimates of the amount of movement they perceived, yet each individual was internally consistent. Interestingly, when Sherif put people together in groups of two or three and asked them to publicly judge the amount of movement, their estimates converged. Thus, even though participants were individually consistent, they changed their judgments when put into a group situation in order to agree with each other. Sherif then went one step further and tested groups comprised of one confederate and one real participant. The confederate's job was to provide estimates that were very different from those of the participant. Slowly but surely, the participant conformed to the confederate's estimates. Sherif's experiments point to the power of the group to influence judgments, even when the judgment itself is an illusion.

Perhaps the best-known studies on conformity are those of Solomon Asch (1952, 1965). In a series of studies, Asch asked his participants to make a simple perceptual judgment concerning the length of lines. As shown in Figure 9.4, each participant was provided with a standard line and three

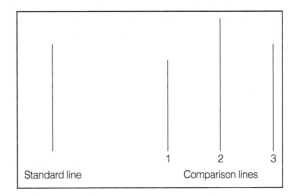

FIGURE 9.4 An example of the type of standard and comparison lines used in Asch's conformity experiments. From Social Psychology by Solomon E. Asch. Copyright © 1987 Oxford University Press. Reprinted by permission of Oxford University Press.

comparison lines, from which the participant was asked to pick the one of equal length to the standard. Most of the line comparisons were easy to make, and the control groups of participants made very few errors.

Imagine for a moment that you are a participant in the following experiment. Seated with a group of six to eight others who, unbeknownst to you, are confederates working with Asch, you are shown the first set of standard and comparison lines. Each participant is asked individually to call out the number of the comparison line that is equal to the standard. Because you are next to last, you have a chance to listen to most of the others respond before you must respond yourself. On the first two trials everyone agrees, and you relax a bit and begin to wonder what could be the purpose of such an absurd experiment!

On the third trial, however, things change. When the standard and comparison lines are shown, you quickly note which are equal; but, to your surprise, everyone in front of you unanimously picks a line different from the one you think is correct. Your turn comes, and you find yourself in a conflict situation. Do you answer as you see it, or do you conform to the answer given by the group? Subjectively you might expect that you would stick with what you believe is the right answer. It is, after all, just a psychology experiment, and the result is of little consequence to you. However, observation of real participants in this experiment revealed that they became very uncomfortable when put in the position of going against the group decision, even when it is obviously wrong.

Asch's original study included 31 real participants who completed 12 trials. In 7 of these trials, they found themselves at odds with the judgment of the confederate majority; the other 5 were control or "neutral" trials. Asch found large individual differences in the amount of conforming behavior seen in the participants of his experiment. Six of the 31 participants (19%) never conformed to the group decision, though generally showing much discomfort in the process. The other 25 participants (81%) conformed at least once and 2 individuals (6%) conformed on all 7 trials!

In postexperimental interviews, participants reported feelings of self-doubt and a desire to agree with the group. Also of some interest is the fact that the participants did not usually question the group judgment but sought within themselves the reasons for their nonconformity. Apparently an individual usually assumes that the majority is correct, even when the majority disagrees with the individual's own judgment. Clearly, then, the presence of others creates in us a motivational state to conform to the group's norms.

Asch found that almost all of the participants who tended to yield to the group's pressure did so in one of two ways. The first was labeled **distortion of judgment** by Asch (often referred to as **informational social influence** in the current literature). In this situation participants realized that their judgment was different from the group's and conformed because they assumed that their judgment was incorrect. Thus, they conformed for information—they wanted to be correct. Presence of the group led to a distortion of individual judgments so that they would conform to the group judgment.[1]

The second major reason for conforming was what Asch called **distortion of action** (also known as **normative social influence**). For these participants, not appearing different from the group seemed of paramount importance. Choosing the correct line was not their primary objective. Rather, conforming to the normative influence of the group motivated their behavior. These participants did not necessarily assume that the group was right. That is, there was no distortion of judgment; they simply felt compelled to conform to the group's response. These participants noted that the conflict they felt between their judgment and that of the group often triggered feelings of inferiority or of being an outsider to the group. These people, then, showed a distortion of actions but not of perceptions or judgments.

---

[1]One participant reported that the group response caused him to change the way he truly perceived the lines, a phenomenon Asch labeled "distortion of perception."

Factors That Affect Conformity Motivation

Asch conducted a number of variations of his initial experiment in order to more precisely determine the conditions that are necessary for conformity to occur. He reasoned that one important factor is the *degree of ambiguity* that is present in the task. Tasks that are inherently ambiguous, such as the autokinetic effect used by Sherif, should produce more conformity than tasks where the majority opinion is clearly in error. To test this idea, Asch increased the disparity between the standard line and the line chosen by the majority (by 7 inches in some cases) and still obtained an overall conformity response of 28%. For a corresponding control group, which was not subject to conformity pressure of the group, the error rate was only 2%. Thus, unambiguous tasks reduce but do not eliminate conformity.

Asch also found that *group size* is positively related to conformity responses—at least up to a point. In a series of experiments that varied the size of the group, Asch found that the conformity effect virtually disappeared if only one other person besides the participant was present. Apparently most people assume their judgments to be just as accurate as anyone else's in a paired situation. When two persons in addition to the participant were added, conforming responses jumped to 12.8%, and with three persons in addition to the participant, conforming responses were approximately 33%. Further increases in group size did not increase conformity for Asch. A meta-analysis of conformity studies has confirmed that conformity is positively related to the size of the majority (Bond & Smith, 1996). In contrast to Asch's findings however, Bond and Smith report that conformity continues to increase along with group size even when the majority is greater than three people. The reason for this disparity in results is unclear. However, it is reasonable to conclude that effect of group size on conformity is complex and is likely moderated by several other variables such as level of task ambiguity and whether or not participants are face to face with the majority when making their responses (Bond, 2005). Because these moderators vary from study to study, more research is needed to address this inconsistency.

Asch also studied the effect of group *unanimity* on conformity motivation. He instructed one of the group to give the correct answer while the rest of the group conformed to the incorrect answer. The effect of only one person deviating from the group's response had a liberating effect on the participants of this experiment. Conforming responses were reduced from 33% to about 5–10%. Observation of the participants during the experiment revealed that they often looked to the deviant and seemed to gain motivation also to deviate. In this regard, Asch pointed out that the nonconformer provided support to the participant—there is someone else who sees it as he or she does—and also broke the unanimity of the group. The presence of just one other individual who differed from the group had a substantial disinhibiting effect on the participants, so that judgments were more likely to be what the individuals actually perceived than a conforming response to the group pressure. It is not surprising then that dissenters are treated harshly in social groups where conformity is highly valued. For example, an individual in a cult or gang who rebels against the norms of the group is very often separated from the group and punished severely. This is done to minimize the disruptive effect that the dissenter might have on the other members.

Criticisms of Conformity Research

All research is subject to the scrutiny of experts in the field, whose job it is to point out possible flaws so that the effect can be more rigorously tested. Critics of conformity research have argued that the laboratory paradigm used by Asch is unrealistic; people simply do not get together, sit around a table, and judge the lengths of lines. Similarly, there is little or no incentive for the participants to produce the correct answer—the task is simply not very important to them. Finally, the Asch studies have been viewed as an historical phenomenon. Perhaps individuals in the US in the 1950s were conformists, but times have changed; people are much more individualistic now. We will briefly examine research relevant to each of these criticisms.

In terms of realism, it is true that most studies of conformity have been conducted in a laboratory environment. However, conformity effects have also been found in many studies conducted in real-life settings. For example, Mann (1977) studied the behavior of people waiting at a bus stop in Jerusalem, where it is customary for people to mill about without formally standing in line. When the bus arrives, people get on without regard to who was at the bus stop first. Mann instructed individual confederates to arrive at the stop as soon as a bus departed. The first confederate stood along the curb, the next stood behind the first, forming an obvious line. The total number of confederates in the line varied from two to eight. Mann recorded whether or not the first non-confederate to arrive at the bus stop conformed by standing in the line. As you can see from Figure 9.5, conformity generally increased as the number of confederates increased, and eight confederates induced almost everyone to conform. Thus, conformity effects certainly occur outside the laboratory.

The effect of task importance on conformity has not received much empirical study. This is surprising when one considers that, if conformity effects only occur for relatively meaningless tasks such as judging line length, it greatly limits our ability to generalize the effect to situations of greater practical significance. However, a growing body of research indicates that conformity occurs in circumstances of the utmost importance. For example, eyewitness accuracy and, presumably, eyewitness testimony as well can be influenced by the motive to conform to the opinion of other witnesses (e.g., Wright, Self, & Justice, 2000). Moreover, Baron, Vandello, and Brunsman (1996) found that eyewitness conformity occurs most often when the task is both important and difficult. Baron et al. interpret this finding to mean that we are most likely to rely on the judgments of others when we are unsure of exactly what we have seen, but when accuracy in our judgment is of paramount importance. Certainly, witnessing a crime fits both these criteria.

The final criticism is that the Asch studies may no longer be relevant; that they occurred many

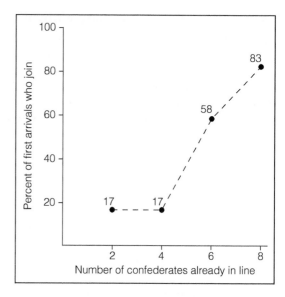

FIGURE 9.5   Percentage of participants who conformed by standing in line at a bus stop as a function of number of confederates comprising the line. From L. Mann, "The Effect of Stimulus Queues on Queue-Joining Behavior." *Journal of Personality and Social Psychology, 35*, p. 437–442. Copyright © 1977 by the American Psychological Association. Reprinted by permission.

years ago at a time and in a place where conformity was much more prevalent than it is today (e.g., Perrin & Spencer, 1980). Indeed, it is very common for students in psychology courses to have such a reaction when they are first exposed to the Asch studies. To test this criticism, Bond and Smith (1996) conducted a meta-analysis of 133 conformity studies and found that conformity is still a robust phenomenon, although the effect sizes in recent studies do tend to be smaller than those of earlier ones. Bond and Smith also report that conformity is a universal phenomenon, occurring in many different countries; however, the degree to which people conform may be related to cultural norms (e.g., Kim & Markus, 1999). Neto (1995) demonstrated the timelessness and universality of conformity motivation when he replicated the Asch study in Portugal in the mid-1990s. He found that 59% of participants conformed at least once. Neto also reported that most of his participants reported that the experimental procedure was very stressful and uncomfortable, and none found it to be a pleasant experience. This is very similar to the reaction that Asch's participants reported almost 50 years earlier. It may also help explain the motive to conform.

Why Do People Conform?

There seems little question that groups exert a strong influence on individuals to conform to group expectations. One reason may be that they produce their effects by subtle, and sometimes not so subtle, behaviors aimed at the deviant. Asch tested this hypothesis by reversing the roles of confederates and participants in his earlier experiments. In this variation the group was comprised of real participants with the exception of one individual—a male confederate of the experimenter who was instructed to give the wrong answer. As expected, the group was not swayed by the lone deviant but became amused at his deviancy, passing knowing glances back and forth, smiling and sometimes laughing. One suspects that these behaviors observed by the deviant in a normal situation would impel a strong desire to conform.

From an evolutionary standpoint, conformity can be adaptive in survival circumstances; those of our ancestors who chose to "go it alone" usually put themselves at a decided disadvantage. Furthermore, our motive for cognitive consistency may also play a role in conformity behavior. If one holds the attitude that one does not like to stand out from the group, one may change their behavior accordingly. Thus, the threat of social ostracism is a powerful force for conformity.

The factors controlling conformity, however, are complex. As Moscovici and Faucheux (1972) pointed out, even the nonconformers in Asch's study were probably conforming but to a different set of rules, such as beliefs concerning the importance of individuality and independence. From a practical viewpoint, we can never really be sure that someone is not conforming because we do not know all the reference groups, attitudes, and beliefs that are influencing that person. Nevertheless, it is certain that groups do exert strong pressures on individuals to conform to group expectations. From the individual's point of view, groups seem to trigger a motivational state that tends to bring the individual into line with the group.

One final point bears mention. Nowhere in any of the conformity studies that we discussed were the participants explicitly asked to change their behavior. In all cases, conformity motivation was induced merely by the presence and the behavior of the confederates. However, social influence can also be exerted via direct requests for compliance, which is a topic we discuss below.

Compliance

Friends ask us for favors, telemarketers and Internet pop-up ads solicit us to buy products, public television stations always seem to be in a pledge drive, and politicians appeal to us to vote for them. We are constantly presented with situations where others seek our **compliance**, or behavior change in response to a direct request. Many factors influence our response to compliance requests, including our relationship to the person making the request, our current mood, the manner in which the request is framed, etc. We will not attempt to present a complete discussion of compliance theory and techniques (see Cialdini, 2009, for such a discussion). Rather, we will present the theory and research on two strategies that are often used to increase compliance motivation: the foot-in-the-door and the door-in-the-face techniques.

Imagine that you hear a knock at the door. You open it and see a stranger with a clipboard, who explains that she is gathering signatures on a petition to save the rainforests. She asks you to sign. Would you do it? If you are like most people, the answer is probably yes. After all, it is a small request and you are probably relieved that she is not trying to sell you anything. Now imagine that a few weeks later, a different person knocks on your door and asks you if you would be willing to spend 8 hours canvassing the neighborhood to gather signatures for the rainforest petition. This is a much larger request to which some people would agree, but many would refuse. Would you agree to do it? Believe it or not, you would be much more likely to agree to canvass the neighborhood if you previously signed the petition.

This idea that people are sometimes more likely to consent to a large request if they had previously agreed to a smaller, related request is known as the **foot-in-the-door effect (FITD)**, and it was first studied by Freedman and Fraser (1966). In one of their experiments, which is conceptually similar to the example described above, an experimenter knocked on doors and asked people to sign a petition to support legislation that promotes safe driving. Two weeks later, a different experimenter asked the same participants if they would allow a very large, rather unattractive sign with the words "Drive Carefully" to be placed on their front lawn. A control group of participants was contacted once and asked only the larger request (i.e., to have the sign placed on their lawn). Only 17% of participants in the control condition agreed to the larger request compared to almost half (48%) of the participants who were asked the smaller request first.

Since Freedman and Fraser's original work, well over 100 studies of the FITD technique have been done. This body of research tells us that FITD technique often does increase compliance. Why does it work? The most common explanation relies on Bem's self-perception theory (e.g., DeJong, 1979; Freedman & Fraser, 1966). According to this view, agreeing to the small request causes a change in how we perceive ourselves. Later, when the larger request is presented to us, we are more likely to agree to it because we are motivated to engage in behavior that is consistent with our self-perception. For example, while signing the petition, the participants in Freedman and Fraser's study may have thought "I am a helpful person" or "I think safe driving is important." Later, when the larger request was made, their decision may have been influenced by their motive to maintain this positive self-perception (e.g., "In the past I have helped to support safe driving, so I should agree.").

There have been challenges to the self-perception explanation (e.g., Dolinski, 2009; Gorassini & Olson, 1995), and it has been noted that there may be other processes involved in the FITD effect (e.g., Burger, 1999). However, researchers have found that agreeing to a small request changes one's self-perception and that this change is responsible for increased compliance to the larger request (Burger & Caldwell, 2003). Thus, self-perception remains the most compelling explanation of the FITD effect.

The FITD effect is a widespread phenomenon and can be used to increase compliance to a variety of desirable behaviors. For example, researchers have employed it successfully to induce individuals to schedule a medical exam (Dolin & Booth-Butterfield, 1995); mothers to have their children vaccinated (Cox, Cox, Sturm, & Zimet, 2010); and homeowners to keep a record of their household waste (Gueguen, Meineri, Martin, & Grandjean, 2010). In addition, a moment's reflection reveals that we can enumerate many examples of the use of the FITD technique in everyday life: trial subscriptions to Web sites, coupons/discounts or "groupons" to get us to try a new product or service, and supermarket tasting samples all involve small requests that are usually followed by larger ones. More ominously, doomsday cults often recruit new members by asking people to accept a brochure or a small gift. Once compliance is gained, successively larger requests are made (e.g., "Would you like to meet some people in the group?" "Would you come to a meeting?" "Would you like to be initiated?"). After all, people like Mrs. Keech would not be very successful if they approach potential members and ask the largest request first (e.g., "Would you like to abandon your loved ones, sell all your possessions, and come to my home to wait for a flying saucer?").

Interestingly though, presenting people with very large requests can sometimes increase compliance motivation, provided that you are seeking compliance to a second, smaller request. This is known as the **door-in-the-face effect (DITF)**, and it was first studied by social psychologist Robert

Cialdini after he had an enlightening encounter with a Boy Scout.

In the early 1970s, Cialdini was walking down a street when a young boy asked him if he would like to buy tickets to a circus sponsored by the Boy Scouts. The tickets were $5 a piece. Having no desire to spend a Saturday night at the Boy Scout Circus, Cialdini declined. The scout then asked if he wanted to buy any candy bars, which were only $1 a piece. Cialdini (2009, p. 36) recounts the rest of the story:

I bought a couple and, right away, realized that something noteworthy had happened. I knew that to be the case because (a) I do not like chocolate bars; (b) I do like dollars; (c) I was standing there with two of his chocolate bars; and (d) he was walking away with two of my dollars.

Shortly thereafter, Cialdini and his associates (Cialdini, Vincent, Lewis, Catalan, Wheeler, & Darby, 1975) designed an experiment to study this phenomenon, which they termed the door-in-the-face effect. The name is derived from the idea that the first request is so large that it will almost certainly be refused—like the proverbial door being slammed in the salesperson's face. Cialdini et al. predicted that participants who refused a large request would be more likely to comply with a smaller request than would participants who were only exposed to the small request. Why should this occur? Cialdini et al. discussed two possible explanations. The first was a motive they called **reciprocal concessions**, which is based on the idea that we tend to treat others the way they treat us. Specifically, participants who refuse the large request and are then asked the smaller one may perceive that the person making the request has given in a little by asking for something less. In order to reciprocate, or give something back in return, the participant may be motivated to comply with the second request. Alternatively, a **contrast effect** may be operating. Participants who only get the small request have nothing with which to compare it. However, participants who are exposed to both requests may perceive the smaller request to be acceptable in contrast to the larger one. According to this explanation, merely exposing participants to

both requests should be enough to cause increased compliance motivation to the smaller one.

Cialdini et al. predicted that the DITF effect was most likely due to reciprocal concessions, but they wanted to evaluate both possible explanations. To do this, they conducted a study with three experimental conditions. In the rejection-moderation condition, which tested the reciprocal concessions explanation, undergraduate students were asked if they would agree to work 2 hours per week for 2 years as a volunteer counselor at the County Juvenile Detention Center (the large request). All refused. They were then asked if they would be willing to chaperone a group of juvenile delinquents on one 2-hour trip to the zoo (the smaller request).

In the exposure control condition, the participants listened to an explanation of both requests and were then asked if they would be willing to do either one. This condition was included to determine if merely exposing the participants to both requests was enough to increase compliance to the smaller one by means of the contrast effect. Note that participants in this condition were not specifically asked to perform the large request; if they complied with the smaller request, it could not be due to reciprocal concessions (because the experimenter did not make a concession). In the control condition, participants were asked only to chaperone the zoo trip. The results of the study are presented in Figure 9.6.

Note that the control and exposure control conditions did not differ substantially. However, the rejection-moderation condition produced significantly more compliance than either control condition. Cialdini et al. concluded that the DITF effect is real and is most likely due to reciprocal concessions. This same conclusion was made by the authors of a study that replicated these results over 30 years later (Lecat, Hilton, & Crano, 2009).

Like the FITD phenomenon, the DITF effect has received much empirical refinement since it was first identified. We have learned that the DITF effect is most likely to occur when both requests are made by the same person (Cialdini, et al., 1975); there is little time delay between the two requests

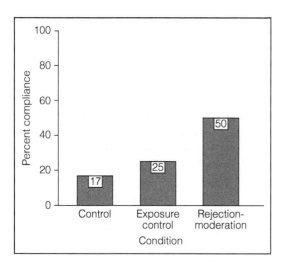

FIGURE 9.6 Percentage of participants who agreed to perform a smaller request depending on degree of exposure to a larger request. Adapted from Cialdini, Vincent, Lewis, Catalan, Wheeler & Darby, 1975.

(Fern, Monroe, & Avila, 1986; O'Keefe & Hale, 2001); the requests involve prosocial behaviors (Dillard, Hunter, & Burgoon, 1984; O'Keefe & Hale, 2001), and the requests are made by members of one's own social group (Lecat, Hilton, & Crano, 2009). Each of these findings supports the adaptive role that reciprocal concessions or the "norm or reciprocity" may have in facilitating the development of bonds between members of social groups.

Are there any practical applications to the DITF technique? Absolutely. The DITF effect can be seen in many real-life bargaining situations. For example, imagine that you are buying a car. The seller of the car typically quotes a sticker or asking price that is higher than they expect to ultimately receive. You make an offer that is less than the asking price, perhaps considerably so. The expectation is that the seller and buyer will adjust their offers and converge on an acceptable sales price—reciprocal concessions at work! This is a hypothetical example, but there is empirical evidence that the DITF technique works for salespeople (Ebster & Neumayr, 2008). More importantly, the DITF technique has also been shown to increase

compliance to medical requests made by health care professionals (Millar, 2001). Millar found that participants were more likely to keep a detailed journal of their eating habits for 4 days if they had first refused a request to keep such a journal for a month.

In general, then, the research on compliance motivation reveals that we often do consent to direct requests made by others, and psychologists have discovered subtle but powerful techniques can be used to increase the motive to comply with such requests. Thus far we have examined the use of implicit pressure (i.e., conformity) and direct requests (i.e., compliance) to influence the motives of others. We will now discuss the most straightforward type of social influence—obedience to orders from authority figures.

Obedience

Though all of us like to think of ourselves as independent and unaffected by the demands of others, we are in fact much more obedient to the authority figures of our society than we generally acknowledge. One of the first people to systematically study **obedience**, or a change in behavior in response to a direct order, was Stanley Milgram. Milgram was trying to explain the brutality of the Holocaust; was it something peculiar about German culture that allowed such atrocities to occur on a grand scale? Or, could such events happen almost anywhere, and be carried out by ordinary people? The results of Milgram's research are both fascinating and frightening.

In a series of studies, Milgram (1963, 1965, 1975) tested participants' willingness to obey commands that for most were unpleasant and morally unjustifiable. Milgram's basic experiment required one participant to teach another participant by delivering increasingly painful electric shocks for incorrect answers in a verbal memory task. In front of the teacher was a shock console with switches indicating varying voltages from 15 to 450 volts in 15-volt steps. Above the switches were labels describing the shocks' characteristics. At the low end the descriptions indicated slight

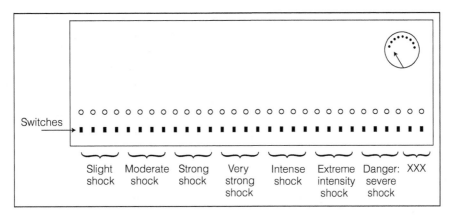

Switches

Slight shock · Moderate shock · Strong shock · Very strong shock · Intense shock · Extreme intensity shock · Danger: severe shock · XXX

FIGURE 9.7 Adapted from "Some Conditions of Obedience and Disobedience to Authority," by S. Milgram, 1965, *Human Relations, 18*, 57–76. Copyright © 1965 by Human Relations. Used by permission.

and moderate shock, while at the upper end descriptions indicated extreme shock, danger: severe shock, and XXX. Figure 9.7 shows the basic layout of the shock console.

Milgram was interested in how far ordinary participants would be willing to go in obeying an experimenter who instructed them to continue delivering shocks of increasing intensity. Before Milgram ran the experiment, he asked several groups of people to predict at what point the participants would defy the experimenter. These groups (including psychiatrists, college sophomores, graduate students, adults, and faculty in behavioral sciences) were all consistent in predicting that the participant serving as teacher would refuse to follow the orders of the experimenter when the shocks became very painful. The psychiatrists in particular predicted that most participants would not go further than 150 volts, that only approximately 4% would go as high as 300 volts, and that less than one in a 1,000 would continue to deliver shocks all the way to 450 volts.

After obtaining these data indicating that most people believed that the majority of persons would not hurt others, even in the name of science, Milgram ran the experiments. He recruited from the New Haven Connecticut area people of varying occupations, ages, and educational levels and asked them to arrive at the lab in pairs. However, one of the pair was always the same—a 47-year-old male confederate. The experimenter, a 31-year-old male who wore a technician's coat, explained to the participants that this was a study of the effect of punishment on learning. One of them was to be assigned the role of teacher and the other the role of learner. Each selected a piece of paper with one of the roles written on it. In reality the drawing was rigged so that the real participant was always assigned the role of teacher and the confederate was the learner.[2]

The teacher then observed as the learner was strapped into a chair and fitted with an electrode. The learner mentioned that he had a slight heart condition and asked if the shocks were dangerous. The experimenter responded that the shocks would be painful, but would not cause damage. The teacher was then led to another room, out of view of the learner, where he was seated in front of the shock generator. The learner responded to each memory task by flipping a switch that indicated his answer to the teacher. Each time the learner made an error, the teacher had to deliver a shock—starting with the mildest level and increasing in 15 volts in intensity each time. In reality, no

---

[2]Milgram ran over 20 versions of studies using this experimental paradigm (Blass, 2009). We discuss Experiment 5 here.

shocks were in fact delivered, and the sequence of correct and incorrect answers as well as the learner's verbal protestations followed a script.

At 75 volts the learner began to make noise. By 120 volts he began to complain about the shock, and at 150 volts he said that his heart was bothering him and started demanding to be released from the experiment. The protestation of the learner to the ever-increasing shock became greater and greater as the shocks continued, until at 285 volts it became a scream of agony.

How did the teachers react to the learner's cries of pain? They were anything but relaxed. As the learner began to protest, they often turned to the experimenter, questioning whether they should continue. The experimenter firmly replied that they must continue, using prods such as "The experiment requires that you go on," "It is absolutely essential that we continue," and so on. Thus, the teachers were quite aware of the learner's plight and were usually distressed at having to continue delivering the painful shock. Nevertheless, 26 of the 40 participants (65%) went all the way to 450 volts. These surprising and unsettling results led Milgram, and many others, to search for an explanation.

Why a Motive to Obey?

Milgram (1974) argued that humans have an innate potential for obedience that can be activated by interaction with the environment under particular conditions. When humans or other animals live in groups, it is adaptive to have a social hierarchy in place. The development of this hierarchy depends on some individuals' willingness to obey others in certain circumstances. Much of Milgram's work was done to explicate the situations under which obedience occurs.

The participants of these experiments were not sadistic persons who got great enjoyment from the pain of others. They were persons just like you and me. But when put into a conflict situation where they had to choose between open defiance of an authority figure and obedience to a personally immoral behavior, the majority of participants chose to obey. Milgram argued that the basis of obedience is one's ability to view oneself as simply an instrument carrying out someone else's wishes. In such a way we cognitively lay the blame for the learner's suffering onto someone else (in this case, the experimenter or perhaps even the learner). Evidence for this type of obedience analysis comes from many sources. For example, the participants' conversations with the experimenter during the experiment often consisted of the teacher's disclaiming any responsibility for the suffering of the learner and frequent checking to see if the experimenter would accept the responsibility for whatever happened.

In one variation of the experiment, the teacher was only required to read aloud the descriptive labels above the switches, while someone else delivered the shocks. Under these conditions 37 of 40 participants continued all the way to the end. When asked about the suffering of the learner, they replied that the person throwing the switches was responsible.

The concept of **detached responsibility** for a person's behavior suggests that increasing the participants' feelings of responsibility should lead to a change in the obedience rate. A number of studies support this concept. For example, in one experiment when participants were allowed to choose their own shock level, the average level chosen was only 60 volts (Milgram, 1975). In the original experiments, the teacher was in one room while the learner was in another. When the teacher was put into the same room with the learner so that responsibility for the teacher's behavior could not easily be denied, obedience rates dropped. Zimbardo (1969) in fact has suggested that the ability to avoid responsibility for one's behavior, which he calls **deindividuation**, is an important component of much violence seen in modern society.

However, the teacher's perceived *personal responsibility* in Milgram's experiments was not the only factor; *characteristics of the authority figure*—for example, the proximity of the experimenter— were also important in increasing obedience. When Milgram had the experimenter deliver instructions to the teacher over a telephone, the obedience rate of the participants who complied all the way to 450 volts dropped to about 30%. It is worth pointing out that even 30% compliance is a huge amount.

The *context* in which the experiment is conducted is also an important factor (Milgram, 1965). When the experiment was conducted at Yale, obedience was high; yet when the experiment was removed from the university context and conducted in a run-down section of town, obedience rates dropped. These results seem to indicate that obedience is also related to our attitudes—we seem to assume that behaving in certain ways for the good of science or country is all right, even though the behavior may transgress our own moral codes.

Milgram also found that a *lack of clear authority* immediately dropped the obedience rate. In this variation of the basic experiment, two experimenters were present and disagreed about whether the learner should continue to be shocked. Under these conditions the teacher quickly stopped shocking the learner.

Finally, Milgram has found that the *obedience of others* to an authority figure leads to the participant's increased obedience, whereas *rebellion of others* leads to rebellion by the participant, who refuses to deliver further shock. This effect is reminiscent of the deviant in Asch's experiments and suggests that conformity to group pressure is also involved in obedience to authority, in the sense that the authority figure represents the head of an accepted group.

Milgram's studies are some of the most well-known in all of psychology, mostly due to the startling results he obtained. But his studies are also famous because many have questioned the ethics of such research. Obviously, participants in these studies were exposed to a tremendous amount of stress. Milgram himself recognized the powerful effect that his research could have on participants and took many steps to minimize negative consequences. The learner greeted every participant immediately after the study in order to show that he was unharmed. In addition, the experimenter extensively discussed the rationale for the study

with each participant during extensive debriefing. All participants were sent a five-page report of the results of the studies with an explanation that whether they chose to obey the experimenter or not, their behavior was not abnormal. They were also sent a follow-up survey on which only 1.3% indicated that they were sorry or very sorry that they had participated in the study, and 84% said that they were glad or very glad. Finally, a psychiatrist interviewed 40 participants who seemed to be at the greatest risk of harm from the studies. He concluded that none showed signs of having been harmed by this experience.

As is the case with Asch's conformity research, many people, when they are exposed to Milgram's results the first time, are tempted to conclude that "things are different now" or that "I wouldn't behave that way." However, Burger (2009) replicated, as much as was ethically allowed, one of Milgram's original studies and found essentially the same results over four decades later. There are even videos posted on YouTube that depict 21st century demonstrations of obedience using Milgram's protocol (see links at the end of this chapter). Finally, a review of the literature on obedience has revealed that obedience in studies using Milgram's paradigm (a) has remained essentially unchanged over time; (b) has been reported in the US and in many other countries; and (c) occurs at the same level for both male and female participants (Blass, 1999).

Milgram's research suggests that most of us have a strong motive to obey the authority figures of our society, even when such obedience seems compromising to our own standards of conduct. Milgram believed that obedience to authority is a basic element of social living. Without obedience to accepted authorities, the very fabric of society would dissolve. Nevertheless, the same obedience that has helped humans to survive in groups can also lead to atrocities such as occurred in the concentration camps of World War II and in such incidents as My Lai during the Vietnam conflict, and more recently Abu Ghraib during the Iraq war. It is frightening to realize that most of us are capable of committing such acts under the right conditions. Although we do not like to admit it, obedience to authority can override our ethics, morals, and sympathies toward our fellow human beings. Our cognitive processes allow us to rationalize away our own responsibilities to the point that we can self-righteously say, "We were only following orders." Finally, the very structure of our society, with its various divisions of labor, works against feelings of personal responsibility for our acts, as Milgram (1975) has so clearly pointed out. The person ordering an execution can disclaim responsibility for the death because he or she did not deliver the lethal injection, while the executioner can likewise disclaim responsibility because he or she was only following the order of the judge. Also, when decisions are made by the state, no one need feel responsible because the responsibility falls on a nonliving entity. In some respects it is perhaps surprising that atrocities are not more frequent.

In general, then, the study of social motivation leads us to consider the situational factors that influence our behavior. As is evident from Milgram's work, psychologists are often interested in determining the motives behind antisocial behaviors so that such behaviors can be minimized. However, psychologists are also intrigued by the motives that underlie prosocial actions. We will now examine the research on one particular prosocial behavior, which is called bystander intervention. As you will see, our discussion of this topic will incorporate many of the ideas that we have examined earlier in this chapter, such as coaction/audience effects and conformity.

Bystander Intervention

Recall that we began this chapter with the story of Tim who, while walking down the stairs, heard a woman trip and fall a few floors below him. Tim chose not to help her. One of Tim's reasons was that there were other people on the stairs and that someone else would probably help. However, suppose everyone else on the stairs used the same logic. Ironically, this would mean that the woman would be more likely to get help if there was only one person nearby than if there were a lot of people around. It turns out that this is often the case. If you have ever had the misfortune of a car breakdown on an interstate highway and you had no cellular telephone, you already know how difficult it can be to get help from passersby. Yet, it isn't because there is no one around. Paradoxically, it may be because there are too many people around.

The topic of bystander intervention has been examined in most detail by Bibb Latané and John Darley. Their book, *The Unresponsive Bystander: Why Doesn't He Help?* (1970), has shed much light on this phenomenon. As Latané and Darley have pointed out, it is not a question of people not helping others—because sometimes they do—but rather of the conditions under which helping behavior is likely to occur. This suggests that the motive to engage in helping behavior depends less on the characteristics of the potential helper than on the characteristics of the emergency situation. Consider the following example from Latané and Darley.

Andrew Mormille is stabbed in the stomach as he rides the A train home in Manhattan. Eleven other riders watch the 17-year-old boy as he bleeds to death; none come to his assistance even though his attackers have left the car. He dies.[3]

Latané and Darley determined to study the conditions leading to helping behavior or the lack of it. One of their first findings was that, in response to a direct request (i.e., a compliance situation), helping behavior depends to a certain extent upon what is being asked of the helper. In an initial study involving nonemergency situations, they had students at Columbia University in New York City walk up to people on the street and ask them for the time of day, directions, a dime, or their name. Results of the experiment showed that minor assistance such as time or directions was rarely

---

[3]The case of Kitty Genovese, a woman who was murdered while some of her neighbors observed the scene, is often cited as a classic example of bystander apathy. However, a review of the evidence indicates that the onlookers may not have been as impassive as was once believed (Manning, Levine, & Collins, 2007).

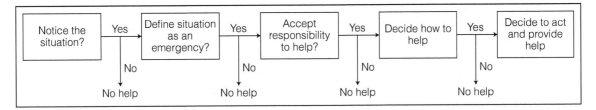

FIGURE 9.8 Schematic diagram of Latané and Darley's model of the intervention process. Data from Latané & Darley, 1970.

refused, and that 85% of those requested provided assistance. Less than 40% of those asked gave the student their names, and only about 30% gave a dime when requested. Thus, it appears that one factor determining helping behavior, at least in nonemergency situations, is the *amount of commitment* that the helper must make. Minor or common requests are usually granted. Less common requests or requests that require the helper to make a larger commitment, such as giving money or one's name, are less likely to be granted unless some reasonable explanation is provided.

The dynamic in emergency situations is more complex. First of all, in an emergency, the commitment by the potential helper can be relatively large, often leading to some reluctance to intervene. Latané and Darley pointed out that the very characteristics of emergency situations make them a no-win situation for the helper. For example, there is sometimes very real possibility of harm. There are also few tangible rewards for helping behavior, other than an occasional citation or news article. Thus, we should not be too surprised that people hesitate to intervene.

A second problem is that most of us are generally unfamiliar with emergency situations, and there is no handy list of how to behave or what to do in a particular emergency, and so we may not help because we simply *don't know what to do*. A third characteristic of emergencies is that they *occur suddenly*; if we are to react, we must do so immediately, without thinking through the best means of responding. We may thus hesitate in a state of indecision while the crucial time for action passes by.

A Model of Intervention

Latané and Darley proposed that whether or not an individual intervenes in an emergency situation can be understood in terms of five factors, as shown in the flowchart of Figure 9.8. The presence of others affects the decision process at each stage but is particularly important in the first three stages.

First we must take note of the situation; obviously we cannot react to an emergency of which we are unaware. Latané and Darley have found that the presence of other people around us, particularly strangers, reduces our attention to the environment so that we take longer to notice a potential emergency situation (stage 1 of the model). In one experiment, participants were asked to report to a room to participate in an interview about urban life. The male students were given the room number and instructed to begin filling out some preliminary forms while they waited to be called to the interview. After the participant had been working alone for a few minutes, smoke began to filter into the room through a vent in one wall. The participants who were waiting alone typically noticed the smoke soon after it began, quickly investigated it, and, finding no reasonable explanation, left the room to report it.

In a second condition, however, a participant, upon arrival at the designated room, found two other participants already there and busily filling out forms (the two participants already present were actually confederates of the experimenter). When the smoke was introduced into the room, the confederates were instructed to look up and notice the smoke but to continue working. Careful observation revealed that 63% of the participants in the alone condition noticed the smoke within 5 seconds of its introduction, while only 26% of the participants in the room with others present noticed the smoke within 5 seconds.

These data indicate that one effect of the presence of others is a reduction in the amount of attention that we pay to our environment. The results suggest that when an emergency exists, we will be slower to notice it if others are present. This reduced attention to our environment may result from a tendency to maintain a certain psychological distance from others by avoiding eye contact. By avoiding looking at others, we also avoid observing much of our environment and thus notice potential emergency situations more slowly.

The smoke-filled room experiment also demonstrates another factor involved in the inhibition of helping behavior (stage 2). Emergency situations are often ambiguous, at least initially, and we are uncertain whether to consider the situation an actual emergency. Recall the results of Sherif's studies of conformity and the autokinetic effect. When we are uncertain, we tend to look to those around us in order to test our ideas about the situation. The problem, in an emergency situation, is that everyone else often takes cues from each other (i.e., conforms). Because we don't want to embarrass ourselves by declaring an emergency when none exists, we tend to have calm, nonemotional expressions on our faces as we look around, and we see that everyone else also appears calm. Therefore we must be wrong; an emergency must not exist. Latané and Darley have labeled this behavior **pluralistic ignorance**. By remaining expressionless and unemotional as we survey the reactions of others, we fool each other into believing that an emergency does not in fact exist. In the study described above, Latané and Darley also recorded how many participants left the room to report the smoke to the experimenter, thus defining the situation as an emergency. In the alone condition, 50% reported the smoke within 2 minutes of its introduction, and 75% reported it within 4 minutes. However, only 10% of the participants waiting with the unresponsive confederates left to report

the smoke during the entire 6-minute test period. Pluralistic ignorance is a compelling explanation for this result.

In another conceptually similar experiment, participants filled out questionnaires in a room either alone or with another person. Some of the participant pairs were strangers, others were friends, and in one condition one participant was a confederate of the experimenter, as in the smoke experiment. A female experimenter, whom the participants had met briefly, was heard to fall in the next room and moan that she had hurt her ankle. Latané and Darley found that 70% of the participants alone in the room came to the aid of the female experimenter, while only 7% of the participants paired with the confederate, who sat passively throughout, came to her aid. These latter participants appeared uneasy and glanced often at the confederate, who continued to fill out the questionnaire.

For participants paired with a stranger, only 8 out of 40 (or 20%) intervened. This demonstrates that the mere presence of an audience, which in this case was one other person, tends to inhibit helping behavior. When two friends were paired in the room, helping behavior was approximately 70%—though friends, too, were slower to intervene than participants in the alone condition. The friend condition, however, did create significantly faster intervention than the stranger conditions.

Latané and Darley believed that the results of this experiment can also be understood in terms of pluralistic ignorance. In both the passive confederate and stranger conditions, participants looked furtively at one another while remaining outwardly calm. They were, in effect, creating a pluralistic ignorance that reduced the chances of their defining the situation as an emergency. Friends, however, were more likely to be open about their feelings, and this led to a reduction of the pluralistic ignorance created—although even in the friend condition the reaction time to providing helping behavior was slower than in the alone condition.

When participants were interviewed after the experiment, noninterveners were consistent in their interpretation of the situation as a nonemergency. Of some interest is that, in both experiments described above, participants were unaware that their behavior had been inhibited by the presence of others. Thus in an ambiguous situation, pluralistic ignorance apparently leads to cognitions that define the situation as a nonemergency, and behavior is inhibited. Referring again to Figure 9.8, the presence of others initially retards our noticing the situation (stage 1), but the presence of others also creates a pluralistic ignorance that retards our defining the situation as an emergency (stage 2).

Many situations, of course, cannot be ignored and are immediately defined as emergencies; yet even under these conditions, people may not intervene. This brings us to the third stage in the intervention model: deciding if you are responsible for intervening.

Anyone who lives in a large metropolitan area and reads the newspaper or watches the news knows how common the examples of nonintervention have become. Why don't more people help? For one reason, the cost of direct intervention can be high. If you intervene, for example, you may be harmed yourself; your prosocial behavior may be misunderstood by the victim, who may not want your help; you may have to testify in court, etc. There are good reasons, then, for not directly intervening. But what about some sort of indirect intervention such as calling 911? Even indirect intervention often does not occur.

Latané and Darley believed that the lack of intervention can be understood as resulting from a **diffusion of responsibility** because of the presence of others. In a situation where a person may already be reluctant to intervene, the presence of others takes the responsibility from the person's shoulders ("Surely someone has already called the police."). The problem is that each person is similarly influenced by this diffusion of responsibility so that many times no one intervenes, as likely occurred in the Andrew Mormille attack.

In order to examine the effect of diffusion of responsibility, Latané and Darley designed an experiment in which participants were recruited to take part in a discussion of personal problems associated with college life. In order to reduce embarrassment, so they were told, the participants were placed in individual booths with headphones and microphones for communicating with each other. After the experiment had begun, the participants heard one of the group fall into an epileptic seizure. In one condition each participant was led to believe that he or she was the only one aware of the seizure, while in a second condition each thought that four other participants could also hear the emergency. The seizure episode was actually a tape recording made to determine what percentage of people would seek help for the seizure victim.

Latané and Darley found that 85% of the participants who thought they were alone sought help for the victim before the tape ended (125 seconds), while only 31% of the participants who thought that four people could hear the seizure responded to the emergency. Eventually, 100% of the participants who thought they were alone sought help, and 62% of those in the second condition eventually reported it.

Those participants who did not report the seizure were, however, anything but apathetic. They were very nervous and concerned about the seizure victim. Apparently, then, apathy and depersonalization resulting from city living are not adequate explanations for nonintervention in emergency situations. Instead, the presence of others diffuses the responsibility felt by any specific individual to the point that no help may be provided. These effects tend to be reduced if we are in the company of friends or are familiar with our surroundings, and they are exaggerated if we are in the company of strangers or are unfamiliar with our environment.

Even if we accept responsibility for helping (stage 3), there are still two more conditions that must be satisfied for intervention to occur. As noted earlier, most people are unfamiliar with emergency situations, so they simply might not know how to help (stage 4). Finally one must decide to provide help (stage 5). This is a decision that could be difficult, given that one could be putting one's self at considerable risk.

Factors That Affect Helping Behavior

The Latané and Darley model of helping has generally been supported by empirical studies of bystander intervention. Indeed, the **bystander effect**, or reduced helping in the presence of others, has even been found to occur in studies in which people communicate online (e.g., Lee & Lee, 2010; Markey, 2000). However, there is evidence that the bystander effect can be reduced or even eliminated under certain circumstances. For example, Fischer, Greitemeyer, Pollozek, and Frey (2006) found that the presence of a confederate bystander did not reduce helping in a serious, violent emergency situation. In this study, participants were asked to view and evaluate interactions between pairs of people (one male and one female in each pair) who had never met one another before. The participants were told that the study measured the degree to which people can misperceive the level of romantic interest others have in them when meeting for the first time. The participants viewed via closed circuit television what they thought were three live interactions taking place in a nearby room. In fact the interactions were on videotape. The first two interactions proceed without incident, but in the third video sequence, the male actor became increasingly suggestive, and ultimately verbally and physically harassed the female actress. He initiated physical contact and blocked the exit to the room when she tried to leave. Soon thereafter the video feed ended, indicating to the participant that the incident could still be going on.

Half the participants watched the interactions alone and half did so with a passive confederate. In addition, the level of danger was manipulated by using two different male actors in the third video. In the high danger condition the male was large and physically imposing; in the low danger condition, he was small and thin. The researchers recorded whether or not the participants attempted to help the victim directly—by attempting to go to the room in which the incident was supposedly taking place. The results were intriguing (see Figure 9.9). Note that in the low danger condition the presence of the confederate reduced the level of helping, which is the traditional bystander effect. However, the confederate had no negative effect on helping in the high danger condition.

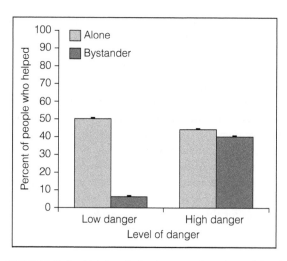

FIGURE 9.9 Helping behavior as a function of level of danger in the situation and presence or absence of a passive bystander. Adapted from Fischer, et al., 2006.

A meta-analysis of research on helping behavior confirms the reduced inhibitory effect of bystanders in dangerous situations (Fischer, Krueger, Greitemeyer, Vogrincic, Kastenmuller, Frey, Heene, Wicher, & Kainbacher, 2011). Fischer et al. (2011) present evidence that this effect could be due to several factors. First, highly dangerous situations are often unambiguous; we are likely to notice them and interpret them as emergencies, thus successfully navigating stages 1 and 2 of the model of intervention. In addition, many people prefer to be around others when fearful or anxious (e.g., Schachter, 1959). Fischer et al. contend that, in dangerous emergencies, being with others provides us with support and the potential for assistance if we decide to intervene.

Researchers have also studied the role that personality characteristics have in helping behavior and the results have been equivocal. Some researchers report that individuals high in **empathy**, or feelings of sympathy or compassion for someone as a result of imagining how you would feel in the same situation, are more likely to help others (e.g., Davis, 1983). However, Latané and Darley found no correlation between five different personality scales and helping behavior in the seizure study. Latané and Darley's results suggest that situational factors such as the presence of other people are crucial determinants of helping behavior, while dispositional characteristics of the individual are less important. This is perhaps not surprising when one considers that helping situations can vary greatly in terms of danger, potential cost, and the presence of bystanders, to name just a few variables.

The dominant role of the situation can be clearly seen in an experiment by Darley and Batson (1976). Seminary students, whom one would assume have personality traits that engender helping behavior, at Princeton University were asked to participate in a study on religious education and vocation. The participants began the experiment in one room but were then asked to go to a building next door to finish the experiment by giving a short talk on either religious vocations or the parable of the Good Samaritan. In addition to varying the topic of the talk to be given, the amount of time the participant had was also manipulated. In the first condition, participants were told that they were late for the second part of the experiment and should hurry across the alley to the second building. A second group of participants was told that they had just time enough to make it to the other building, and a third group of participants was told that they had plenty of time to get to the second part of the experiment.

Participants were directed to the building next door. Getting there required crossing an alley that ran between the buildings. In this alley a confederate of the experimenter was slumped against the wall and instructed to cough twice and groan as participants passed him. The behavior of interest was whether students in training for the ministry would stop to aid the victim and whether the type of talk they were about to give (religious vocation versus the parable of the Good Samaritan) and the degree of hurry (late, on time, or early) would influence the probability of their giving aid.

Results of the experiment are quite fascinating. The type of talk the seminarian was about to give, and thus was presumably thinking about on his way across the alley, had no effect on helping behavior.

Participants asked to talk on the parable of the Good Samaritan were no more likely to stop than those asked to talk on religious vocations. Thus, thinking about helping others did not appear to increase the likelihood of lending aid to a victim. By contrast, the time constraints put on the participants had a large effect on helping behavior. Participants who thought they were late and were thus in a hurry were not very helpful; only 10% stopped to offer the victim aid. Of the participants in the on-time condition, 45% stopped to offer aid, while 63% in the early condition stopped. Clearly the situational factor of time can be crucial in determining helping behavior. Again we see the importance of one's immediate environment in motivating behavior in social situations.

We have just reviewed considerable evidence that people are often reluctant to aid others in need. The factors identified as important in this reluctance have helped us to understand how tragedies such as the Andrew Mormille murder sometimes occur. Although these factors often work against bystander intervention in an emergency, people nevertheless often do help others (Latané & Nida, 1981). Helping is especially likely when the conditions of Latané and Darley's model of intervention are met.

What Motivates Helping?

Researchers have also looked at some of the motivational factors that lead to helping behavior in general, beyond the bystander intervention paradigm (see studies by Batson et al., 1981, 1983; Batson & Gray, 1981; Bauman, Cialdini, & Kenrick, 1981; Coke, Batson, & McDavis, 1978; Hoffman, 1981; Rutkowski, Gruder, & Romer, 1983; Schwartz & Gottlieb, 1980; Senneker & Hendrick, 1983; Toi & Batson, 1982; Weiner, 1980). One question of considerable interest is whether helping can ever be truly **altruistic**; that is, help is provided as a result of an unselfish concern for others and nothing is received in return. Some researchers believe that, under certain circumstances, helping behavior can be motivated solely by altruism (e.g., Batson, Duncan, Ackerman,

Buckley, & Birch, 1981; Toi & Batson, 1982). Others have suggested that helping behavior is never truly altruistic but is, rather, **egoistic** because the helper always gets some type of benefit from their benevolence (e.g., Cialdini, Brown, Lewis, Luce, & Neuberg, 1997). For example, helping another may make us feel good, or it may reduce the distress that occurs when we see another suffer. Alternatively, helping behavior may be viewed as egoistic if it leads to material or social rewards.

Batson and his colleagues have presented evidence that feelings of empathy toward another can trigger altruistic motivation, which in turn, increases the likelihood of helping. By manipulating empathic feelings, Coke, Batson, and McDavis (1978) found that participants who experienced the most empathy also offered the most help. Furthermore, Batson and colleagues (e.g., Batson, Duncan, Ackerman, Buckley, & Birch, 1981; Toi & Batson, 1982) report the results of several studies which, they argue, present evidence for helping that is motivated by altruism rather than egoism. In one such study (Batson et al., 1981, Study 1), female participants were assigned to watch, via closed circuit television, and to evaluate a fellow female student who had to complete 10 trials of a digit-recall task while being randomly shocked while doing so. The fellow student, whose name was Elaine, was actually a confederate whose performance was recorded on videotape and played for each participant. On the tape, Elaine pretended to react so negatively to the shocks that the female experimenter entered Elaine's testing room and momentarily stopped the study during the second of the 10 trials to check Elaine's welfare. The experimenter suggested that Elaine cease participating in the study, but Elaine wanted to continue. The experimenter then went to the room where the real participant was seated and asked her if she would be willing to trade places with Elaine for the remainder of the trials. Her decision was the primary measure of helping in the study.

Two variables were manipulated in this experiment. The first was the level of empathy that the participant was experiencing toward Elaine, which can be influenced by the degree to which one feels similar to another (Stotland, 1969). In the high empathy condition, the participant was led to believe that Elaine's values and interests were very similar to her own; in the low empathy condition, Elaine's profile was very dissimilar to the participant's. Ease of escape from the situation was also manipulated. In the easy escape condition, the participant was told her role as observer was complete after the second trial—she did not have to observe Elaine any longer. In the difficult escape condition, the participant had to watch Elaine be shocked until the 10 trials were completed.

The researchers predicted that the low empathy/easy escape condition would produce the lowest level of helping. These participants feel no connection to Elaine and can remove themselves from the situation, rather than trading places with her. Participants in the low empathy/difficult escape condition must choose between getting shocked themselves or watching Elaine endure the shocks for eight more trials. These individuals should be more likely to help Elaine, but for an egoistic reason—they want to reduce the distress that they feel when watching Elaine get shocked. Participants in both of the high empathy conditions feel a connection to Elaine, so they should be more likely to help her. If participants in the high empathy/difficult escape group decide to help, it could be due to altruism induced by empathy, but it could also be due to a desire to reduce their own distress (remember that they would have to watch Elaine for eight more trials if they don't help). However, if participants in the high empathy/easy escape condition helped Elaine, as the researchers predicted they would, their behavior is likely motivated by altruism because they could easily reduce the distress they feel by leaving.

The results of the study confirm the researchers' predictions (see Figure 9.10).

Although these results are compelling, they have not gone unchallenged. For example, Cialdini and colleagues (Cialdini, Brown, Lewis, Luce, & Neuberg, 1997) conducted several studies in which they manipulated empathy and measured helping. Their results replicated those of Batson et al. (1981). However, their interpretation is quite

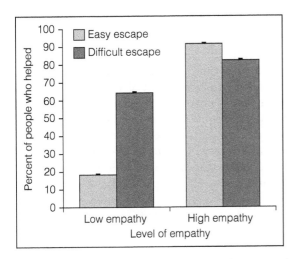

FIGURE 9.10 Helping behavior as a function of empathy and ease of escape. Adapted from Batson, et al., 1981.

different. They argue that manipulations of empathy also produce in people a sense of oneness with the other person. That is, the more of a connection that we feel with another person, the more we feel a "sense of shared, merged or interconnected personal identities" (Cialdini et al., 1997, p. 483). They argue that (a) it is the sense of oneness, rather than level of empathy, that predicts whether or not helping will occur; and (b) if we feel one with another and help them, then we are also helping ourselves. Helping in this case would be egoistic, not altruistic.

In the studies noted above, Cialdini et al. (1997) also included a measure of the level of oneness that the participant felt for the person who needed help. When they statistically controlled for oneness, empathy was no longer related to helping. However, when they removed the effect of empathy, oneness was still significantly related to helping. This led them to conclude that Batson's studies do not provide evidence of altruism.

The egoistic interpretation also receives support from those who try to understand helping from an evolutionary perspective (e.g., Kenrick, 1991; Krebs, 1991). According to this view, empathy may have evolved as a means of communication among individuals who lived in close proximity to

one another. These individuals also tend to be genetically related to each other. It is adaptive to help our relatives because every relative who lives long enough to reproduce will pass on some of our genes to the next generation. Indeed, many studies indicate that we are more likely to help relatives than unrelated individuals, and that close relatives are more likely to receive assistance than distant ones (e.g., Burnstein, Crandall, & Kitayama, 1994). Thus, perhaps an evolutionary link between empathy and helping exists. Such a link might have developed because those with whom we are most likely to empathize, and therefore help, are people who share our genes (Maner & Gailliot, 2007). One can argue that, from an evolutionary standpoint, this is ultimately a way of helping ourselves. The effect of kinship on helping is perhaps best illustrated by the biologist J. B. S. Haldane who quipped that he would lay down his life in order to save two brothers or eight cousins. Because we share 50% of our genes with siblings and 12.5% with cousins, saving either group of relatives would mean that genetic material equal to that which we possess would be preserved.

The egoistic versus altruistic debate continues to interest researchers. Cialdini and associates have presented much empirical work that supports the egoistic interpretation of helping (e.g., Cialdini, Brown, Lewis, Luce, & Neuberg, 1997; Maner, Luce, Neuberg, Cialdini, Brown, & Sagarin, 2002; Neuberg, Cialdini, Brown, Luce, Sagarin, & Lewis, 1997). However, Batson and colleagues have found much evidence in defense of an altruistic view of helping (e.g., Batson & Ahmad, 2001; Batson, Ahmad, Yin, Bedell, Johnson, Templin, & Whiteside, 1999; Batson & Weeks, 1996). From a theoretical and philosophical standpoint, the question of whether pure altruism exists is interesting and has been for quite some time (e.g., Butler, 1726/1991; Hobbes, 1651/1991). But one could argue that, from a practical standpoint, whether or not prosocial behavior can ever be motivated solely by altruism is immaterial (e.g., Hartenian & Lilly, 2009). As a society, we would like to encourage people to help one another, and if both parties receive some benefit from the interaction, then the task is a little easier.

SUMMARY

In this chapter, we have examined a major conception of motivation that emphasizes cognitive structures as important in the determination of behavior. Cognitive consistency theories such as balance theory and cognitive dissonance assume that inconsistencies between attitudes, beliefs, and behavior lead to a state of tension that generates a motivation to reduce or eliminate the inconsistency. Several triadic examples of Heider's balance theory were presented. In each, the overall model was balanced if two people agreed on their evaluation of a third object/person/event/idea. If there was disagreement, the model was out of balance and, according to Heider, this triggers a motive to restore balance. Leon Festinger's cognitive dissonance theory has been the most popular consistency theory to date. Festinger proposed that we strive for consistency or consonance in our cognitions, attitudes, and behaviors. If there is inconsistency among two or more of these elements, we experience a state of dissonance which, like imbalance in Heider's theory, we are motivated to reduce. Dissonance theory has been the subject of thousands of studies in the domains of induced compliance, justification of effort, and postdecision dissonance. However, Daryl Bem and others question the usefulness of dissonance as an explanation of motivation. Bem proposed self-perception theory as an alternative explanation to account for some of the situations formerly explained by dissonance without having to assume the production of a negative motivational state. Bem argues that our attitudes are formed and changed not by dissonance, but by self-observation and attribution. Our present understanding of the processes involved suggests that both cognitive dissonance and self-perception processes may be operating, but under differing conditions.

We have seen in this chapter that motivation due to the presence of others, or social motivation, can have both positive and negative effects on our behavior. Having others perform a task with us as coactors, or watch us as an audience, seems to have an energizing effect and, usually, increases our performance via a physiological challenge response. However, the presence of others can sometimes inhibit our performance due to a physiological threat response, especially if the task we are performing is a novel one.

Pressures to conform to, comply with, and obey the rules of society are also the product of social motivation. Data from Asch's conformity experiments indicate that it is very difficult to go against perceived group pressure, even when the group is obviously wrong. Research on compliance techniques such as the foot-in-the-door and door-in-the-face techniques reveals that there are reasonably simple strategies that one can use to increase the likelihood that others will do what we ask of them. Milgram's obedience experiments point out the difficulty that most of us have in refusing to carry out instructions from authority figures, even if the behaviors we are told to engage in are morally reprehensible to us. These data on obedience are important because they help us understand how atrocities can occur. Because of the tendency to obey authority figures, most of us have the potential to act in ways that we would judge immoral in others. However, conformity, compliance, and obedience have likely had adaptive significance for us in our evolutionary past. Each of these sources of influence can serve to form and strengthen social bonds among members of a group.

Even the likelihood of helping someone in distress is affected by the presence of others. Latané and Darley have found that the presence of others reduces our scanning of the environment so that we are slower to notice emergencies. We also tend to mask our true feelings while observing the expressions of others in an ambiguous situation. Masking our emotions leads to the creation of a pluralistic ignorance, in which we fool each other into defining the situation as a nonemergency, thus reducing the chances of intervention or increasing the time until intervention takes place. The presence of others also diffuses the responsibility for action, so that any specific individual feels less responsibility to act. These factors contribute to the paradoxical finding that the likelihood of a person in need receiving help is often greatest when there is only one potential helper and decreases as the number of people present in the situation increases. This chapter concluded with a discussion of the debate regarding altruistic and egoistic motives for helping. There is evidence that, under some circumstances, people may help one another without receiving any external or internal reward. However, these results have been reinterpreted, and additional data presented, to support the argument that a helper always receives some type of benefit for his or her benevolence.

KEY TERMS

balance theory, *269*
rationalization, *271*
pre-bet bolstering, *274*
self-perception theory, *276*
coaction effect/audience
   effect, *279*
dominant response/challenge
   response/vasodilation/threat
   response, *280*
conformity/autokinetic
   effect, *281*

distortion of judgment
   (informational social
   influence)/distortion of action
   (normative social influence),
   282
compliance, *285*
foot-in-the-door effect (FITD)/
   door-in-the-face effect
   (DITF), *286*
reciprocal concessions/contrast
   effect, *287*

obedience, *288*
detached responsibility/
   deindividuation, *290*
pluralistic ignorance, *294*
diffusion of responsibility, *295*
bystander effect/empathy, *296*
altruistic, *297*
egoistic, *298*

SUGGESTIONS FOR FURTHER READING

Bem, D. (1967). Self-Perception: An alternative explanation of cognitive dissonance phenomena. *Psychological Review, 74*, 183–200. Bem presents his case that the results of dissonance studies can be better explained using self-perception theory, which does not include the motivational state of cognitive dissonance.

Blascovich, J., Mendes, W. B., Hunter, S., & Salomon, K. (1999). Social "facilitation" as challenge and threat. *Journal of Personality and Social Psychology, 77*, 68–77. The authors of this article present evidence that the presence of others can help or hinder one's performance depending on whether a physiological challenge or threat response is elicited.

Cialdini, R. (2009). *Influence: Science and Practice* (5th ed.). Boston, MA: Pearson/Allyn/Bacon. This book describes the research on and practical applications of techniques of social influence, including the foot-in-the-door and door-in-the-face techniques.

Festinger, L., & Carlsmith, J. (1959). Cognitive consequences of forced compliance. *Journal of Abnormal and Social Psychology, 58*, 203–210. This article reports the classic study in which participants who received a small reward for lying exhibited greater attitude change than those who lied for a large reward, presumably because the small reward produced cognitive dissonance which motivated the attitude change.

Festinger, L., Riecken, H. W., & Schachter, S. (1956). *When Prophecy Fails*. Minneapolis: University of Minnesota Press. This small book describes the field observations conducted by Festinger and his colleagues on the group that expected the world to come to an end. It is fascinating reading.

Latané, B., & Darley, J. M. (1970). *The Unresponsive Bystander: Why Doesn't He Help?* New York:

Appleton-Century-Crofts. This book describes many of the initial experiments conducted by Latané and Darley on helping behavior.

Milgram, S. (1974). *Obedience to Authority*. New York: Harper & Row. This book summarizes Milgram's studies of obedience.

WEB RESOURCES

A 21st century demonstration of obedience using the Milgram protocol http://www.youtube.com/watch?v=y6GxIuljT3w

A discussion of the foot-in-the-door and door-in-the-face effects http://healthyinfluence.com/wordpress/steves-primer-of-practical-persuasion-3-0/var/sequential-messages/

A demonstration of Asch's conformity protocol http://www.youtube.com/watch?v=iRh5qy09nNw

A site devoted to theory and research on cognitive dissonance http://cognitive-dissonance.behaviouralfinance.net/

A video demonstration of the bystander effect http://www.youtube.com/watch?v=OSsPfbup0ac&feature=related

CHAPTER 10

Cognitive Motivation: Attribution Approaches

CHAPTER PREVIEW

This chapter is concerned with the following questions:

1. How can we explain the cause-and-effect relationships that people make concerning motivated behavior?

2. What are the major theories of attribution?

3. How are we biased in the attributions that we make?

4. How has attribution theory been applied to research on achievement and learned helplessness?

On Friday July 22, 2011, a 32-year-old Norwegian man named Anders Behring Breivik, who was reportedly upset because his country's population demographics were changing due to lenient immigration policies, detonated a bomb outside the office of Norway's Prime Minister in Oslo. He then traveled to a lake 28 miles from the city. Heavily armed and dressed in a blue uniform, in which he could be mistaken for a police officer, he took a boat to a nearby island. Here he entered a summer camp that was occupied by about 600 youths, who by this time were aware of the bombing. He began shooting. Witnesses said he went from tent to tent firing at whomever he saw. Some youths ran toward him because his clothing led them to believe that he was there to help. He shot and killed them. The horror on the island lasted for approximately 90 minutes until police arrived and he surrendered. In all, 77 people lie dead from the two attacks.

The first question on most people's lips was: "Why?" What explanation would help us understand how such events could occur? We will probably never completely understand why this man felt compelled to act the way he did, but the point of this chapter is that we all try to make sense of the events around us, not only tragic incidents such as those described in the previous paragraph, but also everyday events such as why the driver in the car behind me is so impatient, or why my friend seems very happy today.

The study of how we make decisions concerning the events we experience is called **attribution theory**, and it has been a subject of considerable interest to social psychologists. Indeed, there are over 5000 journal articles with the term *attribution* in the title! Obviously we can only present a fraction of that information here. We will concentrate on some of the major theories of attribution with an emphasis on the motivational components of those theories. We then discuss common biases that occur when we make attributions, followed by some practical applications of research findings in this field. We begin with an overview of attribution theory.

Attribution Theory

Attribution theory, or more correctly, "attribution theories" because there are many different theories of attribution, primarily concerns factors assumed by the general public to cause people's behavior. People thus *attribute* behavior to particular factors—usually either to consistent personality characteristics (termed **dispositions**) or to aspects of the social **situation** of the persons involved. Attribution theory examines the explanations at which we arrive both when we observe someone else's behavior and also when we observe our own behavior and relates these explanations to observable characteristics of the individual and the situation.

Though it is debatable whether the attributions we make are always motivational in nature, it seems clear that attributions, once made, do serve to alter future behavior, rather like motivational variables are thought to do. Before we discuss some of the major theories of attribution that researchers have proposed, we first review the basic assumptions that underlie the study of attribution.

Attribution theory rests on three basic assumptions (Jones, Kanouse, Kelley, Nisbett, Valins, & Weiner, 1972). First, it assumes that *we do attempt to determine the causes of both our own behavior and that of others.* More generally, many theorists believe that we are motivated to seek out information that helps us make attributions about all cause-and-effect relationships. Why? Shermer (1997) proposes that causal reasoning is evolutionarily adaptive; it helps us to understand and consequently control our environment. It certainly would have been an advantage for our ancestors to learn animal migration patterns, which foods are poisonous, the meaning of threat displays in animals, etc. According to Shermer, we are the descendants of those individuals who were best able to correctly attribute cause-and-effect relationships.

Attributions of human behavior also stem from a need to control our environment (e.g., Pittman & Pittman, 1980). Understanding the motive behind another person's action gives us cues as to how to respond. For example, if a friend compliments us on our appearance, we would likely conclude that his or her statement was genuine. However, if a salesperson said the same thing, we might attribute the comment to an ulterior motive and become more cautious in our interaction with him or her. Thus, understanding the behavior of others is very important to us. It may be so adaptive, in fact, that we make rudimentary attempts to do it when we are only 6 months old (Woodward, 1998).

Note that this assumption does not require that we assign causes to all our behaviors or to all the behaviors of others. There are simply too many behaviors about which we can make attributions. Not surprisingly, we seem most likely to attribute behaviors that have some importance to us. For example, acts that are highly unusual or distressing are likely to trigger attributional processes (e.g., Kanazawa, 1992). Certainly the murderous behavior of Anders Behring Breivik meets both of these criteria.

The second assumption underlying attribution theory is that *the assignment of causes to behavior is not done randomly; that is, rules exist that can explain how we come to the conclusions we do about the causes of behavior.* In this regard Beck (1978) has pointed out the conceptual similarity between expectancies and attributions. An expectancy, as he noted, is a belief (cognition) that one thing will follow from another (e.g., "If I put money into the machine, I'll get a soda."). An attribution is also a belief but is often the reverse of an expectancy; that is, an attribution is a belief that one thing has followed as a result of another thing (e.g., "The soda came out because I put money into the machine."). Thus, expectancies and attributions have a good deal in common. What differs is the time at which we consider the linked events. Thus, when the cause has occurred, I expect the effect; after observing the effect, I attribute the cause.

Of course we also have expectancies that do not involve cause and effect. For example, I expect my car to be in the garage when I open the garage door, but I don't believe that my opening of the garage door caused the car to be there. Thus not all expectancies are equivalent to attributions.[1]

Nevertheless, Beck's analysis suggests that much of the research reported in Chapter 8, where expectancy was emphasized as an important factor in behaviors such as achievement, could just as easily be analyzed from an attribution standpoint. That is exactly what has happened, and later in this chapter we will briefly consider an attributional analysis of achievement motivation.

The final assumption that attribution theories rest upon is that *the causes attributed to particular behaviors will influence subsequent emotional and nonemotional behaviors.* The attributions we make, then, may activate other motives. Consider the example of the insincere salesperson discussed previously.

In summary, attribution theories propose that we are motivated to try to understand the environment in which we are immersed. This environment includes people with whom we interact and situations in which those interactions occur. Having obtained sufficient information, we cognitively process it according to relatively standard rules—many of them currently unknown—and make decisions (attributions) concerning how one event is related to another. One of the first people to study this process was Fritz Heider, whose theory we will now explore.

Heider's Naive Psychology

The origin of attribution theory is properly attributed to Fritz Heider. You may recall from Chapter 9 that Heider was also responsible for balance theory which, as we will see, can help to explain the motivation for attributions to occur. Heider (1944) first outlined some of his thoughts on the attribution of behavior in a review paper. Later he formalized his thinking into what he termed a **naive psychology** (1958). Heider chose the term *naive* to emphasize the point of his main

interest—how the average person, who is presumably naive about how behaviors are objectively determined, decides what are the causes of a behavior. Thus he was not interested in how an objectively trained observer might attribute behavior but how you and I in our everyday affairs attribute causality.

Heider pointed out that logically one could attribute behaviors either to forces within the individual (dispositions) or to forces external to the individual (situational factors). Dispositions include such factors as needs, wishes, and emotions, as well as abilities, intentions, and one's willingness to work (exertion). Dispositions have usually been divided into **abilities** and **motivations**, with motivation being further subdivided into **intention** (the cognitive plan to behave in a particular way) and **exertion** (the amount of effort that one is willing to put into the behavior). Situational attributions include **task difficulty** and **luck**. Thus when we judge another's behavior (or our own), we may attribute the observed behavior to ability (or lack thereof), intention, exertion, task difficulty, or luck.

Figure 10.1 depicts Heider's model. To illustrate, consider the following example: You are driving on a crowded highway when another driver cuts in front

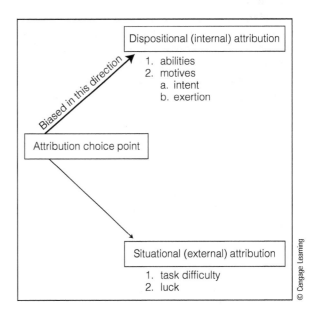

FIGURE 10.1 Diagram of Heider's attribution model.

---

[1] I thank Dr. Mark Lepper for pointing out this distinction to me.

of you without using his turn signal, causing you to slam on your brakes to avoid a collision. According to Heider, we can attribute the other driver's behavior to dispositional factors (e.g., "he is a jerk," or "he is a bad driver"). Alternatively, we could attribute the behavior to situational factors (e.g., "maybe he didn't see me," or "he might have been distracted"). A dispositional attribution could be based on ability (e.g., "he is a bad driver") or motivation, which could involve intention (e.g., "that jerk, he did that on purpose") or exertion (e.g., "he was too lazy to use a turn signal or to look in his mirror"). A situational attribution could be made if we considered task difficulty (e.g., "traffic is really bad today, everyone is impatient") or luck (e.g. "maybe something went wrong with his car").

We might, of course, attribute a behavior to varying degrees of each of these factors, but Heider suggested that as a rule we tend to attribute behavior to dispositional as opposed to situational causes. According to Heider, the attribution rules are biased toward personal causation (Be honest, what type of attribution are you likely to make if someone cuts you off in traffic?).

The tendency to attribute behavior to stable, internal characteristics has been termed the *fundamental attribution error* (Jones, 1979; Ross, 1977) because our attributions clearly tend to be biased against situational explanations (see also Harvey, Town, & Yarkin, 1981; Reeder, 1982). Notice in Figure 10.1 that the attribution choice point represents the point at which the person is trying to decide how to attribute the behavior in question. The heavy arrow pointing toward dispositional attributions indicates the bias that exists toward choosing that alternative. There has been much research on the fundamental attribution error, including work that indicates that it may not be as "fundamental" as we once thought. We will return to this topic later in this chapter.

One final point bears mention. Heider recognized that his balance and attribution theories were related and could be subsumed under a more general theory of social perception. Unfortunately he never made his case explicitly. Decades after Heider's seminal works, Christian Crandall and

colleagues (Crandall, Silvia, N'Gbala, Tsang, & Dawson, 2007) have made a compelling argument on Heider's behalf. They contend that our desire for balance can motivate us to make certain attributions rather than others. For example, if you discover that the person who cut you off in traffic is a close friend, you may change your dispositional attribution (e.g., "he's a jerk") to a situational one (e.g., "he didn't see me") so that your mutually positive relationship with your friend stays in balance. In addition, attributions can motivate behavior that maintains balance. If you consider yourself a good athlete, but you cannot forget how terribly you played in yesterday's game, you may: a) attribute the poor outcome to lack of effort rather than lack of ability; and, b) use this experience to motivate you to practice much harder for the next contest, which should result in better performance, thus maintaining balance with your belief in your ability. Thus, attributions that maintain balance can be both a cause and a consequence of motivation (Crandall, Silvia, N'Gbala, Tsang, & Dawson, 2007).

Like all theories, Heider's attribution model is not perfect. A major problem with his approach was that it did not generate specific hypotheses that were easily testable in the laboratory. His theory was, rather, a general framework that left the specific determinants of attributions unspecified. But it did compel later theorists to build on Heider's foundation.

The Jones and Davis Correspondent Inference Theory

Jones and Davis (1965) agreed with Heider that dispositional attributions are more frequent than situational ones. They expanded Heider's approach in an attempt to make the components of dispositional attributions more specific. They believe that people making a causal attribution observe a person's behavior and its inferred effects in the context in which it occurs. That is, people observe a behavior and then make an *inference* about the intent of the behavior. In making an attribution, Jones and Davis believed that we look for a *correspondence* between the observed behavior, the inferred intent of that behavior, and a person's disposition. For example, suppose you are walking down the street and notice a driver whose car is stuck in the snow. A person named Seth stops his vehicle, gets out, and helps the driver to push her car in order to gain traction. You may make an inference that Seth's intent is to help the stranded woman, which corresponds to both the helpful act as well as to a dispositional attribution that Seth is kind or helpful. But, Jones and Davis believe that there are several other factors that we consider before we make a dispositional attribution such as this one.

First, the person's behavior must reflect some degree of **choice**. This includes not only the choice of engaging in the behavior versus doing nothing but, more importantly, a choice between multiple behaviors that could have been performed. If a person has little or no choice, we are likely to attribute his or her behavior to the situation. For example, suppose Seth's vehicle was blocked by the woman's car on a narrow street, and the only way Seth could have continued on his way was if he helped her. Thus, Seth did not have much choice except to help. In this case, we are less likely to make a dispositional attribution because Seth's choice of behavior was highly constrained by the situation. But now suppose Seth had enough room to drive around the stranded car if he chose to do so. If he decided to help in this situation, a dispositional attribution is more likely because he chose the helpful option over other possible behaviors.

Jones and Harris (1967) conducted several studies that support the contention that freely chosen behaviors lead to dispositional attributions. In one experiment, undergraduate research participants read an essay that critiqued the way Fidel Castro, who was the prime minister of Cuba at the time, was leading his country. Cuba was a Cold War ally of the Soviet Union when this study was conducted, so Castro was quite unpopular among most Americans. The essay, which was supposedly a fellow student's answer to a question on a political science exam, was either pro-Castro or anti-Castro in tone. A second variable that Jones and Harris

manipulated was whether instructions to the exam question *required* the fictitious student to take either the pro- or anti-Castro position (i.e., the No-Choice condition) or if the student was allowed to choose which position to take (i.e., the Choice condition).

After reading the essay, participants were asked to estimate the student's true attitude toward Castro on a 10-item scale. The researchers predicted that participants would be more likely to assume that the essay reflected the student's true attitude when the student could choose which essay to write, and thus would be most likely to make a dispositional attribution in the two Choice conditions. Figure 10.2 displays the results of the study, which supported the researchers' predictions. Participants who read the anti-Castro essay perceived that the student held a negative view of Castro, especially in the Choice condition. This pattern was reversed in the pro-Castro conditions. Thus, participants were more likely to make dispositional attributions when they believed the student chose to engage in the behavior willingly.

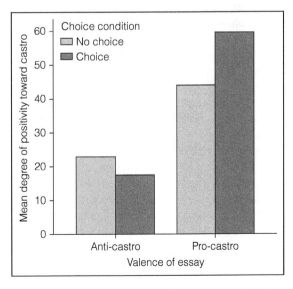

FIGURE 10.2 Attitude toward Castro as a function of level of choice and tone of essay. Data from Jones and Harris, 1967.

Assuming we perceive some level of choice in an actor's behavior,[2] Jones and Davis believe that two other factors are considered in our attribution decision. One is the level of **social desirability** associated with the behavior. A socially desirable behavior is one that is approved of and performed by most people. According to Jones and Davis, because socially desirable behaviors are common, they don't tell us as much about a person's disposition as do less socially desirable behaviors. For example, consider two people, Bill and Jack, who are both opposed to a proposed local zoning law. Bill writes a letter to his representative expressing his opposition. Jack, on the other hand, bursts into a council meeting and begins to scream obscenities at the legislators. Because Bill's behavior was high in social desirability, an observer would have difficulty forming a dispositional attribution about him. The observer would have a much easier time concluding what type of person Jack is. Similarly, helping is socially desirable, so Seth's choice to push the car tells us less about him than if he had chosen to stop his car and throw snowballs at the struggling motorist.

Jones and Davis suggested that another factor we consider when we make decisions about the causes of behavior is what they termed **noncommon effects**. Some parts of most behaviors that we observe are common to several alternative attributions. Other parts of an observed behavior, however, will be unique, and it is these unique aspects that allow us to make our attributions. In Jones and Davis's terms, the noncommon correspondences provide information to us about the causes of the behavior. Consider a football coach who is unhappy with the performance of the offensive line on his team. One effect he wants to accomplish is to get this message to the linemen. He could easily do this by calling a meeting with them to express his displeasure. However, suppose he wishes to accomplish another effect, and that is to motivate them to play and practice harder by challenging them in public. In this case he chooses to "call out" the players in a newspaper interview. Both the private meeting and the newspaper interview would accomplish the first effect. But the second and, in this case, noncommon effect is only accomplished by the interview. Similarly, if Seth simply wanted to leave the situation he could have driven around the woman's car. But if he found her attractive and wanted to exchange phone numbers with her, this noncommon effect is best accomplished by helping her. According to Jones and Davis, the noncommon effects tell us more about the actor's intention, which then allows us to make a correspondent inference about their disposition.

Let us return to the horrific behavior of Anders Behring Breivik. What could have motivated him to kill 77 people? If we apply the correspondent inference theory of Jones and Davis, we could consider several factors, all of which point to a dispositional attribution. First, he has admitted that he chose to perform his action willingly—his behavior was not constrained by the situation. Sadly, few acts are lower in social desirability than his. Finally, although he could have accomplished the effect of making his views known by attending a rally or protesting against the government, his behavior after he was apprehended indicates that he also valued the noncommon effect of becoming famous or, in his case, infamous.

Jones and Davis, then, expanded on Heider's work in an attempt to specify some of the factors involved in making dispositional attributions. Unfortunately, correspondent inference theory did not generate as much research activity as some other theories of motivation, and this makes it difficult to validate the theory empirically. In addition, correspondent inference theory had little to say about attributions that we make about our own behavior. Around the same time that Jones and Davis were working, Harold Kelley developed another theory of attribution, which was also an extension of Heider's ideas. Kelley's theory is presented in the next section.

Kelley's Covariation Theory

Kelley (1967, 1971, 1972, 1973) believed that we have a need to control the environment in which we interact. In order to gain control, we must first

---

[2]In attribution theory, the term *actor* denotes the person who engages in a behavior and the term *observer* refers to someone who is making an attribution about the actor.

gather information and determine what is causing particular changes to occur. In other words, our attributions are attempts to specify how events are causally related to each other.

Causal attributions are regarded as the result of a complex interaction between several possible causal agents. Kelley argued that when we make attributions about events, we choose the explanations that best fit the observations. This is true whether we are making attributions about our own behavior or that of others. For Kelley, making attributions can be likened to generating a series of hypotheses concerning the causes of a particular event, then, through our observations and logical processes, eliminating alternatives until we reach the most logical explanation for the event. Kelley compared the attribution process to the way in which a scientist goes about testing an experimental question. Both attributions and scientific hypotheses are based on the logical elimination of alternatives.

Kelley argued that several principles guide our attribution decisions. A major principle used in the attribution process is that of **covariation**. Covariation (or correlation) across time is an important way in which we are able to make a judgment about causality. Although not all events that correlate with one another reflect a causal relationship, all causal relationships are correlational. Thus, if events do not correlate with each other, they cannot be causally linked. Because there are usually several possible causes for any outcome, only those events that are consistently related to a particular outcome are likely to be causal. For example, suppose you receive an "A" on a test for which you studied very hard. The good grade may have been the result of luck, an easy test, or the fact that you studied. If you then take another test after not studying very hard and get a "C," the causal attribution "good grades result from studying" will be strengthened because studying and good grades covary (i.e., study hard = A; do not study hard = C). According to Kelley, we are sensitive to this covariation of cause and outcome. Across time the alternative hypotheses will be eliminated because they will not be consistently related to the outcome.

What factors do we look for in assessing covariation? Kelley proposed that, when possible,

we look for patterns of past behavior to help us make attributions. For example, suppose we notice that Martin has lost a lot of money on a "get rich quick" scam that he saw on the Internet. Several attributions are possible. Perhaps Martin is easy to fool—a dispositional attribution. Or, maybe the scam was very well-designed and convincing, which would lead to a situational attribution. Kelley articulated three dimensions of past behavior that are particularly relevant in helping us decide what type of attribution to make. The first of these dimensions is **distinctiveness**, which refers to the degree to which the behavior is unique. Does Martin respond to lots of other ads and infomercials that promise more than they deliver? If the answer is "yes," then Martin's behavior is low in distinctiveness (i.e., it is not a unique, distinct event). If the answer is "no," Martin's behavior is high in distinctiveness. Other things held constant, behaviors low in distinctiveness lead to dispositional attributions (e.g., Martin is easy to fool); behaviors high in distinctiveness produce situational attributions (e.g., this must be a good scam—Martin isn't one to fall for these things).

Kelley's second dimension is **consensus**, which means that we examine other people's behavior in the same situation. How many other people have been fooled by this scam? If we know of no one else who has been cheated, then consensus is low and we may be tempted to make a dispositional attribution about Martin. If lots of people were taken in by the scam, then consensus is high, which may lead us to a situational attribution.

The third dimension is **consistency**, which refers to the frequency with which the actor engages in the specific behavior in question. Has Martin been investing in this scam for a long time or was this a "one-shot deal"? If Martin is a first-time investor, the behavior is low in consistency, and the attribution is likely to be situational, other factors held constant. If Martin has been putting money into the scam for a long time, then the behavior is high in consistency. Behaviors that are high in consistency could lead to dispositional or situational attributions, depending on the other information that we have available. For example,

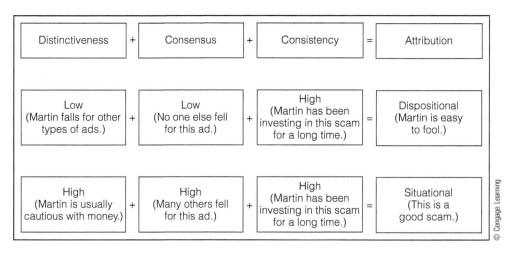

FIGURE 10.3 Attributions in Kelley's covariation model.

if Martin has been investing for a long time but no one else has been doing so (i.e., consensus is low), then a dispositional attribution is likely. However if Martin has been investing along with many others (i.e., consensus is high), we may make a situational attribution.

Because each of Kelley's three dimensions has two possible outcomes ("high" or "low"), there are $2 \times 2 \times 2 = 8$ different possible scenarios involving combinations of distinctiveness, consistency, and consensus. In practice, however, the most straightforward attributions occur under the two scenarios depicted in Figure 10.3. In the scenario depicted in the middle row, we find that Martin falls for all sorts of offers that are too good to be true, so distinctiveness is low; no one else seems to have lost money in this particular scam, so consensus is low; and Martin has been investing money in this scam for quite some time, so consistency is high. In this instance, we are likely to make a dispositional attribution: Martin is easy to fool. In the scenario in the bottom row, however, we find that Martin is usually cautious with his money (distinctiveness is high), lots of other people "fell for" this scam (consensus is high), and Martin had been investing for quite some time (consistency is high). In this case, we are likely to infer that some aspect of the situation, such as a well-orchestrated scam, caused Martin's behavior.

If we apply Kelley's covariation model to the behavior of Anders Behring Breivik, we see that his behavior, although extreme, is low in distinctiveness because he has engaged in other acts of opposition such as joining extremist groups and posting his anti-immigration stance on the Internet. Consensus is low as well—very few Norwegians espouse his extremist position. However, consistency is high—he spent a great deal of time and effort planning the attacks. Thus, a dispositional attribution seems appropriate, according to Kelley's model.

The attribution theories of Heider, Jones and Davis, and Kelley emphasize the information-processing aspects of human behavior. We accumulate information and, based on that information, attribute the causes of behavior in various ways. Thus, these theories focus on the assumptions that a) we do attempt to determine the causes of behavior and b) that we do this based on a series of rules. Recall that these were two of the three assumptions that we mentioned earlier as being common to all attribution theories. But what about the third assumption—that our attributions, once made, will influence our subsequent behavior? The theories we have discussed thus far have concentrated on how attributions are formed and, although they also assume that attributions influence our subsequent behavior, these theories had little to say about this part of the process. Thus, other theories were needed to explain the consequences of our attributions. One of the most influential of these was developed by Bernard Weiner.

Weiner's Attributional Analysis of Achievement Behavior

Weiner and his colleagues developed an attributional theory that was initially used to explain achievement motivation (Frieze, 1976; Weiner, 1972, 1974; Weiner, Frieze, Kukla, Reed, Rest, & Rosenbaum, 1971; Weiner & Kukla, 1970; Weiner, Russell, & Lerman, 1978), but later the theory was applied to a broader range of topics. As we saw in Chapter 9, much research has been conducted in an attempt to understand achievement motivation from an expectancy-value perspective. Recall that in an expectancy-value framework, achievement behavior is explained in terms of several factors, one of which is one's perceived likelihood of future success. Weiner broadened the question to include the attributions that we make when attempting to explain *past* successes and failures and how these attributions influence our emotions, expectancies of future success/failure, and subsequent behavior. In doing so, he incorporated many ideas that we have presented previously, including those of Heider, Atkinson, and Rotter. We present an abbreviated version of Weiner's theory here. For the full model and a description of its evolution, the reader should consult Weiner (1985) and Weiner (2010), respectively.

Weiner argued that at least four elements are important in our interpretation of the outcome of an achievement-related event. The elements are **ability**, **effort**, **task difficulty**, and **luck**. When we engage in achievement-related behavior, we will ascribe our success or failure at the task as a result of one or various combinations of these elements.

Weiner's approach assumed that the inferences we make about our abilities primarily result from earlier experiences. Past successes will lead us to conclude that we have certain abilities in certain areas, while past failures will reduce our beliefs in our abilities. Our inferences about our abilities are

not judged in a vacuum but in relation to the performance of others, a process known as **social comparison**. If we succeed at a task in which others fail, we are likely to perceive ourselves as capable individuals.

We judge the effort that we have put into a task using such factors as time spent, muscular effort, and so on. Interestingly, we tend to perceive ourselves as having expended more effort when we are successful at a task (Weiner & Kukla, 1970). This suggests that we associate effort with a successful outcome because they tend to go together in our experience.

We apparently judge task difficulty primarily via social comparison, though objective characteristics of the task also play a part. We infer the difficulty of a task by observing the percentage of other people who succeed. When many or most others succeed, we judge the task to be easy; observing that most others fail leads us to infer that the task is very difficult.

Luck is assumed to be involved in a task when we have no control over the outcome of the task. For example, we tend to ascribe the attainment of a particular goal to luck when we can detect no relationship between our behavior and the successful attainment of that goal. Likewise, if we fail at a task but the failure seems unrelated to anything we have done, we tend to ascribe it to bad luck.

Weiner argues that these four elements differ along three causal dimensions: **locus**, **stability**, and **controllability**. You may find it helpful to refer to Figure 10.4 while reading the description of these dimensions. Locus refers to whether the cause is believed to be something *internal* or *external* to the individual. Both ability and effort can be regarded as internal characteristics. We tend to regard our abilities and the effort we expend in working toward a goal as dispositional in character. Conversely, the difficulty of the task and luck can be considered situational factors, which are external to the individual. Thus attributions concerning outcomes that involve task difficulty or luck will tend to be situational rather than dispositional.

The second dimension refers to the likelihood that the cause can be altered in the future. If the

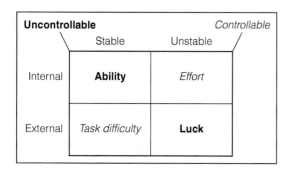

FIGURE 10.4 The causal ascriptions of ability, effort, task difficulty and luck classified according to the dimensions of internal/external, stable/unstable and controllable/uncontrollable causes. Adapted from Weiner, 1985 and Weiner, 2010.

cause is believed to be something that will not change, it is *stable*; if change is possible, it is *unstable*. Abilities do not swing drastically from moment to moment, nor does the difficulty of a task. Effort and luck, on the other hand, are rather unstable. We may work diligently on one project but put little effort into another. Likewise, luck fluctuates from moment to moment.

Finally, some causes are *controllable* and some are *uncontrollable* by one's self or by others. Consider your performance on an algebra exam. You do not have control over your aptitude in math, nor over whether your guess on a particular multiple choice question will be correct or not. Thus, ability and luck are uncontrollable (denoted by the boldface type in Figure 10.4). However, the teacher could make the exam easy or difficult, and you determine how much time you will spend studying. Therefore, task difficulty and effort are under someone's control (denoted by italics in Figure 10.4).

To summarize, each of the four elements has a unique profile of causal dimensions. Ability is internal, stable, and uncontrollable; effort is internal, unstable, and controllable; task difficulty is external, stable, and controllable; and luck is external, unstable, and uncontrollable. As we will see, the level of each of these causal dimensions will determine the emotions and expectancies that an individual experiences, and ultimately their level of motivation.

Weiner has noted that affect plays a multifaceted role in motivation and attribution. First, achievement-related results initially produce what Weiner called *attribution independent* affect. That is, the outcome itself triggers happiness or sadness, depending on whether the person succeeded or failed. No attribution has been made at this point. Once an attribution has been formed, however, a different set of emotions is possible, depending on the causal dimensions that are activated. For example, if one concludes that they succeeded due to their ability, which is internal, stable, and uncontrollable, the resulting emotion should be pride. On the other hand, if one attributes failure to (lack of) effort, which is internal, unstable, and controllable, guilt and regret should result. These more specific emotions are *attribution dependent*; they are determined by the salient causal dimensions which are, in turn, the result of the attribution.

Weiner and colleagues have empirical evidence for their hypothesized relationship between affect, outcomes, and attributions. In one study, Weiner, Russell, and Lerman (1978) presented participants with a brief story concerning success or failure that also contained the reason for the positive or negative outcome. The following is one of the story lines that Weiner used: "Francis studied intensely for a test he took. It was very important for Francis to record a high score on this exam. Francis received an extremely high score on the test. Francis felt that he received this high score because he studied so intensely. How do you think Francis felt upon receiving this score?" (Weiner, Russell, & Lerman, 1978, p. 70).

Participants were asked to indicate the emotional reaction of the individual in the story by selecting emotionally toned words from a list prepared by Weiner. He presented 10 different stories with 10 different reasons for success. The results of the study indicated that some words reappeared in all of the 10 stories of success. These were the attribution-independent emotions such as pleased and happy. Presumably, success usually leads to happiness regardless of why one succeeds. More specific emotions clustered together depending on the attribution that was made. These were the attribution-dependent emotions. For example, success attributed to ability (internal, stable, and uncontrollable) led to choices of words that denoted confidence and competence whereas success attributed to luck (external, unstable, and uncontrollable) led to choices that expressed surprise and astonishment.

In a similar fashion, 11 stories were devised that attributed failure to various causes such as ability, mood, luck, fatigue, and so on. The attribution-independent emotions such as unhappiness and displeasure were common, as predicted. It does not seem to matter why we fail; failing is simply an unpleasant outcome. With respect to attribution-dependent emotions, again it was possible to discriminate between attributions by the emotional words chosen. For example, failure resulting from lack of ability led participants to choose words that reflected incompetence or inadequacy, while failure attributed to lack of effort led to feelings of shame and guilt.

The results of the Weiner et al. study indicate that the relationship between attribution and emotion is complex and that the commonsense view that success at achievement-related activities always leads to feelings of pride and that failure leads to feelings of shame seems oversimplified. One may feel confident and pleased when success is attributed to ability while feeling surprised and astonished when success is attributed to luck. Likewise, failure does not always lead to feelings of shame. Failure resulting from lack of intense effort does elicit guilt and shame as emotionally toned associations, but failure as a result of others' efforts leads to aggressiveness, as evidenced by such words as ferocious, revengeful, and furious.

Weiner argued that the attribution and the associated attribution-dependent affect will influence our expectancies of future success and subsequent motivation. Failure attributed to lack of effort may induce guilt along with increased motivation due to the expectation that greater effort will lead to future success. Conversely, failure due to lack of ability may result in shame, hopelessness, and lack of motivation.

Weiner incorporated the elements, causal dimensions, emotions, and expectancies into his broader attribution theory of achievement motivation, an abbreviated version of which is depicted in Figure 10.5. The progression begins with an achievement-related outcome, which produces a change in attribution-independent emotion. Success produces happiness and failure begets sadness. Next, we look for a cause, especially if the outcome was negative or unexpected, and if the event was important to us. This is where we look to our past successes and failures, and compare our performance to that of others. Based on the result of this process, we attribute our current outcome to ability, effort, task difficulty, or luck. The element chosen in this step will determine the levels of the locus, stability, and controllability dimensions. This profile will produce psychological consequences such as changes in emotions and expectancies and, ultimately, behavioral consequences such as increased exertion or giving up. Refer to Figure 10.5 as you consider the following examples that illustrate Weiner's theory.

Suppose that a married couple, Lorraine and Leon, decide to go on the same diet together. Unfortunately, Leon was unable to strictly follow the diet and thus did not lose any weight. This is a negative outcome that causes him to feel unhappy and to search for the cause of his failure. He recalls that he has failed to stay on other diets no matter how much effort he exerted. He also knows friends who were able to successfully follow this particular diet. He thus attributes his failure to (a lack of) ability—he just does not think he can diet successfully. Recall that ability is an internal, stable, and uncontrollable cause. The psychological consequences of this attribution could include shame and expectancy of failure in the future. Because he does not expect to succeed, a logical but undesirable behavioral consequence would be to stop trying to diet.

Suppose Lorraine also failed to stay on the diet. She too is unhappy, but her search for a cause reveals that she has lost weight every other time she has tried. She notes that on this diet she did not keep track of her food intake as well as she could have because she was preoccupied with

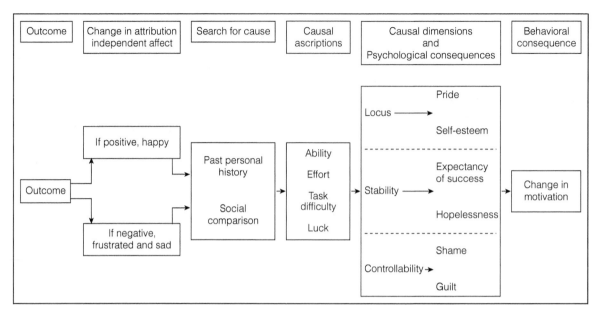

FIGURE 10.5   An abbreviated schematic diagram of Weiner's attribution model. From Weiner, B., "The develop-ment of an attribution-based theory of motivation: A history of ideas," *Educational Psychologist, 45*, 28–36. Copyright © 2010 Taylor & Francis. Reprinted with permission.

work and family issues. Thus, she attributes her fail-ure to a lack of effort, which is an internal, unstable, and controllable cause. In terms of psychological consequences, she may regret the lost opportunity, but she should still expect to succeed the next time she tries. This combination of regret and expec-tancy may cause her to be even more motivated to start the diet anew, which is a positive behavioral consequence. As these examples illustrate, it is pos-sible for two or more people to be subjected to the same outcome, yet experience different affective and motivational consequences.

Given the quantity of attributions that we make each day and the scope and applicability of the attribution theories discussed above, it seems clear then that we expend a good deal of effort trying to explain the behavior of ourselves and others. These attributions can have significant psy-chological and motivational consequences. Unfor-tunately, they can also be incorrect—and often in predictable ways. Some of the most common biases in attribution will now be discussed.

Biases in Attribution

At the beginning of this chapter we listed some assumptions that are common to all theories of attri-bution. Note that there is an important omission from this list: In no case is it assumed that the attri-butions that we make are accurate. Attributions are our perceptions of why a behavior occurred. These perceptions may, but often do not, match reality. Nonetheless, they do help us to explain behavior and they can motivate and guide our future actions. For example, suppose someone cuts you off in traf-fic. A few minutes later your car is sitting next to his at a stoplight, and he opens his window and asks you for directions. The tone of your response will prob-ably depend on the attribution that you just made about him, regardless of whether or not your attri-bution is correct.

Why do we continually make attributions, even though they may be erroneous? One possibil-ity is that we are motivated to understand our surroundings—or at least to think we understand them. Uncertainty can be an uncomfortable feeling, especially if the behavior that we are uncertain about is important to us. The problem is that we rarely have all the information necessary to be sure we are making the correct attribution, which means that our attributions may be biased, often in a way that benefits us.

The Self-Serving Bias Suppose that two teenagers, Mary and Christine, are in the process of obtaining their driver's licenses. They take their driving skills test on the same day. Christine passes and Mary fails. Christine could attribute the result to a disposition (e.g., "I am a good driver") or to the situation (e.g., "the test is very easy"). Mary has the same choice between a dispositional attribution (e.g., "I am a bad driver") and a situational one (e.g., "The test wasn't fair"). Which attributions are more likely? If you predicted that Christine is more likely to make a dispositional attribution, and that Mary is more likely to attribute failure to the situation, you have identified the self-serving attribution bias.

Researchers have long known about the **self-serving bias**, or the tendency to take credit for success and to avoid responsibility for failure (e.g., Heider, 1958; Johnson, Feigenbaum, & Weiby, 1964; Miller & Ross, 1975). For example, participants in the Johnson et al. (1964) study were instructed to teach math to confederates who posed as students. Those teachers whose students performed well attributed the outcome to their teaching ability (disposition); those whose students performed poorly attributed the result to shortcomings of the students (situation).

The self-serving bias is a robust phenomenon (Campbell & Sedikides, 1999; Zuckerman, 1979a), and it has been documented in both Western and non-Western cultures (e.g., Jain & Mal, 1984; Kudo & Numazaki, 2003; Nathawat & Singh, 1997), although the bias is less pronounced in non-Western cultures (Mezulis, Abramson, Hyde, & Hankin, 2004). Mezulis and colleagues (2004) conducted a meta-analysis of over 200 studies and found an overall effect size that was very large, indicating that the self-serving bias is both pervasive and

strong. In addition they found that, although the bias exists in all age groups, it is highest in childhood and late adulthood. Interestingly, people with psychopathologies displayed less of a bias, indicating that self-enhancement may be an adaptive process.

Why does it occur? One explanation involves the motives of **self-assessment** and **self-enhancement** (Duval & Silvia, 2002; Sedikides & Strube, 1997; Silvia & Duval, 2001). We are motivated to accurately assess our abilities, but we are also motivated to maintain a positive self-image. So, if given a choice, we will make attributions that are favorable to our self-image.

Cognitive "information processing" errors may also contribute to the self-serving bias. For example, our expectations may play a role in our attributions in the sense that we usually engage in behaviors at which we expect to succeed. In addition, events that are anticipated have been found to produce dispositional attributions (Miller & Ross, 1975). Thus, if we anticipate that we will succeed, and then achieve success, a dispositional attribution is logical.

Thus, the self-serving bias may be influenced by both motivational and cognitive factors (Shepperd, Malone, & Sweeny, 2008). However, the bias persists even when cognitive factors are controlled (e.g., Miller, 1976; Sedikides, Campbell, Reeder, & Elliot, 1998). Therefore, the self-serving bias appears to have a fundamental motivational component. Furthermore, there is evidence that this process may occur automatically. Krusemark, Campbell, and Clementz (2008) recorded neural activity in people making either self-serving or non-self-serving attributions. They found that the non-self-serving attributions were associated with activity in brain regions responsible for cognitive control and evaluation of outcome expectancies whereas that self-serving attributions did not display this pattern. Thus it appears that unbiased attributions require conscious effort while biased attributions are more reflexive.

In addition to studying the causes of a phenomenon, psychologists are interested in its consequences as well. In the case of the self-serving bias, the possible consequences are intriguing. Chronically denying responsibility for one's failures can protect one's self image, but it can also lead to a sense of unrealistic optimism. On the other hand, the absence of the self-enhancement motive can lead one to depression if one overattributes failures internally and successes externally. Indeed, the self-serving bias is less pronounced in people who are depressed (Mezulis et al., 2004). We will have more to say about this topic when we discuss the phenomenon of learned helplessness below.

The False Consensus Effect Try the following exercise: Think of a television show or musical act that is very popular, but that is one that you absolutely cannot stand to watch or listen to. If you have ever found yourself asking "What can people possibly like about THAT?" you may be exhibiting the **false consensus effect**. This refers to our tendency to believe that most other people think and act the same way that we do.

Like many other topics in psychology, the belief that our evaluations and behaviors are representative of the larger population has been around for quite some time (e.g., Katz and Allport, 1931). However, this effect has only been studied empirically since the 1970s. This line of research began with the studies of Ross, Greene, and House (1977). These researchers asked college students if they would be willing to walk around campus wearing a very large advertising sign. They were then asked to predict the responses of other students to the same request. Both the students who consented to carry the sign and those who refused to do so estimated that approximately 2 out of 3 students would respond the same way that they themselves did. Obviously, both groups cannot be correct.

The false consensus effect has been found to occur across a wide range of behaviors, attitudes, beliefs, and expectations (e.g., Gilovich, Jennings, & Jennings, 1983; Sanders & Mullen, 1983). Although prevalent across many domains, the false consensus effect is especially likely to occur when an individual's attitude or behavior is unpopular or deviant from the majority of his or her reference group (e.g., Henry, Kobus, & Schoeny, 2011; Suls & Wan, 1987). For example, Wolfson (2000)

asked first-year university students to indicate whether they had ever used cannabis (marijuana) or amphetamines. Three categories of participants emerged: a) those who had not used either drug; b) those who had used cannabis only; and, c) those who had used cannabis and amphetamines. Participants were also asked to estimate the percentage of all students who use each drug. The results were intriguing (see Figure 10.6). When estimating cannabis use, nonusers provided the lowest estimate. People who had used cannabis or both cannabis and amphetamines guessed a much higher value. For amphetamines, only the people who had used them estimated a high value. The cannabis-only group and the nonuser group were both nonusers of amphetamines, so they provided lower estimates.

As is the case with the self-serving bias, the false consensus effect is likely influenced by both motivational and cognitive factors. The motives to gain social support and to bolster self-esteem appear to be operating in false consensus estimates, especially

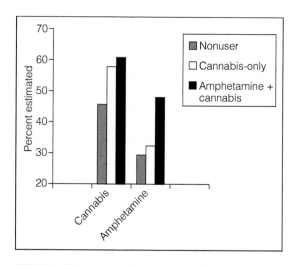

FIGURE 10.6 Estimates of cannabis and amphetamine use made by nonusers, cannabis-only users and amphetamine + cannabis users. From S. Wolfson, "Students' estimates of the prevalence of drug use: Evidence for a false consensus effect." *Psychology of Addictive Behaviors, 14*, 295–298. Copyright © 2000 by the American Psychological Association. Used by permission.

when socially undesirable behaviors or attitudes are involved (Marks & Miller, 1987; Wolfson, 2000). Apparently it makes us feel better to believe that there are others who think and behave the way we do, especially when we are different from the norm. Wolfson (2000) also recognized that there may be cognitive factors influencing this effect. Because we tend to associate with others who share similar interests, it is reasonable to assume that drug users are likely to associate with one another. This **selective exposure** may produce inflated estimates of people who share our interests.

Research on the false consensus effect has led to some changes in the emphasis of public health messages. For example, binge drinking is a problem on college campuses, and many people *perceive* it to be a problem that affects a majority of students.[3] If so, then a public health message that urges students not to conform (e.g., "just because everyone else is doing it doesn't make it right") would be appropriate. However, research has revealed the actual incidence of binge drinking is much lower than what many people perceive it to be (e.g., Marks, Graham, & Hansen, 1992; Perkins, Meilman, Leichliter, Cashin, & Presley, 1999). Thus, many colleges have changed their preventative message to emphasize that binge drinking is the exception rather than the norm. The rationale behind this approach is based on the false consensus effect. If a motive for social support or self-esteem really is important to those who drink heavily, then pointing out that they are a distinct minority should reduce their feeling support/esteem and may cause some binge drinkers to rethink their behavior.

The Actor–Observer Bias   Recall our earlier example in which we asked you to imagine that you were driving along a busy highway and another driver cut you off causing you to slam on your brakes. You are likely to attribute the other driver's behavior to a disposition (e.g., "that guy is a jerk!"). But at one time or another, we have all made errors

while driving. Suppose it had been you who cut off another driver, causing him to brake suddenly to avoid a collision. What attribution might you make about your own behavior? It probably would not be a dispositional attribution (e.g., "I'm a jerk, and I deserve every nasty thing that guy is saying about me right now."). Rather, we are more likely to attribute our own behavior to situational factors (e.g., "I was distracted," or "I didn't see him."). This tendency to infer dispositional attributions of others' behavior but situational attributions of our own behavior is known as the **actor–observer bias**.

Much research has been conducted on this phenomenon (e.g., Jones & Nisbett, 1972). For example, Nisbett, Caputo, Legant, and Marecek (1973) asked male college students to write essays about why they chose to date their current girlfriend and why they picked the college major they did. They were then asked to write similar essays answering the same two questions about their best friend. Responses indicated that participants attributed their own behavior to the situation (e.g., positive characteristics of their girlfriend or their college major), but their friend's behavior to his enduring dispositions (e.g., his likes and dislikes).

Another study by Nisbett et al. (1973) demonstrated the generality of this effect. They found that college students assumed that participants who volunteered to help in one situation would be likely to do so in future, unrelated situations. Thus, the observers generalized from one discrete instance and inferred that the actors' behavior would be consistent across situations. The volunteers themselves, on the other hand, did not rate themselves as more likely to help out in the future. Apparently they were more sensitive to the situational cues that were present. Thus, salience of situational factors is one possible explanation for the actor–observer bias.

Jones and Nisbett pointed out that although behavior is always judged in relation to the situational context, the concept is different for the actor and the observer. The major difference lies, they believed, in the fact that the *actor is aware of his or her own background and past experiences, while the*

---

[3]It should be noted that there is a disagreement about whether the term *binge drinking* is the best way to describe heavy alcohol consumption. See DeJong, 2001 for a discussion.

observer must judge the behavior simply from what is observed. Thus, the guy who cuts you off in traffic may actually be a very nice person, but a few seconds of driving behavior is all you have to go on when making your attribution about him.

Jones and Nisbett also noted that part of the difference between the attributions of the actor and observer results from a *difference in what each attends to within the event.* The actor focuses attention on environmental cues because those are what must be attended to in order to interact successfully. At the same time, the actor will be relatively unaware of his or her own responses, because he or she cannot directly observe them. The observer, however, focuses attention on the actor because the actor is the focal point of the behavior being observed. Thus the observer may be quite unaware of the cues to which the actor is paying attention.

Suppose Shannel is playing tennis while her friend Shianna observes her. Shannel is concentrating her attention on the other player, the ball, the lines of the court, and so forth, because these determine what her next response will be. At the same time, she may be unaware of her stance, movements, and appearance. (My own experience is that attempts to pay such attention to personal details while playing tennis have disastrous results!) Shianna sees Shannel moving back and forth, seemingly always knowing where the ball is going to be, and concludes that she is "a great tennis player"— that is, she makes a dispositional attribution. Shannel in fact had to learn all the various moves and has learned to focus attention on the opponent's eyes, feet, and racket in order to anticipate the next move. Actors will tend to see their own behavior as resulting from these cues rather than from some dispositional characteristic.

Jones and Nisbett's analysis suggests that actors and observers attribute behavior differently because they perceive the behavior from different points of view. Storms (1973) directly tested the perceptual question in an ingenious experiment. Four participants were seated in the configuration depicted in Figure 10.7. Two participants were asked to engage

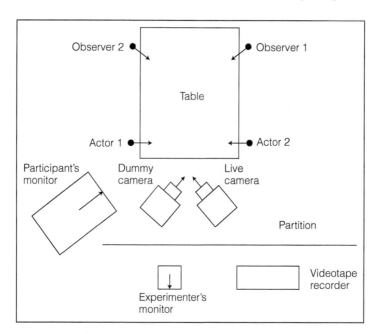

FIGURE 10.7   Seating diagram of Storms' actor-observer study. From M.D. Storms, "Videotape and the attribution process: Reversing actors' and observers' points of view." *Journal of Personality and Social Psychology, 27,* 165–175. Copyright © 1973 by the American Psychological Association. Used by permission.

in a short, unstructured conversation; the other two were instructed to observe the interaction. Consistent with the actor-observer bias, those who participated in the conversation attributed more of their behavior to the situation than did the observers who watched them. Storms, however, also videotaped the conversation from two different points of view (see Figure 10.7). One point of view was what the actor saw during the conversation, while the second was what the observer saw. In a second part of the experiment, a group of actors saw themselves on videotape from the viewpoint of the observer, and a group of observers saw the conversation from the viewpoint of the actor. They were then asked to form attributions about the interaction. Under these conditions the actors attributed more of their own behavior to dispositional characteristics than did the observers.

Apparently the point of view (quite literally) of actor and observer is crucial in the attributions we make. Research has also revealed a more fundamental actor-observer asymmetry: that the perspective of actors and observers may influence the behaviors that they *choose to attend to* and then make attributions about. According to Bertrand Malle and his colleagues (Malle & Knobe, 1997; Malle & Pearce, 2001), actors are more interested in explaining behaviors that are unintentional and unobservable; observers concentrate on behaviors that are intentional and observable. Why should this be so? Actors presumably already know why they performed intentional behaviors (e.g., why they made a phone call), so they are more interested in those that are unintentional (e.g., why they might be blushing). In contrast, observers are most concerned with the intentional behaviors of actors because they can glean more information about the actor from them. Similarly, actors attend less to their observable behaviors (e.g., body language) than they do to their feelings and thoughts. Observers are not privy to an actor's internal states, so they must concentrate on observable behaviors.

It is interesting to note that, unlike the literature on the self-serving bias and the false consensus effect, research reveals that the actor-observer effect

is neither robust nor pervasive. A meta-analysis of over 170 studies found that the overall effect size was very small (Malle, 2006). Malle did find, however, that the effect does appear when certain moderator variables are present. For example, actors are less likely to make dispositional attributions for negative events than are observers, so the valence of the behavior is one moderator of the effect. This led Malle to speculate that the actor–observer asymmetry may simply be a special type of self-serving bias. Because of these results, Malle and colleagues argue that traditional attribution theory may not be the best explanation of actor–observer asymmetry (Malle, Knobe, & Nelson, 2007).

Are the results of actor–observer studies of any practical significance? Martinko and Thomson (1998) believe that actor–observer effects, understood using terms from Kelley's covariation model, can help to explain workplace interactions between supervisors and subordinates. According to Martinko and Thomson, because subordinates (actors) have more knowledge about their own past behavior than supervisors do, they thus have information on the dimension of consistency. Thus, they are more likely to make situational attributions about their workplace behavior, particularly if consistency is low. However, supervisors (observers) are more likely to know how other individuals behave in similar situations, so they have knowledge on the dimension of consensus. Therefore, they are more likely to make dispositional attributions about a worker's behavior, especially when consensus is low.

The Fundamental Attribution Error (Correspondence Bias)   Perhaps the attribution bias that has received the most attention is what has come to be known as the **fundamental attribution error (FAE)**. This refers to our tendency to attribute the behavior of others to stable, internal characteristics, and thus to underestimate the influence of situational factors. Thus, it is related to the actor–observer effect, except that the FAE concentrates on attributions made by observers. It is also sometimes known as the **correspondence bias**

because, when viewed within Jones and Davis' (1965) correspondent inference theory, it refers to an observer's tendency to infer that an actor's behavior *corresponds* to an internal disposition.[4]

We have already presented evidence for the FAE earlier in this chapter. Recall the study by Jones and Harris (1967) in which participants were asked to read essays about Fidel Castro that were supposedly written by fellow college students. The essays were either positive or negative toward Castro, and the participants were led to believe that the student who wrote the essay either took a position freely (Choice condition), or that they were instructed by their professor which position they had to take (No Choice condition). Thus, participants in the No Choice conditions knew that powerful situational factors (i.e., the professor's instructions) constrained what was said in the essay. Refer to the two No Choice conditions in Figure 10.2, which presents the results of this study. Despite knowledge that the writer had no choice of which position to take, the participants used the tone of the essay to infer the writer's true attitude toward Castro, which is evidence for the FAE.

One of the clearest demonstrations of the FAE is presented in a pair of studies by Ross, Amabile, and Steinmetz (1977). In their first experiment they asked same-sex pairs of undergraduates to participate in a quiz game. One participant was assigned the role of "Questioner" and was asked to generate 10 difficult, but not impossible general knowledge trivia questions. The other was the "Contestant" and was asked to answer each of the questions during the game. These roles were assigned randomly by choosing one of two cards placed facedown before the participants. The contestants correctly answered an average of 4 out of the 10 questions, indicating that the items were quite difficult (e.g., "What is the longest glacier in the world?"). After

the game concluded each participant was asked to rate their own level of general knowledge as well as that of the other participant, on a scale of 0–100 where "0" represented "much worse than average" and "100" represented "much better than average."

The results, which are presented on the left and center of Figure 10.8, indicate that the questioners rated themselves and their contestant as relatively average. The contestants, however, viewed the questioners as having more general knowledge than they themselves had. Why? Remember that the roles were assigned at random, so the questioners had a distinct advantage in that they could generate questions on topics with which they were familiar and avoid topics about which they knew little. The contestants failed to take this situational variable into account and attributed greater knowledge to the questioner.

Further evidence for the FAE comes from the second study conducted by Ross et al. (1977). The researchers replicated their first study with a few modifications. First, there were four people present at each "game." One person played the role of

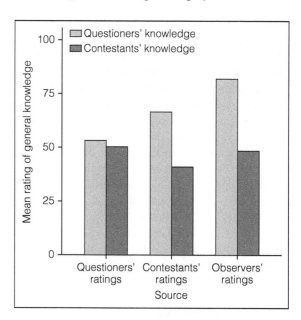

FIGURE 10.8   Ratings of participant's level of general knowledge as a function of their role in a quiz game. Data from Ross, Amabile & Steinmetz, 1977.

---

[4]Krull (2001) and others (e.g., Gawronski, 2004; Hamilton, 1988) have made a distinction between the two phenomena, arguing that correspondence bias is "the tendency to infer that dispositions correspond to behavior" and that the FAE is the "tendency to prefer dispositional attributions over situational attributions." By this definition, then, the FAE is not always an error.

questioner and one was the contestant. In addition, two others served as "observers." The second major change was that, unbeknownst to the observers, the questioner and contestant were both confederates who simulated each of the actual games from the first study. Observers, who believed that all of the roles in the study were assigned at random, provided their ratings of the knowledge of the questioner and contestant at the end of the game. As you can see from the right side of Figure 10.8, the observers' ratings mirrored those of the contestants, indicating that they too failed to consider the constraints of the situation and instead made a dispositional attribution.

Since the 1960s, there have been hundreds of studies on the fundamental attribution error which investigated the prevalence of the FAE when attributions are made about qualities such as attitudes, abilities, emotionality and morality (Gawronski, 2004). We will not attempt to review such a voluminous literature. Rather, we will examine two central themes: the universality of the FAE and the search for its cause(s).

How fundamental is the FAE? One way of addressing this issue is to examine the effect cross-culturally. Is the bias present in people of different cultures? This is a difficult question to answer, in part because there are many different cultures that differ in myriad ways. However, one useful dimension that has helped researchers to study cultural differences is that of individualism-collectivism (Markus & Kitayama, 1994). Theoretically, people from individualistic cultures such as the United States and Australia should be more likely to attribute behaviors to dispositions of the actor, because of the value placed on the individual as the causal agent of behavior. In collectivist cultures, such as India and Japan, the individual is seen as part of a larger social group, and one's individual identity can be subsumed by a group identity. Thus, the FAE should be less likely to occur in collectivist cultures. Is this the case? The short answer is that it depends on how the question is framed.

Krull and his colleagues (1999) draw a distinction between looking for a difference in the frequency of situational vs. dispositional attributions

and assessing the degree to which observers consider situational information when they make a dispositional attribution. In the former case, there is ample evidence that indicates that dispositional inferences are more common in individualistic cultures (e.g., Lee, Hallahan, & Herzog, 1996) and that socialization is responsible for this difference (e.g., Miller, 1984).

However, Krull et al. (1999) contend that it is the latter case that is the true test of the universality of the FAE. That is, when people of different cultures make a dispositional attribution, do the attributions differ in the degree to which they correspond with the actor's behavior? To answer this question, Krull et al. asked students in the United States and Taiwan to participate in a study that was analogous to the Jones and Harris (1967) essay study described earlier. Krull and colleagues found that the FAE occurred, and was equally strong, in both cultures. A similar result was reported by Choi and Nisbett (1998), who studied U.S. and Korean participants. Thus, the FAE is not unique to individualistic cultures.

The cause of the FAE: Why does it occur? One popular explanation relies on the relative **salience** of the actor and the situation. As we have already mentioned, observers tend to focus on the actor's behavior rather than on the situation. Thus, aspects of the situation are less salient and are given less weight when attributions are made. Although this explanation is intuitively appealing, it is not without its critics.

Gilbert and Malone (1995) question exactly what is meant by the term *salience*, and contend that the salience explanation is incomplete and too simplistic. Rather, they view the FAE as being a complicated phenomenon that can be caused by four different factors. These factors correspond to the 4 steps of the attribution process, which are **situation perception, behavioral expectation, behavior perception, and attribution, with or without correction**. According to Gilbert and Malone, the FAE can occur because a) we may not be aware of the situational factors that weigh on the actor (i.e., poor situation perception); b) we may be aware of, but fail to fully appreciate, the magnitude of the situational influences (unrealistic behavioral expectation); c) our experiences may affect our perception of the actor's behavior (biased behavior perception); and d) we may be unable or unwilling to fully consider the impact of the situation (inability to correct an erroneous attribution).

For example, remember that (hypothetical) guy who cut you off in traffic? You were probably not aware of all of the distractions that affect his situation (e.g., he is late for work, he just had a fight with his wife, etc.). Even if you were aware of all those things, you might discount them (e.g., "everyone has problems, but you should still be able to drive a car"). Assuming that you got past steps 1 and 2, you might notice that he is driving a particular type of car (e.g., an SUV), and you may have certain negative stereotypes about people who drive those cars. In this case your expectations match your perception of the driver's behavior. Finally, you are a busy person and you don't have time to consider all of these things for every attribution that you make! According to Gilbert and Malone, we can make the FAE if we do not navigate all four of these steps correctly. Interestingly, the attribution that we make is not immutable—we will sometimes expend the effort to correct it. For example, upon reflection you may consider aspects of the situation that could have caused the driver's behavior (e.g., heavy traffic, sun glare) and conclude that it might have been accidental. Unfortunately, this process takes effort whereas Gilbert and Malone believe that the original dispositional attribution is automatic and requires little mental exertion.

One of Gilbert's earlier studies provides support for the idea that accounting for situational factors necessitates cognitive effort (Gilbert, Pelham, & Krull, 1988). Female participants watched a videotape of a clearly anxious woman discussing either an anxiety-producing topic (e.g., personal failures, sexual fantasies) or an ordinary one (e.g., hobbies, travel) and then rated the woman's level of trait anxiety. As expected, participants who saw an anxious woman discussing an ordinary topic made a dispositional attribution (i.e., that she is an anxious

person). However, participants who thought she was discussing an anxiety-producing topic were able to take the situation into consideration and were less likely to make a dispositional attribution (e.g., "she is anxious because she is being taped while discussing sensitive topics"). This result is depicted on the left side of Figure 10.9.

The participants did not hear the woman's voice on the tape. Rather, they read the discussion via subtitles. This nuance was included to maximize the effect of the second variable in the study, which was the cognitive interference task. Half of the participants were given a memory rehearsal task to do while also reading the subtitles. The memory task was expected to interfere with the participants' ability to correct for situational factors in their attribution decision. The researchers predicted that the participants who were "cognitively busy" due to the memory task would be less able to consider situational factors in their attribution and would likely rate the woman as being an anxious person. As you can see from the right side of Figure 10.9, this is exactly what happened.

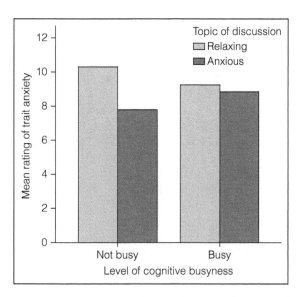

FIGURE 10.9 Trait anxiety ratings as a function of topic of discussion and cognitive busyness of the rater. Data from Gilbert, Pelham & Krull, 1988.

Thus, according to Gilbert and Malone's dual-process model, we are generally biased to an initial dispositional attribution, but sometimes correct for situational factors if we are motivated and able to do so. If we are busy with other cognitive tasks, the dispositional attribution is likely to endure. Since Gilbert and Malone's model was proposed, other researchers have revealed that the dispositional attribution does not necessarily occur first—the processes could be parallel (e.g., Smith & DeCoster, 2000) because they are produced by different neural pathways (e.g., Lieberman, Gaunt, Gilbert, & Trope, 2002).

What Is the Real Fundamental Error?

Before moving on to the practical applications of attribution theory, one important criticism of attribution biases, and of attribution theories in general, bears mention. In a provocative article, Sabini, Seipmann, and Stein (2001) criticize attribution theory at its very foundation. They argue that the conventional distinction between a dispositional and a situational attribution is flawed. Specifically, the epidermis of the actor has been the traditional boundary line for attribution theorists (i.e., anything that happens inside the skin of the actor prompts a dispositional attribution; causes outside the skin lead to situational attributions).

However, Sabini et al. argue that all behavior is the result of an interplay between internal and external factors, as Lewin had noted in his force field theory (1936, 1938). Sabini et al. used the following example to illustrate their point:

> Did Tom eat this piece of candy because he liked sweets or because the candy was sweet? Was his eating the piece of candy internally or externally caused? Typically, both are true. Indeed, it is correct, although awkward, to say that because he liked sweets, he ate the piece of candy because it was sweet, or, conversely to say that because the candy was sweet, he ate it because he liked sweets. (Sabini et al., 2001, p. 8)

In short, all behaviors need both actors and situations to occur; it doesn't make sense to try to tease out one or the other and anoint it as the cause. In a supporting commentary on the Sabini et al. article, Funder (2001) contends that the "really, really fundamental attribution error" is made by psychologists who look for artificially simple causes of complex human behavior.

So what does this mean for the FAE? Sabini et al. argue that there are other interpretations to the classic Jones and Harris (1967) study (and for the FAE in general). Recall that the traditional interpretation is that participants in the No Choice condition underestimated the power of the situation (i.e., the instructions that constrained the essay writer). Sabini et al. contend that there are many possible causes for the essay writer's behavior, both internal (e.g., a desire to follow instructions, or his/her views about Castro) and external (e.g., Castro's behavior, or the instructions given regarding the content of the essay).

The larger issue, according to Sabini et al., is why we choose one cause over another. They contend that we do not have a particular bias toward or away from dispositional causes. Rather, we have a tendency to underestimate the power of certain important motives called **channel factors**. These include a motive to "save face," or to avoid embarrassment of ourselves and others (e.g., if the essay writer had not followed instructions, he/she could have suffered embarrassment). According to Sabini et al., channel factors such as the motive to "save face" underlie the behaviors observed in many of the classic studies of social psychology including research on attribution, conformity, and obedience.

The criticisms of Sabini et al. were certainly not the last word on attribution theory, which remains alive and well. What Sabini and colleagues have done is provide us with a new challenge to improve our understanding of attributions. Ideally, this will lead to more research which has practical applications, such as the work we describe below.

Application of Research on Attributions

Much research has been conducted in an attempt to put our knowledge of the attribution process to practical use. We will briefly discuss the literature on two important topics: achievement motivation and learned helplessness.

Achievement We have already discussed the work of Bernard Weiner, who is one important researcher who studies achievement motivation. Carol Dweck and her colleagues are responsible for another interesting line of research on this topic. Dweck takes a developmental approach to the attributions we make about the causes of our successes and failures. She and colleagues have found that our attributions clearly influence our future expectancies of success as well as the emotions we experience as a result of success and failure (Diener & Dweck, 1978, 1980; Dweck, 1975; Dweck & Reppuci, 1973). The Diener and Dweck studies are particularly interesting.

In the 1978 study, children were tested for mastery orientation or helpless orientation. Individuals with a **mastery orientation** tend to set challenging goals for themselves in order to increase competence. Those with a **helpless orientation** avoid challenging goals and tend to give up easily. Prior to performing a task that they would subsequently fail, there were no differences between the attributions offered by the two types of children. Following the failure experience, however, the attributions made by the two groups were almost completely different. The children classified as helpless attributed their failure to uncontrollable factors; the mastery-oriented children did not appear to have defined themselves as failing at all but, from their verbalizations, appeared to be searching for solutions for their failure.

The emotionality generated by the failure task also differed for the two groups. The mastery-oriented children maintained positive attitudes about the task and continued to believe that they could do well in the future. The helpless children, on the other hand, developed negative attitudes about the task and sought to escape from the situation.

In their 1980 study, Diener and Dweck examined the attributions of helpless children and mastery-oriented children to successful experiences and once again found differences between the two groups. The basic differences concerned how success was interpreted. The helpless children, for example, seemed to remember their successes less than the mastery-oriented children

because they consistently underestimated the number of problems they had correctly solved. Additionally, the helpless children rated their success as lower than what they expected other children would do, while the mastery-oriented children rated their success as higher than that of most other children. This latter finding suggests that the helpless children attributed their success in such a way that it was not an especially rewarding event. Diener and Dweck have proposed that helpless children may compare themselves not to the average child of their peer group but rather to the "best" children. If such is the case, then to be truly successful these children would have to perform better than the best children in their reference group, a clearly difficult task.

Perhaps the most interesting difference between helpless and mastery-oriented children is that helpless children do not assume that present success is predictive of future success. Diener and Dweck suggested that this difference may result from different attributions about the causes of success. Although mastery-oriented children are likely to attribute their successes to ability, helpless children are not. Furthermore, when helpless children experience success followed by failure, they discount the success more than do mastery-oriented children. The helpless children in the study, for example, were more likely to attribute their earlier successes to the ease of the task when asked about those successes after subsequent failure. Additionally, the helpless children lowered their expectancy of future success after failure, while the mastery-oriented children's estimates remained high. Helpless and mastery-oriented children, then, appear to view both success and failure quite differently. The helpless child seems to give more weight to failure in making attributions, while the mastery-oriented child pays more attention to success experiences.

Further research by Dweck and her colleagues has led to the hypothesis that helpless and mastery-oriented individuals differ in the goals they seek. As we noted in Chapter 8, Dweck (1986) and Dweck and Elliot (1983), identified two different goal strategies. Helpless individuals seek **performance goals** (defined as the gaining of favorable judgments of performance), while mastery-oriented individuals seek **learning goals** (defined as increasing one's competence). Their research suggests that these different goals lead to differing patterns of response, with failure in the pursuit of performance goals increasing one's vulnerability to helplessness, and failure at learning goals promoting behavioral strategies to turn the failure into success.

Dweck suggests that the pursuit of these two types of goals stems from differing implicit theories about one's intelligence. Some individuals seem to believe that their intellectual abilities are fixed, whereas others see the possibility for growth. Dweck's research (Dweck & Leggett, 1988; Leggett, 1985) indicates that participants who viewed their intelligence as fixed tended to adopt performance goals in order to prove their ability. Individuals who viewed their intelligence as malleable, on the other hand, tended to adopt learning goals as a way of further developing that intelligence.

In light of Weiner's attribution model that emphasizes effort as one component of the attributions we make, it is also interesting to note that Leggett and Dweck (1986, as cited by Dweck & Leggett, 1988) have found that helpless and mastery-oriented children view effort differently. Helpless children perceive effort as indicating a lack of ability (if I have to work hard I must not be very smart), whereas mastery-oriented children view effort as one strategy for demonstrating their competence.

The research of Dweck and her associates would appear to show that individuals' helpless and mastery-oriented behaviors can be traced to their different views about their abilities, which in turn lead to a focus on different goals. When these goals are not met the individuals' perceptions are quite different, leading to feelings of helplessness in some persons or more active problem solving in others.

Dweck, Hong, and Chiu (1993) further suggest that some people view themselves and others as acting on the basis of fixed traits (such people are called **entity theorists** by Dweck et al. [1993]), while other people view themselves and others as acting on the basis of malleable traits (called

incremental theorists by Dweck et al. [1993]). These two types of individuals view the world quite differently. For example, entity theorists tend to make more global inferences, and tend to rely more on dispositional evidence when making judgments. Incremental theorists, on the other hand, make inferences that are more context-specific in nature. Moreover, incremental theorists are more likely to attribute their failures to unstable factors like effort and to modify these factors in an attempt to increase performance (Hong, Chiu, Dweck, Lin, & Wan; 1999). Ironically, research in this area has revealed that praising children for their intelligence leads them to adopt an entity theory orientation. Because intelligence is uncontrollable, success leads them to view themselves as intelligent. However, failure should then also be attributed to intelligence—in this case a lack thereof. These children should thus seek performance goals and give up more easily if the goal is not reached. Conversely, praising children for their effort is more effective in fostering an incremental orientation a preference for learning goals and increasing task persistence (Dweck, 2002; Kamins & Dweck, 1999; Mueller & Dweck, 1998).

The entity versus incrementalist perspective has also proven useful in explaining social behavior. For example, children with an entity perspective are more likely to desire to seek revenge in response to negative social interactions such as bullying (Yeager, Trzesniewski, Tirri, Nokelainen, & Dweck, 2011). In addition, Haselhuhn, Schweitzer, and Wood (2010) report that students with an incrementalist perspective about morality are more likely to trust another after an apology for untrustworthy past behavior.

Dweck's research program suggests that different persons view behavior in fundamentally different ways and these differences can then influence future behavior. People who believe traits to be fixed will analyze their own behavior and that of others differently from people who believe that traits can be changed. These differences in attribution will then influence future behaviors. Interestingly, it appears as though the entity versus incremental orientation itself is subject to change, at least temporarily. In the aforementioned studies on social behavior, Yeager et al. (2011) were able to reduce desire for revenge and Haselhuhn et al. (2010) were able to induce participants to adopt an incremental view by having them read an essay or a magazine article that espoused an incremental perspective.

Similar encouraging results have been reported in the literature on intelligence and academic performance. Dweck (1975) has shown, for example, that retraining helpless children's failure attributions leads to improved performance in intellectual tasks (Dweck, 1975).

The research of Dweck and her associates points out the importance of the attribution process in evaluating both success and failure—different people can attribute the same events in quite different ways. Further, these attributions will influence future expectancies of success and failure and will thus likely alter future motivation, which could contribute to or protect us from the development of learned helplessness.

Learned Helplessness In Chapter 5 we examined the concept of learned helplessness, which Seligman and his associates believed analogous to depression in humans. Seligman and colleagues have modified his theory (as it relates to depression) to take into account the importance of the attributions one makes about why one's behavior is ineffective (Abramson et al., 1978).

The "old" model of learned helplessness argued that helplessness and depression result from the perceived noncontingency between personal acts and the environment; that is, people become helpless when they believe that they have no control over what happens to them. The early model of helplessness, however, had a number of problems. One was that it could not account for the depressed individual's generally low self-esteem; a second problem was the well-known fact that depressed persons typically blame themselves for their lack of control. The original learned helplessness theory of depression also could explain neither why some depressions are short-lived and others continue for some time, nor why in some cases the observed

helplessness is rather specific while at other times it is quite general.

The reformulated model of learned helplessness relies on the type of attribution that the person makes to overcome these problems. For example, Abramson and associates argued that an individual may attribute his or her own lack of control to either *external* or *internal* events. Some situations over which we have no control are universal; that is, no one else has control over them either. A tornado that destroys our house is beyond our own control and that of others as well, while doing badly on a test may result from an internal characteristic, such as a perceived lack of intelligence. In this latter situation we perceive ourselves to be personally helpless (others do okay on tests), while in the case of the tornado we are universally helpless. Seligman and his associates argued that the type of attribution we make about our lack of control, either universal or personal, affects our self-esteem (Abramson et al., 1978). If we believe that we lack characteristics possessed by others that allow them to control their situations, this **attribution of personal helplessness** will lead to lowered self-esteem.

In attributions of both universal and personal helplessness, there will be motivational deficits, but only when attributions of personal helplessness are made will self-esteem be affected. According to Abramson and associates, depressed individuals tend to attribute their lack of control to personal characteristics, and this attribution leads to feelings of low self-worth. The lowered self-esteem and self-blame of the depressed individual can be understood, Seligman argued, as the result of attributions of personal helplessness.

In a similar fashion, the generality of helpless depression can be understood as a result of the type of attributions that a person makes. When people discover that their behavior has no discernible effect on the outcomes they are seeking, they may attribute it to *specific* circumstances or to a more *global* situation. If the attribution is to a specific circumstance (I don't do well in school), the individual is likely to demonstrate helplessness only in those specific situations. However, if the discovery of uncontrollability leads to a global attribution (failure on a test leading to the attribution that one is totally incompetent), many future behaviors will be affected by this global attribution.

The concept of specific versus global attributions regarding the lack of control over events may help explain why some depressions are characterized by little effort on the part of individuals to change their behavior; the *depressed individuals tend to make global attributions* and come to believe that nothing they do will have any effect on their environment.

The time course of depression can be understood, according to Seligman, by referring to the *stable-unstable* dimension of attributions. An individual, when perceiving no control over events, may attribute this lack of control to stable factors (intelligence) or to unstable factors (I've had a run of bad luck). *Helplessness that is perceived as the result of stable factors will greatly extend the time course of the helplessness,* while attributions to unstable causes will be more transient. According to Seligman, the depressed individual's attributions tend to be stable and thus chronic.

Note that the attributional dimensions of the learned helplessness model are similar to those employed by Weiner, with the exception of the global-specific dimension versus the conceptually similar controllable–uncontrollable dimension. Furthermore, the learned helplessness dimensions are also analogous to Kelley's covariation model. For example, depressed individuals should attribute failure to stable (high consistency), internal (low consensus), and global (low distinctiveness) factors.

Seligman was the first to admit that there are other causes of depression than helplessness. He argued, however, that helpless depression is one type of depression that occurs when people perceive their behavior as independent of the outcomes they seek. He suggested that the attributions made by this type of depressed person will determine whether the depression is long or short, specific to particular situations or more general, and whether he or she expresses feelings of low-esteem and self-blame or lacks these characteristics. Seligman suggested that some depressed individuals tend to make personal (internal), global, stable attributions concerning their lack of control over events. Attributions of this type will lead to self-blame, lowered self-esteem, and to chronic and general depressions.

The attribution model of learned helplessness has generated a great deal of controversy (Alloy & Abramson, 1982; Baum & Gatchel, 1981; Boyd, 1982; Brockner et al., 1983; Danker-Brown & Baucom, 1982; Follette & Jacobson, 1987; Kuhl, 1981; Mikulincer, 1988; Mikulincer & Nizan, 1988; Raps, Peterson, Jonas, & Seligman, 1982). Though it is beyond the scope of this text to examine all the current research on learned helplessness, looking at a few of these studies will be useful.

Wortman and Brehm (1975) proposed that the initial reaction to loss of control is not helplessness but **reactance** (a resistance to the loss of control with subsequent increased effort). If control is not regained as a result of reactance, *then* learned helplessness occurs. Raps and associates (1982) attempted to test this proposal by presenting people (either outpatients or those hospitalized for 1, 3, or 9 weeks) with a number of cognitive tasks. The rationale underlying their procedure was that hospitalization typifies a situation where a person has little control. If Wortman and Brehm's hypothesis is correct, then changes in performance on the cognitive tasks should occur. Patients hospitalized for a short time should show reactance and thus increased performance, while patients hospitalized longer should show increasing amounts of learned helplessness, as evidenced by a decrease in performance on the cognitive tasks. The results of the study indicated a steady decline in performance on the cognitive tasks as the length of stay in the hospital increased but no evidence of reactance. (The outpatients showed very little helplessness.) So these results support the proposed relationship between loss of control and learned helplessness but not between loss of control and reactance. Though Raps and associates conceded that the patient population they studied may have been particularly sensitive to learned helplessness manipulations (the patients were at a VA medical center), they argued that loss of control was the operative factor in the observed changes.

Although Raps and associates (1982) found no support for the reactance model, Mikulincer (1988) obtained evidence of both reactance and learned helplessness. In his study some participants were exposed to one unsolvable problem while others were exposed to four unsolvable problems. For those participants who had an internal attributional style, exposure to a single unsolvable problem led to reactance and better performance on a later task when compared to participants who had an external attributional style. Internal-style participants who were exposed to four unsolvable problems, however, exhibited stronger feelings of incompetence and showed a decrease in performance on a later task, much as learned helplessness would predict. Thus Mikulincer's study would appear to support the Wortman and Brehm reactance model.

In another study, Mikulincer and Nizan (1988) found that global attributions of failure led to an increase in what they termed off-task cognitions. These anxious thoughts interfered with subsequent performance. When instructions were given that discouraged off-task cognitions, the performance-decreasing effects of global attributions were eliminated. These researchers suggest that the performance deficits found with global attributions may result more from anxiety than from a change in motivational state as the learned helplessness model has proposed.

Baltes and Skinner (1983) have taken strong exception to the study by Raps and associates. These researchers point out that while the Raps study does not support the Wortman-Brehm model of learned helplessness, it also does not necessarily support the learned helplessness model of Seligman and his colleagues. Baltes and Skinner noted that at least two other models could explain the deficits observed in the hospitalized patients—**operant learning** and **role theory**.

From an operant perspective, hospitalization presents a situation where reinforcement contingencies are such that independent, active, and control-taking behaviors are discouraged, while passive, dependent behaviors are encouraged. If rewards are consistently tied to passiveness and punishments to active control taking, then it is not surprising that as the length of hospitalization becomes greater, helpless behavior increases.

Role theory proposes that expectations, in the form of rules regarding appropriate behavior, can lead to behaviors appropriate for the role being played. As a result, when people play "patient," their expectations of appropriate patient behavior lead them to act in a passive and dependent way. Thus the participants in the Raps study may have behaved passively because that is what they thought was expected of them.

In 1989 Abramson, Metalsky, and Alloy modified the 1978 learned helplessness theory and termed their revised model the **hopelessness theory of depression**. This model proposes to explain a specific subtype of depression that they call hopelessness depression. This model also plays down the role of attributions in the understanding of this depression subtype. Hopelessness depression is, they believe, typified by two basic expectations: (a) highly valued outcomes are unobtainable or highly aversive outcomes cannot be avoided, and (b) the individual is helpless to change these situations. Thus helplessness becomes a component of hopelessness in the model.

Although the model deemphasizes the role of attributions in the development of hopelessness and depression, it does not eliminate them. Rather, Abramson et al. now view causal attributions as one of several contributory factors that could lead to hopelessness and then to depression. Furthermore, although attributions receive less emphasis as a possible cause of depression, changes in attributions are thought to be a valuable therapeutic tool that can be used to treat depressed individuals (Needles & Abramson, 1990). Specifically, internal, stable, and global attributions of *positive* life events are related to decreased hopelessness and diminished symptoms of depression in psychiatric inpatients (Johnson, Feinstein, & Crofton, 1996; Johnson, Han, Douglas, Johannet, & Russell, 1998). Interestingly, the results of the Johnson et al. studies appear to occur independent of the effect of antidepressant medication.

As you can see, the role of attributions as either a cause or a treatment of learned helplessness/ hopelessness has yet to be fully understood. At present more definitive research is needed before we can determine the usefulness of any model of depression. Attributional approaches in general, however, are very popular. As we have seen, they have been applied to many different psychological phenomena, of which achievement and learned helplessness are only two examples. Attributional approaches tell us that we must understand how a person perceives cause and effect if we are to understand why that person behaves in a particular way. That is of course a difficult problem to solve, but it is one in which many researchers are currently engaged.

SUMMARY

One of the most important things we do is to make judgments or attributions about the causes of behavior. Attribution theory originated with the work of Heider, who believed that most of us attempt to explain behavior informally, through a process he called naïve psychology. Heider's ideas were extended and refined by Jones and Davis, Kelley, Weiner and others. Jones and Davis theorized that we look for a correspondence between the observed behavior and the inferred intent of that behavior. For Kelley, attributions are based on the degree of covariation between causes and effects across the dimensions of distinctiveness, consistency, and consensus. In an effort to explain the consequences of attributions, Weiner postulated that attributions are determined by the degree to which behavior is perceived to result from internal vs. external, stable vs. unstable, and controllable vs. uncontrollable factors. Each of these attribution theories shares the common assumption that we do attempt to understand behavior, but they differ in their emphasis on the processes involved in attribution formation and the consequences of our attributions once they are made.

Unfortunately our attributions are not always correct. Four of the most common biases in attribution are the self-serving bias (i.e., the tendency to take credit for success and avoid responsibility for failure), the false consensus bias (i.e., the tendency to believe that most other people think and act as we do), the actor–observer asymmetry (i.e., the tendency to infer dispositional attributions of our own behavior and situational attributions of others' behavior), and the fundamental attribution error (i.e., the tendency to underestimate the influence of situational causes of other people's behavior).

Recently, critics of attribution research have pointed out that the primary distinction made in attribution theory, whether to infer a dispositional or situational cause, may be a false dichotomy because all behavior has multiple causes. Nonetheless, traditional attribution theory has been successfully applied to many topics in psychology, including achievement motivation and learned helplessness. Weiner, for example, has investigated the various emotional ascriptions given to success and failure in achievement situations. Dweck has shown that the attributions of helpless children and mastery-oriented children differ, and Seligman and his associates have reformulated their theory of learned helplessness to include the kinds of attributions people make when they discover that their behavior is unrelated to outcomes. These attributions in turn may influence the generality, time course, and self-blame that are often observed in depression.

Attribution theory emphasizes cognitive information processing as crucial to the understanding of behavior. Though in a sense nonmotivational, the attribution approaches generally acknowledge the importance of motives in generating attributions and, more importantly, the role of attributions in the future direction of behavior. Thus the attribution of past success to high ability probably serves to motivate future achievement behaviors.

If we are to understand why people behave as they do, we must understand the processes by which people attribute the causes of events, both within themselves and in others. Attribution theory attempts to help us gain such an understanding.

KEY TERMS

attribution theory, *303*
dispositions/situation, *304*
naive psychology/abilities/
   motivations/intention/
   exertion/task difficulty/
   luck, *305*
choice, *307*
social desirability/noncommon
   effects, *308*
covariation/distinctiveness/
   consensus/consistency, *309*
ability/effort/task difficulty/
   luck/social comparison/locus/
   stability/controllability, *311*

self-serving bias/self-assessment/
   self-enhancement, *315*
false consensus effect, *316*
selective exposure/
   actor–observer bias, *317*
fundamental attribution error
   (FAE) (correspondence
   bias), *319*
salience/situation perception/
   behavioral expectation/
   behavior perception/
   attribution, with or without
   correction, *321*

channel factors, *323*
mastery orientation/helpless
   orientation/performance
   goals, *324*
learning goals/entity theorists/
   incremental theorists, *325*
attribution of personal
   helplessness, *326*
reactance, *327*
operant learning/role theory/
   hopelessness theory of
   depression, *328*

SUGGESTIONS FOR FURTHER READING

Abramson, L. Y., Metalsky, G. I., & Alloy, L. B. (1989). Hopelessness depression: A theory-based subtype of depression. *Psychological Review*, *96*, 358–372. The revision of the helplessness model is outlined here along with research support. For the advanced student.

Dweck, C. S., Hong, Y., & Chiu, C. (1993). Implicit theories: Individual differences in the likelihood and meaning of dispositional inference. *Personality and Social Psychology Bulletin*, *19*, 644–656. This article summarizes several lines of reseach showing that people

view traits as fixed or malleable. For the advanced student.

Forsterling, F. 2001. *Attribution: An introduction to theories, research and applications*. Philadelphia, PA: Psychology Press. A good overall summary of the field of attribution.

Martinko, M. J. & Thomson, N. F. (1998). A synthesis and extension of the Weiner and Kelley attribution models. *Basic and Applied Social Psychology, 20*, 271–284. This article presents a synthesized attribution model based on the theories of Kelley and Weiner.

WEB RESOURCES

Interviews with Carol Dweck http://www.iub.edu/%7Eintell/dweck_interview.shtml

A critical review of learned helplessness/hopelessness theories http://www.springerlink.com/content/7myf2qu5qwavbp8n/fulltext.pdf

CHAPTER 11

Cognitive Motivation: Competence and Control

The 15-month-old child tried for the fifth time to pull herself up onto the dining room chair. The seat of the chair, at eye level to the child, proved to be a formidable opponent. At last, after much struggling, the child managed to get a knee onto the seat and was able to push with one leg while pulling with an arm. The maneuver succeeded in getting the child onto "Daddy's" chair.

The child crowed with delight in herself and smiled broadly. Within a minute atop her perch, however, she began to whimper, demanding to be let down off the chair. The father, reading the evening paper, ignored the child's cries until they became louder and more persistent—he had played this game before. Putting down the paper and walking into the dining room from his easy chair, he gently removed the child from her perch and gave her an affectionate pat on the rear, admonishing her to "stay down." No sooner had the child's feet hit the floor, however, than she grabbed the chair and began her effort anew. After some struggle she again managed to pull herself onto the chair, and again her delight in this success quickly turned to demands to be rescued. This game continued until the child tired of the activity but began anew the next day. Eventually climbing the giant chair became easy, and the child lost interest in her conquest and turned to new challenges such as the several buttons on the stereo that controlled the music to which she danced.

This short "day in the life" of a typical 15-month-old child illustrates the major thrust of this chapter. Researchers in the tradition of **humanistic psychology** study the persistent motive within individuals to become competent in dealing with the environment. Successful completion of a task, however, often seems to cause the task to lose some of its value, and new, more difficult challenges are undertaken.

Theorists and researchers in this area have described this persistent motive to test and expand one's abilities by a number of terms. Rogers has described this motive state as an attempt to grow and reach fulfillment, that is, to become a fully functioning individual. Maslow has described the process as a movement toward self-actualization, an attempt to become all that one can possibly become. White has suggested that a motive for competence exists in each of us, while deCharms has emphasized the idea that people strive toward personal causation. Bandura proposes that we are guided by core processes of human agency, and Deci and Ryan's self-determination theory is based on the innate psychological needs of autonomy, competence, and relatedness. According to each of these approaches, all of us, like the child and the chair, strive to reach our potential.

Most of the theories examined in this chapter take the point of view that human behavior cannot fully be understood without some reference to this striving toward actualization or full functioning. We shall see that, although many of these theories are highly similar, each has approached the question from a slightly different point of view. To begin our study of these approaches we turn to the work of Carl Rogers.

Carl Rogers and Positive Regard

Carl Rogers is probably best known for the development of client-centered therapy. His therapeutic approach, however, is firmly based upon his humanistic ideas about the motives of individuals.

Rogers pointed out that life itself is an active, ongoing process and that the most basic characteristic of human behavior is a striving for wholeness. This concept of striving is important because it implies that the process of achieving wholeness is never complete; we change as we grow. Rogers has called this striving to become fully functioning the **actualizing tendency** and argued that it is innate in all living organisms (Arkes & Garske, 1977; Evans, 1975; Rogers, 1951, 1961; Schultz, 1977).

According to Rogers, there is only one motive—the basic motive toward growth. But this motive can be analyzed as consisting of attempts by an organism to maintain, enhance, and reproduce itself. The specific motives that other theorists discuss (hunger, thirst, sex, avoidance of pain) can be regarded as aspects of either maintenance or reproduction of the individual. Though we need to know under what conditions specific behaviors occur, we gain little, according to Rogers, by assuming the existence of specific motive states.

Rogers argued that our striving for fulfillment is importantly influenced by our environment. We are cognitive organisms, and our experiences (and their interpretations) can either help or hinder our attempts to grow. In this regard our interactions with others are particularly important. Rogers argued that experiences learned early in infancy influence our psychological growth. He saw the actualizing tendency as creating both a need for **positive regard** and a need for **positive self-regard**. Our feelings of positive regard from others, as well as from the self, come from interactions with our parents in what Rogers called **unconditional positive regard**. The basic idea is that a person is accepted and loved regardless of behavior; hence we receive experiences that allow us to see that we are loved regardless of what we do. Under these circumstances, the actualizing tendency works toward growth because the person's own concept (the self) is consistent with the feedback received from others. Under these conditions the person is open to change and is nondefensive, so the self can change and grow. In Rogers's terms, this person is a "fully functioning individual."

Too often, however, positive regard is made contingent upon specific behaviors; that is, individuals are made to feel they are worthwhile only if they behave in certain ways. According to Rogers, **conditional positive regard** leads to maladaptive behaviors because it creates anxiety. We feel loved only to the extent that our behavior is correct. Anxiety triggers defenses, so that the individual begins denying or distorting cognitions because they are inconsistent with the self-concept.

When positive regard is made conditional, much energy of the self-actualizing tendency is channeled into the defenses used to protect the self. Because the self is threatened, it is not free to grow and change in an atmosphere of acceptance, and so becomes static. Lack of self-growth is maladjustive and limits the individual's attempts to become fully functioning.

Growth and change, then, are the basics for psychological health. According to Rogers's approach, the basic motive underlying all behavior is the actualizing tendency. To be **fully functioning individuals**, we must have unconditional positive regard so that we can "let down" our defenses and allow the self to change and grow. When we lose our defensiveness, we become aware of what is happening within us and can change. We can also learn to accept ourselves for what we are without the anxiety created by conditional positive regard.

The Fully Functioning Individual

Five basic characteristics define Rogers's concept of full functioning:

1. *Openness to experience*. Fully functioning individuals do not have to defend themselves against certain experiences; thus their perceptions of events are less distorted. They are aware of their own characteristics and are more flexible about altering them. The fully functioning individual is usually more emotional than others, experiencing a wider range of emotions and experiencing them more intensely.

2. *Existential living*. The fully functioning individual lives each moment to the fullest and does not concentrate on either the past or the future. The fully functioning person also has a general interest in life, and all aspects of life are experienced as new and rich. Rogers believed existential living to be the very core of the healthy personality.

3. *Trust in one's own organism*. Rogers described the fully functioning individual as one who often behaves in particular ways because it feels right rather than because it seems intellectually right. Thus, fully functioning individuals are often intuitive because they are open and in touch with their innermost feelings. This trust in one's "gut reactions" may lead to spontaneous and sometimes impulsive behavior, but not at the expense of others. While intellectual decisions may be downgraded in importance, they are not ignored.

4. *Sense of freedom*. Fully functioning persons experience a sense of personal freedom in choosing what happens to them. They see themselves as having the personal power to determine what their future will be. They regard themselves as in control of their lives rather than at the mercy of chance events.

5. *Creativity*. As might be expected, fully functioning persons are highly creative. This creativity is also evidenced by their increased ability to adapt to change and to survive even drastic changes in their environment.

Fully functioning persons, as described by Rogers, have the power to control their own lives because they are free from the denial and distortions that produce rigid behavior. The fully functioning person is not in a "state" but is immersed in a "process," which causes continual striving to enhance the self.

To be fully functioning does not mean that we are in a constant state of ecstasy. Enhancing the self is both difficult and painful as we grow. Full functioning does not promise happiness, although happiness often appears to be a byproduct of the process. The fully functioning person can be expected, however, to be more comfortable with life situations (whether happy or not) and to cope with situations in open and flexible ways.

Criticisms of Rogers's Approach

Rogers's view of human motivation is much more optimistic than most. He sees humans as motivated by the need to become fully functional in order to reach their ultimate potential. When we fail to reach our potential, it is because of experiences we have had in interacting with our parents or others where our self-worth has been made conditional.

Rogers's theory has been criticized on a number of counts (Arkes & Garske, 1977; Schultz, 1977). First, *many of the terms Rogers used are not operationally defined.* For example, what is the self-actualizing tendency in operational terms? Can it be measured? Where does it come from, and how does it promote one behavior as opposed to another? Although a valid criticism of Rogers's model, lack of operational definition for terms is a common problem in psychology.

Second, the environment is regarded as an important source of motivational change; yet *it is unclear which environmental conditions will enhance growth and which will hinder it.* In this regard a clearer distinction between situations that lead to unconditional versus conditional positive regard would help clarify the role of the environment in motivation.

A third criticism of Rogers's approach is that *it implies a "me first" psychology.* Rogers said little about how feelings of responsibility toward others may lead to growth. In light of Maslow's views on self-actualization, which will be discussed shortly, this seems a major omission.

Fourth, Rogers's approach *does not emphasize to any great extent the goals toward which an individual may be striving.* Although he has emphasized the striving, he has largely ignored the end products of that striving as important determinants of behavior. As we saw in the work of Klinger (Chapter 6), the goals toward which we strive can be very important determiners of behavior.

In summary, *Rogers's theory is weak empirically.* He has not specified the components of his theory in a manner that can be easily tested. We might also question the generality of conditional positive regard. We should probably make a distinction between situations in which a parent disapproves of a specific behavior in a child and situations in which the parent "rejects" the child. Disapproval of specific behaviors without rejection of the individual would not necessarily lead to stunting of the growth process. The dividing line between disapproval of specific behaviors and rejection is, however, difficult to determine—particularly from the child's point of view.

Abraham Maslow and Self-Actualization

Abraham Maslow also developed a homeostatic motivational theory that emphasizes the striving to reach one's full potential as basic to human motivation but also includes additional motives besides self-actualization.

Maslow (1943, 1959, 1965, 1971, 1973a, 1973b, 1976) argued that any comprehensive theory of human motivation must take into account the individual as a whole. We cannot hope to understand the complexities of the human condition by reducing behavior to specific responses in specific situations. The wholeness of behavior can also serve several motive states at once. Thus, for example, sexual behavior may serve physiological as well as psychological needs of belongingness and esteem.

Maslow argued that we must seek to understand the **ultimate goals** of behavior rather than the superficial or apparent goals, because the apparent goal for any observed behavior may be quite different from the ultimate goal. This implies, in a fashion similar to Freudian theory, that motivations for much of our behavior may occur at an unconscious level. Unlike Freud, however, Maslow saw the unconscious in much more positive terms. Like Rogers, Maslow also regarded the striving for perfection or **self-actualization** as the ultimate purpose of behavior.

Maslow argued that human motivation can best be studied by observing human rather than animal behavior. His observations led him to the conclusion that human needs can be understood in terms of a **hierarchy of needs**. Needs lower on the hierarchy are prepotent (stronger) and must be satisfied before needs higher on the hierarchy will be triggered. Maslow did not, however, regard the hierarchy as totally rigid: we can partly satisfy lower needs, thus allowing higher needs to become partly active. Maslow regarded the satisfaction of needs on the hierarchy in a probabilistic manner. If a lower need is being satisfied most of the time (perhaps 85%), that need will have little influence on behavior, while other higher needs that are less satisfied will have a

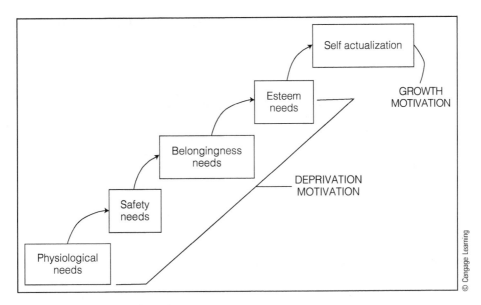

FIGURE 11.1 Maslow's hierarchy of needs.

larger influence on behavior. Figure 11.1 depicts Maslow's hierarchy.

Hierarchy of Needs

Physiological Needs The first level of the hierarchy consists of physiological needs. If needs such as hunger or thirst are not adequately being met, the needs above them on the hierarchy are pushed into the background in terms of controlling behavior. The individual is in an emergency situation and the whole being is dominated by these basic needs. For example, someone in a state of semi-starvation will constantly think, dream, and talk about food (Keys, Brozek, Henschel, Mickelsen, & Taylor, 1950).

Maslow felt that physiological needs are adequately met for most people in our society. When these needs are met, the next need on the hierarchy emerges as a dominant force in controlling and directing behavior.

Safety Needs These needs represent a need for safety or security in our environment. Like the physiological needs, safety needs are triggered primarily in emergency situations. Higher needs

become unimportant when life is endangered, and then behavior reflects attempts to remain secure. An example of this occurred when the remnants of a hurricane caused extensive flooding in my neighborhood. Some of my neighbors sustained thousands of dollars of damage to their homes; yet at the time of the flood their material loss was unimportant to them because escaping the flood was all that mattered.

Safety needs dominate our behavior primarily in times of emergency. Maslow, however, felt that safety needs can also be seen in people's preference for familiar surroundings, secure jobs, savings accounts, and insurance. Safety needs are most evident in young children, as shown when an infant cries if he or she is dropped suddenly or startled by a loud sound, or if a stranger enters the room.

Maslow believed that the safety needs of most adults in Western society are adequately met. These needs do not normally dominate behavior. Some types of disorders, however, can be understood according to Maslow as the nonsatisfaction of these needs. In this nonsatisfied state the person reacts as if continually in a threatening situation. Maslow proposed that obsessive-compulsive disorder exemplifies behavior generated by nonsatisfaction of the safety needs.

Love or Belongingness Needs   When safety needs have been adequately met, they become unimportant in the direction of behavior, and the love or belongingness needs emerge. These needs involve a hunger for affectionate relationships with others, a need to feel part of a group, or a feeling that we "belong." The love needs are not equivalent to sexual needs (which are physiological), though sexual intimacy can serve to satisfy our need to belong. The love needs require both the receiving and giving of love—love from another and someone to love.

We may gain a sense of belonging in a number of ways. Marriage, a job, or admission to a select group such as a fraternity, sorority, or civic group can serve this need. According to Maslow, thwarting of the love needs leads to behavioral maladjustment and pathology and is the most common basis for behavioral problems in our society.

Esteem Needs   If the love needs have been adequately met, they too slip into the background in relation to guiding behavior, and the esteem needs become dominant. These are needs for a positive, high evaluation of self. This evaluation can be broken down into two subcategories—a **need for self-esteem** and a **need for esteem from others**.

The need for self-esteem motivates the individual to strive for achievement, strength, confidence, independence, and freedom. The need for self-esteem seems to have at its core the desire to feel worthwhile and appears highly similar to Rogers's concept of positive regard. The related need of esteem from others involves a desire for reputation, status, recognition, appreciation by others of our abilities, and a feeling of importance.

When the esteem needs are satisfied, we have feelings of self-confidence and self-worth and see ourselves as having a purpose in the world. When these needs are frustrated, maladjustment can occur, typified by feelings of inferiority, weakness, and, helplessness. Lack of esteem leads the individual to feel inconsequential and to have little self-worth.

One suspects that Maslow would regard depression as triggered by inadequate satisfaction of the esteem needs.

Deprivation Motivation   The first four steps on Maslow's hierarchy constitute the needs that must be satisfied before reaching the final level, the level of self-actualization. Maslow considered these needs to result from deficiencies in the person's life; that is, behaviors related to the first four categories are motivated by a deprivation of those things necessary for full development. Behaviors generated in attempts to fill these needs are therefore said to be activated by **deprivation motivation (D-motivation)**.

Maslow pointed out that although the order of these four steps is correct for most people, there are exceptions. The most common exception is that, for some people, esteem needs precede the love needs. For these people it is necessary to feel worthwhile before they can satisfy the love needs.

Maslow also believed that for some individuals chronically deprived at the physiological level, the higher needs might never emerge. For these people it is sufficient simply to get enough to eat. On the other hand, Maslow also believed that people who have always had their basic needs satisfied will be less influenced by these needs later if the needs are suddenly no longer being met. This might explain the behavior of martyrs who suffer deprivation because of lofty ideals. Maslow suggested that martyrs may be able to withstand deprivation better because their needs had usually been well met early in life, thus insulating them against these needs later. In this regard, he felt that the first four years of life are particularly important in building resistance to later deprivation.

As mentioned earlier, each level of the hierarchy does not have to be perfectly satisfied. As lower needs are partly met, higher needs partly emerge. As the lower needs become more and more satisfied, the higher needs become more and more prominent in the control of behavior. Finally, Maslow suggested that most people are unaware of the need hierarchy; their needs are mostly unconscious.

Self-Actualization When we have satisfied the first four levels of need, the final level of development—which Maslow termed **self-actualization**—can be reached. At the self-actualization level, the person's behavior is motivated by different conditions than at the lower levels.

The self-actualized individual has satisfied all the deprivation needs of the first four levels of the hierarchy. The behavior of the self-actualized person is, as a result, motivated by a new set of needs, which Maslow termed the **being needs (B-motivation, or metamotivation)**. These B-motives are values such as truth, honesty, beauty, and goodness, and they provide meaning to the life of the self-actualized individual.

The picture Maslow gives us of the self-actualized person is a very positive one. Self-actualized individuals are no longer motivated by deficiencies but are motivated to grow and become all that they are capable of becoming. Self-actualization constantly stimulates people to test their abilities and expand their horizons.

Maslow suggested that the process of growth leading to self-actualization takes considerable time and that most self-actualizing persons are 60 or more years old. Maslow also believed that few people in our society reach self-actualization, estimating that fewer than 1% of the population could be considered self-actualized (Goble, 1970).

The self-actualized person, then, is a person apart. He or she has mastered the deficiency needs and is motivated by what Maslow called growth motivation. These persons seek to solve problems outside themselves and reach for truth, beauty, justice, and other high values. One should not, however, consider the self-actualized as perfect. Maslow pointed out that self-actualized individuals also have many of the lesser failings common to us all. They can be silly, wasteful, and thoughtless. They can also be boring, stubborn, and irritating. Self-actualized people often show superficial vanity concerning their own products and can occasionally exhibit ruthlessness. Because of their extreme abilities to concentrate, they sometimes appear absent-minded and can be impolite when thinking about a problem. They also feel guilt, anxiety, sadness, and

conflict, but these arise from their realization that they are not all that they could be—rather than from psychopathology.

In his later writing, Maslow (1971) came to the conclusion that there are actually two types of self-actualizing people, differentiated in regard to peak experiences. A peak experience is a short but intense feeling of awe or ecstasy often accompanied by a sense of fulfillment, insight, and oneness with something larger than one's self. Some self-actualized persons rarely have peak experiences, while others experience peaks much more often. Those self-actualized individuals who experienced peaks were called **transcenders** or **peakers**, and those who did not were called **nontranscenders** or **nonpeakers**. Both peakers and nonpeakers share all the characteristics of self-actualization with the exception of the frequency of peak experiences.

Maslow's description of the two types of actualizers suggests that self-actualization itself may contain two levels. The transcendent self-actualizers seem, if possible, more self-actualized than the nontranscendent. For example, peak experiences for the transcenders become the most important aspect of their lives. They are more consciously motivated by the B-values, and they think and talk in language concerned with honesty, truth, beauty, perfection, and so on. Transcenders see more fully the sacredness of all things and are more likely to be profoundly religious. They are also more holistic in their approach to the world than nontranscenders and are more likely to be held in awe by others. Interestingly, Maslow believed that transcenders may be less happy than nontranscenders. He suggested that this is because of their ability to see the stupidity of people more clearly and to experience a kind of cosmic sadness for the failings of others.

Failure to Self-Actualize If self-actualization is the ultimate level of being toward which we all strive, then why do most people fall short of this goal? First, Maslow believed that the *tendency toward growth is weaker than the deficiency motives* and can easily be stunted by poor environment or poor education. Second, Maslow believed that Western culture, with its emphasis on the negative nature of human motivation, has worked against our trusting of our inner nature. Our culture has emphasized that inner nature is bad (e.g., Freudian theory) and has been concerned with mechanisms of control. This has led many people to reject their inner experiences altogether.

Third, Maslow noted that *growth requires the taking of chances*, a stepping away from the secure and comfortable. It is not easy to take that step, which we must do again and again to grow, and many people choose security over growth. Finally, Maslow believed that people are afraid of their own abilities. To become all that one is capable of becoming is frightening to many, and so people reject opportunities for growth. Maslow dubbed this phenomenon the **Jonah complex** after the Old Testament story of Jonah, who tried to run away from the purpose that God had planned for him.

Most people fall short of self-actualization for one or all of these reasons. Nevertheless, Maslow believed that to understand the potentialities of human behavior, one must study the truly exceptional individual rather than the average person. Only in the self-actualized person can one see the full range of human motivation.

Criticisms of Self-Actualization   Maslow's theory has not been free of criticism (Schultz, 1977; Geller, 1982). Perhaps the most common and damaging criticism concerned the self-actualized individuals whom Maslow studied. Maslow began his study of self-actualization in an attempt to understand two friends whom he greatly admired. In talking with them he discovered that they shared many common attributes. This led him to study self-actualization more fully by examining friends, acquaintances, and public and historical figures. Many of the living individuals he studied preferred to remain anonymous, so other psychologists could not check the accuracy of Maslow's perceptions of these people. Also, the historical figures were dead, requiring reliance on written accounts, which are often self-serving. *The major problem is one of replicability.* We are asked to take Maslow's word

that the people he studied had the characteristics he described.

Second, Maslow's theory has sometimes been criticized as elitist. People confined by poor education, dead-end jobs, or societal expectations are unlikely to become self-actualized persons. The elite seem to have a distinct advantage in obtaining self-actualization, and, as a result, *the theory may not describe people in general.*

That so many people fail to become self-actualized has also suggested to some researchers that *a motivation toward growth may not be as general as Maslow proposed.* Perhaps the need to become all that one can become is idiosyncratic to some persons rather than present in all of us.

Finally, Maslow's theory has been criticized because of *its vagueness in language and concepts and its general lack of evidence* (Cofer & Appley, 1964).

Research on Self-Actualization   Several research efforts have been completed since Cofer and Appley's criticisms, and to this research we now briefly turn.

Everett Shostrom (1964, 1966) developed an inventory designed to discriminate between self-actualized and non–self-actualized individuals. The inventory consisted of 150 two-choice value and behavior judgments; items were scored on two major scales plus ten subscales. Shostrom (1964) has shown that his inventory discriminates between people judged as self-actualized, normal, and non–self-actualized. His results indicate that self-actualized individuals appear to be less restricted by social pressures or conformity. The self-actualized person also appears to live in the present but can meaningfully tie past or future events to the present. One aspect of this **time competence**, as Shostrom terms it, is that the self-actualized individual's aspirations are tied to the goals toward which he or she is striving in the present.

Several studies have examined the characteristics of peak experiences (Mathes, Zevon, Roter, & Joerger, 1982; Privette, 1983). Privette, for example, compared the construct of peak experience with the constructs of **peak performance** and **flow**. Peak performance has been defined as an episode of superior functioning, while flow has been defined as an intrinsically enjoyable experience. Peak experiences are largely passive; that is, one does not create a peak experience but rather senses them when they occur. Peak experiences would therefore appear to be largely perceptual, requiring no behavior of the individual and often leading to a reorganization of our thoughts. Peak performance, however, is active, involving interaction with another person or with the environment. Flow, like peak performance, is active, but like peak experience it is intrinsically enjoyable and leads to a fusion with the experience and subsequent loss of self.

In surveying the literature on these three concepts, Privette found many similarities and some differences among them. One quality common to all three is **absorption**. In peak experience, peak performance, and flow, an individual intensely focuses attention to the exclusion of other perceptual events. Further, in all three situations the individual spontaneously and effortlessly experiences events as they occur without trying to influence them in any way.

Privette has noted, however, that each concept also describes situations that have unique properties. Peak experiences, for example, usually have a mystical or transpersonal aspect that does not typically occur in either peak performance or flow. Indeed, in peak performance there is a strong awareness of oneself rather than a loss. "Flow is fun" (Privette, 1983, p. 1364)—people engage in activities that create a sense of flow because they are enjoyable. Additionally, people make some attempt to engage in activities that create flow, whereas peak experiences and peak performances are unplanned. Privette's topology is interesting and helps us sort out both the similarities and differences among these three constructs.

A study by Davis, Lockwood, and Wright (1991) examined why people are reluctant to report peak experiences. These researchers found that 79% of the 246 people they studied reported having had a peak experience; however, there was a reluctance to tell other people about those experiences. More than 50% of their sample had told no more than two other people about the experience, and about 20% of the sample reported that they had told no one else about the experience. Their participants reported that they were reluctant to tell others about their experiences because the experiences were special, intimate, or personal. They also mentioned a concern that telling others might cause the experience to be devalued. Finally, they noted that the experiences were not easy to describe to someone else in words. Davis and colleagues' research suggests that most people do have peak experiences but, for the reasons noted earlier, are not very likely to share them with others.

On a more basic level, researchers have tried to determine if self-actualization is indeed the fundamental human need that Maslow believed it to be. For example, Sheldon, Elliot, Kim, and Kasser (2001) asked participants to recall the "single most personally satisfying event" that they experienced. After doing so, participants rated their level of agreement with a series of statements designed to measure self-actualization, self-esteem, and several other constructs. Interestingly, self-actualization was not among the concepts that were most strongly related to the salience of the most satisfying events. This result was consistent across different time periods (e.g., the most satisfying event in the past month vs. during the entire semester) and was found in both U.S. and South Korean participants. Somewhat surprisingly, self-esteem was significantly associated with these "most satisfying" events, as was autonomy, relatedness and, competence. We will have more to say about the latter three needs when we discuss self-determination theory later.

Research on, and criticism of, Maslow's theory continues (see Mittelman, 1991; Neher, 1991; Sheldon, Elliot, Kim, & Kasser, 2001; Sumerlin & Norman, 1992). Although the evidence for some of the constructs proposed by Maslow is mixed, his ideas have proven popular and durable as is evident from an extensive reformulation of the theory which was published in 2010.

A Revised Hierarchy of Needs

Kenrick and colleagues (Kenrick, Griskevicius, Neuberg, & Schaller, 2010) have proposed a reformulated hierarchical structure of needs that retains much of Maslow's original model, but changes it in significant ways to include advances that have occurred since the publication of the original work in 1943. Kenrick et al. believe, as Maslow did, that different needs are driven by different motivational systems. In order to fully understand each of these systems, their revised model includes analyses of each need on three levels: (a) evolutionary significance, (b) developmental trajectory, and (c) the specific environmental stimuli that trigger each need at any given moment. For example, consider the motive to attain status/esteem. One could analyze this need in terms of its adaptive significance. Individuals who earn status/esteem within their social group are accorded evolutionary advantages such as greater access to resources and potential mating partners. One could also trace developmental changes in the need for status/esteem across the life span. Finally, the specific environmental situations that activate status-seeking behavior could also be analyzed.

Recall that Maslow believed that there are five fundamental needs. Furthermore he argued that, on some occasions, two needs could be active at one time. As you can see from Figure 11.2, Kenrick et al. have extended both of these ideas. First, they include many of Maslow's original five needs as well as three additional ones. In addition, the overlapping circles indicate that any of the needs could potentially be active at a given point in a person's life (e.g., basic physiological needs never go away entirely).

If you take a close look at Figure 11.2 you will see that one of Maslow's needs that is not listed is his most important one: self-actualization! Kenrick et al. do not dismiss this motive entirely, but they do argue that it is not a fundamental human need. Rather, they believe that it is part of other needs such as status/esteem and, ultimately, the needs that govern mating. By this they mean that

self-actualized people often attain status by virtue of their accomplishments, creativity, and so on. Because status can be a source of reproductive advantage, they argue that self-actualization can be one way to progress up the hierarchy to the three mating-related needs.

Why then are the three mating needs at the top of the hierarchy? Because from an evolutionary standpoint, successful propagation of one's genes is the ultimate goal. Kenrick et al. invoke their three levels of analysis to elaborate on this point. They argue that evolution has provided all animals with a developmental trajectory that best fits their day-to-day environment and maximizes reproductive success. For humans, this means that as infants physiological and safety needs are paramount. We must satisfy them before we move up the hierarchy, but these basic needs can still motivate behavior throughout the life span. In early childhood, affiliation needs become more dominant, followed by a motive to gain status/esteem in the eyes of the people with whom we have become affiliated. When we reach adolescence, our evolutionary history dictates that sexual needs become strong motivators of behavior. This urge to find a mate or mates continues into adulthood. Once a suitable mate has been found the motive to retain him or her becomes prominent and both positive (e.g., emotional bonding) and negative (e.g., jealousy) factors can help us satisfy this need. Individuals who have met each of the first six needs are in the best position to become parents and to nurture their offspring, and hence their genes, through the same process.

Kenrick and colleagues realize that this model does not fully account for the large differences both between and within the sexes in terms of how individuals choose to navigate these stages. Indeed, they stress that choice is an important factor in how each of us satisfies each motive and thus exercises some control over our environment. Thus, the reformulated model is more of a general blueprint with lots of room for individual variation. But it is precisely this variation that psychologists are trying to understand. Thus,

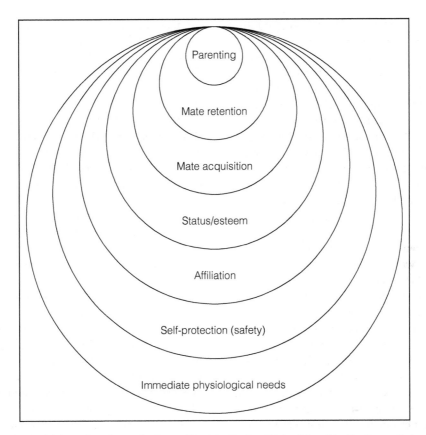

FIGURE 11.2 Revised hierarchy of needs. From Kenrick, D. T., Griskevicius, V., Neuberg, S. L., & Schaller, M., "Renovating the pyramid of needs: Contemporary extensions built upon ancient foundations," *Perspectives on Psychological Science, 5*, 292–314. Copyright © 2010 Sage Publications. Reprinted with permission.

Kenrick et al. argue that the model can serve as a useful tool in guiding research on many positive aspects of human behavior including topics such as emotional bonding, caregiving, courtship, affiliation, and the development of competence.

Rogers's concept of full functioning and Maslow's construct of self-actualization both contain the idea that actualized individuals are free to control what happens to them. The concept of control is central to both theories and coincides with ideas generated by other theorists of human motivation. Control aspects of human motivation have been termed competence (White, 1959), personal causation (deCharms, 1968), and human agency (Bandura, 2001, 2002). Competence is also

a major part of a more general theory of self-determination (Deci & Ryan, 1980, 1985, 2000). These theories imply that the basis for much of human behavior is the need to be effective in controlling one's environment. We will briefly discuss the seminal work of White and deCharms before turning to the more extensive theories of Bandura and Deci and Ryan.

Competence

Robert White (1959) argued persuasively for the concept of **competence** motivation. As he defined it, competence is the capacity to interact effectively with one's environment. In a review of the theories popular in 1959, he showed how several lines of evidence from animal behavior, psychoanalysis, and related areas of psychology all pointed toward a motive that activated a striving for competence. White noted that this **effectance motivation**, as he termed it, was most clearly seen in the behavior of young children. The example at the beginning of this chapter concerning the child repeatedly climbing onto a chair can be viewed as the child's striving to gain control over her environment. In White's view the play behavior of children is serious business; it is triggered by the child's attempt to master the environment effectively.

White suggested that effectance motivation is normally seen when other homeostatic motives are at low levels. When, for example, children are neither thirsty nor cold, they will play in order to increase control over their world.

In the child, effectance motivation is rather global, and the child's behavior is directed toward whatever aspect of the environment catches his or her attention. So, for example, the child may play with television remote control, but a few moments later climb the stairs to turn the light off and on. These repeated behaviors can be quite exasperating to parents who are trying to keep the child away from the remote, but they take on a new perspective if seen as motivated by the need to control one's environment. In the adult, competence behavior can become quite differentiated, so that one might even consider achievement behavior (as noted in previous chapters) as energized by effectance motivation, the control aspect in this case being to excel intellectually.

The goal of effectance motivation, according to White, is a feeling of efficacy (effectiveness), which satisfies much as physical goals satisfy physical needs. White also argued that competence behavior is adaptive. While the goal of effectance motivation is simply to have an effect on the environment and in turn discover how the environment affects us, the relationships we learn can serve us usefully later. For example, the child learning to climb a chair does so simply to be able to do it, yet he or she may use the information later to get a piece of fruit from a bowl. Clearly, learning occurs during episodes of effectance motivation, and we can put this learning to good use at a later time.

Personal Causation

The concept of control suggested by White has been further extended by deCharms (1968). DeCharms argued that the primary motive in humans is to "be effective in producing changes in [their] environment" (p. 269). In other words, we strive for **personal causation**, such that we can be causal agents in our environment.

Personal causation is not strictly a motive but a guiding principle upon which all other motives are built. As deCharms noted, we typically describe motivation in relation to the goals toward which a behavior leads: when hungry, we seek food; when thirsty, we seek water; and so on. Though we speak of the hunger motive, personal causation is the force requiring that we be able to respond in ways that will get us food. Thus, deCharms saw personal causation as the underlying principle of all motivated behaviors.

Origins and Pawns   DeCharms argued that people may be categorized as origins or pawns. An **origin** believes that our behavior is controlled by our own choices. A **pawn**, on the other hand, perceives our behavior as being controlled by external forces over which we have no control. As you might guess, origins have strong feelings of personal causation, and much of their behavior is directed by these feelings of control. Pawns feel powerless, and their behavior is related to their perception of lack of control.

The work of both White and deCharms was important in elucidating humans' motive for growth; unfortunately, neither theory inspired much empirical research. We now discuss two theories of the control aspects of human motivation that have generated a great deal of supporting data—those of Bandura and Deci and Ryan.

Bandura's Social Cognitive Theory of Human Agency

According to Albert Bandura, human agency, or the "capacity to exercise control over the nature and quality of one's life" is "the essence of humanness" (Bandura, 2001, p. 1). In Bandura's social cognitive theory, humans are active rather than reactive organisms, and our behavior is shaped by internal factors as much as by our environment. Bandura argues that understanding can best be achieved by studying the complex interplay between behavior, cognition, and environmental factors which interact with one another via **reciprocal causation**. The essence of reciprocal causation is that our behavior (B), environment (E), and personal (P) factors (such as cognitive, affective and biological events) influence and are influenced by one another as depicted in the following illustration:

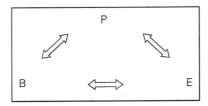

Bandura takes the holistic perspective that events should be understood in their entirety, not broken down into component parts. Thus, both negative behaviors (e.g., eating disorders, alcohol abuse) and positive behaviors (e.g., athletic functioning, career development) are the result of the environmental factors, and internal cognitive, affective, and biological events. What's more, the planning and performance of these behaviors subsequently influence one's environment and internal milieu. Bandura argues that reciprocal causation should not be approached from a reductionist perspective. To try to understand an experience by breaking it down (e.g., reducing it to reinforcement history or neural activity) is to lose the essence of the event. Like water, human experience is more

than the sum of its parts, as Bandura (1997, p. 4) notes:

> the emergent properties of water, such as fluidity, viscosity, and transparency, are not simply the aggregate properties of its microcomponents, oxygen and hydrogen.

Core Features of Human Agency According to Bandura (2001), human agency has four core features, the first of which is **intentionality**, or a proactive commitment to bring about a future course of action. Intentionality is a necessary first step, but it is just the beginning. For example, suppose you notice someone to whom you feel attracted. You decide to ask him or her out on a date (intentionality). You have made a commitment to follow a course of action. However, where this course of action leads is anyone's guess. Your offer may be declined. Or, if your offer is accepted, the date may go very well (or not) and perhaps even lead to a happy (or unhappy) long-term relationship.

In order to maximize your chances of a successful outcome, intentionality is not enough; **forethought** is needed. Forethought is your action plan, or your anticipation of future events and their likely consequences. Consider the planning that you must do for a first date: What to wear? Where to go? What topics of conversation to discuss? Each of these decisions is made with some of the potential consequences anticipated. For example, because the way you dress says a lot about you on a first date, people typically put more forethought into their choice of clothing on a first date than they do on subsequent dates. Later, when you have gotten to know one another better, what one wears is less important.

Because forethought involves anticipation of future events, it is, by definition, not an easy thing to accomplish. It is impossible to anticipate all of the things that may occur and how you might react to them. Events like getting stuck in traffic, running into a former lover, or becoming violently ill are all things that occasionally occur on dates, yet most people don't have an "action plan" in place for them. Furthermore, forethought is needed for both short-term events like those mentioned earlier as well as longer-term events, such as when to go on a trip together or to meet one another's family.

According to Bandura, even when we have our intention and action plan in place, we still cannot rest. We engage in **self-reactiveness**, or the motivation and self-regulation necessary to maintain a course of action and to evaluate it with respect to our goals and standards. What are your short-term and long-term goals for a relationship? Are they likely to be met with this person? Do your friends "approve" of him or her, or do you find yourself drifting away from other people that you value? Self-reactiveness also involves a moral component that keeps our behavior in line with our ideas of right and wrong. What if you were to learn that your new partner is married? Or is involved in an illegal activity such as drug trafficking? What each of these questions has in common is that our decision to maintain, or to deviate from a course of action is in some way dependent upon its relationship to our personal goals and standards.

The final core feature of Bandura's theory is **self-reflectiveness**, or the ability to evaluate how effective we are at exercising our capacity for human agency. By engaging in the first three processes of human agency, we will learn something about ourselves. What do we want out of life? How successful are we at attaining the goals we set for ourselves? This result of this evaluation of *self-efficacy* is very important because it has an impact on many aspects of our lives including how we feel about ourselves, what types of challenges we will seek out (and which we will avoid), whether we feel optimism or pessimism about future events, and so on.

In these core features of human agency, we can see the reciprocal determinism inherent in Bandura's theory. Our decision to engage in or not to engage in a given behavior is shaped by forces in the environment and internal factors.

Once a course of action has been chosen, our behavior is then both influenced by and becomes a causal factor in the environment in which we behave. We then evaluate our behavior according to our internal standards and goals. Finally, through the process of self-reflectiveness, we develop perceptions of self-efficacy that influence our future decisions regarding the environments and behaviors that we seek out and those we avoid.

Personal, Proxy, and Collective Agency   Bandura has identified what he calls three modes of human agency. **Personal agency** includes the four features discussed earlier, and is concerned with agency from the perspective of an individual. However, according to Bandura, there are two other modes of agency that are important and they both stem from the fact that human beings are social creatures by nature.

Like many other animals, humans live in groups. One of the advantages to living in a society is that labor can be divided among group members; it is not necessary for everyone to be an expert at every conceivable task. When we take advantage of each other's areas of expertise, we are relying on **proxy agency**. For example, a friend or family member who works for a computer manufacturer or in an automobile dealership comes in very handy when we need advice about the purchase of a new computer or car. Another example of proxy agency is the type of government employed in most modern republics. In the United States, for example, citizens do not vote directly on legislation or other matters of interest. Instead, elected representatives, or proxies, vote for us. One advantage of proxy agency is that we can each specialize in our own area of interest, providing that we can locate a proxy who will share his or her expertise with us when the need arises. Another advantage is that we do not have to be responsible for decisions that we are ill-informed to make. For example, our elected representatives are, in essence, being paid to stay informed and to make decisions for us.

The third mode of Bandura's theory is **collective agency**. This refers to the ability of groups to accomplish more than can be done by the same number of individuals working alone, provided that they work together and share the belief that they can achieve their goal (Bandura, 2000). Recall from our discussion of social loafing in Chapter 8 that individual productivity does not automatically increase just because people work together on a task. Rather, coordination of effort and a shared belief that a valued goal can be achieved are necessary for individuals to give their all in a group setting. According to Bandura, this feeling that the group can attain its goal, or group efficacy is a major factor (along with knowledge and skill of group members) in determining whether or not the group goal is met (collective agency). Once again applying the concept of reciprocal determinism, Bandura contends that the perception of collective efficacy lives within the group members and that it both influences and is influenced by their behavior and the surrounding environment.

Applying the Social Cognitive Theory of Human Agency

Beliefs about efficacy, which are a fundamental component of Bandura's social cognitive theory, have been found both to predict and to have a causal impact on many aspects of human functioning. For example, Bandura, Barbaranelli, Caprara, and Pastorelli (1996) found evidence that both children's and parents' beliefs about efficacy are important predictors of children's academic success. From a collective agency perspective, there is evidence that teachers' beliefs about their collective efficacy to educate students generally declines as the child's grade level increases (Bandura, 1993), and teachers' efficacy beliefs are related to children's perceived performance and expectancies for success in school (e.g., Midgley, Feldlaufer, & Eccles, 1989). Thus, improving the perceived collective efficacy of teachers is one approach to improving student performance.

In the health care domain, feelings of personal efficacy are positively related to the development and maintenance of healthy behaviors. For example, Clark, Ghandour, Miller, Taylor, Bandura, and DeBusk (1997) found that a self-efficacy based treatment program resulted in at least a 5% reduction in blood cholesterol levels in participants across five separate studies. DeBusk and colleagues (1994) found that an intervention program that included self-efficacy training was more successful than the standard medical treatment in helping cardiac patients to quit smoking, reduce cholesterol, and increase cardiovascular capacity. In people with diabetes, self-efficacy beliefs have been found to predict adherence to dietary guidelines and blood glucose levels (Nouwen, Ford, Balan, Twisk, Ruggiero, & White, 2011) as well as level of physical activity (Plotnikoff, Lippke, Courneya, Birkett, & Sigal, 2008).

In addition to academic performance and health care, Bandura's social cognitive theory of human agency has been successfully applied to the treatment of eating disorders, phobias, depression, athletic performance, and organizational decision-making (see Bandura, 1997; 2006 for reviews of this literature). Thus, there is a great deal of research that suggests that feelings of competence induced by self-efficacy training can improve the quality of one's life. However, competence may not be the only variable that is important for healthy functioning. Edward Deci and Richard Ryan have developed a theory that postulates that competence is necessary but not sufficient for optimal functioning. In their view, we must satisfy our needs for autonomy and relatedness as well.

Self-Determination Theory

Deci and Ryan have developed a theory of motivation that postulates three basic needs that all humans strive to satisfy: competence, relatedness, and autonomy (Deci & Ryan, 1980, 1985, 2000). **Competence** refers to our need to have some control over our environment and is similar to Bandura's concept of agency. **Relatedness** is our need to feel a sense of belongingness with others. **Autonomy** is our need to freely integrate our experiences with our sense of self (Deci & Ryan, 2000). According to their self-determination theory, these three needs are *psychological* in nature, yet they are *innate*, rather than learned. Thus, self-determination theory is different from most traditional theories of motivation that are typically concerned either with innate physiological needs (e.g., Hull, 1943) or learned psychological needs (e.g., Murray, 1938). Because these three needs are innate, they are shared by people of all cultures and backgrounds. However, the way these needs are met may differ from culture to culture.

According to Deci and Ryan, satisfaction of all three needs is necessary for healthy functioning. We cannot maintain psychological health if we satisfy only one or two (or worse, none) of the three basic needs. What's more, if one's attempt to satisfy these psychological needs is thwarted, we may become more determined to meet the need, just as one would if a physiological need such as hunger was not being met. However, continued thwarting of attempts to meet a psychological need such as autonomy may result in *fewer* attempts to satisfy the need and may cause maladaptive consequences such as feelings of helplessness and/or misdirected attempts at need satisfaction (e.g., development of an eating disorder).

Why might initial failure to satisfy a physiological need increase motivation, but continued thwarting of a psychological need produce the opposite effect? According to Deci and Ryan, this occurs because physiological needs such as hunger occur when we experience a deficit that must be satisfied. Once the deficit has been met, the organism can rest. However, psychological needs are not deficits; they are needs that spur us toward growth. Thus, thwarting a psychological need may result in a lack of activity or decreased motivation toward personal development. Although such a circumstance does not place us in immediate physical danger, it can have serious psychological consequences. One possible consequence is learned helplessness. As you may recall from the data presented in Chapters 5 and 10, considerable evidence exists that animals and humans "give up" when they perceive that they have no control over their environment. In a sense, learned helplessness and perceived control are two sides of the same coin: lack of control has a demotivating effect on behavior,

while perceived control (whether the perception is correct or not) has a motivating effect.

There is quite a bit of evidence that all three needs specified by self-determination theory are important for growth and development. For example, recall the study by Sheldon and colleagues (2001) discussed earlier. Participants who were asked to describe how they felt when they experienced their "most satisfying events" consistently reported feelings of autonomy, relatedness, and competence as being associated with these important experiences. There is also a good deal of research that indicates that self-determination theory can help explain the development of intrinsic motivation.

Psychological Needs and the Development of Intrinsic Motivation According to self-determination theory, satisfaction of the basic psychological needs is conducive to the development of **intrinsic motivation**, or the value or pleasure associated with an activity as opposed to the goal toward which the activity is directed (Staw, 1976). Thus, we engage in intrinsically motivated behaviors because we *want* to do so, not because we are expecting a reward or trying to avoid a punishment. **Extrinsic motivation**, by contrast, emphasizes the external goals toward which the activity is directed.

Intrinsic motivation is important because it is associated with overall psychological health and functioning (e.g., Kasser & Ryan, 1996; Ryan & Deci, 2000), yet as children our behavior is largely determined by extrinsic factors. How then does intrinsic motivation develop? According to Deci and Ryan (2000), the development of intrinsic motivation is mediated by the fulfillment of the three basic psychological needs postulated by self-determination theory. Furthermore, intrinsic motivation can be undermined by the presence of rewards for performing a behavior (e.g., Deci, Koestner, & Ryan, 1999). According to self-determination theory, this occurs because the rewards reduce the individual's sense of autonomy. Consider the hypothetical example of a young child named Melissa who likes to read. Her parents notice her interest in books and want to encourage it, so they offer Melissa a monetary reward for every 30 minutes she spends reading. According to self-determination theory, the parents' good intentions may reinforce Melissa's reading behavior, but may actually undermine Melissa's *desire* to read. Why? Because Melissa may attribute her behavior to the reward contingencies (i.e., the money), rather than to her volition. Melissa will not feel as though she is freely choosing to read and her need for autonomy is not being met under these circumstances.

The need for competence may also mediate the development of intrinsic motivation, because we are more likely to enjoy activities if we are proficient at them. How can a sense of competence be fostered such that intrinsic motivation can develop? According to self-determination theory, positive feedback is one technique that, under certain conditions, can increase feelings of competence and produce intrinsic motivation for an activity (e.g., Vallerand & Reid, 1984). However, positive feedback alone is not enough. Among other things, the feedback must be perceived to be sincere (e.g., Henderlong & Lepper, 2002) and must not override one's sense of autonomy (e.g., Deci & Ryan, 2000). Consider our example of Melissa once again. If Melissa's parents praise her for her interest in reading, Melissa should develop feelings of competence provided that she perceives the praise to be sincere and noncontrolling. Sincerity is important because Melissa must believe that the praise has been earned and that her parents are not just trying to make her feel good (e.g., Henderlong & Lepper, 2002). The praise must be administered in a manner such that Melissa can maintain her sense of autonomy (e.g., "You are a good reader."). She should not feel controlled by conditional praise (e.g., "You are a good reader, just like we want you to be.").

Finally, self-determination theory holds that meeting one's need for relatedness is an important facilitating factor in the development of intrinsic motivation (e.g., Ryan & La Guardia, 2000), although this need may not be as fundamental as are the needs of autonomy and competence (Deci & Ryan, 2000). Feeling a sense of connectedness to others, as is the case when one experiences the caring environment provided by parents and teachers, can foster intrinsic motivation (e.g., Ryan, Stiller, & Lynch, 1994). Thus, if Melissa perceives that her parents and teachers love and care for her, she can feel free to pursue her interest in reading.

Moving From Extrinsic to Intrinsic Motivation According to self-determination theory, behavior that was once the result of extrinsic factors can become intrinsically motivated, provided that the external motives become internalized, or integrated into one's sense of self. There are different levels of internalization, and they are represented along the continuum of motivation depicted in Figure 11.3. At the far left of Figure 11.3 is the state of **amotivation**, which occurs when an individual either does not engage in a behavior, or does so but only "goes through the motions" (Ryan & Deci, 2000). Amotivation can occur when our basic needs of competence and autonomy are not met. For example, Melissa may not read at all if she feels that she is an incompetent reader. Or, she may "go through the motions" and pretend to read if she is forced to do so by parents or teachers.

The center section of Figure 11.3 labeled "Extrinsic Motivation" depicts the different levels of internalization. As we move from left to right, the behavior becomes more internalized, and the perceived locus of causality changes from external to internal. **External regulation** occurs when we engage in a behavior in order to receive rewards or avoid punishments that are controlled by others. Thus, if Melissa were to read in order to earn money or to avoid a punishment, she would be engaging in external regulation. **Introjection** is similar to external regulation in that the behavior is still motivated by rewards and punishments. However, introjection involves contingencies that are administered by individuals themselves. If Melissa were to put *herself* on a reinforcement schedule (e.g., she allows herself one hour of television for every 30 minutes that she reads), she would be engaging in introjection.

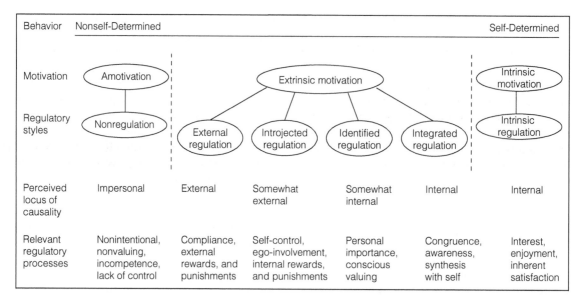

FIGURE 11.3 Types of motivation and their regulatory processes, according to Deci and Ryan's self-determination theory. From R. M. Ryan and E. L. Deci, "Self-Determination Theory and the Facilitation of Intrinsic Motivation, Social Development, and Well-Being." *American Psychologist, 55,* 68–78. Copyright © American Psychological Association. Reprinted with permission.

Identified regulation occurs when we begin to see the value of the activity for its own sake, but are still motivated by external factors. For example, Melissa may recognize that reading is an important lifetime skill, and may thus exercise her autonomy and choose to do more of it. In this case, the motivation is still external, but the goal is now something that is more personal than a simple reward or punishment. The final type of extrinsic motivation is called **integrated regulation**. This type of motivation occurs when individuals have not only identified the behavior as valuable, but have integrated it into their sense of self. For example, Melissa may aspire to be a generally knowledgeable and educated person. A healthy desire to read will help her attain this goal. Ryan and Deci (2000) point out that integrated regulation is similar to intrinsic motivation in many respects. However, individuals engaged in integrated regulation are not truly intrinsically motivated because they are not yet performing the behavior for its own sake (i.e., the behavior is still a means to an end). The final section of Figure 11.3 is labeled intrinsic motivation. True intrinsic motivation involves performing a behavior for the inherent satisfaction of the activity. Melissa is intrinsically motivated when she desires to read for the pleasure of reading.

As you may have noticed, the theories of Rogers, Maslow, White, deCharms, Bandura, and Deci and Ryan share several characteristics, the most obvious of which is the focus on human growth. This theme has not always been so apparent in the history of psychological theory and research. As a matter of fact, some psychologists have argued that psychology has neglected to focus on the more positive aspects of the human condition for far too long.

The Rise of Positive Psychology

Martin Seligman and Mihaly Csikszentmihalyi (2000) note that, prior to World War II, psychology had three primary foci: (1) to treat individuals with mental illness, (2) to improve the productivity and functioning of all people, and (3) to determine how to best foster the development of individuals with exceptional abilities. According to Seligman and Csikszentmihalyi, psychology has focused most of its energy on the first goal and has seriously neglected the other two. In short, psychology has become dominated by attempts to treat disease and has not focused enough on nurturing healthy individuals to avoid disorders and to grow to their full potential.

Seligman and Csikszentmihalyi are not advocating the abandonment of clinical research and treatment. This will always be a primary focus of psychology. However, they argue that studying healthy development is as important as studying disease for at least two reasons. First, it is important to learn the processes that control positive growth so that it can best be nurtured in all people. A second benefit is that much can be learned about disorders if we understand how they differ from healthy development. For example, studying competence and autonomy can tell us a great deal about learned helplessness; learning about the development of happiness and subjective well-being can enhance our understanding of depression, and other conditions.

Building on the work of humanistic psychologists such as Maslow and Rogers, researchers in the field of positive psychology have attempted toempirically study the antecedents and consequences of various aspects of positive human functioning. These include **positive emotions, positive individual traits and virtues**, and **positive institutions** (Seligman, 2002; Seligman & Csikszentmihalyi, 2000). Seligman (2002) divides positive emotions based on their temporal sequence: past, future, and present. He believes that each type is distinct and can be altered to improve our overall happiness or well-being (terms he uses interchangeably). Past emotions include contentment, pride, and satisfaction and we can improve them through gratitude and forgiveness. Future emotions such as optimism and hope are more likely if we retrain ourselves to notice and limit pessimistic cognitions.

Present emotions are further divided into pleasures and gratifications. **Pleasures** (sometimes referred to as **hedonia** in the literature) include both *bodily pleasures* such as sexual gratification and eating savory food as well as what Seligman calls *higher pleasures* such as excitement, glee, and amusement, which are more complex than bodily pleasures. Unfortunately, both types of pleasures are fleeting and we quickly habituate to stimuli that trigger them. Thus, they are not a viable path to long-lasting happiness. However, pleasures can be enhanced by depriving ourselves of stimuli that activate them or through **mindfulness**, which is focusing one's attention on the moment rather than engaging in a pleasure-inducing activity automatically or reflexively. **Gratifications** (also known as **eudaimonia**) are activities that are characterized by immersion, intense concentration, effortless involvement, and a loss of a sense of time. Thus, gratifications share some characteristics with Maslow's peak experiences. If you have ever been so immersed in an activity that you lose track of time or forget to eat, you have experienced gratification. Activities that trigger gratification vary from person to person, but can include things like getting lost in a good book, engaging in athletic activity, and creative activities such as painting, composing or playing music, and writing. In contrast to pleasures, gratifications can help lead us to long-term happiness. They occur when we exercise our positive individual traits in order to attain virtue, which is the second pillar of positive human functioning.

Seligman (2002) draws a distinction between *virtues* and *positive traits or strengths*. He and his colleagues (Dahlsgaard, Peterson, & Seligman, 2005) set out to classify virtues, which are aspects of human character that are valued universally. They read texts from Athenian philosophy, Islam, Judaism, Christianity, and major Eastern philosophies/religions such as Hinduism, and Buddhism. They discovered six core virtues that were mentioned or alluded to in the written works of all or nearly all traditions. They are *wisdom, courage, humanity, justice, temperance* (protection against excess), and *transcendence* (a sense of connection to something larger than one's self). Because these different cultures, philosophies, and religions value the same virtues, Seligman and colleagues argue that they are universal aspects of positive human character and thus should be cultivated.

Thus, Seligman (2002) identified a list of 24 positive traits or strengths that can be exercised to help individuals to develop virtues. His original list has been modified slightly but remains largely intact (see Peterson & Park, 2011 and Peterson & Seligman, 2004 for a complete description of the updated version). We present an abbreviated description of the 24 traits in the revised list here. The first virtue, wisdom, grows out of curiosity, creativity, open-mindedness, a love of learning, and perspective (the ability to provide sound guidance to another). Courage stems from honesty, persistence, bravery, and zest (enthusiasm about life). Humanity develops by exercising kindness, love, and social intelligence (sensitivity to the emotions and motives of others). Individuals can cultivate the virtue of justice by exhibiting teamwork, leadership, and fairness. One can develop temperance by exhibiting modesty, forgiveness, prudence, and self-regulation of affect and behavior. Finally, hope, gratitude, humor, an appreciation of beauty, and belief in a higher purpose/meaning in life can lead to transcendence. Seligman argues that not everyone possesses all of the traits on his list. Thus, he advocates that each of us concentrates on those that we enjoy using and that we feel are characteristic of our true selves. He terms these traits *signature strengths*, and it is our signature strengths that will contribute to the development of positive institutions.

The final pillar of positive psychology, positive institutions, has received substantially less attention from researchers than have positive emotions and positive traits/virtues (Biswas-Diener, Linley, Govindji, & Woolston, 2011; Dutton, Roberts, & Bednar, 2011; Gable & Haidt, 2005). Positive institutions develop when individuals use their strengths in the service of the greater good, such as an artist exhibiting his creativity or a judge exercising her sense of fairness. In this context, the term *institution* is broadly defined and includes, but is not limited to, community, workplace, education, and family. Thus, the potential application of positive psychology to the broader social realm is wide indeed, but researchers have yet to determine the mechanisms by which this can occur.

Criticisms of Positive Psychology Positive psychology has been criticized on both theoretical and practical grounds. Humanistic psychologists have pointed out that positive psychology has adopted many core principles of their domain such as well-being and optimism without proper recognition of the roots of those ideas and that positive psychology has applied a reductionist research methodology to these principles, which is in opposition to the holistic approaches used in humanistic psychology (Taylor, 2001; Wong, 2011). From a practical standpoint, some (e.g., Miller, 2008) have argued that positive psychology is prescriptive rather than descriptive; meaning that, rather than trying to understand optimism and happiness, positive psychology is telling us that we should be optimistic and happy. Put another way, it is prescribing what choices we should make and how we should live our lives.

SUMMARY

In this chapter we have reviewed data and theories suggesting that one very basic motive of human behavior is the need to develop the competence necessary to control our environment. Various theorists have approached this idea in slightly different ways, but all seem to share the conviction that healthy individuals need to perceive that they can affect their surroundings. In many respects the data and theories on learned helplessness also support the importance of perceptions of control.

Carl Rogers proposed that an individual is constantly striving for enhancement and growth. He argued that only one motive underlies all behavior—a motive for growth. Abraham Maslow proposed a very similar approach but also noted that certain deficiency needs must first be met before we can become all that we are capable of becoming. Nevertheless, the growth of the individual is the underlying theme of Maslow's theory too. In a revision of Maslow's theory, Kenrick and colleagues agree that growth of the individual begins with basic needs and progresses to social needs. However, they contend that the highest stage of development is not self-actualization, but mating and parenting such that we can help to guide our children (and thus our genes) through the very same process. Though not stated explicitly, the theory of both Rogers and the original theory of Maslow seem to imply that the fully functioning or self-actualized person is both competent and in control of his or her environment.

Robert White and Richard deCharms have separately proposed models of human behavior emphasizing a striving for competence and personal causation as basic motives of human behavior. For Albert Bandura, the essential feature of human functioning is agency, which includes the core features of intentionality, forethought, self-reactiveness, and self-reflectiveness. According to Bandura, human agency can be exercised on an individual, proxy, or collective level. Edward

Deci and Richard Ryan have proposed self-determination theory. They contend that all humans have innate needs for autonomy, competence, and relatedness and that all three of these needs must be satisfied for growth to occur. What's more, the satisfaction of these needs mediates the development of intrinsic motivation.

Positive psychology has become very popular since the turn of the 21st century. It is, in many ways, a reaction to the extreme degree to which psychology had previously concerned itself with the treatment of disorders and had neglected the study of how to nurture positive functioning. Positive psychology is based on three general concepts. These are the study of positive emotions, positive traits and virtues, and positive institutions.

Recall that we began this chapter with an example of a 15-month-old child trying vigorously to pull herself up onto a dining room chair. In the remainder of the chapter we learned that the need to be competent, self-determining, in control, fully functioning, and self-actualizing is an important motivation of behavior. Although the terminology differs from theorist to theorist, all would agree that the child climbed the chair due to a need to believe that she has an effect on the world around her.

KEY TERMS

humanistic psychology, *331*
actualizing tendency/positive regard/positive self-regard/unconditional positive regard/conditional positive regard, *332*
fully functioning individuals/openness to experience/existential living/trust in one's own organism/sense of freedom/creativity, *333*
ultimate goals/self-actualization/hierarchy of needs, *334*

physiological needs/safety needs, *335*
love or belongingness needs/esteem needs/need for self-esteem/need for esteem from others/deprivation motivation (D-motivation), *336*
self-actualization/being needs/B-motivation/metamotivation/transcenders/peakers/nontranscenders/nonpeakers, *337*

Jonah complex/time competence/peak performance/flow, *338*
absorption, *339*
competence, *341*
effectance motivation/personal causation/origin/pawn, *342*
reciprocal causation/intentionality/forethought, *343*
self-reactiveness/self-reflectiveness/personal agency/proxy agency/collective agency, *344*

SUGGESTIONS FOR FURTHER READING

Bandura, A. (1997). *Self-efficacy: The exercise of control.* New York W. H. Freeman. A comprehensive book that includes an outline of Bandura's theory and its many applications.

Deci, E. L. & Ryan, R. M. (2000). The "what" and "why" of goal pursuits: Human needs and the self-determination of behavior. *Psychological Inquiry, 11,* 227–268. An overview of self-determination theory and the relationship of the goals of autonomy, competence and relatedness to the development of intrinsic motivation.

Henderlong, J. & Lepper, M. R. (2002). The effects of praise on children's intrinsic motivation: A review and synthesis. *Psychological Bulletin, 128,* 774–795. A comprehensive summary of the somewhat inconsistent literature on the effect of praise on intrinsic motivation. The authors provide a cogent argument for when praise is beneficial and when it can be detrimental.

Rogers, C. R. (1961). *On becoming a person: A therapist's view of psychotherapy.* Boston Houghton Mifflin. This book provides a good overview of Rogers's ideas concerning full functioning.

Seligman, M. E. P. & Csikszentmihalyi, M. (2000). Positive psychology: An introduction. *American Psychologist, 55,* 5–14. The original call for the development of positive psychology.

WEB RESOURCES

A site devoted to the work of Albert Bandura: http://www.des.emory.edu/mfp/bandurabio.html

The home page of the Positive Psychology Center: http://www.ppc.sas.upenn.edu/index.html

A site devoted to self-determination theory: http://www.psych.rochester.edu/SDT/

PART V

EMOTION AND MOTIVATION

CHAPTER 12
The Emotions as Motivators

CHAPTER 12

The Emotions as Motivators

As an avid amateur athlete, I have watched various Olympic events with great interest and have vicariously experienced some of the emotional impact that success and failure brought to the participants. I have seen athletes receive gold medals with tears rolling down their cheeks. Are they sad? Hardly. Emotional? Definitely.

This chapter is about emotion. How can we explain both the emotionality of the successful athlete and our own emotional reactions? Do emotions result from internal visceral changes, as suggested by James and Lange (see later in this chapter), or do they result from cognitive appraisal of ongoing events? Are emotions innate and of limited number, or are they learned and multitudinous? These are a few of the questions research on emotion has attempted to answer. As we shall discover, the answers to such questions are difficult to obtain, and opinions differ widely.

Originally the word **emotion** meant to move, as in migrating from one place to another; however, the term later came to mean a moving or agitation in the physical sense. This usage was later broadened to include social and political agitation. Finally, the term came to mean an agitated or aroused state in an individual (Young, 1975). Thus the idea of emotion seems to imply that a person is moved—that is, changed—from one state to another, as in from happy to sad or from nonemotional to emotional.

Researchers interested in the concept have attempted numerous definitions of emotion, but as noted by Mandler (1984), no commonly accepted definition has been provided. As we examine the various models of emotion presented in this chapter, it will become apparent that emotion can be conceptualized in many different ways, from physiological changes to cognitive appraisals to innate, fundamental facial expressions. Each approach has something to offer, and the lack of a generally acceptable definition of emotion probably results in part from the fact that emotion is multifaceted. We will use, as a working definition of emotion, the following quote from Damasio (2001, p. 781): "An emotion, be it happiness or sadness, embarrassment or pride, is a patterned collection of chemical and neural responses that is produced by the brain when it detects the presence of an emotionally competent stimulus—an object or situation for example." Damasio further makes a distinction between an emotion and its participative experience: "Feelings are the mental representation of the physiological changes that characterize emotions" (Damasio, 2001, p. 781). It is worth noting that researchers better understand emotions than they do feelings.

Over the years several traditions have developed in the study of emotion. One tradition is biological. Begun by Darwin (1872), the biological approach was further developed by James, Lange, and Cannon, and more recently by the ethologists (as well as by many others too numerous to mention). In the first section of this chapter we will examine emotion from this biological perspective.

A second tradition has emphasized the role of learning processes in emotion. The drive-like qualities of emotion have been noted by Spence and Taylor, and the modeling of emotional behavior has been noted by Bandura. In the second section of this chapter we will briefly review some of the ways in which learning is involved with emotion.

In the third section of the chapter we will examine cognitive approaches to emotion. Theorists in this tradition have often emphasized cognitive appraisal as important to the experience of emotion. Several cognitive models will be examined.

At the end of this chapter, we will examine the idea that a limited number of emotions are universal. The theories typically propose that a small number of innate emotions have evolved because of their adaptive value to the individual. Further, facial musculature changes are often suggested as the way in which emotions are communicated to others and, indeed, to ourselves. The fundamental emotions may be blended to produce an almost unlimited range of emotional experience.

As is evident from this short introduction, research on emotion has provided no easy answers, and the disputes between theorists have sometimes been severe. In fact, one explanation has tended to replace another about every 20 years (Averill, 1983). In this chapter we will examine many of the approaches noted by Averill that have influenced our concepts about emotion. Let's start out at the beginning of modern approaches to the topic, that is, with Darwin.

Emotion from a Biological Perspective

Darwin's Principles of Emotion

If you were to read Darwin's book *The Expression of the Emotions in Man and Animals* (1872), you would be struck by how modern much of it sounds. For example, he was aware that body movements and facial expressions (today called body language or nonverbal communication) communicate meaning between individual members of a species. He argued that much of this nonverbal communication transmits information about the organism's emotional state.

Darwin believed that both emotions and their expression are innate, though he allowed for the possibility that some types of emotional expression may be learned. Much of his analysis of emotion revolved around the manner in which emotions are expressed. He proposed three principles for understanding the expression of emotion in both humans and animals: **serviceable associated habits, antithesis,** and **direct action of the nervous system**.

Serviceable Associated Habits

In the principle of serviceable associated habits, Darwin proposed that the ways in which organisms express emotion have had survival value in the past. Thus a dog may bare its teeth when defending its master because, in the evolutionary past of canines, such behaviors increased the survival value of dogs that behaved that way. Baring the teeth should be adaptive for several reasons; for example, it can signal motivational readiness to attack, which in turn often causes the opposing animal to leave, and second, it prepares the dog for biting if necessary.

Darwin believed that emotional expressions were originally learned but had become innate over many generations; thus serviceable associated habits were learned behaviors that became innate because of their usefulness. Because he did not know of the genetic work of Mendel, Darwin did not know how characteristics are passed from one generation to another, so he proposed that emotional expressions evolved from learned habits to hereditary traits over many generations. Today we know that evolution does not work that way. However, to bring Darwin's principle in line with modern knowledge of genetics, we need only note that certain genes predispose the development of particular emotional behaviors and that emotional expression (the dog baring its teeth) had survival value for organisms that possessed those genes.

Antithesis

In the principle of antithesis, Darwin proposed that the expression of opposite emotions (anger and calm) involves opposite kinds of behavior. The "angry" cat crouches down, flattens its ears against its head, extends its claws, and opens its mouth to bite. The calm, "friendly" cat rubs against your leg with its tail and ears erect, mouth closed, and claws retracted. The behavioral expression of these two emotional states is very different and, in many respects, opposite. Thus the principle of antithesis notes that behaviors associated with opposite kinds of feelings are often expressed in opposite kinds of behavior (consider the upturned smile of the happy person and the downturned mouth of the sad person).

Direct Action of the Nervous System

Darwin realized that he could not categorize all emotional behavior under the first two principles because some emotional behaviors appear useless to the organism and, in addition, often have no opposites. He therefore proposed the principle of direct action of the nervous system, which says that some emotional expressions occur simply because of changes in nervous system activity. Trembling when fearful or screaming when in agony might be considered as examples of this principle.

Darwin's first two principles seem more relevant today than his third. It is generally believed that emotions and their expressions have been adaptive and are present today because they serve to communicate internal states from one individual to another. For example, how often have you glanced at someone and, without a word being spoken, known that something was wrong? Your recognition that something is amiss probably results from emotional signals you observed in the person's facial expression. Many modern theorists, following the lead of Darwin, also believe that emotions can be understood as consisting of polar opposites such as happy–sad, angry–calm, excited–bored, and so forth. As we shall see, however, there is much debate concerning unipolar versus bipolar dimensions in emotion. Darwin's third principle is currently not very popular. Trembling in fear, for example, can be understood as the result of activation of the sympathetic nervous system, and though activation of this system often accompanies emotion, it may not be the same as emotion. The trembling and the fear may result from activation of different systems. Likewise, screaming in agony may be an innate response to pain that is separate from concurrently experienced emotion.

Recognition of Emotional States

One way in which emotional behavior would have survival value for an individual is if it provided "clues" of that individual's emotional state to other members of its species. Darwin believed that expressive movements are recognized as being associated with particular emotional states by members of a species and that this recognition is itself innate. In other words, we recognize certain behaviors as indicating that an individual is in a particular emotional state, and we can alter our behavior accordingly (when Dad starts frowning and clenching his teeth, he is angry, so do as he says). Interestingly, Darwin noted that movements of the eyebrows, forehead, and mouth are important signals of emotional state (the next time someone "gets mad" at you, note these facial regions).

Other Formulations of Emotion after Darwin

Prior to the 1884 publication of William James's article on emotion, it was felt that the arousal of behavior was the last step in a three-step process that began with the perception of some stimulus (e.g., a barking dog), which led to the development of an emotion (e.g., fear), and culminated in behavior (e.g., running away). Figure 12.1a depicts the sequence of events leading from perception to behavior as they were understood prior to 1884.

The James-Lange Theory

James in 1884 and Lange in 1885 independently proposed that the feelings of emotion did not occur immediately after the perceptions of some event in the environment but as a result of our bodily responses to the object. Their approach became known as the James-Lange theory of emotion. For James the experience of emotion occurs as follows: the perception of an environmental stimulus (a barking dog) leads to changes in the body (increased heart rate, rapid breathing), which, in turn, are fed back to the brain, indicating a "changed state." The change in the physical state (particularly of the internal organs) is the experience of emotion. In other words, our perception of changes in our body leads to an emotional experience. The sequence of events leading from perception to behavior is noted in Figure 12.1b.

For example, if an automobile almost runs us down as we are jogging along the roadside, we react by changes in muscle tension and glandular

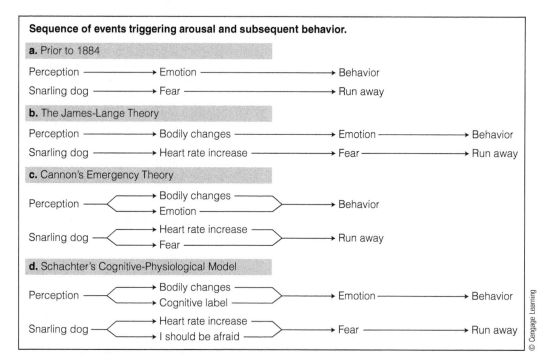

FIGURE 12.1   Four models of the relationships between events, emotion, and behavior.

secretion, and we become angry (perhaps making an obscene gesture)—in that order.

James thought that without the bodily changes, emotions would not exist or, at most, would be cold or intellectualized (e.g., "I know I should feel angry, but I don't.").

The James-Lange theory of emotion was very popular because it agreed with common sense, and it was generally regarded as "truth" until W. B. Cannon (1929, 1968) began to question it experimentally. Based on his own research and that of others, he criticized the James-Lange theory on five counts. (But see a review by Friedman [2010] indicating that the Jamesian perspective is still very much alive and well.)

First, Cannon argued that the bodily changes supposed to provide feedback to the brain and thus provide emotional quality to experience could be completely eliminated without disturbing the emotions of an organism. He denervated cats so that no changes in the body could occur. These cats, however, still showed normal rage behavior in the presence of a barking dog.

Second, Cannon noted that the bodily changes occurring in emotional states are very nearly the same regardless of the emotion shown. For example, he noted that in both fear and rage the heart accelerates, blood sugar levels increase, the pupils of the eyes dilate, and hair stands erect. Thus feedback from these kinds of changes could not be determining the emotional state of the organism. He further noted that these same bodily changes occur in response to changes in temperature (exposure to extreme cold or heat).

Third, Cannon claimed that the internal organs (viscera) supposed to provide feedback to the brain for the experience of emotion are not very sensitive structures. The number of sensory nerve fibers (afferents) coming from these structures (stomach, intestines, heart, and so on) are often only one-tenth the number of motor nerve fibers coming to them from the brain (efferents). Cannon noted that we are usually unaware of the movements and changes of our internal organs (e.g., what is your small intestine

doing at this moment?). He noted that one can cut, tear, crush, or even burn the components of the digestive system with no discomfort to unanesthetized humans—which suggests that these organs do not play a prominent role in providing feedback.

Fourth, Cannon felt that the changes occurring in the internal organs are too slow to provide the experience of emotion. He observed that the experience of emotion is sometimes immediate, but the triggering of the internal organs and feedback to the brain concerning their change may take several seconds. Cannon believed, therefore, that the state of emotion exists before feedback from the viscera can occur.

Fifth, Cannon noted that artificial induction of an aroused emotional state does not lead to an emotional "feeling." Thus injections of adrenaline (a hormone released by the adrenal glands during an emotional episode) did not typically make injected persons emotional, even though adrenaline alters bodily functioning in ways associated with emotionality. About 70% of injected participants reported feeling "as if" they should be emotional but without the emotional experience itself (Marañon, 1924; see also Cornelius, 1991, for a review of Marañon's research). In about 30% of the cases studied by Marañon, real emotions were produced, but only when the individuals had been induced into an emotional state by talking about their sick children or dead parents after they had been injected.

These five criticisms of the James-Lange theory led Cannon to propose an alternative theory of emotion termed the **emergency theory**. To understand Cannon's theory fully, we must briefly examine the autonomic nervous system.

The Autonomic Nervous System The **autonomic nervous system** (ANS) is basically involved with the regulation of vegetative processes (Carlson, 2002); that is, the ANS controls those processes that we do not voluntarily control, such as heartbeat, blood vessel constriction or dilation, glandular secretion, and so on. The ANS is composed of two subsystems, the sympathetic and parasympathetic nervous systems, which tend to have opposite effects on the body.

The **sympathetic nervous system** (SNS) is most active when energy stores of the body are being expended. When activated, the SNS causes increased blood flow to the muscles, secretion of adrenaline (today the term *epinephrine* is more commonly used) from the adrenal glands, increased heart rate, and release of additional blood sugar by the liver. The SNS in general prepares the organism to deal with emergency situations such as attack or flight.

The **parasympathetic nervous system** (PNS) is most active when the body is in the process of storing energy for future use. It decreases heart rate, dilates blood vessels, and causes saliva flow to the mouth when one is eating food. It also increases stomach and intestinal activity and directs the flow of blood away from the muscles to the digestive system. It is the system most active when we are quiet and relaxed after a large holiday meal.

The ANS also controls the endocrine system, which consists of glands that secrete their hormones directly into the bloodstream (the pituitary, thyroid, and adrenal glands for example). This system will be discussed later when we examine its relationship to stress.

The SNS and PNS do not work in strict opposition to one another; however, it is a useful simplification to view them as opposing one another from a motivational point of view, and this is essentially what Cannon did.

Cannon believed that emotion is associated with activation of the SNS. He argued that the control of emotion is based on a brain structure called the *thalamus*, which receives information from the various senses throughout the body and is located as shown in Figure 12.2. Although today we believe that the thalamus is only one of several structures involved in emotional behavior, a structure located very close to it called the *hypothalamus* (Figure 12.2) seems to be especially important. The

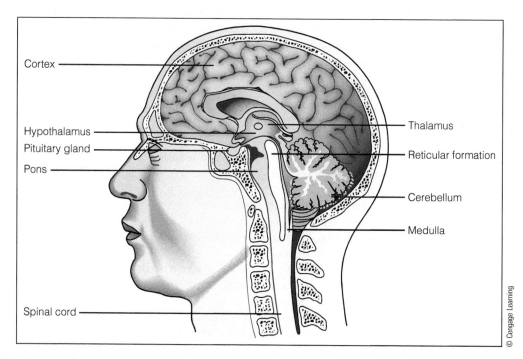

FIGURE 12.2 Major structures of the brain. Note the locations of the thalamus, hypothalamus, and recticular formation.

motivational role of the hypothalamus was examined in Chapters 3 and 4.

Cannon proposed that various emotional response patterns (e.g., anger and fear) are activated by the thalamus when the external sensory information it received is relayed to the cortex. He argued that the emotional behaviors activated by the thalamus are held in check by the cortex (see Figure 12.2). When the cortex receives appropriate sensory information, it releases the thalamus to trigger emotional responses. Cannon thought the thalamus was also responsible for SNS activation leading to the bodily changes considered so important by the James-Lange theory. Thus Cannon saw the expression of emotion as simultaneous with activation of the body, not the result of it (Figure 12.1c).

The Cognitive-Physiological Theory of Emotion

Stanley Schachter proposed the **cognitive-physiological theory of emotion** that proposes that both physiological arousal and cognitive attributions are necessary for the full experience of emotion (Schachter, 1964; Schachter & Singer, 1962). If either is absent, the participative state experienced will be incomplete. As noted by Cornelius (1991), Schachter's model is very similar to a model of emotion proposed by Marañon in 1924 that was largely ignored by the psychologists of his day.

Schachter and Singer devised a novel experiment to test the idea that both arousal and cognitive labeling are necessary for the experience of emotion. In most everyday circumstances the physiological arousal that occurs is clearly defined by the situation, so that we do not perceive the cognitive label and the arousal as distinct. What would happen, Schachter and Singer wondered, if some participants were artificially aroused through the injection of a substance normally present when a person is in an aroused state? They surmised that participants experiencing physiological arousal for which there was no adequate explanation would search their environment for cues to help them label (attribute) the arousal they felt.

Male participants were told that the experiment involved the effects of a new vitamin supplement on vision. This supplement was to be given by injection, after which the participants would wait 20 minutes for it to begin to act and then would be given a vision test. Actually the injections were either epinephrine (a chemical released by the body during arousal that leads to changes in heart rate, breathing, flushing, and hand tremors) or a harmless salt solution (saline placebo). Some participants were correctly told what to expect from the injection of epinephrine, while another group was misinformed that their feet would feel numb and that they might experience itching and a slight headache. A third group of participants was given no information about what to expect from the epinephrine injection. Participants in the placebo condition were also given no information concerning the injection.

In order to provide an experimentally induced cognitive label, half of the participants in each group waited to take the eye test in a room with another participant (actually a confederate of the experimenter) who acted either euphoric (sailing paper airplanes, shooting paper wads, using a hula hoop) or angry (at being asked to take an injection, at filling out a questionnaire, and finally tearing up the questionnaire and storming from the room). The seven groups and the conditions under which they were run were as follows:

Euphoria Condition	Anger Condition
epinephrine informed	epinephrine informed
epinephrine ignorant	epinephrine ignorant
epinephrine misinformed*	placebo
placebo	

*Note that this group was run only in the euphoria condition. From "Cognitive, Social, and Psychological Determinants of Emotional State," by S. Schachter and J. E. Singer, 1962, *Psychological Review*, 69, 379–399. Copyright © by the American Psychological Association. Reprinted by permission.

Schachter and Singer expected that the epinephrine-informed condition would not lead to the experience of the emotions of euphoria or anger because these participants should already have been able to attribute the bodily changes they experienced to the epinephrine injection. Likewise, the placebo condition should not have led to much emotional experience because there should have been no physiological arousal. Both the epinephrine-ignorant and the epinephrine-misinformed groups, however, could be expected to search their environment for cues concerning the bodily reactions they would feel. The presence of a euphoric or angry companion (whom the participant thought also had been injected) should have led the participant to attribute his own experiences to either euphoria or anger. In other words, the confederate should have provided cues that would have allowed the participant cognitively to label the feeling he was experiencing as either euphoric or angry.

The results of the experiment supported Schachter and Singer's hypothesis. The euphoria or anger experienced by the epinephrine-ignorant group was greater than for the epinephrine-informed condition. Likewise, the epinephrine-misinformed group showed more euphoria than the epinephrine-informed group. One problem with the results was that the participants of the placebo condition experienced emotion intermediate to the epinephrine-ignorant and the epinephrine-informed conditions and did not differ from the epinephrine-ignorant condition. Schachter and Singer believed that the lack of difference between the epinephrine-ignorant and the placebo conditions resulted from the fact that some participants in the epinephrine-ignorant condition attributed their feelings to the injection, even though they had not been specifically told that the injection would have an effect. These "self-informed" participants should therefore have been less influenced by the euphoric or angry model, and the effect of the confederate on their emotion would tend to be reduced. Schachter and Singer were able to determine which participants were self-informed by their answers to an open-ended question. When these participants were eliminated from the analysis, the epinephrine-ignorant

group and the placebo group differed significantly in emotionality.

Schachter and Singer's data support the notion that participative feelings of emotion require both physiological arousal and a cognitive label that attributes the aroused state to particular causes. Normally the cues for labeling the aroused state are clear to us; however, if a physiological state is aroused and we have no ready explanation for it, we then search our environment for cues that will help us attribute (label) the arousal we experience.

Schachter's analysis of emotion suggests that if a cognitive label exists in the absence of physiological arousal, the experience of emotion should also be incomplete. Such an experience would perhaps resemble a cold anger or an "as if" state; that is, the person might feel "as if" he or she should be angry or sad but the participative state would lack the full-blown feeling of true emotion.

One way in which to test the contribution of physiological arousal to emotionality would be to interview patients with spinal cord damage. The nearer the break in the spinal cord to the brain, the less information will be available to judge one's state of arousal. Schachter (1964) cited a study conducted by Hohmann (1962) revealing that the closer a spinal break was to the brain, the greater was the decrease in emotion. This decrease in emotionality applied to sexual excitement, fear, anger, and grief, but not to sentimentality. Several of the accident victims also reported that their feelings of emotionality were more cognitive or "mental" than before. However, a study by Chwalisz, Diener, and Gallagher (1988) obtained results with spinal cord patients that contradict those of Hohmann. Chwalisz et al. found that the spinal-cord-injured participants in their study often reported stronger emotional feelings, especially the emotion of fear. As they note (Chwalisz et al., 1988, p. 825), "Our results do not support strong forms of autonomic arousal-based theories of emotion. Those theories maintain that the perception of autonomic arousal is an essential component of emotion and that the experience of emotion cannot occur without it."

In many respects Schachter's model of emotion is a combination and modification of the James–Lange theory and Cannon's emergency theory of emotion. Schachter's theory, like the James-Lange theory, proposes that bodily changes are involved in the experience of emotion. In a fashion similar to Cannon, however, Schachter also proposes that the interpretation of an event is important for the full experience of emotion. But Schachter goes beyond the earlier theories in proposing that both physiological change and cognitive labeling are necessary for the full experience of emotion. Schachter's model has proven enormously popular since its introduction in 1964. In addition to its initial purpose as an explanation of emotion, the theory has also spawned a large body of literature on the misattribution of arousal, particularly as misattribution relates to the reduction of fear and anxiety.

Although Schachter's theory has both generated and suggested several lines of research, the support for the theory itself is modest (Reisenzein, 1983). Cotton (1981) reviewed research on the model and noted that the original study on which the model was based (Schachter & Singer, 1962) has been criticized on both methodological and empirical grounds (see, e.g., Plutchik & Ax, 1967). Additionally, several attempts to replicate the Schachter and Singer study have been unsuccessful (Marshall & Zimbardo, 1979; Maslach, 1979; Rogers & Deckner, 1975), although Erdmann and Janke (1978) have provided support for the model as a result of their research. Research by Lazarus (1968) and Weiner, Russell, and Lerman (1978) suggests that the cognitive component alone may be both necessary and sufficient for the arousal of emotion (see also the extensive review of Reisenzein, 1983, on this point). As should be evident at this point, there has been considerable debate among psychologists concerning the conditions necessary for the instigation of emotion. Over the past several decades, analyses of emotion have increasingly emphasized a cognitive component.

Ethology

Following the lead of Darwin, ethologists have concentrated primarily on the study of the expressive movements of organisms. In fact the index of Eibl-Eibesfeldt's book *Ethology: The Biology of Behavior* (1970) does not contain *emotion* as a separate term. For the ethologists, motivation and emotion are seen as two names for the same concept: the buildup of action-specific energy.

Intention Movements Ethological research has focused on the information conveyed by the expressive movements that accompany emotion. For example, Eibl-Eibesfeldt provided the following definition: "Behavior patterns that have become differentiated into *signals* are called **expressive movements**" (1970, p. 91, *italics* and **bolding** added). According to ethological analysis, these innate expressions of an animal's emotional state have evolved from intention movements, which you may recall are indicators of a behavior that an organism is about to make (see Chapter 2). Thus a dog's baring of the teeth is an expressive movement indicative of emotion and preparatory to biting. These expressive behaviors are often seen when opposing emotions are present and tend to be a mixture of behaviors involved in the conflicting states. For example, a male cat defending its territory against an intruding male may hiss and raise its fur and shortly thereafter turn away from the intruder. These expressive movements might indicate hostility mixed with fear.

Intention movements will be informative to the extent that other members of the individual's group recognize them as a signal of behavior that may occur. Recognition of anger, for example, would help an individual avoid damaging fights; a fear response such as a cry could quickly bring an adult to the aid of an infant; and sensitivity to emotional cues could help males avoid wasting energy in making sexual overtures to unreceptive females. Intention movements thus serve the adaptive purpose of coordinating behavior between individuals so that they can exist in close proximity to others of their species and interact efficiently. Animals that live in groups, this also suggests, may have evolved ways of recognizing emotionally loaded signals and acting appropriately. Because humans as well as other primates typically live in small groups, it would not be surprising if both we and monkeys proved to be sensitive to emotional signals. Analysis of such nonverbal cues is considered in the following section.

Nonverbal Cues Among primates, facial expressions, gestures, and calls often accompany emotional behavior (Buck, 1976). Do these expressions, calls, and gestures serve as **nonverbal cues** to the emotional state of an individual animal? Robert Miller and his colleagues have examined this idea in a series of experiments (Miller, Caul, & Mirsky, 1967). We will look at just one of them, as representative.

Miller put rhesus monkeys into an experimental situation in which they had to avoid shock by pressing a key whenever a light came on. This is an avoidance learning situation, and the monkeys had no trouble learning to avoid the shock. After he had shown that they could learn to avoid the shock, Miller altered the situation so that one monkey could see the lighted stimulus but could not avoid the shock directly because it had no key to press. A second monkey had the key but could not see the stimulus. This second monkey, however, could see the first monkey via a closed circuit TV monitor that showed the first monkey's face. The question was: Would the first monkey alter its facial expression when the light came on? And could the second monkey perceive that change, press the key, and thus avoid shock for both of them?

The answer is yes. The first monkey's facial expression changed when the light came on, and the second monkey observed that change and learned to press the key to avoid the shock. Thus these monkeys could both "send" appropriate facial expressions and "receive" these expressions and alter their behavior as a result.

It should be noted that the sending monkey was not consciously trying to send information to the observing monkey. The sending monkey simply reacted to the light with a change of facial expression because the light indicated that shock was about to occur. The observing monkey was able to use this change in expression to press the key in order to avoid the shock. Likewise, the second monkey was not being altruistic by pressing the key so that both could avoid shock; it was simply pressing the key so that it would not get shocked. This experiment indicates that rhesus monkeys are sensitive to facial movements that may be expressions of emotion and can alter their behavior accordingly. If they can use this "emotional" communication in the sterile environment of the laboratory, they can probably also make use of facial expression in the natural environment.

In another part of this experiment, Miller, Caul, and Mirsky paired monkeys raised in isolation with normally reared monkeys and ran all combinations of senders and receivers. We have long known that monkeys isolated from other members of their species develop behavioral abnormalities, including self-clasping, rocking, and avoidance of social interaction. Miller found the isolates incapable as both reliable senders and observers. One effect of isolation, then, may be disruption of the ability to use nonverbal, emotion-produced cues. This disruption could be related to the bizarre behavior exhibited by isolated monkeys.

The ability to send and receive emotional cues may involve an interaction between innate and acquired patterns of behavior. Mason (1961) has suggested that many behaviors used by monkeys in communication are species-specific (and therefore innate) but that the proper development of these behaviors depends on adequate experience. Thus, isolated monkeys may be deficient in emotional communication because their innate abilities have not had the proper social atmosphere to develop. If monkeys can communicate emotional states by facial movements, gestures, and calls, what about humans? Do they also communicate feelings through nonverbal cues?

Ross Buck attempted to answer this question by adapting Miller's sender–observer methods for use with humans (Buck, 1976; Buck, Miller, & Caul, 1974; Buck et al., 1972). In Buck's experiments a participant viewed a series of slides that fell into various categories in relation to the emotional responses the participant was likely to feel when viewing them. The categories might include sexual, scenic, maternal, disgusting, and ambiguous slides.

Another participant observed the facial reactions of the person viewing the slides and attempted to predict what type of slide the first person was viewing and whether the emotion experienced was pleasant or unpleasant. If humans express emotion through facial movements, the observer should have been able to predict with some accuracy what type of slide the first person was watching and whether the person experienced it as pleasurable or unpleasurable.

In one study Buck found that an observer could predict at levels greater than chance the category of the slide that the sender was viewing. Although the prediction accuracy was statistically significant, it was not overwhelming, probably because different people reacted differently to the same stimuli. For example, one person might find nude photos pleasant, while another might find them distasteful. Accuracy of predicting categories of emotion, then, was marginal. In terms of pleasantness and unpleasantness, however, prediction was much better. Apparently we are pretty good at sending and receiving signals that reflect our general mood but not so good at indicating nonverbally why we feel the way we do (the reasons for our pleasure or displeasure).

In all his studies Buck found that women communicated emotion nonverbally better than men—they were better senders—because they were more facially expressive (they made more facial movements). Buck has suggested that in our society little girls are taught that it is all right to express emotion openly, while little boys are taught that they must inhibit their expression of feelings. Thus women may be better at expressing emotion nonverbally because they are allowed to externalize their feelings, while boys are taught to internalize theirs. In a fashion parallel to the monkey data, the research by Buck implies that emotional expression is innate but can be altered by experience.

How early does emotional expression occur? Buck (1975) found that children as young as age 4 reliably communicate emotion through facial expression. At this age, however, no reliable differences appeared between the sexes in sending ability, though girls still had a slight edge. Buck also found

that the mothers of these children were most accurate at judging the categories and also the pleasantness of the emotion, though undergraduate observers also had some success in interpreting the children's facial expressions.

In all these studies the observers were better at judging the pleasantness or unpleasantness of the expressed emotion than they were at judging the particular category of the emotion. Emotional expression through facial movements, then, seems generally to indicate emotional mood but not the causes (category of slide) of that mood. In the last section of this chapter we will examine additional evidence that different facial expressions can accurately indicate specific emotions.

Robert Rosenthal has also been interested in understanding nonverbal communication. Rosenthal and his associates at Harvard developed a device that they believe allows them to measure a person's sensitivity to nonverbal cues (Rosenthal et al., 1974). They measured reaction to such nonverbal cues as facial movement, body movement, voice tone, and so on, by having people choose from a set of answers the emotion they believed was being conveyed. Their research indicated that most people can correctly identify various emotional states, even when given only very brief exposures (1/24 of a second) to the nonverbal cues.

In agreement with Buck's research, Rosenthal and associates found that women were more sensitive than men to nonverbal cues, particularly body cues. According to the findings of Buck and Rosenthal, women are apparently better than men at both sending nonverbal information and detecting it in others. Although these researchers do not rule out learning, they suggest that some aspects of the ability to send and detect emotional nonverbal cues may be innate.

A study of very young infants also bears on the question of the innateness of emotional expression (Haith, Bergman, & Moore, 1977). In Haith's experiment the visual fixation of faces by infants was examined. Infants 3 to 5 weeks old fixated the face of an adult only 22% of the time during testing, whereas 7-week-old infants fixated the face of an adult more than 87% of the time. The researchers also examined which facial features were fixated and found that the eyes attracted the most attention from 7 weeks on. This was true even when the adult was talking (although one might have predicted that the infant would fixate the mouth region). Haith and his coworkers argued that the eyes become important fixation points because they serve as the source of signals or cues in social situations. Although this study does not show that gazing at the face is an innate response, it does suggest that fixating the face, particularly the eyes, begins at a very early age and may have some innate components (see also Field et al., 1982, for evidence that imitation of adult facial responses can occur as early as 36 hours after birth).

The studies of Haith, Rosenthal, and Buck indicate that humans are sensitive to the nonverbal expression of emotion and that, while learning is undoubtedly involved in much of this ability, some components of emotional expression and recognition of the same are probably innate. Like other primates, humans apparently communicate affect nonverbally and "read" the nonverbal emotional signals of others.

Brain Mechanisms of Emotion

Numerous bodily changes are associated with emotionality. You may also recall from Chapter 4, on mechanisms of regulation, that James Papez (1937) proposed a system of structures within the brain that was concerned with emotional expression. Papez suggested that the hypothalamus, anterior thalamic nuclei, cingulate gyrus, and hippocampus were involved with emotion. Later research confirmed many of Papez's ideas and added the importance of an additional structure, the amygdala (Kluver & Bucy, 1939; Rosvold, Mirsky, & Pribram, 1954). These interconnected structures have become known as the **limbic system**. Although structures within the limbic system are involved with emotion, the limbic system also does many other things, and structures outside of the limbic system are also involved with emotion

(LeDoux, 2000). As a result, current research has focused on specific structures that are involved with emotion such as the amygdala, cingulate cortex, and orbital frontal cortex (see, e.g., Adolphs, Tranel, & Damasio, 2001; Anderson, Spencer, Fulbright, & Phelps, 2000; Cardinal, Parkinson, Hall, & Everitt, 2002; Cohen, Paul, Zawacki, Moser, Sweet, & Wilkinson, 2001; Mlot, 1998; Whalen, Shin, McInerney, Fischer, Wright, & Rauch, 2001).

In particular, the amygdala has been strongly implicated as the primary structure concerned with the production and governance of the expression of emotions. The following overview is based on summaries of research by Cardinal, Parkinson, Hall, and Everitt (2002), Carlson (2010), Kalat (2009), and LeDoux (1994, 2000).

According to Carlson (2010), an emotional response consists of three components: emotional behaviors, autonomic changes, and hormonal changes. Emotional behaviors are composed of muscular changes that are appropriate to the environmental context in which those behaviors occur. For example, someone who is very angry will often clench his or her fists. Such behavior could be thought of as preparatory to fighting if the situation were to continue to escalate. Autonomic changes make additional energy available quickly and prepare the individual for more intense behaviors, such as rapid movements or stronger responses. Hormonal responses, such as the production of epinephrine and norepinephrine by the adrenal medulla, help sustain the autonomic changes. Carlson suggests that the integration of muscular, autonomic, and hormonal changes is performed by the amygdala.

The Amygdala, Orbital Frontal Cortex, and Cingulate Cortex

The **amygdala** is a complex structure located within the temporal lobes and consists of approximately 12 different nuclei (groups of cells) (LeDoux, 2000). The major divisions, and those most relevant to emotion, are the medial nucleus, the lateral and basolateral nuclei, the central nucleus, and the basal nucleus (Carlson, 2001).

At the present time there appears to be considerable support for the role of the amygdala in theintegration of the components of emotion (Carlson, 2010; LeDoux, 1994, 1996, 2000). Inputs to the amygdala come from many different sources, such as the thalamus and sensory cortex, that provide sensory information to the amygdala that would be relevant emotionally. Some of these inputs come directly to the amygdala, and provide a means whereby sensory information could stimulate emotional responding without cortical processing (LeDoux, 2000)—that is, automatically. Additional inputs to the amygdala from the hippocampus provide a route through which cortical associations could also influence emotional responsiveness and provide a route whereby contextual conditioning of fear may occur (LeDoux, 2000). Figure 12.3 shows some of the basic input and output routes of the major regions of the amygdala.

Thus, the circuitry exists for the rather direct expression of emotion to sensory events as well as the expression of emotion as the result of associations. Inputs to and from the **orbital frontal cortex (OFC)** (a brain region close to the eye sockets—thus the term orbital) provide information to the amygdala that may be important for emotionality produced by social situations (Carlson, 2002).

The importance of the orbital frontal regions (a subsection of the larger prefrontal cortex) has been known for some time. Perhaps the most famous case of a profound change in emotionality following frontal lobe damage is that of **Phineas Gage**. Gage suffered damage to his brain when a powder charge he was tamping into a hole in a rock exploded, driving the tamping iron upward through his left cheek, through his brain, and out the top of his head (Damasio et al., 1994). Incredibly, Gage survived the accident and in most ways recovered

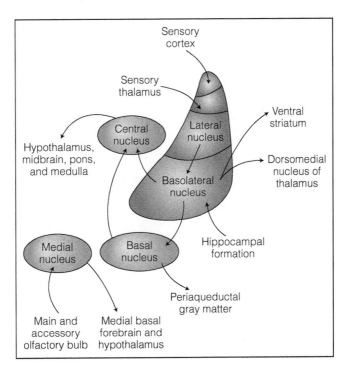

FIGURE 12.3 Major cell groups and major connections of the amygdala associated with emotion. Adapted from Beil R. Carlson, Foundations of Physiological Psychology, 5th ed. Published by Allyn and Bacon, Boston, MA. Copyright © 2001 by Pearson Education. Reprinted by permission of the publisher.

fully. Although his intellect and motor abilities remained intact, he suffered profound changes in personality. Before the accident he had been a very responsible and socially well-adjusted person. After the accident he was irresponsible and unconcerned with social conventions. A modern analysis of Gage's skull (who died in 1861) by Damasio and others (1994) confirms that the orbital frontal regions of his brain were damaged by the rod. The changes in personality observed in Gage are also consistent with changes in behavior reported by Damasio and associates (1994, see note 12) in a modern group of patients with orbital frontal damage. These patients have trouble making rational decisions about personal and social matters and show changes in their processing of emotion. The orbitofrontal cortex and the **anterior cingulate cortex** together are often designated as the **ventromedial prefrontal cortex (vmPFC),** and it is thought that this area integrates complex, abstract computations of the neocortex with more basic bodily and emotional information (Vanderkerckhove & Cludts, 2010). The neurotransmitter serotonin appears to be a major player in the modulation of PFC neuronal activity (Zhong & Yan, 2011) as is dopamine (Jocham, Klein, & Ullsperger, 2011).

Finally, the anterior cingulate cortex also has connections with the amygdala (Carlson, 2010; LeDoux, 2000). The anterior cingulate cortex has been implicated in cognitive-emotional interactions (see Cohen, Paul, Zawacki, Moser, Sweet, & Wilkinson, 2001, for a short review of research on the role of the cingulate cortex in cognition and emotion).

Of the various areas just noted, by far the most research has been devoted to studying the role of the amygdala in emotion. This research is consistent in showing that the amygdala appears to exert control over many of the changes that are produced when emotions occur (Viviani et al. 2011). For example, the amygdala has connections to the hypothalamus that could provide the necessary pathway for autonomic changes as a result of emotional situations (Carlson, 2002; LeDoux, 2000). The amygdala also connects to the brain stem (LeDoux, 2000), providing a route through which

the amygdala can influence behaviors associated with emotionality. Finally, as previously noted, the amygdala has connections to the orbital frontal cortex and anterior cingulate cortex, which could provide a means whereby cognition and emotion interact (see Carlson, 2010, for a more in-depth discussion of cognition and emotion as they relate to mechanisms within the amygdala, frontal and anterior cingulate cortices).

The amygdala has also been implicated in the recognition of facial expressions of emotion (see the section later in this chapter on the facial expression of emotion). In particular, the amygdala appears to be important in the recognition of the facial expressions of fear (Adolphs, Tranel, & Damasio, 2001; Anderson, Spencer, Fulbright, & Phelps, 2000; Calder, Lawrence, & Young, 2001; Whalen, Shin, McInerney, Fischer, Wright, & Rauch, 2001). Whalen (1998, p. 184; see also animal research by Kapp's laboratory, for example, Silvestri & Kapp, 1998) has proposed that in humans amygdala activation "is related to attempts to resolve biologically relevant, associative ambiguity, that is, to process stimuli that have some biologically relevant, but presently unclear, predictive value." He proposes that the amygdala attempts to do this by modulating **vigilance** in order to gain additional information to resolve the situation. For example, sensitivity to facial expressions of fear ought to lead to the processing of additional cues from the environment in order to understand the situation. Thus, based on neuroimaging research in humans, Whalen suggests that the amygdala has a more general function, beyond just fear processing, of modulating vigilance in ambiguous, but biologically important situations.

To summarize, the research evidence currently available is consistent in showing that the amygdala is crucial to the behavioral, autonomic, and hormonal changes that occur in emotional situations and appears to contribute to the cognitive aspects of emotion as well. For a fuller discussion of the original studies that led to these conclusions, see Carlson (2010), Cohen et al. (2001), LeDoux (1994, 1996, 2000), and Whalen (1998).

Emotion from a Learning Perspective

In this section we will briefly look at some of the ways in which learning may contribute to emotionality. As noted in Chapter 5, classical conditioning situations can lead to the development of emotional responses to formerly neutral stimuli. It is also clear that emotions such as fear can lead to new instrumental behaviors that reduce or remove the organism from the emotion-producing situation.

Classical Conditioning and Emotion

Considerable research in both animals and humans provides evidence for the importance of classical conditioning in the production of emotion (summaries of such work can be found in Carlson, 2010; LeDoux, 2000; Whalen, 1998). As we saw in Chapter 5, classical conditioning can result in new motivation as in Watson and Rayner's (1920) conditioning of Little Albert to avoid a white rat associated with a loud noise. Not only did little Albert want to escape from the presence of the white rat, he also acted fearful toward it (e.g., by crying in its presence).

It seems likely that many emotions that we experience result from the accidental pairing of stimuli in the environment with things that happen to us. Both positive and negative emotions could be acquired in just such a way and could lead us to at least partially reexperience the emotion when presented with those stimuli. For example, classical conditioning might explain why some old songs make us feel good (and nostalgic)—the song has been associated with good experiences in the past. Similarly, stimuli associated with unpleasant experiences in the past may call up some of the negative emotionality previously associated with those stimuli a situation termed **conditioned fear**. A child frightened by a freely roaming large dog will appear fearful around that dog in the future even when it is on a leash. Additionally, as noted in Chapter 5, the classically conditioned response typically generalizes to other similar stimuli, so that a child frightened by a large dog will also be fearful around dogs in general.

Of some interest in this regard is research indicating that conditioned fear is associated with activity in the amygdala. LeDoux (1994, 1996, 2000) has summarized a large body of research that shows the amygdala to be crucial in the development of emotional learning. In particular, the amygdala appears to be crucial in the classical conditioning of the emotional responses associated with fear. As noted by Cardinal, Parkinson, Hall, and Everitt (2002) and LeDoux (2000), the **basolateral nucleus of the amygdala (BLA)** appears to be important for the association of conditioned stimulus (CS) and unconditioned stimulus (UCS) in conditioned fear situations. This association enables a CS to call forth the emotional or motivational value of the UCS to which it is connected (Cardinal et al., 2002). Other research suggests that the BLA is also important "in the emotional modulation of memory storage" (Cardinal et al., 2002, p. 331) and is a part of the circuitry that may improve memory in emotionally arousing situations (see Cahill, 2000; McGaugh, Ferry, Vazdarjanova, & Roozendaal, 2000).

The **central nucleus of the amygdala (CeA)** is involved with the control of the hypothalamus, midbrain, and brain stem areas concerned with arousal and responding; however, it has also been shown to be involved in some types of conditioned responses (CRs). As summarized by Cardinal et al. (2002, p. 333), "The simplest analysis at present seems to be that the CeA does form simple CS-UR [i.e., conditioned stimulus-unconditioned response] ('sensorimotor') associations, which do not depend upon a specific US [i.e., unconditioned stimulus]: that is, they are independent of the identity and current motivational value of the US." Still other types of CRs appear to require both BLA and CeA involvement (Cardinal et al., 2002).

Operant/Instrumental Conditioning and Emotion

The largest proportion of research conducted on the role of learning in emotion has examined classical conditioning. It is clear from information we just covered, and earlier in Chapter 5, that classical conditioning is an important component in learned motives and emotions. The question of concern for us in this section is how operant/instrumental conditioning might contribute to the learning of emotions.

In operant/instrumental conditioning, the consequences of a response (i.e., reinforcement or punishment) alter the future probability of that response. Reinforcement makes the response more likely to occur again while punishment makes the response less likely to occur. The question is, does such a relationship between a response and its consequence also have an emotional component? A moment's reflection would seem to yield a qualified "yes" to that question.

When a response is followed by "something good" (i.e., a reinforcer), we are not only likely to repeat the response, we also find it to be an emotionally positive experience. Similarly when a response we have made is followed by "something bad" (i.e., a punisher) we not only are less likely to behave that way in the future, we also find it to be an unpleasant experience emotionally. So, from a commonsense point of view, it would seem that response-consequence contingencies both motivate us (as noted in Chapter 5) and alter our emotional experience. Given what we know about the brain systems underlying emotion and those concerned with reinforcement/punishment, it seems reasonable that there should be such a relationship between response-consequence contingencies and emotion.

As noted earlier, the amygdala and its associated areas such as the orbital frontal cortex and the anterior cingulate cortex are intimately involved in the processes of emotion. As it turns out, all three of these areas are also connected to the **nucleus accumbens (Acb)** either directly or indirectly (Cardinal et al., 2002). The Acb has been shown to be crucial for the reinforcing effects of natural reinforcers such as food, water, and sex, as well as artificial reinforcers such as drugs of abuse like cocaine and amphetamine (see Cardinal et al., 2002, and Carlson, 2010, for an overview of nucleus accumbens circuitry and for a review of

this literature). Both natural and artificial reinforcers stimulate the release of **dopamine (DA)** in the Acb and are thought by some researchers to produce the pleasurable effects of reinforcement, however, aversive stimuli can also cause the release of DA in the nucleus accumbens (Salamone, 1992). In addition, Baldwin, Sadeghian, and Kelley (2002) have found that DA and NMDA glutamate receptors in the **medial prefrontal cortex (mPFC)** of rats also play a crucial role in producing operant/instrumental conditioning. The mPFC also appears to be part of a network of brain regions concerned with both learning and motivation (Baldwin et al., 2002; Cardinal et al., 2002). Figure 12.4 summarizes some of the connections of the various brain regions just discussed.

It seems, therefore, that circuitry including frontal areas of the cortex (OFC, ACC, mPFC), the amygdala (especially BLA and CeA), and the nucleus accumbens (Acb) are importantly involved in the association of responses and their consequences, and the value of those consequences in operant/instrumental conditioning. As noted earlier, these regions also appear to be involved with the classical conditioning of emotions.

Emotional Modeling

The research just discussed suggests that emotion, motivation, and learning go hand in hand—at least with respect to classical conditioning and operant/instrumental conditioning processes. Bandura (1971) has argued that emotionality also can be learned through just the observation of others. Such learning is usually called **observational learning** or **modeling**. According to Bandura, we are sensitive to the facial, vocal, and postural indications of emotional arousal in others, and we note them. If we later find ourselves in circumstances similar to those we have observed, we are likely to react in emotionally similar ways. As might be expected, we seem to be influenced more by the emotionality of models who are important to us—though probably part of the appeal of motion pictures, television, and plays is the actors' ability to arouse in us the emotions that we are observing.

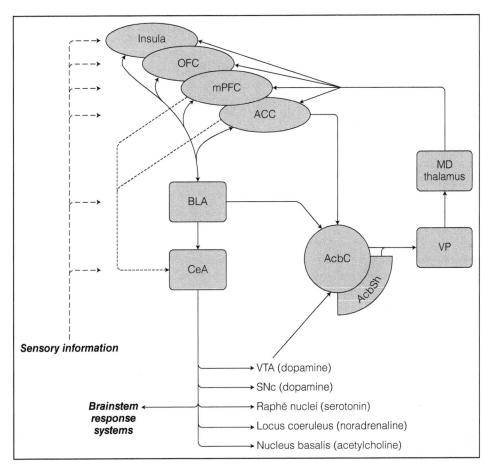

FIGURE 12.4 A diagram showing the major connections between the amygdala, frontal cortical regions, nucleas accumbens, and various other structures.

OFC = orbital frontal cortex
mPFC = medial prefrontal cortex
ACC = anterior cingulate cortex
BLA = basolateral nucleus of the amygdala
CeA = central nucleus of the amygdala
VTA = ventral tegmental area
SNc = substantia nigra pars compacta
AcbC = nucleus accumbens core
AcbSH = nucleus accumbens shell
VP = ventral pallidum
MD = medial dorsal nucleus of the thalamus

From Cardinal et al., "Emotion and motivation: The role of the amygdala, ventral striatum, and prefrontal cortex," *Neuroscience and Biobehavioral Reviews*, *26*, 321–352. Figure 3, p. 329. Copyright © 2002 by Elsevier. Reprinted with permission.

This emotional learning via observation appears to occur very early in development. Mumme and Fernald (2003) found that 12-month-old infants avoided an object and showed negative emotion toward the object after they had seen an adult on a television screen react negatively toward the object. Ten-month-old infants however, did not respond consistently in this situation. Thus it would seem that the ability to learn emotional responses observationally first occurs at about a year of age.

Bandura (1969) has suggested that people may sometimes develop phobias not from direct experience but from seeing a model behave fearfully toward, or be injured by, some object (see the following discussion on the preparedness of some phobias for a somewhat different perspective). Bandura also pointed out that people may sometimes learn prejudices toward certain groups by observing a model who shows intense negative emotionality toward a particular group.

Though we may learn emotional behavior directly through classical or operant procedures, Bandura's analysis also makes it clear that, through simple observation of emotional behavior, we can incorporate the emotionality into our own patterns of responding. We will now examine the idea that organisms have been specially adapted by evolution to associate emotion with certain classes of events.

The Preparedness of Emotional Learning

For many years theorists assumed that the rules by which learning occurs are fundamentally the same across organisms. This approach, termed **general process learning theory**, assumes that one response can be learned just as easily as any other. It now is clear that the assumptions of general process theory have to be modified. The type of response that we ask an organism to learn makes a difference (Seligman, 1970; Seligman & Hager, 1972). Some responses are learned very easily, while others are learned only with considerable difficulty, and still others may be unlearnable. Such thinking was foreshadowed by Breland and Breland (1961); after many years of conditioning and observing thousands of animals, these researchers

reluctantly concluded that you cannot adequately understand, control, or predict an organism's behavior unless you know something about its instinctive patterns, evolutionary history, and ecological niche.

Seligman (1970) suggested that the associability of events in the environment can be described as a continuum. At one end of the continuum are events that can be easily and quickly associated; these are said to be **prepared associations**. At the other extreme are associations that an organism apparently cannot learn; these are called **contraprepared associations**. Between these two extremes are said to be **unprepared associations**; these can be learned, but numerous experiences with the events are necessary for an association to be formed. The **preparedness hypothesis** argues that different species will have evolved different prepared, unprepared, and contraprepared associations as a result of the selective pressures of evolution. Thus one species may quickly learn a response to one set of environmental circumstances but not to another set because evolution has prepared one type of association to be easily formed while, at the same time, making other associations difficult or impossible.

Seligman (1971) has proposed that the development of phobias is just such an example of prepared learning in humans. A **phobia** can be defined as an unreasonable fear of some object, situation, or symbol that has no basis in fact. The presence of a phobic object leads to highly emotional behavior usually described as irrational fear. Many theorists have regarded the development of phobic behavior as an instance of classical conditioning. For example, neutral stimuli within the inside of an elevator might become associated with intense anxiety reactions triggered by the elevator becoming stuck between floors. Subsequently, when an elevator door opens the stimulus cues from the inside come to elicit a conditioned anxiety reaction too.

As noted by Seligman, however, several problems exist with this type of interpretation. First, phobias are very resistant to extinction, while normal laboratory conditioning of fear often extinguishes more easily (Seligman, 1971). Exposure to a stimulus that has elicited conditioned fear in the past without the fear now being present weakens conditioned fear. Presentation of phobic objects, on the other hand, usually does not diminish fear and may even enhance it.

A second problem with the conditioning explanation of phobias is that sometimes phobic reactions appear to have been learned in as little as one exposure, while conditioned fear in the laboratory usually takes somewhere between three and six trials to become established. Thus some phobias appear to be acquired much more quickly than is typical of conditioned fear reactions.

Third, conditioned stimuli are supposed to be arbitrary. Any neutral stimulus can (theoretically) become a conditioned stimulus if paired with some UCS, in the example an anxiety-producing UCS. But most common phobias appear to represent a nonarbitrary set of conditions (fear of snakes and spiders, fear of heights, fear of the dark, and fear of enclosed spaces).

Fourth, most phobic reactions are to objects of natural origin. The reasoning is that evolution has adapted us to be particularly sensitive to forming relationships between fearfulness and natural phenomena such as darkness and heights or organisms such as spiders and snakes because fearfulness of such things can be useful (some snakes and spiders are poisonous; darkness and heights increase the possibility of injury). This is not to say that all phobias are examples of prepared associations; some people are phobic of airplanes and even of symbols, like the number 13 (White, 1964).

Phobias, then, apparently have many of the characteristics of prepared behaviors. Both phobias and prepared behaviors can be learned in one trial, both concern a nonarbitrary set of situations, both are very resistant to extinction, and both are probably noncognitive in nature. The overlap in the characteristics of phobias and prepared behavior is strong, and certain common phobias may develop because humans are prepared to make associations between fear and particular situations. Because phobias involve emotionally charged situations, one wonders whether, in a more general sense, humans are prepared to make associations that contain an emotional element. Perhaps emotion has its impact precisely because it is easily associated with other events. Certainly, emotion contributes to the

acquisition and retrieval of information (Cahill, 2000; Cardinal et al., 2002; McGaugh, Ferry, Vazdarjanova, & Roozendaal, 2000).

Although some aspects of emotion are clearly biological while others are just as clearly learned, many emotions also seem to have a cognitive component. That is, how we react emotionally seems to depend in part on how we interpret particular situations. In the next section we will examine research on this aspect of emotional experience.

Emotion from a Cognitive Perspective

The idea that cognitive processes are important in the experience of emotion has been around at least since the time of Aristotle. However, until the middle of the 20th century, cognition played a limited role in most theories of emotion, including those of James, Lange, and Cannon discussed earlier. Much has changed. In the past 60 years, a large number of theories that include cognitive processes as an integral part of emotional experience have emerged.

Cognitive approaches to the understanding of emotion stress the importance of cognitive appraisal (Lazarus, 1982, 1984). According to this view, bodily changes are insufficient for the experience of true emotion; we must assess a situation as emotion producing before we experience emotion. Schachter's model was one of the first to suggest the importance of some sort of appraisal process. Recall that Schachter proposed that when arousal occurs a cognitive label is attached to the arousal, and that both are necessary for the experienced emotion. Thus when we are aroused and the cues suggest pleasantness, we are happy; but the same arousal in the presence of different cues can make us feel angry. In Schachter's model the critical element determining the particular emotion experienced is the cognitive label; although arousal was deemed necessary, it was not thought to differentiate among the various emotions one could feel. Schachter's model has been criticized on a number of counts and some cognitive theorists have argued that cognition alone may be sufficient for the experience of emotion. For example, altering the appraisal process of participants before viewing a gruesome film affected the quality and intensity of the emotions produced by the film (Lazarus, 1968). Emotional reaction to the film could be intensified by a soundtrack that emphasized the harmful consequences or decreased by a sound-track that emphasized intellectual detachment. Lazarus's data argue for the primacy of cognition in the perception of emotion. Indeed Lazarus (1982, 1984) has strongly argued this point with Zajonc (1980, 1984), whose point of view we will examine in the next section.

The emphasis on the appraisal process in the experience of emotion is very similar to attribution approaches to motivation examined in Chapter 10. It should come as no surprise, then, that attribution theory has also been applied to the study of emotion. A study by Valins will serve as example.

Attribution of Emotion

Valins (1966) asked male college students to view slides of seminude females. While viewing the slides, the men were told that their heart rate was being monitored; in addition, they were given auditory feedback such that they could hear their heart beating as the slides were presented. The participants did not realize that the heart rate feedback they were hearing was false; it was being controlled by the experimenter to indicate large increases or decreases for some slides and no change for others. When participants were later asked to rate the slides in terms of attractiveness, they judged the slides associated with a heart rate change (either up or down) to be more attractive than those associated with no change. In addition, Valins let his participants take some of the slides home and found that the ones chosen were primarily those that had been associated with the heart rate changes.

Valins's data suggest that, at least for ratings of liking, we form a hypothesis and then attempt to test it by searching for relevant cues in ourselves or our environment. If this attribution process is an active one, as Valins suggested, then the rating

may have been arrived at somewhat as follows: "My heart rate changed. Why? Because the person in this photo is attractive." In a later study (Valins, 1974) participants were debriefed and told that the heart rate feedback was false. Nevertheless, even after debriefing, the participants still rated pictures associated with bogus heart rate changes as more attractive than others not so associated. As is the case with attributions in general, once formed, emotions appear difficult to change. Valins's research has generated a number of additional studies and debate—for his data seem to show that only the belief that one is aroused is necessary for the experience of emotion.

In a study conceptually similar to Valins's research, Goldstein, Fink, and Mettee (1972) showed male participants pictures of male nudes and provided false heart rate information, but, unlike Valins, they also recorded actual heart rates. These researchers expected the pictures to be disliked by most participants because of implicit homosexual connotations. The researchers found that the false heart rate information was not related to the dislike of the slides as rated by the participants, but the participants' actual heart rate was. This result suggests that the attractiveness scores in Valins's studies may have resulted not only from the false feedback but also from actual physiological changes.

Further, Beck and Matteson (1982) have reported results suggesting that the false feedback effect may result from subtle cues provided by the experimenter that indicate to the participant how to respond. These experimenter **demand characteristics**, rather than an attribution that one is aroused, may therefore be responsible for the effects obtained in false feedback situations. Additionally, Parkinson and Manstead (1981) have provided evidence that attentional processes are important for Valins's effect. Participants in this study were asked to view unpleasant slides while listening to either false heart rate feedback or to a series of electronic "bleeps," both of which were increased and decreased by the experimenter. In addition, half the participants were told to attend both to the slides and to the auditory feedback, and the other half were told to try to ignore the feedback and attend only to the slides. Interestingly, Parkinson and Manstead found that the type of feedback had no effect on participants' ratings; that is, the heartbeat feedback did not change ratings any more than the bleeps did. However, focus of attention did affect ratings. Participants who were told to pay attention to the auditory feedback displayed the Valins effect; participants who were told to ignore the feedback were unaffected.

One possible reason for these inconsistent results is that people differ in the degree to which they are motivated to behave according to internal or external cues. Snyder (1974; Snyder & Gangestad, 1986) developed a scale that measures a personality trait he called **self-monitoring**. People who are high self-monitors are motivated to change their behavior to meet the demands of a situation. These individuals analyze their surroundings and tend to alter their behavior such that it is appropriate to the circumstances. They are good role players and they can appear to be very different people in different situations. Low self-monitors are also aware of their surroundings. However, they are motivated to engage in behavior that is consistent with their internal states (e.g., attitudes and feelings), even if their behavior is incongruous with the demands of the situation. Low self-monitors tend to behave more consistently across different situations than do high self-monitors. Graziano and Bryant (1998) nicely summarized the distinction. According to them, high self-monitors ask the question "What does the situation want me to be, and how can I be that person?" whereas low self-monitors ask "Who am I and how can I be me in this situation?"

Graziano and Bryant (1998) predicted that high self-monitors are more sensitive to external emotional cues than are low self-monitors. To test this prediction, they replicated Valins's original study, but they also asked participants to complete Snyder's Self-Monitoring Scale. As predicted, high self-monitors attributed the bogus feedback to their liking for the slide with which it was paired; the low self-monitors were not affected by the false heart rate feedback. Thus, Valins's findings about the attribution of emotion were replicated, but

only for individuals who are motivated to behave according to the demands of the situation.

Attribution theory has become important as theorists attempt to develop models describing how emotionality is influenced by the causes that we ascribe to events. Recall from Chapter 10 that emotion is a primary component of Weiner's attribution theory (Weiner, 1985; Weiner et al., 1987). Weiner argues that the perceived stability and locus of the causes for behavior will influence one's expectancy of future success. In addition, our perceptions of the degree to which an event was controllable will influence the emotions we feel. Finally, expectancies and emotion are seen as guiding motivated behavior.

Consider the following example. Nicole is supposed to meet her coworker Kathryn for lunch but fails to show up. According to Weiner's theory, the reason Nicole later gives for breaking the engagement should influence Kathryn's emotions, and her future behavior toward Nicole. The excuse "I missed our luncheon date because I went to lunch with Alexis instead" suggests that the reason for the missed date was internal and controllable (Nicole decided that she would rather go to lunch with someone else). Weiner's research has shown that internal and controllable excuses tend to produce aversive emotional reactions (Kathryn might become angry with Nicole) and a desire for reduced social contact (she might not invite Nicole out to lunch again). On the other hand, in the excuse "I missed our luncheon date because I had an accident and got a concussion," the cause was external to the person, and uncontrollable. As a result of the second excuse, Kathryn is much less likely to feel negative emotionality toward her friend, and her future desire for social contact will probably not be diminished.

Weiner and associates (1987) studied the excuses people give and found support for the analysis just mentioned. It would seem that attribution theory can help us understand why our emotional reactions to various situations occur and, further, how these emotional reactions influence future behavior. Additional research on causal ascriptions and emotions is likely to help us understand, at least in part, the generation of emotion.

Because many theories of emotion now include a cognitive component, the precise nature of the interplay between cognition and emotion has become an interesting field of inquiry. The remainder of this chapter is devoted to the study of this relationship. Next, we present some of the major cognitive theories of emotion within the context of several lively debates about the structure of affect. We will discuss whether discrete emotions exist (or are they merely semantic categories), whether or not emotions are universal, and the most fundamental debate of all: can emotion occur independent of cognition?

Emotion as Primary and Universal

Not all psychologists were pleased when cognitive approaches to emotion became popular. Robert Zajonc has argued for the primacy of affect; that is, he has argued that *emotion is independent of, and can occur prior to, any cognition*. Zajonc and Lazarus argued this point in several articles published in the *American Psychologist* (Lazarus, 1982, 1984; Zajonc, 1980, 1984). As we saw in the last section, Lazarus proposed that cognition must precede emotion, and indeed much research supports the idea that cognition is often involved in the experience of emotion. Zajonc proposed, however, that although cognition is often associated with emotion, emotion can occur without cognition and prior to any cognitive processing.

Zajonc argued that *affect is basic*, that is, that emotion is universal among animal species. Because it is difficult to know whether animals other than humans cognitively process information, Zajonc reasoned that the system that generates affect must be independent of cognitive processing. Indeed, as Zajonc noted, a rabbit would rarely have time to assess all the attributes of a snake in order to decide whether to fear it; the rabbit feels fear and reacts. Such reactions may also occur in people. For example, you may react to a dark leaf falling on your arm as if it were a feared insect when the movement is seen unclearly. Though we cannot rule out cognition in the human example, the fear and subsequent

behavior generated by it are very quick, and closer analysis of the situation often seems to occur *after* the emotion is triggered.

A second argument in favor of the primacy of emotion is that *emotions are inescapable*. Affective reactions seem to occur whether we want them to or not. As noted by Zajonc, we can sometimes learn to control the expression of emotion (and society often demands this of us), but we do not seem able to control the feeling. Third, once an affective reaction occurs, subsequent instances of the emotion are very *hard to alter*. Zajonc suggested that we encounter great difficulty in trying to change an emotional reaction because emotional judgments feel *right*. Emotional reactions do not seem open to logic; if we don't like a particular piece of music, we simply do not like it, period. Similarly, an individual who finds oysters repugnant is not easily persuaded to eat them. According to Zajonc, if cognitive processing occurs prior to emotion, then logic should affect our emotional judgments.

Zajonc also noted that *emotional reactions are difficult to verbalize*. For example, when meeting someone for the first time, we usually form a positive or negative impression of the person very quickly, but we often cannot say why we feel the way we do. Several lines of research suggest that the communication of emotion is largely nonverbal. Work reviewed in this chapter on intention movements and nonverbal cues represents part of that evidence. We will shortly examine research on the facial feedback hypothesis, which also bears on this issue. Zajonc proposed that our difficulty in verbalizing emotions suggests that emotion lies outside the cognitive system.

By what mechanism might emotion occur without cognition? Zajonc (1998) notes that there is a direct link between the thalamus and the amygdala (see LeDoux, 1995). Because it is possible for higher cortical structures to be bypassed via this link, Zajonc contends that this may be the physiological substrate that allows emotion to sometimes occur very quickly and without cognition.

The points mentioned above are representative of Zajonc's view, but they are certainly not the only issues that have been raised during the debate (see Zajonc, 1998, 2000). Moreover, Lazarus (1982, 1984, 1991, 1999) has expressed a cogent rebuttal to Zajonc's claim of affective primacy. Rather than enumerate Lazarus's response to each of the points listed above, we will summarize Lazarus's (1999, p. 8) general conclusion that "emotion is always a response to meaning." In this view, emotion should not be viewed separately from cognition and motivation. Rather, emotion should be understood as the meaning (cognition) of a circumstance that is relevant to our personal motives. Thus, Lazarus maintains that the debate over the "primacy" of cognition vs. emotion is not the most productive approach to understanding the relationship between them. Just as Bandura proposes a reciprocal interaction between the person, environment, and behavior (see Chapter 11), Lazarus (1999, pp. 8–9) argues that there is a continuous interplay between cognition, motivation, and emotion:

> In any complex and continuing transaction, an emotion can certainly come before a subsequent cognition or emotion in the continuous flow of cognitive, motivational and emotional processes. But this emotion also includes within it the thoughts and goals that aroused it in the first place. To see this clearly, it helps to use the metaphor of a motion picture rather than a still photo in thinking about human behavior, since the still photo captures only a single response to a given stimulus.

Although there is some disagreement over the primacy issue, Zajonc's view of emotion has been presented in some detail here because it represents a good overview of a particular approach to understanding emotion—the idea that emotions are evolutionarily adaptive, fundamental, and innate reactions. These reactions are usually seen as preprogrammed within the organism and consisting of a limited number of specific affective states. This view of emotion is ably represented by models developed by Tomkins and Izard.

The Tomkins Model

Sylvan Tomkins (1962, 1963, 1979, 1981) proposed that we have a limited set of discreet emotions, which are genetically programmed into the brain and initiated by changes in stimulation. Specifically, changes in stimulation presumably cause changes in the neural firing pattern of circuits within the brain. These changed patterns in turn generate specific emotional states. Thus, increased neural firing will lead to interest, fear, or surprise as the firing rate increases, while enjoyment is assumed to occur when the pattern of neural firing decreases. Distress and anger result from sustained levels of firing above some optimum level, with anger resulting from a higher sustained level than distress (Tomkins, 1979).

Although changes in the neural firing pattern are the triggering mechanism for innately programmed emotional reactions, our communication and experience of emotion result from feedback from facial expressions and voice. There is a preprogrammed set of facial muscle responses associated with each specific emotion. Similarly, for each emotion there is also a specific set of vocalizations such that there are "cries of joy, cries of distress, cries of anger, cries of excitement, cries of fear, and so on" (Tomkins, 1981, p. 315). Thus, we communicate our emotional state to others through facial expressions and voice inflections; however, we also *experience* emotion as a result of feedback from these responses. Although he originally emphasized facial musculature as important for the experience of emotion, Tomkins later proposed that the important feedback signals for emotion come from changes in the stimulation of sensory receptors in the facial skin, in a manner analogous to the experience of orgasm resulting from changes in stimulation of skin receptors in the genital region.

One of the most interesting aspects of Tomkins' theory is his proposal that emotions serve to amplify drives. Although we may be aware of such drive states as hunger, thirst, and the need for sex, according to Tomkins their urgency is provided by the emotional amplification of these conditions. In a very real sense for Tomkins, emotion provides the intensity factor in motivation and is necessary for the activation of behavior.

One final aspect of the theory deserves mention. Tomkins makes a distinction between innate emotion and what he calls **backed-up emotion**. The points we have examined above refer to innate emotion; however, as noted by Tomkins, every society puts constraints on the free expression of emotion because of its contagious quality and its power to generate behavior. As a result, many of the emotional reactions we observe in others are not innate but backed up—that is, voluntarily modified in some way. Often the modification of emotional expression is suppression, but people also feign anger, surprise, joy, and other emotions when they do not feel them. Tomkins argued that the backed-up expression of emotions is particularly common when we experience anger.

Because we can suppress, augment, and disguise the emotional reactions we make, it is difficult for layperson and scientist alike to distinguish clearly between true and backed-up emotion. This confusion may partly account for the many different models of emotion that currently exist.

Izard's Differential Emotions Theory

A model closely related to Tomkins's has been developed by Carroll Izard (1977, 1979, 2007), who, in agreement with Tomkins, argued that the discreet emotions are innately programmed. Izard's **differential emotions theory (DET)** emphasizes the idea that specific emotions have distinct experiential qualities. As noted by Izard (2011), the theory has been revised multiple times since its inception to account for new research findings, however many of its core tenets have remained unchanged. We present the original theory (omitting facets of it that have been substantially revised or discarded) along with some of the major revisions that reflect Izard's (2009, 2011) later thinking.

The original version of DET is based on five assumptions (Izard, 1977). The first assumption is that each emotion has three components—its own neural substrate, a characteristic expressive pattern (usually involving facial expressions), and a distinct participative quality or feeling associated with it. None of these components by itself is an emotion;

all three are required. For example, the emotion of sadness is characterized by a pattern of neural activity in the brain, facial expressions such as frowning, and a negative feeling state.

Izard's second assumption is that each *emotion is inherently adaptive*; that is, each emotion has unique motivational properties that are important for survival of either the individual or the species. Third, *emotions are discreet*. That is, different emotions produce different inner experiences and are associated with different behaviors. Fourth, *emotions interact with each other*. Thus, one emotion may activate, amplify, or reduce another. This assumption is important because it means that a particular emotional state may consist of a complex blend of individual emotions. Consider a person who is about to move to a new city. He may be experiencing a cluster of emotions such as excitement and anxiety about his new surroundings as well as sadness and regret about leaving his old ones. Because emotions can interact, the number of possible participative emotional states is quite large.

Finally, according to Izard, *emotions interact with and influence other important bodily processes such as homeostasis, drive, perception, cognition, and motor responses*. This interplay makes emotion the principal motivational system for behavior. As is apparent in the following quote, emotion also provides the basis for personality. "The emotions are viewed not only as the principal motivational system but, even more fundamentally, as the personality processes which give meaning and significance to human existence" (Izard, 1977, p. 44).

Differential emotions theory argues that neurochemical activity, occurring in innate programs within the brain, causes facial and bodily changes. As these changes are fed back to the brain and made conscious, they produce a discreet emotion. Because positive emotions such as interest or joy increase a person's sense of well-being, contact with the object or person generating the emotion is continued. Negative emotions such as fear or disgust, on the other hand, are aversive and generate withdrawal of contact if possible.

Other characteristics noted by Izard can also help us understand his conception of emotion. First of all, emotion is noncyclical. There does not appear to be any rhythm to emotions—for example, we do not typically become interested or disgusted at certain times of the day independent of environmental stimulation. Second, emotions have almost unlimited generality. Although a relatively limited number of items will satisfy hunger or thirst, for example, we can react with fear, joy, disgust, and so forth to an apparently unlimited number of things. The diversity of human personality structure may result in part from the flexibility with which associations can be formed between emotions and events. Third, according to Izard, the emotions serve as important regulators. In this regard an important function of emotion is to amplify or reduce the action of other motivational systems. Thus, on the one hand, the sex drive can recruit an emotion such as interest-excitement and greatly increase sexual motivation, while on the other hand, the presence of fear can inhibit the sex drive completely.

As noted earlier, Izard has revised DET multiple times. One of the most significant revisions occurred when Izard noted that some of the disagreement among researchers in the field is due to the fact that there is no consensus on the exact definition of the term *emotion* (Izard, 2007). Researchers often use the term in a very general sense, thus obscuring some important distinctions among concepts, such as the one between **basic emotions** and **emotion schemas**. According to Izard (2007), basic emotions are innate, evolutionarily adaptive, automatic responses to stimuli, and are generally short in duration. They require only the perception of a stimulus; no higher order conscious processing is necessary. For example, little thought is required to experience fear when one notices a scorpion crawling up one's arm. Izard identified six basic emotions: interest, joy/happiness, sadness, anger, disgust, and fear.

Abe and Izard (1999) argue that basic emotions are necessary for the process of human development to occur. Applying differential emotions theory to early development, Abe and Izard propose that both positive and negative basic emotions are adaptive and motivational in nature. In infancy, for example, four basic emotions predominate: joy, interest, sadness, and anger (Izard, Fantauzzo, Castle, Haynes, Rayias, & Putnam, 1995, Study 1). According to differential

emotions theory, joy and interest serve to maintain interactions with the caregiver and to facilitate the bonding process; anger and sadness, which often occur during infant-caregiver separation, signal the caregiver to return (Abe & Izard, 1999). As we progress through childhood, adolescence, and adulthood, the influence of positive and negative basic emotions generally decreases, however basic emotions do not completely disappear (Izard, 2011). Positive basic emotions, in particular, remain adaptive as they motivate and guide our immediate behavior in response to novel stimuli. Negative basic emotions occur infrequently in most adults except in cases of emergency or danger. If negative basic emotions (e.g., anger) occur too regularly, they may contribute to maladaptive behavior (e.g., aggression) or undesirable personality characteristics (e.g., emotional reactivity).

Emotion schemas are more complex than basic emotions, are generally longer in duration, and involve an interaction between emotion and cognitive processes such as appraisal or attribution. For example, the emotion schema of jealousy can involve several discreet emotions (e.g., anger, sadness, disappointment) as well as cognitive processes such as attributions, memories, appraisal, and decision-making, among others. In this example, the emotions and cognitions interact and influence one another to form the emotion schema of jealousy. Izard (2007) argues that emotion schemas such as jealousy or pity can arise during life span development from combinations of the feeling component of emotions and cognitive processes. As an example of the distinction between Izard's two types of emotions, consider that infants can experience the basic emotion of fear but they do not have the cognitive capacity to feel the emotion schema of jealousy.

As we progress out of early childhood to later stages of life, emotion schemas become our primary motivators (Izard, 2007). Because emotion schemas are part of the developmental process, we accrue more of them as we progress through the life span and have more experience associating feelings with cognitions.

Indeed, Izard argues that most research on emotion is done on emotion schemas rather than basic emotions.

It is important to note that any feelings, including those associated with basic emotions, can develop into emotion schemas, provided they interact with cognitive processes. For example, if a person experiences an event that produces feelings of sadness and then attributes that event to internal causes, an emotion schema is developing. If this occurs often and also triggers other sad memories which intensify the feelings of sadness, the schema can become a part of the person's personality and could perhaps develop into a disorder such as depression.

Because emotions (both basic and emotion schema) are so important to development, perhaps emotion-based interventions can be employed to foster healthy development and minimize negative psychological and behavioral consequences in children (e.g., Mostow, Izard, Fine, & Trentacosta, 2002). Izard (2002) has proposed just such an approach. According to him, because both positive and negative emotional energy is necessary for healthy development, interventions should focus on regulating the intensity of the emotions and on directing the emotional energy toward positive growth. For example, intense and prolonged feelings of shame can lead to behavioral and psychological problems. However, shame can also be constructive if it is moderate in intensity and results in energy directed toward self-improvement (see Izard 2002 for a complete discussion).

From this brief survey of Izard's approach, it should be apparent that he believes that emotion is the primary motivator of behavior; it influences and is in turn influenced by the other systems. For Izard the emotions are fundamental and adaptive. Blends of emotions can and often do occur, making the possible number of emotional experiences quite large and varied. However, this wide variety of emotional experiences has led some researchers to look for basic similarities among them. We will examine one such approach in the next section.

The Circumplex Model of Affect

One major theoretical approach to the study of emotion has been to regard emotion as divisible into discreet independent factors, where each emotion represents a separate unipolar dimension (e.g., one is either happy or not happy). The theories of Tomkins and Izard are representative of this view. Russell (1980, 2003) is not a proponent of this approach. He contends that there is too much variability within emotions for them to be discreet entities. He uses the concept of "fear" as an example. Is the fear that you experience if you are chased by a bear the same emotion as the fear you experience when you watch a horror movie in the safety of a theater? Is it the same as fear of failing a test? Of missing a plane? Of making the wrong career decision? Clearly these fears have something in common, but they are not identical. According to Russell, finding the commonality necessitates a different methodology—breaking emotions into their component parts (dimensions).

Russell views emotions as *consistently related to one another rather than discreet and independent.* He proposed that emotions can be classified along two dimensions (pleasantness-unpleasantness and high arousal-low arousal), with emotional words describing a circle around these dimensions (Russell, 1980). Further, he argued that emotional labels represent a relationship that is a bipolar continuum (e.g., one can be very happy, happy, sad, very sad) rather than unipolar (e.g., happy versus not happy). Russell arrived at this model after conducting a series of studies to determine how participants classified 28 words that represented the range of emotionality. He presented participants with the words (e.g., relaxed, bored, delighted, satisfied) and asked them to put each into a category that varied on the dimensions of pleasantness (e.g., pleasure-misery) and arousal (e.g., excitement-sleepiness). Participants were then asked to arrange the categories according to similarity. Using sophisticated statistical scaling techniques, Russell found that the ordering of the words was best represented as falling along a circular path based on these two dimensions: pleasantness and arousal. Figure 12.5 shows the clustering of the 28 words along the pleasantness (horizontal) and arousal (vertical) dimensions of the **circumplex**. A circumplex is a circular pattern around a vertical and a horizontal axis in which items that are positively correlated tend to cluster together, items that are unrelated are at 90 degree

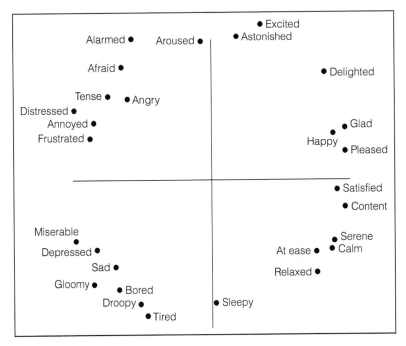

FIGURE 12.5   Circumplex arrangement of 28 affect words. Adapted from "A circumplex model of affect" by J. A. Russell, 1980, *Journal of Personality and Social Psychology, 39*, 1161–1178. Copyright © 1980 by the American Psychological Association. Used by Permission.

angles to one another, and items that are negatively correlated are at opposite ends of the circle (180 degrees apart). This is precisely the relationship depicted by Figure 12.5. Notice that words expressing similar emotions tend to be near each other (e.g., satisfied, content), those expressing unrelated emotions are at approximate 90 degree angles (e.g., satisfied, sleepy) and those expressing opposite emotional experiences tend to fall about 180 degrees from each other (e.g., satisfied, frustrated). The finding that opposite emotions fall at opposite points along the circumplex supports the notion that emotions can be regarded as bipolar (e.g., happy, sad).

Another interesting finding in Russell's results was that people sometimes placed a particular emotional word in more than one category and that these placements tended to be adjacent to each other. This suggests that an affective term (e.g., *pleased*) is essentially a label for a category

that is not discreet but is one in which the transition from membership to nonmembership is gradual. Such a category has been called a **fuzzy set** and appears generally characteristic of language categories. As noted by Russell, it is probably reasonable to consider the labeling of emotions as a mapping process whereby an internal emotional state is specified according to its degree of membership within a fuzzy set. Thus, for example, we can be a little happy, happy, or extremely happy—each term describing a different degree of membership within the fuzzy set "happy."

Since Russell's 1980 paper, several other researchers have developed models of emotion based on two primary dimensions of pleasantness and arousal (Larsen & Diener, 1992; Thayer, 1996; Watson & Tellegen, 1985). Yik, Russell, and Feldman Barrett (1999) examined the structure of each of these representations, along with that of Russell (1980) and found them to be similar enough to be

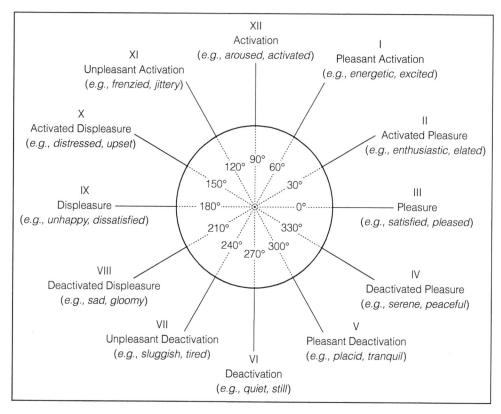

FIGURE 12.6   Two-dimensional circumplex of core affect. From M. Yik, J. A. Russell and J. H. Steiger, "A 13-point circumplex structure of core affect," *Emotion, 11,* 705–731. Copyright © 2011 by the American Psychological Association. Reprinted with permission.

integrated into a single circumplex model, which Russell (2003) calls **core affect**. The original model (Yik, Russell, & Feldman Barrett, 1999) was updated by Yik, Russell, and Steiger in 2011. We present the revised version in Figure 12.6.

According to Russell (2003), core affect is that aspect of an emotional experience that can be mapped on the dimension of pleasantness (pleasure-displeasure) and arousal (activation-deactivation). It is a state "experienced simply as feeling good or bad, energized or enervated" (Russell, 2003, p. 145). Thus, core affect is a basic feeling state that is necessary, but rarely sufficient, for an emotion. The different levels of core affect are presented in Figure 12.6, which, interestingly enough, looks somewhat like a clock. The pleasantness dimension

is depicted on the 3 o'clock–9 o'clock axis and the arousal dimension runs along the 12 o'clock–6 o'clock axis. In between are gradations of change as you move along each dimension. For example, moving from 12 o'clock to 3 o'clock, activation (arousal) decreases while pleasantness (pleasure) increases. As we move from 9 o'clock to 12 o'clock, activation increases and displeasure decreases (or, one could also say that pleasure increases, because pleasure-displeasure is a bipolar continuum). Analogous relationships are depicted on the bottom half of the "clock."

According to Russell, core affect is always with us; our levels of pleasure and activation are forever moving around in the circumplex of Figure 12.6. However, we are not always experiencing an emotion. So what is missing? According to Russell, emotion usually involves at least a) *core affect*; b) *an object*; c) *affective quality*; and d) *attributed affect*. In order for emotion to be experienced, there must be an object identified as its cause (e.g., a snake or a sunset). We must then perceive the affective quality of the object, which is the ability of the object to cause a change in core affect (e.g., we need to perceive the snake as frightening or the sunset as beautiful). Finally, we must attribute our core affect to the object (i.e., I feel the way I do because of the snake or the sunset).

According to this model, all emotional experiences are not alike. What we commonly think of as discrete emotions such as fear or anger are actually experiences in which core affect is attributed to a causal object. This can occur in many different ways, which accounts for the various experiences that receive the same label, such as the varieties of "fear" discussed above. Note that Russell's model operates on a different level of analysis from that of Tomkins and Izard. For Russell, discrete emotional categories such as "fear" are the illusory products of language, rather than unchanging entities that have been instilled in us by evolution or culture. However, evolution has bequeathed to us the two dimensions of core affect, which is the common substrate of all emotional experiences (Russell, 2003).

Additional support for Russell's circumplex model of core affect can be found in many other studies (e.g., Daly, Lancee, & Polivy, 1983; Russell, 1983; Watson, Clark, & Tellegen, 1984). For example, Russell (1983) found that emotional labels yield circular patterns in Gujarati, Croatian, Japanese, and Chinese, as well as in English. Thus, there seems to be cross-cultural evidence for the circular arrangement of emotion-related words. Watson, Clark, and Tellegen (1984), in a carefully conducted study, examined Japanese and American mood terms and found a remarkable convergence in the structure of emotion within the two languages. Further, their study supported a two-factor structure (which they labeled *positive affect* and *negative affect*). Although the two factors identified by Watson and coworkers are labeled

differently than Russell's, and although these researchers argued for a simple two-factor model rather than a circular one, their data support the notion that emotion-related words may be reasonably described with only two dimensions (see also Mayer & Gaschke, 1988; Watson & Tellegen, 1985). Their data would also seem to support the idea that emotion-related words represent categories that define emotional states. The close similarity between these categories across Japanese and American cultures, together with the cross-cultural similarities found by Russell, suggest the interesting possibility that the categories of emotional experience may be universal in humans.

Russell (1991b) has extended his research on the categorization of emotions cross-culturally (for related reviews of the role of culture on emotion, see Markus & Kitayama, 1991, and Mesquita & Frijda, 1992). Drawing on a large body of evidence from psychology, linguistics, and anthropology, Russell shows that while there is considerable agreement across various cultures in categories and concepts concerning the emotions (as noted above and summarized more fully in Russell, 1991b), there are also numerous differences (Russell, 1991a). For example, some languages have no words for emotional terms used in English and some emotional terms in other languages have no English equivalents. Additionally, Russell points out that the way in which one categorizes various emotions appears to differ from culture to culture. Based on his review of the literature, Russell (1991b, p. 444) concludes that although there is "great similarity in emotion categories across different cultures and languages ... people of different cultures and speaking different languages categorize the emotions somewhat differently." As Russell points out, however, the fact that people in different cultures categorize emotions somewhat differently does not mean that emotional experiences could not still be universal.

The debate over the existence of a finite number of discrete emotions versus a more general form of core affect is not limited to the theorists discussed earlier. Ortony and Turner (1990) argue that the evidence for a relatively small set of discreet emotions is not convincing, while Ekman (1992a, 1992b) and Panksepp (1992) contend that there is considerable evidence for a biologically based, limited set of basic emotions. This controversy concerning the concept of "basic emotions" has often been played out in an area of research that concerns the role of facial expression in the production of emotion. We now focus on some of that research.

Facial Expression and Emotion

The theories of Tomkins and Izard have especially stressed the importance of facial changes in both the experience and communication of emotion. Unlike theorists who have stressed autonomic feedback as the source of differentiation between the various emotions, Tomkins and Izard have suggested that facial changes tell us what we are feeling. Tomkins originally proposed that feedback from the facial muscles provides the information necessary for the experience of the different emotions; later, however, he proposed that the essential information comes from changes in the facial skin (Tomkins, 1981a). Izard has maintained the position that facial musculature changes are the feedback for emotional experience. The modern emphasis on facial changes in emotion is often traced to Darwin's (1872) book *The Expression of the Emotions in Man and Animals*, although others such as Sir Charles Bell and French physiologist Duchenne had commented on facial changes and emotion earlier.

For both Tomkins and Izard, the existence of a fundamental set of emotions suggests that emotional expression should be similar across cultures. Although there has been considerable controversy concerning the universality of facial expression (Ekman, 1972, 1999a; Russell, 1994; Russell, Bachorowski, Fernandez-Dols, 2003), it now appears that some expressions are universal and thus support the concept of innate, fundamental emotions. (As we will see, however, some aspects of facial expressions are clearly culture specific.) Early evidence for a correspondence between

emotion and facial changes was provided by Tomkins and McCarter (1964), who found that observers could show high agreement in judging the emotion depicted in carefully selected photographs representing the fundamental emotions proposed by Tomkins.

Much of the initial work on the universality of facial expression was conducted by Ekman and his colleagues (see Ekman, 1972, 1999b; Ekman & Oster, 1982, for reviews) and by Izard (1971). Ekman gathered data on the interpretation of facial expressions from five different cultures, while Izard gathered data from nine cultures. As noted by Ekman and Oster (1982, p. 147), "The majority of observers in each culture interpreted the facial expressions as conveying the same emotions."

People from diverse cultures not only judge specific facial expressions similarly, they also produce the same facial movements when asked to portray particular emotions. For example, Ekman and Friesen (1971) found that members of a preliterate New Guinea group showed the same facial movements as people in literate cultures when asked to pose specific emotions. Further, Ekman (1972) and Friesen (1972; as reported in Ekman, Friesen, & Ellsworth, 1982) found that Japanese and American individuals asked to watch films (some of which were stressing) showed the same facial expressions if they watched the film alone.

Ekman and 12 other scholars from around the world (Ekman et al., 1987) have gathered additional evidence for the universal nature of facial expressions of emotion. Participants from 10 different cultures (Estonia, Germany, Greece, Hong Kong, Italy, Japan, Scotland, Sumatra, Turkey, and the United States) were asked to judge the emotions depicted in pictures of a face. Participants judged the primary emotion expressed and also secondary emotions that might be present. In addition, participants were asked to judge the intensity of the emotional expressions. Results of the study showed very good agreement across cultures in the interpretation of the emotions shown. Cross-culturally, participants consistently agreed on which emotion was the strongest; they also agreed on which secondary emotion was being expressed for those pictures where more than one emotion was present; finally, there was also good agreement concerning the relative intensities of the emotions expressed. Ekman and associates view this study as providing strong evidence for the universal nature of facial expressions because many of the criticisms of earlier cross-cultural studies were controlled in their study. Ekman's conclusion is further supported by the results of a meta-analysis of 97 different studies of cross-cultural emotion recognition, which found strong support for the universality of emotions, and limited support for the influence of culture (Elfenbein & Ambady, 2002). In addition to the research on culture, Sauter, LeGuen, and Haun (2011) found that perception of emotion does not depend on language, and these researchers conclude that an evolutionary mechanism is the most plausible explanation for their results.

One noteworthy aspect of emotion recognition that does appear to vary based on culture is the judgment of emotional intensity. Although Ekman et al., (1987) found agreement on the judgment of *relative* intensities of expressed emotions (i.e., if more than one emotion is present, which emotion is more intense?), Ekman et al. and others have also found that judgment of *absolute* emotional intensity (i.e., how strong is the emotion being depicted?) differs between cultures (e.g., Biehl et al., 1997; Ekman et al., 1987; Matsumoto, Kasri, & Kooken, 1999). For example, Matsumoto et al. (1999) presented Japanese and American participants with photographs that depicted seven common emotions and asked them to rate the intensity of the *external* display of emotion and their perception of the *internal* state of the person in the photograph. As Matsumoto and colleagues predicted, Americans rated the external display as more intense than did the Japanese participants. The results were reversed for the rating of the internal experience of emotion. Matsumoto et al. attributed this difference to the fact that people in collectivist cultures like Japan are socialized to modify their expression of emotion to fit what is acceptable in the situation, even though they may feel differently inside. The fact that people often alter their display of emotion based on social rules is a topic to which we now turn.

Display Rules Recall the studies of Ekman (1972) and Friesen (1972) in which participants watched films and their facial expressions were monitored. When an authority figure was present during the viewing of the films, differences in the facial expressions of the Japanese and American participants became apparent. In particular, the Japanese participants showed greater control over their facial expressions (though they also smiled more than the American participants under similar circumstances). The differences in facial responsiveness in the presence of an authority figure suggested to Ekman that although universal facial expressions are associated with specific emotional states, these expressions can be modified by what he calls **display rules**. Display rules are presumably learned early in life, and they determine which emotional expressions are appropriate in particular situations (e.g., Safdar et al., 2009). An example of a display rule noted by Ekman is the masking of sadness in public by white urban males in the United States. (Similarly, women usually mask anger in public.) The modification of the fundamental emotional expressions by display rules is conceptually similar to Tomkins's concept of backed-up emotion. Ekman's research therefore supports both Tomkins's concept of primary emotions and his idea that primary emotions are often disguised.

The operation of display rules will vary from culture to culture and even within cultures to a degree. As Ekman (1972) pointed out, the contradictory findings of early studies on facial expression may have resulted from observation of facial changes that were modified, in part, by different display rules from one culture to another.

The role of facial expression in emotion has been pursued even further. Ekman, Friesen, and Ancoli (1980) presented films to participants depicting happy events (a puppy playing with a flower, a gorilla in a zoo, ocean waves) and recorded the movements of the participants' faces. In particular they wanted to determine if smiling associated with the action of the zygomatic major muscles corresponds with happiness. They based their analysis of this particular muscle group on observation, hunch, and the suspicion that it is involved with smiles of happiness, while other muscle groups are involved with other types of smiles.

Their results supported their predictions. Movement of the zygomatic major muscles was associated with self-reports of happiness. Seven of the participants watching the films showed no movements of these muscles, and, interestingly, their happiness ratings were significantly lower than those of the participants who showed zygomatic major muscle smiles. Further, the intensity of the zygomatic major muscle movements was an accurate predictor of which film was best liked by the participants, indicating that movement of this muscle system is associated not only with positive feelings but also with the intensity of those feelings.

Ekman, Friesen, and O'Sullivan (1988) examined the physical differences between smiles people give when genuinely happy and the smiles they give when they are not happy. In particular these researchers were interested in the subtle differences in muscle contraction that occur when people are asked to deliberately lie about their feelings of happiness.

Student nurses were shown either nature films designed to elicit pleasant feelings or gruesome films of amputations and burns. Participants viewing the pleasant film were asked to describe their feelings honestly to an interviewer, while participants viewing the gruesome film were told that it was important to mask their true feelings and to try to convince the interviewer that they had in fact just seen a pleasant film. They were told being able to mask their true feelings was important because they would encounter situations in their nursing career similar to those in the gruesome film and that revealing their true feelings to these patients would be unprofessional. Participants' faces were videotaped during the sessions and their facial responses scored according to the Facial Action Coding System (FACS) developed by Ekman and Friesen (1976, 1978).

Results of the experiment showed that true smiles involved contraction of the outer muscles that orbit the eye (the orbicularis oculi) in addition to the contraction of the zygomatic major muscles. Smiles made while lying about their true feelings, however, showed a "leakage" (Ekman and Friesen's term) of other facial muscle activity (in addition to the zygomatic major muscle contractions) associated with the participants' true feelings. For example, in some participants minor muscle contractions associated with disgust were seen; in others, traces of sadness were observed. Ekman and Friesen's data show that measurable differences can be found between true happy smiles and masking smiles produced to cover true feelings (see also Ekman & O'Sullivan, 1991).

The above data suggest that our true emotional state can influence the facial expressions that we portray, despite our attempts to mask our feelings. There is also evidence that this relationship works in reverse.

The Facial Feedback Hypothesis   The **facial feedback hypothesis** proposes that the emotion we experience is influenced by feedback from facial muscles or skin. In an attempt to test the facial feedback hypothesis, Kraut (1982) designed an experiment in which he presented both pleasant and disgusting odors to participants. The participants smelled the odors over several trials during which their facial expressions were videotaped. Some trials recorded the participants' spontaneous reactions to the smells. On other trials the participants were instructed to compose their faces as if the odors were pleasant, and on still other trials they were told to act as if the odors were unpleasant. Participants also rated each odor after each trial so that the experimenters could determine whether posing influenced the emotional evaluation of the odors.

Analysis of the data revealed that posing pleasant or unpleasant expressions led to evaluations consistent with the posed expression. In other words, the posed expressions influenced the emotion experienced, supporting the facial feedback hypothesis. Additionally, posing pleasant expressions increased the evaluation of an odor over its evaluation after nonposed trials; similarly, posing unpleasant expressions decreased the odor evaluations relative to nonposed trials. Kraut's study therefore provides limited support for the facial feedback hypothesis; however, as he has noted, the posing effect was small—the actual odors had a much larger effect on the participants' emotional evaluations than did the posed facial expressions.

A study by Strack and associates (1988) is ingenious in its attempt to test the facial feedback hypothesis in an unobtrusive way. Participants were asked to hold a pen in their mouths in one of two different ways while viewing and rating cartoons for their humor content. One group held the pen between their teeth with their lips open so that they did not touch the barrel of the pen. Holding the pen in this manner contracts the zygomatic major and the risorius muscles that are involved in smiling. A second group held the pen with their lips only. Holding the pen in this manner contracts the orbicularis oris muscle, which should effectively prevent the contraction of the zygomatic major and risorius muscles. A third group of participants served as a control by rating the cartoons while holding the pen in their nondominant hand.

A cover story concerning the use of pens by disabled individuals was developed in order to make the three varying tasks appear reasonable to the participants. Although the two experiments were considerably more complicated than presented here, the general outcome of the study was that participants required to hold the pen between their teeth (and thus contract the muscles associated with smiling) rated the cartoons as more humorous than the control group, who held the pen with their nondominant hand. Those participants asked to hold the pen with their lips (which prevented contraction of the muscles involved in smiling) rated the cartoons as less humorous than the control group. Thus the evidence suggests that the affective reaction to an emotional stimulus was intensified or weakened when the facial muscles associated with smiling were facilitated or inhibited, respectively.

Similar results have been obtained by Larsen, Kasimatis, and Frey (1992) using unpleasant affect. They had participants contract their corrugator supercilii muscles, which are located above the eyes and act to wrinkle the forehead when one frowns, in order to touch two golf tees together that had been attached to their brow region. Participants reported more sadness when viewing photos in this condition than a group inhibited from contracting these muscles. Soussignan (2002) extended the research on the facial feedback hypothesis to include the genuine and deceptive smiles that Ekman, Friesen, and O'Sullivan (1988) reported.

Using a cover story similar to the one employed by Strack et al. (1988), Soussignan asked participants to hold pens in their mouths in a manner that mimicked a genuine smile (called a **Duchenne smile**), a fake smile (called a non-Duchenne smile), or two non smiling expressions (see Figure 12.7). Participants then watched positive and negative video clips, which they were asked to rate. Results indicated that the Duchenne smiling group rated the video clips as more positive than the other three groups. Taken together, these findings provide support for the facial feedback hypothesis and further suggest that recognizing the emotional meaning of the facial responses is not necessary in order for the emotion to be influenced.

When we consider the variety of theories and methodologies that have been used to study the relationship between cognition and emotion, it is clear that there is considerable disagreement in the field and much that is still to be discovered. However, there are some themes emerging. First, cross-cultural research indicates that certain aspects of emotion are universal. Second, most researchers agree that emotional experience is at least partly (if not entirely) shaped by evolution. Finally, the sheer number of researchers working in this field indicates the degree of importance that science places on understanding the developmental, cognitive, physiological and social aspects of emotional experience.

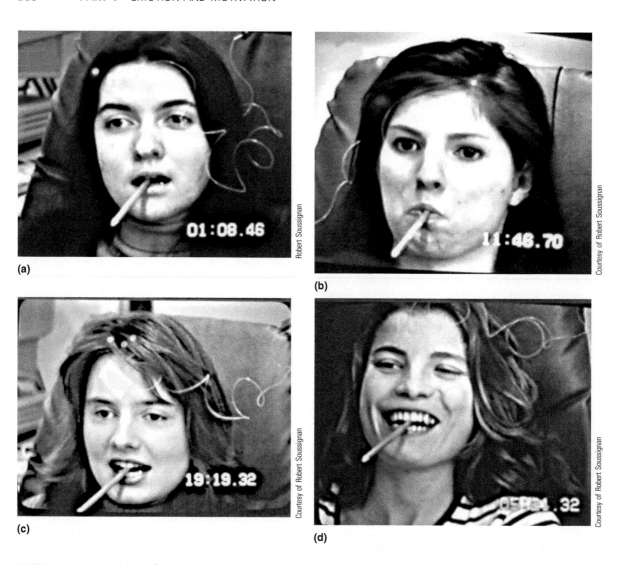

(a)

(b)

(c)

(d)

Robert Soussignan

Courtesy of Robert Soussignan

Courtesy of Robert Soussignan

Courtesy of Robert Soussignan

FIGURE 12.7 Facial configurations used in Soussignan's study: panels (a) and (b) are non-smiling control conditions; (c) non-Duchenne smile; (d) Duchenne smile. From "Duchenne Smile, Emotional Experience, and Autonomic Reactivity: A Test of the Facial Feedback Hypothesis," by R. Soussignan, 2002, *Emotion, 2,* 52–74. Copyright © 2002 by the American Psychological Association. Used by permission.

SUMMARY

In this chapter we have examined theories and research on emotion. As we discovered, Darwin's early emphasis on facial expression and body posture has its modern counterparts in the study of intention movements by the ethologists and research on the universality of facial movements by theorists such as Tomkins, Izard, and Ekman. Biological explanations of emotion, first popularized by the James-Lange theory and modified by research conducted by Cannon, eventually led to a better understanding of the brain mechanisms underlying emotion. Brain circuitry encompassing the amygdala, orbital frontal cortex, and cingulate cortex seem especially important in the experience of emotion.

Learning is an integral component of emotion. Classical conditioning provides a mechanism through which new emotions are quickly learned in a relatively automatic fashion. Biologically, the amygdala appears crucial to the development of conditioned fears. Emotions can also be learned as a result of instrumental/operant conditioning processes. Reinforcement and punishment appear to influence emotional behaviors in the same way that they influence other, nonemotional behaviors. Biologically, the nucleus accumbens and the medial prefrontal cortex have been implicated in the effects of reinforcement and punishment. The neurotransmitter dopamine also plays a pivotal role in these processes. Emotions can also be learned through observation of others. Perhaps many of the emotions we feel as adults were initially learned from the observation of family members earlier in life. There are however, some constraints on what we learn to fear. Some fears (e.g., snakes, spiders, heights, and enclosed spaces) are more common than would be expected by chance. We seem prepared to learn some fears more easily than others. Whether the preparedness of emotional learning also applies to other emotions in addition to fear remains to be explored.

Schachter's proposal that physiological changes by themselves are insufficient for the full experience of emotion has led to the development of several more fully cognitive explanations of the experience of emotion. These appraisal models, developed by researchers such as Lazarus, suggest that the cognitive component of emotion is primary and occurs before the full experience of emotion. This emphasis on cognitive appraisal has led some researchers to study how our causal attributions influence the emotions we experience.

In contrast to strictly cognitive models of emotion, Zajonc has argued that emotion can precede and occur independent of cognitive appraisal processes. His argument for the primacy of emotion is supported by the research of Izard, Ekman, and others. In a sense the study of emotion has come full circle, starting with an emphasis on the bodily expression of emotion by Darwin and returning to similar analyses by theorists such as Tomkins and Izard, both of whom argue that there are a relatively small number of innate, discrete emotions.

However, Russell sees a great deal of variability in apparently discrete emotional categories such as "fear." Russell argues that, in order to account for this variability, we should study emotions by reducing them to their primary components, one of which he calls core affect. Studies of the words we use when expressing emotional states have provided evidence for Russell's circumplex model that describes a circular pattern of emotions around the two major dimensions of pleasantness and arousal.

Cross-cultural research has provided strong evidence for the universality of some aspects of emotional expression and recognition. However, emotions are also influenced by cultural display rules that govern what is considered appropriate in a situation.

It should be obvious by now that the study of emotion is terribly complex and that theoretical explanations can and do differ widely. One reason for such divergence of opinion is that our emotional experiences are undoubtedly multiply determined. Some emotional feelings and their expression are probably innate and shared by all humans regardless of culture. Other emotional experiences may consist of subtle interactions of the more primary emotions or may require consciousness of the self as suggested by Lewis (see Suggestions for Further Reading). Finally, still other emotional experiences may be altered by learned cultural display rules that limit emotional expression in many ways. Cognition must also play a part in our emotional lives, although the argument over the primacy of cognition is far from resolved. It is also clear that emotionality is strongly associated with physiological changes. Although our thinking has changed somewhat since James and Lange first suggested the importance of physiological change, alterations in the autonomic nervous system (particularly the sympathetic branch) usually accompany the experience of emotion. If emotion is multiply determined, as the evidence presented in this chapter seems to suggest, we should probably not expect one theory to encompass all we know. Rather, like motivation, emotion may be triggered by physiological change, learning, cognition, and perhaps by factors as yet undiscovered.

KEY TERMS

emotion, *355*

serviceable associated habits/
   antithesis/direct action of the
   nervous system, *356*

emergency theory/autonomic
   nervous system, *359*

sympathetic nervous system/
   parasympathetic nervous
   system, *360*

cognitive-physiological theory
   of emotion, *361*

expressive movements, *363*

nonverbal cues, *364*

limbic system/amygdala, *366*

orbital frontal cortex (OFC)/
   Phineas Gage, *367*

anterior cingulate cortex/
   ventromedial prefrontal
   cortex (vmPFC)/vigilance,
   368

conditioned fear/basolateral
   nucleus of the amygdala
   (BLA)/central nucleus of the
   amygdala (CeA), *369*

nucleus accumbens (Acb)/
   dopamine (DA)/medial
   prefrontal cortex (mPFC)/
   observational learning/
   modeling, *370*

general process learning theory/
   prepared associations/
   contraprepared associations/
   unprepared associations/

preparedness hypothesis/
   phobia, *372*

demand characteristics, *374*

self-monitoring, *375*

backed-up emotion/
   differential emotions
   theory (DET), *378*

basic emotions/emotion
   schemas, *379*

circumplex, *380*

fuzzy set, *381*

core affect, *382*

display rules, *385*

facial feedback hypothesis, *386*

Duchenne smile, *387*

SUGGESTIONS FOR FURTHER READING

Cardinal, R. N., Parkinson, J. A., Hall, J., & Everitt, B. J. (2002). Emotion and motivation: The role of the amygdala, ventral striatum, and prefrontal cortex. *Neuroscience and Biobehavioral Reviews, 26,* 321–352. This article provides a very complete overview of the role of the amygdala and other structures in emotion. For the advanced student.

Ekman, P. (1999b). Facial Expressions. In T. Dalgleish & M. J. Power (Eds.), *Handbook of cognition and emotion*, pp. 301–320. West Sussex, England: John Wiley & Sons. A thorough discussion of the debate about the universality of facial expressions.

Lewis, M. (1995). Self–conscious emotions. *American Scientist, 83,* 68–78. Lewis provides an interesting analysis of emotions such as shame, guilt, pride, and hubris that appear to require self-awareness for their experience.

Mumme, D. L., & Fernald, A. (2003). The infant as onlooker: Learning from emotional reactions observed in a television scenario. *Child Development, 74,* 221–337. This article provides evidence that infants as young as 12 months are sensitive to emotion in others.

Russell, J. A. (2003). Core affect and the psychological construction of emotion. *Psychological Review, 110,* 145–172. Russell presents a revised version of his circumplex model and argues that core affect is the necessary substrate for emotional experience.

WEB RESOURCES

The Center for the Study of Emotion and Attention: http://csea.phhp.ufl.edu/ The homepage of an organization dedicated to the study of emotion, physiology, behavior and motivation.

Stanford University: http://www-psych.stanford.edu/ ~tsailab/index.htm. This site at Stanford University provides information about various cross-cultural projects associated with the study of emotion.

The Tomkins Institute: http://www.behavior.net/ orgs/ssti/. This is the official site for the Tomkins Institute for the study of emotion.

University of Michigan: http://selfcontrol.psych.lsa .umich.edu/index.php. This site at the University of Michigan examines presents information on emotion and self-control.

PART VI ENDVIEW

CHAPTER 13
Conclusions

CHAPTER 13

Conclusions

How does one pull together the research in a field as complex and diverse as motivation? Not easily. The difficulty in drawing conclusions is due in part to the fact that the research findings stretch from instincts to attitudes with many stops in between. The understanding of the activation and direction of behavior by motivational mechanisms is so complex because the relevant information cuts across all subareas within psychology. As a result, motivational explanations have varied depending on the subarea within psychology from which the data were drawn. In order to attempt some conclusions, however, it seems worthwhile to return to concepts originally outlined in the beginning of this text.

Chapter 1 introduced the idea that motivational processes in all animals could be regarded as "in the service of" a more general principle of all living things—the need to continue one's genetic information on to the next generation. We dubbed this the primary operating principle (POP). Consequently, the motives discussed in the chapters following the first, while operating on their own principles, seem understandable as promoting the POP. One could argue, therefore, that in general, motivation exists to promote the continuance of life.

Furthermore, evolution—especially natural selection—decrees which motivated behaviors are useful. In Chapter 2 we examined research on genetically programmed motives as an example of one way in which evolutionary processes have shaped the behavior of various species including our own. Clearly, some motives are built into the organism and are triggered by appropriate circumstances without any need for understanding the purpose of the behavior or any awareness of why the behavior is activated.

Motive states such as hunger, thirst, aggression, and sexual activity are reasonably viewed from a physiological perspective.

Neural circuits deep within the brain trigger appropriate motivation when internal changes are detected by monitoring systems or environmental conditions demand it. This neural circuitry often appears to be homeostatic, activating behavior to keep the body at an optimal level as discussed in Chapter 4. We reviewed much of the research pertaining to this view of motivation. Can a biological perspective explain all that we know about hunger, thirst, and sexual behavior? Certainly not. Each of these motives is also known to be influenced by learning, and in humans, cognitive processes also seem to play a role. Even the most basic motives have been shown to result from complicated combinations of factors.

We covered a different type of physiological explanation in Chapter 3. There we examined research suggesting that arousal mechanisms located within the brain stem are important for motivated activity. Researchers within this realm agree that understanding arousal mechanisms provides us with insight into motivated behavior, and behaviors as disparate as sleep and stress can be viewed as different points on an arousal continuum. But once again we find that arousal can be influenced by a variety of factors, including physiology, social interactions, and even attitude. Clearly, arousal theory alone cannot explain all that we know about the activation and direction of behavior.

Although physiological analysis can help us to understand some types of motivated states, physiological explanations alone are inadequate. Humans clearly can override homeostatic mechanisms as a result of experience. Anorexics voluntarily starve, while bulimics gorge and then purge. History is full of examples of individuals who have denied physiological needs for political, philosophical, or religious purposes. Such examples suggest that other mechanisms must play a large role in the motivation of behavior.

Learning is certainly one such mechanism. In Chapters 5 and 6 we examined the role of learning in the motivation of behavior, and discovered that learning can result in the development of new motives not only through classical and operant conditioning but also through modeling. Further, and perhaps more important, learning plays a large role in the goals that we pursue. For humans, learning processes lead to the development of incentive motivation, which in turn provides an important way in which environmental objects or goals stimulate and guide our behavior. Although learning mechanisms by themselves cannot explain all of motivation, they do add an essential element to our overall understanding. Some motives are clearly learned. To understand why people behave the way that they do, we need to better understand the role that learning plays in the motivation of behavior.

Why do people pursue external goals? Chapter 7 suggested that one reason is that the characteristics of stimuli can be rewarding (or punishing). Thus, reinforcement and punishment processes shape how we are motivated to respond in particular situations. Further, the underlying neural basis for these processes seems to be closely tied to circuitry that is also concerned with emotion. In particular the amygdala, various areas in the frontal cortex, and the nucleus accumbens in the basal forebrain contribute to emotional learning, as well as reward/punishment. The neurotransmitter dopamine also seems to be a major player in these processes.

Cognitive mechanisms concerned with active information processing also provide an important source of motivation in humans. In Chapters 8 through 11 we examined these sources of motivation. In Chapter 8, for example, we noted the importance of expectancy in guiding behavior. In Chapter 9 we explored the important role that others play in socially motivating conformity and compliance in an individual. Additionally, we reviewed the concept of cognitive consistency. Consistency approaches propose that inconsistencies in our thoughts trigger motivation that brings those thoughts back into consistent relationships with one another. Consistency models, as represented by such theories as cognitive dissonance, suggest that our attitudes about ourselves, others, and events are an important source of motivation. Like research on learning and motivation, research on cognition and motivation has added an important dimension to our understanding. Once again, however, we find that cognitive explanations by themselves are not sufficient to explain all that we know about why people behave.

In Chapter 10 we explored a line of evidence for attitudinal influences on motivation known as attribution theory. As noted, our attributions do alter our motivation; further, we appear to be biased in how we make those attributions. Clearly we cannot hope to understand human behavior unless we also understand both how attributions are made and how they change our motivation to behave in the future. Additionally, both social motivation and attribution approaches agree that our motivation is heavily influenced by the behavior of others.

In Chapter 11 we examined a somewhat different approach, one that might be considered as occurring at a more philosophical level of analysis. The concepts of the fully functioning individual and self-actualization introduced in Chapter 11 are based on a positive point of view about human motivation—that we strive to become all that we can become. Because of difficulties in operationally defining such terms as *self-actualization*, data concerned with these approaches are often difficult to interpret. Nevertheless, these approaches have helped us describe some human behaviors not easily accounted for by homeostatic or learned motives. As the title of Chapter 11 suggests, a common thread that seems to run through many human behaviors is the need to control one's environment. Research on intrinsic motivation and perceived control suggests that competence in controlling the events of life is an important source of motivation. Perhaps self-actualization can be understood as a person's lifelong struggle to maintain and increase control over the events of life. If we have good control over such basic needs as food, water, shelter, and so forth, then we can focus more attention on gaining control over less immediate goals, such as those proposed by Maslow in his hierarchy of needs.

In Chapter 12, we used information gained in earlier chapters to examine several theoretical approaches to emotion. Research explored in this chapter suggests that emotion, like motivation, is multidimensional. Physiological changes associated with the sympathetic nervous system and feedback from facial regions have both been implicated in the experience of emotion. Several brain regions, and especially the amygdala, appear to be responsible for much of the integration of the various components of emotional experience. Further, cross-cultural evidence supports the notion that some basic emotions are universal but can be overridden by culturally learned display rules. Analysis of emotional terms suggests that a model of emotionality incorporating the dimensions of arousal and pleasantness may be able to account for much of emotional experience, although much more research clearly must be done to test the viability of such a model. Additionally, motivation and emotion interact to produce behavior. The mechanisms of this interaction, however, are poorly understood. As noted at the beginning of this book, no single theory can account for all that we know about the motivation of behavior. Even a seemingly simple motivation like hunger can be influenced by physiological, cultural, learned, and social factors. Human motives appear to be multiply determined.

In thinking about motivational processes in a more general way, we might consider the following. At its base, motivation can be influenced by genetic predispositions that bias an individual to be more likely to behave one way rather than another. These predispositions exist today because they helped our ancestors to survive (and reproduce) in the environment in which they lived. Many of these biases are outside of awareness and so motivate us unconsciously.

Arranged on top of these genetic biases is a large repertoire of learned behaviors that can vary from one person to the next depending upon what each individual has experienced during his or her lifetime. Our interaction with the environment shapes our motives. These learned motives can become habitual and virtually automatic given enough repetitions.

Because we are social animals, the presence of others also heavily influences what motivates us and might be depicted as sitting on top of the individually learned motives. Social motives are probably a complex interaction of genetics and learning functioning together.

Our cognitive capacities allow us to make inferences about why others (and ourselves) behave the way that they do and that promotes motivation via expectancies and attributions. Cognitive motivation sitting on top of the genetic, learned, and social processes surely interacts with each in complex and poorly understood ways.

Because survival in a hostile environment is increased by the ability to control that environment to some extent, we seem motivated to attempt to control what happens to us. Lack of control often produces feelings of helplessness and depressed motivation. Control has obvious survival value, but how to control one's environment is probably learned during development, during social interactions, and is also a function of the decisions we make using cognitive processes.

Motivation, then, could be regarded as a series of multilayered processes woven together by genetics, learning, sociality, and cognition to produce behavior. Problems within any of these processes or their interactions could result in maladaptive behaviors; in fact, it is surprising how well these systems typically work in concert to produce adaptive behavior.

Much of the complex interaction between the various factors that motivate us remains to be worked out. Some of the most pressing problems that face us as humans—health changes due to stress; eating disorders such as anorexia, bulimia, and obesity; indiscriminate aggression against family members; atrocities committed in the name of nationalism or religion; drive-by shootings; as well as a host of other problems—will require a better understanding of what motivates people to behave as they do if we are to solve these problems. It is our hope that this text may motivate you to help science find some of those solutions.

References

Abe, J. A., & Izard, C. E. (1999). The developmental functions of emotions: An analysis in terms of differential emotions theory. *Cognition and Emotion, 13,* 523–549.

Abelson, R. P., Aronson, E., McGuire, W. J., Newcomb, T. M., Rosenberg, M. J., & Tannenbaum, P. H. (Eds.). (1968). *Theories of cognitive consistency: A source book.* Chicago, IL: Rand McNally.

Abramson, E. E., & Lucido, G. M. (1991). Childhood sexual experience and bulimia. *Addictive Behaviors, 16,* 529–532.

Abramson, L. Y., Metalsky, G. I., & Alloy, L. B. (1989). Hopelessness depression: A theory-based subtype of depression. *Psychological Review, 96,* 358–372.

Abramson, L. Y., Seligman, M. E., & Teasdale, J. D. (1978). Learned helplessness in humans: Critique and reformulation. *Journal of Abnormal Psychology, 87,* 49–74.

Abu-Elheiga, L., Matzuk, M. M., Abo-Hashema, K. A. H., & Wakil, S. J. (2001). Continuous fatty acid oxidation and reduced fat storage in mice lacking acetyl-CoA carboxylase 2. *Science, 291,* 2613–2616.

Adelman, H. M., & Maatsch, J. L. (1955). Resistance to extinction as a function of the type of response elicited by frustration. *Journal of Experimental Psychology, 50,* 61–65.

Ader, R. (Ed.). (1981). *Psychoneuroimmunology.* New York: Academic Press.

Ader, R. (2001). Psychoneuroimmunology. *Current Directions in Psychological Science, 10,* 94–98.

Ader, R., & Cohen, N. (1975). Behaviorally conditioned immune suppression. *Psychosomatic Medicine, 37,* 333–340.

Adler, N., & Matthews, K. (1994). Health psychology: Why do some people get sick? In L. W. Porter & M. R. Rosenzweig (Eds.), *Annual review of psychology* (pp. 229–259). Palo Alto, CA: Annual Reviews.

Adler, R., & Hogan, J. A. (1963). Classical conditioning and punishment of an instinctive response in *Betta splendens. Animal Behavior, 11,* 351–354.

Adler, T. (1989, August). Shy monkeys are born, not made. *American Psychological Association Monitor,* p. 5.

Adolfsson, B., Andersson, I., Elofsson, S., Rossner, S., & Unden, A. (2005). Locus of control and weight reduction. *Patient Education and Counseling, 56,* 55–61.

Adolphs, R., Tranel, D., & Damasio, H. (2001). Emotion recognition from faces and prosody following temporal lobectomy. *Neuropsychology, 15,* 396–404.

Aggarwal, P., & O'Brien, C. L. (2008). Social loafing on group projects: Structural antecedents and effect on student satisfaction. *Journal of Marketing Education, 30,* 255–264.

Agmo, A. (1999). Sexual motivation–An inquiry into the events determining the occurrence of sexual behavior. *Behavioural Brain Research, 105,* 129–150.

Ahsanuddin, K. M., & Nyeem, R. (1983). Fourth ventricle tumors and anorexia nervosa. *International Journal of Eating Disorders, 2,* 67–72.

Ajzen, I. (1988). *Attitudes, personality, and behavior.* Chicago, IL: Dorsey.

Ajzen, I. (1991). The theory of planned behavior. *Organizational Behavior and Human Decision Processes, 50,* 179–211.

Albarracin, D., Johnson, B. T., Fishbein, M., & Muellerleile, P. A. (2001). Theories of reasoned action and planned behavior as models of condom use: A meta-analysis. *Psychological Bulletin, 127,* 142–161.

Alberts, B., Bray, D., Lewis, J., Raff, M., Roberts, K., & Watson, J. D. (1989). *Molecular biology of the cell* (2nd ed.). New York: Garland.

Alcock, J. (1975). *Animal behavior: An evolutionary approach.* Sunderland, MA: Sinauer.

Alloy, L. B., & Abramson, L. Y. (1982). Learned helplessness, depression, and the illusion of control. *Journal of Personality and Social Psychology, 42,* 1114–1126.

Allport, G. W. (1937). *Personality: A psychological interpretation.* New York: Holt, Rinehart and Winston.

American Psychiatric Association. (1994). *Diagnostic and statistical manual of mental disorders* (4th ed.). Washington, DC: American Psychiatric Association.

American Psychiatric Association. (2000). *Diagnostic and statistical manual of mental disorders* (4th ed., Text revision). Washington, DC: American Psychiatric Association.

Amico, M. C. (2010). *The association between father-child relationship, locus of control, and sensation-seeking* (UMI 3426506). Unpublished doctoral dissertation, Capella University.

Amsel, A. (1972). Behavioral habituation, counter conditioning, and a general theory of persistence. In A. H. Black & W. F. Prokasy (Eds.), *Classical conditioning II: Current research and theory*. New York: Appleton-Century-Crofts.

Amsel, A., & Roussel, J. (1952). Motivational properties of frustration: I. Effect on a running response of the addition of frustration to the motivational complex. *Journal of Experimental Psychology, 43,* 363–368.

Anand, B. K., & Brobeck, J. R. (1951). Hypothalamic control of food intake in rats and cats. *Yale Journal of Biological Medicine, 24,* 123–140.

Ancoli-Israel, S., & Kripke, D. F. (1991). Prevalent sleep problems in the aged. *Biofeedback and Self-Regulation, 16,* 349–359.

Anderson, A. K., Spencer, D. D., Fulbright, R. K., & Phelps, E. (2000). Contribution of the anteromedial temporal lobes to the evaluation of facial emotion. *Neuropsychology, 14,* 526–536.

Andersson, B. (1971). Thirst and brain control of water balance. *American Scientist, 59,* 408–415.

Andrew, R. J. (1965). The origins of facial expressions. *Scientific American, 213,* 88–94.

Angier, N. (2002). The importance of grandma. *The New York Times.* Retrieved November 5, 2002, from http://www.nytimes.com/2002.GRAN.html

Appley, M. H., & Trumbull, R. (1967). On the concept of psychological stress. In M. H. Appley & R. Trumbull (Eds.), *Psychological stress*. New York: Appleton-Century-Crofts.

Arkes, H. R., & Garske, J. P. (1977). *Psychological theories of motivation*. Monterey, CA: Brooks/Cole.

Armitage, C. J., & Conner, M. (2001). Efficacy of the theory of planned behaviour: A meta-analytic review. *British Journal of Social Psychology, 40,* 471–499.

Arnold, M. B. (1967). Stress and emotion. In M. H. Appley & R. Trumbull (Eds.), *Psychological stress*. New York: Appleton-Century-Crofts.

Aronson, E. (1968). Dissonance theory: Progress and problems. In R. P. Abelson et al. (Eds.), *Theories of cognitive consistency: A source book*. Chicago, IL: Rand McNally.

Aronson, E. (1992). The return of the repressed: Dissonance theory makes a come back. *Psychological Inquiry, 3,* 303–311.

Aronson, E., & Carlsmith, J. (1963). Effect of the severity of threat on the devaluation of forbidden behavior. *Journal of Abnormal and Social Psychology, 66,* 584–588.

Aronson, E., & Mills, J. (1959). The effect of severity of initiation on liking for a group. *Journal of Abnormal and Social Psychology, 59,* 177–181.

Arterberry, M. E., Cain, K. M., & Chopko, S. A. (2007). Collaborative problem solving in five-year-old children: Evidence of social facilitation and social loafing. *Educational Psychology, 27,* 577–596.

Asch, S. E. (1952). *Social psychology*. Englewood Cliffs, NJ: Prentice Hall.

Asch, S. E. (1965). Interpersonal influence. In H. Proshansky & B. Seidenberg (Eds.), *Basic studies in social psychology*. New York: Holt, Rinehart and Winston.

Aserinsky, E. (1987, November 9). This week's citation classic. *Current Contents, 22.*

Aserinsky, E., & Kleitman, N. (1955). A mobility cycle in sleeping infants as manifested by ocular and gross bodily activity. *Journal of Applied Physiology, 8,* 11–19.

Aston-Jones, G., & Bloom, F. E. (1981). Activity of norepinephrine-containing locus coeruleus neurons in behaving rats anticipates fluctuations in the sleep-waking cycle. *Journal of Neuroscience, 1,* 876–886.

Aston-Jones, G., Rajkowski, J., Kubiak, P., & Alexinsky, T. (1994). Locus coeruleus neurons in monkey are selectively activated by attended cues in a vigilance task. *Journal of Neuroscience, 14,* 4467–4480.

Atkinson, J. W., & Birch, D. (1978). *An introduction to motivation* (2nd ed.). New York: Van Nostrand.

Atkinson, J. W., & Litwin, G. H. (1960). Achievement motive and test anxiety conceived as motive to approach success and motive to avoid failure. *Journal of Abnormal and Social Psychology, 60,* 52–63.

Averill, J. R. (1983). Studies on anger and aggression: Implications for theories of emotion. *American Psychologist, 38,* 1145–1160.

Ayllon, T., & Azrin, N. H. (1968). *The token economy: A motivational system for therapy and rehabilitation*. New York: Appleton-Century-Crofts.

Azrin, N. H., Hutchinson, R. R., & Sallery, R. D. (1964). Pain aggression toward inanimate objects. *Journal of the Experimental Analysis of Behavior, 7,* 223–227.

Baerends, G. P. (1976). The functional organization of behavior. *Animal Behavior, 24,* 726–738.

Bailey, P., & Davis, E. W. (1969). Effects of lesions of the periaqueductal gray matter in the cat. In K. H. Pribram (Ed.), *Brain and behavior 1: Mood, states and mind.* Baltimore, MD: Penguin.

Baldwin, A. E., Sadeghian, K., & Kelley, A. E. (2002). Appetitive instrumental learning requires coincident activation of NMDA and dopamine D1 receptors within the medial prefrontal cortex. *The Journal of Neuroscience, 22,* 1063–1071.

Baltes, M. M., & Skinner, E. A. (1983). Cognitive performance deficits and hospitalization: Learned helplessness, instrumental passivity, or what? Comment on Raps, Peterson, Jonas, and Seligman. *Journal of Personality and Social Psychology, 45,* 1013–1016.

Balthazart, J., Stamatakis, A., Bacola, S., Absil, P., & Dermon, C. R. (2001). Effects of lesions of the medial preoptic nucleus on the testosterone-induced metabolic changes in specific brain areas in male quail. *Neuroscience, 108,* 447–466.

Bandler, R. J., & Flynn, J. P. (1974). Neural pathways from thalamus associated with regulation of aggressive behavior. *Science, 183,* 96–99.

Bandura, A. (1969). *Principles of behavior modification.* New York: Holt, Rinehart & Winston.

Bandura, A. (1971). *Social learning theory.* Morristown, NJ: General Learning Press.

Bandura, A. (1973). *Aggression: A social learning analysis.* Englewood Cliffs, NJ: Prentice Hall.

Bandura, A. (1977). *Social learning theory.* Englewood Cliffs, NJ: Prentice Hall.

Bandura, A. (1993). Perceived self-efficacy in cognitive development and functioning. *Educational Psychologist, 28,* 117–148.

Bandura, A. (1997). *Self efficacy: The exercise of control.* New York: Freeman.

Bandura, A. (2000). Exercise of human agency through collective efficacy. *Current Directions in Psychological Science, 9,* 75–78.

Bandura, A. (2001). Social cognitive theory: An agentic perspective. In S. Fiske, D. L. Schacter, & C. Zahn-Waxler (Eds.), *Annual review of psychology* (p. 52). Palo Alto, CA: Annual Reviews.

Bandura, A. (2002). Growing primacy of human agency in adaptation and change in the electronic era. *European Psychologist, 7,* 2–16.

Bandura, A. (2006). Toward a psychology of human agency. *Perspectives on Psychological Science, 1,* 164–180.

Bandura, A., Barbaranelli, C., Caprara, G. V., & Pastorelli, C. (1996). Multifaceted impact of self-efficacy beliefs on academic functioning. *Child Development, 67,* 1206–1222.

Bandura, A., O'Leary, A., Taylor, C. B., Gauthier, J., & Gossard, D. (1987). Perceived self-efficacy and pain control: Opioid and non-opioid mechanisms. *Journal of Personality and Social Psychology, 53,* 563–571.

Bandura, A., Ross, D., & Ross, S. A. (1961). Transmission of aggression through imitation of aggressive models. *Journal of Abnormal and Social Psychology, 63,* 575–582.

Bandura, A., Ross, D., & Ross, S. A. (1963). Imitation of film mediated aggressive models. *Journal of Abnormal and Social Psychology, 66,* 3–11.

Barber, N. (1995). The evolutionary psychology of physical attractiveness: Sexual selection and human morphology. *Ethology and Sociobiology, 16,* 395–424.

Bard, P. (1928). A diencephalic mechanism for the expression of rage with special reference to the sympathetic nervous systems. *American Journal of Physiology, 84,* 490–515.

Bard, P., & Mountcastle, V. B. (1964). Some forebrain mechanisms involved in expression of rage with special reference to suppression of angry behavior. In R. L. Isaacson (Ed.), *Basic readings in neuropsychology.* New York: Harper & Row.

Barfield, R. J., Wilson, C., & McDonald, P. G. (1975). Sexual behavior: Extreme reduction of post ejaculatory refractory period by midbrain lesions in male rats. *Science, 189,* 147–149.

Barker, R. H., Dembo, T., & Lewin, K. (1941). Frustration and regression: An experiment with young children. *University of Iowa Studies in Child Welfare, 18,* 1–314.

Baron, R. A. (1974a). The aggression-inhibiting influence of heightened sexual arousal. *Journal of Personality and Social Psychology, 30,* 318–322.

Baron, R. A. (1974b). Sexual arousal and physical aggression: The inhibiting influence of "cheese cake" and nudes. *Bulletin of Psychonomic Society, 3,* 337–339.

Baron, R. A., & Bell, P. A. (1977). Sexual arousal and aggression by males: Effect of type of erotic stimuli and prior provocation. *Journal of Personality and Social Psychology, 35,* 79–87.

Baron, R. S., Vandello, J. A., & Brunsman, B. (1996). The forgotten variable in conformity research: Impact of task importance on social influence. *Journal of Personality and Social Psychology, 71,* 915–927.

Bartoshuk, L. M., & Beauchamp, G. K. (1994). Chemical senses. *Annual Review of Psychology, 45,* 419–449. Palo Alto, CA: Annual Reviews.

Basil, D. Z., & Herr, P. M. (2006). Attitudinal balance and cause-related marketing: An empirical application of balance theory. *Journal of Consumer Psychology, 16,* 391–403.

Bateson, P. P. G., & Reese, E. P. (1969). The reinforcing properties of conspicuous stimuli in the imprinting situation. *Animal Behavior, 17,* 692–699.

Bator, R. J., & Cialdini, R. B. (2006). The nature of consistency motivation: Consistency, aconsistency, and anticonsistency in a dissonance paradigm. *Social Influence, 1,* 208–233.

Batson, C. D., & Ahmad, N. (2001). Empathy-induced altruism in a prisoner's dilemma II: What if the target of empathy has defected? *European Journal of Social Psychology, 31,* 25–36.

Batson, C. D., Ahmad, N., Yin, J., Bedell, S. J., Johnson, J. W., Templin, C. M., & Whiteside, A. (1999). Two threats to the common good: Self-interested egoism and empathy induced altruism. *Personality and Social Psychology Bulletin, 25,* 3–16.

Batson, C. D., Duncan, B. D., Ackerman, P., Buckley, T., & Birch, K. (1981). Is empathic emotion a source of altruistic motivation? *Journal of Personality and Social Psychology, 40,* 290–302.

Batson, C. D., & Gray, R. A. (1981). Religious orientation and helping behavior: Responding to one's own or to the victim's needs? *Journal of Personality and Social Psychology, 40,* 511–520.

Batson, C. D., O'Quin, K., Fultz, J., Vanderplas, M., & Isen, A. M. (1983). Influence of self-reported distress and empathy on egoistic versus altruistic motivation to help. *Journal of Personality and Social Psychology, 45,* 706–718.

Batson, C. D., & Weeks, J. L. (1996). Mood effects of unsuccessful helping: Another test of the empathy altruism hypothesis. *Personality and Social Psychology Bulletin, 22,* 148–157.

Baum, A., & Gatchel, R. J. (1981). Cognitive determinants of reaction to uncontrollable events: Development of reactance and learned helplessness. *Journal of Personality and Social Psychology, 40,* 1078–1089.

Baum, A., & Posluszny, D. M. (1999). Health psychology: Mapping biobehavioral contributions to health and illness. *Annual Review of Psychology, 50,* 137–163.

Baum, M. J. (2002). Neuroendocrinology of sexual behavior in the male. In J. B. Becker, S. M. Breedlove, D. Crews, & M. M. McCarthy (Eds.), *Behavioral endocrinology* (2nd ed., pp. 153–203). Cambridge, MA: MIT Press.

Baumann, D. J., Cialdini, R. B., & Kenrick, D. T. (1981). Altruism as hedonism: Helping and self-gratification as equivalent responses. *Journal of Personality and Social Psychology, 40,* 1039–1046.

Baumeister, R. F., & Steinhilber, A. (1984). Paradoxical effects of supportive audiences on performance under pressure: The home field disadvantage in sports championships. *Journal of Personality and Social Psychology, 47,* 85–93.

Beach, F. A. (1955). The descent of instinct. *Psychological Review, 62,* 401–410.

Beach, F. A. (1967). Cerebral and hormonal control of reflexive mechanisms involved in copulatory behavior. *Physiological Review, 47,* 289–316.

Beach, F. A. (1976). Sexual attractivity, proceptivity, and receptivity in female mammals. *Hormones and Behavior, 7,* 105–138.

Beck, A. T. (1967). *Depression: Clinical, experimental, and theoretical aspects.* New York: Harper & Row.

Beck, R. C. (1978). *Motivation: Theories and principles.* Englewood Cliffs, NJ: Prentice Hall.

Beck, R. C. (1983). *Motivation: Theories and principles* (2nd ed.). Englewood Cliffs, NJ: Prentice Hall.

Beck, R. C. (2000). *Motivation: Theories and principles* (4th ed.). Upper Saddle River, NJ: Prentice Hall.

Beck, R. C., & Matteson, N. (1982). *False physiological feedback and emotion: An experimental artifact?* Paper presented at the annual convention of the Southeastern Psychological Association, New Orleans.

Bedell, J. R., Giordani, B., Amour, J. L., Tavormina, J., & Boll, T. (1977). Life stress and the psychological and medical adjustment of chronically ill children. *Journal of Psychosomatic Research, 21,* 237–242.

Beebe-Center, J. G. (1932). *The psychology of pleasantness and unpleasantness.* New York: Russell & Russell. (Reissued 1966)

Beecher, H. K. (1959). *Measurement of subjective responses: Quantitative effects of drugs.* New York: Oxford University Press.

Bem, D. J. (1967). Self-perception: An alternative interpretation of cognitive dissonance phenomena. *Psychology Review, 74,* 183–200.

Bem, D. J. (1970). *Beliefs, attitudes, and human affairs.* Monterey, CA: Brooks/Cole.

Bemis, K. M. (1978). Current approaches to the etiology and treatment of anorexia nervosa. *Psychological Bulletin, 85,* 593–617.

Benedetti, F. (1996). The opposite effects of the opiate antagonist naloxone and the cholecystokinin antagonist proglumide on placebo analgesia. *Pain, 64,* 535–543.

Bennett, A. M. H. (1961). Sensory deprivation in aviation. In P. Solomon et al. (Eds.), *Sensory deprivation.* Cambridge, MA: Harvard University Press.

Benson, H. (1975). *The relaxation response.* New York: Avon.

Benson, H., Kotch, J. B., Crassweller, K. D., & Greenwood, M. M. (1977). Historical and clinical considerations of the relaxation response. *American Scientist, 65,* 441–445.

Beretvas, S. N., Suizzo, M. A., Durham, J. A., & Yarnell, L. M. (2008). A reliability generalization study of scores on Rotter's and Nowicki-Strickland's locus of control scales. *Educational and Psychological Measurement, 68,* 97–119.

Berkowitz, L. (1974). Some determinants of impulsive aggression: Role of mediated associations with reinforcements for aggression. *Psychological Review, 81,* 165–176.

Berkowitz, L., & Geen, R. G. (1966). Film violence and the cue properties of available targets. *Journal of Personality and Social Psychology, 3,* 525–530.

Berkowitz, L., & LePage, A. (1967). Weapons as aggression eliciting stimuli. *Journal of Personality and Social Psychology, 7,* 202–207.

Berlyne, D. E. (1951). Attention to change. *British Journal of Psychology, 42,* 269–278.

Berlyne, D. E. (1958a). The influence of the albedo and complexity of stimuli on visual fixation in the human infant. *British Journal of Psychology, 49,* 315–318.

Berlyne, D. E. (1958b). The influence of complexity and novelty in visual figures on orienting responses. *Journal of Experimental Psychology, 55,* 289–296.

Berlyne, D. E. (1960). *Conflict, arousal, and curiosity.* New York: McGraw-Hill.

Berlyne, D. E. (1963). Motivational problems raised by exploratory and epistemic behavior. In S. Koch (Ed.), *Psychology: A study of a science* (Vol. 5). New York: McGraw-Hill.

Bermant, G. (1976). Sexual behavior: Hard times with the Coolidge Effect. In M. H. Siegel & H. P. Ziegler (Eds.), *Psychological research: The inside story.* New York: Harper & Row.

Bernard, R. S., Cohen, L. L., & Moffett, K. (2009). A token economy for exercise adherence in pediatric cyctic fibrosis: A single subject analysis. *Journal of Pediatric Psychology, 34,* 354–365.

Bernstein, I. L. (1978). Learned taste aversions in children receiving chemotherapy. *Science, 200,* 1302–1303.

Bernstein, I. L. (1991). Aversion conditioning in response to cancer and cancer treatment. *Clinical Psychology Review, 11,* 185–191.

Berscheid, E., & Walster, E. (1974). A little bit about love. In T. L. Huston (Ed.), *Foundations of interpersonal attraction.* New York: Academic Press.

Berthoud, H.-R., & Morrison, C. (2008). The brain, appetite, and obesity. *Annual Review of Psychology, 59,* 55–92.

Bertini, M. (1973). REM sleep as a psychophysiological "agency" of memory organization. In W. P. Koella & P. Levin (Eds.), *Sleep: Physiology, biochemistry, psychology, pharmacology, clinical implications.* New York: Karger.

Bexton, W. H., Heron, W., & Scott, T. H. (1954). Effects of decreased variation in the sensory environment. *Canadian Journal of Psychology, 8,* 70–76.

Bickman, L. (1972). Environmental attitudes and actions. *The Journal of Social Psychology, 87,* 323–324.

Biehl, M., Matsumoto, D., Ekman, P., Hearn, V., Heider, K., Kudoh, T., & Ton, V. (1997). Matsumoto and Ekman's Japanese and Caucasian facial expressions of emotion (JACFEE): Reliability data and cross-national differences. *Journal of Nonverbal Behavior, 21,* 3–21.

Bieliauskas, L. A., & Strugar, D. A. (1976). Sample size characteristics and scores on the social readjustment rating scale. *Journal of Psychosomatic Research, 20,* 201–205.

Bieliauskas, L. A., & Webb, J. M. (1974). The social readjustment rating scale: Validity in a college population. *Journal of Psychosomatic Research, 18,* 115–123.

Bindra, D. (1968). Neuropsychological interpretation of the effects of drive and incentive-motivation on general activity and instrumental behavior. *Psychological Review, 75,* 1–22.

Bindra, D. (1969). The interrelated mechanisms of reinforcement and motivation, and the nature of their influence on response. In W. J. Arnold & D. Levine (Eds.), *Nebraska symposium on motivation.* Lincoln, NE: University of Nebraska Press.

Bindra, D. (1972). A unified account of classical conditioning and operant training. In A. H. Black & W. F. Prokasy (Eds.), *Classical conditioning II: Current research and theory.* New York: Appleton-Century-Crofts.

Bindra, D. (1974). A motivational view of learning, performance, and behavior modification. *Psychological Review, 81,* 199–213.

Birch, D., Atkinson, J. W., & Bongort, K. (1974). Cognitive control of action. In B. Weiner (Ed.), *Cognitive views of human motivation.* New York: Academic Press.

Biswas-Diener, R., Linley, P. A., Govindji, R., & Woolston, L. (2011). Positive psychology as a force for social change. In K. M. Sheldon, T. B. Kashdan, & M. F. Steger (Eds.), *Designing positive psychology*. New York: Oxford University Press.

Bjorklund, D. F., & Shackelford, T. K. (1999). Differences in parental investment contribute to important differences between men and women. *Current Directions in Psychological Science, 8*, 86–89.

Black, R. W. (1969). Incentive motivation and the parameters of reward in instrumental conditioning. In W. J. Arnold & D. Levine (Eds.), *Nebraska symposium on motivation*. Lincoln, NE: University of Nebraska Press.

Blagrove, M. (1996). Effects of length of sleep deprivation on interrogative suggestibility. *Journal of Experimental Psychology: Applied, 2*, 48–59.

Blankenship, V. (1992). Individual differences in resultant achievement motivation and latency to and persistence at an achievement task. *Motivation and Emotion, 16*, 35–63.

Blascovich, J., Mendes, W. B., Hunter, S., & Salomon, K. (1999). Social "facilitation" as challenge and threat. *Journal of Personality and Social Psychology, 77*, 68–77.

Blass, E. M. (1968). Separation of cellular from extracellular controls of drinking in rats by frontal brain damage. *Science, 162*, 1501–1503.

Blass, E. M., & Kraly, F. S. (1974). Medial forebrain bundle lesions: Specific loss of feeding to decreased glucose utilization in rats. *Journal of Comparative and Physiological Psychology, 86*, 679–692.

Blass, T. (1999). The Milgram paradigm after 35 years: Some things we know about obedience to authority. *Journal of Applied Social Psychology, 29*, 955–978.

Blass, T. (2009). From New Haven to Santa Clara: A historical perspective on the Milgram obedience experiments. *American Psychologist, 64*, 37–45.

Blaustein, J. D. (2008). Neuroendocrine regulation of feminine sexual behavior: Lessons from rodent models and thoughts about humans. *Annual Review of Psychology, 59*, 93–118.

Blaustein, J. D., & Erskine, M. S. (2002). Feminine sexual behavior: Cellular integration of hormonal and afferent information in the rodent forebrain. In D. W. Pfaff, A. P. Arnold, A. M. Ergen, S. E. Fahrbach, & R. T. Rubin (Eds.), *Hormones, brain and behavior* (pp. 139–214). New York: Academic.

Blodgett, H. C. (1929). The effect of the introduction of reward upon maze behavior in rats. *University of California Publications in Psychology, 4*, 113–134.

Blouin, A., Blouin, J., Aubin, P., Carter, J., Goldstein, C., Boyer, H., & Perez, E. (1992). Seasonal patterns of

bulimia nervosa. *American Journal of Psychiatry, 149*, 73–81.

Bolles, R. C. (1967). *Theory of motivation*. New York: Harper & Row.

Bolles, R. C. (1974). Cognition and motivation: Some historical trends. In B. Weiner (Ed.), *Cognitive views of human motivation*. New York: Academic Press.

Bolles, R. C. (1975). *Theory of motivation* (2nd ed.). New York: Harper & Row.

Bolles, R. C., & Moot, S. A. (1972). Derived motives. In P. H. Mussen & M. R. Rosenzweig (Eds.), *Annual review of psychology, 23*, 51–72.

Bond, R. (2005). Group size and conformity. *Group Processes & Intergroup Relations, 8*, 331–354.

Bond, R., & Smith, P. B. (1996). Conformity and culture: A meta-analysis of studies using Asch's (1952b, 1956) line judgment task. *Psychological Bulletin, 119*, 111–137.

Boring, E. G. (1950). *A history of experimental psychology* (2nd ed.). New York: Appleton-Century-Crofts.

Borsook, D., Upadhyay, J., Chudler, E. H., & Becerra, L. (2010). A key role of the basal ganglia in pain and analgesia-insights gained through human functional imaging. *Molecular Pain, 6*, 27–43.

Bowlby, J. (1973). *Attachment and loss, vol. 11: Separation.* New York: Basic Books.

Bowlby, J., & Parkes, C. M. (1970). Separation and loss within the family. In E. J. Anthony & C. Koupernik (Eds.), *The child in his family*. New York: Wiley.

Boyd, T. L. (1982). Learned helplessness in humans: A frustration-produced response pattern. *Journal of Personality and Social Psychology, 42*, 738–752.

Brecher, G., & Waxler, S. (1949). Obesity in albino mice due to single injections of gold thio glucose. *Proceedings of the Society for Experimental Biology and Medicine, 70*, 498.

Breedlove, S. M. (1994). Sexual differentiation of the human nervous system. *Annual Review of Psychology, 45*, 389–418.

Brehm, J. W. (1956). Post decision changes in the desirability of alternatives. *Journal of Abnormal and Social Psychology, 52*, 384–389.

Breland, R., & Breland, M. (1961). The misbehavior of organisms. *American Psychologist, 16*, 681–684.

Bremer, F. (1937). L'activité cerebral eau cours dus ommeilet de la narcose. Contributional' étud edu mechanism edu sommeil. *Bulletin de l'Académie Royale de Belgique, 4*, 68–86.

Breslin, F. C., Sobell, M. B., Cappell, H., Vakili, S., & Poulos, C. X. (1999). The effects of alcohol, gender, and sensation seeking on the gambling choices of social drinkers. *Psychology of Addictive Behaviors, 13,* 243–252.

Bridgeman, B. (2003). *Psychology and evolution: The origins of mind.* Thousand Oaks, CA: Sage.

Brockner, J., Gardner, M., Bierman, J., Mahan, T., Thomas, B., Weiss, W., Winters, L., & Mitchell, A. (1983). The roles of self-esteem and self-consciousness in the Wortman-Brehm model of reactance and learned helplessness. *Journal of Personality and Social Psychology, 45,* 199–209.

Brot, M. D., Braget, D. J., & Berstein, I. L. (1987). Flavor, not post ingestive, cues contribute to the salience of proteins as targets in a version conditioning. *Behavioral Neuroscience, 101,* 683–689.

Broughton, R., & Gastaut, H. (1973). Memory and sleep. In W. P. Koella & P. Levin (Eds.), *Sleep: Physiology, biochemistry, psychology, pharmacology, clinical implications.* New York: Karger.

Brown, J. S., Kalish, H. I., & Farber, I. E. (1951). Conditioned fear as revealed by magnitude of startle response to an auditory stimulus. *Journal of Experimental Psychology, 41,* 317–328.

Brown, M. E., Trevino, L. K., & Harrison, D. A. (2005). Ethical leadership: A social learning perspective for construct development and testing. *Organizational Behavior and Human Decision Processes, 97,* 117–134.

Brown, R. (1965). *Social psychology.* New York: Free Press.

Brownmiller, S. (1975). *Against our will: Men, women, and rape.* New York: Simon & Schuster.

Brownstein, A. L., Read, S. J., & Simon, D. (2004). Bias at the race track: Effects of individual expertise and task importance on predecision reevaluation of alternatives. *Personality and Social Psychology Bulletin, 30,* 891–904.

Bruch, H. (1973). *Eating disorders.* New York: Basic Books.

Bruner, J. S. (1961). The cognitive consequences of early sensory deprivation. In P. Solomon et al. (Eds.), *Sensory deprivation.* Cambridge, MA: Harvard University Press.

Brunner, H. G., Nelen, M., Breakefield, X. O., Ropers, H. H., & van Oost, B. A. (1993). Abnormal behavior associated with a point mutation in the structural gene for mono amine oxidase A. *Science, 262,* 578–580.

Brunstrom, J. M., Tribbeck, P. M., & Mac Rae, A. W. (2000). The role of mouth state in the termination of drinking behavior in humans. *Physiology and Behavior, 68,* 579–583.

Buck, R. (1975). Non verbal communication of affect in children. *Journal of Personality and Social Psychology, 31,* 644–653.

Buck, R. (1976). *Human motivation and emotion.* New York: Wiley.

Buck, R., Losow, J. I., Murphy, M. M., & Costanzo, P. (1992). Social facilitation and inhibition of emotional expression and communication. *Journal of Personality and Social Psychology, 63,* 962–968.

Buck, R., Miller, R. E., & Caul, W. F. (1974). Sex, personality, and physiological variables in the communication of affect via facial expression. *Journal of Personality and Social Psychology, 30,* 587–596.

Buck, R., Savin, V. J., Miller, R. E., & Caul, W. F. (1972). Communication of affect through facial expression in humans. *Journal of Personality and Social Psychology, 23,* 362–371.

Bulkeley, K., Broughton, B., Sanchez, A., & Stiller, J. (2005). Earliest remembered dreams. *Dreaming, 15,* 205–222.

Bullen, B. A., Reed, R. B., & Mayer, J. (1964). Physical activity of obese and nonobese adolescent girls, appraised by motion pictures ampling. *American Journal of Clinical Nutrition, 14,* 211–223.

Bunnell, D. E., Bevier, W., & Horvath, S. M. (1983). Effects of exhaustive exercise on the sleep of men and women. *Psychophysiology, 20,* 50–58.

Burger, J. M. (1999). The foot-in-the-door compliance procedure: A multiple-process analysis and review. *Personality and Social Psychology Review, 3,* 303–325.

Burger, J. M. (2009). Replicating Milgram: Would people still obey today. *American Psychologist, 64,* 1–11.

Burger, J. M., & Caldwell, D. F. (2003). The effects of monetary incentives and labeling on the foot-in-the-door effect: Evidence for a self-perception process. *Basic and Applied Social Psychology, 25,* 235–241.

Burghardt, G. M. (1973). Instinct and innate behavior: Toward an ethological psychology. In J. A. Nevin (Ed.), *The study of behavior: Learning, motivation, emotion, instinct.* Glenview, IL: Scott, Foresan.

Burish, T. G., & Carey, M. P. (1986). Conditioned aversive responses in cancer chemotherapy patients: Theoretical and developmental analysis. *Journal of Consulting and Clinical Psychology, 54,* 593–600.

Burish, T. G., Carey, M. P., Krozely, M. G., & Greco, F. A. (1987). Conditioned side effects induced by cancer chemotherapy: Prevention through behavioral treatment. *Journal of Consulting and Clinical Psychology, 55,* 42–48.

Burnstein, E., Crandall, C., & Kitayama, S. (1994). Some neo-Darwinian decision rules for altruism: Weighing cues for inclusive fitness as a function of the biological importance of the decision. *Journal of Personality and Social Psychology, 67,* 773–789.

Bushwick, N. L. (2001). Social learning and the etiology of autism. *New Ideas in Psychology, 19,* 49–75.

Buss, D. M. (1988). The evolution of human intrasexual competition: Tactics of mate attraction. *Journal of Personality and Social Psychology, 54,* 616–628.

Buss, D. M. (1994). The strategies of human mating. *American Scientist, 82,* 238–249.

Buss, D. M. (1999). *Evolutionary psychology: The new science of the mind.* Boston, MA: Allyn & Bacon.

Buss, D. M. (2004). *Evolutionary psychology: The new science of the mind* (2nd ed.). Boston, MA: Allyn & Bacon.

Buss, D. M. (2005). *The handbook of evolutionary psychology.* Hoboken, NJ: Wiley.

Buss, D. M. (2008). *Evolutionary psychology: The new science of the mind* (3rd ed.). Boston, MA: Allyn & Bacon.

Butler, J. (1726/1991). *Fifteen sermons preached at the Rolls Chapel.* Indianapolis, IN: Hackett. (Reprinted in part in D. D. Raphael's *British Moralists 1650–1800*)

Butler, R. K., Nilsson-Todd, L., Cleren, C., Lena, I., Garcia, R., & Finn, D. P. (2011). Molecular and electrophysiological changes in the prefrontal cortex-amygdala-dorsal peri aqueductal grey pathway during persistent pain state and fear-conditioned analgesia. *Physiology and Behavior, 104,* 1075–1081.

Buxton, C. E. (1940). Latent learning and the goal gradient hypothesis. *Contributions to Psychological Theory (Duke University), 2*(6).

Buysse, D. J., Browman, K. E., Monk, T. H., Reynolds, C. F., Fasiczka, A. L., & Kupfer, D. J. (1992). *Journal of the American Geriatrics Society, 40,* 779–786.

Cahill, L. (2000). Modulation of long-term memory storage in humans by emotional arousal: Adrenergic activation and the amygdala. In J. P. Aggleton (Ed.), *The amygdala: A functional analysis* (2nd ed., pp. 425–445). New York: Oxford University Press.

Calder, A. J., Lawrence, A. D., & Young, A. W. (2001). Neuro psychology of fear and loathing. *Nature Reviews/Neuroscience, 2,* 352–363.

Campbell, W. K., & Sedikides, C. (1999). Self-threat magnifies the self-serving bias: A meta-analytic integration. *Review of General Psychology, 3,* 23–43.

Cannon, W. B. (1929). *Bodily changes in pain, hunger, fear and rage* (2nd ed.). New York: Appleton.

Cannon, W. B. (1934). Hunger and thirst. In C. Murchinson (Ed.), *Handbook of General Experimental Psychology.* Worchester, MA: Clark University Press.

Cannon, W. B. (1968). The James-Lange theory of emotion: A critical examination and an alternative theory. In M. B. Arnold (Ed.), *The nature of emotion.* Baltimore: Penguin.

Cannon, W. B., & Washburn, A. L. (1912). An explanation of hunger. *American Journal of Physiology, 29,* 444–454.

Cantwell, D. P., Sturzenberger, S., Borroughs, J., Salkin, B., & Green, J. K. (1977). Anorexia nervosa–An affective disorder? *Archives of General Psychiatry, 34,* 1087–1093.

Caplan, R. D. (1975). A less heretical view of life change and hospitalization. *Journal of Psychosomatic Research, 19,* 247–250.

Cardinal, R. N., Parkinson, J. A., Hall, J., & Everitt, B. J. (2002). Emotion and motivation: The role of the amygdala, ventral striatum, and prefrontal cortex. *Neuroscience and Biobehavioral Reviews, 26,* 321–352.

Carlson, N. R. (1977). *Physiology of behavior.* Boston, MA: Allyn & Bacon.

Carlson, N. R. (1994). *Physiology of behavior* (5th ed.). Boston, MA: Allyn & Bacon.

Carlson, N. R. (2001). *Physiology of behavior* (7th ed.). Boston: Allyn & Bacon.

Carlson, N. R. (2002). *Foundations of physiological psychology.* Boston: Allyn & Bacon.

Carlson, N. R. (2007). *Physiology of behavior* (9th ed.). Boston: Allyn & Bacon.

Carlson, N. R. (2010). *Physiology of behavior* (10th ed.). Boston: Allyn & Bacon.

Carver, C. S., & Scheier, M. F. (2000). On the structure of behavioral self-regulation. In M. Boekaerts, P. R. Pintrich, & M. H. Zeidner (Eds.), *Handbook of self-regulation.* San Diego, CA: Academic Press.

Caspari, E. W. (1965). The evolutionary importance of sexual processes and of sexual behavior. In F. A. Beach (Ed.), *Sex and behavior* (pp. 34–52). New York: Wiley.

Cassel, J. C. (1976). The contribution of the social environment to host resistance. *American Journal of Epidemiology, 104,* 107–123.

Center for Disease Control. (2004). Trends in intake of energy and macronutrients–United States, 1971–2000. *Morbidity and Mortality Weekly Report, 2*(53), 80–82.

Center for Disease Control. (2010). *Clinical guidelines on the identification, evaluation, and treatment of overweight and obesity in adults: The evidence report.* Retrieved from http://www.nhlbi.nih.gov/guidelines/obesity/bmi_tbl.pdf

Chakraborty, K., Basu, D., & Vijaya Kumar, K. G. (2010). Internet addiction: Consensus, controversies, and the way ahead. *East Asian Archives of Psychiatry, 20,* 123–132.

Charles, S. T., Gatz, M., Kato, K., & Pedersen, N. L. (2008). Physical health 25 years later: The predictive ability of neuroticism. *Health Psychology, 27,* 369–378.

Chemelli, R. M., Willie, J. T., Sinton, C. M., Elmquist, J. K., Scammell, T., Lee, C., Richardson, J. A., Williams,

S. C., Xiong, Y., Kisanuki, Y., Fitch, T. E., Nakazato, M., Hammer, R. E., Saper, C. B., & Yanagisawa, M. (1999). Narcolepsy in orexin knock out mice: Molecular genetics of sleep regulation. *Cell, 98,* 437–451.

Chen, M. K., & Risen, J. L. (2010). How attitude choice affects and reflects preferences: Revisiting the free-choice paradigm. *Journal of Personality and Social Psychology, 99,* 573–594.

Chicurel, M. (2000). The sand man's secrets. *Nature, 407,* 554–556.

Choi, I., & Nisbett, R. E. (1998). Situational salience and cultural differences in the correspondence bias and actor observer bias. *Personality and Social Psychology Bulletin, 24,* 949–960.

Chwalisz, K., Diener, E., & Gallagher, D. (1988). Autonomic arousal feedback and emotional experience: Evidence from the spinal cord injured. *Journal of Personality and Social Psychology, 54,* 820–828.

Cialdini, R. B. (2008). *Influence: Science and practice* (5th ed.). Boston, MA: Allyn & Bacon.

Cialdini, R. B., Brown, S. L., Lewis, B. P., Luce, C., & Neuberg, S. (1997). Reinterpreting the empathy-altruism relationship: When one into one equals oneness. *Journal of Personality and Social Psychology, 73,* 481–494.

Cialdini, R. B., Trost, M. R., & Newsom, J. T. (1995). Preference for consistency: The development of a valid measure and the discovery of surprising behavioral implications. *Journal of Personality and Social Psychology, 69,* 318–328.

Cialdini, R. B., Vincent, J. E., Lewis, S. K., Catalan, J., Wheeler, D., & Darby, B. L. (1975). Reciprocal concessions procedure for inducing compliance: The door-in-the-face technique. *Journal of Personality and Social Psychology, 31,* 206–215.

Clark, M., Ghandour, G., Miller, N. H., Taylor, C. B., Bandura, A., & DeBusk, R. F. (1997). Development and evaluation of a computer-based system for dietary management of hyperlipidemia. *Journal of the American Dietetic Association, 97,* 146–150.

Clark, T. K., Caggiula, A. R., McConnell, R. A., & Antelman, S. M. (1975). Sexual inhibition is reduced by rostral midbrain lesions in the male rat. *Science, 190,* 169–171.

Cleary, P. J. (1981). Problems of internal consistency and scaling in life event schedules. *Journal of Psychosomatic Research, 25,* 309–320.

Cobb, S. (1976). Social support as a moderator of life stress. *Psychomatic Medicine, 38,* 300–314.

Cofer, C. N., & Appley, M. H. (1964). *Motivation: Theory and research.* New York: Wiley.

Cohen, R. A., Paul, R., Zawacki, T. M., Moser, D. J., Sweet, L., & Wilkinson, H. (2001). Emotional and personality changes following cingulotomy. *Emotion, 1,* 38–50.

Cohen, S., & Wills, T. A. (1985). Stress, social support, and the buffering hypothesis. *Psychological Bulletin, 98,* 310–357.

Coke, J. S., Batson, C. D., & McDavis, K. (1978). Empathic mediation of helping: A two-stage model. *Journal of Personality and Social Psychology, 36,* 752–766.

Cole, H. W., Figler, M. H., Parente, F. J., & Peeke, H. V. S. (1980). The relationship between sex and aggression in convictcichlids (*Cichlasoma* nigrofasciatum *Gunther*). *Behavior, 75,* 1–21.

Cooper, J., & Fazio, R. H. (1984). A new look at dissonance theory. In L. Berkowitz (Ed.), *Advances in experimental social psychology* (Vol. 17). Orlando, FL: Academic Press.

Cooper, W. H. (1983). An achievement motivation nomological network. *Journal of Personality and Social Psychology, 44,* 841–861.

Cornelius, R. R. (1991). Gregorio Maranon's two-factor theory of emotion. *Personality and Social Psychology Bulletin, 17,* 65–69.

Cornwell, R. E., Boothroyd, L., Burt, D. M., Feinberg, D. R., Jones, B. C., Little, A. C., Pitman, R., Whiten, S., & Perrett, D. I. (2004). Concordant preferences for opposite-sex signals? Human pheromones and facial characteristics. *Proceedings of the Royal Society of London, 271,* 635–640.

Costello, C. G. (1978). A critical review of Seligman's laboratory experiments on learned helplessness and depression in humans. *Journal of Abnormal Psychology, 87,* 21–31.

Cotton, J. L. (1981). A review of research on Schachter's theory of emotion and the misattribution of arousal. *European Journal of Social Psychology, 11,* 365–397.

Cottrel, N. B. (1968). Performance in the presence of other human beings: Mere presence, audience, and affiliation effects. In E. C. Simmel, R. A. Hoppe, & G. A. Milton (Eds.), *Social facilitation and imitative behavior.* Boston, MA: Allyn & Bacon.

Cowles, J. T. (1937). Food-tokens as incentive for learning by chimpanzees. *Comparative Psychology Monographs, 14*(5).

Cowley, M. A., Smart, J. L., Rubinstein, M., Cerdan, M. G., Diano, S., Horvath, T. L., Cone, R. D., & Low, M. J. (2001). Leptin activates anorexigenic POMC neurons through a neural network in the arcuate nucleus. *Nature, 411,* 480–484.

Cox, D. S., Cox, D. C., Sturm, L., & Zimet, G. (2010). Behavioral interventions to increase HPV vaccination acceptability among mothers of young girls. *Health Psychology, 29*, 29–39.

Craig, W. O. (1918). Appetites and aversions as constituents of instincts. *Biological Review, 34*, 91–107.

Crandall, C. S. (1988). Social contagion of binge eating. *Journal of Personality and Social Psychology, 55*, 588–598.

Crandall, C. S., Silvia, P. J., N'Gbala, A. N., Tsang, J.-A., & Dawson, K. (2007). Balance theory, unit relations, and attribution: The underlying integrity of Heiderian theory. *Review of General Psychology, 11*, 12–30.

Crawford, C. B., & Krebs, D. L. (1998). *Handbook of evolutionary psychology: Ideas, issues, and applications.* Mahwah, NJ: Erlbaum.

Crespi, L. P. (1942). Quantitative variation of incentive and performance in the white rat. *American Journal of Psychology, 55*, 467–517.

Creswell, J. D., Welch, W. T., Taylor, S. E., Sherman, D. K., Gruenewald, T. L., & Mann, T. (2005). Affirmation of personal values buffers neuroendocrine and psychological stress responses. *Psychological Science, 16*, 846–851.

Cummings, D. E. (2006). Ghrelin and the short- and long-term regulation of appetite and body weight. *Physiology and Behavior, 89*, 71–84.

Cunningham, M. R. (1986). Measuring the physical in physical attractiveness: Quasi-experiments on the sociobiology of female facial beauty. *Journal of Personality and Social Psychology, 50*, 925–935.

Cutler, W. B., Friedmann, E., & McCoy, N. L. (1998). Pheromonal influences on socio sexual behavior in men. *Archives of Sexual Behavior, 27*, 1–13.

Czeisler, C. A., Kronauer, R. E., Allan, J. S., Duffy, J. F., Jewett, M. E., Brown, E. N., & Ronda, J. M. (1989). Bright light induction of strong (Type O) resetting of the human circadian pacemaker. *Science, 244*, 1328–1333.

Dahlsgaard, K., Peterson, C., & Seligman, M. E. P. (2005). Shared virtue: The convergence of valued human strengths across culture and history. *Review of General Psychology, 9*, 203–213.

Daly, E. M., Lancee, W. J., & Polivy, J. (1983). A conical model for the taxonomy of emotional experience. *Journal of Personality and Social Psychology, 45*, 443–457.

Damasio, A. (2001). Fundamental feelings. *Nature, 413*, 781.

Damasio, H., Grabowski, T., Frank, R., Galaburda, A. M., & Damasio, A. R. (1994). The return of Phineas Gage: Clues about the brain from the skull of a famous patient. *Science, 264*, 1102–1105.

Danker-Brown, P., & Baucom, D. H. (1982). Cognitive influences on the development of learned helplessness. *Journal of Personality and Social Psychology, 43*, 793–801.

Dantzer, R., Bluthe, R. M., Ghensi, G., Cremona, S., Laye, S., Parnet, P., & Kelley, K. W. (1998). Molecular basis of sickness behavior. *Annals of the New York Academia of Science, 856*, 132–138.

Darley, J. M., & Batson, C. D. (1976). From Jerusalem to Jericho: A study of situational and dispositional variables in helping behavior. In M. P. Golden (Ed.), *The research experience.* Itasca, IL: Peacock.

Darwin, C. R. (1871). *The descent of man, and selection in relation to sex.* New York: Appleton.

Darwin, C. R. (1872). *The expression of the emotions in man and animals.* New York: Appleton.

Darwin, C. R. (1899). *On the origin of species by means of natural selection* (6th ed.). Akron, OH: Werner.

Davenport, W. H. (1976). Sex in cross-cultural perspective. In F. A. Beach (Ed.), *Human sexuality in four perspectives*, 115–163. Baltimore: Johns Hopkins University Press.

Davidson, J. M. (1980). Hormones and sexual behavior in the male. In D. T. Krieger & J. C. Hughes (Eds.), *Neuroendocrinology*, 232–238. Sunderland, MA: Sinauer.

Davis, H., & Hurwitz, H. M. B. (Eds.). (1977). *Operant-Pavlovian interactions.* Hillsdale, NJ: Erlbaum.

Davis, J., Lockwood, L., & Wright, C. (1991). Reasons for not reporting peak experiences. *Journal of Humanistic Psychology, 31*, 86–94.

Davis, M. H. (1983). Empathic concern and the Muscular Dystrophy Telethon: Empathy as a multidimensional construct. *Personality and Social Psychology Bulletin, 9*, 223–229.

Dawkins, R. (1976). *The selfish gene.* New York: Oxford University Press.

Dawkins, R. (1996). *The blind watch maker.* New York: Norton.

DeBusk, R. F., Miller, N. H., Superko, H. R., Dennis, C. A., Thomas, R. J., Lew, H. T., Berger, W. E., Heller, R. S., Rompf, J., Gee, D., Kraemer, H. C., Bandura, A., Ghandour, G., Clark, M., Shah, R. V., Fisher, L., & Taylor, C. B. (1994). A case management system for coronary risk factor modification after acute myocardial infarction. *Annals of Internal Medicine, 120*, 721.

deCastro, J. M., & Brewer, E. M. (1992). The amount eaten in meals by humans is a power function of the number of people present. *Physiology and Behavior, 51*, 121–125.

deCharms, R. (1968). *Personal causation: The internal affective determinants of behavior.* New York: Academic Press.

Deci, E. L., Koestner, R., & Ryan, R. M. (1999). A meta analytic review of experiments examining the effects of extrinsic rewards on intrinsic motivation. *Psychological Bulletin, 125,* 627–668.

Deci, E. L., & Ryan, R. M. (1980). The empirical exploration of intrinsic motivational processes. In L. Berkowitz (Ed.), *Advances in experimental social psychology* (Vol. *13*). New York: Academic Press.

Deci, E. L., & Ryan, R. M. (1985). *Intrinsic motivation and self determination in human behavior.* New York: Plenum.

Deci, E. L., & Ryan, R. M. (2000). The "what" and "why" of goal pursuits: Human needs and the self-determination of behavior. *Psychological Inquiry, 11,* 227–268.

Deery, H. A., & Fildes, B. N. (1999). Young novice driver subtypes: Relationship to high-risk behavior, traffic accident record, and simulator driving performance. *Human Factors, 41,* 628–643.

DeJong, W. (1979). An examination of self-perception mediation of the foot-in-the-door effect. *Journal of Personality and Social Psychology, 37,* 2221–2239.

DeJong, W. (2001). Finding common ground for effective campus-based prevention. *Psychology of Addictive Behaviors, 15,* 292–296.

Delgado, J. M. R., Roberts, W. W., & Miller, N. E. (1954). Learning motivated by electrical stimulation of the brain. *American Journal of Physiology, 179,* 587–593.

Dement, W. C. (1972). *Some must watch while some must sleep.* San Francisco, CA: Freeman.

Dermon, C. R., Stamatakis, A., Tlemcani, O., & Balthazart, J. (1999). Performance of appetitive or consummatory components of male sexual behavior is mediated by different brain areas: A2-deoxyglucose autoradiographic study. *Neuroscience, 94,* 1261–1277.

DeWaal, F. B. M. (1995). Bonobo sex and society. *Scientific American, 272,* 82–88.

Dewan, E. M. (1970). The programming (P) hypothesis for REM sleep. In E. R. Hartmann (Ed.), *Sleep and dreaming.* Boston, MA: Little, Brown.

Dhabhar, F. S., McEwen, B. S. (1997). Acute stress enhances while chronic stress suppresses cell-mediated immunity in vivo: A potential role for leukocyte trafficking. *Brain, Behavior, and Immunity, 11,* 286–306.

Dickerson, S. S., & Kemeny, M. E. (2004). Acute stressors and cortisol responses: A theoretical integration and synthesis of laboratory research. *Psychological Bulletin, 130,* 355–391.

Diener, C. I., & Dweck, C. S. (1978). An analysis of learned helplessness: Continuous changes in performance, strategy, and achievement cognitions following failure. *Journal of Personality and Social Psychology, 36,* 451–462.

Diener, C. I., & Dweck, C. S. (1980). An analysis of learned helplessness: II. The processing of success. *Journal of Personality and Social Psychology, 39,* 940–952.

Dillard, J. P., Hunter, J. E., & Burgoon, M. (1984). Sequential request persuasive strategies: Meta-analysis of foot-in-the-door and door-in-the-face. *Human Communication Research, 10,* 461–488.

DiMarzo, V., Goparaju, S. K., Wang, L., Liu, J., Batkai, S., Jarai, Z., Fezza, F., Miura, G. I., Palmiter, R. D., Sugiura, T., & Kunos, G. (2001). Leptin-regulated endo cannabinoids are involved in maintaining food intake. *Nature, 410,* 822–825.

Dohrenwend, B. S., & Dohrenwend, B. P. (1974). A brief historical introduction to research on stressful life events. In B. S. Dohrenwend & B. P. Dohrenwend (Eds.), *Stressful life events: Their nature and effects.* New York: Wiley.

Dolan, B. (1991). Cross-cultural aspects of anorexia nervosa and bulimia: A review. *International Journal of Eating Disorders, 10,* 67–78.

Dolin, D. J., & Booth-Butterfield, S. (1995). Foot-in-the-door and cancer prevention. *Health Communication, 7,* 55–66.

Dolinski, D. (2009). People in a freezer. Self-perception as an explanatory mechanism for the effectiveness of the foot-in-the-door technique. *Polish Psychological Bulletin, 40,* 113–116.

Dollard, J. C., Doob, L., Miller, N., Mowrer, O., & Sears, R. (1939). *Frustration and aggression.* New Haven, CT: Yale University Press.

Domhoff, G. W. (2001). A new neuro cognitive theory of dreams. *Dreaming, 11,* 13–33.

Domjan, M., Blesbois, E., & Williams, J. (1998). The adaptive significance of sexual conditioning: Pavlovian control of sperm release. *Psychological Science, 9,* 411–415.

Domjan, M., & Burkhard, B. (1982). *The principles of learning and behavior.* Monterey, CA: Brooks/Cole.

Domjan, M., Miller, V., & Gemberling, G. A. (1982). Note on aversion learning to the shape of food by monkeys. *Journal of the Experimental Analysis of Behavior, 38,* 87–91.

Donnerstein, E., Donnerstein, M., & Evans, R. (1975). Erotic stimuli and aggression: Facilitation or inhibition. *Journal of Personality and Social Psychology, 32,* 237–244.

Donohew, L., Zimmerman, R., Cupp, P. S., Novak, S., Colon, S., & Abell, R. (2000). Sensation seeking, impulsive decision-making, and risky sex: Implications for risk taking and design of interventions. *Personality and Individual Differences, 28,* 1079–1091.

Dorland's illustrated medical dictionary (24th ed.). (1965). Philadelphia, PA: Saunders.

Duffy, E. (1966). The nature and development of the concept of activation. In R. N. Haber (Ed.), *Current research in motivation*. New York: Holt, Rinehart & Winston.

Duke, M. P., Shaheen, J., & Nowicki, S. (1974). The determination of locus of control in a geriatric population and a subsequent test of the social learning model for interpersonal distances. *Journal of Psychology: Interdisciplinary and Applied, 86*, 277–285.

Dunham, P. J. (1968). Contrasted conditions of reinforcement: A selective critique. *Psychological Bulletin, 69*, 295–315.

Dusek, J. A., Otu, H. H., Wohlhueter, A. L., Bhasin, M., Zerbini, L. F., Joseph, M. G., Benson, H., & Libermann, T. A. (2008). Genomic counter-stess changes induced by the relaxation response. *Plos ONE, 3*, 1–8.

Dutton, J., Roberts, L. M., & Bednar, J. (2011). Using a positive lens to complicate the positive in identity research. *The Academy of Management Review, 36*, 427–431.

Duval, T. S., & Silvia, P. J. (2002). Self-awareness, probability of improvement, and the self-servingbias. *Journal of Personality and Social Psychology, 82*, 49–61.

Dweck, C. S. (1975). The role of expectations and attributions in the alleviation of learned helplessness. *Journal of Personality and Social Psychology, 31*, 674–685.

Dweck, C. S. (1986). Motivational processes affecting learning. *American Psychologist, 41*, 1040–1048.

Dweck, C. S. (2002). Messages that motivate: How praise molds students' beliefs, motivation, and performance. In J. Aronson (Ed.), *Improving academic achievement: Impact of psychological factors on education*. San Diego, CA: Academic Press.

Dweck, C. S., & Elliott, E. S. (1983). Achievement motivation. In P. Mussen & E. M. Hetherington (Eds.), *Handbook of child psychology: Socialization, personality, and social development*. New York: Wiley.

Dweck, C. S., Hong, Y., & Chiu, C. (1993). Implicit theories: Individual differences in the likelihood and meaning of dispositional inference. *Personality and Social Psychology Bulletin, 19*, 644–656.

Dweck, C. S., & Leggett, E. L. (1988). Asocial-cognitive approach to motivation and personality. *Psychological Review, 95*, 256–273.

Dweck, C. S., & Repucci, N. D. (1973). Learned helplessness and reinforcement responsibility in children. *Journal of Personality and Social Psychology, 25*, 109–116.

Ebster, C., & Neumayr, B. (2008). Applying the door-in-the-face technique to retailing. *The International Review of Retail, Distribution and Consumer Research, 18*, 121–128.

Egan, V., Charlesworth, P., Richardson, C., Blair, M., & McMurran, M. (2001). Sensational interests and sensation seeking in mentally disordered offenders. *Personality and Individual Differences, 30*, 995–1007.

Eibl-Eibesfeldt, I. (1961). The fighting behavior of animals. *Scientific American, 205*, 112–122.

Eibl-Eibesfeldt, I. (1970). *Ethology: The biology of behavior* (Erich Klinghammer, Trans.). New York: Holt, Rinehart & Winston.

Eibl-Eibesfeldt, I. (1972). *Love and hate: The natural history of behavior patterns* (Geoffrey Strachan, Trans.). New York: Holt, Rinehart & Winston.

Eibl-Eibesfeldt, I. (1977). Evolution of destructive behavior. *Aggressive Behavior, 3*, 127–144.

Eibl-Eibesfeldt, I. (1979). *The biology of peace and war*. Britain: Thames and Hudson.

Eibl-Eibesfeldt, I. (1989). *Human ethology*. New York: Aldine DeGruyter.

Ekman, P. (1972). Universals and cultural differences in facial expressions of emotion. In J. K. Cole (Ed.), *Nebraska symposium on motivation* (pp. 207–283). Lincoln, NE: University of Nebraska Press.

Ekman, P. (1992a). Are there basic emotions? *Psychological Review, 99*, 550–553.

Ekman, P. (1992b). Facial expressions of emotion: New findings, new questions. *Psychological Science, 3*, 34–38.

Ekman, P. (1999a). Basic emotions. In T. Dalgleish & M. J. Power (Eds.), *Handbook of cognition and emotion* (pp. 45–60). West Sussex, England: John Wiley & Sons.

Ekman, P. (1999b). Facial expressions. In T. Dalgleish & M. J. Power (Eds.), *Handbook of cognition and emotion* (pp. 301–320). West Sussex, England: John Wiley & Sons.

Ekman, P., & Friesen, W. V. (1971). Constants across cultures in the face and emotion. *Journal of Personality and Social Psychology, 17*, 124–129.

Ekman, P., & Friesen, W. V. (1976). Measuring facial movement. *Environmental Psychology and Nonverbal Behavior, 1*, 56–75.

Ekman, P., & Friesen, W. V. (1978). *Facial action coding system*. Palo Alto, CA: Consulting Psychologists Press.

Ekman, P., Friesen, W. V., & Ancoli, S. (1980). Facial signs of emotional experience. *Journal of Personality and Social Psychology, 39*, 1125–1134.

Ekman, P., Friesen, W. V., & Ellsworth, P. (1982). What are the similarities and differences in facial behavior across cultures? In P. Ekman (Ed.), *Emotion in the human face* (2nd ed., pp. 128–143). New York: Cambridge University Press.

Ekman, P., Friesen, W. V., & O'Sullivan, M. (1988). Smiles when lying. *Journal of Personality and Social Psychology, 54,* 414–420.

Ekman, P., Friesen, W. V., O'Sullivan, M., Chan, A., Diacoyanni-Tarlatzis, I., Heider, K., Krause, R., LeCompte, W. A., Pitcairn, T., Ricci-Bitti, P. E., Scherer, K. Tomita, & M. Tzavaras, A. (1987). Universals and cultural differences in the judgments of facial expressions of emotion. *Journal of Personality and Social Psychology, 53,* 712–717.

Ekman, P., Levenson, R. W., & Friesen, W. V. (1983). Autonomic nervous system activity distinguishes among emotions. *Science, 221,* 1208–1210.

Ekman, P., & Oster, H. (1982). Review of research, 1970–1980. In P. Ekman (Ed.), *Emotion in the human face* (2nd ed., pp. 147–173). New York: Cambridge University Press.

Ekman, P., & O'Sullivan, M. (1991). Who can catch a liar? *American Psychologist, 46,* 913–920.

Elfenbein, H. A., & Ambady, N. (2002). On the universality and cultural specificity of emotion. *Psychological Bulletin, 128,* 203–235.

Elliot, A. J. (1999). Approach and avoidance motivation and achievement goals. *Educational Psychologist, 34,* 169–189.

Elliot, A. J., & Church, M. A. (1997). A hierarchical model of approach and avoidance achievement motivation. *Journal of Personality and Social Psychology, 72,* 218–232.

Elliot, A. J., & McGregor, H. A. (2001). A 2 x 2 achievement goal framework. *Journal of Personality and Social Psychology, 80,* 501–519.

Elliot, A. J., & Murayama, K. (2008). On the measurement of achievement goals: Critique, illustration, and application. *Journal of Educational Psychology, 100,* 613–628.

Elliott, M. A., Armitage, C. J., & Baughan, C. J. (2005). Exploring the beliefs underpinning drivers' intentions to comply with speed limits. *Transportation Research Part F, 8,* 459–479.

Elliott, M. H. (1928). The effect of change of reward on the maze performance of rats. *University of California Publications in Psychology, 4,* 19–30.

Ellis, B. J. (1992). The evolution of sexual attraction: Evaluative mechanisms in women. In J. Barkow, L. Cosmides, & J. Tooby (Eds.), *The adapted mind* (pp. 267–288). New York: Oxford.

Ellman, S. J., Spielman, A. J., & Lipschutz-Brach, L. (1991). Update: REM deprivation. In S. J. Ellman & J. S. Antrobus (Eds.), *The mind insleep: Psychology and psychophysiology* (pp. 369–376). New York: Wiley.

Ellman, S. J., Spielman, A. J., Luck, D., Steiner, S. S., & Halperin, R. (1991). REM deprivation: A review. In S. J. Ellman & J. S. Antrobus (Eds.), *The mind in sleep: Psychology and psychophysiology* (pp. 329–369). New York: Wiley.

Ellsworth, P. C., Carlsmith, J. M., & Henson, A. (1972). The stare as a stimulus to flight in human subjects: A series of field experiments. *Journal of Personality and Social Psychology, 21,* 302–311.

El Mansari, M., Sakai, K., & Jouvet, M. (1989). Unitary characteristics of presumptive cholinergic tegmental neurons during the sleep-waking cycle in freely moving cats. *Experimental Brain Research, 76,* 519–529.

Encarta Encyclopedia. (1996). CD-ROM, Microsoft.

Engberg, L. A., Hansen, G., Welker, R. L., & Thomas, D. (1972). Acquisition of key pecking via autoshaping as a function of prior experience: Learned laziness? *Science, 178,* 1002–1004.

Entwisle, D. R. (1972). To dispel fantasies about fantasy-based measures of achievement motivation. *Psychological Bulletin, 77,* 377–391.

Epel, E., Lapidus, R., McEwen, B., & Brownell, K. (2001). Stress may add bite to appetite in women: A laboratory study of stress-induced cortisol and eating behavior. *Psychoneuroendocrinology, 26,* 37–49.

Epley, N., & Gilovich, T. (1999). Just going along: Non conscious priming and conformity to social pressure. *Journal of Experimental Social Psychology, 35,* 578–589.

Epstein, A. N. (1982). The physiology of thirst. In D. W. Pfaff (Ed.), *The physiological mechanisms of motivation.* New York: Springer-Verlag.

Epstein, A. N., Fitzsimons, J. T., & Rolls, B. J. F. (1970). Drinking induced by injection of angiotensin into the brain of the rat. *Journal of Physiology (London), 210,* 457–474.

Epstein, A. N., & Teitelbaum, P. (1967). Specific loss of hypoglycemic control of feeding in recovered lateral rats. *American Journal of Physiology, 213,* 1159–1167.

Epstein, L. H., Temple, J. L., Bouton, M. E., & Roemmich, J. N. (2009). Habituation as a determinant of human food intake. *Psychological Review, 116,* 384–407.

Epstein, S. M. (1967). Toward a unified theory of anxiety. In B. A. Maher (Ed.), *Progress in experimental personality research* (Vol. 4). New York: Academic Press.

Erdmann, G., & Janke, W. (1978). Interaction between physiological and cognitive determinants of emotions: Experimental studies on Schachter's theory of emotions. *Biological Psychology, 6,* 61–74.

Eron, L. D., & Huesmann, L. R. (1984). The control of aggressive behavior by changes in attitudes, values, and the conditions of learning. In R. J. Blanchard & D. C. Blanchard (Eds.), *Advances in the study of aggression* (Vol. 1, pp. 139–171). New York: Academic Press.

Ershler, W., & Keller, E. (2000). Age-associated increased interleukin-6 gene expression, late-life diseases, and frailty. *Annual Review of Medicine, 51,* 245–270.

Evans, R. I. (1975). *Carl Rogers: The man and his ideas.* New York: Dutton.

Everson, C. A. (1995). Functional consequences of sustained sleep deprivation in the rat. *Behavioural Brain Research, 69,* 43–54.

Exton, M. S., von Auer, A. K., Buske-Kirschbaum, A., Stockhorst, U., Gobel, U., & Schedlowski, M. (2000). Pavlovian conditioning of immune function: Animal investigation and the challenge of human application. *Behavioural Brain Research, 110,* 129–141.

Fairburn, C. G., & Cooper, P. J. (1989). Eating disorders. In K. Hawton, P. M. Salkovskis, J. Kirk, & D. M. Clark (Eds.), *Cognitive behavior therapy for psychiatric problems: A practical guide* (pp. 277–314). Oxford: Oxford Medical Publications.

Faust, I. M., Johnson, P. R., & Hirsch, J. (1977a). Adipose tissue regeneration following lipectomy. *Science, 197,* 391–393.

Faust, I. M., Johnson, P. R., & Hirsch, J. (1977b). Surgical removal of adipose tissue alters feeding behavior and the development of obesity in rats. *Science, 197,* 393–396.

Fazio, R. H., Zanna, M. P., & Cooper, J. (1977). Dissonance and self-perception: An integrative view of each theory's proper domain of application. *Journal of Experimental Social Psychology, 13,* 464–479.

Feather, N. T. (1961). The relationship of persistence at a task to expectations of success and achievement-related motives. *Journal of Abnormal and Social Psychology, 63,* 552–561.

Feder, H. H. (1984). Hormones and sexual behavior. In M. R. Rosenzweig & L. W. Porter (Eds.), *Annual Review of Psychology, 35,* 165–200.

Feingold, A. (1992). Gender differences in mate selection preferences: A test of the parental investment model. *Psychological Bulletin, 112,* 125–139.

Fenollar, P., Roman, S., & Cuestas, P. J. (2007). University students' academic performance: An integrative conceptual framework and empirical analysis. *British Journal of Educational Psychology, 77,* 873–891.

Fern, E. F., Monroe, K. B., & Avila, R. A. (1986). Effectiveness of multiple request strategies: A synthesis of research results. *Journal of Marketing Research, 23,* 144–152.

Festinger, L., & Carlsmith, J. (1959). Cognitive consequences of forced compliance. *Journal of Abnormal and Social Psychology, 58,* 203–210.

Festinger, L., Riecken, H. W., & Schachter, S. (1956). *When prophecy fails.* Minneapolis: University of Minnesota Press.

Festinger, L. A. (1957). *A theory of cognitive dissonance.* Stanford, CA: Stanford University Press.

Field, T. M., Woodson, R., Greenberg, R., & Cohen, D. (1982). Discrimination and imitation of facial expressions by neonates. *Science, 218,* 179–181.

Figler, M. H. (1973). The effects of chlordiazepoxide (Librium) on the intensity and habituation of agonistic behavior in male Siamese fighting fish. *Psychopharmacologia, 33,* 277–292.

Figler, M. H., Klein, R. M., & Thompson, C. S. (1975). Chlordiazepoxide (Librium) induced changes in intra specific attack and selected non-agonistic behaviors in male Siamese fighting fish. *Psychopharmacologia, 42,* 139–145.

Figler, M. H., Mills, C. J., & Petri, H. L. (1974). Effects of imprinting strength on stimulus generalization in chicks (Gallusgallus). *Behavioral Biology, 12,* 541–545.

Figler, M. H., Twum, M., Finkelstein, J. E., & Peeke, H. V. S. (1995). Maternal aggression in red swamp crayfish (Procambarus Clarkii, Girard): The relation between reproductive status and outcome of aggressive encounters with male and female conspecifics. *Behaviour, 132,* 107–125.

Fillingim, R. B., King, C. D., Ribeiro-Dasilva, M. C., Rahim-Williams, B., & Riley, J. L. (2009). Sex, gender, and pain: A review of recent clinical and experimental findings. *The Journal of Pain, 10,* 447–485.

Fillion, T. J., & Blass, E. M. (1986). Infantile experience with suckling odors determines adult sexual behavior in male rats. *Science, 231,* 729–731.

Fischer, P., Greitemeyer, T., Pollozek, F., & Frey, D. (2006). The unresponsive bystander: Are bystanders more responsive in dangerous emergencies? *European Journal of Social Psychology, 36,* 267–278.

Fischer, P., Krueger, J. I., Greitemeyer, T., Vogrincic, C., Kastenmuller, A., Frey, D., Heene, M., Wicher, M., & Kainbacher, M. (2011). The bystander-effect: A meta-analytic review on bystander intervention in dangerous and non-dangerous emergencies. *Psychological Bulletin, 137,* 517–537.

Fishbein, M., & Ajzen, I. (1975). *Belief, attitude, intention, and behavior: An introduction to theory and research.* Reading, MA: Addison-Wesley.

Fisher, K. (1988, December). Researchers debate lifestyle, health links. *American Psychological Association Monitor,* 13–14.

Fitzsimons, J. T. (1973). Some historical perspectives in the physiology of thirst. In A. N. Epstein et al. (Eds.), *The neuropsychology of thirst.* Washington, DC: V. H. Winston.

Fitzsimons, J. T., & LeMagnen, J. (1969). Eating as a regulatory control of drinking in the rat. *Journal of Comparative and Physiological Psychology, 67,* 273–283.

Fitzsimons, J. T., & Simons, B. J. (1969). The effect on drinking in the rat of intravenous infusion of angiotensin, given alone or in combination with other stimuli of thirst. *Journal of Physiology (London), 203,* 45–57.

Flaherty, C. F. (1982). Incentive contrast: Are view of behavioral changes following shifts in reward. *Animal Learning and Behavior, 10,* 409–440.

Flaherty, J., & Richman, J. (1989). Gender differences in the perception and utilization of social support: Theoretical perspectives and an empirical test. *Social Science and Medicine, 28,* 1221–1228.

Flynn, J. P. (1969). Neural aspects of attack behavior in cats. *Experimental approaches to the study of emotional behavior. Annals of the New York Academy of Sciences, 159,* 1008–1012.

Flynn, J. P., Vanegas, H., Foote, W., & Edwards, S. (1970). Neural mechanisms involved in a cat's attack on a rat. In R. E. Whalen, R. F. Thompson, M. Verzeano, & N. M. Weinberger (Eds.), *The neural control of behavior* (pp. 138–173). New York: Academic Press.

Follette, V. M., & Jacobson, N. S. (1987). Importance of attributions as a predictor of how people cope with failure. *Journal of Personality and Social Psychology, 52,* 1205–1211.

Ford, C. S., & Beach, F. A. (1951). *Patterns of sexual behavior.* New York: Harper & Row.

Forthun, L. F., Bell, N. J., Peek, C. W., & Sun, S.-W. (1999). Religiosity, sensation seeking, and alcohol/drug use in denominational and gender contexts. *Journal of Drug Issues, 29,* 75–90.

Fossi, L., Faravelli, C., & Paoli, M. (1984). The ethological approach to the assessment of depressive disorders. *Journal of Nervous and Mental Disease, 172,* 332–341.

Foster-Schubert, K. E., Overduin, J., Prudom, C. E., Liu, J., Callahan, H. S., Gaylinn, B. D., Thorner, M. O., & Cummings, D. E. (2008). Acyl and total ghrelin are suppressed strongly by ingested proteins, weakly by lipids, and biphasically by carbohydrates. *Journal of Clinical Endocrinology and Metabolism, 93,* 1971–1979.

Foulkes, D. (1966). *The psychology of sleep.* New York: Scribner's.

Fowler, H. (1967). Satiation and curiosity: Constructs for a drive and incentive-motivational theory of exploration. In K. W. Spence & J. T. Spence (Eds.), *The psychology of learning and motivation* (Vol. 1). New York: Academic Press.

Fox, D. K., Hopkins, B. L., & Anger, W. K. (1987). The long-term effects of a token economy on safety performance in open pit mining. *Journal of Applied Behavior Analysis, 20,* 215–224.

Franken, R. E. (1982). *Human motivation* (3rd ed.). Monterey, CA: Brooks/Cole.

Franklin, J. C., Hessel, E. T., Aaron, R. V., Arthur, M. S., Heilbron, N., & Prinstein, M. J. (2010). The functions of non-suicidal self-injury: Support for cognitive-affective regulation and opponent processes from a novel psychophysiological paradigm. *Journal of Abnormal Psychology, 119,* 850–862.

Franklin, M. S., & Zyphur, M. J. (2005). The role of dreams in the evolution of the human mind. *Evolutionary Psychology, 3,* 59–78.

Freedman, J. L., & Fraser, S. C. (1966). Compliance without pressure: The foot-in-the-door technique. *Journal of Personality and Social Psychology, 4,* 195–202.

Freeman, G. L. (1940). The relationship between performance level and bodily activity level. *Journal of Experimental Psychology, 26,* 602–608.

French, D. P., & Hankins, M. (2003). The expectancy-value muddle in the theory of planned behaviour—And some proposed solutions. *British Journal of Health Psychology, 8,* 37–55.

Freud, S. (1957). *The standard edition of the complete psychological works of Sigmund Freud* (Vol. 14) (James Strachey, Trans.). London: Hogarth.

Friedman, B. H. (2010). Feelings and the body: The Jamesian perspective on autonomic specificity of emotion. *Biological Psychology, 84,* 383–393.

Friedman, M. I., & Stricker, E. M. (1976). The physiological psychology of hunger: A physiological perspective. *Psychological Review, 83,* 409–431.

Friesen, W. V. (1972). *Cultural differences in facial expression in a social situation: An experimental test of the concept of display rules.* Unpublished doctoral dissertation, University of California, San Francisco.

Frieze, I. H. (1976). Causal attributions and information seeking to explain success and failure. *Journal of Research in Personality, 10,* 293–305.

Frye, C. A. (2001a). The role of neurosteroids and non-genomic effects of progestins and androgens in mediating sexual receptivity of rodents. *Brian Research Reviews, 37,* 201–222.

Frye, C. A. (2001b). The role of neurosteroids and non-genomic effects of progestins in the ventral tegmental area in mediating sexual receptivity of rodents. *Hormones and Behavior, 40,* 226–233.

Funder, D. C. (2001). The really, really fundamental attribution error. *Psychological Inquiry, 12,* 21–23.

Funk, S. C. (1992). Hardiness: A review of theory and research. *Health Psychology, 11,* 335–345.

Gable, S. L., & Haidt, J. (2005). What (and why) is positive psychology? *Review of General Psychology, 9,* 103–110.

Gackenbach, J., & Kuruvilla, B. (2008). The relationship between video game play and threat simulation dreams. *Dreaming, 18,* 236–256.

Gangestad, S. W., Thornhill, R., & Yeo, R. A. (1994). Facial attractiveness, developmental stability, and fluctuating asymmetry. *Ethology and Sociobiology, 15,* 73–85.

Garcia, J., Ervin, F. R., & Koelling, R. A. (1966). Learning with prolonged delay of reinforcement. *Psychonomic Science, 5,* 121–122.

Garcia, J., & Koelling, R. A. (1966). Relation of cue to consequence in avoidance learning. *Psychonomic Science, 4,* 123–124.

Garcia-Velasco, J., & Mondragon, M. (1991). The incidence of the vomeronasal organ in 1000 human subjects and its possible clinical significance. *Journal of Steroid Biochemistry and Molecular Biology, 39,* 561–563.

Gardner, B., & Abraham, C. (2010). Going green? Modeling the impact of environmental concerns and perceptions of transportation alternatives on decisions to drive. *Journal of Applied Social Psychology, 40,* 831–849.

Gardner, L. I. (1972). Deprivation dwarfism. *Scientific American, 227*(1), 76–82.

Garrity, T. F., Marx, M. B., & Somes, G. W. (1977a). The influence of illness severity and time since life change on the size of the life change-health change relationship. *Journal of Psychosomatic Research, 21,* 377–382.

Garrity, T. F., Marx, M. B., & Somes, G. W. (1977b). Langner's 22-item measure of psycho physiological strain as an intervening variable between life change and health outcome. *Journal of Psychosomatic Research, 21,* 195–199.

Gawronski, B. (2004). Theory-based bias correction in dispositional inference: The fundamental attribution error is dead, long live the correspondence bias. *European Review of Social Psychology, 15,* 183–217.

Geary, N. (2004). Endocrine controls of eating: CCK, leptin, and ghrelin. *Physiology & Behavior, 81,* 719–733.

Geen, R. G. (1972). *Aggression.* Morristown, NJ: General Learning Press.

Geen, R. G., & Pigg, R. (1970). Acquisition of an aggressive response and its generalization to verbal behavior. *Journal of Personality and Social Psychology, 15,* 165–170.

Geller, L. (1982). The failure of self-actualization theory: A critique of Carl Rogers and Abraham Maslow. *Journal of Humanistic Psychology, 22,* 56–73.

Gibbons, A. (1993). Evolutionists take the long view on sex and violence. *Science, 261,* 987–988.

Gibbs, J., Young, R. G., & Smith, G. P. (1973). Cholecystokinin decreases food intake in rats. *Journal of Comparative and Physiological Psychology, 84,* 488–495.

Gigerenzer, G., & Selten, R. (2001). *Bounded rationality: The adaptive tool box.* Cambridge, MA: The MIT Press.

Gilbert, D. T., & Malone, P. S. (1995). The correspondence bias. *Psychological Bulletin, 117,* 21–38.

Gilbert, D. T., Pelham, B. W., & Krull, D. S. (1988). On cognitive busyness: When person perceivers meet persons perceived. *Journal of Personality and Social Psychology, 54,* 733–740.

Gilovich, T., Jennings, D. L., & Jennings, S. (1983). An examination of the false-consensus effect. *Journal of Personality and Social Psychology, 45,* 550–559.

Girl recants testimony, freeing man from jail. (1990, January 28). Baltimore Sun, p. 15A.

Glaser, R., & Kiecolt-Glaser, J. K. (2005). Stress-induced immune dysfunction: Implications for health. *Nature Reviews Immunology, 5,* 243–251.

Glassman, T., Braun, R. E., Dodd, V., Miller, J. M., & Miller, E. M. (2010). Using the theory of planned behavior to explain the drinking motivations of social, high-risk, and extreme drinkers on game day. *Journal of Community Health, 35,* 172–181.

Goble, F. G. (1970). *The third force: The psychology of Abraham Maslow.* New York: Grossman.

Goggin, K., Murray, T. S., Malcarne, V. L., Brown, S. A., & Wallston, K. A. (2007). Do religious and control cognitions predict risky behavior? I. Development and validation of the Alcohol-related God Locus of Control Scale for Adolescents (AGLOC-A). *Cognitive Therapy and Research, 31,* 111–122.

Gold, R. M. (1973). Hypothalamic obesity: The myth of the ventro medial nucleus. *Science, 182,* 488–490.

Goldberger, L., & Holt, R. R. (1961). Experimental interference with reality contact: Individual differences.

In P. Solomon et al. (Eds.), *Sensory deprivation* (pp. 130–142). Cambridge, MA: Harvard University Press.

Goldbloom, D. S., & Garfinkel, P. E. (1990). The serotonin hypothesis of bulimia nervosa: Theory and evidence. *Canadian Journal of Psychiatry, 35,* 741–744.

Goldstein, D., Fink, D., & Mettee, D. R. (1972). Cognition of arousal and actual arousal as determinants of emotion. *Journal of Personality and Social Psychology, 21,* 41–51.

Goodenough, D. R. (1991). Dream recall: History and current status of the field. In S. J. Ellman & J. S. Antrobus (Eds.), *The mind in sleep: Psychology and psychophysiology* (2nd ed., pp. 143–171). New York: Wiley.

Goodison, T., & Siegel, S. (1995). Learning and tolerance to the intake suppressive effect of cholecystokinin in rats. *Behavioral Neuroscience, 109,* 62–70.

Goodwin, D. V. (1978, September 24). Dwarfism: The victim child's response to abuse. *Baltimore Sun,* p. K2.

Gorassini, D. R., & Olson, J. M. (1995). Does self-perception change explain the foot-in-the-door effect? *Journal of Personality and Social Psychology, 69,* 91–105.

Gorski, R. A., Gordon, J. H., Shryne, J. E., & Southam, A. M. (1978). Evidence for a morphological sex difference within the medial preoptic area of the rat brain. *Brain Research, 148,* 333–346.

Gottlieb, G. (1972). Imprinting in relation to a parental and species identification by avian neonates. In M. E. P. Seligman & J. L. Hager (Eds.), *Biological boundaries of learning* (pp. 279–298). New York: Appleton-Century-Crofts.

Graham, S., & Weiner, B. (1996). Theories and principles of motivation. In D. C. Berliner & R. C. Calfee (Eds.), *Handbook of educational psychology* (pp. 63–84). New York: Macmillan.

Grammer, K., Fink, B., & Neave, N. (2005). Human pheromones and sexual attraction. *European Journal of Obstetrics and Gynecology and Reproductive Biology, 118,* 135–142.

Grammer, K., Kruck, K., Juette, A., & Fink, B. (2000). Non-verbal behavior as courtship signals: The role of control and choice in selecting partners. *Evolution and Sociobiology, 21,* 371–390.

Gray, J. A. (1971). *The psychology of fear and stress.* New York: McGraw-Hill.

Graziano, W. G., & Bryant, W. H. (1998). Self-monitoring and the self-attribution of positive emotions. *Journal of Personality and Social Psychology, 74,* 250–261.

Graziano, W. G., & Habashi, M. M. (2010). Motivational processes underlying both prejudice and helping. *Personality and Social Psychology Review, 14,* 313–331.

Greenberg, R. (1970). Dreaming and memory. In E. Hartmann (Ed.), *Sleep and dreaming* (pp. 258–267). Boston, MA: Little, Brown.

Greenberg, R., Pearlman, C., Schwartz, W. R., & Grossman, H. Y. (1983). Memory, emotion, and REM sleep. *Journal of Abnormal Psychology, 92,* 378–381.

Greene, E. (1989). A diet-induced developmental polymorphism in a caterpillar. *Science, 243,* 643–646.

Griffin, D. R. (1984). *Animal thinking.* Cambridge, MA: Harvard University Press.

Griffin, D. R. (1992). *Animal minds.* Chicago, IL: University of Chicago Press.

Griffin, D. R. (2001). *Animal minds: Beyond cognition to consciousness.* Chicago, IL: University of Chicago Press.

Griffin, M. (2001). The phenomenology of the alone condition: More evidence for the role of aloneness in social facilitation. *Journal of Psychology, 135,* 125–127.

Griffin, M., & Kent, M. V. (1998). The role of aloneness in social facilitation. *Journal of Social Psychology, 138,* 667–669.

Grinker, J. A. (1982). Physiological and behavioral basis of human obesity. In D. W. Pfaff (Ed.), *The physiological mechanisms of motivation* (pp. 145–164). New York: Springer-Verlag.

Grossman, M. I., & Stein, I. F., Jr. (1948). Vagotomy and the hunger producing action of insulin in man. *Journal of Applied Physiology, 1,* 263–269.

Grossman, S. P. (1976). Neuroanatomy of food and water intake. In D. Novin et al. (Eds.), *Hunger: Basic mechanisms and clinical implications* (pp. 51–59). New York: Raven Press.

Gueguen, N., Meineri, S., Martin, A., & Grandjean, I. (2010). The combined effect of the foot-in-the-door technique and the "but you are free" technique: An evaluation on the selective sorting of household wastes. *Ecopsychology, 2,* 231–237.

Guhl, A. M. (1956). The social order of chickens. *Scientific American, 194,* 42–46.

Guillemin, R., & Burgus, R. (1976). The hormones of the hypothalamus. In R. F. Thompson (Ed.), *Progress in psychobiology* (pp. 132–141). San Francisco, CA: Freeman.

Gull, W. W. (1874). Anorexia nervosa. *Transactions of the Clinical Society of London, 7,* 22–28.

Hager, J. C., & Ekman, P. (1979). Long-distance transmissions of facial affect signals. *Ethology and Sociobiology, 1,* 77–82.

Hagger, M. S., & Chatzisarantis, N. L. D. (2009). Integrating the theory of planned behaviour and self-determination theory in health behaviour: A meta-analysis. *British Journal of Health Psychology, 14*, 275–302.

Hailman, J. P. (1969). How an instinct is learned. *Scientific American, 221*(6), 98–106.

Haith, M. M., Bergman, T., & Moore, M. J. (1977). Eye contact and face scanning in early infancy. *Science, 198*, 853–855.

Halmi, K. A., Falk, J. R., & Schwartz, E. (1981). Binge-eating and vomiting: A survey of a college population. *Psychological Medicine, 11*, 697–706.

Hamilton, D. L. (1998). Dispositional and attributional inferences in person perception. In J. M. Darley & J. Cooper (Eds.), *Attribution and social interaction* (pp. 99–114). Washington, DC: American Psychological Association.

Harkins, S. G. (1987). Social loafing and social facilitation. *Journal of Experimental Social Psychology, 23*, 1–18.

Harlow, H. F. (1953). Mice, monkeys, men and motives. *Psychological Review, 60*, 23–32.

Harlow, H. F. (1958). The nature of love. *American Psychologist, 13*, 673–685.

Harlow, H. F., & Harlow, M. K. (1962). Social deprivation in monkeys. *Scientific American, 207*(5), 136–146.

Harlow, H. F., & Harlow, M. K. (1966). Learning to love. *American Scientist, 54*, 244–272.

Harlow, H. F., Harlow, M. K., & Meyer, D. R. (1950). Learning motivated by a manipulation drive. *Journal of Experimental Psychology, 40*, 228–234.

Harlow, H. F., & Suomi, S. J. (1970). Nature of love—Simplified. *American Psychologist, 25*, 161–168.

Harmatz, M. G., & Novak, M. A. (1983). *Human sexuality*. New York: Harper & Row.

Harmon-Jones, E., Brehm, J. W., Greenberg, J., Simon, L., & Nelson, D. E. (1996). Evidence that the production of aversive consequences is not necessary to create cognitive dissonance. *Journal of Personality and Social Psychology, 70*, 5–16.

Harris, B. (1979). Whatever happened to little Albert? *American Psychologist, 34*, 151–160.

Harris, J. A., Gorissen, M. C., Bailey, G. K., & Westbrook, R. F. (2000). Motivational state regulates the content of learned flavor preferences. *Journal of Experimental Psychology: Animal Behavior Processes, 26*, 15–30.

Hart, B. L. (1967). Sexual reflexes and mating behavior in the male dog. *Journal of Comparative and Physiological Psychology, 66*, 388–399.

Hart, B. L. (1974). Gonadal androgen and socio sexual behavior of male mammals: A comparative analysis. *Psychological Bulletin, 81*, 383–400.

Hartenian, L. S., & Lilly, B. (2009). Egoism and commitment: A multidimensional approach to understanding sustained volunteering. *Journal of Managerial Issues, 21*, 97–118.

Hartmann, E. L. (1973). *The functions of sleep*. New Haven, CT: Yale University Press.

Harvey, J. H., Town, J. P., & Yarkin, K. L. (1981). How fundamental is "the fundamental attribution error"? *Journal of Personality and Social Psychology, 40*, 346–349.

Haselhuhn, M. P., Schweitzer, M. E., & Wood, A. M. (2010). How implicit beliefs influence trust recovery. *Psychological Science, 21*(5), 645–648.

Hayashi, Y., & Endo, S. (1982). All-night sleep polygraphic recordings of healthy aged persons: REM and slow-wave sleep. *Sleep, 5*, 277–283.

Heatherton, T. F., & Baumeister, R. F. (1991). Binge eating as escape from self-awareness. *Psychological Bulletin, 110*, 86–108.

Hebb, D. O. (1949). *The organization of behavior*. New York: Wiley.

Hebb, D. O. (1955). Drives and the conceptual nervous system. *Psychological Review, 62*, 243–253.

Hebb, D. O. (1966). *A textbook of psychology* (2nd ed.). Philadelphia, PA: Saunders.

Heider, F. (1944). Social perception and phenomenal causality. *Psychological Review, 51*, 358–374.

Heider, F. (1946). Attitudes and cognitive organization. *Journal of Psychology, 21*, 107–112.

Heider, F. (1958). *The psychology of interpersonal relations*. New York: Wiley.

Heimer, L., & Larsson, K. (1966/1967). Impairment of mating behavior in male rats following lesions in the preoptic hypothalamic continuum. *Brain Research, 3*, 248–263.

Heine, S. J., & Lehman, D. R. (1997). Culture, dissonance and self-affirmation. *Personality and Social Psychology Bulletin, 23*, 389–400.

Heitland, K., & Bohner, G. (2010). Reducing prejudice via cognitive dissonance: Individual differences in preference for consistency moderate the effects of counter-attitudinal advocacy. *Social Influence, 5*, 164–181.

Helmuth, L. (2001). Beyond the pleasure principle. *Science, 294*, 983–984.

Henderlong, J., & Lepper, M. R. (2002). The effects of praise on children's intrinsic motivation: Are view and synthesis. *Psychological Bulletin, 128*, 774–795.

Henry, D. B., Kobus, K., & Schoeny, M. E. (2011). Accuracy and bias in adolescents' perceptions of friends' substance use. *Psychology of Addictive Behaviors, 25*, 80–89.

Herman, S., & Shows, W. D. (1984). How often do adults recall their dreams? *Journal of Aging and Human Development, 18,* 243–254.

Heron, G., & Johnson, D. (1976). Hypothalamic tumor presenting as anorexia nervosa. *American Journal of Psychiatry, 133,* 580–582.

Heron, W. (1957). The pathology of boredom. *Scientific American, 196*(1), 52–56.

Heron, W. (1961). Cognitive and physiological effects of perceptual isolation. In P. Solomon et al. (Eds.), *Sensory deprivation* (pp. 6–33). Cambridge, MA: Harvard University Press.

Heron, W., Doane, B. K., & Scott, J. H. (1956). Visual disturbances after prolonged perceptual isolation. *Canadian Journal of Psychology, 10,* 13–18.

Herzog, D. B., & Copeland, P. M. (1985). Eating disorders. *New England Journal of Medicine, 313,* 295–303.

Hess, E. H. (1962). Ethology: An approach toward the complete analysis of behavior. In R. Brown, E. Galanter, E. H. Hess, & G. Mandler (Eds.), *New directions in psychology* (pp. 157–265). New York: Holt, Rinehart & Winston.

Hetherington, A. W., & Ranson, S. W. (1940). Hypothalamic lesions and adiposity in the rat. *Anatomical Record, 78,* 149–172.

Hetherington, M. M., & Rolls, B. J. (1996). Sensory-specific satiety: Theoretical frame works and central characteristics. In E. D. Capaldi (Ed.), *Why we eat what we eat: The psychology of eating* (pp. 267–290). Washington, DC: American Psychological Association.

Heyes, C., & Huber, L. (Eds.). (2000). *The evolution of cognition.* Cambridge, MA: MIT Press.

Hilgard, E. R., & Bower, G. H. (1975). *Theories of learning* (4th ed.). Englewood Cliffs, NJ: Prentice Hall.

Hinde, R. A. (1966). *Animal behavior.* New York: McGraw-Hill.

Hinde, R. A. (1971). Critique of energy models of motivation. In D. Bindra & J. Stewart (Eds.), *Motivation* (2nd ed., p. 36). Baltimore, MD: Penguin.

Hinkle, L. E. (1974). The effect of exposure to culture change, social change, and changes in interpersonal relationships on health. In B. S. Dohrenwend & B. P. Dohrenwend (Eds.), *Stressful life events: Their nature and effects* (pp. 9–44). New York: Wiley.

Hinton, B. L. (1968). Environmental frustration and creative problem solving. *Journal of Applied Psychology, 52,* 211–217.

Hinz, L. D., & Williamson, D. A. (1987). Bulimia and depression: Are view of the affective variant hypothesis. *Psychological Bulletin, 102,* 150–158.

Hinz, V. B., Matz, D. C., & Patience, R. A. (2001). Does women's hair signal reproductive potential? *Journal of Experimental Social Psychology, 37,* 166–172.

Hiroto, D. S. (1974). Locus of control and learned helplessness. *Journal of Experimental Psychology, 102,* 187–193.

Hirsch, H. V. B., & Spinelli, D. N. (1970). Visual experience modifies distribution of horizontally and vertically oriented receptive fields in cats. *Science, 168,* 869–871.

Hirsch, H. V. B., & Spinelli, D. N. (1971). Modification of the distribution of receptive field orientation in cats by selective visual exposure during development. *Experimental Brain Research, 13,* 509–527.

Hirsch, J., & Knittle, J. L. (1970). Cellularity of obese and nonobese human adipose tissue. *Federation Proceedings, 29,* 1516–1521.

Hobbes, T. (1651/1991). *Leviathan.* Indianapolis, IN: Hackett. (Reprinted in part in D. D. Raphael's British Moralists 1650–1800).

Hoffman, H. S., & Boskoff, K. J. (1972). Control of aggressive behavior by an imprinted stimulus. *Psychonomic Science, 29,* 305–306.

Hoffman, H. S., Eiserer, L. A., Ratner, A. M., & Pickering, V. L. (1974). Development of distress vocalization during withdrawal of an imprinting stimulus. *Journal of Comparative and Physiological Psychology, 86,* 563–568.

Hoffman, H. S., & Ratner, A. M. (1973). A reinforcement model of imprinting: Implications for socialization in monkeys and men. *Psychological Review, 80,* 527–544.

Hoffman, H. S., Searle, J. L., Toffey, S., & Kozma, F., Jr. (1966). Behavioral control by an imprinted stimulus. *Journal of the Experimental Analysis of Behavior, 9,* 177–189.

Hoffman, H. S., & Solomon, R. L. (1974). An opponent-process theory of motivation: III. Some affective dynamics in imprinting. *Learning and Motivation, 5,* 149–164.

Hoffman, J. W., Benson, H., Arns, P. A., Stainbrook, G. L., Landsberg, L., Young, J. B., & Gill, A. (1982). Reduced sympathetic nervous system responsivity associated with the relaxation response. *Science, 215,* 190–192.

Hoffman, M. L. (1981). Is altruism a part of human nature? *Journal of Personality and Social Psychology, 40,* 121–137.

Hogben, M., & Byrne, D. (1998). Using social learning theory to explain individual differences in human sexuality. *Journal of Sex Research, 35,* 58–71.

Hohmann, G. W. (1962). *The effect of dysfunctions of the autonomic nervous system on experienced feelings and emotions.*

Paper presented at the Conference on Emotions and Feelings New School of Social Research, New York.

Hokanson, J. E. (1969). *The psychological bases of motivation.* New York: Wiley.

Holden, C. (2001). "Behavioral" addictions: Do they exist? *Science, 294,* 980–982.

Holden, C. (2007). Our ancestral brains. *Science, 318,* 25.

Holland, A. J., Sicotte, N., & Treasure, J. (1988). Anorexia nervosa: Evidence for a genetic basis. *Journal of Psychosomatic Research, 32,* 561–571.

Holmes, T. H., & Masuda, M. (1974). Life change and illness susceptibility. In B. S. Dohrenwend & B. P. Dohrenwend (Eds.), *Stressful life events: Their nature and effects* (pp. 45–72). New York: Wiley.

Holmes, T. H., & Rahe, R. H. (1967). The social readjustment rating scale. *Journal of Psychosomatic Research, 11,* 213–218.

Hong, T. B., Oddone, E. Z., Dudley, T. K., & Bosworth, H. B. (2006). Medication barriers and anti-hypertensive medication adherence: The moderating role of locus of control. *Psychology, Health and Medicine, 11,* 20–28.

Hong, Y., Chiu, C., Dweck, C. S., Lin, D. M.-S., & Wan, W. (1999). Implicit theories, attributions, and coping: A meaning system approach. *Journal of Personality and Social Psychology, 77,* 588–599.

Houpt, T. R., Anika, S. M., & Wolff, N. C. (1978). Satiety effects of cholecystokinin and caerulein in rabbits. *American Journal of Physiology, 235,* 23–28.

House, J. S., Landis, K. R., & Umberson, D. (1988). Social relationships and health. *Science, 241,* 540–544.

Hoyenga, K. B., & Hoyenga, K. T. (1984). *Motivational explanations of behavior: Evolutionary, physiological, and cognitive ideas.* Monterey, CA: Brooks/Cole.

Hsu, L. K. G. (1982). Is there a disturbance in body image in anorexia nervosa? *Journal of Nervous and Mental Disease, 170,* 305–307.

Hsu, L. K. G., & Zimmer, B. (1988). Eating disorders in old age. *International Journal of Eating Disorders, 7,* 133–138.

Hudson, J. I., Pope, H. G., Jonas, J. M., Yurgelun-Todd, D., & Frankenburg, F. R. (1987). A controlled family history of bulimia. *Psychological Medicine, 17,* 883–890.

Hull, C. L. (1930). Knowledge and purpose as habit mechanisms. *Psychological Review, 37,* 511–525.

Hull, C. L. (1931). Goal attraction and directing ideas conceived as habit phenomena. *Psychological Review, 38,* 487–506.

Hull, C. L. (1943). *Principles of behavior: An introduction to behavior theory.* New York: Appleton-Century-Crofts.

Hull, C. L. (1951). *Essentials of behavior.* New Haven, CT: Yale University Press.

Hull, C. L. (1952). *A behavior system: An introduction to behavior theory concerning the individual organism.* New Haven, CT: Yale University Press.

Hulleman, C. S., Durik, A. M., Schweigert, S. A., & Harackiewicz, J. M. (2008). Task values, achievement goals, and interest: An integrative analysis. *Journal of Educational Psychology, 100,* 398–416.

Hulleman, C. S., Schrager, S. M., Bodmann, S. M., & Harackiewicz, J. M. (2010). A meta-analytic review of achievement goal measures: Different labels for the same constructs or different constructs with similar labels? *Psychological Bulletin, 136,* 422–449.

Hulse, S. H. (1958). A mount and percentage of reinforcement and duration of goal confinement in conditioning and extinction. *Journal of Experimental Psychology, 56,* 48–57.

Hulse, S. H., Fowler, H., & Honig, W. K. (Eds.). (1978). *Cognitive processes in animal behavior.* Hillsdale, NJ: Erlbaum.

Ingham, A. G., Levinger, G., Graves, J., & Peckham, V. (1974). The Ringelmann effect: Studies of group size and group performance. *Journal of Experimental Social Psychology, 10,* 371–384.

Isaacson, R. L. (1964). Relation between achievement, test anxiety, and curricular choices. *Journal of Abnormal and Social Psychology, 68,* 447–452.

Isherwood, J., & Adam, K. S. (1976). The social readjustment rating scale: A cross-culture study of New Zealanders and Americans. *Journal of Psychosomatic Research, 20,* 211–214.

Iwata, K., Yamamoto, M., Nakao, M., & Kimura, M. (1999). A study on polysomnographic observations and subjective experiences under sensory deprivation. *Psychiatry and Clinical Neurosciences, 53,* 129–131.

Izard, C. E. (1971). *The face of emotion.* New York: Appleton Century-Crofts.

Izard, C. E. (1977). *Human emotions.* New York: Plenum.

Izard, C. E. (1979). Emotions as motivations: An evolutionary-developmental perspective. In R. A. Dienstbier (Ed.), *1978 Nebraska symposium on motivation* (pp. 163–200). Lincoln, NE: University of Nebraska Press.

Izard, C. E. (2002). Translating emotion theory and research into preventive interventions. *Psychological Bulletin, 128,* 796–824.

Izard, C. E. (2007). Basic emotions, natural kinds, emotion schemas, and a new paradigm. *Perspectives on Psychological Science, 2,* 260–280.

Izard, C. E. (2009). Emotion theory and research: Highlights, unanswered questions, and emerging issues. *Annual Review of Psychology, 60,* 1–25.

Izard, C. E. (2011). Forms and functions of emotions: Matters of emotion-cognition interaction. *Emotion Review, 3,* 371–378.

Izard, C. E., Fantauzzo, C. A., Castle, J. M., Haynes, O. M., Rayias, M. F., & Putnam, P. H. (1995). The ontogeny and significance of infants' facial expressions in the first 9 months of life. *Developmental Psychology, 31,* 997–1013.

Jackson, J. M., & Williams, K. D. (1985). Social loafing on difficult tasks: Working collectively can improve performance. *Journal of Personality and Social Psychology, 49,* 937–942.

Jacobs, B. L., & Fornal, C. A. (1997). Serotonin and motor activity. *Current Opinion in Neurobiology, 7,* 820–825.

Jain, U., & Mal, S. (1984). Effect of prolonged deprivation on attribution of causes of success and failure. *Journal of Social Psychology, 124,* 143–149.

James, W. (1884). What is an emotion? *Mind, 9,* 188–205. (Reprinted in M. Arnold (Ed.), *The nature of emotion.* Baltimore, MD: Penguin, 1968)

James, W. (1890). *Principles of psychology.* New York: Holt.

James, W. (1994/1936). *The varieties of religious experience.* New York: The Modern Library.

Jennings-White, C. (1995). Perfumary and the sixth sense. *Perfumer Flavorist, 20,* 1–9.

Jenson, W. R., Paoletti, P., & Peterson, B. P. (1984). Self monitoring plus a reinforcement contingency to reduce a chronic throat clearing tic in a child. *Behavior Therapist, 7,* 192.

Jimerson, D. C., Lesem, M. D., Kaye, W. H., & Brewerton, T. D. (1992). Low serotonin and dopamine metabolite concentrations in cerebrospinal fluid from bulimic patients with frequent binge episodes. *Archives of General Psychiatry, 49,* 132–138.

Jocham, G., Klein, T. A., & Ullsperger, M. (2011). Dopamine-mediated reinforcement learning signals in the striatum and ventromedial prefrontal cortex underlie value-based choices. *Journal of Neuroscience, 31,* 1606–1613.

Johnson, C., & Larson, R. (1982). Bulimia: An analysis of moods and behavior. *Psychosomatic Medicine, 44,* 341–351.

Johnson, C. L., Stuckey, M. K., Lewis, L. D., & Schwartz, D. M. (1982). Bulimia: A descriptive survey of 316 cases. *International Journal of Eating Disorders, 2,* 3–16.

Johnson, J. G., Feinstein, S., & Crofton, A. (1996). Attributions for positive life events and increased hopefulness predict recovery from depression among psychiatric in patients. *Depression and Stress, 2,* 3–14.

Johnson, J. G., Han, Y.-S., Douglas, C. J., Johannet, C. M., & Russell, T. (1998). Attributions for positive life events predict recovery from depression among psychiatric inpatients: An investigation of the Needles and Abramson model of recovery from depression. *Journal of Consulting and Clinical Psychology, 66,* 369–376.

Johnson, J. H., & Sarason, I. G. (1978). Life stress, depression and anxiety: Internal-external control as a moderator variable. *Journal of Psychosomatic Research, 22,* 205–208.

Johnson, L. C. (1983). Sleep deprivation and performance. In W. B. Webb (Ed.), *Biological rhythms and performance* (pp. 111–141). West Sussex, England: Wiley.

Johnson, P. M., & Kenny, P. J. (2010). Dopamine D2 receptors in addiction-like reward dysfunction and compulsive eating in obese rats. *Nature Neuroscience, 13,* 635–641.

Johnson, R. N. (1972). *Aggression in man and animals.* Philadelphia, PA: Saunders.

Johnson, T. J., Feigenbaum, R., & Weiby, M. (1964). Some determinants and consequences of the teachers' perceptions of causation. *Journal of Educational Psychology, 55,* 237–246.

Johnston, V. S., Hagel, R., Franklin, M., Fink, B., & Grammer, K. (2001). Male facial attractiveness: Evidence for hormone-mediated adaptive design. *Evolution and Human Behavior, 22,* 251–267.

Jones, A. P., & Friedman, M. I. (1982). Obesity and adipocyte abnormalities in offspring of rats under nourished during pregnancy. *Science, 215,* 1518–1519.

Jones, E. E. (1979). The rocky road from acts to dispositions. *American Psychologist, 34,* 107–117.

Jones, E. E., & Davis, K. E. (1965). From acts to dispositions: The attribution process in person perception. In L. Berkowitz (Ed.), *Advances in experimental social psychology* (Vol. 2, pp. 219–266). New York: Academic Press.

Jones, E. E., & Harris, V. A. (1967). The attribution of attitudes. *Journal of Experimental Social Psychology, 3,* 1–24.

Jones, E. E., Kanouse, D. E., Kelley, H. H., Nisbett, R. E., Valins, S., & Weiner, B. (Eds.). (1972). *Attribution: Perceiving the causes of behavior.* Morristown, NJ: General Learning Press.

Jones, E. E., & Nisbett, R. E. (1972). The actor and the observer: Divergent perceptions of the causes of behavior. In E. E. Jones et al. (Eds.), *Attribution: Perceiving the causes of behavior* (pp. 79–94). Morristown, NJ: General Learning Press.

Jones, M. C. (1924). A laboratory study of fear: The case of Peter. *Pedagogical Seminary, 31,* 308–315.

Jordan, N. (1953). Behavioral forces that area function of attitudes and cognitive organization. *Human Relations, 6,* 273–287.

Jouvet, M. (1976). The states of sleep. In R. F. Thompson (Ed.), *Progress in psychobiology*. San Francisco: Freeman.

Kagan, H. (1951). Anorexia and severe inanition associated with a tumor involving the hypothalamus. *Archives of Diseases in Childhood, 26*, 274.

Kagan, J., Reznick, J. S., & Snidman, N. (1988). Biological bases of childhood shyness. *Science, 240*, 167–171.

Kalat, J. W. (2001). *Biological psychology* (7th ed.). Belmont, CA: Wadsworth.

Kalat, J. W. (2009). *Biological psychology* (10th ed.). Belmont, CA: Wadsworth.

Kamins, M. L., & Dweck, C. S. (1999). Person versus process praise and criticism: Implications for contingent self worth and coping. *Developmental Psychology, 35*, 835–847.

Kampe, K. K. W., Frith, C. D., Dolan, R. J., & Frith, U. (2001). Reward value of attractiveness and gaze. *Nature, 413*, 589.

Kanazawa, S. (1992). Outcome or expectancy? Antecedent of spontaneous causal attribution. *Personality and Social Psychology Bulletin, 18*, 659–668.

Kaplan, A., & Bartner, S. (2005). Reciprocal communication between the nervous and immune systems: Crosstalk, back-talk, and motivational speeches. *International Review of Psychiatry, 17*, 439–441.

Kaplan, H. S. (1978). *Disorders of sexual desire*. New York: Simon & Schuster.

Karaoglu, A., Aydin, S., Dagli, A. F., Cummings, D. E., Ozercan, I. H., Canatan, H., & Ozkan, Y. (2009). Expression of obestatin and ghrelin in papillary thyroid carcinoma. *Molecular and Cellular Biochemistry, 323*, 113–118.

Karau, S., & Williams, K. (1993). Social loafing: A meta-analytic review and theoretical integration. *Journal of Personality and Social Psychology, 65*, 681–706.

Karni, A., Tanne, D., Rubenstein, B. S., Askenasy, J. J. M., & Sagi, D. (1994). Dependence on REM sleep of overnight improvement of a perceptual skill. *Science, 265*, 679–682.

Kashima, Y., Siegal, M., Tanaka, K., & Kashima, E. S. (1992). Do you believe behaviours are consistent with attitudes? Towards a cultural psychology of attribution processes. *British Journal of Social Psychology, 31*, 111–124.

Kasser, T., & Ryan, R. M. (1996). Further examining the American dream: Differential correlates of intrinsic and extrinsic goals. *Personality and Social Psychology Bulletin, 22*, 280–287.

Katz, D., & Allport, F. H. (1931). *Student attitudes: Are port of the Syracuse University reaction study*. Syracuse, NY: Craftsman Press.

Kaye, W. (2008). Neurobiology of anorexia and bulimia nervosa. *Physiology and Behavior, 94*, 121–135.

Kaye, W. H., Frank, G. K., Meltzer, C. C., Price, J. C., McConaha, C. W., Crossan, P. J., Klump, K. L., & Rhodes, L. (2001). Altered serotonin 2a receptor activity in women who have recovered from bulimia nervosa. *American Journal of Psychiatry, 158*, 1152–1155.

Kaye, W. H., & Weltzin, T. E. (1991a). Neurochemistry of bulimia nervosa. *Journal of Clinical Psychiatry, 52*(10, Suppl.), 21–28.

Kaye, W. H., & Weltzin, T. E. (1991b). Serotonin activity in anorexia and bulimia nervosa: Relationship to the modulation of feeding and mood. *Journal of Clinical Psychiatry, 52*(12, Suppl.), 41–48.

Keating, C. F., Randall, D. W., Kendrick, T., & Gutshall, K. A. (2003). Do baby faced adults receive more help? The (cross-cultural) case of the lost resume. *Journal of Nonverbal Behavior, 27*, 89–109.

Keeling, L. J., & Hurnik, J. F. (1993). Chickens show socially facilitated feeding behavior in response to a video image of a conspecific. *Applied Animal Behaviour Science, 36*, 223–231.

Keesey, R. E., Boyle, P. C., Kemnitz, J. W., & Mitchell, J. S. (1976). The role of the lateral hypothalamus in determining the body weight set point. In D. Novin et al. (Eds.), *Hunger: Basic mechanisms and clinical implications* (pp. 243–255). New York: Raven Press.

Keesey, R. E., & Powley, T. L. (1975). Hypothalamic regulation of body weight. *American Scientist, 63*, 558–565.

Kelley, H. H. (1967). Attribution theory in social psychology. In D. Levine (Ed.), *Nebraska symposium on motivation* (Vol. 15, pp. 192–238). Lincoln, NE: University of Nebraska Press.

Kelley, H. H. (1971). *Attribution in social interaction*. Morristown, NJ: General Learning Press.

Kelley, H. H. (1972). Attribution in social interaction. In E. E. Jones et al. (Eds.), *Attribution: Perceiving the causes of behavior* (pp. 1–26). Morristown, NJ: General Learning Press.

Kelley, H. H. (1973). The processes of causal attribution. *American Psychologist, 28*, 107–128.

Kemeny, M. E. (2003). The psychobiology of stress. *Current Directions in Psychological Science, 12*, 124–129.

Kenrick, D. T. (1991). Proximate altruism and selfishness. *Psychological Inquiry, 2*, 135–137.

Kenrick, D. T., Griskevicius, V., Neuberg, S. L., & Shaller, M. (2010). Renovating the pyramid of needs: Contemporary extensions built upon ancient foundations. *Perspectives on Psychological Science, 5,* 292–314.

Kerr, N. L. (1983). Motivation loss in small groups: A social dilemma analysis. *Journal of Personality and Social Psychology, 45,* 819–828.

Keys, A., Brozek, J., Henschel, A., Mickelsen, O., & Taylor, H. L. (1950). *The biology of human starvation.* St. Paul, MN: University of Minnesota Press.

Kiecolt-Glaser, J. K. (2009). Psychoneuroimmunology: Psychology's gateway to the biomedical future. *Perspectives on Psychological Science, 4,* 367–369.

Kiecolt-Glaser, J. K., Belury, M. A., Porter, K., Beversdorf, D., Lemeshow, S., & Glaser, R. (2007). Depressive symptoms, omega-6: Omega-3 fatty acids, and inflammation in older adults. *Psychosomatic Medicine, 69,* 217–224.

Kiecolt-Glaser, J. K., Glaser, R., Gravenstein, S., Malarky, W. B., & Sheridan, J. (1996). Chronic stress alters the immune response to influenza virus vaccine in older adults. *Proceedings of the National Academy of Sciences, 93,* 3043–3047.

Kiecolt-Glaser, J. K., McGuire, L., Robles, T. F., & Glaser, R. (2002). Emotions, morbidity, and mortality: New perspectives from psychoneuroimmunology. *Annual Review of Psychology, 53,* 83–107.

Kiecolt-Glaser, J. K., Preacher, K. J., MacCallum, R. C., Atkinson, C., Malarky, W. B., & Glaser, R. (2003). Chronic stress and age related increases in the proinflammatory cytokine IL-6. *Proceedings of the National Academy of Sciences, 100,* 9090–9095.

Kim, H., & Markus, H. R. (1999). Deviance or uniqueness, harmony or conformity? A cultural analysis. *Journal of Personality and Social Psychology, 77,* 785–800.

Kissileff, H. R. (1969). Food-associated drinking in the rat. *Journal of Comparative and Physiological Psychology, 67,* 284–300.

Kissileff, H. R. (1973). Nonhomeostatic controls of drinking. In A. N. Epstein et al. (Eds.), *The neuropsychology of thirst: New findings and advances in concepts* (pp. 163–198). Washington, DC: V. H. Winston.

Kissileff, H. R., & Epstein, A. N. (1969). Exaggerated prandial drinking in the "recovered lateral" rat without saliva. *Journal of Comparative and Physiological Psychology, 67,* 301–308.

Klein, R. M., Figler, M. H., & Peeke, H. V. S. (1976). Modification of consummatory (attack) behavior resulting from prior habituation of appetitive (threat) components of the agonistic sequence in male *Betta Splendens* (Pisces, Belongtiidae). *Behaviour, 58,* 1–25.

Kleinginna, P. R., & Kleinginna, A. M. (1981). A categorized list of motivation definitions, with a suggestion for a consensual definition. *Motivation and Emotion, 5,* 263–291.

Kleinke, C. L. (1986). Gaze and eye contact: Are search review. *Psychological Bulletin, 100,* 78–100.

Kleitman, N. (1963). *Sleep and wakefulness* (2nd ed.). Chicago, IL: University of Chicago Press.

Kline, J. P., Blackhart, G. C., & Williams, W. C. (2007). Anterior EEG asymmetries and opponent process theory. *International Journal of Psychophysiology, 63,* 302–307.

Klinger, E. (1966). Fantasy need achievement. *Psychological Bulletin, 66,* 291–306.

Klinger, E. (1975). Consequences of commitment to and disengagement from incentives. *Psychological Review, 82,* 1–25.

Klinger, E. (1977). *Meaning and void: Inner experience and the incentives in people's lives.* Minneapolis, MN: University of Minnesota Press.

Klopfer, P. H. (1971). Mother love: What turns it on? *American Scientist, 59,* 404–407.

Kluver, H., & Bucy, P. C. (1939). Preliminary analysis of functions of the temporal lobes in monkeys. *Archives of Neurology and Psychiatry, 42,* 979–1000.

Knowles, J. B., MacLean, A. W., & Cairns, J. (1982). REM sleep abnormalities in depression: A test of the phase-advance hypothesis. *Biological Psychiatry, 17,* 605–609.

Knox, R. E., & Inkster, J. A. (1968). Post decision dissonance at post time. *Journal of Personality and Social Psychology, 8,* 319–323.

Kobasa, S. C. (1979). Stressful life events, personality, and health: An inquiry into hardiness. *Journal of Personality and Social Psychology, 37,* 1–11.

Kobasa, S. C., Maddi, S. R., & Puccetti, M. C. (1982). Personality and exercise as buffers in the stress–illness relationship. *Journal of Behavioral Medicine, 5,* 391–404.

Kobashi, M., & Adachi, A. (1992). Effect of hepatic portal infusion of water on water intake by water-deprived rats. *Physiology and Behavior, 52,* 885–888.

Koh, K., Joiner, W. J., Wu, M. N., Yue, Z., Smith, C. J., & Sehgal, A. (2008). Identification of SLEEPLESS, a sleep-promoting factor. *Science, 321,* 372–376.

Köhler, W. (1925). *The mentality of apes* (E. Winter, Trans.). New York: Harcourt, Brace & World.

Kojima, M., Hosoda, H., Date, Y., Nakazato, M., Matsuo, H., & Kangawa, K. (1999). Ghrelin is a growth-hormone-releasing acylated peptide from stomach. *Nature, 402,* 656–660.

Konishi, M. (1971). Ethology and neurobiology. *American Scientist, 59*, 56–63.

Korman, A. R. (1974). *The psychology of motivation.* Englewood Cliffs, NJ: Prentice Hall.

Kozlowski, S., & Drzewiecki, K. (1973). The role of osmoreception in portal circulation in control of water intake in dogs. *Acta Physiologica Polonica, 24*, 325–330.

Kraly, F. S. (1981). A diurnal variation in the satiating potency of cholecystokinin in the rat. *Appetite: Journal of Intake Research, 2*, 177–191.

Kraly, F. S. (1983). Histamine plays a part in induction of drinking by food intake. *Nature, 301*, 65–66.

Kraly, F. S. (1984). Physiology of drinking elicited by eating. *Psychological Review, 91*, 478–490.

Kraly, F. S. (1990). Drinking elicited by eating. In A. N. Epstein & A. Morrison (Eds.), *Progress in psychobiology and physiological psychology* (Vol. *14*, pp. 67–133). New York: Academic Press.

Kraly, F. S., & Blass, E. M. (1974). Motivated feeding in the absence of glucoprivic control of feeding in rats. *Journal of Comparative and Physiological Psychology, 87*, 801–807.

Kraly, F. S., Carty, W. J., Resnick, S., & Smith, G. P. (1978). Effect of cholecystokinin on meal size and intermeal interval in the sham-feeding rat. *Journal of Comparative and Physiological Psychology, 92*, 697–707.

Kraly, F. S., & Corneilson, R. (1990). Angiotensin II mediates drinking elicited by eating in the rat. *American Journal of Physiology, 258*, R436–R442.

Kraly, F. S., & Specht, S. M. (1984). Histamine plays a major role for drinking elicited by spontaneous eating in the rat. *Physiology and Behavior, 33*, 611–614.

Kramer, A., Yang, F.-C., Snodgrass, P., Li, X., Scammell, T. E., Davis, F. C., & Weitz, C. J. (2001). Regulation of daily locomotor activity and sleep by hypothalamic EGF receptor signaling. *Science, 294*, 2511–2515.

Krantz, D. S., Grunberg, N. E., & Baum, A. (1985). Health psychology. *Annual Review of Psychology, 36*, 349–383.

Krasner, L. (1988). In memoriam: Mary Cover Jones 1896-1987. *The Behavior Analyst, 11*, 91–92.

Kraut, R. E. (1982). Social presence, facial feedback, and emotion. *Journal of Personality and Social Psychology, 42*, 853–863.

Kravitz, D. A., & Martin, B. (1986). Ringelmann rediscovered: The original article. *Journal of Personality and Social Psychology, 50*, 936–941.

Krebs, D. L. (1991). Altruism and egoism: A false dichotomy? *Psychological Inquiry, 2*, 137–139.

Krebs, J. R., & Davies, N. B. (1993). *An introduction to behavioural ecology* (3rd ed.). Boston, MA: Blackwell.

Krull, D. S. (2001). On partitioning the fundamental attribution error: Dispositionalism and the correspondence bias. In G. B. Moskowitz (Ed.), *Cognitive social psychology* (pp. 211–227). Mahwah, NJ: Lawrence Erlbaum Associates Inc.

Krull, D. S., Loy, M. H.-M., Lin, J., Wang, C.-F., Chen, S., & Zhao, X. (1999). The fundamental fundamental attribution error: Correspondence bias in individualist and collectivist cultures. *Personality and Social Psychology Bulletin, 25*, 1208–1219.

Krusemark, E. A., Campbell, W. K., & Clementz, B. A. (2008). Attributions, deception, and event related potentials: An investigation of the self-serving bias. *Psychophysiology, 45*, 511–515.

Kubzansky, P. E., & Leiderman, P. H. (1961). Sensory deprivation: An overview. In P. Solomon et al. (Eds.), *Sensory deprivation* (pp. 221–238). Cambridge, MA: Harvard University Press.

Kuczmarski, R. J., Flegal, K. M., Campbell, S. M., & Johnson, C. L. (1994). Increasing prevalence of overweight among U.S. adults: The national health and nutrition examination surveys, 1960 to 1991. *Journal of the American Medical Association, 272*, 205–211.

Kudo, E., & Numazaki, M. (2003). Explicit and direct self-serving bias in Japan: Reexamination of self-serving bias for success and failure. *Journal of Cross-Cultural Psychology, 34*, 511–521.

Kuhl, J. (1981). Motivational and functional helplessness: The moderating effect of state versus action orientation. *Journal of Personality and Social Psychology, 40*, 155–170.

Kuo, Z. Y. (1921). Giving up instincts in psychology. *Journal of Philosophy, 17*, 645–664.

Kupfer, D. J. (1976). REM latency: A psycho biologic marker for primary depressive disease. *Biological Psychiatry, 11*, 159–174.

Kwan, B. M., & Bryan, A. D. (2010). Affective response to exercise as a component of exercise motivation: Attitudes, norms, self-efficacy, and temporal stability of intentions. *Psychology of Sport and Exercise, 11*, 71–79.

LaBar, K. S., Gitelman, D. R., Parrish, T. B., Kim, Y.-H., Nobre, A. C., & Mesulam, M.-M. (2001). Hunger selectively modulates corticolimbic activation to food stimuli in humans. *Behavioral Neuroscience, 115*, 493–500.

Labott, S. M., & Martin, R. B. (1987, Winter). The stress moderating effects of weeping and humor. *Journal of Human Stress, 13*, 159–164.

LaBrie, J. W., Huchting, K., Pedersen, E. R., Hummer, J. F., Shelesky, K., & Tawalbeh, S. (2007). Female college drinking and the social learning theory: An examination of the developmental transition period from high school to college. *Journal of College Student Development, 48,* 344–356.

Lacey, J. H., & Dolan, B. M. (1988). Bulimia in British Blacks and Asians: A catchment area study. *British Journal of Psychiatry, 152,* 73–79.

Lacey, J. I. (1967). Somatic response patterning and stress: Some revisions of activation theory. In M. H. Appley & R. Trumbull (Eds.), *Psychological stress* (pp. 14–37). New York: Appleton-Century-Crofts.

Laessle, R. G., Kittl, S., Fichter, M. M., Wittchen, H.-U., & Pirke, K. M. (1987). Major affective disorder in anorexia nervosa and bulimia: A descriptive diagnostic study. *British Journal of Psychiatry, 151,* 785–789.

Lalasz, C. B., & Weigel, D. J. (2011). Understanding the relationship between gender and extra dyadic relations: The mediating role of sensation seeking on intentions to engage in sexual infidelity. *Personality and Individual Differences, 50,* 1079–1083.

Lalumiere, M. L., & Quinsey, V. L. (1998). Pavlovian conditioning of sexual interests in human males. *Archives of Sexual Behavior, 27,* 241–252.

Lan, W. Y., & Repman, J. (1995). The effects of social learning context and modeling on persistence and dynamism in academic activities. *Journal of Experimental Education, 64,* 53–67.

Lange, C. (1885). One leuds beveegelser (I. A. Haupt, Trans.). In K. Dunlap (Ed.), *The emotions.* Baltimore, MD: Williams & Wilkins.

Langlois, J. H., & Roggman, L. A. (1990). Attractive faces are only average. *Psychological Science, 1,* 115–121.

Larsen, R. J., & Diener, E. (1992). Promises and problems with the circumplex model of emotion. In M. S. Clark (Ed.), *Review of personality and social psychology: Emotion* (Vol. 13, pp. 25–59). Newbury Park, CA: Sage.

Larsen, R. J., Kasimatis, M., & Frey, K. (1992). Facilitating the furrowed brow: An unobtrusive test of the facial feedback hypothesis applied to unpleasant affect. *Cognition and Emotion, 6,* 321–338.

Laségue, C. (1873). On hysterical anorexia. *Medical Times and Gazette, 2,* 265–266, 367–369.

Latané, B., & Darley, J. M. (1970). *The unresponsive bystander: Why doesn't he help?* New York: Appleton-Century-Crofts.

Latané, B., & Nida, S. (1981). Ten years of research on group size and helping. *Psychological Bulletin, 89,* 308–324.

Latané, B., Williams, K., & Harkins, S. (1979). Many hands make light the work: The causes and consequences of social loafing. *Journal of Personality and Social Psychology, 37,* 822–832.

Lavie, P. (2001). Sleep-wake as a biological rhythm. *Annual Review of Psychology, 52,* 277–303.

Lazarus, R. S. (1968). Emotions and adaptation: Conceptual and empirical relations. In W. J. Arnold (Ed.), *Nebraska symposium on motivation* (pp. 175–266). Lincoln, NE: University of Nebraska Press.

Lazarus, R. S. (1982). Thoughts on the relations between emotion and cognition. *American Psychologist, 37,* 1019–1024.

Lazarus, R. S. (1984). On the primacy of cognition. *American Psychologist, 39,* 124–129.

Lazarus, R. S. (1991). Progress on a cognitive-motivational relational theory of emotion. *American Psychologist, 46,* 819–834.

Lazarus, R. S. (1999). The cognition-emotion debate: A bit of history. In T. Dalgleish & M. J. Power (Eds.), *Handbook of cognition and emotion* (pp. 3–19). West Sussex, England: John Wiley & Sons.

Lecat, B., Hilton, D. J., & Crano, W. D. (2009). Group status and reciprocity norms: Can the door-in-the-face effect be obtained in an out-group context? *Group Dynamics: Theory Research and Practice, 13,* 178–189.

LeDoux, J. E. (1994). Emotion, memory and the brain. *Scientific American, 270,* 50–57.

LeDoux, J. E. (1995). Emotion: Clues from the brain. *Annual Review of Psychology, 46,* 209–235.

LeDoux, J. E. (1996). *The emotional brain: The mysterious underpinnings of emotional life.* New York: Touchstone.

LeDoux, J. E. (2000). Emotion circuits in the brain. *Annual Review of Neuroscience, 23,* 155–184.

Lee, F., Hallahan, M., & Herzog, T. (1996). Explaining real life events: How culture and domain shape attributions. *Personality and Social Psychology Bulletin, 22,* 732–741.

Lee, G., & Lee, W. J. (2010). Altruistic traits and organizational conditions in helping online. *Computers in Human Behavior, 26,* 1574–1580.

Lee, S. (1991). Anorexia nervosa in Hong Kong: A Chinese perspective. *Psychological Medicine, 21,* 703–711.

Lee, S., Lee, A. M., Ngai, E., Lee, D. T., & Wing, Y. K. (2001). Rationales for food refusal in Chinese patients with Anorexia Nervosa. *International Journal of Eating Disorders, 29,* 224–229.

Lefcourt, H. M. (1966). Internal versus external control of reinforcement: A review. *Psychological Bulletin, 65,* 206–220.

Leggett, E. L. (1985, March). *Children's entity and incremental theories of intelligence: Relationships to achievement behavior.* Paper presented at the annual meeting of the Eastern Psychological Association, Boston.

Leggett, E. L., & Dweck, C. S. (1986). *Individual differences in goals and inference rules: Sources of causal judgments.* Manuscript submitted for publication.

Lehrman, D. S. (1970). Semantic and conceptual issues in the nature-nuture problem. In L. R. Aronson, E. Tobach, D. S. Lehrman, & J. S. Rosenblatt (Eds.), *Development and evolution of behavior.* San Francisco: Freeman.

Leibowitz, S. F., & Shor-Posner, G. (1986). Brain serotonin and eating behavior. *Appetite, 7*(Suppl.), 99–103.

Leknes, S., Brooks, J. C. W., Wiech, K., & Tracey, I. (2008). Pain relief as an opponent process: A psychophysical investigation. *European Journal of Neuroscience, 28,* 794–801.

Lenneberg, E. H. (1960). Language, evolution, and purposive behavior. In S. Diamond (Ed.), *Culture in history: Essays in honor of Paul Radin* (pp. 869–893). New York: Columbia University Press.

Lenneberg, E. H. (1967). *Biological foundations of language.* New York: Wiley.

Leonard, B. E. (2001). The immune system, depression and the action of antidepressants. *Progress in Neuro-Psychopharmacology and Biological Psychiatry, 25,* 767–780.

Leone, C., & D'Arienzo, J. (2000). Sensation-seeking and differentially arousing television commercials. *Journal of Social Psychology, 140,* 710–720.

Lepper, M. R., & Greene, D. (1978). *The hidden costs of reward: New perspectives on the psychology of human motivation.* Hillsdale, NJ: Erlbaum.

Levine, F. M. (1975). *Theoretical readings in motivation: Perspectives on human behavior.* Chicago, IL: Rand McNally.

Levine, S. (1966). Sex differences in the brain. *Scientific American, 214*(4), 84–90.

Levine, S. (1971). Stress and behavior. *Scientific American, 224*(1), 26–31.

Levinger, G., & Breedlove, J. (1966). Interpersonal attraction and agreement: A study of marriage partners. *Journal of Personality and Social Psychology, 3,* 367–372.

Lewin, I., & Singer, J. L. (1991). Psychological effects of REM ("dream") deprivation upon waking mentation. In S. J. Ellman & J. S. Antrobus (Eds.), *The mind in sleep: Psychology and psychophysiology* (2nd ed., pp. 396–412). New York: Wiley.

Lewin, K. (1936). *Principles of topological psychology.* New York: McGraw-Hill.

Lewin, K. (1938). *The conceptual representation and the measurement of psychological forces.* Durham, NC: Duke University Press.

Liberman, A. M., & Mattingly, I. G. (1989). A specialization for speech perception. *Science, 243,* 489–494.

Libet, J. M., & Lewisohn, P. M. (1973). Concept of social skill with special reference to the behavior of depressed persons. *Journal of Consulting and Clinical Psychology, 40,* 304–312.

Liddell, H. S. (1954). Conditioning and emotions. *Scientific American, 190*(1), 48–57.

Liden, R. C., Wayne, S. J., Jaworski, R. A., & Bennett, N. (2004). Social loafing: A field investigation. *Journal of Management, 30,* 285–304.

Lieberman, M. D., Gaunt, R., Gilbert, D. T., & Trope, Y. (2002). Reflexion and reflection: A social cognitive neuroscience approach to attributional inference. In M. Zanna (Ed.), *Advances in experimental social psychology* (Vol. 34, pp. 199–249). New York: Elsevier.

Lima, S. L., Rattenborg, N. C., Lesku, J. A., & Amlaner, C. J. (2005). Sleeping under the risk of predation. *Animal Behaviour, 70,* 723–736.

Lin, L., Faraco, J., Li, R., Kadotani, H., Rogers, W., Lin, X., Qiu, X., deJong, P. J., Nishino, S., & Mignot, E. (1999). The sleep disorder canine narcolepsy is caused by a mutation in the hypocretin (orexin) receptor 2 gene. *Cell, 98,* 365–376.

Lindsley, D. (1950). Emotions and the electro encephalogram. In M. L. Reymert (Ed.), *Feelings and emotions.* New York: McGraw-Hill.

Lindsley, D. (1951). Emotion. In S. S. Stevens (Ed.), *Handbook of experimental psychology* (pp. 473–516). New York: Wiley.

Linville, P. W. (1987). Self-complexity as a cognitive buffer against stress-related illness and depression. *Journal of Personality and Social Psychology, 52,* 663–676.

Lockard, J. S., Allen, D. J., Schielle, B. J., & Wiemer, M. J. (1978). Human postural signals: Stance, weight-shifts and social distance as intention movements to depart. *Animal Behavior, 26,* 219–224.

Logan, F. A. (1968). Incentive theory and changes in reward. In K. W. Spence & J. T. Spence (Eds.), *The psychology of learning and motivation* (Vol. 2, pp. 1–30). New York: Academic Press.

Long, M. E. (1987, December). What is this thing called sleep? *National Geographic,* 787–821.

Lopez, H. H., & Ettenberg, A. (2002). Sexually conditioned incentives: Attenuation of motivational impact during dopamine receptor antagonism. *Pharmacology, Biochemistry and Behavior, 72,* 65–72.

Lopez-Bonilla, J. M., & Lopez-Bonilla, L. M. (2010). Sensation seeking and the use of the internet: A confirmatory analysis of the brief sensation seeking scale

(BSSS) by gender. *Social Science Computer Review, 28,* 177–193.

Lorenz, K. (1950). The comparative method of studying innate behavior patterns. In *Symposia of the society of experimental biology.* Cambridge, MA: Cambridge University Press.

Lorenz, K. (1967). *On aggression.* New York: Bantam.

Lorenz, K. (1970). The establishment of the instinct concept. In *Studies in animal and human behavior* (Vol. *1*) (Robert Martin, Trans.). Cambridge, MA: Harvard University Press.

Lorenz, K. (1971a). Part and parcel in animal and human societies. In *Studies in animal and human behavior* (Vol. *2*) (Robert Martin, Trans.). Cambridge, MA: Harvard University Press.

Lorenz, K. (1971b). A scientist's credo. In *Studies in animal and human behavior* (Vol. *2*) (Robert Martin, Trans.). Cambridge, MA: Harvard University Press.

Lorenz, K., & Tinbergen, N. (1938). Taxis und instinkthandlung in der eirollbewegung der graugens. I. *Zeitschrift fur Tierpsychologie, 2,* 1–29.

Lortie-Lussier, M., Cote, L., & Vachon, J. (2000). The consistency and continuity hypotheses revisited through dreams of women at two periods of their lives. *Dreaming, 2,* 67–76.

Lu, X. Y., Kim, C. S., Fraser, A., & Zhang, W. (2006). Leptin: A potential novel antidepressant. *Proceedings of the National Academy of Sciences, USA, 103,* 1593–1598.

Lubow, R. E., Rosenblatt, R., & Weiner, I. (1981). Confounding of controllability in the triadic design for demonstrating learned helplessness. *Journal of Personality and Social Psychology, 41,* 458–468.

Luria, Z., Friedman, S., & Rose, M. D. (1987). *Human sexuality.* New York: Wiley.

Lutter, M., & Nestler, E. J. (2009). Homeostatic and hedonic signals interact in the regulation of food intake. *The Journal of Nutrition, 139,* 629–632.

Lutter, M., Sakata, I., Osborne-Lawrence, S., Rovinsky, S. A., Anderson, J. G., Jung, S., Birnbaum, S., Yanagisawa, M., Elmquist, J. K., Nestler, E. J., & Zigman, J. M. (2008). The orexigenic hormone ghrelin defends against depressive symptoms of chronic stress. *Nature Neuroscience, 11,* 752–753.

Lyamin, O. I., Manger, P. R., Ridgway, S. H., Mukhametov, L. M., & Siegel, J. M. (2008). Cetacean sleep: An unusual form of mammalian sleep. *Neuroscience and Biobehavioral Reviews, 32,* 1451–1484.

Maddi, S. R., Bartone, P. T., & Puccetti, M. C. (1987). Stressful events are indeed a factor in physical illness:

Reply to Schroeder and Costa (1984). *Journal of Personality and Social Psychology, 52,* 833–843.

Maddi, S. R., Khoshaba, D. M., Persico, M., Lu, J., Harvey, R., & Bleecker, F. (2002). The personality construct of hardiness II. Relationships with comprehensive tests of personality and psychopathology. *Journal of Research in Personality, 36,* 72–85.

Magoun, H. W. (1963). *The waking brain.* Springfield, IL: Thomas.

Maier, S. F. (1970). Failure to escape traumatic shock: Incompatible skeletal motor responses or learned helplessness? *Learning and Motivation, 1,* 157–170.

Maier, S. F., Anderson, C., & Lieberman, D. S. (1972). Influence of control of shock on subsequent shock-elicited aggression. *Journal of Comparative and Physiological Psychology, 81,* 94–100.

Malcolm-Smith, S., & Solms, M. (2004). Incidence of threat in dreams: A response to Revonsuo's threat simulation theory. *Dreaming, 14,* 220–229.

Malle, B. F. (2006). The actor-observer asymmetry in attribution: A (surprising) meta-analysis. *Psychological Bulletin, 132,* 895–919.

Malle, B. F., & Knobe, J. (1997). Which behaviors do people explain? A basic actor-observer asymmetry. *Journal of Personality and Social Psychology, 72,* 288–304.

Malle, B. F., Knobe, J. M., & Nelson, S. E. (2007). Actor-observer asymmetries in explanations of behavior: New answers to an old question. *Journal of Personality and Social Psychology, 93,* 491–514.

Malle, B. F., & Pearce, G. E. (2001). Attention to behavioral events during interaction: Two actor-observer gaps and three attempts to close them. *Journal of Personality and Social Psychology, 81,* 278–294.

Malvin, R. L., Mouw, D., & Vander, A. J. (1977). Angiotensin: Physiological role in water-deprivation-induced thirst of rats. *Science, 197,* 171–173.

Mandler, G. (1967). Invited commentary on adaptive stress behavior. In M. H. Appley & R. Trumbull (Eds.), *Psychological stress* (pp. 307–310). New York: Appleton-Century-Crofts.

Mandler, G. (1984). *Mind and body: Psychology of emotion and stress.* New York: Norton.

Maner, J. K., & Gailliot, M. T. (2007). Altruism and egoism: Prosocial motivations for helping depend on relationship context. *European Journal of Social Psychology, 37,* 347–358.

Maner, J. K., Luce, C., Neuberg, S. L., Cialdini, R. B., Brown, S. L., & Sagarin, B. J. (2002). The effects of perspective taking on motivations for helping: Still no evidence for altruism. *Personality and Social Psychology Bulletin, 28,* 1601–1610.

Mann, L. (1977). The effect of stimulus queues on queue joining behavior. *Journal of Personality and Social Psychology, 35,* 437–442.

Manning, R., Levine, M., & Collins, A. (2007). The Kitty Genovese murder and the social psychology of helping: The parable of the 38 witnesses. *American Psychologist, 62,* 555–562.

Maquet, P. (2001). The role of sleep in learning and memory. *Science, 294,* 1048–1052.

Marañon, G. (1924). Contributionàl' étudede l'action emotive de l'adrenaline. *Revue Française D'endocrinologie, 2,* 301–325.

Marean, C. W., Bar-Matthews, M., Bernatchez, J., Fisher, E., Goldberg, P., Herries, A. I. R., Jocobs, Z., Jerardino, A., Karkanas, P., Minichillo, T., Nilssen, P. J., Thompson, E., Watts, I., & Williams, H. M. (2007). Early human use of marine resources and pigment in South Africa during the Middle Pleistocene. *Nature, 449,* 905–908.

Margules, D. L. (1979). Beta-endorphin and endoloxone: Hormones of the autonomic nervous system for the conservation or expenditure of bodily resources and energy in anticipation of famine or feast. *Neuroscience and Biochemical Reviews, 3,* 155–162.

Margules, D. L., Moisset, B., Lewis, M. J., Shibuya, H., & Pert, C. B. (1978). Beta-endorphin is associated with overeating in genetically obese mice (ob/ob) and rats (fa/fa). *Science, 202,* 988–991.

Markey, P. M. (2000). Bystander intervention in computer mediated communication. *Computers in Human Behavior, 16,* 183–188.

Markowitz, S. M., & Arent, S. M. (2010). The exercise and affect relationship: Evidence for a dual-mode model and a modified opponent process theory. *Journal of Sport and Exercise Psychology, 32,* 711–730.

Marks, G., Graham, J. W., & Hansen, W. B. (1992). Social projection and social conformity in adolescent alcohol use: A longitudinal analysis. *Personality and Social Psychology Bulletin, 18,* 96–101.

Marks, G., & Miller, N. (1987). Ten years of research on the false-consensus effect: An empirical and theoretical review. *Psychological Bulletin, 102,* 72–90.

Markus, H. R., & Kitayama, S. (1991). Culture and the self: Implications for cognition, emotion, and motivation. *Psychological Review, 98,* 224–253.

Markus, H. R., & Kitayama, S. (1994). A collective fear of the collective: Implications for selves and theories of selves. *Personality and Social Psychology Bulletin, 20,* 568–579.

Marler, P. (1970). Bird song and speech development: Could there be parallels? *American Scientist, 58,* 669–673.

Marshall, G. D., & Zimbardo, P. G. (1979). Affective consequences of inadequately explained physiological arousal. *Journal of Personality and Social Psychology, 37,* 970–988.

Marshall, J. F., & Teitelbaum, P. (1974). Further analysis of sensory in attention following lateral hypothalamic damage in rats. *Journal of Comparative and Physiological Psychology, 86,* 375–395.

Martin, R. J., Usdan, S., Nelson, S., Umstattd, M. R., LaPlante, D., Perko, M., & Shaffer, H. (2010). Using the theory of planned behavior to predict gambling behavior. *Psychology of Addictive Behaviors, 24,* 89–97.

Martinko, M. J., & Thomson, N. F. (1998). A synthesis and extension of the Weiner and Kelley attribution models. *Basic and Applied Social Psychology, 20,* 271–284.

Masek, K., Petrovicky, P., Sevcik, J., Zidek, Z., & Frankova, D. (2000). Past, present and future of psycho neuroimmunology. *Toxicology, 142,* 179–188.

Maslach, C. (1979). Negative emotional biasing of unexplained arousal. *Journal of Personality and Social Psychology, 37,* 953–969.

Maslow, A. H. (1943). A theory of motivation. *Psychological Review, 50,* 370–396.

Maslow, A. H. (1959). *New knowledge in human values.* New York: Harper & Row.

Maslow, A. H. (1965). *Eupsychian management: A journal.* Homewood, IL: Dorsey.

Maslow, A. H. (1971). *The farther reaches of human nature.* New York: Viking.

Maslow, A. H. (1973a). Self-actualizing people: A study of psychological health. In R. J. Lowry (Ed.), *Dominance, self-esteem, self-actualization: Germinal papers of A. H. Maslow* (pp. 177–201). Monterey, CA: Brooks/Cole.

Maslow, A. H. (1973b). Theory of human motivation. In R. J. Lowry (Ed.), *Dominance, self-esteem, self-actualization: Germinal papers of A. H. Maslow* (pp. 153–173). Monterey, CA: Brooks/Cole.

Maslow, A. H. (1976). *Religion, values, and peak experiences.* Harmondsworth, England: Penguin.

Mason, W. A. (1961). The effects of social restriction on the behavior of rhesus monkeys: II. Tests of gregariousness. *Journal of Physiological and Comparative Psychology, 54,* 287–290.

Masters, W. H., & Johnson, V. E. (1966). *Human sexual response.* Boston, MA: Little, Brown.

Masters, W. H., & Johnson, V. E. (1970). *Human sexual inadequacy.* Boston, MA: Little, Brown.

Masters, W. H., & Johnson, V. E. (1974). *The pleasure bond: A new look at sexuality and commitment.* Boston, MA: Little, Brown.

Mathes, E. W., Zevon, M. A., Roter, P. M., & Joerger, S. M. (1982). Peak experience tendencies: Scale development and theory testing. *Journal of Humanistic Psychology, 22,* 92–108.

Matson, J. L., & Boisjoli, J. A. (2009). The token economy for children with intellectual disability and/or autism: A review. *Research in Developmental Disabilities, 30,* 240–248.

Matsumoto, D., Kasri, F., & Kooken, K. (1999). American Japanese cultural differences in judgements of expression intensity and subjective experience. *Cognition and Emotion, 13,* 201–218.

Mattingly, I. G. (1972). Speech cues and sign stimuli. *American Scientist, 60,* 327–337.

Maturana, H. R., Lettvin, J. Y., McCulloch, W. S., & Pitts, W. H. (1960). Anatomy and physiology of vision in the frog (Ranapipiens). *Journal of General Physiology, 43,* 129–175.

Matuszewich, L., Lorrain, D. S., & Hull, E. M. (2000). Dopamine release in the medial preoptic area of female rats in response to hormonal manipulation and sexual activity. *Behavioral Neuroscience, 114,* 772–782.

Mayer, J. (1955). Regulation of energy intake and the body weight: The glucostatic theory and the lipostatic hypothesis. *Annals of the New York Academy of Science, 63,* 15–43.

Mayer, J. D., & Gaschke, Y. N. (1988). The experience and meta-experience of mood. *Journal of Personality and Social Psychology, 55,* 102–111.

Mayr, E. (1974). Behavior programs and evolutionary strategies. *American Scientist, 62,* 650–659.

McBrearty, S., & Stringer, C. (2007). The coast in color. *Nature, 449,* 793–794.

McCarley, R. W. (1982). REM sleep and depression: Common neurobiological control mechanisms. *American Journal of Psychiatry, 139,* 565–570.

McCarthy, M. M., & Becker, J. B. (2002). Neuroendocrinology of sexual behavior in the female. In J. B. Becker, S. M. Breedlove, D. Crews, & M. M. McCarthy (Eds.), *Behavioral endocrinology* (2nd ed., pp. 117–151). Cambridge, MA: MIT Press.

McClelland, D. C., & Atkinson, J. W. (1948). The projective expression of needs: I. The effect of different intensities of hunger drive on perception. *Journal of Psychology, 25,* 205–222.

McClelland, D. C., Clark, R. A., Roby, T. B., & Atkinson, J. W. (1949). The projective expression of needs: IV. The effect of the need for achievement on thematic apperception. *Journal of Experimental Psychology, 39,* 242–255.

McClintock, M. K. (1971). Menstrual synchrony and suppression. *Nature, 229,* 244–245.

McCoy, N. L., & Pitino, L. (2002). Pheromonal influences on sociosexual behavior in young women. *Physiology and Behavior, 75,* 367–375.

McDermott, C. M., LaHoste, G. J., Chen, C., Musto, A., Bazan, N. G., & Magee, J. C. (2003). Sleep deprivation causes behavioral, synaptic, and membrane excitability alterations in hippocampal neurons. *The Journal of Neuroscience, 23,* 9687–9695.

McDougall, W. (1970). The nature of instincts and their place in the constitution of the human mind. In W. A. Russell (Ed.), *Milestones in motivation* (pp. 18–33). New York: Appleton-Century-Crofts.

McGaugh, J. L., Ferry, B., Vazdarjanova, A., & Roozendaal, B. (2000). Amygdala: Role in modulation of memory storage. In J. P. Aggleton (Ed.), *The amygdala: A functional analysis* (2nd ed., pp. 391–423). New York: Oxford University Press.

McGuire, W. J. (1966). The current status of cognitive consistency theories. In S. Feldman (Ed.), *Cognitive consistency: Motivational antecedents and behavioral consequents* (pp. 1–46). New York: Academic Press.

McKinley, M. J. (2009). Thirst. In G. G. Berntson & J. T. Cacioppo (Eds.), *Handbook of neuroscience for the behavioral sciences* (Vol. 2). Hoboken, NJ: Wiley.

Mechanic, D. (1974). Discussion of research programs on relations between stressful life events and episodes of physical illness. In B. S. Dohrenwend & B. P. Dohrenwend (Eds.), *Stressful life events: Their nature and effects* (pp. 87–97). New York: Wiley.

Mechoulam, R., & Fride, E. (2001). A hunger for cannabinoids. *Nature, 410,* 763–765.

Meddis, R. (1975). On the function of sleep. *Animal Behavior, 23,* 676–691.

Meece, J. L., Blumenfeld, P. C., & Hoyle, R. H. (1988). Students' goal orientations and cognitive engagement in classroom activities. *Journal of Educational Psychology, 80,* 514–523.

Melzack, R. (1961, February). The perception of pain. *Scientific American,* 3–12.

Melzack, R., & Wall, P. D. (1965). Pain mechanisms: A new theory. *Science, 150,* 971–979.

Mesquita, B., & Frijda, N. H. (1992). Cultural variations in emotions: A review. *Psychological Bulletin, 112,* 179–204.

Metzger, R., Cotton, J. W., & Lewis, D. J. (1957). Effect of reinforcement magnitude and order of presentation of different magnitudes on runway behavior. *Journal of Comparative and Physiological Psychology, 50,* 184–188.

Mezulis, A. H., Abramson, L. Y., Hyde, J. S., & Hankin, B. L. (2004). Is there a universal positivity bias in attributions? A meta-analytic review of individual, developmental, and cultural differences in the self-serving attributional bias. *Psychological Bulletin, 130,* 711–747.

Mialon, H. M., & Mialon, S. H. (2006). Violence against women, social learning, and deterrence. *Journal of Evolutionary Economics, 16,* 367–382.

Miczek, K. A., Brykczynski, T., & Grossman, S. P. (1974). Differential effects of lesions in the amygdala, periamygdaloid cortex, and striaterminalis on aggressive behavior in rats. *Journal of Comparative and Physiological Psychology, 87,* 760–771.

Midgley, C., Arunkumar, R., & Urdan, T. C. (1996). "If I don't do well tomorrow, there's a reason": Predictors of adolescents' use of academic self-handicapping strategies. *Journal of Educational Psychology, 88,* 423–434.

Midgley, C., Feldlaufer, H., & Eccles, J. S. (1989). Change in teacher efficacy and student self and task-related beliefs in mathematics during transition to junior high school. *Journal of Educational Psychology, 81,* 247–258.

Mikulincer, M. (1988). Reactance and helplessness following exposure to unsolvable problems: The effects of attributional style. *Journal of Personality and Social Psychology, 54,* 679–686.

Mikulincer, M., & Nizan, B. (1988). Causal attribution, cognitive interference, and the generalization of learned helplessness. *Journal of Personality and Social Psychology, 55,* 470–478.

Mileykovskiy, B. Y., Kiyashchenko, L. I., & Siegel, J. M. (2005). Behavioral correlates of activity in identified hypovretin/orexin neurons. *Neuron, 46,* 787–798.

Milgram, S. (1963). Behavioral study of obedience. *Journal of Abnormal and Social Psychology, 67,* 371–378.

Milgram, S. (1965). Some conditions of obedience and disobedience to authority. *Human Relations, 18,* 57–76.

Milgram, S. (1974). *Obedience to authority.* New York: Harper & Row.

Milgram, S. (1975). The perils of obedience. In S. Milgram (Ed.), *Psychology in today's world.* Boston, MA: Little, Brown.

Millar, M. G. (2001). Promoting health behaviors with door-in-the-face: The influence of the beneficiary of the request. *Psychology, Health and Medicine, 6,* 115–119.

Miller, A. (2008). A critique of positive psychology–or "the new science of happiness." *Journal of Philosophy of Education, 42,* 591–608.

Miller, A. H. (1998). Neuro endocrine and immune system interactions in stress and depression. *Psychiatric Clinical of North America, 21,* 443–463.

Miller, D. T. (1976). Ego involvement and attributions for success and failure. *Journal of Personality and Social Psychology, 34,* 901–906.

Miller, D. T., & Ross, M. (1975). Self-serving biases in the attribution of causality: Factor fiction? *Psychological Bulletin, 82,* 213–225.

Miller, J. G. (1984). Culture and the development of everyday social explanation. *Journal of Personality and Social Psychology, 46,* 961–978.

Miller, L. C., Putcha-Bhagavatula, A., & Pedersen, W. C. (2002). Men's and women's mating preferences: Distinct evolutionary mechanisms? *Current Directions in Psychological Science, 11,* 88–93.

Miller, N. E. (1948). Studies of fear as an acquirable drive: I. Fear as motivation and fear-reduction as reinforcement in the learning of new responses. *Journal of Experimental Psychology, 38,* 89–101.

Miller, N. E. (1963). Some reflections on the law of effect produce a new alternative to drive reduction. In M. R. Jones (Ed.), *Nebraska symposium on motivation* (pp. 65–112). Lincoln, NE: University of Nebraska Press.

Miller, N. E., & Dollard, J. (1941). *Social learning and imitation.* New Haven, CT: Yale University Press.

Miller, R. E., Caul, W. F., & Mirsky, I. A. (1967). Communication of affects between feral and socially isolated monkeys. *Journal of Personality and Social Psychology, 7,* 231–239.

Miller, T. W. (1988). Advances in understanding the impact of stressful life events on health. *Hospital and Community Psychiatry, 39,* 615–622.

Miller, W. R., & Seligman, M. E. P. (1975). Depression and learned helplessness in man. *Journal of Abnormal Psychology, 84,* 228–238.

Mineka, S. (1975). Some new perspectives on conditioned hunger. *Journal of Experimental Psychology, 104,* 134–148.

Mineka, S., & Kihlstrom, J. F. (1978). Unpredictable and uncontrollable events: A new perspective on experimental neurosis. *Journal of Abnormal Psychology, 87,* 256–271.

Mineka, S., & Suomi, S. J. (1978). Social separation in monkeys. *Psychological Bulletin, 85,* 1376–1400.

Mineka, S., Suomi, S. J., & Delizio, R. (1981). Multiple separations in adolescent monkeys: An opponent-process interpretation. *Journal of Experimental Psychology: General*, *110*, 56–85.

Mischel, W. (1973). Towards a cognitive social learning reconceptualization of personality. *Psychological Review*, *80*, 252–283.

Mishkin, M., & Petri, H. L. (1984). Memories and habits: Some implications for the analysis of learning and retention. In L. R. Squire & N. Butters (Eds.), *Neuropsychology of memory* (pp. 287–296). New York: Guilford.

Mittelman, W. (1991). Maslow's study of self-actualization: A reinterpretation. *Journal of Humanistic Psychology*, *31*, 114–135.

Mlot, C. (1998). Probing the biology of emotion. *Science*, *280*, 1005–1007.

Mogenson, G. J. (1976). Neural mechanisms of hunger: Current status and future prospects. In D. Novin et al. (Eds.), *Hunger: Basic mechanisms and clinical implications* (pp. 473–485). New York: Raven Press.

Moltz, H. (1965). Contemporary instinct theory and the fixed action pattern. *Psychological Review*, *72*, 27–47.

Money, J. (1977). The syndrome of abuse dwarfism (psychosocial dwarfism or reversible hyposomatotropinism). *American Journal of Disabled Children*, *131*, 508–513.

Money, J., & Ehrhardt, A. A. (1972). *Man, woman, boy, girl.* Baltimore, MD: Johns Hopkins University Press.

Money, J., & Wolff, G. (1974). Late puberty, retarded growth and reversible hyposomatotropinism (psychosocial dwarfism). *Adolescence*, *9*, 121–134.

Montgomery, K. C. (1953). Exploratory behavior as a function of "similarity" of stimulus situations. *Journal of Comparative and Physiological Psychology*, *46*, 129–133.

Moore, M. M. (1985). Nonverbal courtship patterns in women: Context and consequences. *Ethology and Sociobiology*, *6*, 237–247.

Morell, V. (1993). Evidence found for a possible "aggression gene." *Science*, *260*, 1722–1723.

Morgan, C. T. (1943). *Physiological psychology.* New York: McGraw-Hill.

Morgan, C. T., & Morgan, J. T. (1940). Studies in hunger: II. The relation of gastric denervation and dietary sugar to the effect of insulin upon food-intake in the rat. *Journal of Genetic Psychology*, *57*, 153–163.

Morris, D. (1967). *The naked ape.* New York: Dell.

Morrissette, J. O. (1958). An experimental study of the theory of structural balance. *Human Relations*, *11*, 239–254.

Morrone, J. V., Depue, R. A., Scherer, A. J., & White, T. L. (2000). Film-induced incentive motivation and positive activation in relation to agentic and affiliative components of extraversion. *Personality and Individual Differences*, *29*, 199–216.

Morrongiello, B. A., Sandomierski, M., & Valla, J. (2010). Early identification of children at risk of unintentional injury: A sensation seeking scale for children 2-5 years of age. *Accident Analysis and Prevention*, *42*, 1332–1337.

Mortenson, F. J. (1975). *Animal behavior: Theory and research.* Monterey, CA: Brooks/Cole.

Moruzzi, G., & Magoun, H. W. (1949). Brain stem reticular formation and activation of the EEG. *Electroencephalography and Clinical Neurophysiology*, *1*, 455–473.

Moscovici, S., & Faucheux, C. (1972). Social influence, conformity bias, and the study of active minorities. In L. Berkowitz (Ed.), *Advances in experimental social psychology* (Vol. 6, pp. 149–202). New York: Academic Press.

Mostow, A. J., Izard, C. E., Fine, S., & Trentacosta, C. J. (2002). Modeling emotional, cognitive, and behavioral predictors of peer acceptance. *Child Development*, *73*, 1775–1787.

Mowrer, O. H. (1947). On the dual nature of learning: A reinterpretation of "conditioning" and "problem solving." *Harvard Educational Review*, *17*, 102–148.

Mowrer, O. H. (1960). *Learning theory and behavior.* New York: Wiley.

Moyer, K. E. (1971). *The physiology of hostility.* Chicago, IL: Markham.

Mueller, C. M., & Dweck, C. S. (1998). Praise for intelligence can undermine children's motivation and performance. *Journal of Personality and Social Psychology*, *75*, 33–52.

Mullen, B. (1983). Operationalizing the effect of the group on the individual: A self-attention perspective. *Journal of Experimental Social Psychology*, *19*, 295–322.

Mumme, D. L., & Fernald, A. (2003). The infant as onlooker: Learning from emotional reactions observed in a television scenario. *Child Development*, *74*, 221–237.

Murray, H. A. (1936). Techniques for a systematic investigation of fantasy. *Journal of Psychology*, *3*, 115–143.

Murray, H. A. (1938). *Explorations in personality.* New York: Oxford University Press.

Myer, J. S. (1964). Stimulus control of mouse-killing rats. *Journal of Comparative and Physiological Psychology*, *58*, 112–117.

Myer, J. S., & White, R. T. (1965). Aggressive motivation in the rat. *Animal Behavior*, *13*, 430–433.

Myers, H. H., & Siegel, P. S. (1985). The motivation to breast feed: A fit to the opponent-process theory? *Journal of Personality and Social Psychology*, *49*, 188–193.

Nash, L. T. (1978). The development of mother-infant relationship in wild baboons (Papioanubis). *Animal Behavior, 26,* 746–759.

Nathawat, S. S., & Singh, R. (1997). The effect of need for achievement on attributional style. *Journal of Social Psychology, 137,* 55–62.

National Safety Council. (1986). *Accident facts.* Chicago, IL: National Safety Council.

National Task Force on the Prevention and Treatment of Obesity. (1994). Weight cycling. *Journal of the American Medical Association, 272,* 1196–1202.

Nauta, W. J. H. (1946). Hypopthalamic regulation of sleep in rats: Experimental study. *Journal of Neurophysiology, 9,* 285–316.

Needles, D. J., & Abramson, L. Y. (1990). Positive life events, attributional style, and hopefulness: Testing a model of recovery from depression. *Journal of Abnormal Psychology, 99,* 156–165.

Neher, A. (1991). Maslow's theory of motivation: A critique. *Journal of Humanistic Psychology, 31,* 89–112.

Nelson, K. G. (2010). Exploration of classroom participation in the presence of a token economy. *Journal of Instructional Psychology, 37,* 49–56.

Nemme, H. E., & White, K. M. (2010). Texting while driving: Psychosocial influences on young people's texting intentions and behaviour. *Accident Analysis and Prevention, 42,* 1257–1265.

Neria, Y., Solomon, Z., Ginzburg, K., & Dekel, R. (2000). Sensation seeking, wartime performance, and long-term adjustment among Israeli war veterans. *Personality and Individual Differences, 29,* 921–932.

Neto, F. (1995). Conformity and independence revisited. *Social Behavior and Personality, 23,* 217–222.

Neuberg, S. L., Cialdini, R. B., Brown, S. L., Luce, C., Sagarin, B. J., & Lewis, B. P. (1997). Does empathy lead to anything more than superficial helping? Comment on Batson et al. (1997). *Journal of Personality and Social Psychology, 73,* 510–516.

New, J., Cosmides, L., & Tooby, J. (2007). Category-specific attention for animals reflects ancestral priorities, not expertise. *Proceedings of the National Academy of Sciences, 104,* 16598–16603.

Nisbett, R. E., Caputo, C., Legant, P., & Marecek, J. (1973). Behavior as seen by the actor and as seen by the observer. *Journal of Personality and Social Psychology, 27,* 154–164.

Nouwen, A., Ford, T., Balan, A. T., Twisk, J., Ruggiero, L., & White, D. (2011). Longitudinal motivational predictors of dietary self-care and diabetes control in adults with newly diagnosed Type 2 diabetes Mellitus. *Health Psychology, 30,* 771–779.

Novin, D. (1976). Visceral mechanisms in the control of food intake. In D. Novin et al. (Eds.), *Hunger: Basic mechanisms and clinical implications.* New York: Raven Press.

Nowicki, S., & Strickland, B. R. (1973). A locus of control scale for children. *Journal of Consulting and Clinical Psychology, 40,* 148–154.

Oakley, D. A. (1983). The varieties of human memory: A phylogenetic approach. In A. Mayes (Ed.), *Memory in humans and animals* (pp. 20–82). Wokingham, England: Van Nostrand Reinhold.

Ogilvie, R. D. (2001). The process of falling asleep. *Sleep Medicine Reviews, 5,* 247–270.

O'Keefe, D. J., & Hale, S. L. (2001). An odds-ratio-based metaanalysis of research on the door-in-the-face influence strategy. *Communication Reports, 14,* 31–38.

Oken, D. (1967). The psychophysiology and psychoendocrinology of stress and emotion. In M. H. Appley & R. Trumbull (Eds.), *Psychological stress* (pp. 43–62). New York: Appleton-Century-Crofts.

Olds, J., & Milner, P. (1954). Positive reinforcement produced by electrical stimulation of septal area and other regions of rat brain. *Journal of Comparative and Physiological Psychology, 47,* 419–427.

Olff, M. (1999). Stress, depression and immunity: The role of defense and coping styles. *Psychiatry Research, 85,* 7–15.

Oliver, J. E., Jose, P. E., & Brough, P. (2006). Confirmatory factor analysis of the Work Locus of Control scale. *Educational and Psychological Measurement, 66,* 835–851.

Olvera, R. L. (2002). Intermittent explosive disorder: Epidemiology, diagnosis and management. *CNS Drugs, 16,* 517–526.

Oomura, Y. (1976). Significance of glucose, insulin, and free fattyacid on the hypothalamic feeding and satiety neurons. In D. Novin et al. (Eds.), *Hunger: Basic mechanisms and clinical implications.* New York: Raven Press.

Ortony, A., & Turner, T. J. (1990). What's basic about basic emotions? *Psychological Review, 97,* 315–331.

Overholser, J. C. (1992). Sense of humor when coping with life stress. *Personality and Individual Differences, 13,* 799–804.

Overmier, J. B. (1968). Interference with avoidance behavior. *Journal of Experimental Psychology, 78,* 340–343.

Overmier, J. B., & Lawry, J. A. (1979). Pavlovian conditioning and the mediation of behavior. In

G. H. Bower (Ed.), *The psychology of learning and motivation* (Vol. *13*, pp. 1–55). New York: Academic Press.

Overmier, J. B., & Seligman, M. E. P. (1967). Effects of inescapable shock upon subsequent escape and avoidance learning. *Journal of Comparative and Physiological Psychology*, *63*, 23–33.

Ozkan, T., & Lajunen, T. (2005). Multidimensional Traffic Locus of Control Scale (T-LOC): Factor structure and relationship to risky driving. *Personality and Individual Differences*, *38*, 533–545.

Padgett, W. L., Garcia, H. D., & Pernice, M. B. (1984). A travel training program: Reducing wandering in a residential center for developmentally disabled persons. *Behavior Modification*, *8*, 317–330.

Palca, J. (1989). Sleep researchers awake to possibilities. *Science*, *245*, 351–352.

Panksepp, J. (1992). A critical role for "affective neuroscience" in resolving what is basic about basic emotions. *Psychological Review*, *99*, 554–560.

Panksepp, J., & Trowill, J. (1971). Positive and negative contrast in licking with shifts in sucrose concentration as a function of food deprivation. *Learning and Motivation*, *2*, 49–57.

Papez, J. W. (1937). A proposed mechanism of emotion. *Archives of Neurological Psychiatry*, *38*, 725–743.

Pappenheimer, J. R. (1976). The sleep factor. *Scientific American*, *235*(2), 24–29.

Parkinson, B., & Manstead, A. S. R. (1981). An examination of the roles played by meaning of feedback and attention to feedback in the "Valins effect." *Journal of Personality and Social Psychology*, *40*, 239–245.

Parmentier, R., Ohtsu, H., Djebbara-Hannas, Z., Valatx, J.-L., Watanabe, T., & Lin, J.-S. (2002). Anatomical, physiological, and pharmacological characteristics of histidine decarboxylase knock-out mice: Evidence for the role of brain histamine in behavioral and sleep-wake control. *The Journal of Neuroscience*, *22*, 7695–7711.

Patton, R. G., & Gardner, L. I. (1963). *Growth failure in maternal deprivation*. Springfield, IL: Thomas.

Pavlov, I. P. (1960). *Conditioned reflexes*. New York: Dover.

Payne, J., D., & Kensinger, E. A. (2010). *Current Directions in Psychological Science*, *19*, 290–295.

Pearce, J. M. (1997). *Animal learning and cognition*. East Sussex, UK: Psychology Press.

Pearlman, C. A. (1970). The adaptive function of dreaming. In E. Hartmann (Ed.), *Sleep and dreaming* (pp. 329–334). Boston, MA: Little, Brown.

Pearsall, M. J., Christian, M. S., & Ellis, A. P. J. (2010). Motivating interdependent teams: Individual rewards, shared rewards, or something in between? *Journal of Applied Psychology*, *95*, 183–191.

Peck, M. S. (1978). *The road less traveled: A new psychology of love, traditional values and spiritual growth*. New York: Touchstone.

Peeke, H. V. S. (1969). Habituation of con-specific aggression in the three-spined stickle-back (*Gasterosteuaculeatus L.*). *Behaviour*, *35*, 137–156.

Peets, J. M., & Pomeranz, B. (1978). CXBK mice deficient in opiate receptors show poor electro acupuncture analgesia. *Nature*, *273*, 675–676.

Pennisi, E. (1997). Tracing molecules that make the brain body connection. *Science*, *275*, 930–931.

Pepitone, A. (1966). Problems of consistency models. In S. Feldman (Ed.), *Cognitive consistency*. New York: Academic Press.

Perkins, H. W., Meilman, P. W., Leichliter, J. S., Cashin, J. R., & Presley, C. A. (1999). Misperceptions of the norms for the frequency of alcohol and other drug use on college campuses. *Journal of American College Health*, *47*, 253–258.

Perrin, S., & Spencer, C. P. (1980). The Asch effect–A child of its time? *Bulletin of the British Psychological Society*, *32*, 405–406.

Peterson, C., & Park, N. (2011). Character strengths and virtues: Their role in well-being. In S. I. Donaldson, M. Csikszentmihalyi, & J. Nakamura (Eds.), *Applied positive psychology: Improving everyday life, health, schools, work, and society* (pp. 49–62). New York: Psychology Press.

Peterson, C., & Seligman, M. E. P. (2004). *Character strengths and virtues: A handbook and classification*. New York: Oxford University Press.

Peterson, C., Seligman, M. E. P., & Vaillant, G. E. (1988). Pessimistic explanatory style is a risk factor for physical illness: A thirty-five-year longitudinal study. *Journal of Personality and Social Psychology*, *55*, 23–27.

Petri, H. L., & Mills, C. J. (1977). Effects of imprinting and isolation on aggressive responses in chicks. *Aggressive Behavior*, *3*, 173–183.

Petri, H. L., & Mishkin, M. (1994). Behaviorism, cognitivism and the neuro psychology of memory. *American Scientist*, *82*, 30–37.

Peyron, C., Faraco, J., Rogers, W., Ripley, B., Overeem, S., Charnay, Y., Nevsimalova, S., Aldrich, M., Reynolds, D., Albin, R., Li, R., Hungs, M., Pedrazzoli, M., Padigaru, M., Kucherlapati, M., Fan, J., Maki, R., Lammers, G. J., Bouras, C., Kucherlapati, R., Nishino, S., & Mignot, E. (2000). A mutation in a case of early onset narcolepsy and a generalized absence of hypocretin peptides in human narcoleptic brains. *Nature Medicine, 6,* 991–997.

Pfaff, D. W., & Pfaffmann, C. (1969). Behavioral and electro physiological responses of male rats to female rat urine odors. In C. Pfaffmann (Ed.), *Olfaction and taste.* New York: Rockefeller University Press.

Pfaffmann, C. (1960). The pleasures of sensation. *Psychological Review, 67,* 253–268.

Pfaus, J. G., Kippin, T. E., & Centeno, S. (2001). Conditioning and sexual behavior: A review. *Hormones and Behavior, 40,* 291–321.

Picazo-Vela, S., Chou, S. Y., Melcher, A. J., & Pearson, J. M. (2010). Why provide an online review? An extended theory of planned behavior and the role of Big Five personality traits. *Computers in Human Behavior, 26,* 685–696.

Piliavin, J. A., Callero, P. L., & Evans, D. E. (1982). Addiction to altruism? Opponent-process theory and habitual blood donation. *Journal of Personality and Social Psychology, 43,* 1200–1213.

Pinheiro, A., Root, T., & Bulik, C. M. (2009). The genetics of anorexia nervosa: Current findings and future perspectives. *International Journal of Child and Adolescent Health, 2,* 153–163.

Pintrich, P. R., & DeGroot, E. V. (1990). Motivational and self-regulated learning components of classroom academic performance. *Journal of Educational Psychology, 82,* 33–40.

Pi-Sunyer, F. X. (1994). The fattening of America. *Journal of the American Medical Association, 272,* 238.

Pittman, T. S., & Pittman, N. L. (1980). Deprivation of control and the attribution process. *Journal of Personality and Social Psychology, 39,* 377–389.

Platania, J., & Moran, G. P. (2001). Social facilitation as a function of theme represence of others. *The Journal of Social Psychology, 141,* 190–197.

Ploog, D. W., & Pirke, K. M. (1987). Psychobiology of anorexia nervosa. *Psychological Medicine, 17,* 843–859.

Plotnik, J. M., deWaal, F. B. M., & Reiss, D. (2006). Self-recognition in an Asian elephant. *Proceedings of the National Academy of Sciences, 103,* 17053–17057.

Plotnikoff, R. C., Lippke, S., Courneya, K. S., Birkett, N., & Sigal, R. J. (2008). Physical activity and social cognitive theory: A test in a population sample of adults with Type 1 or Type 2 diabetes. *Applied Psychology: An International Review, 57,* 628–643.

Plutchik, R., & Ax, A. (1967). A critique of "determinants of emotional states" by Schachter and Singer (1962). *Psychophysiology, 4,* 79–82.

Polivy, J., & Herman, C. P. (2002). Causes of eating disorders. *Annual Review of Psychology, 53,* 187–213.

Pomeranz, B. (1981). Neural mechanisms of acupuncture analgesia. In S. Lipton (Ed.), *Persistent pain: Modern methods of treatment.* London: Academic Press.

Pomeranz, B., Cheng, R., & Law, P. (1977). Acupuncture reduces electro physiological and behavioral responses to noxious stimuli. *Experimental Neurology, 54,* 172–178.

Pool, R. (1989). Illuminating jetlag. *Science, 244,* 1256–1257.

Popkin, M. K., Stillner, V., Pierce, C. M., Williams, M., & Gregory, P. (1976). Recent life changes and outcome of prolonged competitive stress. *Journal of Nervous and Mental Disease, 163,* 302–306.

Porkka-Heiskanen, T. (1999). Adenosine in sleep and wakefulness. *Annals of Medicine, 31,* 125–129.

Porkka-Heiskanen, T., Strecker, R. E., Thakkar, M., Bjorkum, A. A., Greene, R. W., & McCarley, R. W. (1997). Adenosine: A mediator of the sleep-inducing effects of prolonged wakefulness. *Science, 276,* 1265–1268.

Povinelli, D. J., Gallup, G. G., Jr., Eddy, T. J., Bierschwale, D. T., Engstrom, M. C., Perilloux, H. K., & Toxopeus, I. B. (1997). Chimpanzees recognize themselves in mirrors. *Animal Behaviour, 53,* 1083–1088.

Powell, J., Dawkins, L., & Davis, R. E. (2002). Smoking, reward responsiveness, and response inhibition: Tests of an incentive motivational model. *Biological Psychiatry, 51,* 151–163.

Powley, T. L., & Keesey, R. E. (1970). Relationship of body weight to the lateral hypothalamic feeding syndrome. *Journal of Comparative and Physiological Psychology, 70,* 25–36.

Pressman, M. R. (1986). Sleep and sleep disorders: An introduction. *Clinical Psychology Review, 6,* 1–9.

Price, D. D., Finniss, D. G., & Benedetti, F. (2008). A comprehensive review of the placebo effect: Recent advances and current thought. *Annual Review of Psychology, 59,* 565–590.

Price, D. D., Milling, L. S., Kirsch, I., Duff, A., Montgomery, G. H., & Nicholls, S. S. (1999). An analysis of factors that contribute to the magnitude of placebo analgesia in an experimental paradigm. *Pain, 83,* 147–156.

Privette, G. (1983). Peak experience, peak performance, and flow: A comparative analysis of positive human experiences. *Journal of Personality and Social Psychology, 45,* 1361–1368.

Probst, M., VanCoppenolle, H., Vandereycken, W., & Goris, M. (1992). Body image assessment in anorexia nervosa patients and university students by means of video distortion: Are liability study. *Journal of Psychosomatic Research, 36,* 89–97.

Rachlin, H. (1976). *Behavior and learning.* San Francisco, CA: Freeman.

Rachman, S. (1966). Sexual fetishism: An experimental analogue. *Psychological Record, 16,* 293–296.

Rachman, S., & Hodgson, R. J. (1968). Experimentally induced "sexual fetishism": Replication and development. *Psychological Record, 18,* 25–27.

Rahe, R. H. (1974). The pathway between subjects' recent life change and their near-future illness reports: Representative results and methodological issues. In B. S. Dohrenwend & B. P. Dohrenwend (Eds.), *Stressful life events: Their nature and effects.* New York: Wiley.

Rainnie, D. G., Grunze, H. C. R., McCarley, R. W., & Greene, R. W. (1994). Adenosine inhibition of mesopontine cholinergic neurons: Implications for EEG arousal. *Science, 263,* 689–692.

Rajecki, D. W., Ivins, B., & Reins, B. (1976). Social discrimination and aggressive pecking in domestic chicks. *Journal of Comparative and Physiological Psychology, 90,* 442–452.

Ramirez, J., Bryant, J., & Zillmann, D. (1982). Effects of erotica on retaliatory behavior as a function of level of prior provocation. *Journal of Personality and Social Psychology, 43,* 971–978.

Ramos, S. M., & DeBold, J. F. (2000). Fos expression in female hamsters after various stimuli associated with mating. *Physiology and Behavior, 70,* 557–566.

Ramsay, A. D., & Hess, E. H. (1954). A laboratory approach to the study of imprinting. *Wilson Bulletin, 66,* 196–206.

Rand, C. S. W., & Kuldau, J. M. (1992). Epidemiology of bulimia and symptoms in a general population: Sex, age, race, and socio economic status. *International Journal of Eating Disorders, 11,* 37–44.

Raps, C. S., Peterson, D., Jonas, M., & Seligman, M. E. P. (1982). Patient behavior in hospitals: Helplessness, reactance, or both? *Journal of Personality and Social Psychology, 42,* 1036–1041.

Rasch, B., & Born, J. (2008). Reactivation and consolidation of memory during sleep. *Current Directions in Psychological Science, 17,* 188–192.

Rastam, M., Gillberg, C., & Wahlstrom, J. (1991). Chromosomes in anorexia nervosa. A study of 47 cases including a population-based group: A research note. *Journal of Child Psychology and Psychiatry, 32,* 695–701.

Rattenborg, N. C., Lima, S. L., & Amlaner, C. J. (1999). Facultative control of avian unihemispheric sleep under the risk of predation. *Behavioral Brain Research, 15,* 163–172.

Ravelli, G. P., Stein, Z. A., & Susser, M. W. (1976). Obesity in young men after famine exposure in utero and early infancy. *New England Journal of Medicine, 295,* 349–353.

Ray, J. J. (1982). Achievement motivation and preferred probability of success. *Journal of Social Psychology, 116,* 255–261.

Raybould, H. E. (2007). Sensing of glucose in the gastrointestinal tract. *Autonomic Neuroscience: Basic and Clinical, 133,* 86–90.

Raybould, H. E., Glatzle, J., Freeman, S. L., Whited, K., Darcel, N., Liou, A., Bohan, D. (2006). Detection of macronutrients in the intestinal wall. *Autonomic Neuroscience, 30,* 28–33.

Raynor, H. A., & Epstein, L. H. (2001). Dietary variety, energy regulation, and obesity. *Psychological Bulletin, 127,* 325–341.

Raynor, J. O. (1969). Future orientation and motivation of immediate activity: An elaboration of the theory of achievement motivation. *Psychological Review, 76,* 606–610.

Raynor, J. O. (1970). Relationship between achievement related motives, future orientation and academic performance. *Journal of Personality and Social Psychology, 15,* 28–33.

Raynor, J. O. (1974). Future orientation in the study of achievement motivation. In J. W. Atkinson & J. O. Raynor (Eds.), *Motivation and achievement.* Washington, DC: V. H. Winston.

Razran, G. (1961). The observable unconscious and the inferable conscious in current Soviet psychophysiology: Interoceptive conditioning, semantic conditioning and the orienting reflex. *Psychological Review, 68,* 81–147.

Rechtschaffen, A. (1967). Dream reports and dream experiences. *Experimental Neurology,* (Suppl. 4), 4–15.

Rechtschaffen, A., & Bergmann, B. M. (1995). Sleep deprivation in the rat by the disk-over-water method. *Behavioural Brain Research, 69,* 55–63.

Rechtschaffen, A., Bergmann, B. M., Everson, C. A., Kushida, C. A., & Gilliland, M. A. (1989). Sleep deprivation in the rat: X. Integration and discussion of the findings. *Sleep, 12,* 68–87.

Rechtschaffen, A., Gilliland, M. A., Bergmann, B. M., & Winter, J. B. (1983). Physiological correlates of prolonged sleep deprivation in rats. *Science, 221,* 182–184.

Redd, M., & deCastro, J. M. (1992). Social facilitation of eating: Effects of social instruction on food intake. *Physiology and Behavior, 52*, 749–754.

Reeder, G. D. (1982). Let's give the fundamental attribution error another chance. *Journal of Personality and Social Psychology, 43*, 341–344.

Reisenzein, R. (1983). The Schachter theory of emotion: Two decades later. *Psychological Bulletin, 94*, 239–264.

Reiss, D., & Marino, L. (2001). Mirror self-recognition in the bottlenose dolphin: A case of cognitive convergence. *Proceedings of the National Academy of Sciences, 98*, 5937–5942.

Restle, F. (1957). Discrimination of cues in mazes: A resolution of the "place-vs.-response" question. *Psychological Review, 64*, 217–228.

Reynolds, G. S. (1975). *A primer of operant conditioning* (Rev. ed.). Glenview, IL: Scott, Foresman.

Ridley, M. (1993). *The red queen: Sex and the evolution of human nature.* New York: Penguin.

Riesen, A. H. (1961). Excessive arousal effects of stimulation after early sensory deprivation. In P. Solomon et al. (Eds.), *Sensory deprivation* (pp. 34–40). Cambridge, MA: Harvard University Press.

Rise, J., Sheeran, P., & Hukkelberg, S. (2010). The role of self-identity in the theory of planned behavior: A meta-analysis. *Journal of Applied Social Psychology, 40*, 1085–1105.

Rissman, E. (1995). An alternative animal model for the study of female sexual behavior. *Current Directions in Psychological Science, 4*, 6–10.

Roberts, J. L., Chen, C. C., Dionne, F. T., & Gee, C. E. (1982). Peptide hormone gene expression in heterogeneous tissues. *Trends in Neurosciences, 5*, 314–317.

Roberts, S. B., Fuss, P., Heyman, M. B., Evans, W. J., Tsay, R., Rasmussen, H., Fiatarone, M., Cortiella, J., Dallal, G. E., & Young, V. R. (1994). Control of food intake in older men. *Journal of the American Medical Association, 272*, 1601–1606.

Robinson, T. E., & Berridge, K. C. (2000). The psychology and neurobiology of addiction: An incentive-sensitization view. *Addiction, 95*(Suppl. 2), s91–s117.

Robinson, T. E., & Berridge, K. C. (2001). Incentive-sensitization and addiction. *Addiction, 96*, 103–114.

Robinson, T. E., & Berridge, K. C. (2003). Addiction. *Annual Review of Psychology, 54*, 25–53.

Rodin, J. (1981). Current status of the internal-external hypothesis for obesity: What went wrong? *American Psychologist, 36*, 361–372.

Rogers, C. R. (1951). *Client-centered therapy: Its current practice, implication, and theory.* Boston, MA: Houghton Mifflin.

Rogers, C. R. (1961). *On becoming a person: A therapist's view of psychotherapy.* Boston, MA: Houghton Mifflin.

Rogers, R. W., & Deckner, D. W. (1975). Effects of fear appeals and physiological arousal upon emotion, attitudes and cigarette smoking. *Journal of Personality and Social Psychology, 32*, 222–230.

Rolls, B. J., van Duijvenvoorde, P. M., & Rolls, E. T. (1984). Pleasantness changes and food intake in a varied four course meal. *Appetite, 5*, 337–348.

Romanes, G. J. (1888). *Animal intelligence.* New York: Appleton.

Roos, P. E., & Cohen, L. H. (1987). Sex roles and social support as moderators of life stress adjustment. *Journal of Personality and Social Psychology, 52*, 576–585.

Roselli, C. E., Handa, R. J., & Resko, J. A. (1989). Quantitative distribution of nuclear androgen receptors in micro dissected areas of the rat brain. *Neuro Endocrinology, 49*, 449–453.

Rosenthal, R., Archer, D., DiMatteo, M. R., Koivumaki, J. H., & Rogers, P. L. (1974). The language without words. *Psychology Today, 8*, 64–68.

Roskies, E., Iida-Miranda, M., & Strobel, M. G. (1975). The applicability of the life events approach to the problems of immigration. *Journal of Psychosomatic Research, 19*, 235–240.

Ross, L. (1977). The intuitive psychologist and his short comings: Distortions in the attribution process. In L. Berkowitz (Ed.), *Advances in experimental social psychology* (Vol. 10, pp. 173–220). New York: Academic Press.

Ross, L., Greene, D., & House, P. (1977). The false consensus effect: An egocentric bias in social perception and attributional processes. *Journal of Experimental Social Psychology, 13*, 279–301.

Ross, L. D., Amabile, T. M., & Steinmetz, J. L. (1977). Social roles, social control, and biases in social-perception processes. *Journal of Personality and Social Psychology, 35*, 485–494.

Ross, R. R. (1964). Positive and negative partial-reinforcement extinction effects carried through continuous reinforcement, changed motivation and changed response. *Journal of Experimental Psychology, 68*, 492–502.

Rossano, M. J. (2003). *Evolutionary psychology: The science of human behavior and evolution.* Hoboken, NJ: Wiley.

Rosvold, H. E., Mirsky, A. F., & Pribram, K. H. (1954). Influence of amygdalectomy on social behavior in monkeys. *Journal of Comparative and Physiological Psychology, 47,* 173–178.

Rotter, J. B. (1954). *Social learning and clinical psychology.* Englewood Cliffs, NJ: Prentice Hall.

Rotter, J. B. (1966). Generalized expectancies for internal versus external control of reinforcement. *Psychological Monographs, 80,* 1–28.

Rotter, J. B. (1975). Some problems and misconceptions related to the construct of internal versus external control of reinforcement. *Journal of Consulting and Clinical Psychology, 43,* 36–67.

Revonsuo, A. (2000). The reinterpretation of dreams: An evolutionary hypothesis of the function of dreaming. *Behavioral and Brain Sciences, 23,* 793–1121.

Rowland, W. J. (1989a). The effects of body size, aggression and nuptial coloration on competition for territories in male three spine stickle backs (*Gasterosteusaculeatus*). *Animal Behavior, 37,* 282–289.

Rowland, W. J. (1989b). The ethological basis of mate choice in male three-spine stickle backs (*Gasterosteusaculeatus*). *Animal Behavior, 38,* 112–120.

Rowland, W. J. (1989c). Mate choice and the super normality effect in female stickle backs (*Gasterosteusaculeatus*). *Behavioral Ecology and Sociobiology, 24,* 433–438.

Roy-Byrne, P. P., Uhde, T. W., & Post, R. M. (1986). Effects of one night's sleep deprivation on mood and behavior in panic disorder. *Archives of General Psychiatry, 43,* 895–899.

Rozin, P., Dow, S., Moscovitch, M., & Rajaram, S. (1998). What causes humans to begin and end a meal? A role for memory for what has been eaten, as evidenced by a study of multiple meal eating in amnesiac patients. *Psychological Science, 9,* 392–396.

Rozin, P., & Kalat, J. W. (1971). Specific hungers and poison avoidance as adaptive specializations of learning. *Psychological Review, 78,* 459–486.

Ruch, L. O., & Holmes, T. H. (1971). Scaling of life change: Comparison of direct and indirect methods. *Journal of Psychosomatic Research, 15,* 221–227.

Ruff, G. E., & Korchin, S. J. (1967). Adaptive stress behavior. In M. H. Appley & R. Trumbull (Eds.), *Psychological stress* (pp. 297–306). New York: Appleton-Century-Crofts.

Russell, J. A. (1980). A circumplex model of affect. *Journal of Personality and Social Psychology, 39,* 1161–1178.

Russell, J. A. (1983). Pan cultural aspects of the human conceptual organization of emotions. *Journal of Personality and Social Psychology, 45,* 1281–1288.

Russell, J. A. (1991a). The contempt expression and the relativity thesis. *Motivation and Emotion, 15,* 149–184.

Russell, J. A. (1991b). Culture and the categorization of emotions. *Psychological Bulletin, 110,* 426–450.

Russell, J. A. (1994). Is there universal recognition of emotion from facial expression? A review of the cross-cultural studies. *Psychological Bulletin, 115,* 102–141.

Russell, J. A. (2003). Core affect and the psychological construction of emotion. *Psychological Review, 110,* 145–172.

Russell, J. A., Bachorowski, J. A., & Fernandez-Dols, J. M. (2003). Facial and vocal expressions of emotion. *Annual Review of Psychology, 54,* 329–349.

Russell, R. J. H., Wells, P. A., & Rushton, J. P. (1985). Evidence for genetic similarity detection in human marriage. *Ethology and Sociobiology, 6,* 183–187.

Russell, W. A. (1970). *Milestones in motivation: Contributions to the psychology of drive and purpose.* New York: Appleton Century-Crofts.

Rutkowski, G. K., Gruder, C. L., & Romer, D. (1983). Group cohesiveness, social norms, and bystander intervention. *Journal of Personality and Social Psychology, 44,* 545–552.

Ryan, A. M., & Pintrich, P. R. (1997). "Should I ask for help?" The role of motivation and attitudes in adolescents' help seeking in math class. *Journal of Educational Psychology, 89,* 329–341.

Ryan, R. M., & Deci, E. L. (2000). Self-determination theory and the facilitation of intrinsic motivation, social development, and well-being. *American Psychologist, 55,* 68–78.

Ryan, R. M., & LaGuardia, J. G. (2000). What is being optimized? Self-determination theory and basic psychological needs. In S. H. Qualls & N. Abeles (Eds.), *Psychology and the aging revolution: How we adapt to longer life.* Washington, DC: American Psychological Association.

Ryan, R. M., Stiller, J. D., & Lynch, J. H. (1994). Representations of relationships to teachers, parents, and friends as predictors of academic motivation and self esteem. *Journal of Early Adolescence, 14,* 226–249.

Sabini, J., Siepmann, M., & Stein, J. (2001). The really fundamental attribution error in social psychological research. *Psychological Inquiry, 12,* 1–15.

Sackett, G. P. (1967). Some persistent effects of different rearing conditions on preadult social behavior of monkeys. *Journal of Comparative and Physiological Psychology, 64,* 363–365.

Safdar, S., Friedlmeier, W., Matsumoto, D., Hee Yoo, S., Kwantes, C. T., Kakai, H., & Shigemasu E. (2009,

January). Variations of emotional display rules within and across cultures: A comparison between Canada, USA, and Japan. *Canadian Journal of Behavioural Science/Revue Canadienne Des Sciences Du Comportement, 41*(1), 1–10. [serial online]. Retrieved March 14, 2012, from PsycINFO, Ipswich, MA.

Saito, A., Williams, J. A., Waxler, S. H., & Goldfine, I. D. (1982). Alterations of brain cholecystokinin receptors in mice made obese with gold thioglucose. *Journal of Neurochemistry, 39*, 525–528.

Salamone, J. D. (1992). Complex motor and sensorimotor function of striatal and accumbens dopamine: Involvement in instrumental behavior processes. *Psychopharmacology, 107*, 160–174.

Saltmarsh, M. (2001). Thirst: Or, why do people drink? *Nutrition Bulletin, 26*, 53–58.

Sanders, G. S. (1981). Driven by distraction: An integrative review of social facilitation theory and research. *Journal of Experimental Social Psychology, 17*, 227–251.

Sanders, G. S., & Baron, R. S. (1975). The motivating effects of distraction on task performance. *Journal of Personality and Social Psychology, 32*, 956–963.

Sanders, G. S., & Mullen, B. (1983). Accuracy in perceptions of consensus: Differential tendencies of people with majority and minority positions. *European Journal of Social Psychology, 13*, 57–70.

Sansone, C., & Harackiewicz, J. M. (Eds.). (2000). *Intrinsic and extrinsic motivation: The search for optimal motivation and performance.* San Diego, CA: Academic Press.

Saper, C. B., Fuller, P. M., Pedersen, N. P., Lu, J., & Scammell, T. E. (2010). Sleep state switching. *Neuron, 68*, 1023–1042.

Sapolsky, B. S., & Zillmann, D. (1981). The effect of soft-core and hard-core erotica on provoked and unprovoked hostile behavior. *Journal of Sex Research, 17*, 319–343.

Sauter, D., LeGuen, O., Haun, D. (2011, December). Categorical perception of emotional facial expressions does not require lexical categories. *Emotion, 11*(6), 1479–1483. [serial online]. Retrieved March 14, 2012, from PsycINFO, Ipswich, MA

Sawyer, C. H. (1969). Regulatory mechanisms of secretion of gonadotrophic hormones. In W. Haymaker et al. (Eds.), *The hypothalamus* (pp. 389–430). Springfield, IL: Thomas.

Schachter, S. (1959). *The psychology of affiliation: Experimental studies of the sources of gregariousness.* Stanford CA: Stanford University Press.

Schachter, S. (1964). The interaction of cognitive and physiological determinants of emotional state.

In L. Berkowitz (Ed.), *Advances in experimental social psychology* (Vol. 1, pp. 49–80). New York: Academic Press.

Schachter, S., & Singer, J. E. (1962). Cognitive, social, and physiological determinants of emotional state. *Psychological Review, 69*, 379–399.

Schallert, T., Pendergrass, M., & Farrar, S. B. (1982). Cholecystokinin-octapeptide effects on eating elicited by "external" versus "internal" cues in rats. *Appetite: Journal for Intake Research, 3*, 81–90.

Schein, M. W., & Hale, E. B. (1965). Stimuli eliciting sexual behavior. In F. Beach (Ed.), *Sex and behavior* (pp. 440–482). New York: Wiley.

Scherag, S., Hebebrand, J., & Hinney, A. (2010). Eating disorders: The current status of molecular genetic research. *European Child and Adolescent Psychiatry, 19*, 211–226.

Schildkraut, J. J., & Kety, S. S. (1967). Biogenic amines and emotion. *Science, 156*, 21–30.

Schmid, D. A., Held, K., Ising, M., Uhr, M., Weikel, J. C., & Steiger, A. (2005). Ghrelin stimulates appetite, imagination of food, GH, ACTH, and cortisol, but does not affect leptin in normal controls. *Neuro-psychopharmacology, 30*, 1187–1192.

Schmitt, M. (1973). Influences of hepatic portal receptors on hypothalamic feeding and satiety centers. *American Journal of Physiology, 225*, 1089–1095.

Schneiderman, N. (1973). *Classical (Pavlovian) conditioning.* Morristown, NJ: GeneralLearning Press.

Schneiderman, N., Antoni, M. H., Saab, P. G., & Ironson, G. (2001). Health psychology: Psycho social and biobehavioral aspects of chronic disease management. *Annual Review of Psychology, 52*, 555–580.

Schroeder, D. H., & Costa, P. T. (1984). Influence of life event stress on physical illness: Substantive effects or methodological flaws? *Journal of Personality and Social Psychology, 46*, 853–863.

Schroeder, M. A., Young, J. R., & Braun, C. E. (1999). Sage Grouse (Centrocercus urophasianus): In A. Poole, P. Stettenheim, & F. Gill (Eds.), *The Birds of North America 425* (pp. 1–28). Philadelphia, PA: The Birds of North America, Inc.

Schultz, D. (1977). *Growth psychology: Models of the healthy personality.* New York: Van Nostrand.

Schwartz, S. H., & Gottlieb, A. (1980). Bystander anonymity and reactions to emergencies. *Journal of Personality and Social Psychology, 39*, 418–430.

Scrima, L. (1982). Isolated REM sleep facilitates recall of complex associative information. *Psychophysiology, 19*, 252–259.

Sedikides, C., Campbell, W. K., Reeder, G., & Elliot, A. J. (1998). The self-serving bias in relational context. *Journal of Personality and Social Psychology, 74,* 378–386.

Sedikides, C., & Strube, M. J. (1997). Self-evaluation: Tothine own self be good, tothine own self be sure, tothine own self be true, and tothine own self be better. *Advances in Experimental Social Psychology, 29,* 206–269.

Segerstrom, S. C., & Miller, G. E. (2004). Psychological stress and the human immune system: A meta-analytic study of 30 years of inquiry. *Psychological Bulletin, 130,* 601–630.

Seligman, M. E. P. (1970). On the generality of the laws of learning. *Psychological Review, 77,* 406–418.

Seligman, M. E. P. (1971). Phobias and preparedness. *Behavior Therapy, 2,* 307–320.

Seligman, M. E. P. (1975). *Helplessness: On depression, development, and death.* San Francisco: Freeman.

Seligman, M. E. P. (1976). *Learned helplessness and depression in animals and man.* Morristown, NJ: General Learning Press.

Seligman, M. E. P. (2002). *Authentic happiness.* New York, NY: Free Press.

Seligman, M. E. P., & Csikszentmihalyi, M. (2000). Positive psychology: An introduction. *American Psychologist, 55,* 5–14.

Seligman, M. E. P., & Hager, J. L. (1972). *Biological boundaries of learning.* New York: Appleton-Century-Crofts.

Seligman, M. E. P., & Maier, S. F. (1967). Failure to escape traumatic shock. *Journal of Experimental Psychology, 74,* 1–9.

Seligman, M. E. P., Maier, S. F., & Geer, J. (1968). The alleviation of learned helplessness in the dog. *Journal of Abnormal and Social Psychology, 73,* 256–262.

Selye, H. (1950). *Stress.* Montreal: Acta.

Selye, H. (1956). *The stress of life.* New York: McGraw-Hill.

Selye, H. (1973). The evolution of the stress concept. *American Scientist, 61,* 692–699.

Senneker, P., & Hendrick, C. (1983). Androgyny and helping behavior. *Journal of Personality and Social Psychology, 45,* 916–925.

Sevenster, P. (1961). A causal analysis of a displacement activity (fanning in *Gasterosteusaculeatus*). *Behavior Supplements, 9,* 1–170.

Seward, J. P. (1949). An experimental analysis of latent learning. *Journal of Experimental Psychology, 39,* 177–186.

Shapiro, C. M. (1982). Energy expenditure and restorative sleep. *Biological Psychology, 15,* 229–239.

Shapiro, C. M., Bortz, R., Mitchell, D., Bartel, P., & Jooste, P. (1981). Slow-wave sleep: A recovery period after exercise. *Science, 214,* 1253–1254.

Shaw, P. J., Cirelli, C., Greenspan, R. J., & Tononi, G. (2000). Correlates of sleep and waking in *Drosophilamelanogaster. Science, 287,* 1834–1837.

Sheffield, F. D., & Roby, T. B. (1950). Reward value of a nonnutritive sweet taste. *Journal of Comparative and Physiological Psychology, 43,* 471–481.

Sheffield, F. D., Roby, T. B., & Campbell, B. A. (1954). Drive reduction versus consummatory behavior as determinants of reinforcement. *Journal of Comparative and Physiological Psychology, 47,* 349–354.

Sheldon, K. M., Elliot, A. J., Kim, Y., & Kasser, T. (2001). What is satisfying about satisfying events? Testing 10 candidate psychological needs. *Journal of Personality and Social Psychology, 80,* 325–339.

Shepherd, S., Fitch, T. J., Owen, D., & Marshall, J. L. (2006). Locus of control and academic achievement in high school students. *Psychological Reports, 98,* 318–322.

Shepperd, J., Malone, W., & Sweeny, K. (2008). Exploring causes of the self-serving bias. *Social and Personality Psychology Compass, 2,* 895–908.

Shepperd, J. A. (1993). Productivity loss in performance groups: A motivation analysis. *Psychological Bulletin, 113,* 67–81.

Shepperd, J. A., & Taylor, K. M. (1999). Social loafing and expectancy-value theory. *Personality and Social Psychology Bulletin, 25,* 1147–1158.

Sherif, M. (1947). Group influences upon the formation of norms and attitudes. In T. M. Newcomb & E. L. Hartley (Eds.), *Readings in social psychology.* New York: Holt.

Shermer, M. (1997). *Why people believe weird things: Pseudoscience, superstition and other confusions of our time.* New York: W. H. Freeman.

Sherrington, C. (1947). *The integrative action of the nervous system.* New Haven, CT: Yale University Press.

Shettleworth, S. J. (1998). *Cognition, evolution and behavior.* New York: Oxford University Press.

Shettleworth, S. J. (2001). Animal cognition and behaviour. *Animal Behavior, 61,* 277–286.

Shiue, Y.-C., Chiu, C.-M., & Chang, C.-C. (2010). Exploring and mitigating social loafing in online communities. *Computers in Human Behavior, 26,* 768–777.

Shostrom, E. L. (1964). An inventory for the measurement of self-actualization. *Educational and Psychological Measurement, 24,* 207–216.

Shostrom, E. L. (1966). *Manual for the personal orientation inventory.* San Diego, CA: Educational and Industrial Testing Service.

Siegel, A., Roeling, T. A. P., Gregg, T. R., & Kruk, M. R. (1999). Neuro pharmacology of brain-stimulation-evoked aggression. *Neuroscience and Biobehavioral Reviews, 23*, 359–389.

Siegel, J. M. (1999). Narcolepsy: A key role for hypocretins (orexins). *Cell, 98*, 409–412.

Siegel, J. M. (2001). The REM sleep-memory consolidation hypothesis. *Science, 294*, 1058–1063.

Siegel, S. (1975). Evidence from rats that morphine tolerance is a learned response. *Journal of Comparative and Physiological Psychology, 89*, 498–506.

Siegel, S. (1977). Morphine tolerance acquisition as an associative process. *Journal of Experimental Psychology: Animal Behavior Processes, 3*, 1–13.

Siegel, S., Sherman, J. E., & Mitchell, D. (1980). Extinction of morphine analgesic tolerance. *Learning and Motivation, 11*, 289–301.

Silvestri, A. J., & Kapp, B. S. (1998). Amygdaloid modulation of mesopontine peri brachial neuronal activity: Implications for arousal. *Behavioral Neuroscience, 112*, 571–588.

Silvia, P. J., & Duval, T. S. (2001). Predicting the interpersonal targets of self-serving attributions. *Journal of Experimental Social Psychology, 37*, 333–340.

Simmonds, M. (1914). Ueber embolische prozesse in der hypophysis. *Archiv fuer Pathologische, Anatomie, und Physiologie und fuer Klinische Medicin, 217*, 226.

Simmons, R. (1924). The relative effectiveness of certain incentives in animal learning. *Comparative Psychology Monographs, 2*(7), 1–79.

Simon, G. E., Von Korff, M., Saunders, K., Miglioretti, D. L., Crane, P. K., van Belle, G., & Kessler, R. C. (2006). Association between obesity and psychiatric disorders in the US adult population. *Archives of General Psychiatry, 63*, 824–830.

Simpson, J. B., & Routtenberg, A. (1973). Subfornical organ: Site of drinking elicitation by angiotension II. *Science, 181*, 1172–1175.

Simpson, M. J. A., & Simpson, A. E. (1982). Birth sex ratios and social rank in rhesus monkey mothers. *Nature, 300*, 440–441.

Singer, J. E. (1966). Motivation of consistency. In S. Feldman (Ed.), *Cognitive consistency: Motivational antecedents and behavioral consequents* (pp. 48–73). New York: Academic Press.

Singh, D. (1993). Adaptive significance of female physical attractiveness: Role of waist-to-hip ratio. *Journal of Personality and Social Psychology, 65*, 293–307.

Skinner, B. F. (1938). *The behavior of organisms: An experimental analysis.* New York: Appleton-Century-Crofts.

Slanger, E., & Rudestam, K. E. (1997). Motivation and disinhibition in high risk sports: Sensation seeking and self-efficacy. *Journal of Research in Personality, 31*, 355–374.

Sluckin, W. (1973). *Imprinting and early learning.* Chicago, IL: Aldine.

Smith, D. E., King, M. B., & Hoebel, B. G. (1970). Lateral hypothalamic control of killing: Evidence for a cholinoceptive mechanism. *Science, 167*, 900–901.

Smith, E. R., & DeCoster, J. (2000). Dual-process models in social and cognitive psychology: Conceptual integration and links to underlying memory systems. *Personality and Social Psychology Review, 4*, 108–131.

Smith, G. P., & Jerome, C. (1983). Effects of total and selective abdominal vagotomies on water intake in rats. *Journal of the Autonomic Nervous System, 9*, 259–271.

Smith, O. (2000). Sleep, eat and be merry. *Science, 289*, 1706.

Snyder, M. (1974). Self-monitoring of expressive behavior. *Journal of Personality and Social Psychology, 30*, 526–537.

Snyder, M., & Gangestad, S. (1986). On the nature of self monitoring: Matters of assessment, matters of validity. *Journal of Personality and Social Psychology, 51*, 125–139.

Soares, J.-B., & Leite-Moreira, A. F. (2008). Ghrelin, des-acyl ghrelin and obestatin: Three pieces of the same puzzle. *Peptides, 29*, 1255–1270.

Sohlberg, S., & Norring, C. (1992). A three-year prospective study of life events and course for adults with anorexia nervosa/bulimia nervosa. *Psychosomatic Medicine, 54*, 59–70.

Solbrig, O. T. (1966). *Evolution and systematics.* New York: Macmillan.

Solomon, R. L. (1977). An opponent-process theory of motivation: V. Affective dynamics of eating. In L. M. Barker, M. R. Best, & M. Domjan (Eds.), *Learning mechanisms in food selection.* Dallas: Baylor University Press.

Solomon, R. L. (1980). The opponent-process theory of acquired motivation: The costs of pleasure and the benefits of pain. *American Psychologist, 35*, 691–712.

Solomon, R. L., & Corbit, J. D. (1974). An opponent-process theory of motivation. *Psychological Review, 81*, 119–145.

Sommer, R., Wynes, M., & Brinkley, G. (1992). Social facilitation effects in shopping behavior. *Environment and Behavior, 24*, 285–297.

Soussignan, R. (2002). Duchennesmile, emotional experience, and autonomic reactivity: A test of the facial feedback hypothesis. *Emotion, 2,* 52–74.

Spector, P. E. (1988). Development of the Work Locus of Control Scale. *Journal of Occupational Psychology, 61,* 335–340.

Spence, K. W. (1956). *Behavior theory and conditioning.* New Haven, CT: Yale University Press.

Spence, K. W. (1960). *Behavior theory and learning.* Englewood Cliffs, NJ: Prentice Hall.

Spielman, A., & Herrera, C. (1991). Sleep disorders. In S. J. Ellmanand & J. S. Antrobus (Eds.), *The mind in sleep: Psychology and psycho physiology* (2nd ed., pp. 25–80). New York: Wiley.

Spitz, R. A. (1946). *The psycho analytic study of the child, II.* New York: International University Press.

Spurzheim, J. G. (1908). *Phrenology* (Rev. ed.). Philadelphia, PA: Lippincott.

Squire, L. R. (1992). Memory and the hippo campus: A synthesis from findings with rats, monkeys, and humans. *Psychological Review, 99,* 195–231.

Staddon, J. E. R. (1970). Temporal effects of reinforcement: A negative "frustration" effect. *Learning and Motivation, 1,* 227–247.

Stangler, R. S., & Printz, A. M. (1980). DSMIII: Psychiatric diagnosis in a university population. *American Journal of Psychiatry, 137,* 937–940.

Starr, M. D. (1978). An opponent-process theory of motivation: VI. Time and intensity variables in the development of separation-induced distress calling in ducklings. *Journal of Experimental Psychology: Animal Behavior Processes, 4,* 338–355.

Staw, B. M. (1976). *Intrinsic and extrinsic motivation.* Morristown, NJ: General Learning Press.

Stedman's medical dictionary (26th ed.). (1995). Baltimore, MD: Williams & Wilkins.

Steers, R. M., & Porter, L. W. (1983). *Motivation and work behavior.* New York: McGraw-Hill.

Stellar, E. (1954). The physiology of motivation. *Psychological Review, 61,* 5–22.

Stellar, E., Hyman, R., & Samet, S. (1954). Gastric factors controlling water and salt solution drinking. *Journal of Comparative and Physiological Psychology, 47,* 220–226.

Steppan, C. M., Bailey, S. T., Bhat, S., Brown, E. J., Banerjee, R. R., Wright, C. M., Patel, H. R., Ahima, R. S., & Lazar, M. A. (2001). The hormone resist in links obesity to diabetes. *Nature, 409,* 307–312.

Sterman, M. B., & Clemente, C. D. (1962a). Forebrain inhibitory mechanisms: Cortical synchronization induced by basal forebrain stimulation. *Experimental Neurology, 6,* 91–102.

Sterman, M. B., & Clemente, C. D. (1962b). Forebrain inhibitory mechanisms: Sleep patterns induced by basal forebrain stimulation in the behaving cat. *Experimental Neurology, 6,* 103–117.

Stern, G. S., McCants, T. R., & Pettine, P. W. (1982). Stress and illness: Controllable and uncontrollable life events' relative contributions. *Personality and Social Psychology Bulletin, 8,* 140–145.

Stern, K., & McClintock, M. K. (1998). Regulation of ovulation by human pheromones. *Nature, 392,* 177–179.

Stern, P. (2001). Sweet dreams are made of this. *Science, 294,* 1047.

Stern, W. C. (1970). The relationship between REM sleep and learning: Animal studies. In E. Hartmann (Ed.), *Sleep and dreaming* (pp. 249–257). Boston, MA: Little, Brown.

Sternberg, E. M. (1992) The Stress response and the regulation of inflammatory disease. *Annals of Internal Medicine, 117,* 854–866.

Sternglanz, S. H., Gray, J. L., & Murakami, M. (1977). Adult preferences for infantile facial features: A nethological approach. *Animal Behavior, 25,* 108–115.

Stevenson, J. A. F. (1969). Neural control of food and water intake. In W. Haymaker et al. (Ed.), *The hypothalamus* (pp. 524–621). Springfield, IL: Thomas.

Stice, E., Chase, A., Stormer, S., & Appel, A. (2001). A randomized trial of a dissonance-based eating disorder prevention program. *International Journal of Eating Disorders, 29,* 247–262.

Stickgold, R. (2005). Sleep-dependent memory consolidation. *Nature, 437,* 1272–1278.

Stickgold, R., Hobson, J. A., Fosse, R., & Fosse, M. (2001). Sleep, learning, and dreams: Off-line memory reprocessing. *Science, 294,* 1052–1057.

Stoeckel, L. E., Weller, R. E., Cook, E. W., Tweig, D. B., Knowlton, R. C., & Cox, J. E. (2008). Widespread reward-system activation in obese women in response to pictures of high-calorie foods. *Neuroimage, 41,* 636–647.

Stoleru, S., Gregoire, M. C., Gerard, D., Decety, J., Lafarge, E., Cinotti, L., Lavenne, F., LeBars, D., Vernet-Maury, E., Rada, H., Collet, C., Mazoyer, B., Forest, M. G., Magnin, F., Spira, A., & Comar, D. (1999). Neuro anatomical correlates of visually evoked sexual arousal in human males. *Archives of Sexual Behavior, 28,* 1–21.

Stone, J., Aronson, E., Crain, A. L., Winslow, M. P., & Fried, C. B. (1994). Inducing hypocrisy as a means of encouraging young adults to use condoms. *Personality and Social Psychology Bulletin, 20,* 116–128.

Stone, J., & Cooper, J. (2001). A self-standards model of cognitive dissonance. *Journal of Experimental Social Psychology, 37*, 228–243.

Stone, T. H., Jawahar, I. M., & Kisamore, J. L. (2010). Predicting academic misconduct intentions and behavior using the theory of planned behavior and personality. *Basic and Applied Social Psychology, 32*, 35–45.

Storms, M. D. (1973). Videotape and the attribution process: Reversing actors' and observers' points of view. *Journal of Personality and Social Psychology, 27*, 165–175.

Stotland, E. (1969). Exploratory investigations of empathy. In L. Berkowitz (Ed.), *Advances in experimental social psychology* (Vol. 4, pp. 271–313). New York, NY: Academic Press.

Stoyva, J., & Kamiya, J. (1968). Electrophysiological studies of dreaming as the prototype of a new strategy in the study of consciousness. *Psychological Review, 75*, 192–205.

Strack, F., Martin, L. L., & Stepper, S. (1988). Inhibiting and facilitating conditions of the human smile: A non-obtrusive test of the facial feedback hypothesis. *Journal of Personality and Social Psychology, 54*, 768–777.

Straumann, C., & Anderson, J. R. (1991). Mirror-induced social facilitation in stump-tailed macaques (*Macacaarctoides*). *American Journal of Primatology, 25*, 125–132.

Straus, E., & Yalow, R. S. (1979). Cholecystokinin in the brains of obese and nonobese mice. *Science, 203*, 68–69.

Stricker, E. M., Friedman, M. I., & Zigmond, M. J. (1975). Gluco regulatory feeding by rats after intraventricular 6 hydroxy dopamine or lateral hypothalamic lesions. *Science, 189*, 895–897.

Stricker, E. M., & Sved, A. F. (2000). Thirst. *Nutrition, 16*, 821–826.

Stricker, E. M., & Zigmond, M. J. (1976). Brain catecholamines and the lateral hypothalamic syndrome. In D. Novin et al. (Eds.), *Hunger: Basic mechanisms and clinical implications*. New York: Raven Press.

Striegel-Moore, R. H., Silberstein, L. R., & Rodin, J. (1986). Toward an understanding of risk factors for bulimia. *American Psychologist, 41*, 246–263.

Strober, M., Freeman, R., Lampert, C., Diamond, J., & Kaye, W. (2000). Controlled family study of anorexia nervosa and bulimia nervosa: Evidence of shared liability and transmission of partial syndromes. *American Journal of Psychiatry, 157*, 393–401.

Stuart, R. B., & Davis, B. (1972). *Slim chance in a fat world*. Champaign, IL: Research Press.

Suedfeld, P. (1975). The benefits of boredom: Sensory deprivation reconsidered. *American Scientist, 63*, 60–69.

Suedfeld, P. (1977). Using environmental restriction to initiate long-term behavior change. In R. B. Stuart (Ed.), *Behavioral self-management: Strategies, techniques and outcomes* (pp. 230–257). New York: Brunner/Mazel.

Suedfeld, P. (1980). *Restricted environmental stimulation: Research and clinical applications*. New York: Wiley.

Suedfeld, P., & Ikard, F. F. (1974). The use of sensory deprivation in facilitating the reduction of cigarette smoking. *Journal of Clinical and Consulting Psychology, 42*, 888–895.

Suedfeld, P., & Kristeller, J. L. (1982). Stimulus reduction as a technique in health psychology. *Health Psychology, 1*, 337–357.

Suls, J., & Mullen, B. (1981). Life change and psychological distress: The role of perceived control and desirability. *Journal of Applied Social Psychology, 11*, 379–389.

Suls, J., & Wan, C. K. (1987). In search of the false-uniqueness phenomenon: Fear and estimates of social consensus. *Journal of Personality and Social Psychology, 52*, 211–217.

Sumerlin, J. R., & Norman, R. L. (1992). Self-actualization and homelessmen: A known-groups examination of Maslow's hierarchy of needs. *Journal of Social Behavior and Personality, 7*, 469–481.

Swan, I. (1977). Anorexia nervosa, a difficult diagnosis. *The Practitioner, 218*, 424–427.

Symons, D. (1979). *The evolution of human sexuality*. New York: Oxford University Press.

Szymusiak, R., Alam, N., Steininger, T. L., & McGinty, D. (1998). Sleep-waking discharge patterns of ventro lateral preoptic/anterior hypothalamic neurons in rats. *Brain Research, 803*, 178–188.

Takahashi, J. S. (1999). Narcolepsy genes wake up the sleep field. *Science, 285*, 2076–2077.

Takahashi, K., Lin, J.-S., & Sakai, K. (2006). Neuronal activity of histaminergic tuberomammillary neurons during wake–sleep states in the mouse. *The Journal of Neuroscience, 26*, 10292–10298.

Tanner, O. (1976). *Stress*. New York: Time-Life Books.

Tarpy, R. M., & Mayer, R. E. (1978). *Foundations of learning and memory*. Glenview, IL: Scott, Foresman.

Taubes, G. (2001). The soft science of dietary fat. *Science, 291*, 2536–2545.

Taylor, E. (2001). Positive psychology and humanistic psychology: A reply to Seligman. *Journal of Humanistic Psychology, 41*, 13–29.

Taylor, T. (1997). *The prehistory of sex*. New York: Bantam. (Quote reprinted in *Science, 275*, 1894)

Teegarden, S. L., & Bale, T. L. (2008). Effects of stress on dietary preference and intake are dependent on access and stress sensitivity. *Physiology and Behavior, 93,* 713–723.

Teitelbaum, P., & Stellar, E. (1954). Recovery from the failure to eat produced by hypothalamic lesions. *Science, 120,* 894–895.

Thayer, R. E. (1996). *The origin of everyday moods: Managing energy, tension, and stress.* New York: Oxford.

Thiessen, D., & Gregg, B. (1980). Human assortative mating and genetic equilibrium: An evolutionary perspective. *Ethology and Sociobiology, 1,* 111–140.

Thompson, B., & Thornton, B. (2007). Exploring mental-state reasoning as a social-cognitive mechanism for social loafing in children. *The Journal of Social Psychology, 147,* 159–174.

Thompson, W. R., & Melzack, R. (1956). Early environment. *Scientific American, 194*(1), 38–42.

Thorens, B. (2008). Glucose sensing and the pathogenesis of obesity and type 2 diabetes. *International Journal of Obesity, 32,* 562–571.

Thorndike, E. L. (1913). *Educational psychology* (Vol. 2). New York: Teachers College.

Tinbergen, E. A., & Tinbergen, N. (1972). Early childhood autism: An ethological approach. *Beiheftezur Zeitschrift Tierpsychologie, 10,* 7–53.

Tinbergen, N. (1948). Social releasers and the experimental method required for their study. *Wilson Bulletin, 60,* 6–52.

Tinbergen, N. (1951). *The study of instinct.* New York: Oxford University Press.

Tinbergen, N. (1977). On war and peace in animals and man. In T. E. McGill (Ed.), *Readings in animal behavior* (3rd ed., pp. 452–467). New York: Holt, Rinehart & Winston.

Tinklepaugh, O. L. (1928). An experimental study of representative factors in monkeys. *Journal of Comparative Psychology, 8,* 197–236.

Toi, M., & Batson, C. D. (1982). More evidence that empathy is a source of altruistic motivation. *Journal of Personality and Social Psychology, 43,* 281–292.

Tolman, E. C. (1923). The nature of instinct. *Psychological Bulletin, 20,* 200–218.

Tolman, E. C. (1959). Principles of purposive behavior. In S. Koch (Ed.), *Psychology: A study of a science* (Vol. 2, pp. 92–157). New York: McGraw-Hill.

Tolman, E. C. (1967). *Purposive behavior in animals and men.* New York: Appleton-Century-Crofts.

Tolman, E. C., & Honzik, C. H. (1930). Introduction and removal of reward, and maze performance in rats.

University of California Publications in Psychology, 4, 257–275.

Tolman, E. C., Ritchie, B. F., & Kalish, D. (1946). Studies in spatial learning: II. Place learning versus response learning. *Journal of Experimental Psychology, 36,* 221–229.

Tolman, E. C., Ritchie, B. F., & Kalish, D. (1947). Studies in spatial learning: V. Response learning vs. place learning by the non-correction method. *Journal of Experimental Psychology, 37,* 285–292.

Tomkins, S. S. (1962). *Affect, imagery, consciousness: Vol. I. The positive affects.* New York: Springer.

Tomkins, S. S. (1963). *Affect, imagery, consciousness: Vol. II. The negative affects.* New York: Springer.

Tomkins, S. S. (1979). Script theory: Differential magnification of affects. In R. A. Dienstbier (Ed.), *1978 Nebraska symposium on motivation* (pp. 201–236). Lincoln, NE: University of Nebraska Press.

Tomkins, S. S. (1981). The quest for primary motives: Biography and autobiography of an idea. *Journal of Personality and Social Psychology, 41,* 306–329.

Tomkins, S. S., & McCarter, R. (1964). What and where are the primary affects? Some evidence for a theory. *Perceptual and Motor Skills, 18,* 119–158.

Tonetti, L., Adan, A., Caci, H., De Pascalis, V., Fabbri, M., & Natale, V. (2010). Morningness-eveningness preference and sensation seeking. *European Psychiatry, 25,* 111–115.

Tony, T. S. K. (2003). Locus of control, attributional style and discipline problems in secondary schools. *Early Child Development and Care, 173,* 455–466.

Trapold, M. A., & Overmier, J. B. (1972). The second learning process in instrumental learning. In A. H. Black & W. F. Prokasy (Eds.), *Classical conditioning II: Current research and theory* (pp. 427–452). New York: Appleton-Century-Crofts.

Triplett, N. (1898). The dynamogenic factors in pacemaking and competition. *The American Journal of Psychology, 9,* 507–533.

Trivers, R. (1972). Parental investment and sexual selection. In B. Campbell (Ed.), *Sexual selection and the descent of man* (pp. 136–179). Chicago, IL: Aldine.

Trivers, R. (1985). *Social Evolution.* Menlo Park, CA: Benjamin/Cummings.

Troland, L. T. (1932). *The principles of psychophysiology.* New York: VanNostrand.

Tschop, M., Smiley, D. L., & Heiman, M. L. (2000). Ghrelin induces adiposityin rodents. *Nature, 407,* 908–912.

Turner, J. E., & Schallert, D. L. (2001). Expectancy-value relationships of shame reactions and shame resiliency. *Journal of Educational Psychology, 93*, 320–329.

Udwin, O., & Yule, W. (1984). Spelling remediation: A single case study. *Educational Psychology, 4*, 285–296.

Ulrich, R., & Azrin, N. H. (1962). Reflexive fighting in response to aversive stimulation. *Journal of the Experimental Analysis of Behavior, 5*, 511–520.

Urdan, T. C., & Maehr, M. L. (1995). Beyond a two-goal theory of motivation and achievement: A case for social goals. *Review of Educational Research, 65*, 213–243.

Vaglio, S., Minicozzi, P., Bonometti, E., Mello, G., & Chiarelli, B. (2009). Volatile signals during pregnancy: A possible chemical basis for mother-infant recognition. *Journal of Chemical Ecology, 35*, 131–139.

Vale, W., Spiess, J., Rivier, C., & Rivier, J. (1981). Characterization of a 41-residue ovine hypothalamic peptide that stimulates secretion of cortico tropin and B-endorphin. *Science, 213*, 1394–1397.

Valins, S. (1966). Cognitive effects of falseheart-rate feedback. *Journal of Personality and Social Psychology, 4*, 400–408.

Valins, S. (1974). Persistent effects of information about internal reactions: In effectiveness of debriefing. In H. London & R. E. Nisbett (Eds.), *The cognitive alteration of feeling states* (pp. 116–126). Chicago, IL: Aldine.

Vallerand, R. J., & Reid, G. (1984). On the causal effects of perceived competence on intrinsic motivation: A test of cognitive evaluation theory. *Journal of Sport Psychology, 6*, 94–102.

Valli, K., Lenasdotter, S., Macgregor, O., & Revonsuo, A. (2007). A test of the threat simulation theory— Replication of results in an independent sample. *Sleep and Hypnosis, 9*, 30–46.

Valli, K., Revonsuo, A., Palkas, O., Ismail, K. H., Ali, K. J., & Punamaki, R. L. (2005). *Consciousness and Cognition, 14*, 188–218.

Vandekerckhove, M., & Cluydts, R. (2010). The emotional brain and sleep: An intimate relationship. *Sleep Medicine Reviews, 14*, 219–226.

Vanderweele, D. A., & Sanderson, J. D. (1976). Peripheral glucosensitive satiety in the rabbit and the rat. In D. Novin et al. (Eds.), *Hunger: Basic mechanisms and clinical implications*. New York: Raven Press.

Van Der Werf, Y., Altena, E., Schoonheim, M. M., Sanz-Arigita, E. J., Vis, J. C., De Rijke, W., & Van Someren, E. J. W. (2009). Sleep benefits subsequent hippo campal functioning. *Nature Neuroscience, 12*, 122–123.

van Dick, R., Stellmacher, J., Wagner, U., Lemmer, G., & Tissingyon, P. A. (2009). Group membership salience and task performance. *Journal of Managerial Psychology, 24*, 609–626.

VanHemel, P. E. (1972). Aggression as a reinforcer: Operant behavior in the mouse killing rat. *Journal of the Experimental Analysis of Behavior, 17*, 237–245.

Van Orden, K. A., Witte, T. K., Cukrowicz, K. C., Braithwaite, S. R., Selby, E. A., & Joiner, T. E. (2010). The interpersonal theory of suicide. *Psychological Review, 117*, 575–600.

van Veen, V., Krug, M. K., Schooler, J. W., & Carter, C. S. (2009). Neural activity predicts attitude change in cognitive dissonance. *Nature Neuroscience, 12*, 1469–1474.

Vanwesenbeeck, I. (2001). Psychosexual correlates of viewing sexually explicit sex on television among women in the Netherlands. *The Journal of Sex Research, 38*, 361–368.

Vargas-Perez, H., Ting-A-Kee, R. A., Heinmiller, A., Sturgess, J. E., & van der Kooy, D. (2007). A test of the opponent-process theory of motivation using lesions that selectively block morphine reward. *European Journal of Neuroscience, 25*, 3713–3718.

Vauclair, J. (1996). *Animal cognition: An introduction to modern comparative psychology*. Cambridge, MA: Harvard University Press.

Verney, E. B. (1947). The anti diuretic hormone and the factors which determine its release. *Proceedings of the Royal Society (London), Series B, 135*, 25–106.

Vernon, W., & Ulrich, R. (1966). Classical conditioning of pain-elicited aggression. *Science, 152*, 668–669.

Veroff, J., Wilcox, S., & Atkinson, J. W. (1953). The achievement motive in high school and college-age women. *Journal of Abnormal and Social Psychology, 48*, 103–119.

Vincent, N., Sande, G., Read, C., & Giannuzzi, T. (2004). Sleep locus of control: Report on a new scale. *Behavioral Sleep Medicine, 2*, 79–93.

Viviani, D., Charlet, A., van den Burg, E., Robinet, C., Hurni, N., Abatis, M., Magara, F., & Stoop, R. (2011). Oxytocin selectively gates fear responses through distinct outputs from the central amygdala. *Science, 333*, 104–107.

Volicer, L., & Lowe, C. G. (1971). Penetration of angiotensin II into the brain. *Neuropharmacology, 10*, 631–636.

Volkow, N. D., & Wise, R. A. (2005). How can drug addiction help us understand obesity? *Nature Neuroscience, 8*, 555–560.

Wade, T. D., Bulik, C. M., Neale, M., & Kendler, K. S. (2000). Anorexia nervosa and major depression: Shared genetic and environmental risk factors. *American Journal of Psychiatry, 157,* 469–471.

Wagner, A. R. (1961). Effects of amount and percentage of reinforcement and number of acquisition trials on conditioning and extinction. *Journal of Experimental Psychology, 62,* 234–242.

Walker, M. P., & van der Helm, E. (2009). Overnight therapy? The role of sleep in emotional brain processing. *Psychological Bulletin, 135,* 731–748.

Wallston, K. A., Wallston, B. S., & DeVellis, R. (1978). Development of the Multidimensional Health Locus of Control (MHLC) scales. *Health Education Monographs, 6,* 160–170.

Wang, G.-J., Volkow, N. D., Pappas, N. R., Netusil, N., Wong, C. T., Logan, J., Fowler, J. S., & Zhu, W. (2001). Brain dopamine and obesity. *Lancet, 357,* 354–358.

Wang, Z., Nudelman, A., & Storm, D. R. (2007). Are pheromones detected through the main olfactory epithelium? *Molecular Neurobiology, 35,* 317–323.

Warga, C. (1987, August). Pain's gatekeeper. *Psychology Today,* 51–56.

Waterman, D. (1991). Aging and memory for dreams. *Perceptual and Motor Skills, 73,* 355–365.

Waters, A., Hill, A., & Waller, G. (2001). Bulimics' responses to food cravings: Is binge-eating a product of hunger or emotional state? *Behaviour Research and Therapy, 39,* 877–886.

Watson, D., Clark, L. A., & Tellegen, A. (1984). Cross-cultural convergence in the structure of mood: A Japanese replication and a comparison with U.S. findings. *Journal of Personality and Social Psychology, 47,* 127–144.

Watson, D., & Tellegen, A. (1985). Toward a consensual structure of mood. *Psychological Bulletin, 98,* 219–235.

Watson, J. B. (1914). *Behavior, an introduction to comparative psychology.* New York: Holt, Rinehart & Winston.

Watson, J. B., & Rayner, R. (1920). Conditioned emotional reactions. *Journal of Experimental Psychology, 3,* 1–14.

Webb, W. B. (1982). The sleep of older subjects fifteen years later. *Psychological Reports, 50,* 11–14.

Webb, W. B. (1986). Sleep deprivation and reading comprehension. *Biological Psychology, 22,* 169–172.

Webb, W. B., & Agnew, H. W. (1968). Measurement and characteristics of nocturnal sleep. In L. E. Abt & B. F. Riess (Eds.), *Progress in clinical psychology* (Vol. 8). New York: Grune & Stratton.

Webb, W. B., & Agnew, H. W. (1973). *Sleep and dreams.* Dubuque, Iowa: Brown.

Webster, H. H., & Jones, B. E. (1988). Neurotoxic lesions of the dorso lateral pontomesencephalic tegmentum cholinergic cell area in the cat. II. Effects upon sleep waking states. *Brain Research, 458,* 285–302.

Weiner, B. (1972). *Theories of motivation: From mechanism to cognition.* Chicago: Markham.

Weiner, B. (1974). An attributional interpretation of expectancy-value theory. In B. Weiner (Ed.), *Cognitive views of human motivation* (pp. 51–69). New York: Academic Press.

Weiner, B. (1980). A cognitive (attribution) - emotion-action model of motivated behavior: An analysis of judgments of help giving. *Journal of Personality and Social Psychology, 39,* 186–200.

Weiner, B. (1985). An attributional theory of achievement motivation and emotion. *Psychological Review, 92,* 548–573.

Weiner, B. (1991). Metaphors in motivation and attribution. *American Psychologist, 46,* 921–930.

Weiner, B. (2010). The development of an attribution-based theory of motivation: A history of ideas. *Educational Psychologist, 45,* 28–36.

Weiner, B., Amirkhan, J., Folkes, V. S., & Verette, J. A. (1987). An attributional analysis of excuse giving: Studies of a naïve theory of emotion. *Journal of Personality and Social Psychology, 52,* 316–324.

Weiner, B., Frieze, I., Kukla, A., Reed, L., Rest, S., & Rosenbaum, R. M. (1971). Perceiving the causes of success and failure. In E. E. Jones et al. (Eds.), *Attribution: Perceiving the causes of behavior* (pp. 95–120). Morristown, NJ: General Learning Press.

Weiner, B., & Kukla, A. (1970). An attributional analysis of achievement motivation. *Journal of Personality and Social Psychology, 15,* 1–20.

Weiner, B., Russell, D., & Lerman, D. (1978). Affective consequences of causal ascriptions. In J. H. Harvey et al. (Eds.), *New directions in attribution research* (Vol. 2). Hillsdale, NJ: Erlbaum.

Weinstein, M. S. (1969). Achievement motivation and risk preference. *Journal of Personality and Social Psychology, 13,* 153–172.

Weiss, J. M., Krieckhaus, E. E., & Conte, R. (1968). Effects of fear conditioning on subsequent avoidance behavior. *Journal of Comparative and Physiological Psychology, 65,* 413–421.

Wershow, H. J., & Reinhart, G. (1974). Life change and hospitalization: A heretical view. *Journal of Psychosomatic Research, 18,* 393–401.

West, P. M., & Packer, C. (2002). Sexual selection, temperature, and the lion's mane. *Science, 297,* 1339–1343.

Wexler, B. E., Gottschalk, C. H., Fulbright, R. K., Prohovnik, I., Lacadie, C. M., Rounsaville, B. J., & Gore, J. C. (2001). Functional magnetic resonance imaging of cocaine craving. *American Journal of Psychiatry, 158,* 86–95.

Whalen, P. J. (1998). Fear, vigilance, and ambiguity: Initial neuroimaging studies of the human amygdala. *Current Directions in Psychological Research, 7,* 177–188.

Whalen, P. J., Shin, L. M., McInerney, S. C., Fischer, H., Wright, C. I., & Rauch, S. L. (2001). A functional MRI study of human amygdale responses to facial expressions of fear versus anger. *Emotion, 1,* 70–83.

White, R. W. (1959). Motivation reconsidered: The concept of competence. *Psychological Review, 66,* 297–333.

White, R. W. (1964). *The abnormal personality* (3rd ed.). New York: Ronald Press.

Wicklund, R. A., & Brehm, J. W. (1976). *Perspectives on cognitive dissonance.* Hillsdale, NJ: Erlbaum.

Wiebe, D. J. (1991). Hardiness and stress moderation: A test of proposed mechanisms. *Journal of Personality and Social Psychology, 60,* 89–99.

Wiebe, D. J., & Williams, P. G. (1992). Hardiness and health: A social psychophysiological perspective on stress and adaptation. *Journal of Social and Clinical Psychology, 11,* 238–262.

Wiggins, J. S., Wiggins, N., & Conger, J. C. (1968). Correlates of heterosexual somatic preference. *Journal of Personality and Social Psychology, 10,* 32–90.

Wilcox, P. M., Fetting, J. H., Nettesheim, K. M., & Abeloff, M. D. (1982). Anticipatory vomiting in women receiving cyclophosphomide, methotrexate, and 5-FU (MF) adjuvant chemotherapy for breast carcinoma. *Cancer Treatment Reports, 66,* 1601–1604.

Wilcoxon, H. C., Dragoin, W. B., & Kral, P. A. (1971). Illness induced aversions in rat and quail: Relative salience of visual and auditory cues. *Science, 171,* 826–828.

Williams, C. E., Povey, R. C., & White, D. G. (2008). Predicting women's intentions to use pain relief medication during childbirth using the theory of planned behavior and self-efficacy theory. *Journal of Reproductive and Infant Psychology, 26,* 168–179.

Williams, G. C. (1975). *Sex and evolution.* Princeton, NJ: Princeton University Press.

Williams, H. L., Holloway, F. A., & Griffiths, W. J. (1973). Physiological psychology: Sleep. In P. H. Mursen & M.

R. Rosenzweig (Eds.), *Annual Review of Psychology, 24,* 279–307.

Williams, P. G., Wiebe, D. J., & Smith, T. W. (1992). Coping processes as mediators of the relationship between hardiness and health. *Journal of Behavioral Medicine, 15,* 237–255.

Wilson, J. F. (2003). *Biological foundations of human behavior.* Belmont, CA: Wadsworth.

Wilson, M. A., & McNaughton, B. L. (1994). Reactivation of hippo campal ensemble memories during sleep. *Science, 265,* 676–679.

Wing, R. R. (1992). Weight cycling in humans: A review of the literature. *Annals of Behavioral Medicine, 14,* 113–119.

Withgott, J. (2002). Cool cats lose out in the mane event. *Science, 297,* 1255–1256.

Witt, E. D., Ryan, C., & Hsu, L. K. G. (1985). Learning deficits in adolescents with anorexia nervosa. *Journal of Nervous and Mental Disease, 173,* 182–184.

Wolfe, J. B. (1936). Effectiveness of token rewards for chimpanzees. *Comparative Psychology Monographs, 12*(60), 72.

Wolff, G., & Money, J. (1973). Relationship between sleep and growth in patients with reversible somatotropin deficiency (psychosocial dwarfism). *Psychological Medicine, 3,* 18–27.

Wolfson, S. (2000). Students' estimates of the prevalence of drug use: Evidence for a false consensus effect. *Psychology of Addictive Behaviors, 14,* 295–298.

Wolgin, D. L., Cytawa, J., & Teitelbaum, P. (1976). The role of activation in the regulation of food intake. In D. Novin et al. (Eds.), *Hunger: Basic mechanisms and clinical implications* (pp. 179–191). New York: Raven Press.

Wolpe, J. (1958). *Psychotherapy by reciprocal inhibition.* Stanford, CA: Stanford University Press.

Wolpe, J. (1973). *The practice of behavior* (2nd ed.). New York: Pergamon.

Wong, P. T. P. (2011). Reclaiming positive psychology: A meaning-centered approach to sustainable growth and radical empiricism. *Journal of Humanistic Psychology, 51,* 408–412.

Woodbridge, F. J. E. (1958). *Hobbes selections.* New York: Scribner.

Woodruff, D. S. (1985). Arousal, sleep and aging. In J. E. Birren & K. W. Schaie (Eds.), *Handbook of the psychology of aging* (pp. 261–295). New York: VanNostr and Reinhold.

Woods, S. C., Schwartz, M. W., Baskin, D. G., & Seeley, R. J. (2000). Food intake and the regulation of body weight. *Annual Review of Psychology, 51,* 255–277.

Woodward, A. L. (1998). Infants selectively encode the goal object of an actor's reach. *Cognition, 69*, 1–34.

Woodworth, R. S. (1918). *Dynamic psychology*. New York: Columbia University Press.

Wookey, P. J., Lutz, T. A., & Andrikopoulos, S. (2006). Amylin in the periphery II: An updated mini-review. *Scientific World Journal, 6*, 1642–1655.

Wortman, C. B., & Brehm, J. F. (1975). Responses to uncontrollable outcomes: An integration of reactance theory and the learned helplessness model. In L. Berkowitz (Ed.), *Advances in experimental social psychology* (Vol. *8*, pp. 278–336). New York: Academic Press.

Wright, D. B., Self, G., & Justice, C. (2000). Memory conformity: Exploring misinformation effects when presented by another person. *British Journal of Psychology, 91*, 189–202.

Yamada, M., Miyakawa, T., Duttaroy, A., Yamanaka, A., Moriguchi, T., Makita, R., Ogawa, M., Chou, C. J., Xia, B., Crawley, J. N., Felder, C. C., Deng, C.-X., & Wess, J. (2001). Mice lacking them 3 muscarinic acetylcholine receptor are hypophagic and lean. *Nature, 410*, 207–212.

Yeager, D. S., Trzesniewski, K. H., Tirri, K., Nokelainen, P., & Dweck, C. S. (2011). Adolescents' implicit theories predict desire for vengeance after peer conflicts: Correlational and experimental evidence. *Developmental Psychology, 47*, 1090–1107.

Yik, M., Russell, J. A., & Steiger, J. H. (2011). A 12-point circumplex structure of core affect. *Emotion, 11*, 705–731.

Yik, M. S., Russell, J. A., & Feldman Barrett, L. (1999). Structure of self-reported affect: Integration and beyond. *Journal of Personality and Social Psychology, 77*, 600–619.

Yoo, S.-S., Hu, P. T., Gujar, N., Jolesz, F. A., & Walker, M. P. (2007). A deficit in the ability to form new human memories without sleep. *Nature Neuroscience, 10*, 385–392.

Young, P. T. (1959). The role of affective processes in learning and motivation. *Psychological Review, 66*, 104–125.

Young, P. T. (1961). *Motivation and emotion*. New York: Wiley.

Young, P. T. (1973). *Emotion in man and animal* (2nd ed.). Huntington, NY: Robert E. Krieger.

Young, P. T. (1975). *Understanding your feelings and emotions*. Englewood Cliffs, NJ: Prentice Hall.

Young, P. T., & Falk, J. L. (1956). The relative acceptability of sodium chloride solutions as a function of concentration and water need. *Journal of Comparative and Physiological Psychology, 49*, 569–575.

Young, P. T., & Greene, J. T. (1953). Quantity of food in gested as a measure of relative acceptability. *Journal of Comparative and Physiological Psychology, 46*, 288–294.

Youngsteadt, E. (2008). Simple sleepers. *Science, 321*, 334–337.

Zacny, J. P. (2010). A possible link between sensation-seeking status and positive subjective effects of oxycodone in healthy volunteers. *Pharmacology, Biochemistry and Behavior, 95*, 113–120.

Zajonc, R. B. (1965). Social facilitation. *Science, 149*, 269–274.

Zajonc, R. B. (1972). *Animal social behavior*. Morristown, NJ: General Learning Press.

Zajonc, R. B. (1980). Feeling and thinking: Preferences need no inferences. *American Psychologist, 35*, 151–175.

Zajonc, R. B. (1984). On the primacy of affect. *American Psychologist, 39*, 117–123.

Zajonc, R. B. (1998). Emotions. In D. T. Gilbert, S. T. Fiske, & G. Lindzey (Eds.), *Handbook of social psychology* (Vol. *1*, pp. 591–632). Boston, MA: McGraw-Hill.

Zajonc, R. B. (2000). Feeling and thinking: Closing the debate over the independence of affect. In J. P. Forgas (Ed.), *Feeling and thinking: The role of affect in social cognition* (pp. 31–58). New York: Cambridge.

Zajonc, R. B., Heingartner, A., & Herman, E. M. (1969). Social enhancement and impairment of performance in the cockroach. *Journal of Personality and Social Psychology, 13*, 83–92.

Zeaman, D. (1949). Response latency as a function of the amount of reinforcement. *Journal of Experimental Psychology, 39*, 466–483.

Zeliger, H. P., & Karten, H. J. (1974). Central trigeminal structures and the lateral hypothalamic syndrome in the rat. *Science, 186*, 636–638.

Zentall, T. R. (2010). Justification of effort by humans and pigeons: Cognitive dissonance or contrast? *Current Directions in Psychological Science, 19*, 296–300.

Zhang, Y. Y., Procenca, R., Maffei, M., Barone, M., Leopold, L., & Friedman, J. M. (1994). Positional cloning of the mouse obese gene and its human homologue. *Nature, 372*, 425–432.

Zhong, P., & Yan, Z. (2011). Differential regulation of the excitability of prefrontal cortical fast-spiking interneurons and pyramidal neurons by serotonin and fluoxetine. *PLoS ONE, 6*, 1–7.

Zilbergeld, B., & Ellison, C. R. (1980). *Principles and practice of sex therapy*. New York: Guilford.

Zillmann, D., & Bryant, J. (1982). Pornography, sexual callousness, and the trivialization of rape. *Journal of Communication, 32,* 10–21.

Zimbardo, P. G. (1969). The human choice: Individuation, reason, and order versus deindividuation, impulse, and chaos. In W. J. Arnold & D. Levine (Eds.), *Nebraska symposium on motivation* (pp. 237–307). Lincoln, NE: University of Nebraska Press.

Zornetzer, S. F., Gold, M. S., & Boast, C. A. (1977). Neuroanatomic localization and the neurobiology of sleep and memory. In R. R. Drucker-Colin & J. L. McGaugh (Eds.), *Neurobiology of sleep and memory* (pp. 185–226). New York: Academic Press.

Zuckerman, M. (1979a). Attribution of success and failure revisited, or: The motivational bias is alive and well in attributional theory. *Journal of Personality, 47,* 245–287.

Zuckerman, M. (1979b). *Sensation seeking: Beyond the optimal level of arousal.* Hillsdale, NJ: Erlbaum.

Zuckerman, M. (1994). *Behavioral expressions and biosocial bases of sensation seeking.* New York: Cambridge University Press.

Zuckerman, M., Kolin, I., Price, L., & Zoob, I. (1964). Development of a sensation seeking scale. *Journal of Consulting Psychology, 28,* 477–482.

Name Index

Subject Index

('f' indicates a figure, 't' indicates a table)